HTML
CGI
SGML
VRML
JAVA

Web Publishing

UNLEASHED

William Robert Stanek

201 West 103rd Street
Indianapolis, IN 46290

This book is dedicated to all the teachers who have helped me to understand networking and life in general. May the clarity bestowed upon me help and empower you in your work.

Copyright © 1996 by Sams.net Publishing

International Standard Book Number: 1-57521-051-7

Library of Congress Catalog Card Number: 95-71482

99 98 97 96   4   3   2

Interpretation of the printing code: the rightmost double-digit number is the year of the book's printing; the rightmost single-digit, the number of the book's printing. For example, a printing code of 96-1 shows that the first printing of the book occurred in 1996.

Composed in AGaramond and MCPdigital by Macmillan Computer Publishing

Printed in the United States of America

Trademarks

President, Sams Publishing	Richard K. Swadley
President, Sams.net Publishing	George Bond
Publishing Manager	Mark Taber
Managing Editor	Cindy Morrow
Marketing Manager	John Pierce

Acquisitions Editor
Beverly M. Eppink

Development Editor
Fran Hatton

Software Development Specialist
Merle Newlon

Production Editor
Carolyn Linn

Copy Editor
Mary Ann Faughnan

Technical Reviewers
Sue Charlesworth
John W. Nelsen
Dennis Teague

Editorial Coordinator
Bill Whitmer

Technical Edit Coordinator
Lynette Quinn

Formatter
Frank Sinclair

Editorial Assistant
Carol Ackerman

Cover Designer
Tim Amrhein

Book Designer
Alyssa Yesh

Production Team Supervisors
Brad Chinn, Elizabeth Lewis

Production
Mary Ann Abramson,
Stephen Adams, Carol Bowers,
Michael Brumitt,
Brian Buschkill, Jason Carr,
Bryan Flores, Trey Frank,
DiMonique Ford, Sonja Hart,
Damon Jordan, Clint Lahnen,
Stephanie Layton, Michelle Lee,
Paula Lowell, Nancy Price,
Julie Quinn, Laura Robbins,
Josette Starks, Michael Thomas,
Todd Wente, Colleen Williams

Indexers
Ginny Bess, Chris Cleveland

Contents

Part II Web Publishing with HTML

Part III Interactive Web Publishing

Part V   Multimedia and Beyond

Acknowledgments

Thanks to the team at Sams.net who put their hearts into their work and helped make this one of the best Web publishing books on the market. Beverly, Carolyn, Fran and everyone else at Sams.net are a delight to work for and with.

Special thanks to my wife and family, who've put up with the tappety-tap of my keyboard at all hours of the day and night. Without your support, *Web Publishing Unleashed* wouldn't have been possible.

Apologies to all the folks whose e-mail I didn't answer during the writing of *Web Publishing Unleashed*. I really meant to get back to all of you, honest. But sometimes, the dragon wins.

—William Robert Stanek

Thanks to Lauren and my family for their love and support.

—Gregory Stenstrom

About the Authors

William Robert Stanek, Author

William Robert Stanek (director@tvp.com) is the publisher and founder of The Virtual Press (http://tvp.com/ and mirror site http://www.tvpress.com/), a nontraditional press established in March 1994. As a publisher and writer with more than 10 years experience on networks, he brings a solid voice of experience on the Internet and electronic publishing to his many projects. He has been involved in the commercial Internet community since 1991 and was first introduced to Internet e-mail in 1988 when he worked for the government.

His years of practical experience as a network manager are backed by a solid education: a bachelor's degree in computer science and a master's degree in information systems. While his press publishes electronic books under four imprints, the core business is shifting and the time that isn't spent writing such hits as Sam's *Electronic Publishing Unleashed* is spent consulting with corporate clients and developing hot new Web sites.

William served in the Persian Gulf War as a combat crew member on an electronic warfare aircraft. During the war, he flew on numerous combat missions into Iraq and was awarded 9 medals for his wartime service including one of our nation's highest flying honors, the Air Force Distinguished Flying Cross. He has written many books, articles, and essays. His book-length projects include nine fiction titles and five nonfiction titles. When he's not writing or working, he spends time with his family, his favorite time of the day being when he reads to the youngest. **(Part I, "Getting Started and Planning," Part II, "Web Publishing with HTML," Part III, "Interactive Web Publishing," Chapter 25, "Designing and Publishing a Web Document," Chapter 26, "Designing and Publishing a Web Site," and Chapter 28, "The Future of Web Publishing." William also coauthored Chapters 15-18.)**

Contributing Authors

Steven J. DeRose (sjd@ebt.com) earned a doctorate in computational linguistics from Brown University in 1989 and served as director of the early FRESS hypertext system there. He has worked as a technical writer and design consultant for the CDWord hypertext system and a variety of other systems in computational linguistics, hypermedia, and related fields. Steven has published a variety of papers on markup systems, hypertext, natural language processing, artificial intelligence, and other topics, plus a book with David Durand entitled *Making Hypermedia Work: A User's Guide to HyTime*. He is now senior system architect at Electronic Book Technologies, whose DynaText product is the leading SGML-based software for delivering large-scale electronic books on CD-ROM, disk, LAN, and the Internet. He is very active in standards development, serving with groups including the ANSI and ISO SGML and HyTime groups, the Text Encoding Initiative, and several Internet and Web-related groups. He lives, works, and ice skates in Rhode Island with his wife, Laurie, and two-year-old son, Todd. **(Chapter 19, "Should You Upgrade to SGML?")**

Mary Jo Fahey (mjfahey@interport.net) wrote *Macintosh Visiref System 7.5 Edition* (Macmillan Computer Publishing) and *Web Publisher's Design Guide* (the Coriolis Group, Macintosh, and Windows editions). She is a contributor to *HOW Magazine*, a graphic design publication. Mary Jo is a hardware and software consultant who has taught computer graphics at Pratt Institute, graphic design firms, advertising agencies, and book publishers in New York City. **(Chapter 21, "Multimedia Presentation Tools," and Chapter 27, "Designing and Publishing a Multimedia Presentation")**

John J. Kottler (73157.335@compuserve.com, jkottler@aol.com, or jay_kottler@msn.com) has been programming for fourteen years and has spent the past six years developing applications for the Windows platform. In addition to Windows development, John has been programming multimedia applications for more than two years and has spent this past year developing for the Web. His knowledge includes C/C++, Visual Basic, Lotus Notes, PowerBuilder, messaging-enabled applications, multimedia and digital video production, and Internet Web page development. He has published numerous articles in a computer magazine, writing original programs and instructing developers on programming techniques. John has been recently published in Sams.net's *Netscape Unleashed* and Sams Publishing's *Programming Windows 95 Unleashed*. He was also a co-developer of the shareware application Virtual Monitors. A graduate of Rutgers University with a degree in computer science, he enjoys roller-blading, cycling, or playing digital music in his spare time. **(Chapter 24, "Writing Java Applets")**

Adrian Scott, Ph.D., (scotta@rpi.edu) is founder and CEO of Aereal Inc. (http://www.aereal.com), the first company to have a corporate VRML home world. He has helped Hewlett Packard with its marketing on the Internet and advised one of the U.S. presidential campaigns on Internet campaigning. He is a former visiting professor in the department of management at Hong Kong Polytechnic University and vice-president of marketing for a corporate accounting and finance software developer. He earned his doctorate in mathematics, with applications to DNA research, from Rensselaer Polytechnic Institute. **(Chapter 22, "Creating VRML Worlds," Chapter 23, "Using 3-D Modeling Tools to Create VRML Worlds," and Appendix E "VRML Resource Directory")**

Gregory Stenstrom (gstenstr@stentut.com) is a senior computer scientist at Computer Sciences Corporation. He specializes in the design, coding, and implementation of large, open architecture, client/server MIS systems, and integrated CALS technologies. **(Chapter 15, "Building and Managing a Web-Based Information System," Chapter 16, "Designing Web Documents Using Your Favorite Word Processor," Chapter 17, "Other Document Systems," Chapter 18, "Desktop Publishing," Chapter 20, "Image, Sound, and Video Formats," and Appendix C, "SGML")**

Richmond Tuttle (rtuttle@stentut.com) is a senior computer scientist at Computer Sciences Corporation. He specializes in the design, coding, and implementation of client/server enterprise document management systems, and integrated CALS technologies. **(Chapters 15-18 and Chapter 20)**

Sandra Tuttle (stuttle@stentut.com) is a consultant and technical writer. She designs, programs, and implements large hypertext and SGML-based online help systems for corporations and government agencies. **(Chapters 15-18 and Chapter 20)**

Introduction

Web Publishing Unleashed is probably the only Web publishing book you will ever need. This book covers every major Web publishing issue. It is designed to unleash the topic of Web publishing and help you become one of the thousands of successful Web publishers providing ideas, services, and products to millions of Web users. Not only can you reach these millions of consumers on the Web, you can do so in mind-blowing proportions and in ways that are limited only by your imagination.

Whether your Web publishing plans are large or small, you don't want to wait any longer to get into the action. By the end of 1998, more than 100 million people will have access to the global Internet and to the World Wide Web. What this means is that for a few dollars a month, you can reach a potential audience of millions. If you think this is hype, think again. The World Wide Web has caught the eye of the media, businesses, entrepreneurs, and governments. Media coverage of the Internet and related issues grows every day. Thousands of articles related to the Internet are published every month in books, magazines, newspapers, and newsletters. You will find discussions about the Internet and the Web on TV shows, radio, and the news. You will also find addresses to Web pages in all forms of advertising, from magazine ads to television commercials.

As you read this book, you will learn about the things the Web has to offer. I have taken great care to provide invaluable tips and pour my expertise into every page of *Web Publishing Unleashed*. Today's Web publishers have powerful resources at their fingertips and this book will show you how to use every one of them. Here are the major topics covered in this book:

- Issues to consider before you start Web publishing
- Plotting your course to success
- Creating Web documents with HTML
- In-depth coverage of the up-and-coming HTML 3.0 specifications
- Adding sound, video, and graphics to your Web documents
- Creating Web publications for the hottest browsers, including Netscape and Internet Explorer
- Designing documents with hot features such as tables and frames
- Writing CGI scripts
- Designing interactive documents with forms and image maps
- Using search engines and building indexed databases
- Creating live documents with client pull/server push
- Building and managing Web-based information systems
- Using your favorite word processor to create Web documents
- Upgrading to SGML
- VRML and creating VRML worlds
- 3-D modeling

- Java and writing Java applets
- Building a perfect Web site

How This Book Is Organized

This book is designed to be the most comprehensive Web publishing resource available anywhere. Chapter by chapter, you will learn everything you need to know to create, design, and publish dazzling Web publications.

Part I, "Getting Started and Planning," covers everything you need to know to get started as a Web publisher. Chapter 1 explores the issues you should consider before publishing on the Web. Coverage of these issues is intended to save you time, money, and resources. Chapter 2 answers the questions about why you should publish on the Web, what you can publish on the Web, and who is already publishing on the Web. Then, the book takes you on a tour through all that is wonderful, wild, bizarre, and truly amazing on the Web. The final chapter of Part I helps you plot your course to success in Web publishing. Not only will you learn about HTML, SGML, VRML, Java, and Netscape and Internet Explorer extensions to HTML, you will also learn how, when, and why to use these powerful Web publishing resources.

Part II, "Web Publishing with HTML," explores every facet of the HyperText Markup Language and includes extensive coverage of the hottest and latest issues. Chapter 5 is a power primer for creating Web documents with HTML 2.0. You will find useful tips, expert advice, and a strong emphasis on sound design. Chapter 6 is a comprehensive guide to HTML 3.0 with a focus on its features and enhancements to the HTML standard. The chapter also covers how to transition to HTML 3.0 from HTML 2.0. Chapter 7 covers the specifics of adding multimedia (pictures, sound, and video) to Web publications written in HTML 2.0 and HTML 3.0. The chapter tells you when, how, and why to use pictures, sound, and video. Chapter 8 tells you how to use key Netscape and Internet Explorer extensions, including backgrounds, font enhancements, inline motion video, sound tracks, and Netscape plug-ins. Chapter 9 explores two of the hottest elements in Web publishing: tables and frames. Not only do leading browsers, such as Netscape and Internet Explorer, support tables and frames, but these elements are also a part of the new HTML specification.

Interactivity is the main attraction on the Web, and Part III, "Interactive Web Publishing," provides you with everything you need to know to create truly interactive publications. Chapter 10 is designed to help you put together the ultimate Web publishing toolkit. Chapter 11 provides a top-notch introduction to CGI scripts that won't leave you confused and wondering how it all works. Chapter 12 tells you in a very straightforward way how to use forms and image maps, and more importantly, how to design good forms and image maps. The chapter also discusses HTML 3.0 enhancements and hot extensions for forms and image maps. Chapter 13 shows you firsthand how to use the hypertext facilities of the Web to put the world's most powerful search engines at your fingertips. The chapter also provides in-depth coverage on how to build an indexed database. Finally, Chapter 14 is for anyone who wants to create fully animated documents fast, with powerful and simple techniques you can use immediately.

Part IV, "Web Publishing Production Systems," explores topics that will help you access and use Web technologies in new and innovative ways. Chapter 15 tells you how to create a corporate intranet that uses Web technology to build a Web-based information system. If using your favorite word processor to create Web publications is appealing, you won't want to miss the next chapter. In Chapter 16, you'll find out how to use your favorite applications, such as Word, WordPerfect, InterLeaf, FrameMaker, and TeX, to create perfect HTML publications. Chapter 17 discusses other document systems that will ease the transition to Web publishing. Featured applications include Common Ground, FrameMaker, Adobe Acrobat, and Adobe Amber. Chapter 18 discusses how you can take the core experience you'll gain as a Web publisher and apply it to desktop publishing. Chapter 19 explores upgrading to SGML—one of the most powerful and versatile markup languages.

Part V, "Multimedia and Beyond," is a power tour of multimedia concepts related to Web publishing. Chapter 20 provides an in-depth discussion of image, sound, and video formats, and what is more important, tells you why and when you should use one format over another. Chapter 21 explores multimedia presentation tools and how you can use them to create more dynamic Web presentations. If you've dreamed of creating 3-D worlds, Chapters 22 and 23 are for you. Chapter 22 discusses the Virtual Reality Modeling Language (VRML) and how you can use it. Chapter 23 discusses 3-D modeling tools and how to use them to create images in 3-D. The final chapter in Part V is the starting point for the fast track to Java and writing Java applets.

Practical application of this book's many topics is the subject of Part VI, "Putting It All Together." Every success story has a beginning, and in Web publishing the first step is creating a Web page. Chapter 25 covers everything you need to know to build a terrific Web page—publishing strategies, page structure, creating the page, adding features, proofing the page, testing the page, and publishing the page. Creating and publishing your first Web page is only a starting point—the next chapter tells you how to build a cool Web site. But Chapter 26 doesn't stop there, it goes on to tell you how to publicize your Web site as well. The final chapter in Part VI tells you how to build a multimedia presentation that will dazzle the masses.

Fittingly, Part VII, "Looking Ahead," discusses things to come. Chapter 28 provides a hint of what you can expect to see as the Web comes of age. Some of the innovations coming to the Web you will truly have to see in print to believe.

The final section of the book puts the reference resources you need into your hands. Appendix A, "An HTML Reference," is an invaluable at-a-glance resource for HTML. Appendix B, "Netscape and Internet Explorer Extensions," finally puts all those tough-to-track-down Netscape and Internet Explorer extensions to HTML in an easy-to-use reference resource. Appendix C, "SGML," is a companion resource to Chapter 19, "Should You Upgrade to SGML?" We anticipated that you might want to upgrade to SGML and put everything you need to get started right here in this appendix. Appendix D, "Sources for Additional Information," is a collection of URLs for all kinds of information. Appendix E, "VRML Resource Directory," is a resource for anyone wanting to create VRML worlds.

Who Should Read this Book?

Web Publishing Unleashed is for anyone who wants to publish on the Web or has considered publishing on the Web. Although this book is intended for those with a casual to accomplished knowledge of the Internet or the World Wide Web, the plain English approach makes this book perfect for just about anyone. I truly hope you find this book to be invaluable as you plot your course to success in Web publishing.

Getting Started and Planning

PART

I

Before You Start: Issues to Consider

1

by William Robert Stanek

The World Wide Web is rapidly evolving into a medium that rivals television for information content and entertainment value. Millions of people and thousands of businesses around the world are racing to get connected to the global Internet and the World Wide Web because the Web is the most powerful and least expensive medium you have ever published in. Whether you are an information provider or simply a creative person who wants to publish your own work, you will find there is no other medium that empowers the individual like the World Wide Web does. The Web levels the playing field, allowing a one-person operation to compete head-to-head with corporate conglomerates that employ thousands of people.

To publish successfully on the Web, you do not have to be a computer guru with insider secrets, a programmer, or a genius. What you need are the practical advice, tips, and techniques you will find throughout this book. Many books on Internet and Web publishing discuss theories, cover key subjects, and show basic examples, but rarely follow a practical approach to Web publishing. Books without practical examples and genuinely useful information can leave you wondering where to start, how to start, and what to do when you do finally manage to start. This chapter, like all the chapters in the book, is filled with useful information designed to unleash the topic of Web publishing and help you become one of the thousands of successful Web publishers providing ideas, services, and products to millions of Web users.

This chapter provides an overview of some basic information you need to know and decisions you need to make before you start publishing on the Web.

Overview of Web Publishing's Past

The World Wide Web is an open-ended information system designed specifically with ease of use and ease of document interchange in mind. In early 1989, Tim Berners-Lee of the European Laboratory for Particle Physics (CERN) proposed the Web as a way for scientists around the world to collaborate using a global information system based on hypertext. Work on the World Wide Web project proceeded slowly but amazingly, and near the end of 1990 the pieces started to fall into place.

In the fall of 1990, the first text-only browsers were implemented and CERN scientists could access hypertext files and other information at CERN. However, the structure of hypertext documents and the way they would be transferred to remote sites still had to be further defined. Based on proposals by Tim Berners-Lee, the structure of hypertext documents was defined by a new language called the HyperText Markup Language (HTML). HTML was based on a subset of the Standard Generalized Markup Language (SGML) that was already in wide use at the time. To transfer HTML documents to remote sites, a new protocol was devised. This protocol is called the HyperText Transfer Protocol (HTTP).

HTTP offers a means of moving from document to document and indexing within documents. The power of hypertext is in its simplicity and transparency. Users can navigate through a global network of resources at the touch of a button. Hypertext documents are linked together through keywords or specified hot areas within the document. These hot areas could be graphical icons or even parts of indexed maps. When a new word or idea is introduced, hypertext makes it possible to jump to another document containing complete information on the new topic. Readers see links as highlighted keywords or images displayed graphically. They can access additional documents or resources by selecting the highlighted keywords or images.

In the fall of 1991, conference-goers around the world started hearing about the promise and ease of hypertext. A few people started talking about hypertext and its potential, but sparks still weren't flying. In early 1993 there were only about 50 Web sites worldwide. Then a wonderful thing happened. A browser enabling users to exploit the graphical capabilities of the Web was developed at the National Center for Supercomputing Applications (NCSA). NCSA called the browser Mosaic. For a time, it seemed the Web and Mosaic were synonymous. Interest in the Web began to grow, at first a trickle of interest, then a great flood of enthusiasm. Looking back, it seems the Web sprang to life overnight. Today, the Web is the hottest and fastest growing area of the Internet and Mosaic is only one of the dozens of available browsers.

While you undoubtedly have used a browser before, you may not have thought about the processes that make a browser work the way it does. The purpose of a browser is to request and display information. Another term for a browser is a client. Clients make requests to servers. Servers process requests made by clients based on a set of rules for communicating on the network called a protocol. Protocols specify how the programs talk to each other and what meaning to give to the data they receive. Many protocols are in use on the Internet and the Web makes use of them all. However, the primary protocol in use on the Web is HTTP.

Generally, HTTP processes are transparent to users. To initiate a request for information from a server, all the user has to do is activate a hypertext reference. The user's browser takes care of interpreting the hypertext transfer commands and communicating requests. The mechanism on the receiving end, which is processing the requests, is a program called the Hypertext Transfer Protocol Daemon (HTTPD). A *daemon* is a UNIX term for a program that processes requests. If you have used a UNIX system, you have probably unknowingly sent requests to the Line-Printer Daemon (LPD) to print material to a printer using the commands lp or lpr. The HTTP daemon resides on the Web server, which is at the heart of your connection to the Web.

Using the hypertext facilities of the Web, you have the freedom to provide information to readers in powerfully innovative ways. The entrepreneurs who fostered the growth of the Web started by creating small publications that used few of the Web's graphical and multimedia capabilities. This changed dramatically in a few short years, and today's Web publications use many of the graphical, interactive, and multimedia features of the Web. New ways to publish on the Web are constantly being defined, and the features that tomorrow's publications will have may amaze you.

A recent development in HTML publishing is the specification for HTML 3.0. Using HTML 3.0, Web publishers finally have advanced control over the layout of their documents using the simple and easy-to-use facilities of the hypertext markup language. HTML 3.0 supports tables, mathematical equations, banners, and much more. (See Chapter 6, "Designing with HTML 3.0," for the complete inside scoop on HTML 3.0.)

Yet, the Web is not defined by the HyperText Markup Language alone. Many Web publishers are going back to the standard language that HTML is based upon. SGML is an advanced markup language that, although complex, offers better control over the layout of documents than HTML. SGML is also the basis for many page definition languages used by publishing production systems such as Adobe Acrobat and CorelVENTURA. (For more information on SGML, see Chapter 19, "Should You Upgrade to SGML?")

While some Web publishers are looking at the origins of Web publishing, others are taking giant leaps forward. These giant leaps forward are possible in part due to innovators such as Netscape Communications Corporation, Microsoft Corporation, and Sun Microsystems Incorporated. In the fall of 1994, Netscape Corporation released the first browser to support unique extensions to HTML. The Netscape Navigator took the Internet community by storm and quickly became the most popular browser on the Net. Netscape Navigator 2.0 and Netscape Navigator Gold 2.0 are featured in Figure 1.1.

FIGURE 1.1.

The Netscape Navigator: a hot Web browser.

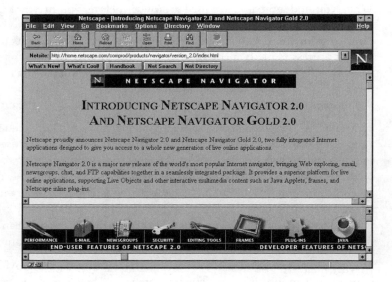

The browser that may replace top-dog Netscape Navigator is Microsoft's Internet Explorer. Microsoft's Web site is featured in Figure 1.2 and as you can imagine, the site showcases the Internet Explorer. Internet Explorer features extensions that enable Web publishers to add soundtracks and live video segments to their Web publications. When a reader accesses a publication with a soundtrack or a live video segment, the sound or video plays automatically if the reader's browser supports these extensions. (See Chapter 8, "Netscape and Internet Explorer Extensions," for more information on using Netscape and Internet Explorer extensions.)

FIGURE 1.2.

Microsoft's Web site featuring the Internet Explorer.

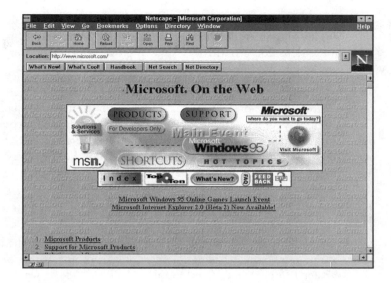

Sun Microsystems Incorporated has been a leading supporter of Web innovation. Recently, Sun Microsystems released the HotJava browser, which is written entirely in the Java programming language developed by Sun. The Java language is similar to C and C++, but is unique in that it is platform-independent. Using Java, you can add programs called applets to your Web publications. Applets are self-running applications that readers of your Web publications can preview and play automatically. Sun has set up several Web servers to handle requests related to Java. One of those servers is featured in Figure 1.3. (See Chapter 24, "Writing Java Applets," for more information on creating and using applets.)

FIGURE 1.3.

Sun's Web site featuring Java.

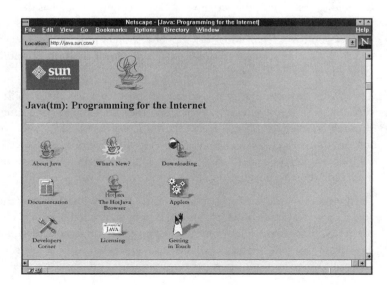

Innovations by Netscape, Sun, and Microsoft represent only a small part of the changes that are revolutionizing the way information is provided to millions of people around the world. These innovations, coupled with the explosive growth and enthusiasm in the World Wide Web, make now a more exciting time than ever to be a Web publisher.

As a Web publisher, you can publish information that will be seen by people in dozens of countries around the world, but the best news is that you as an individual can compete solely on the merits of your ideas, products, and services—not the size of your bank account. In Web publishing, you can reach the same audience using a $25 basic account as you can with your own Web server and leased lines costing $5,000 a month. Web users will judge your publications based on their information content and entertainment value.

Internet Standards and Specifications

Many standards are in place on the Web to enable information to be transferred the way it is. Many of these standards relate to specifications for protocols that predate the Web, such as File Transfer Protocol (FTP) and Gopher. FTP provides a way to access files on remote systems. Using FTP, you can log onto a FTP server, search for a file within a directory structure, and download the file. FTP also enables you to upload files to the FTP server. Searching the file structures on FTP servers is time-consuming, especially if you do not know the directory of the file you are looking for. The basic functions of FTP have been extended in various ways. The most popular extension is Archie. Using Archie, you can search file archives easily using keywords.

The Gopher protocol is similar to HTTP, but not as powerful or versatile. Using Gopher, you can search and retrieve information that is presented as a series of menus. Menu items are linked to the files containing the actual text. Gopher is most useful as the basis protocol for its more powerful and recent extensions, including Gopher Jewels, Jughead, and Veronica. Gopher Jewels enables you to search catalogs of Gopher resources indexed by category. Jughead enables you to search Gopher indexes according to specified information. Veronica enables you to search Gopher menus by keyword.

The major shortcoming of early Internet protocols was the inability to access information through a common interface. Generally, files available via one interface were not available through another interface. To access information on a FTP server, you used FTP. To access information on a Gopher server, you used Gopher. For files that weren't available through either FTP or Gopher, you could try to initiate a remote login to a host using telnet. Sometimes you went from host to host looking for the information you needed.

Even with this simplified scenario, you can probably imagine how time-consuming and frustrating it was to track down the information you needed. Consequently, a major design issue for the Web was to provide a common easy-to-use interface to access information on the Internet. To ensure that information available through previous protocols is accessible on the Web as well, the Web was built upon existing standards and specifications like those related to FTP and Gopher. You will find that using these other protocols in your Web documents is easy. You simply specify the protocol in a reference to a Uniform Resource Locator (URL). URLs provide a uniform way to access and retrieve files. Without a single way to retrieve files, Internet publishers and users would still be pulling their hair out.

While the specification for URLs is an extremely important specification for finding files on the Web, many other specifications play a major role in defining the World Wide Web. Specifications for the hypertext transfer protocol define how hypertext documents are transferred. Specifications for markup languages define the structure of Web documents. Specifications for multipurpose Internet mail extensions define the type of data being trans-ferred and enable you to transfer any type of data on the Web. Finally, specifications for the Common Gateway Interface (CGI) make it possible for you to create dynamic documents. The following sections look briefly at each of these specifications with emphasis on how they affect you as the Web publisher.

Transferring Files Using HTTP

The HyperText Transfer Protocol is the primary protocol used to distribute information on the Web. HTTP is a powerful and fast protocol that allows for easy exchange of files. HTTP is evolving along with other Web technologies. The original specification for HTTP is HTTP/ 0.9. HTTP Version 0.9 has many shortcomings. Two major shortcomings are that it does not allow for content typing and does not have provisions for providing meta-information in requests and responses.

Content typing enables the computer receiving the data to identify the type of data being transferred. The computer can then use this information to display or process the data. Meta-information is supplemental data, such as environment variables that identify the client's computer. Being able to provide information about the type of data transferred as well as supple-mental information about the data is extremely important.

To address the shortcomings of HTTP/0.9, the current version of HTTP, HTTP/1.0, allows for headers with a Content-Type field and other types of meta-information. The type of data being transferred is defined in the Content-Type field. You can also use meta-information to provide additional information about the data, such as the language, encoding of the data, and state information. (See Chapter 5, "Creating Web Documents with HTML," for a preliminary discussion on using meta-information in HTML documents.)

An issue that most Web users and publishers want HTTP to address is security. Web publishers and users want to be able to conduct secure transactions. The key issue in security that needs to be addressed to promote the widespread use of electronic commerce is the ability to authenticate and encrypt transactions. Currently, there are several proposals for secure versions of HTTP. When one of these specifications is embraced, secure transaction using HTTP will become a reality for mainstream Web users.

HTTP is a powerful protocol because it is fast and light, yet extremely versatile. To achieve this speed, versatility, and robustness, HTTP is defined as a connectionless and stateless protocol. What this means is that generally, the client and server do not maintain a connection or state information related to the connection.

Connectionless Versus Connection-Oriented Protocols

HTTP is a connectionless protocol. Connectionless protocols differ from connection-oriented protocols in the way requests and responses to requests are handled. With a connectionless protocol, clients connect to the server, make a request, get a response, then disconnect. With a connection-oriented protocol, clients connect to the server, make a request, get a response, then maintain the connection to service future requests.

An example of a connection-oriented protocol is FTP. When you connect to an FTP server, the connection remains open after you download a file. The maintenance of this connection requires system resources. A server with too many open connections quickly gets bogged down. Consequently, many FTP servers are configured to allow only 250 open connections at one time. What this means is that only 250 users can access the FTP server at once. Additionally, processes that are not disconnected cleanly can cause problems on the server. The worst of these processes run out of control, use system resources, and eventually crash the server. The best of these processes simply eat up system resources.

In contrast, HTTP is a connectionless protocol. When clients connect to the server, they make a request, get a response, then disconnect. Because a connection is not maintained, no system resources are used after the transaction is completed. Consequently, HTTP servers are only limited by active connections and can generally service thousands of transactions with low system overhead. The drawback to connectionless protocols is that when the same client requests additional data, the connection must be reestablished. To Web users, this means a delay whenever additional data is requested.

Stateless Versus Stateful Protocols

HTTP is a stateless protocol. Stateless protocols differ from stateful protocols in the way information about requests is maintained. With a stateless protocol, no information about a transaction is maintained after a transaction has been processed. With a stateful protocol, state information is maintained after a transaction has been processed.

Servers using stateful protocols maintain information about transactions and processes, such as the status of the connection, the processes running, the status of the processes running, and so on. Generally, this state information is resident in memory and uses up system resources. When a client breaks a connection with a server running a stateful protocol, the state information has to be cleaned up and is often logged as well.

Stateless protocols are light. Servers using stateless protocols maintain no information about completed transactions and processes. When a client breaks a connection with a server running a stateless protocol, there is no data that has to be cleaned up or logged. By not tracking state information, there is less overhead on the server and the server can generally handle transactions swiftly. The drawback for Web publishers is that if you need to maintain state information for your Web documents, you must include this as meta-information in the document header.

Determining the Structure of Web Documents

The way you can structure documents is largely determined by the language you use to layout the document. Some languages are advanced and offer you rich control over document layout. Other languages are basic and offer ease of use and friendliness instead of advanced features. The following sections take a look at commonly used languages, including

- Standard Generalized Markup Language (SGML)
- Virtual Reality Modeling Language (VRML)
- HyperText Markup Language (HTML)
- Page definition

SGML

Most Web documents are structured using a markup language that is based on the Standard Generalized Markup Language (SGML). SGML defines a way to share complex documents using a generalized markup that is described in terms of standard text. Describing complex structures in terms of plain text ensures the widest distribution to any type of computer and presents the formatting in a human-readable form called markup. Because the markup contains standard characters, this also means anyone can create documents in a markup language without needing special software.

SGML is an advanced language with few limitations. In SGML, you have full control over the positioning of text and images. This means text and images will be displayed by the user's SGML browser in the precise location you designate. Although SGML is a powerful markup language, it is not widely used on the Web. However, this is changing as more publishers become aware of the versatility of SGML. Two of the most common markup languages that SGML forms the basis for are the Virtual Reality Modeling Language (VRML) and the HyperText Markup Language (HTML).

VRML

Technology on the Web is growing at an explosive pace and one of the most recent developments is VRML. VRML enables you to render complex models and multidimensional documents using a standardized markup language. The implications of virtual reality for Web publishers are far reaching.

Using VRML, you can reduce calculations and data points that would have filled 10MB of disk space to a few hundred lines of markup code. Not only does this drastically reduce the download time for VRML files and save network bandwidth, it also presents complex models in a readable and—gasp—understandable format. While VRML is not yet widely used on the Web, it is attracting tremendous interest within the Internet community and within the world community as well. The current version of VRML is VRML 1.0.

HTML

HTML is the most commonly used markup language. HTML's popularity stems in large part from its ease of use and friendliness. With HTML, you can quickly and easily create Web documents and make them available to a wide audience. HTML enables you to control many of the layout aspects for text and images. You can specify the relative size of headings and text as well as text styles, including bold, underline, and italics. There are extensions to HTML that enable you to specify font type, but standard HTML specifications do not give you that capability.

Although many advanced layout controls for documents are not available using HTML, HTML is still the publishing language of choice on the vast majority of Web sites. Remember, the limitations are a way to drastically reduce the complexity of HTML. Currently, three specifications are associated with HTML: HTML 1.0, HTML 2.0, and HTML 3.0. Each level of the specification steadily introduces more versatility and functionality.

In addition to these specifications, several Internet developers have created extensions to HTML. While the extensions are nonstandard, many extensions have been embraced by Web publishers. Some extensions, like Netscape's, are so popular that they seem to be standard HTML.

Page Definition Languages

Some Web documents are formatted using page definition languages instead of markup languages. Page definition languages often use formats that are specific to a particular commercial page layout application, such as Adobe Acrobat or CorelVENTURA. Page layout applications are popular because they combine rich control over document layout with user-friendly graphical interfaces. While the formats these applications use are proprietary, most of the formats are based on the standards set forth by SGML.

Identifying Data Types with MIME

Using HTTP, you can transfer full-motion video sequences, stereo sound tracks, high-resolution images, and any other type of media you can think of. The standard that makes this possible is Multipurpose Internet Mail Extensions (MIME). HTTP uses MIME to identify the type of object being transferred across the Internet. Object types are identified in a header field that comes before the actual data for the object. Under HTTP, this header field is the Content-Type header field. By identifying the type of object in a header field, the client receiving the object can appropriately handle the object.

For example, if the object is a GIF image, the image will be identified by the MIME type image/gif. When the client receiving the object of type image/gif can handle the object type directly, it will display the object. When the client receiving the object of type image/gif cannot handle the object directly, it will check a configuration table to see if an application is configured to handle an object of this MIME type. If an application is configured for use with the client and available, the client will call the application. The application called will then handle the object. Here, the application would display the GIF image.

Not only is MIME typing extremely useful to HTTP, it is useful to other protocols as well. MIME typing was originally developed to allow e-mail messages to have multiple parts with different types of data in each part. In this way, you can attach any type of file to an e-mail message. The MIME standard is described in detail in RFCs 1521 and 1522. (See Chapter 11, "Writing CGI Scripts," for a complete listing of MIME types and their uses in your Web documents.)

NOTE

Many Internet standards and specifications are described in Requests For Comments (RFCs). RFCs are a collection of documents pertaining to the Internet that cover everything from technical issues to nontechnical issues.

Accessing and Retrieving Files Using URLs

To retrieve a file from a server, a client must know three things. The client must know the address of the server, where on the server the file is located, and which protocol to use to access and retrieve the file. This information is specified as a Uniform Resource Locator, commonly called a URL. URLs can be used to find and retrieve files on the Internet using any valid protocol.

Although you normally use the hypertext transfer protocol to transfer your Web documents, you can include references to other protocols in your documents. For example, you can specify the address to a file available via FTP simply by naming the protocol in a URL. Most URLs you will use in your documents look something like this:

```
protocol://server_host:port/path_to_resource
```

The first part of the URL scheme names the protocol the client will use to access and transfer the file. The protocol name is generally followed by a colon and two forward slashes. The second part of the URL indicates the address of the server and terminates with a single slash. The server host may be followed by a colon and a port address. The third part of the URL indicates where on the server the resource is located and may include a path structure. In a URL, double slash marks indicate that the protocol uses the format defined by the Common Internet Scheme Syntax. Colons are separators. In this example, a colon separates the protocol from the rest of the URL scheme; the second colon separates the host address from the port number.

> **NOTE**
>
> The Common Internet Scheme Syntax is a common syntax for URL schemes that involves the direct use of Internet Protocol-based protocols. IP-based protocols specify a particular host on the Internet by a unique numeric identifier called an IP address or by a unique name that can be resolved to the IP address. Non-CISS URL schemes do not name a particular host computer. Therefore, the host is implied to be the computer providing services for the client. (See Chapter 3, "Publishers' Tour of the Web," for detailed information on URL schemes.)

Here's a URL using HTTP to retrieve a file called `index.html` on the Macmillan Computer Publishing Web server:

```
http://www.mcp.com/index.html
```

URLs, which are defined in RFC 1738, are powerful because they provide a uniform way to retrieve multiple types of data. The most common protocols you can specify using URLs are

FTP	File Transfer Protocol
Gopher	Gopher Protocol
HTTP	Hypertext Transfer Protocol
mailto	Electronic mail address
Prospero	Prospero Directory Service
news	Usenet news
NNTP	Usenet news accessed with Network News Transfer Protocol
telnet	Remote login sessions
WAIS	Wide Area Information Servers
file	Files on local host

Using these protocols in your Web documents is explored in Chapter 5, "Creating Web Documents with HTML."

Creating Dynamic Documents with CGI

The popularity of the Web stems in large part from interactivity. Web users click on hypertext links to access Web documents, images, and multimedia files. Yet the URLs in your hypertext links can lead to much more than static resources. URLs can also specify programs that process user input and return information to the user's browser. By specifying programs on the Web server, you can make your Web publications highly interactive and extremely dynamic. You can create customized documents on demand based on the user's input and on the type of browser being used.

Programs specified in URLs are called gateway scripts. The term gateway script comes from UNIX environments. Gateways are programs or devices that provide an interface. Here, the gateway or interface is between your browser and the server. Programs written in UNIX shell are called scripts by UNIX programmers. This is because UNIX shells, such as Bourne, Korn, and C-shell, aren't actual programming languages. Because UNIX shells are easy to use and learn, most gateway scripts are written in UNIX shells.

The specification that describes how gateway scripts pass information to servers is called the Common Gateway Interface (CGI). CGI provides the basis for creating dynamic documents, which can include interactive forms, graphical menus called image maps, and much more. The power of CGI is that it provides Web publishers with a common interface to programs on Web servers. Using this common interface, Web publishers can provide dynamic documents to Web users without regard to the type of system the publisher and user are using.

The Evolution of Standards and Specifications

The standards and specifications you read about in the previous section are the result of coordinated efforts by standards organizations and the working groups associated with these organizations. Generally, these organizations approve changes to existing standards and specifications and develop new standards and specifications. Three primary standards groups develop standards and specifications that pertain to the Internet and to networked computing in general. These groups are

- ISO—the International Organization for Standardization
- IETF—the Internet Engineering Task Force
- W3C—the World Wide Web Consortium

The International Organization for Standardization

The International Organization for Standardization is one of the most important standards-making bodies in the world. The ISO doesn't generally develop standards specifically for the Internet; rather, the organization develops standards for networked computing in general. One of the most important developments by the organization is the internationally recognized seven-layer network model. The seven-layer model is commonly referred to as the Open Systems Interconnection (OSI) Reference Model.

Most Internet specifications and protocols incorporate standards developed by the ISO. For example, ISO standard 8859 is used by all Web browsers to define the standard character set. ISO 8859-1 defines the standard character set called ISO-Latin-1. The ISO-Latin-1 character set has been added to and the addition is called the ISO-Added-Latin-1 character set. You will refer to these character sets whenever you want to add special characters—such as &, ©, or ®—to your Web documents.

The Internet Engineering Task Force

The Internet Engineering Task Force is the primary organization developing Internet standards. All changes to existing Internet standards and proposals for new standards are approved by the IETF. The IETF meets three times a year to set directions for the Internet.

Changes to existing specifications and proposals for new ones are approved by formal committees that meet to discuss and propose changes. These formal committees are called working groups. The IETF has dozens of working groups. Each group generally focuses on a specific topic within an area of development. Some areas of development include

- Applications
- Internet Protocol: Next generation
- Internet
- Network management
- Operational requirements
- Routing
- Security
- Transport
- User services

NOTE

The process for approving and making changes to specifications within the working groups is standardized. The working groups propose Internet Draft specifications. The specifications for HTML and HTTP are currently draft specifications. Internet Drafts are valid for six months after they are formalized. If the Internet Draft has not been approved in six months, the draft expires and is no longer valid. If the Internet Draft is approved, it becomes an RFC.

Requests For Comments are permanently archived and are valid until they are superseded by a later RFC. RFCs, as the name implies, are made available to the general Internet community for discussion and suggestions for improvements.

Many RFCs eventually become Internet Standards, but the process isn't a swift one. For example, URLs were introduced by the World Wide Web global information initiative in 1990. While URLs have been in use ever since, the URL specification did not become an RFC until December 1994 and was only recently approved as an Internet standard.

Figure 1.4 shows IETF's site on the Web. At the IETF, you can find information on current IETF initiatives, which include the latest standards and specifications pertaining to the Internet.

FIGURE 1.4.

The Internet Engineering Task Force Web site.

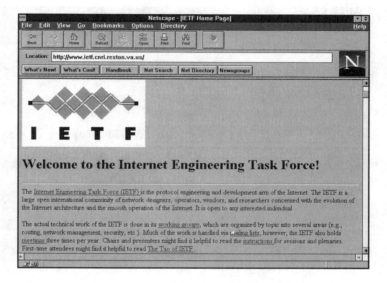

Membership in the IETF is open to anyone. The directors of the working group areas handle the internal management of the IETF. These directors, along with the Chair of the IETF, form the Internet Engineering Steering Group (IESG). The IESG, under the direction of the Internet Society, handles the operational management of the IETF.

You can find more information on the Internet Society and membership in the Internet Society at the Web site:

```
http://www.isoc.org/
```

The World Wide Web Consortium

The World Wide Web Consortium is managed by the Laboratory for Computer Science at the Massachusetts Institute of Technology. The W3 Consortium exists to develop common standards for the evolution of the World Wide Web. It is a joint initiative between MIT, CERN, and INRIA. The U.S. W3C center is based at and run by MIT. The European W3C center is at INRIA, the French National Institute for Research in Computing and Automation. CERN and INRIA cooperate to manage the European W3C center.

The W3C was formed in part to help develop common standards for the development of Web technologies. One of the W3C's major goals is to provide Web developers and users with a repository of information concerning the Web. Toward that end, the W3C has sites available where you can find the most current information related to Web development. At the W3C Web site shown in Figure 1.5, you can find the most recent drafts of specifications, including those for HTML 3.0 and HTTP 1.0.

FIGURE 1.5.

The World Wide Web Consortium Web site.

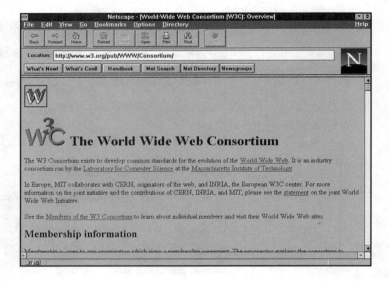

Another goal of the W3C is to provide prototype applications that use new technologies proposed in Internet Drafts. At the W3C Web site, you can find the Arena browser. Arena is fully compliant with HTML 3.0 and is intended to enable Web publishers to test the new features of HTML 3.0.

The W3C works with its member organizations to propose specifications and standards to the IETF. Member organizations pay a fee based on their membership status. Full members pay $50,000 and affiliate members pay $5,000 for a one-year membership. Current member organizations in the W3C include such major companies as AT&T, Adobe Systems Incorporated, America Online, Bellcore, CompuServe, Delphi Internet, Digital Equipment Corporation, Eastman Kodak Company, Electricité de France, Hewlett Packard, IBM, Lotus Development Corporation, MCI Telecommunications, Michelin, Microsoft Corporation, Mitsubishi Electric Corporation, NCSA, NEC Corporation, Netscape Communications Corporation, NeXT Computer Inc., Novell Inc., Open Software Foundation Research Institute, Oracle Corporation, O'Reilly & Associates, Inc., Prodigy Services Company, Silicon Graphics Inc., Softquad, Sony Corporation, Spry Inc., Spyglass Inc., and Sun Microsystems.

Evaluating Your Access Needs

Before you start publishing on the Web, you must evaluate your access needs so you can determine what type of account will meet your needs as a Web publisher and can obtain the level of access to the Web that is right for you. If you plan to provide Internet-related services or products specifically for Internet-smart consumers, you will want your own domain. A domain address is a unique address that only you will have. Web users can use programs, such as Whois, to obtain information about your domain.

> **NOTE**
>
> Whois is a basic protocol to find information on Internet users and domains. If you have an account with an Internet Service Provider with access to a UNIX shell, you can type whois at the shell prompt. For example, to find more information on my domain, tvp.com, you would type the following at the shell prompt:
>
> ```
> whois tvp.com
> ```

Having your own domain plays a key role in establishing a presence on the Web. Many users make specific judgments about you based on the address URL to your Web pages. Most people believe that you must set up a Web server to obtain your own domain. This is not true. Web publishers who want their own domain have several options to make this possible.

Most people do not need to set up their own Web server. If you plan to go through an Internet Service Provider and obtain an account with Web publishing privileges, you do not need to set up your own Web server. You will use your ISP's Web server to publish your Web documents. If you already have an account with an Internet service provider, you may already have all you need to publish on the Web.

Your access options are the following:

- Installing your own Web server
- Using an Internet Service Provider's Web Server with a standard account
- Using a commercial online service's Web server with a standard account
- Getting a phantom domain

Installing Your Own Web Server

Installing your own Web server is the most expensive option for Web publishing, yet with this expense comes significant advantages. With a dedicated connection, you can provide 24-hour Web services to users worldwide. You will have complete control over your Web server and can publish whatever you wish. You can configure the server to handle other services as well, such as FTP, gopher, telnet and CGI scripts. You will also have your own domain, which will establish a clear presence on the Web for you or your company. Your URL will look something like the following:

```
http://www.your_company.com/
```

Server Software and Platform Options

Web server software is available for almost every platform, including Amiga, Macintosh, Windows and UNIX systems. A few commercial options, such as the Netscape Commerce Server, are extremely expensive, but most server software is available free or for a nominal fee. Server software is widely available for downloading on the Internet. You can even get evaluation versions of commercial software that will allow you to try the server software free. Typically, these trial periods are for 90 days and afterward, if you want to continue using the commercial server software, you are obligated to pay a fee.

For an individual or small company wanting to set up a Web server, the best server software for you is most likely the software that will run on the computer system you are most familiar with. For a company with an installed computer network, you may want to use one of the computers already available as your Web server, but before you install the Web server you will want to carefully consider security options such as a firewall to shield your internal network from illegal activities.

If you do not have a computer capable of providing Web services, you will need to purchase one at a cost of $3,000 to $25,000 or lease one at a cost of $75 to $500 per month. Before buying or leasing a computer, you must determine what platform the Web server runs on. Again, the best server software for you is most likely the software that runs on a platform familiar to you or your support staff. However, before you make any decision, examine carefully how and for what purpose the company plans to use the Web server.

Commercial options are usually the easiest to install, support, and maintain; however, the primary reason for using commercial Web server software is support. If you believe you will need outside software support to keep the server alive, commercial software is the best choice.

Most shareware servers run on UNIX systems. UNIX servers are typically the best maintained and supported. As a result, UNIX servers are some of the most reliable and secure servers available. If you have a strong need for reliability and security, you should look at UNIX Web server software. However, you may need an experienced team to compile the source code and to configure the server parameters.

Internet Connection Options

You will also need to obtain an Internet connection. Generally, you will obtain an Internet connection for a fee from an Internet Service Provider or a commercial online service. The speed of the connection will drive the monthly fees. To determine the best connection speed for you, you will need to estimate the volume of traffic for the site. A good way to estimate traffic is to visit a site similar in content and structure to your intended site. As most popular sites provide some historical information on the usage of the site, you can use the data to make a better estimate of traffic for your site.

A Web site with an anticipated high-volume of traffic, such as daily network traffic over 50MB or approximately 10,000 hits per day, will want to consider using a high-speed T1 connection to the Internet. Leasing a T1 line will cost you $2,500 to $5,000 per month, plus an installation fee of $2500 to $5,000.

Most Web sites do not need a T1 connection to the Internet. In fact, the average site needs only a 56-Kbps line. A 56-Kbps connection can adequately handle daily network traffic over 10MB or approximately 2,000 hits per day, and the really good news is that the cost of a 56-Kbps connection to the Internet is only $300 to $500 per month, plus a startup fee of up to $500.

The Basics of Installing a Server

You may be amazed at how easy it is to install server software, especially if you plan to use a commercial server. Commercial server software is nearly trouble-free and includes automatic installation processes. Some commercial servers, such as Webstar for the Macintosh, even claim you can install the server in five minutes.

Freeware server software is not a bad choice either. You can find precompiled versions of most freeware server software. The availability of a precompiled version optimized for your platform makes installation very easy and drastically reduces the level of technical expertise required to install the server.

If you have selected a platform for your server, you can visit the sites listed in Table 1.1 to download free or trial versions of the software. At the sites, you will also find comprehensive information for installing the server software. Usually, you will also find guides that help you with special configuration parameters and troubleshooting problems you may encounter during installation.

Table 1.1. Places to obtain server software on the Web.

Platform	*Server Software*	*Web Site to Obtain Software*
Amiga	AWS	http://www.phone.net/aws/
Macintosh	WebStar	http://www.starnine.com/
UNIX	W3C HTTPD	http://www.w3.org/pub/WWW/Daemon/
	NCSA HTTPD	http://hoohoo.ncsa.uiuc.edu/docs/ Overview.html
	Netscape Servers	http://home.netscape.com/comprod ➥/server_central/index.html

continues

Table 1.1. continued

Platform	Server Software	Web Site to Obtain Software
	WN	http://hopf.math.nwu.edu/docs/overview.html
Windows	Windows HTTPD	http://www.city.net/win-httpd/
Windows 95	WebSite	http://website.ora.com/
	Purveyor	http://www.process.com/
Windows NT	EMWAC HTTPS	http://emwac.ed.ac.uk/html/ internet_toolchest ➥/https/contents.htm
	Netscape Servers	http://home.netscape.com/comprod ➥/server_central/index.html
	Purveyor	http://www.process.com/

NOTE

Table 1.1 has code continuation characters. You will find code continuation characters used throughout this book to signify that a single line of code was split into two lines so it would fit on the page. When you use an URL referenced in Table 1.1, be sure to enter the URL all on one line, such as

```
http://emwac.ed.ac.uk/html/internet_toolchest/https/contents.htm
```

Using an Internet Service Provider's Web Server with a Standard Account

Obtaining an Internet account with Web publishing privileges is an inexpensive option. Typical costs for such an account are $20 to $50 per month, plus a start-up fee of up to $50. The account should include at least 2 to 3 MB of storage space on the service provider's computer. Most ISPs offer unlimited access time to the Internet, meaning whether you log on for 40 or 400 hours a month, you will generally pay the same monthly fee. While your e-mail, standard files, and Web-published files will use this space, 2 to 3 MB is usually adequate to maintain a modest-sized site. If you currently have an account with an ISP that allows SLIP or PPP access to the Web, you may already have Web publishing privileges!

Your account with an ISP is available on a dial-up basis. A dial-up connection requires a computer, which may or may not be dedicated to networking, with communications software and a modem. The good news about a dial-up connection is that it uses a regular phone line with speeds ranging from 9.6 Kbps to 28.8 Kbps. Your computer is used to establish a connection over the modem and phone line for a temporary period and at the end of use, the connection to the Internet is broken. You will use the connection to browse the Web, navigate around the Net, or to check on your site published on the ISP's Web server.

Before you set up an account, check with your ISP for specifics on storage space; additional fees for storage space that should not be more than $2 per MB, and possible additional fees if you have a popular site. You will also want to check on the availability of additional services such as FTP, gopher, telnet, and CGI scripts, which should be available for use free if they are available at all.

While an account with an ISP is an inexpensive option, it is also a very basic option. You do not have control over the Web server. You will be at the mercy of the ISP for additional services, including CGI scripts. You will not have your own domain and people will know this immediately because your URL will look something like this:

```
http://www.your_service_provider.com/~you
```

Using a Commercial Online Service's Web Server with a Standard Account

America Online, CompuServe, Genie, and Prodigy all offer or plan to offer Web publishing privileges to their customer's. Publishing on the Web through a commercial online service is your least expensive alternative if you use your account wisely. Typical costs for such an account are $10 to $20 per month, plus a small additional fee for maintaining your Web pages on the online service's Web server. Most commercial online services provide only a few hours of connection time free each month. After you use your free connection time allotted each month, you will have to pay additional connection charges. If you currently have an account with a commercial online service, you may already be able to publish on the Web!

Your account with a commercial online service is available on a dial-up basis. You will use the connection to browse the Web, navigate around the Net, or to check on your site published on the online service's Web server. Before you set up an account, check with the commercial online service for specifics on storage space and possible additional fees if you have a popular site.

While an account with a commercial online service is the least expensive option, it is also the most basic option. Many online services are fairly new to Web publishing themselves and do not offer the access to essential additional services. While this, of course, will change in time and probably quickly, you should ask your online service about additional services, such as FTP, gopher, and CGI, and find out when they will be available. You will not have your own domain and people will know this immediately because your URL will look something like this:

```
http://www.commercial_online_service.com/~you
```

TIP

If you are interested in Web publishing with a Commercial Online Service, visit these
Web sites, where you will find current rates and publishing options:

America Online	`http://www.aol.com/`
CompuServe	`http://www.compuserve.com/`
Genie	`http://www.genie.com/`
Prodigy	`http://www.prodigy.com/`

Getting a Phantom Domain

Getting a phantom domain is often the best option available for anyone wanting to Web publish. With a phantom domain, you get most of the benefits of having your own Web server
and affordability. When you have your own domain, Web users can use programs, such as
Whois, to learn additional information about you.

Typical costs for a phantom domain are only slightly more than a basic account with an Internet
Service Provider and range from $25 to $75. The primary advantage of a phantom domain is
that you will have your own domain and your URL will look something like this:

`http://www.your_company.com/`

This address URL above is easier to type and remember than an address URL containing the
tilde. Instead of telling people your URL is www.yourserviceprovider.com/~yourcompany, you
can tell them your URL is www.yourcompany.com. You may be surprised to learn that many
users try to find sites based on the company name. For example, when I look for a site associated with a major company, I usually type http://www.companyname.com in my browser's
URL window. If the URL is valid, I am at the company's Web site without having to look up
the URL in a Web database that may or may not have the site's URL.

Some ISPs call this service Web server hosting. By hosting, the ISP generally means they are
creating a phantom domain for you on their system. Maintaining a phantom domain is no
more taxing on the ISP's server than your standard account and is, in fact, little more than
clever linking to make the outside world think you have your own domain. With a phantom
domain, you still have no control over the Web server or additional services. However, most
ISPs that offer phantom domains include as part of the deal additional services, and these
additional services are the only real justification for higher fees.

PHANTOM DOMAINS

Phantom domains are the wave of the future in Web publishing. If you already have an account with an ISP, check to see if they offer phantom domains. Many ISPs provide phantom domains to their users because it is an easy way to generate extra revenues.

You can obtain a phantom domain from an Internet Service Provider, a commercial service provider, or an Internet presence provider. Internet presence providers specialize in setting up Web sites. Most of the sites that presence providers set up are phantom domains. A typical presence provider will service hundreds of phantom domains off one or more Web servers. While servicing hundreds of businesses off one server may sound like a lot, the power and capacity of the server and the speed of its connection to the Internet are more important than anything else.

As Internet presence providers specialize in servicing businesses instead of individual users, business-oriented sites may do better with an Internet presence provider. Dozens of presence providers are available. One such provider is Colossus Incorporated.

Colossus Incorporated specializes in providing services to business. They offer several types of accounts geared toward large, medium, and small businesses. Monthly rates start at $35 per month for maintaining domains with average traffic. The fee includes telnet access to your account, 5MB of space, FTP, and WWW services. You can find Colossus Incorporated on the Web at `http://www.colossus.net/`, or you can contact them via e-mail at `colossus@colossus.net`.

For more information on service providers, visit

`http://www.isoc.org/~bgreene/nsp1-5c.html`

To find a comprehensive list of Internet Service Providers, visit Cyberspace Today's Web site. They maintain one of the best ISP listings. You'll be able to access lists of service providers organized alphabetically, geographically, and by services offered at their site:

`http://www.cybertoday.com/ISPs/ISPinfo.html`

Summary

The Web was built upon existing protocols and intended to provide a common interface to other protocols. Because of this design, you can use any valid protocol to transfer files. While you will primarily use HTTP to access your Web documents, you can use other protocols, such as Gopher and FTP, to enhance the usability of your documents. The face of Web publishing is changing rapidly and the way you can specify the structure of Web documents is changing just as rapidly. The most common way to structure Web documents is with the HyperText

Markup Language. You can also use the Standard Generalized Markup Language, the Virtual Reality Modeling Language, and page layout applications to structure documents you provide on the Web.

The mechanism that enables you to provide access to any type of document on the Web is the MIME standard. Using multipurpose Internet mail extensions, you can provide information about documents in the Content-Type header field. Browsers will use the content type to take appropriate action on the document, such as displaying an image or calling another application. The mechanism that enables you to access and retrieve files on the Web is the URL standard. With Uniform Resource Locators, you can locate files and retrieve files using the appropriate protocol. The final specification of interest to Web publishers is the CGI specification. Using CGI, you can create dynamic documents.

To stay current with the latest developments on the Web, you should follow the Internet standards and specifications proposed by Internet standards groups, such as the IETF and the W3C. While you should consider all these issues before you start Web publishing, you should also evaluate your own access needs. This is true even if you already have an Internet account. By evaluating your access needs, you can determine what type of account will meet your needs as a Web publisher.

Why Publish on the Web?

2

by William Robert Stanek

IN THIS CHAPTER

This chapter explores the primary reasons you should publish on the Web. An entire universe is growing in cyberspace and you may not even know it. The Internet connects 50 thousand computer networks and 6 million host computers worldwide. Almost every country in the world has computers that access the Internet and by the end of 1996, 50 million people will have access to the Internet. What is even more incredible is that in two years, the number of users is expected to double, meaning more than 100 million people will have access to the global Internet by the end of 1998. The segment of the Internet driving this tremendous growth is the World Wide Web. Not only can you reach these millions of consumers on the Web, you can do so in mind-blowing proportions and in ways that are limited only by your imagination.

In 1995 alone, more than 8 million people gained access to the Web. The source of this great influx of new users was primarily commercial online services such as CompuServe, Prodigy, and America Online, which provide their users with full access to the Internet. When these figures are added to a conservative growth rate of 10 percent per month for new users accessing the Web, this means that 25 to 50 million people will have access to the Web by the end of 1996.

Consumers aren't the only ones caught up in the excitement surrounding the Internet and Web technology in general. The Internet and the Web have caught the eye of the media, businesses, entrepreneurs, and governments. While the Web is a tool and the Internet a vehicle under which the tool operates, very often these sources equate the Internet with the Web and discuss them as if they are the same thing. Worldwide media coverage of the Internet and related issues grows every day. Thousands of articles related to the Internet are published every month in books, magazines, newspapers, and newsletters. You will find discussions about the Internet and the Web on TV shows, the radio, and sometimes on your nightly news.

Who's Publishing on the Web?

The Web was born at CERN and it should be no surprise that universities, colleges, and research institutes represent one of the largest segments of Web publishers. Some of the most wonderful Web sites are created by college students and research scientists. These same students and researchers also represent most of the innovators creating new technologies for the Web.

While Web sites created by research and educational organizations are plentiful, their presence has been dwarfed in recent months by commercial sites. Thousands of businesses are already plugged in to the Internet. These businesses have built some of the hottest sites on the Web and are attracting thousands of visitors every day.

Not all the companies running commercial sites are multibillion dollar conglomerates with thousands of employees. Many commercial sites are run by startup companies who represent small groups of entrepreneurs with big dreams. Many more commercial sites are mom and pop businesses from down the street and home businesses run from the kitchen table.

Behind the massive wave of companies and entrepreneurs carving their niche in cyberspace, the governments of the world watch. They know what commerce without national borders, tariffs, and taxes means to global markets and aren't sure how to regulate it—or even if they can regulate it. Many governments are doing much more than watching; they are taking active roles in the development of the Internet and fostering its growth with funding. Government agencies are publishing their own Web sites loaded with useful information and are among the first organizations to publish on the Web. U.S. government agencies publishing on the Web include the Environmental Protection Agency, the Central Intelligence Agency, the National Security Agency, and the Census Bureau.

While many Web publishers represent organizations, this is not always the case. A growing number of Web publishers are individuals who want to share their ideas and interests with the world. These individuals aren't publishing on the Web to make a profit. They are publishing on the Web because it's fun to create something people around the world will see, challenging to test new publishing techniques, and exciting to build something dozens, hundreds, and often thousands of people start talking about.

Conducting Business

On the Web, your business is never closed. Consumers have access to your site 24 hours a day, 7 days a week, 365 days a year. They don't have to worry about fighting traffic to get to the mall. They don't have to race to the store after work and hope that it's not closed. They don't have to talk to a sales representative who's having a bad day and doesn't want to answer their questions. They can access information related to your products and services at their own pace and when it's most convenient for them, even if it's 3 o'clock on Christmas morning.

Businesses are striving to establish a presence on the Web for many different reasons. Some businesses are experimenting and trying to discover the benefits of Web publishing. They are promoting their company's product and service online. Often, they try to gauge consumer interest areas and figure out the directions the Web site should grow in to best serve customers.

Other businesses focus strictly on profits from Web publishing. They expect to make direct sales to customers and are interested in little else. These businesses are often disappointed when their Web publishing operation does not generate thousands of new sales. What these businesses fail to realize is that benefits of Web publishing are not always tangible.

While advertising agencies would undoubtedly argue to the contrary, you cannot precisely gauge the sales generated from a $100,000 television commercial. You can estimate the potential sales based on the estimated size of the viewing audience, but you cannot directly relate sales to a particular 30-second television commercial. The same is true in Web publishing. If your consumers aren't purchasing your product at your online order center, that does not mean they aren't reading about the product online and purchasing the product locally.

While increasing the bottom line because of Web publishing can be a goal, it should not be the only goal. Internet savvy businesses have many goals for their Web publishing operations and know the Web is best used for

- Providing enhanced customer service
- Providing enhanced technical support
- Public relations
- Marketing to global audiences
- Direct sales

Enhanced Customer Service

What do you do when the customer has questions and wants answers at 3 a.m.? Most customer service departments are not open 24 hours a day, primarily because of the tremendous expense of providing around-the-clock service. The best time to reach customers is at their leisure and when they have questions about your products or services.

One of the biggest customer complaints is the wait to get service. Nothing frustrates customers more than waiting on the phone or in a line to get service. Some companies solve this problem by hiring additional customer service representatives during peak periods. Other companies simply cannot afford the additional expense of hiring extra personnel, and the result is poor customer service and long waits for service.

On the Web, there is no wait to get customer support. Customers access the Web site, follow your links to your customer support area, and find the information they need. Ideally, the customer service area would have search facilities so customers could search for specific information quickly.

The Web dramatically reduces the cost of publishing product information. Not only can you provide product information to customers, but you can do so on a scale that would be prohibitively expensive through traditional mediums. You can turn your one-page ad for a leading magazine into a 20-page exposé on your product for a fraction of the cost of publishing in the magazine. In fact, for the same cost as publishing a one-page ad in a leading magazine, you can probably publish detailed information on your entire product line.

Quick access to information is often critical to the success of your products and services. The Web dramatically reduces the lag time for access to new product information. Instead of having to wait days for product information to arrive in the mail, customers can access new product information at your Web site within seconds after you publish it.

Documentation for products is a key area customers focus on. Manuals delivered with products aren't always detailed enough for customers. Poor manuals are sometimes the result of a rush to get the product to market or publishing constraints that limit the size of the manual to reduce costs. Many manuals also contain typos and inconsistencies. Correcting these inconsistencies is costly and not practical when products have already been shipped to wholesalers, retailers and customers. You can correct the deficiencies of your printed manual by providing a deluxe version of the manual online.

The Web dramatically reduces the costs of distributing upgrades to customers. Not only can you provide information on patches for software products, you can make the patches available for downloading online. Providing customers with free upgrades to your products is good business, especially since most minor upgrades fix bugs in the original product. The company saves money because disks and documentation do not have to be published and shipped to the customer.

To provide quality service and ensure you are meeting the needs of the customer, you need feedback from customers. Your Web pages can have forms that customers fill out and submit online via e-mail. In this way, you can keep in touch with the needs of your customers. Fill-out forms can also be used to obtain customer opinions on your latest products and services. You can compile these opinion surveys and use the statistics to identify areas for improvement in future product releases.

Enhanced Technical Support

Providing enhanced technical support to your customers is one of the primary reasons to publish on the Web. Most technical support departments are not open 24 hours a day. However, most customers don't have problems between the convenient hours of 9 a.m. to 5 p.m. They have problems installing products in the evening after the kids are in bed and they've finally found time to tinker with the PC. They have problems on the weekend because it's the only time when they can set aside a few hours to assemble the latest gizmo. They have problems Christmas morning putting together Johnny's new bicycle. Wouldn't it be wonderful if they could access your Web site and find the step-by-step instructions in living color and at a level of detail you just couldn't afford to publish and mass produce to include with the product?

While customers needing technical support also complain about long waits to get service, sometimes the wait in line to reach a technician is the least of the customer's worries. Often technicians cannot solve the customer's problem because the technician doesn't have expertise on a particular product. Sometimes, the technician passes the customer off to another technician, which means another wait to get service. In the worst of cases, the technician tries to solve the problem and wastes the customer's time.

A traditional solution to this problem is to hire more and better-qualified technicians. However, this is not always practical, even if the company can afford it. For example, the specialists for most of your new products are the personnel you trained in-house before the release of a product. If you hire additional technicians after the release of the product, you must train them on the product and this requires time you may not have.

On the Web, there is no wait to get technical support and you can provide customers with access to many levels of information that can help them solve their problems. You can provide product-by-product solutions to frequently encountered problems, troubleshooting guides that detail the steps to take to resolve difficult problems, and access to patches that fix compatibility problems your software products have with certain systems. When you couple this support with simple search facilities to let customers quickly search your technical support area, customers will have a quick and easy way to find solutions to their problems.

For the few answers that cannot be solved online, you can provide access to online forms for detailing problems. Forms can be tailored to prompt the user with specific questions that will let technicians easily solve the problems. Completed forms can be e-mailed to your technical support staff. Instead of having to explain solutions to customers who may or may not understand what the technician is saying, the technician can e-mail the customer a file containing detailed instructions to fix the problem.

Ideally, the solutions to most problems would be saved on the system somewhere so all the technician has to do is select a file and mail the solution back to the customer. Not only does this approach handle problems more efficiently and reduce the workload on the company's technicians, but it also allows technicians to respond to problems whenever they have time without customers having to wait on hold to get answers.

The interactive nature of the Web also makes it possible to fully automate the technical support process. You could pinpoint the user's problem by combining a question and answer session with an artificial intelligence program. The AI program running on your server could lead customers to a solution for their problems.

Public Relations

Building the image of your business is extremely important. One of the best ways to build your company's image is through press coverage. Savvy businesses with Web sites have the Web equivalent of neon signs leading the press to special areas of the site set up for the press.

Often these areas contain lists of contacts for key personnel in the company, such as the marketing director, the public relations manager for hardware issues, or the public relations manager for new product releases. On the Web, you can do much more than simply list names, you can include color photos of the company representatives and executive officers. You can include their phone numbers, fax numbers, and e-mail numbers. You can even include online forms for quick submission of public relations questions.

Along with contact information, these areas often contain press releases. Press releases on your business's products and services are free advertising. Many Web sites publish current and past press releases as well as information to be freely distributed by the press. Coverage in the press shows interested parties what your company has done in the past and is doing now. Press releases aren't only for the press, however. You should also provide access to press releases in areas frequented by your customers. In this way, customers can also see what the company has done in the past and is doing now.

You can also provide demos and screen shots of your products for downloading. In this way, people who interested in your products can see them firsthand. If they are interested, they can test the demo. If they need screen shots for publication in a book, magazine, or newspaper, they can download and use the material you provide.

Marketing to Global Audiences

Selling your products and services to consumers is accomplished through marketing. The interactive and dynamic nature of the Web makes it a powerful tool for marketing. If you don't market your products, they won't sell. If you don't tell people about your services, no one is going to hire you. Large corporations spend millions of dollars on marketing every year. Most of this money is spent building the company's image or that of the company's products and services through direct advertising. Traditional advertising mediums include television and radio commercials, display advertising in magazines and newspapers, and mass marketing through direct mail.

Direct advertising is expensive. A typical 30-second television commercial costs $100,000 and may reach one million viewers. A typical full-page ad in a magazine costs $10,000 and may reach 100,000 readers. By direct mail, the number of consumers you reach is determined by the number of fliers you send out. If you mail 10,000 fliers through direct mail at a cost of $3,000, you will reach 10,000 consumers.

The problem with direct marketing is that there is no guarantee your product will sell based on the advertisement or that you will actually make sales to the consumers you reach. For example, the typical response rate for direct mailings is 3 to 4 percent. This means if you distribute 10,000 flyers to a targeted mailing list, you will generally make 300 to 400 sales.

Another problem with direct advertising is the lack of interaction with customers. Studies have shown that the more interactive the marketing medium, the higher the sales will be. Personal sales visits yield the highest sales of any marketing method. This is because there is a high level of interaction with customers. The members of the sales team can answer the customer's questions and provide detailed information about the products relative to the customer's needs.

While personal sales visits are the ideal marketing method, such visits are extremely expensive and not always practical. Few companies can afford to hire the massive sales force necessary to reach a global market. The companies that can afford to market through personal sales visits to customers often don't because it simply isn't cost effective to spend more money trying to sell the product than would be made from the sale of the product.

In recent years, many companies have been turning to marketing mediums that are more interactive than direct advertising and less expensive than personal sales visits. Companies are using telemarketing to reach potential customers by phone. Companies are also using the long, documentary-style commercials called infomercials to provide customers with information about products in a setting that seems interactive. While telemarketing and infomercials are more interactive than traditional forms of marketing, they also have drawbacks.

Many people view telemarketing as an invasion of their privacy and when telemarketers get through to a person willing to listen, they only have a few minutes to make a sale. Infomercials, like personal sales visits, are not always practical. Infomercials are produced television programs that cost hundreds of thousands of dollars to produce and televise. To produce a successful infomercial, you need the right type of product.

The wonderful thing about Web marketing is that it is right for all types of products and provides a level of interaction with customers that is on a par with personal sales visits. You don't have to spend $100,000 or even $10,000 to reach a global audience. You can publish on the Web for $100 a month or less.

Your Web pages can help you establish connections with new customers and build relationships with your current customers. Web users reach businesses in the world market at the click of a button. One click of the mouse button can take them to a business in London, England. Another click of the mouse button can take them to a business in Albuquerque, New Mexico. The image you present through your Web site is often all the potential customer will know about your business; thus, you can gain substantial competitive advantage in a global market simply by projecting a strong image.

Web marketing is not a replacement for traditional marketing and is best used in combination with other types of marketing. However, Web marketing can certainly help companies of any size meet their marketing needs. The following sidebar presents some comparisons you may want to consider.

TELEVISION ADVERTISING COMPARED TO SETTING UP AND MAINTAINING A COMMERCIAL WEB SITE

Option A: Television commercial
Audience: One million television viewers
Cost: $125,000
Breakdown of costs:
Development and production: $50,000
Broadcast expense: $75,000
Duration: 30 seconds
Recurring costs for broadcasting same commercial to similar-sized audience: $75,000

Option B: Web site with 100s of megabytes of data available
Audience: 10,000 hits per day for 365 days (3.65 million hits)
Cost: $120,000
Breakdown of costs:
Purchase high-capacity Web Server: $20,000
One-year salary for server administrator: $50,000
Professional site design: $20,000

One-year T-1 connection to Internet: $25,000
Installation fees for T-1: $5,000
Average duration of exposure to advertising: 3-5 minutes/hit
Recurring costs for maintaining a Web site: $75,000

MAGAZINE ADVERTISING COMPARED TO RUNNING A WEB SITE FROM AN INTERNET SERVICE PRODUCER'S WEB SERVER

Option A: One-page magazine advertisement
Audience: 100,000 readers
Cost: $18,000
Breakdown of costs:
Development and design: $8,000
Publication expense: $10,000
Average duration of exposure to advertising: 30-60 seconds
Recurring costs for running same advertisement in other magazines: $10,000

Option B: Web Site on ISP's Web Server with 10-20MB of Available Data
Audience: 2,500 hits per day for 365 days (912,500 hits)
Cost: $11,300
Breakdown of costs:
Professional site design: $10,000
One-year account fee: $1200
Phantom domain set up and registration: $100 (includes $50 annual fee for domain registration)
Average Duration of exposure to advertising: 3-5 minutes/hit
Recurring annual costs: $1250 minimum, additional $2-5,000 for site maintenance

DIRECT MAIL ADVERTISING COMPARED TO PRODUCING A WEB PUBLICATION

Option A: Mass marketing campaign through direct mailings
Audience: 10,000 consumers
Cost: $2000
Breakdown of costs:
10,000 sheets paper: $75
10,000 envelopes: $125
10,000 envelope labels: $50
Printer supplies for laser printer: $100
Mail expense (Bulk Rate): $1400
Targeted mailing list: $250
Average duration of exposure to advertising: 0-60 seconds
Recurring costs for subsequent mailings: $1750-2000

Option B: Web publication with 2-3MB of data
Audience: 500 hits per day for 365 days (182,500 hits)
Cost: $650
Breakdown of costs:
One-year account fee: $600
Set up: $50
Average Duration of exposure to advertising: 3-5 minutes/hit
Recurring annual costs: $600

Electronic Commerce

Making direct sales on the Web is not only a possibility, it is a reality, and the interactive nature of the Web is largely responsible for making these sales. Businesses all over the world have online order centers. Primarily, their customers use fill-out forms to directly submit orders for processing.

CAUTION

Online ordering has tremendous potential. Dozens of Internet-savvy businesses have increased revenues 200 to 300 percent through online ordering. However, for every success story there are several companies who fail miserably. The primary reason companies don't generate sales online is that they don't take the time to learn about the market. Traditional advertising and marketing schemes simply do not work on the Web.

The company I founded, The Virtual Press Inc., offers many services to businesses wanting to establish a presence on the Web. When I wear my Internet consulting hat, the advice I often offer new businesses is this: Don't measure the success of your Web site by the revenues generated from online orders.

The Web is best viewed as an extremely powerful advertising medium and marketing tool. Television commercials don't generate sales that can be specifically correlated to a single commercial either. You wouldn't pull the plug on your television commercials when 10,000 viewers fail to run out and buy your latest gizmo immediately after the commercial. So why would you pull the plug on your Web site?

As electronic commerce is in its infancy on the Internet, the mechanism behind direct ordering differs greatly from site to site. A growing number of businesses have set up ways for customers to make secure transfers. In this way, sensitive information, like credit card numbers, is protected by encryption. More businesses will adopt secure transfer methods when true security standards are implemented.

Currently, businesses with online order centers use a variety of methods to secure transfers. Many businesses have customers set up an account with the business before ordering online. Customers are assigned an account number that can be used for online ordering at the customer's convenience. Normally, any orders placed using the account number can only be shipped to the address the customer specified when the account was set up.

Some businesses allow customers to place orders online and then ask them to confirm the order by phone or fax. Customers would typically get an order reference number that they could provide to a sales representative or automated voice mail system along with their credit card number. Because the customer would have already provided all the essential information online, the whole confirmation process by phone or fax would usually take less than a minute.

Spreading the Word About Your Ideas

Often the focus of Web publishing is on the business benefits, yet the Web is much more than a place to conduct marketing and advertising. You don't have to publish on the Web for profit. For every business publishing on the Web to increase the bottom line, someone somewhere is publishing on the Web simply to spread the word about his or her ideas.

The Web is an open repository for information. Research institutes, universities, colleges, non-profit organizations, and individual Web publishers alike freely publish information. One of the primary reasons to Web publish is to gain recognition for your ideas, research findings, and projects. Yet, you can Web publish simply because you want to share information and ideas with others. Knowledge is power and the key to freedom for all the peoples of the world.

Spreading the word about ideas you have published on the Web is easy and what is more important, free. Dozens of Web sites specialize in indexing and cataloging information that is available on the Web. Some of these sites maintain specialized lists of popular, new, and cool documents. Other sites maintain comprehensive lists.

Web users rely on these databases to find resources on the Web. To add your documents to a list, all you have to do is register your documents. This generally means filling out a form and submitting it online, which takes only a few minutes. The key information you enter into a fill-out form includes your name, business address, e-mail address, URL, and a brief description of your document. You can find a comprehensive list of catalog sites in Chapter 26, "Designing and Publishing a Web Site."

The original catalog site on the Web is maintained by the National Center for Supercomputing Applications (NCSA). NCSA's What's New list introduces new sites on the Web. You can find What's New at

```
http://www.ncsa.uiuc.edu/SDG/Software/Mosaic/Docs/whats-new.html
```

What's New is featured in Figure 2.1.

FIGURE 2.1.

Finding What's New on the Web is easy if you visit NCSA.

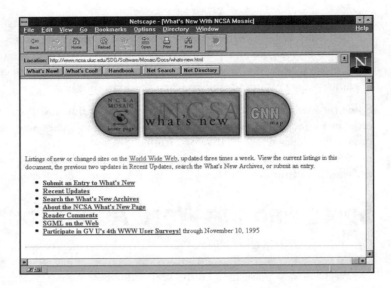

The What's New list maintained by NCSA is so popular there is a What's New Too list. What's New Too offers powerful search features and friendly graphics. You can find What's New Too at

`http://newtoo.manifest.com/WhatsNewToo/`

What's New Too is featured in Figure 2.2.

FIGURE 2.2.

The What's New Too list.

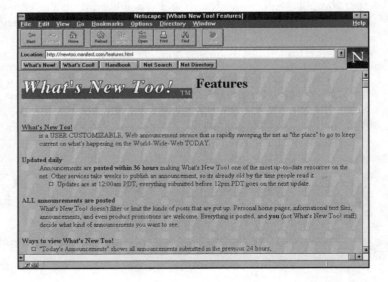

Features of the Web

The Web is the most dynamic medium you will ever publish in. Using the rich features of the Web, you have virtually limitless possibilities for publishing your ideas. Some features you may want to include in your Web publications are

- Text and images
- Interactivity
- Multimedia
- 3-D images and virtual reality

Combining Text and Images

Much has changed since the early days of the Web. While the first Web publications were largely textual in nature and limited in multimedia features, today's Web publications are highly graphical in nature and rich in multimedia features. Using the facilities of the Web, you can easily incorporate images into your publication.

By combining text and images on your Web pages, you can unleash the power of your Web publications. Small images are used to create highlights and navigation mechanisms. Images are used as logos, page titles, illustrations, and links to other Web publications.

Web publishers use images to convey their messages in ways more powerful than text alone. For example, you can use digitized photos in your publications in a variety of ways. Using digitized photos, you can show readers:

- What your products look like
- What your place of business looks like
- What you look like

Traditional publishers worry about the cost of adding extra colors to images they plan to use. The more colors an image uses, the more expensive the image is to publish. Consequently, most traditional publishers use black-and-white pictures whenever possible to reduce production costs. Web publishers can use 4, 16, 256, or even 16.7 million colors in their images if they want to, and the images will not cost the publisher a penny extra to publish.

Interactive Documents

Interactivity is a key ingredient for making connections with readers. Highly interactive documents invite readers to become participants. When your readers are actively involved, they are no longer simply watching as you unfold ideas in page after page. They are deciding how they want to unfold the story and choosing their own path through it. While the Web is not the only medium you can use to create interactive publications, it is the most versatile and least expensive publishing medium available.

You don't have to spend $799 on the latest developer's toolkit to create interactive publications for use on the World Wide Web. The Web has built-in facilities to create highly interactive documents. You can access these facilities by putting a hypertext reference or link in your Web publication. Most Web documents contain hypertext links that act as pointers to resources. Using links within your documents, you can provide readers with access to anything published on the Internet.

Multimedia Documents

Creating multimedia documents for use on the Web is easier than you may think. In fact, the Web is the easiest publishing medium to create multimedia documents in. You can include the following types of multimedia in your Web documents at little or no additional expense:

- Animation
- Digitized video
- Digitized voice
- Java applets
- Music and Sound effects

> **NOTE**
>
> Java applets are written in the Java programming language and are self-running, interactive programs that can be previewed on any Java-capable browser. If you're eager to learn firsthand how you can add applets to your Web publications, hang in there. You will learn more about Java and Java applets in Chapter 24, "Writing Java Applets."

At the Web publisher's fingertips is the world's greatest multimedia library—the Internet and all its archives. Not only does this library have thousands of multimedia clips that you can obtain free or for a small fee, it is complete with a multimedia developer's toolkit that you can obtain free or for a small fee as well. As if free clips and tools weren't enough to persuade you that Web publishing is your best choice for creating multimedia publications, the wonderful thing about Web technology is that it is advancing at an explosive pace. Already you can incorporate directly supported animation, soundtracks, and video into your publications without needing any special tools at all.

The key to using directly supported animation, soundtracks, and video in your publications is that the reader must have a browser that supports these features. For example, to create simple animation and extremely dynamic documents, you can use client pull/server push technology. Client pull/server push can be used with most popular browsers including the Netscape Navigator, the Internet Explorer, Spry Air Mosaic, Spyglass Mosaic and NCSA Mosaic. For more information on this technological breakthrough, see Chapter 14, "Dynamic Documents with Client Pull/Server Push."

VR Documents

Virtual reality is the latest craze. Dozens of companies are pouring millions of dollars into VR research. A handful of companies have recently released VR gaming systems. These systems offer primitive 3-D representation compared to the powerful 3-D images, virtual malls, and even virtual worlds you can create on the Web.

To create VR documents on the Web, you will probably use VRML, the virtual reality modeling language. You can obtain VRML world-building tools on the Web free. While currently readers of your VR documents will need a VRML browser to view the document, several popular browsers, including Netscape Navigator and Internet Explorer, will soon directly support VRML.

What Can You Publish?

If you've Web surfed before, you know there are no real limits to what can be published on the Web. Web publishers are producing electronic versions of traditional print publications and even inventing their own categories of publications.

Some traditional publications that are being published electronically on the Web include

- Books
- Comics and Comic Books
- Magazines
- Newsletters
- Newspapers

Books

Web-published books are called e-books. On the Web, you will find the full text of hundreds of electronic books. E-books are not limited to any category or genre. You will find nonfiction works in dozens of categories and fiction works in any genre you can think of. There are even virtual libraries for browsing the lists and text of the available e-books.

AT DREAM'S END: A WEB-PUBLISHED SUCCESS

Many writers spend years writing their first book only to find that no publisher wants to publish it. I should know; I spent ten years developing a fantasy series called *The Destiny Chronicles*. Two of those years I spent chronicling the history of the fantastic world I was creating. When I was finished, I started work on a book that would become *At Dream's End*. To date I have written four books in the planned eight-book cycle: *At Dream's End: A Kingdom in the Balance*, *Unraveling Paths: Dreamers and Mystics*, *Chaos Path: The Hands of Over-Earth*, and *Mid-Path: The Fourth Realm*.

I worked on the series for five years, from 1986 to 1991, before I ever tried to get the work published. For more than two years, I tried to get traditional publishers and agents interested in the series. I received hundreds of rejection letters. Among those rejections were dozens of personal letters from agents and editors alike. These editors and agents praised the characters, the rich world setting, and the plot, yet still declined to publish the book because in their eyes it was a midlist book. My frustration soared, especially since I had written other projects that were getting the same praise but no offers.

Instead of surrendering, I set out to do what I had wanted to do for years, and that was to start my own press. In March 1994, I founded The Virtual Press. My focus wasn't on profits. I wanted to create a company that would help launch the careers of aspiring writers—and profits be damned. However, you can't launch careers without sales to measure success. In early 1994, I pre-released *At Dream's End* to test my publishing program at TVP. The rest, as they say is history, because by Christmas 1995 the book no one wanted to publish sold more than 5,000 copies on a shoestring advertising budget of $75. I attribute nearly all of the sales to spreading the word about the book to online users and of course, good writing.

You never know what awaits you at the top of a mountain, until you climb it one cautious step at a time. If you have ideas or information that others may be interested in, why not Web-publish it? You have nothing to lose and everything to gain.

Comics and Comic Books

Comics are extremely popular on the Web. The chances are very good that you can find your favorite Sunday comic on the Web. Some publishers of comics maintain daily and weekly updated comics as well as archives that you can search. More importantly, if you would like to be a cartoonist and are looking for a place to start, you may want to publish your comics or samples of your comics on the Web.

Dozens of newspapers, newsletters, and magazines published on the Web could benefit from the right type of comic strip. Publishing giants like United Media provide many Web newspapers with comic strips for a low weekly rate. You could develop a Web site to showcase your talents and offer your comic strip to Web newspapers as well.

The Web is also the place where your comic book can get its start. You could publish samples of your work on the Web or even an entire issue of your comic book.

Magazines

Most magazines are published on a quarterly or monthly basis. Web-published magazines are called zines or e-zines. On the Web, you will find thousands of zines published in every imaginable category. Most zines are small literary or experimental publications that are distributed freely to readers. Successful zines have strong followings on the Internet.

With the flood of zines available, you may wonder how you could successfully publish a zine as well. But the demand for fresh ideas and new zines is always growing, especially as the Internet itself grows. By the end of 1998, one hundred million people will be looking for something interesting to read on the Internet.

Newsletters

Most newsletters are published on a semiannual, quarterly, or monthly basis. The Web is a great place to publish your corporate or special interest newsletter. In general, company newsletters do not contain sensitive information. More often than not, the company newsletter is used to disseminate general information and to provide employees with recognition for their efforts. By publishing the corporate newsletter on the Web, you allow the world to get a glimpse inside the walls of the corporation.

You could also publish a special interest newsletter or news bulletin on the Web. Special interest newsletters cover a very specific category of information and are generally only a few pages in length.

Newspapers

Most newspapers are published daily or weekly. Many Web users spend their mornings reading their favorite newspaper online. They have a cup of Java in one hand and the mouse pointer in the other hand. When they are done reading one newspaper, they can jump to the pages of another newspaper. They can follow the headlines around the country and get a better idea of the whole story. They can peruse the help wanted ads on the West Coast and on the East Coast. Or they can tune in to specialized newspapers covering news in a specific industry or interest area. Is there a newspaper covering your industry? If not, why not publish one?

Beyond Traditional Publications

The Web contains much more than electronic versions of traditional print publications. Web publishers are publishing any type of information that has ever been written down and many types of information that have never before been written down. On the Web you will find virtual corporations complete with products and services that you can access right online, virtual shopping malls where hundreds of businesses show their wares, and virtual libraries with hundreds of creative works.

Not everything Web-published is on such a grand scale, however. Many documents published on the Web are pages created just for fun or to share hobbies and interests with others. These documents often contain collections of resources or links to resources available elsewhere. The resource collections were published because the publisher thought others would see their value as well. If you've browsed the Web for a while, why not share a list of your favorite sites and Web resources with others?

Summary

The most exciting time to publish on the Web is right now. You have a ground floor opportunity to be a part of something truly wonderful and for once, it isn't going to cost you a bundle to join in. People all around the world are publishing on the Web for fun, profit—and because they can.

The Web levels the playing field and empowers you to inexpensively and effectively:

- Market your products and services to a global audience
- Conduct electronic commerce and allow customers to place order online
- Compete head-to-head with corporations
- Spread the word about something you believe in
- Share your ideas, research, and findings with the world

The Web is the most versatile medium you will ever publish in. Web publishers have proven time and time again that there are no real limits to what can be published on the Web. Not only are they publishing every imaginable type of document that has ever been created, they are doing it successfully and helping to build the most powerful information system in the world: the World Wide Web. So, what are you waiting for?

Publishers' Tour of the Web

3

by William Robert Stanek

Even if you surf the Web regularly, there are probably thousands of Web sites you have never ventured to before. After scouring the farthest corners of cyberspace, I put together a virtual tour of some of the hottest, zaniest, and most useful Web sites. These sites are more than examples of the hidden gems waiting for you in cyberspace, however; they are terrific resources to search and study as you begin your quest to publish on the Web.

The tour begins with a brief explanation of how to navigate the Web and use URLs. Afterward, the tour shifts into high gear and propels you headlong into this highly visual arena, empowering you to play powerball in the majors. You will find tips for navigating the Web, using URLs and see where it all started.

Navigating the Web

If you have browsed the Web before, you know that navigating the Web can be as easy as activating a hypertext link. You activate the link by moving your mouse pointer to the area of the link and clicking the left mouse button. Text containing a hypertext link is underlined and generally displayed in a different color from other text on the page. By default, most browsers display links that you have not visited in blue and links that you have visited in purple or light red.

When you move your mouse pointer over a link, most browsers display the URL path to the file or object that will be retrieved if you activate the link. This is useful to identify the type of file referenced by the link. For example, most Web documents written in HTML have the .htm or .html extension.

> **NOTE**
>
> Some browsers let you select the color of text on the page. The four basic color definitions you can assign to text pertain to the color of ordinary text, unvisited links, active links, and visited links. Under HTML 3.0, you as the Web publisher can define the color of text on the page. These color definitions generally override color definitions defined in the user's HTML 3.0 compliant browser.

While following text-based links on Web pages is easy, following links embedded in graphic objects is not always easy. Some clickable images are displayed on the page with a distinctive blue border. This type of clickable image is easy to identify. Other clickable images have no borders around them at all, primarily because of extensions to HTML that enable Web publishers to suppress the border around images. Yet there are other extensions to HTML that enable Web publishers to place borders around nonclickable images. So, how do you know when an image is clickable and when it isn't if it has no distinctive border?

One way to tell if the image is clickable is to move your mouse pointer over the image. If your browser shows that a URL path is associated with the image, you can click on it. I need some cybercash for this Virtual tour anyway, so first we'll hop over to DigiCash, pick up some e-cash, and use the DigiCash home page to show you what I'm talking about.

FIGURE 3.1.

Navigating with images.

The images on DigiCash's home page, shown in Figure 3.1, form a graphical menu to other pages at the site. While there are no distinctive blue borders identifying the images as clickable, all the images shown, except the logo, are clickable. As I needed some e-cash, I went straight to the e-cash image. When I move my mouse pointer over the image, the URL path associated with the image is displayed by my browser. You'll find the following URL at the bottom of Figure 3.1:

```
http://www.digicash.com/ecash/ecash-home.html
```

As you point and click your way through the Web, you probably don't stop to think about the URLs you are using to access Web resources. However, as a Web publisher, you should stop and think about the URLs you use. The URL in the preceding example tells the browser to use the hypertext transfer protocol to obtain a file called `ecash-home.html` in the `ecash` directory on the `www.digicash.com` Web server. URLs are much more powerful and complex than this simple example. The next section takes a closer look at the structure of URLs and how they are used on the Web.

Using URLs

Uniform Resource Locators provide a uniform way of identifying resources that are available using Internet protocols. To better understand URLs, you need to know about URL schemes and formats, how URLs are defined, and how to use escape codes in URLs.

URL Schemes and Formats

The basic mechanism that makes URLs so versatile is the standard naming scheme. URL schemes name the protocol the client will use to access and transfer the file. Web clients use the name of the protocol to determine the format for the information that follows the protocol name. The protocol name is generally followed by a colon and two forward slashes. The colon is a separator. The double slash marks indicate that the protocol uses the format defined by the Common Internet Scheme Syntax.

The Common Internet Scheme Syntax is a common syntax for URL schemes that involve the direct use of Internet Protocol-based protocols. IP-based protocols specify a particular host on the Internet by a unique numeric identifier called an IP address or by a unique name that can be resolved to the IP address. The information following the double slash marks follows a format that is dependent on the protocol type referenced in the URL. Here are two general formats:

```
protocol://hostname:port/path_to_resource
protocol://username:password@hostname:port/path_to_resource
```

> **NOTE**
>
> If you use a DOS/Windows-based system, you normally type a backslash to change directories and maneuver around the system. Consequently, you may have to remind yourself that the Web follows the UNIX syntax for slashes and the slashes you type for URLs should be forward slashes.

Defining Host Information in URLs

Hostname information used in URLs identifies the address to a host and is broken down into two or more parts separated by periods. The periods are used to separate domain information from the hostname. Common domain names for Web servers begin with www, such as www.tvp.com, which identifies the Web server called tvp in the commercial domain. Domains you can specify in your URLs include

COM   Commercial sites
EDU   Education sites

GOV	Nonmilitary government sites
MIL	Military sites
NET	Network sites (developers, ISPs, and so on)
ORG	Organizational sites

Defining Port Information in URLs

Ports are rather like telephone jacks on the Web server. The server has certain ports allocated for certain things, like Port 80 for your incoming requests for hypertext documents. The server listens on a particular port. When it hears something, it in essence picks up the phone and connects the particular port.

Port information used in URLs identifies the port number to be used for the connection. If you don't specify a port number, a default value is assumed as necessary. Generally, you don't have to specify port numbers in your URLs unless the connection will be made to a port other than the default. Default values for ports are defined in the URL specification as follows:

FTP	Port 21
Gopher	Port 70
HTTP	Port 80
NNTP	Port 119
Prospero	Port 1525
telnet	Port 23
WAIS	Port 210

Defining Username and Password information in URLs

By specifying the username and password information in a URL, you enable users to log in to a system automatically. The two protocols that use both username and password information are FTP and telnet. In a FTP session, the username and password information is often used to allow users to log in to FTP servers anonymously. When a connection is made to a FTP server and username and password information is not specified, the following default values are assumed: anonymous for username and the user's e-mail address as the password.

In telnet, there are no default values. If you do not supply the username and password, the user will be prompted for this information. To avoid this, you could enable users to log in automatically by specifying a user and password in your URL. However, you generally do not want to specify a personal password in a URL. Therefore, if you want users to be able to log in automatically using telnet, you should create a guest account with a generic password.

Defining Path Information in URLs

The final part of a URL is the path to the resource. This path generally follows the directory structure from the root or slash directory to the resource specified in the URL. A completely specified path to a resource is called an absolute path. You can also specify a path to a resource relative to the current directory. You will learn more about specifying paths to resources in Chapter 5, "Creating Web Documents with HTML."

Protocol Schemes Defined

Most protocol schemes follow the two general forms of URLs discussed earlier. Protocol schemes conforming to the CISS standard use the double slashes. CISS-compliant protocols are FTP, Gopher, HTTP, NNTP, WAIS, and File. Protocols that do not conform to the CISS standard omit the double slashes. Noncompliant protocols include Mailto and News. Table 3.1 shows the URL schemes associated with each protocol.

Table 3.1. URL Schemes and Formats.

Scheme	Description/Protocol	URL Format

FTP	File Transfer Protocol	`ftp://`
		`username:password@hostname:port/`
		`path_to_resource`

Gopher	Gopher Protocol	`gopher://hostname:port/` `path_to_resource`
HTTP	Hypertext Transfer Protocol	`http://hostname:port/` `path_to_resource`
Mailto	Electronic mail address	`mailto:username@host`
Prospero	Prospero Directory Service	`prospero://hostname:port/` `hsoname;field=value`
News	Usenet news	`news:newsgroup-name` `news:message-number`
NNTP	Usenet news accessed with Network News Transfer Protocol	`nntp://hostname/newsgroup-name`
telnet	Remote login sessions	`telnet:/` `username:password@hostname:port`
WAIS	Wide Area Information Servers	`wais://hostname:port/database`
File	Files on local host	`file://hostname/path_to_resource`

> **NOTE**
>
> Although the URL specification defines the Prospero protocol, Prospero is generally not supported directly by browsers. Prospero is a protocol used by Archie to access FTP archives. The unique identifiers associated with the Prospero directory service are: hsoname, field, and value. The hsoname identifies the host-specific object to be retrieved using the prospero protocol. The field and value help to further identify the object.

How URLs Are Defined

URLs consist of characters defined by the ASCII character set. The URL specification allows for the use of uppercase and lowercase letters. However, uppercase letters used in URLs are interpreted in the same way as lowercase letters. For example, these URLs would all be treated the same:

```
http://tvp.com/vpfound.html
HTTP://Tvp.Com/Vpfound.Html
HTTP://TVP.COM/VPFOUND.HTML
```

> **TIP**
>
> Because URLs typed in uppercase are generally treated the same as URLs typed in lowercase, most Web publishers use only lowercase letters in their URLs. A fall out of this is that most Web documents and object files are named in lowercase letters as well. If you are on a system that has case-sensitive file naming, such as UNIX, you will find naming your files in lowercase is extremely useful in avoiding possible conflicts.

Although URLs consist of characters defined by the ASCII character set, you cannot use all ASCII characters in your URLs. You can use the letters a-z, the numerals 0-9, and a few special characters, including

- asterisks
- dollar signs
- exclamation points
- hyphens
- parentheses (left and right)
- periods
- plus signs
- single quotation marks
- underscores

You are limited to these characters because other characters used in URLs have specific meanings, as shown in Table 3.2.

Table 3.2. The meaning of characters used in URLs.

Character	Meaning	Example
:	The colon is a separator.	
	Separates protocol from the rest of the URL scheme.	`http://tvp.com/vpfound.html`
	Separates hostname from the port number.	`http://www.tvp.com:80/`
	Separates username from the password.	`ftp://anonymous:william@tvp.com/vpinfo.txt`
//	The double slash marks indicate that the protocol uses the format defined by the Common Internet Scheme Syntax.	
	This protocol follows the CISS format.	`ftp://tvp.com/vpinfo.txt`
	This protocol does not follow the CISS format.	`news:newsgroup-name`
/	The slash is a separator and is used to separate the path from hostname and port.	`http://tvp.com/vphp.html`
	The slash is also used to denote the directory path to the resource named in the URL.	`/usr/cgi-bin/useit.pl`
~	The tilde is generally used at the beginning of the path to indicate that the resource is in the specified user's public html directory.	`http://www.aloha.com/~william`
%	Identifies an escape code. Escape codes are used to specify special characters	`gopher://unm.edu/books/english/Book%20Table%20of%20Contents`

Character	Meaning	Example
	in URLs that otherwise have a special meaning or are not otherwise allowed.	
@	The at symbol is used to separate username and/or password information from the hostname in the URL.	`mailto:william@tvp.com`
?	The question mark is used in the URL path to specify the beginning of a query string. Query strings are passed to CGI scripts. All the information following the question mark is data the user submitted and is not interpreted as part of the file path.	`/usr/cgi-bin/useit.pl?keyword`
+	The plus sign is used in query strings as a placeholder between words. Instead of using spaces to separate words the user has entered in the query, the browser substitutes the plus sign.	`/usr/cgi-bin/useit.pl?word1+word2+word3`
=	The equal sign is used in query strings to separate the key assigned by the publisher from the value entered by the user. In the sample URL, username is the key assigned by the publisher and the value entered by the user is `william`.	`/usr/cgi-bin/useit.pl?username=william`
&	The ampersand is used in query strings to separate sets of keys and values.	`/usr/cgi-bin/query.pl?name=william&question=why+not`

continues

Table 3.2. continued

Character	Meaning	Example
	In the sample URL, name is the first key assigned by the publisher and the value entered by the user is william. The second key assigned by the publisher is question and the value entered by the user is why+not.	
^	Reserved for future use.	
{}	Reserved for future use.	
[]	Reserved for future use.	

Using Escape Codes in URLs

To make URLs even more versatile, the specification enables you to use escape codes in URLs. Escape codes are used to specify special characters in URLs that are either reserved or not otherwise allowed. This is particularly useful for protocols (such as Gopher) that allow resources to be defined with spaces between words. For example, to use the Gopher resource:

```
Book Table of Contents
```

You would have to rewrite the resource name using the escape code for spaces. The percent sign identifies an escape code. The number following the percent sign identifies the character being escaped. The escape code for a space is a percent sign followed by the number 20. To use the preceding resource name in a URL, you would rewrite it as follows:

```
Book%20Table%20of%20Contents
```

Using the ISO Latin 1 character set, you can determine the values for characters you need to escape. To do this, you convert the decimal value defined in the character set to a hexadecimal value. The decimal value for a space is 32. When you convert this decimal value to hexadecimal, the resulting value is 20. Table 3.3 shows common character values from the ISO Latin 1 character set and the associated escape codes.

Table 3.3. Common character values and their associated escape codes.

Numeric Value	Character Description	Escape Code
09	Tab	%09
32	Space	%20
35	Number sign (#)	%23
37	Percent sign (%)	%25
38	Ampersand (&)	%26
39	Apostrophe (')	%27
63	Question mark (?)	%3f
64	At symbol (@)	%40
95	Caret symbol (^)	%5f

TIP

When you use escape codes such as %09 for a tab, be sure to include the zero. 09 is a hexadecimal value that the computer will interpret as a tab.

Where It All Started

The Web is a powerful interface to everything the Internet has to offer. Today when most people think of the Internet, they think of the dynamic environment that enables them to search through and access complex webs of text, graphics, sound, and video. In short, they equate the Web with the Internet—and that's because the Web has swallowed the Net. Yet it wasn't always that way. In 1969, the Internet was a tiny project of the US Department of Defense (DOD) Advanced Research Project Agency (ARPA) that involved four computers spread over a wide area. The project was designed to demonstrate the feasibility of wide area networking.

Obviously the project was a smashing success, but it took more than 25 years to get to where we are today in global networking. During those years, the Net was largely the domain of research, education, and government sites. So, it is fitting that this tour of the Web starts with the sites that represent the origins of the Internet. The Internet has changed greatly since the early days. The useful but basic resources published in those early days have grown into invaluable resources of tremendous proportions.

One of the most valuable educational resources on the Web is the AskERIC Web site shown in Figure 3.2. Maintained by the Educational Resources Information Center (ERIC) headquartered at the ERIC Clearinghouse on Information & Technology at Syracuse University,

AskERIC is a treasure trove of information for educators and anyone doing research. The ERIC database has information, including current research papers, from 16 subject-specific clearing-houses that can be searched online. The ERIC database alone makes AskERIC a must visit, but AskERIC has lots of other features.

FIGURE 3.2.

AskERIC: A resource for educators and researchers.

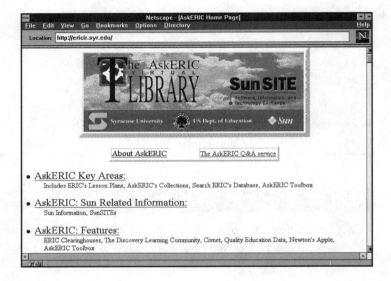

The U.S. Library of Congress maintains over 70 million documents. The Library of Congress Web server shown in Figure 3.3 is a gateway to dozens of other services offered by the Library of Congress. From the site, you can access the Library of Congress Gopher and FTP servers. You can telnet to the Library of Congress Information System to search for government documents, newspapers, and periodicals. Other services let you view and search the complete text of current bills and the Congressional Record, the Library of Congress card catalog system, and the enormous digitized historical collection called American Memory. The Library of Congress Web site is served to the public via a myriad of Web servers, including the following:

http://lcweb.loc.gov/   Main Library of Congress Web Server

http://www.loc.gov/   Alternate Library of Congress Web Server

http://thomas.loc.gov/   Library of Congress Web Server for Thomas, legislative information

http://lcweb2.loc.gov/   Library of Congress Web Server primarily for the American Memory collection

FIGURE 3.3.

The U.S. Library of Congress on the Web.

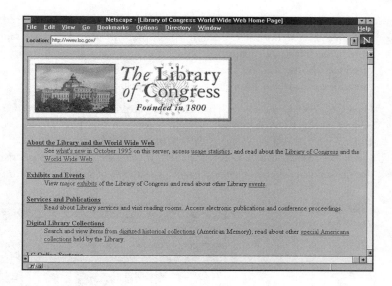

The Smithsonian Institute is America's museum, and the goal of the Smithsonian Institute's Web site is to be one of the richest, most exciting, and most informative places on the Web. The Smithsonian Institute Web site shown in Figure 3.4 is quickly living up to its goal. You can explore more than 150 resources at the site, including the many publications the Smithsonian Institute publishes every year.

FIGURE 3.4.

The Smithsonian Institute on the Web.

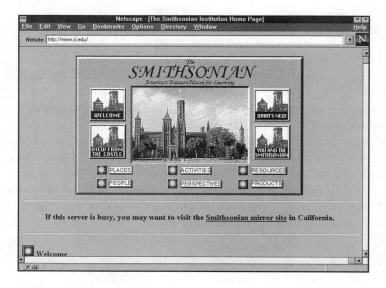

While the early Internet was largely based in the United States, today's Internet is a global initiative on a stellar scale. Take for example, the World Lecture Hall, where you can find a worldwide initiative to promote education and the sharing of information. The World Lecture Hall's home site is at the University of Texas. At the lecture hall, shown in Figure 3.5, you can access the course information in over 50 subject areas.

Have you ever wondered what a class in Virology would be like? Or are you doing research related to the Ebola outbreak in Zaire? You can use The World Lecture Hall as your jump station to the University of Wisconsin's Institute for Molecular Virology (`http://www.bocklabs.wisc.edu/Welcome.html`). At the University of Wisconsin site, you'll find one of the most comprehensive resources on the subject of virology available in the world.

FIGURE 3.5.

The World Lecture Hall.

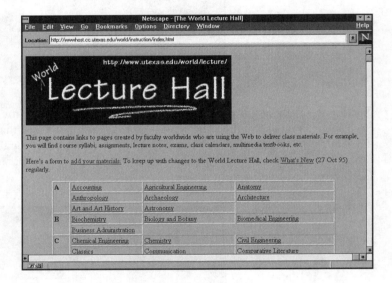

Finding government resources on the Internet for the world community at large is not easy, especially if you are looking for small government agencies that may not have their own Internet presence. Well, not easy unless you know about the one-stop index to government resources on the Net maintained by the University of Michigan's Document Center. The home page for the list, fittingly called Government Resources on the Net, is shown in Figure 3.6. This definitive list has links to government sites the world over. If the government of any country in the world has a site on the Net, you will find the links to it in this list. Here is a sample of what is available for the U.S. federal government:

> General information
> Bibliographies of publications
> Civil service positions
> Directories of agencies and Web sites

Grants
Executive Branch information
Executive Branch Web sites
Administrative regulations
Presidential documents
Legislative Branch information
Directories of Congress and committees
Links for bills, bill status, Congressional Record, floor schedules, and legislative
background
Congressional research guide
Congressional support agencies (GAO, GPO, LC, OTA)
Judicial Branch
Supreme Court decisions and biographies
Links to Circuit Court opinions
Laws and regulations
Code of Federal Regulations and Federal Register
Constitution and U.S. Legal Code
Office of Management and budget circulars
Patent, trademark, and copyright information
Tax forms

FIGURE 3.6.
*Government Resources
on the Web.*

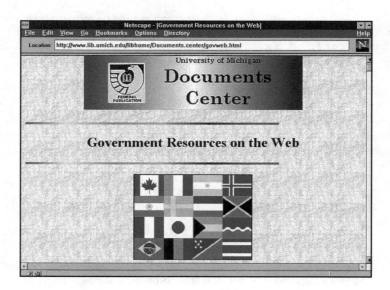

Wouldn't it be great if there were a one-stop index to the cities of the world? Sometimes you
are looking for information on a country, region, or city and can't find what you're looking for
by traditional means. Don't worry, there is just such a resource. It's called City.Net. The home

page for City.Net is shown in Figure 3.7. At the City.Net Web site, you'll find a comprehensive guide to more than 1100 cities and 200 countries. The index is organized alphabetically by region, country, and city. If you want to quickly search for information, you can do a keyword search on all the information available at the site.

FIGURE 3.7.

City.Net: a comprehensive guide to cities, regions, and countries.

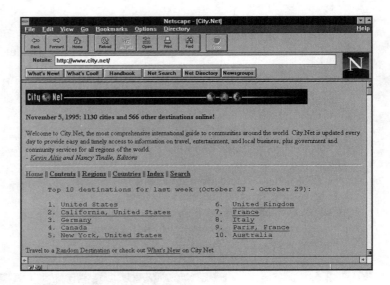

That's Entertainment

Whether you are looking for the latest best seller to curl up with, the hottest movie to watch this weekend, the stats on your favorite team, or hit singles off the billboard charts, the Web is the place to go to find it all. At times, it seems the entire entertainment industry is online doing business in cyberspace. Hundreds of traditional publishers from major conglomerates to small presses have a presence on the Web, along with every major movie, television, and recording studio.

Books, Magazines, and Newspapers on the Web

This tour of entertainment sites starts with the mainstay of the publishing business: books. If you are awed by the superstores, wait till you see the Web's superstores. The largest bookstore on the Web is undoubtedly BookStacks Unlimited. At the Book Stacks Unlimited Web site, shown in Figure 3.8, you can search, browse, and place orders for any of more than 330,000 books. If that's not enough, you can send e-mail to featured authors at the Book Cafe or get a glimpse of upcoming releases in Fresh Ink.

FIGURE 3.8.

Book Stacks Unlimited: find information on 330,000 books.

A Web superstore for magazines and newspapers is the Electronic Newsstand. At the Electronic Newsstand's Web site, shown in Figure 3.9, you can browse the current editions of over 300 magazines and newspapers. Publishers that participate in the Electronic Newsstand provide the table of contents and several articles from the current editions of their publications. You can read these articles free, search through archives of previous editions, and place an order for publications—all online. A sample of the magazines you'll find includes

Air & Space/Smithsonian
American Journalism Review
Atlanta Review
Barron's
The Boston Book Review
Business Week
Byte
Computer Gaming World
Computer Shopper
Computerworld
Cyberspace Today
Discover: The World of Science
Education Week
Entertainment Weekly
FamilyPC
Fantasy and Science Fiction
Field & Stream
Financial World

Game Developer
GamePro
Harvard International Review
HotWired
Internet World
The Journal of Commerce
Journal of Democracy
Kiplinger's Personal Finance Magazine
LAN: The Network Solutions Magazine
The Literary Review
MacUser
Money
Multimedia World
New Age Journal
The New Yorker
Oil & Gas Journal
OS/2 Developer
PC Magazine
PC World
People
Quantum: The Magazine of Math and Science
Reviews in American History
St. Petersburg Press
Software Digest
Technology Review
Telecommunications Week
U.S.—Mexico Free Trade Reporter
Video Technology News
The Village Voice
Virtual Reality Special Report
The Washington Quarterly
Yoga Journal

While superstores for books, magazines, and newspapers are plentiful on the Web, you can also find sites maintained by the publishers themselves. If you are looking for financial information on the Web, the place to go is the *Money and Investing Update* site shown in Figure 3.10. *Money and Investing Update* is the electronic version of *The Wall Street Journal*. Not only does the magazine cover financial news, its does so better than anyone else. You can access *Money and Investing Update* any time of the business day and find current financial news and analysis as the market is shifting. You can also find articles from the *Dow Jones Newswire, The Asian Wall Street Journal,* and *The Wall Street Journal Europe.*

FIGURE 3.9.

The Electronic Newsstand.

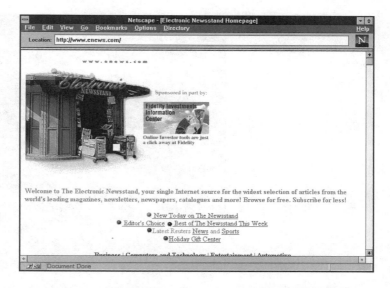

FIGURE 3.10.

Money & Investing Update *from* The Wall Street Journal.

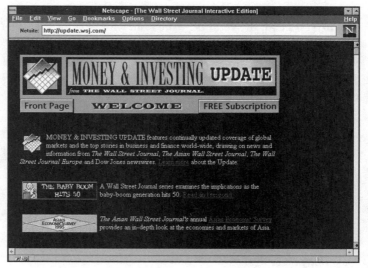

The place to find news about the United States on the Web is *USA Today*'s Web site. At the site, you can find the complete text of articles featured in the current edition of *USA Today*. The weather page for *USA Today*, shown in Figure 3.11, has a clickable map that you can use to find weather forecasts for your area.

FIGURE 3.11.

*The Weather section of
USA Today's online
edition.*

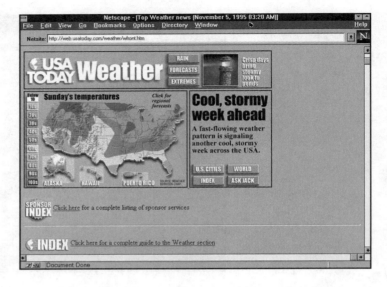

Undoubtedly, one of the hottest publisher sites on the Web is Time Warner's Pathfinder site. The front page for the Pathfinder site is shown in Figure 3.12. You can spend days wandering through gigabyte after gigabyte of the useful and dazzling information Time Warner has to offer at the site. Time Warner publishes an amazing number of books and magazines. At the Pathfinder site, you can find information on current articles from the following publications:

> *Asiaweek*
> *Digital Pulse*
> *Digital Pulse for Kids*
> *Encyclopedia Britannica*
> *Entertainment Weekly*
> *Fortune*
> *Home PC*
> *Hoover's Business Profiles*
> *In, Around and Online*
> *Interactive Age*
> *Life*
> *Money*
> *Information Week*
> *People*
> *People Daily*
> *Progressive Farmer*
> *Sports Access*
> *Sports Illustrated*

Sports Illustrated For Kids
Technology Review
The Daily Spectrum
Time
Time Daily
Time For Kids
Time Magazine
Windows Magazine

One of my favorite places at Pathfinder is the Time Life Photo Site. The Time Life Photo Site features samples from the 20 million photographs gathered or taken on assignment by Time Inc. photographers. The gallery contains a rotating collection of pictures you can view online. When last I visited, featured categories of photographs included animals, space, the 50s, WWII, and celebrities. The photo collection is a must-see.

FIGURE 3.12.

The Time Warner Pathfinder Site.

Wonderful photography is at the core of the Condé Nast Traveler site as well. If you've ever dreamed of traveling the world or are planning a dream vacation, the Condé Nast Traveler Web site is a must see. At the sites shown in Figure 3.13, you will find breathtaking photography combined with terrific articles that will make you yearn to get away from it all. The site features a searchable database of vacation paradises that you can wander for hours. You can search the database by keyword or interactively using an atlas with clickable hot spots that can transport you to any resort location in the world.

FIGURE 3.13.

Find great escapes using the Condé Nast Traveler's Web site.

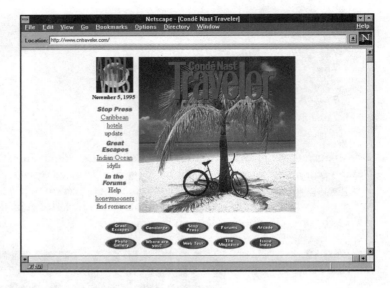

Movies, Television, and Music

The heart of the entertainment industry is in movies, television, and music. The Web is the place to find information on the latest releases, the classic oldies, and new work by hopefuls. Movie producers go all out when it comes to producing Web sites. Time Warner created an entire site just to promote *Batman Forever* (www.batmanforever.com). And that's just the beginning. You can visit all the studios in Hollywood without ever leaving the comfort of your easy chair.

The Lion's Den at Metro Goldwyn Mayer United Artists Studios features the latest hits from MGM/UA movies, television, home video, and interactive entertainment. At the Lion's Den site, shown in Figure 3.14, you can find much more than sneak previews and movie information. MGM/UA has made the site a feast for the eyes and ears. In the multimedia room, you will find dozens of movie clips and hundreds of digitized photographs and sound clips that you can download. For the latest news in the entertainment industry, head off to the Executive Suite. To order souvenirs and memorabilia, visit the MGM/UA Studio Store.

Buena Vista is Disney's production company and as you can imagine, the Buena Vista Web site is one of the best sites on the Web. As shown in Figure 3.15, you can browse the site in text-only mode or in living color by turning the graphic features on or off. I highly recommend turning on the graphics if you have a high-speed modem or the patience to wait for images to download. The site contains a wealth of information on Buena Vista's movie studios, including Hollywood Pictures Productions, Touchstone Productions, and Buena Vista International. The site is also the home of Buena Vista Television and Touchstone Television, where you can find the latest information on hit television series like "Nowhere Man."

FIGURE 3.14.

The Lion's Den at Metro Goldwyn Mayer United Artists Studio.

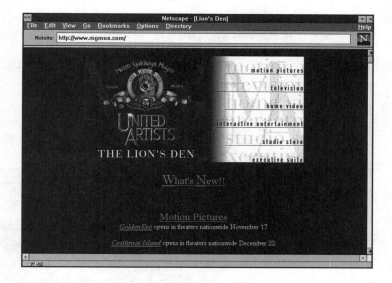

FIGURE 3.15.

Buena Vista's site on the Web.

The Buena Vista site has regular events as well. When I last visited Buena Vista Television, the featured event at the site was the Tool Time Girl Calendar. But the reason you should visit Buena Vista's site isn't for the hundreds of image-laden pages of previews alone, it is for the multimedia you will find there. Featured movies have video clips, still photographs, and trailers that you can access online. Buena Vista's movie clips in QuickTime format are some of the best I've seen anywhere—the best except for those of its parent corporation, Disney.

Walt Disney Picture's Web site is organized just like the Buena Vista site. The primary difference between the sites is in who's running the show. At the Disney site, shown in Figure 3.16, you have access to the Disney Studio's feature films and full-length animation. You can download animation sequences and movies in QuickTime format from Disney's latest releases. You will also still find photographs, trailers, and teasers.

As Figure 3.17 shows, Disney set up an entire Web site at www.toystory.com so the world could preview *Toy Story*. *Toy Story* is a full-length animation that was five years in the making. The geniuses at Disney created the movie in its entirety with computer-generated graphics.

FIGURE 3.16.

Walt Disney Pictures' front door on the Web.

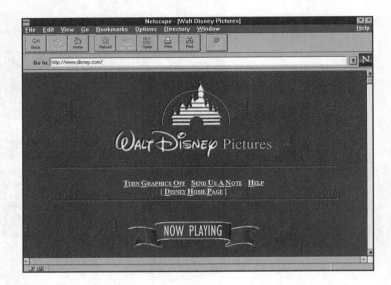

FIGURE 3.17.

Disney goes all out for the debut of Toy Story.

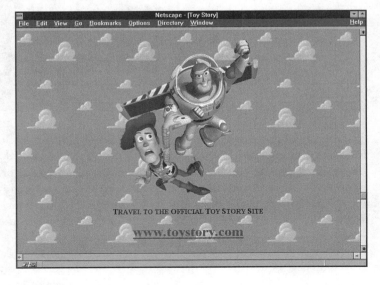

A hidden gem on the Web is *Filmmaker Magazine*, the magazine of independent film, whose site is maintained by New York University. If you didn't know to take a jaunt over to NYU, you would miss a treat for anyone who wants to include digitized video in their Web publications. Although *Filmmaker* is a magazine for independent filmmakers, it goes into depth on many issues related to creating and digitizing video. You'll find invaluable insight into video production and links to industry resources for filmmakers large and small. The *Filmmaker* site is shown in Figure 3.18.

FIGURE 3.18.

Filmmaker Magazine *is an unexpectedly good resource for video production.*

Sci-fi fans everywhere will want to visit Dominion, the Sci-Fi Channel's presence on the Web. The front door to the site alone, shown in Figure 3.19, is worth the trip. If you have a browser that is client pull/server push enabled, you'll see flashing lights, moving objects, and an up-to-date program schedule that scrolls across the middle of your screen. The site features much more than programming information for the Sci-Fi channel. You'll find news and reviews on current TV shows, movies, and anything else related to science fiction.

An area of the site you won't want to miss is the Free Zone. At the Free Zone, you will find digitized videos in the increasingly popular QuickTime format, sound files in Sun's AU format, and images in GIF/JPEG formats. (For more information on these formats or using multimedia in your Web publications, see Chapter 7, "Adding Multimedia Features with HTML.")

The music industry, not to be outdone by the movie industry, has its moguls on the Web as well. If you're into music and want the latest information, the place to go is Rocktropolis. Rocktropolis is a virtual city on the Web where you'll find unsigned bands and industry giants. Everything you see on the main street featured in Figure 3.20 is a doorway to the sights of Rocktropolis. Within Rocktropolis, you'll find opportunities to chat with industry legends and newcomers alike, concert news, and dozens of other things that are sure to distract you for hours. Be sure to check out the clubs, the chat lounge, and the Jim Morrison Hotel.

FIGURE 3.19.

Dominion: the Sci-Fi Channel's ominous Web site.

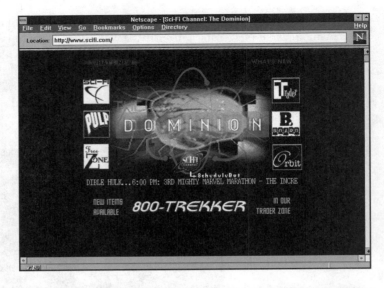

FIGURE 3.20.

Rocktropolis: a city in cyberspace.

Bizarre yet Wonderful

The Web is home to some of the strangest things you will ever find anywhere. Where else but the Web would you find collections of bizarre yet wonderful resources like the Peeping Tom Homepage or the virtual voyage in search of Elvis? The Peeping Tom Homepage is one of those Web pages you would never find unless you stumble across it, yet once you find it, you find yourself irresistibly drawn to it.

The Peeping Tom Homepage, featured in Figure 3.21, isn't what you think it is—well, maybe it is and maybe it isn't. The page is a collection of links to video cameras with live feeds to the Web. Who would've thought that so many video cameras around the world were providing live feeds to the Net? If I hadn't seen the collection all in one place, I would have never believed it. And just what is the value of watching a live feed from the 77th floor of the Empire State Building or Steve's ant farm as the ants tunnel their way through the sand? I don't know, but it's just weird enough to attract thousands of viewers every day.

The availability of camera feeds tends to change frequently, but the Peeping Tom page keeps good track of them. A sample of the live feeds you can access from the page includes this collection of sights:

> The view from the 77th floor of the Empire State Building
> San Diego Bay
> Santa Monica Beach
> Maui
> Ocean front in Santa Cruz
> Boulder, Colorado
> Nob Hill, San Francisco
> Cambridge, Massachusetts
> Sydney, Australia
> Mountains in Scotland
> Vail, Colorado
> The South Shore of Lake Tahoe
> Honolulu, Hawaii
> Sorrento Valley Canyon, San Diego, California
> The Space Needle, Seattle, Washington
> Netscape's Amazing Fish Cam

The virtual voyage in search of Elvis is another bizarre yet wonderful attraction on the Web. Produced by the Houston Chronicle Interactive (`http://www.chron.com/`) as part of their Virtual Voyager series, the virtual voyage in search of Elvis is a collection of Web resources and memorabilia devoted to Elvis. But you don't have to be a fan of the King to get caught up in the excitement.

The Virtual Voyager search for Elvis, shown in Figure 3.22, is only one of several virtual voyages produced by the Houston Chronicle Interactive. To find other voyages, you can go to the Virtual Voyage home page at

`http://www.chron.com/voyager/`

FIGURE 3.21.

The Peeping Tom Homepage isn't what you think it is.

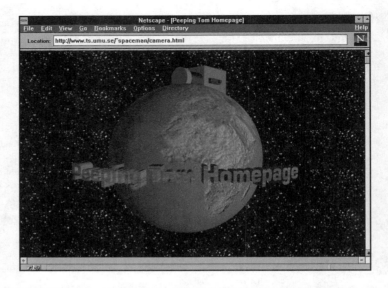

FIGURE 3.22.

A virtual voyage in search of the king of rock and roll.

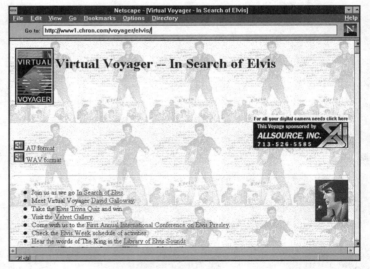

Business in Cyberspace

Business is driving the phenomenal growth of the Web. More than 70 percent of all the resources on the Web are in the commercial domain. The hope for the future of business on the Web is electronic commerce. The businesses of the world want full-scale electronic commerce without any glitches, and they are pouring millions of dollars every year into research.

This research money is rapidly taking electronic commerce from its infancy to the next level, where you can conduct all your banking, financial, and commerce needs online any time of the day or night.

The one-stop index to business on the Net is the Internet Business Center shown in Figure 3.23. Maintained by the Aloha Internet Group (`http://tsunami.tig.com/`), the Internet Business Center has a wealth of useful resources and statistics on Internet business. The timelines, profiles, and presentations will help you understand Internet business and the business directories will lead you to the best business resources on the Net.

FIGURE 3.23.

The Internet Business Center: a one-stop index to business on the Net.

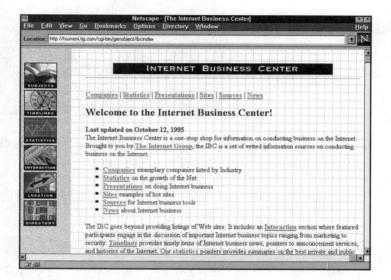

To conduct business on the Web successfully, you need the advice of experts. The place on the Web to learn how to market and advertise online is *Advertising Age*. Each issue of the magazine is filled with essential information that can help drive the success of your Internet marketing efforts and as the slogan for *Advertising Age* says, it's all about marketing. The front door to the *Advertising Age* Web site is shown in Figure 3.24.

The key to selling and buying products online is cybercash. Over a dozen companies from DigiCash (`www.digicash.com`) to First Virtual Holdings (`www.fv.com`) have invented ways to make electronic money transactions on the Internet. While hundreds of businesses have adopted these transfer methods, thousands of businesses are waiting in the sidelines to see what develops next because almost every major credit card company and bank in the world is actively pursuing ways to make full-scale electronic commerce a reality. The goal is to find common ways to make secure money transfers easily, affordably, and effectively.

FIGURE 3.24.

Advertising Age: *your Internet marketing strategist.*

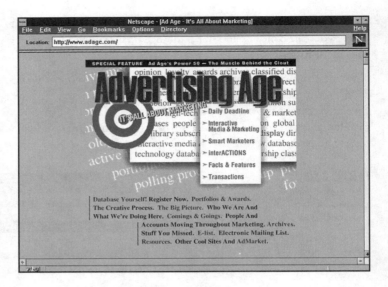

On the Web you will find electronic commerce projects by credit card giants, like MasterCard and Visa. You will also find innovative companies like First Union Corporation striving to put cyberbanking at the forefront of Web technology. First Union's site on the Web is depicted in Figure 3.25. First Union is making a concerted effort to be the first bank to let Web users conduct all their banking needs online.

FIGURE 3.25.

Cyberbanking is coming to the Web.

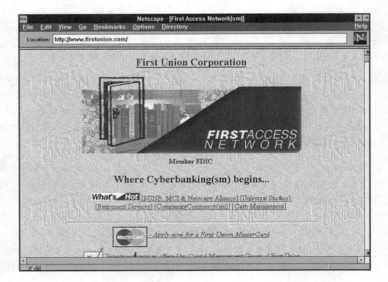

The major success stories in electronic commerce are the shopping malls. The first Internet shopping mall to promote cybershopping on a stellar scale is the Internet Shopping Network (www.internet.net). With the muscle of a billion-dollar parent company backing them, ISN was sure to be a smashing success story and it is. Today ISN has nearly a half-dozen Web servers servicing hundreds of thousands of customers. But ISN is more than an arm of the Home Shopping Network; ISN is the success story that started the race to build shopping malls in cyberspace.

In recent months, the Internet Shopping Network has scaled back its early design that featured a 60,000-byte graphical greeting and gave everyone what they wanted, quick and easy access to bargain-priced products. The redesigned home page is shown in Figure 3.26. The new design is simple, yet much more effective.

FIGURE 3.26.

The Internet Shopping Network: a cybermall.

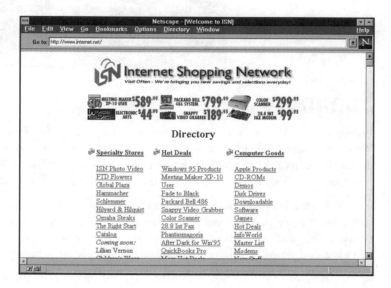

With over 10,000 products, free shipping, and a low-price guarantee, Cybershop is definitely a must-see to complete your Web tour experience. While ISN is scaling back the graphics, the relative newcomer to the cybermall business, Cybershop, is serving graphics up in heaping proportions. As you can see from Figure 3.27, Cybershop greets the world with a graphical menu featuring more than 40 hot spots that you can click on.

FIGURE 3.27.

Cybershop: a growing mall in cyberspace.

Summary

Navigating the Web is easy if you understand the principles of hypertext linking and URLs. While hypertext references can be text- or graphics-based, they are all defined by URLs that define the path to the resources to be accessed and retrieved. As the Web provides a common interface to the Internet, you can use any Internet protocol to access and retrieve Web resources.

The Web has a wealth of resources to visit, study, and learn from. As you start on the journey to become a successful Web publisher, you should visit the sites featured in this tour. Note the sites you liked and the sites you didn't like, then ask yourself what it was about those sites that you liked or disliked. The features you liked, you may want to incorporate into your own Web publications. The features you disliked, you may want to avoid.

Plotting Your Course

4

*by William
Robert Stanek*

If you've browsed the Web lately, you probably noticed that the Web has come a long way in a few short years. With the introduction of HTML 3.0, Java, VRML, and many other powerful Web publishing resources, the simple publications of yesterday have grown into dazzling productions that may leave you wondering "How did they do that?" You may also be wondering if you could create Web publications that would be just as dazzling. The answer is an unequivocal yes.

Plotting your course to success in Web publishing is easy if you know your options. If you do, you will know when and why to use one Web resource over another Web resource and that is exactly what this chapter is all about.

What Is HTML?

When Tim Berners-Lee envisioned the Web, he envisioned it having a common and easy-to-use interface that would enable anyone to Web publish. To accomplish this, he and others at CERN developed the HyperText Markup Language. HTML is based on a subset of the Standard Generalized Markup Language. Using SGML as the basis of HTML ensured that the new markup language for the Web was rooted in a solid standard that was already proven to be a cross-platform solution.

Only the essential elements of SGML were adopted to form the original specification for HTML. Using only the essential elements of SGML drastically reduced the complexity of the original HTML specification and reduced the overhead for transferring hypertext documents over the network. Another advantage of using SGML as the basis for HTML was that SGML document type definitions (DTDs) provided an easy way to extend the HTML standard. Thus, it was the intent of the developers of HTML to create a language for Web documents that was initially simple, yet could grow more complex over time.

What Are the Features of HTML?

The HTML specification has come a long way since the early days. Presently, three specifications for HTML are defined. Each new specification is fully backwards-compatible with previous specifications and includes many enhancements to the HTML standard. In addition to these specifications, many Web publishers are using extensions to the standard. These extensions offer Web publishing solutions that current HTML specifications do not support.

The following sections take a look at the HTML standard and extensions to the standard, including

- HTML 1.0
- HTML 2.0
- HTML 3.0

- Netscape Extensions
- Internet Explorer Extensions
- Java Extensions

HTML 1.0

HTML Version 1 is the original specification for the HyperText Markup Language. Because of the limited capabilities of the specification, documents created with HTML 1.0 have very basic designs. The primary features of HTML 1.0 documents include

> Multiple levels of headings
> Paragraphs
> Hypertext references
> Special formatting for lists of items

Although all HTML browsers can display HTML 1.0 documents, few Web publishers produce documents written exclusively in HTML 1.0 because of the significant improvements offered by later HTML specifications. Consequently, if you plan to publish HTML documents, you should look to the later specifications described below.

HTML 2.0

HTML Version 2 offers better control over the layout and highlighting of text within Web documents and is based on the features and extensions Web publishers were using in their documents before June 1994. The primary enhancements HTML 2.0 provides to the HTML standard are

> Inline images
> Fill-out forms

Being able to display images with the text on the page finally enabled Web publishers to tap into the multimedia capabilities of the Web. Fill-out forms provided Web publishers with a quick and easy way to get participation from users.

When the final draft of HTML 2.0 was ratified recently, the HTML 2.0 specification became a Request For Comments. Most HTML documents on the Web meet the specification for HTML 2.0. You will find dozens of HTML browsers that are HTML 2.0-compliant. If you plan to publish HTML documents on the Web, HTML 2.0 should be your basic publishing solution.

HTML 3.0

Even before the HTML 2.0 draft was ratified, Web publishers eager to create better and more powerful documents started looking to the advanced features offered by HTML 3.0. HTML 3.0 is the next level in HTML publishing and offers powerful features such as

Advanced layout control
Banners
Client-side handling of hot spots in images
Customized lists
Dynamic documents with client pull/server push
Mathematical equations
Style sheets
Tables
Tables within forms

While HTML Version 3 is an emerging standard still being defined, several browsers, including the Netscape Navigator, Internet Explorer, and NCSA Mosaic, already support key enhancements. A growing number of HTML documents have features defined in the HTML Version 3 specification. You will find thousands of documents featuring tables, client-side image maps, and client pull/server push. If you plan to publish HTML documents on the Web, you should strongly consider using HTML 3.0 enhancements.

HTML Extensions for Netscape

Netscape Communications Corporation developed the most popular extensions to the HTML standard. Netscape has many unique extensions. These extensions, like the HTML specification itself, are changing. Many Web users confuse Netscape extensions and HTML 3.0 enhancements. While it is true Netscape created extensions to HTML that are being incorporated into currents draft specifications for HTML 3.0, Netscape adopted key features, like tables, from early drafts of the HTML 3.0 standard.

Netscape implemented the following unique extensions with the release of Netscape Navigator 1.0:

Layout extras like center and blink
Horizontal rule extensions for width, length, and shading
Control over relative font sizes
Control over font color
Use of images or colors to form a background for a document

Although these extensions were once unique to the Netscape Navigator Version 1.0, other companies are adopting these extensions for use in their browsers as well. For example, when Microsoft released the Internet Explorer browser for the Web, the browser featured full support for most Netscape Navigator 1.0 extensions. The development team at Netscape didn't stop with the original extensions. Netscape introduced the following extensions with the release of Netscape Navigator 2.0:

Additional control over font sizes
Support for multiple windows in a document called frames
Netscape scripting language for client-side scripts

The capability to embed multimedia objects and use an add-on module for the browser called a plug-in

Netscape extensions offer terrific solutions for your advanced Web publishing needs. Keep in mind that if you use Netscape extensions, only browsers capable of handling Netscape extensions will display your document as you intended. As approximately 50 percent of Web users have at least a Netscape Version 1.0-capable browser, using Netscape extensions in your publications is something you should seriously consider.

HTML Extensions for Internet Explorer

Until recently, if you used video or sound in your Web publications, users had to select and download the files to preview them. Yet before they could play the sound or video, they needed to have a helper application configured and available for use with their browser. This requires an extra step that not all Web users are willing to take. Yet even the countless millions of users who want to play sound and video files have to install a video or audio player on their system, which isn't always easy.

To solve this problem, Web programmers and developers looked at ways to play multimedia files directly in a user's browser. The first results of this effort came from the computer industry giant, Microsoft. Microsoft's Internet Explorer is the premier browser that directly supports internal multimedia. Using the Internet Explorer, you can

Specify font types and colors
Use scrolling marquees
Use dynamic sources to create inline motion video
Create documents with sound tracks

Internet Explorer extensions are powerful multimedia solutions for your advanced Web publishing needs. However, only browsers capable of handling Internet Explorer extensions can use these features. Currently, Internet Explorer extensions support video in Microsoft AVI format and sound in WAV, AU, and MIDI formats. If you plan to incorporate sound and video into your Web publications, you should seriously consider using Internet Explorer extensions in addition to hypertext references to the multimedia files.

HTML Extensions for Java

Java is Sun Microsystem's contribution to Web publishing. With Java you can create extremely dynamic documents that feature inline applications called applets. Not only are Java applets displayed on the page, they are self-running, interactive programs that can be previewed on any Java-capable browser. The Java language is simple, easy to learn, and like HTML, Java provides a common language that can be used on any computer platform. The implications of a common language for creating applications are so far-reaching that Java became an instant hit with Web publishers and users.

Java introduces only a single extension to HTML: the applet tag. However, the applications you can create with Java are limitless. Already hundreds—perhaps thousands—of Web sites feature Java applets. You can use Java to create games, product demos, utilities, and business applications. Because of the tremendous demand for Java-enhanced publications, many browsers already support or plan to support Java applets. However, keep in mind that only users with a Java-capable browser can view or use an applet. Two browsers currently support applets. The HotJava browser, created by Sun to showcase Java, directly supports applets. The Netscape Navigator 2.0 can use Java applets as an embedded application. You should use Java applets as feature attractions, but not as the only attractions at your Web site.

When to Use HTML and Why

Your Web site can be a collection of pages, publications, and documents that reside on your own Web server, a phantom domain, or a service provider's Web server. While these pages, publications, and documents can be formatted in any single format or a variety of formats, you should use HTML for your home page and all primary pages at the site. This will enable the millions of Web users to easily access and take advantage of your Web site.

HTML should be more than your publishing solution of choice. HTML should be the language you consider first for formatting any new material you plan to publish on the Web. For new publications or documents, you should consider four things:

- The features you want to include
- The style of the document
- The audience for the document
- The format the material is currently in

To get an idea of the features you can include in Web publications, look at the lists of features for HTML and for extensions to HTML, SGML, and VRML found throughout this chapter. When you look at features, you should write down the types of multimedia you would like to include as well as the actual features. Often features you will want to include in your publication take advantage of a particular form of multimedia.

When you look at the style of the document, you should sketch out on paper how you want the material to be organized and the format the material will take on screen. Keep in mind, HTML limits your control over the organization of material based on the level and/or extensions you use. HTML 1.0 offers you limited formatting controls that all Web users, including those with text-only browsers, can take advantage of. HTML 2.0 offers you basic formatting controls that the vast majority of Web users can take advantage of.

While HTML 2.0 is the current standard in Web publishing, Web technology is quickly moving away from HTML 2.0 and toward HTML 3.0. HTML 3.0 offers you more advanced control over document layout and features. HTML extensions offer you unique ways to improve your documents for certain groups of users.

Defining the audience for your Web publications is extremely important. If you know your audience, you can tailor your documents to meet the needs of the audience. For example, if the users you are trying to reach are techno-wizards who seek out cutting-edge sites, you certainly don't want to greet them with pages designed for beginners.

Another thing you should consider when using HTML is the format your documents are currently in. As illustrated in later chapters, you can convert many document formats to HTML and vice versa. However, if the document is already in a form the reader may be able to use, you should consider adding the document in its current format as a hypertext reference on one of your HTML pages.

Many Web publishers provide links to lengthy supplemental documents in both postscript and ASCII text format. Postscript format is used because it is a highly structured format that users can print or view online. If users are unable to print or view postscript files, they can download the files in the no-frills ASCII format. ASCII text files are readable on any computer platform. This enables visitors to the site to access documents you otherwise would not Web publish and saves you the time of having to convert them to a more usable form.

The checklist outlined in Table 4.1 can help you decide which version of the HTML specification or extension to use to meet your Web publishing needs. While you can use the checklist as a guideline, keep in mind that users must have compliant browsers to take advantage of these features.

Table 4.1. A checklist of HTML features and extensions.

Feature	HTML 1.0	HTML 2.0	Netscape 1.0	Netscape 2.0	IE 1.0	IE 2.0	HTML 3.0
Backgrounds	No	No	Yes	Yes	Yes	Yes	Yes
Banners	No	No	No	No	No	No	Yes
Blink	No	No	Yes	Yes	No	No	No
Center (see also text and image alignment)	No	Yes	Yes	Yes	Yes	No	
client pull server push	No	No	No	Yes	No	No	Yes/
Embed multimedia objects	No	No	No	Yes	No	No	No
Font color	No	No	Yes	Yes	Yes	Yes	Yes
Font size, relative	No	No	Yes	Yes	Yes	Yes	Yes
Font type	No	No	No	No	Yes	Yes	No

continues

Table 4.1. continued

Feature	HTML 1.0	HTML 2.0	Netscape 1.0	Netscape 2.0	IE 1.0	IE 2.0	HTML 3.0
Forms	No	Yes	Yes	Yes	Yes	Yes	Yes
Frames	No	No	No	Yes	No	No	Yes
Headings	Yes	Yes	Yes	Yes	Yes	Yes	Yes
Horizontal rule	Yes	Yes	Yes	Yes	Yes	Yes	Yes
Horizontal rule extensions	No	No	Yes	Yes	Yes	Yes	Yes
Image alignment (left, right, center)	No	No	Yes	Yes	Yes	Yes	Yes
Image maps, client-side	No	No	No	Yes	Yes	Yes	Yes
Images, inline	No	Yes	Yes	Yes	Yes	Yes	Yes
Images, aligning (left, right, center)	No	No	No	No	No	No	Yes
Scripts, client-side	No	No	No	Yes	No	No	No
Links, hypertext	Yes	Yes	Yes	Yes	Yes	Yes	Yes
Lists	Yes	Yes	Yes	Yes	Yes	Yes	Yes
Lists, customized	No	No	Yes	Yes	Yes	Yes	Yes
Marquees, scrolling	No	No	No	No	No	Yes	No
Mathematical equations	No	No	No	No	No	No	Yes
Paragraphs	Yes	Yes	Yes	Yes	Yes	Yes	Yes
Paragraphs, center	No	No	Yes	Yes	Yes	Yes	Yes
Sound Tracks, inline	No	No	No	No	No	Yes	No
Style sheets	No	No	No	No	No	No	Yes
Tables	No	No	Yes	Yes	Yes	Yes	Yes
Tables within forms	No	No	No	No	No	No	Yes
Text alignment (left, right, center)	No	No	No	No	No	No	Yes
Video, inline	No	No	No	No	No	Yes	No

What Is SGML?

The Standard Generalized Markup Language was designed to solve compatibility issues for the exchange of strictly formatted documents between different computer platforms. Before SGML, there were limited options for the electronic exchange of documents in a format consistently usable by the recipient. You could reduce the formatting of the document to its most basic form using the standard ASCII text format, or you could try to convert one proprietary format to another proprietary format if a converter was available. Generally, the ASCII formatted or converted document didn't look anything like the creator intended, and this was a major problem.

To solve this problem, the authors of SGML developed a platform-independent format for documents. This means computer systems can exchange SGML documents without regard to the type of receiving computer system. Using SGML, the receiving computer can display or print the document in the precise format and style of the original document. Interestingly enough, the cross-platform solution achieved with SGML was accomplished by distributing the documents as ASCII text with special formatting called markup included with the text in the document.

While the format of SGML documents is defined in terms of standard ASCII text, the documents are not restricted to the formatting offered by ASCII text. The authors of SGML recognized that formatting changes according to the component parts of a publication. Generally, the font type, color, and size are consistent with the way the text is used in a document: A Level One heading has a consistent font type and size; a Level Two heading has a consistent font type and size; and so on.

SGML differentiates between component parts and objects to be displayed or printed using unique characters that identify document tags and entities. Tags define parts of the document and include an element name enclosed by brackets, such as <P>, which indicates the beginning of a paragraph. Entities are generally special components of the document, such as special characters. Special character entities are described by an entity name preceded by an ampersand and ending with a semicolon, such as & for an ampersand. Tags and entities used in SGML documents are called markup.

What Are the Features of SGML?

Using SGML markup, you can create extremely complex document structures. The structure of SGML documents is defined by declaring a document type and defining all assignments and entities associated with the document type. The document type is formally called a document type definition. A single DTD can define hundreds or thousands of assignments and entities. After you have defined a DTD, you can apply it to a single document or a group of related documents.

SGML DTDs are so powerful and versatile that you can create an entirely new way to publish documents if you so desire. When Tim Berners-Lee and the team at CERN looked for a solution for Web publishing, they turned to SGML and defined the structure for HTML 1.0 using a SGML DTD. Today, all the specifications for the HyperText Markup Language are defined with SGML DTDs. But the potential of SGML doesn't stop there. Dozens of companies have created turnkey publishing systems using SGML. Other companies have used SGML as the model for their proprietary page definition languages.

Thus, the main advantage to SGML is that you define the features your documents will contain. You define what a heading will look like, what paragraph text will look like, what quotations will look like, and any other component parts of the document. As demonstrated in later chapters of this book, there are many tools you can use to dramatically reduce the complexity of creating SGML documents. These tools give you as much or as little control over document formatting elements as you need for your publications.

When to Use SGML and Why

As you have seen, SGML is powerful. The power SGML affords publishers does not come without disadvantages, however. If you create a SGML DTD for your Web-published documents, the DTD must be transferred with the document. This means additional downloading time. Users view your Web-published SGML documents with a SGML browser. Currently there are over a dozen SGML browsers available. These browsers range from commercial products like Interleaf 5 <SGML> to freeware products like SoftQuad's Panorama Free. Besides browser support for SGML, some page layout tools will also display SGML documents.

Despite the power of SGML and the widespread availability of SGML-capable applications, use of SGML on the Web is limited. Primarily, this is because the Web community has wholeheartedly adopted the HTML standard. SGML is also not widely used because SGML is a complex language with many nuances. Remember, a goal of the authors of HTML was to drastically reduce the complexity of current publishing solutions and to make HTML the tool for all would-be Web publishers no matter their skill level. The basic premise of HTML was to create an easy and straightforward way to produce generic documents.

While the first specification for HTML accomplished this goal, it did so at great expense to functionality. The authors of HTML decided to overcome the loss of functionality in the long term by continuing to develop HTML. Each new specification for HTML has increased the level of complexity in the HTML standard. Although the enhancements introduced by HTML 2.0 and HTML 3.0 are significant, SGML has always supported these features. The HTML standard is in fact slowly working toward a level of functionality equivalent to what SGML already supports. However, no matter how advanced HTML gets, you will never be able to define a true DTD using HTML. Thus, you should use SGML when you need the freedom it offers or when you cannot meet your publishing needs with HTML or VRML.

SGML documents are used by Web publishers to supplement the primary HTML documents at Web sites. Instead of or in addition to providing lengthy supplement documents in postscript and ASCII format, you could provide the documents in SGML format. This gives users an advanced option for viewing certain types of documents at your Web site. Additionally, as an increasing number of businesses are choosing SGML as their in-house publishing solution, you may already have some of your documents in SGML format.

What Are Page Layout Applications?

Page layout applications are commercial tools for structuring documents. The popularity of page layout applications stems largely from their friendliness, ease of use, and rich control over document structure. Using the friendly graphical interface of your favorite page layout application, you can easily create advanced documents with structures rivaling those of the hottest print magazines.

The primary disadvantage of using a page layout application is that for the most part these applications use a proprietary format. To view a document created in a proprietary format, the end-user must have a compatible reader. Some companies that create page layout applications provide readers free. Other companies charge a fee or royalty for the use of the reader.

Each page layout application offers unique features. These features can strongly influence your decision to use an application to meet your publishing needs. The three most popular layout applications are

> Adobe Acrobat
> CorelVENTURA
> Common Ground

Adobe Acrobat

Adobe Acrobat is a suite of applications that together are a cross-platform solution for distributing electronic documents. As the makers of Adobe Acrobat, Adobe Systems Incorporated, invented PostScript, Adobe Acrobat uses a PostScript-based file format called Portable Document Format. PDF is used to describe the structure of documents created with Adobe Acrobat. The Adobe Acrobat package includes four applications:

- Acrobat Distiller, a program to convert PostScript files and images to Acrobat PDF
- Acrobat Exchange, the main application in the package that is used to view, print, copy, and annotate PDF files
- Acrobat PDF Writer, a platform-specific printer driver that is used to print PDF files or create electronic documents that can be viewed later
- Acrobat Reader, the primary tool used by end-users to view and print PDF files

Once you create a PDF file, end-users can view the file using Acrobat Exchange or Acrobat Reader. Using the same applications, end-users can also print your PDF files on a PostScript or non-PostScript printer. While end-users cannot edit your PDF files, the files can be annotated, searched, and separated into component pages.

Versions of Adobe Acrobat are available for Macintosh, Microsoft Windows, and UNIX systems. Using Adobe Acrobat, you can create documents with hypertext links and inline graphics. However, the hypertext links must be internal links within a single document and cannot extend to other documents. A key advantage of Adobe Acrobat is that the application can interpret and convert to PDF format almost any graphic file format.

A key disadvantage of PDF files is their size. PDF files tend to grow very quickly, and a document of only a few pages can easily exceed 1MB. Additionally, current implementations of PDF require that the entire file be downloaded before any of the file can be displayed. This means if you have a 100-page catalog that contains a hypertext-linked index, users must download the entire catalog before they can make any selections.

CorelVENTURA

CorelVENTURA is a turnkey publishing solution that enables you to create powerful documents. Ventura is extremely popular with desktop publishers because of its versatility. Using CorelVENTURA's suite of products designed for desktop and electronic publishing, you can easily integrate text and graphics from popular word processor, spreadsheet, database, and graphic programs into your documents.

Ventura directly supports dozens of text formats. Not only can you import documents into CorelVENTURA, you can also export documents to any of the formats it supports, including

> AmiPro
> ASCII
> Excel
> Lotus 123
> Microsoft Word for DOS
> Microsoft Word for Macintosh
> Microsoft Word for Windows
> RTF
> SGML
> Word Perfect
> WordStar
> XyWrite

Ventura also supports dozens of graphic formats, including

> Adobe Illustrator
> Apple PICT

AutoCAD
CorelDRAW
DOS/Windows BMP, CGM, and PCX
GIF
JPEG

Corel Corporation distributes different packages for CorelVENTURA. The Corel Ventura 5 package includes almost a dozen applications: Adobe Acrobat Reader, Corel Capture, Corel Database Editor, Corel Mosaic, Corel Ventura, CorelKern, CorelQuery, Corel Photo-Paint, MathType Equation Editor, and Zandar TagWrite. While some of these applications, such as Acrobat Reader and Zandar TagWrite, are not created by Corel, together these applications form one of the most complete publishing solutions available. As an added bonus, the Ventura 5 package includes fonts, clip art, digitized photos, style sheets, and document templates.

You should consider using CorelVENTURA when you want to create an advanced publication that will be used in both print and electronic formats. You should also consider using CorelVENTURA when the documents you plan to use as the basis for the publication are in multiple formats for a variety of applications such as word processors, spreadsheets, and databases. The utilities provided in the Ventura package offer terrific facilities for merging documents from a wide variety of applications. Additionally, Ventura has excellent facilities for importing images. Once these documents and images are merged into a Ventura publication, you can save the publication for viewing electronically as an Adobe PDF file.

Common Ground

Common Ground from Common Ground Software is a high-quality product designed specifically for electronic publishing. Common Ground Software produces several software packages. The basic package includes programs for creating electronic documents: a Common Ground viewer for use with a browser called MiniViewer, ProViewer/Linker, and Maker. The basic package is available for Microsoft Windows and Macintosh systems. The Common Ground Web Publishing package includes server software, MiniViewer, ProViewer/Linker, and Maker. While the Common Ground server software is designed for SunOS or Sun Solaris environments, the publishing package is designed to provide services to Windows and Macintosh clients.

Using Common Ground, you can create advanced document layouts that work better than those used in any printed medium. Common Ground uses a proprietary format called DigitalPaper. After you create a DigitalPaper document, end-users can view the document using a Common Ground viewer. The MiniViewer uses minimal system resources and is designed to be launched as a helper application for your browser. MiniViewer is limited in its capabilities, but the ProViewer is full-featured and user-friendly. Using MiniViewer or ProViewer, end-users can also print your DigitalPaper documents. Although end-users cannot edit your DigitalPaper documents, the documents can be annotated and searched.

Unlike some other electronic document formats, DigitalPaper documents can contain advanced linking to multiple documents. DigitalPaper documents can also be indexed using Common Ground's built-in indexing facilities. Common Ground also features full support for foreign language and other non-Roman characters, enabling you to easily create text in Kanji, Cyrillic, Greek, or other character sets.

The DigitalPaper format takes advantage of innovations in electronic document technology such as TrueDoc and PixelGrade. Bitstream's TrueDoc is a font imaging process that eliminates the necessity to transmit font data with the file. Common Ground's PixelGrade is a technology to enhance the resolution and readability of text on the page. Both processes work together to increase the quality of your documents while reducing the file size.

Common Ground has some of the best facilities for creating electronic publications. You should consider using Common Ground when you want to create an advanced publication that will be used primarily in electronic format. You should also consider using Common Ground when the documents you plan to use as the basis for the publication are in popular word processor or graphics formats.

What Is VRML?

Virtual Reality is not a new idea. People have been fantasizing about VR worlds for decades. Some of the most forward thinkers of our time have been trying to create true VR applications. Other forward thinkers were trying to think of ways to integrate VR technology into the real world. Today, VR and 3-D modeling are moving into the mainstream. Dozens of companies produce applications for rendering 3-D images. The era of Computer-Aided Design is upon us. Corporations, large and small, use CAD/CAM to reduce costs for developing and testing products as well as to create better products.

The Virtual Reality Modeling Language is an outgrowth of the strong interest in VR and 3-D modeling technologies, yet bringing VR to the Web was a major undertaking. While the rest of the Internet community was eagerly downloading the Mosaic browser in October 1993 and heading out into two-dimensional cyberspace, a group of forward thinkers were already considering how the Web could be transformed by VR. These forward thinkers put their heads together at a special meeting during the First International Conference on the World Wide Web in March of 1994. An objective of the meeting was to launch an effort to create a common VR language for the Web, and launch an effort they did.

VRML became a buzzword on the Net. By October 1994, the draft specification for VRML 1.0 was ready to present at the Second International Conference on the World Wide Web. By May 1995, the VRML 1.0 specification was already in its third and final draft. What Mark Pesce, Tony Parisi, Gavin Bell, and the other authors of VRML created was a 3-D modeling language.

What VRML brings to the Web is the capability to render complex 3-D images using simple markup instructions. Like HTML, VRML is designed to be platform-independent and extendible, and use limited network bandwidth. VRML does this using a language that is based on Silicon Graphics' Open Inventor File Format. The authors of VRML chose the Open Inventor File Format because it was a versatile ASCII-based format for rendering 3-D objects. Defining 3-D objects in terms of ASCII characters was the key to ensuring that anyone who wanted to use or create VRML documents could.

What Are the Features of VRML?

Although VRML was developed to be independent of HTML, VRML depends on the structure of hypertext to transfer files across the network. Thus, everything you learned about HTTP and URLs also applies to VRML. You access VRML documents with a VRML browser or a HTML browser with a VRML add-on module. The URLs to VRML documents look just like the URLs to HTML documents except for the extension. HTML documents use the .htm or .html extension, and VRML documents use the .wrl extension. The .wrl extension is used to identify VRML documents called world files.

The power of VRML is that you no longer need a $20,000 workstation or a $500 graphics application to build 3-D models. VRML enables you to create complex 3-D scenes using a basic PC and monitor. You create 3-D scenes with VRML using markup code that defines polygonally rendered objects and special effects for lighting, ambiance, and realism.

VRML documents are entirely graphical in nature. The only text in a VRML document is represented as an object or within a VRML image. The VRML 1.0 specification concentrates on how 3-D scenes are rendered in cyberspace. The intent was to create an easy-to-use solution that, like HTML, would be extended over time. Consequently, VRML 1.0 includes only the most basic facilities for linking VRML objects and scenes.

While the linking facilities in the current implementation of VRML are basic, the model rendering facilities are anything but basic. In VRML, the objects you render are called nodes. VRML 1.0 defines 36 types of nodes. Using these nodes, you can easily create 3-D cones, cylinders, cubes, and spheres. Once you define a shape for an object, you can add texture, lighting, camera effects, and object transformations using a few lines of markup code.

When to Use VRML and Why

The possibilities for Web publishing with VRML are anything but limited. Once you've seen VRML in action on the Web, you will have no doubts that a technology and information revolution is sweeping the planet. Many Web publishers see VRML as the future of Web publishing and indeed, the future of all publishing may be in graphics-based mediums that users can interact with.

When most people think of virtual reality, they think of alternate realities. Yet VRML can be used to render any type of object. You should use VRML whenever you want to model an object that you want users to be able to interact with. The time to experiment with VRML is now, while the technology is young. Here are some example uses for VRML world files:

- Create a VRML model of a VCR and TV that users can interact with to teach people how to program their VCRs.

- Create a VRML model of downtown Los Angeles to show people LA's hot spots.

- Create a VRML model of a college campus to show visitors, students, and teachers how to find the campus resources.

- Create a VRML model of a building to demonstrate your design skills.

- Create a VRML model of the new layout for the office to sell the idea to the boss and to show the rest of the staff where their cubicles will be located.

- Create a VRML model of the solar system as a teaching tool that visitors can actually explore.

While the previous examples are all great reasons to use VRML, you should use VRML when it will enhance the information content or entertainment value of your Web site. VRML should be a feature that supplements material at your existing site. If you are creating your first Web publication or site, the primary documents should be created with HTML. You will do well to create and publish the primary HTML documents before you try to tackle VRML. Once you have your publication or site up and running, you can start creating your VR masterpiece.

Languages Used on the Web: Summing It All Up

The comparison of markup and page layout languages shown in Table 4.2 is meant to help you decide what language to use for your Web publishing efforts. You should use the table as a rough guideline and not an absolute.

As discussed in this chapter and given the current state of Web publishing, HTML 2.0 is best used for the primary documents at your site. HTML 3.0 and extensions to HTML should be used in alternate documents or as alternate features in addition to your HTML 2.0 features. Documents formatted with SGML, page layout applications, or VRML should be supplemental documents. Although supplemental documents could be Web publications in and of themselves, they are linked to your primary HTML pages, and Web users generally access these documents from your primary HTML pages.

The level of support for text layout and style is a major issue you should consider when Web publishing. Most markup and page layout languages support text. However, VRML wasn't designed with textual pages in mind; VRML was designed to render 3-D images.

In Table 4.2, text layout refers to the actual positioning of text within the document and text style refers to the other design elements like font type, color, and size. Using HTML 2.0, you can create documents with basic layout and style. HTML 3.0 enables you to create documents with a more advanced layout and style. HTML extensions like Netscape frames provide you with an advanced way to layout text, but do not resolve advanced style issues. Although SGML gives you advanced control over the style and layout of text, you will either have to use a generic DTD or one that you create yourself. Keep in mind, using a generic SGML DTD reduces your creative freedom and creating your own DTD is time intensive. Because page layout applications are the only applications that give you maximum control over text layout and style, they are rated superior in these areas. Finally, VRML supports basic features for the layout and style of text.

Designing pages with multiple columns using text, graphics, or a combination of text and graphics is something that is high on most Web publishers' wish list. This is because in HTML the only way to create multiple columns is to use a clever workaround. In HTML 2.0, you can use preformatted text to create multiple columns of text. To create multiple columns of graphics in HTML 2.0, your only option is to align the images side by side or use clever spacing techniques such as transparent images for spacing. Additionally, in HTML 2.0 there is no way to align text and graphics into distinct columns. In HTML 3.0, you can use tables to create multiple columns of text, images, or combinations of text and images. HTML 3.0 also enables you to align an image in one column and text in another column. With Netscape frame extensions, you can create multiple window frames on the screen and thus create multiple columns. In SGML, you can create columns, if you make column definitions in the DTD for your documents. The only real way to create multiple columns of text, graphics, or combinations of text and graphics is with page layout applications. Finally, in a 3-D VRML environment, columns for text and graphics are not directly applicable.

Table 4.2 offers a comparison of the capabilities of markup and page layout languages to support text layout and style.

Table 4.2. Comparison of markup and page layout languages.

	HTML 2.0	HTML 3.0	HTML Extensions	SGML	Page Layout	VRML 1.0
Best use	primary	alt	alt	suppl	suppl	suppl
Text support	yes	yes	yes	yes	yes	limited
Layout	basic	inter.	adv.	adv.	v. adv.	basic
Style	basic	inter.	inter.	adv.	v. adv.	basic
Multiple columns text	limited	limited	limited	yes	yes	n/a

continues

Table 4.2. continued

	HTML 2.0	HTML 3.0	HTML Extensions	SGML	Page Layout	VRML 1.0
Multiple columns graphics	limited	limited	limited	yes	yes	n/a
Multiple columns text & graphics	no	limited	limited	yes	yes	n/a
Hypertext support	yes	Yes	yes	yes	limited	limited
Hypertext options	advanced	v adv.	advanced	advanced	n/a	basic

Multimedia is a powerful aspect of any Web publication. As a Web publisher, you must understand the multimedia options available. As Table 4.3 shows, markup and page layout applications have different levels of support for multimedia. Table 4.3 is meant to help you decide what language to use to meet your multimedia needs. You should use the table as a rough guideline and not an absolute.

HTML and SGML browsers support external multimedia using helper applications. The browser calls the helper application and the helper application enables the user to preview the image, sound, or video you have added to the document as an external resource. The page layout applications featured in this chapter do not support external multimedia. While VRML supports multimedia, the support is limited. Current VRML browsers do not support helper applications. A reader of your VRML document must have launched the VRML browser as a helper application from their HTML browser. If the reader did this, the helper application table in the reader's HTML browser will be used to determine what helper application to use.

The level of support for inline graphics is a major issue you should consider when Web publishing. Most markup and page layout languages support inline graphics. However, the level of support varies greatly.

In Table 4.3, layout for graphics refers to the actual positioning of graphics within the document and options for graphics refers to support for multiple graphic formats, features for altering image size, and so on. HTML 2.0 applications support basic layout for graphics and few options for image formats and manipulation. HTML 3.0 applications and applications using extensions to HTML support more advanced layout for graphics and many options for image manipulation. SGML applications support advanced layout for graphics and many options for manipulating images, provided the definitions are made in the document's DTD. Page layout applications support the most advanced layout for graphics and the most options for image formats and manipulation. Finally, VRML offers advanced layout and many options for manipulating 3-D images.

The final multimedia features Table 4.3 includes are inline sound and video. Inline sound and video are relatively new developments in Web publishing. While inline sound and video are gaining support, the options at this time are limited. Internet explorer extensions directly support inline video in Microsoft AVI format and sound in WAV, AU, and MIDI formats. Netscape 2.0 extensions support the embedding of multimedia objects. To use embedded objects, users must have a Netscape plug-in or have a helper application configured in their browser and installed on their system.

Table 4.3. Multimedia support in markup and page layout applications.

	HTML 2.0	*HTML 3.0*	*HTML Extensions*	*SGML*	*Page Layout*	*VRML 1.0*
External graphics support	Yes	Yes	Yes	Yes	No	Limited
External sound support	Yes	Yes	Yes	Yes	No	Limited
External video support	Yes	Yes	Yes	Yes	No	Limited
Inline graphics support	Yes	Yes	Yes	Yes	Yes	Yes
Layout	Basic	Inter	Inter	Adv.	Superior	(3-D)
Options	Few	Many	Many	Many	Most	(3-D)
Inline sound support	No	No	Yes	No	No	No
Inline video support	No	No	Yes	No	No	No

Summary

Plotting your course to success in Web publishing is an extremely important step. As you have seen in this chapter, the face of Web publishing has changed dramatically since the early days. While HTML was once the only option available, Web publishers now have a fleet of options. You can Web publish with HTML 2.0, HTML 3.0, Netscape 1.0 extensions, Netscape 2.0 extensions, Internet Explorer extensions, Java extensions, and SGML, VRML and Page Layout applications. Successful Web publishers understand the options available and use those options to meet their needs.

PART

IN THIS PART

Web Publishing with HTML

Creating Web Documents with HTML

5

by William Robert Stanek

While you can easily create documents with HTML, it is your design that will help sell your ideas, products, or services to a global audience. You do not have to be a programmer or a computer wizard to design dazzling HTML documents. What you need is a firm understanding of HTML design concepts and the pointers you will find in this and other chapters in this book. As discussed in Chapter 4, "Plotting Your Course," the HyperText Markup Language is a markup language based on the Standard Generalized Markup Language. While SGML markup code is complex, HTML markup code is easy to learn and use. HTML enables you to format information in ways that are friendly, interactive, and visually appealing.

Creating HTML Documents

The formatting of HTML documents depends on markup codes called tags. Tags define the structure of the document and include an element name enclosed by brackets, such as <H1>, that indicates the start of a Level One heading. HTML is not case sensitive. This means <h1> and <H1> both denote the same thing.

Most tags are used in pairs. A tag called the begin tag tells the browser a document element is beginning. Another tag called the end tag tells the browser an element is ending. The only difference between a begin tag and an end tag is the end tag contains a forward slash before the element name. For example, the begin heading tag <H1> is paired with the end heading tag </H1>. The initial <H1> tag tells the browser a Level One heading is starting and the end tag </H1> tells the browser the heading is ending.

> **TIP**
>
> Typically, when you create documents in a word processor or text editor, the documents contain text formatting such as tabs, spacing, paragraph markings, or page breaks. A key concept to keep in mind as you create your first Web page is that ASCII text formatting is normally ignored. When your browser sees any of these text formatting techniques, no matter how many times you repeat them, the browser interprets them as a single space. Generally, any of the following will be displayed by your browser as a single space:
>
> Single tab/Multiple tabs
>
> Single space/Multiple spaces
>
> Single paragraph markings/Multiple paragraph markings
>
> Single page breaks/Multiple page breaks

In HTML, you can also define a special character to display. Special characters are described by an element name preceded by an ampersand and ending with a semicolon, such as & for the ampersand symbol. When a browser sees a special character, the browser interprets the special character and displays the corresponding symbol if possible.

Defining the Document Structure

Every HTML document should begin with the markup tag <HTML> and end with the markup tag </HTML>. The begin tag <HTML> tells the browser the document is an HTML-formatted document and marks the beginning of the document. The end tag </HTML> marks the end of the document and is always the last item in any HTML document.

While you may find HTML documents on the Web that do not include the begin and end <HTML> tags, it is poor design style not to use these tags. As explained in Chapter 4, "Plotting Your Course," HTML is not the only markup language in use on the Web. Without identifying your document as an HTML document, you may confuse the reader's browser.

Every HTML document should also have a header and a body. The header immediately follows the first <HTML> tag. The header is used to specify key aspects of the document, such as the title of the document. The beginning of the header is specified with the begin header tag <HEAD> and the end of the header is specified with the end tag </HEAD>.

Following the header is the main section of the document called the body. The body contains the text and objects you want to display in the reader's browser. Like the header, the body has a begin tag <BODY> and an end tag </BODY>.

> **NOTE**
>
> The examples throughout this book generally show markup in capital letters. While using capital letters in markup code is good form and helps to clearly differentiate between code and text, capital letters are not necessary. HTML is not case-sensitive. Thus, <BODY>, <body>, <Body> and <BoDy> all mean the same thing.

While most current HTML browsers can infer the header and body sections of HTML documents, it is good form to include the HEADER and BODY elements in all your HTML documents. Using the three tags discussed in this section, you can create the framework for an HTML document as follows:

```
<HTML>
<HEAD>
. . .
</HEAD>
<BODY>
. . .
</BODY>
</HTML>
```

In the example, the ellipses are used to show where additional information would go in an actual document. Now that we have the framework for an HTML document, let's look at components and concepts for the header and body elements.

HTML Header Design

The header section is primarily used to provide information about the document to the Web server. Everything in the header section is located between the begin and end header tags. Six HTML tags are reserved specifically for the header:

`<TITLE>`	The title of the document
`<BASE>`	Identifies the base URL for the document
`<ISINDEX>`	Provides a way to turn on the browser's textual search mechanism
`<LINK>`	Identifies the document's relationship to other documents
`<META>`	Enables you to identify general or meta-information about the document
`<NEXTID>`	Identifies the next identifier to be generated

NOTE

The `<BASE>`, `<LINK>`, `<META>`, and `<NEXTID>` tags do not display when the document is loaded into the reader's browser and are used primarily by Web publishers with large sites to manage. While these tags are used infrequently, this may stem from a lack of understanding about the purpose of the tags. The tags provide information about the document to the Web server and to anyone who reads the HTML source code for the document.

Using Document Titles

The most commonly used header tag is the `<TITLE>` tag. The begin title tag `<TITLE>` identifies the beginning of the document title, and the end title tag `</TITLE>` identifies the ending of the document title. Each document can only have one title. Because a limited number of characters will be displayed, your title should be short but descriptive. A general rule to follow for the length of the title is 65 characters or less. Additionally, the title can contain no extra formatting or markup. This means the title should contain only plain ASCII characters.

Because the title may be referenced separately from your document by the user, the title should provide insight into the contents or topic of the document. A good title for the extreme sports service in Australia could be

```
<TITLE>Extreme Sports Australia</TITLE>
```

Depending on the focus of the document, a better title might be

```
<TITLE>Extreme Sports in Australia and New Zealand</TITLE>
```

or

```
<TITLE>Extreme Sport Experiences in Australia and New Zealand</TITLE>
```

The title could be added to the framework of a Web document as follows:

```
<HTML>
<HEAD>
<TITLE>Extreme Sport Experiences in Australia and New Zealand</TITLE>
</HEAD>
<BODY>
. . .
</BODY>
</HTML>
```

Using Base Links

Normally, you access files on a local Web server using a relative file path. When you use a relative path to locate a file, you are locating the file in relation to the current file. Although this is the normal way to use relative paths, you can define a base path for all relative links in your document. Using a base path, you can tell the browser to locate files in relation to a specific path that could actually point to a remote server.

The `<BASE>` tag can only appear within the `<HEAD>` element. The only valid attribute for the `<BASE>` tag is HREF.

You could define a base path as follows:

`<BASE HREF="http://tvp.com/">`

The base path example tells the browser to add `http://tvp.com/` to all relative links in the document. You will find that defining a base path is most useful when your document is available at two different locations and you want to relate them to documents at a specific location. For example, you could publish your home page at a free Web mall without changing relative addresses to absolute addresses. Listing 5.1 shows how you would do it.

Listing 5.1. `tvphome.htm`.

```
<HTML>
<HEAD>
<TITLE>The Virtual Press — A Hot Spot on the Web</TITLE>
<BASE HREF="http://tvp.com/">
</HEAD>
<BODY>
<P> <A HREF="vpbg.html"><IMG SRC="vpttl11.gif" ALT=""></A></P>
<H2><IMG SRC="bboard.gif" ALIGN="BOTTOM" ALT="* ATTN *">
The Original Virtual Press — Hot contests for writers &amp; artists,
job information, electronic publishing information and much more!</H2>
<P><STRONG><A HREF="vphp.html">Experience the explosive features we've
created especially for you.</A></STRONG></P>
. . .
</BODY>
</HTML>
```

Whenever a user accessed the example document, no matter where the document was actually located on the Web, any links the user followed would lead them to pages at the tvp.com Web site. The base path also ensures other relative paths on the page are valid at the new site, including the path to the images on your page.

Using the base path defined above, the relative references in the document—`vpbg.html`, `vpttl11.gif`, `bboard.gif`, and `vphp.htm`—would be interpreted as

`http://tvp.com/vpbg.html`

`http://tvp.com/vpttl11.gif`

`http://tvp.com/bboard.gif`

`http://tvp.com/vphp.html`

Using *<ISINDEX>*

The <ISINDEX> tag is used with interactive searches of your document. To activate an ISINDEX query, a user must first access a gateway script that generates an HTML document containing the <ISINDEX> tag. When the user enters information requested by the query, a special URL containing the path to the original script and the information the user typed in is sent back to the gateway script for processing. The specification that describes how gateways pass information to the server is called Common Gateway Interface (CGI). CGI enables HTML documents to call external programs called gateway scripts. By calling gateway scripts, you can make your Web documents highly interactive and extremely dynamic. CGI provides the basis for creating the interactive forms and image maps discussed in Chapter 12, "Form and Image Map Creation and Design."

Using *<LINK>*

Although header links are defined in the HTML 2.0 standard, no HTML 2.0-compliant browsers support this powerful and versatile element. Possible uses for the <LINK> tag are discussed in detail in the next chapter.

Using *<META>*

When a client application requests an HTML document, a Web server normally passes the document with a response header prepended. This header is separate from the HTML HEAD element and contains information the client needs to interpret the document. Sometimes you will want to modify the standard header or create your own header for special situations. Other times, you will want to provide information to the client that you could not pass using standard HTML elements. Using the <META> tag, you could pass this extra or specialized information in the HEAD element of a document. The server retrieving the document would include this information in the response header for the client's use.

The <META> tag has three attributes:

```
CONTENT
HTTP-EQUIV
NAME
```

Generally, these three attributes are used with each other. You can specify information to be included in the response header using the HTTP-EQUIV attribute. To do this you should use a valid HTTP header name and supply a value for it using the CONTENT attribute. If you do not know the valid HTTP header name or do not supply a header name using HTTP-EQUIV, you should use the NAME attribute to identify the value you are referencing with the CONTENT attribute.

In general, you would use the `<META>` tag only when there wasn't another HTML tag you could use to provide the information. Header names are not case-sensitive. You could use meta-information to specify an expiration date for your document as follows:

```
<META HTTP-EQUIV="expires" CONTENT="Mon, 31 Dec 1998 10:00:00 HST">
```

A Web server would add this meta-information to the document's response header as

```
Expires: Mon, 31 Dec 1998 10:00:00 HST
```

You could use meta-information to set keywords for the document. Here, the keywords are publishing, books, and magazines:

```
<META HTTP-EQUIV="keywords" CONTENT="Publishing, Books, Magazines">
```

A Web server would add this meta-information to the document's response header as

```
Keywords: Publishing, Books, Magazines
```

You could use meta-information to specify a time interval that the client should request the file again. Here, the client will re-request the file every thirty seconds:

```
<META HTTP-EQUIV="refresh" CONTENT="30">
```

If you use the NAME attribute, the server will not generate a response header. Some information you may want to pass in this way includes an e-mail address as the document's author, the date the document was published, and other information not specifically addressed by other HTML tags. You could specify the document's author as follows:

```
<META NAME="author" CONTENT="william@tvp.com">
```

You could specify the document's publication date as follows:

```
<META NAME="published" CONTENT="Mon, 15 Nov 1995">
```

Your HTML documents can have several `<META>` tags. The meta-information used as examples in this section could be added to the HEAD element of an HTML document as shown in Listing 5.2.

Listing 5.2. `metasamp.htm`.

```
<HTML>
<HEAD>
<TITLE>The Web Book</TITLE>
<META HTTP-EQUIV="expires" CONTENT="Mon, 31 Dec 1998 10:00:00 HST">
<META HTTP-EQUIV="keywords" CONTENT="Publishing, Books, Magazines">
<META HTTP-EQUIV="refresh" CONTENT="30">
<META NAME="author" CONTENT="william@tvp.com">
<META NAME="published" CONTENT="Mon, 15 Nov 1995">
```

```
</HEAD>
<BODY>
  . . .
</BODY>
</HTML>
```

Using *<NEXTID>*

The <NEXTID> tag is used only by HTML editors that generate identifiers for elements. Using <NEXTID>, the editor tracks the next ID value to assign to an element. In this way, the editor uses unique identifiers for elements.

The <NEXTID> tag has only one attribute: N

The value of the N attribute is the next identifier for an element. This identifier should be alphanumeric. You must use the N attribute and specify a value as follows:

```
<NEXTID N="alphanumeric value">
```

In this example, the ID value of the next element you create would be alpha7:

```
<NEXTID N="alpha7">
```

The <NEXTID> tag is used only by HTML editors. Browsers do not use the <NEXTID> tag in any way.

HTML Body Design

The main section of a Web document is the body. Everything in the body is located between the begin and end body tags. Dozens of HTML tags can be used in the body. These tags are defined throughout this chapter and in other chapters that explore HTML. As you design your document, focus on the structure of the elements you plan to include in the body section.

Well-designed documents look effortless and achieve their impact from simplicity of design. They are organized in a way that is coherent and flowing. Yet designs that seem simple and natural to the reader are often the result of intense efforts to make them seem this way. You can use many techniques to structure the document in powerful yet uncomplicated ways.

Sometimes it is not what you have on the page that helps convey your message, but what you do not have on the page. Empty space on the page makes material easier to read and helps focus the reader's attention on your ideas. Interestingly enough, it is the separation of the material that creates the emphasis and draws the reader's attention. Two key components of the page that can help you create white space are paragraphs and headings.

Browsers typically display an empty space between paragraphs, so a page with many paragraphs will have more white space. You should use short paragraphs the most and long paragraphs the least. A short paragraph has fewer than six lines. A long paragraph has 10 or more lines. Varying the length of paragraphs is a key technique to keep the reader's attention. If you use the same paragraph length repeatedly, even the most lively material seems monotonous.

Browsers also display an empty space between headings. Using headings, you can divide the document into sections or topics. A document broken into topics looks more manageable and interesting. Headings help the reader identify the main points of the document at a glance. They also help the reader quickly find topics of interest.

Color is another key feature you can add to the document. Most browsers display your document on a gray background. Netscape includes an extension for the <BODY> tag that enables you to add images and color to the background. Other extensions enable you to specify the color of text and links. If you plan to enhance your documents specifically for users with a browser that uses Netscape extensions, this can be a good extension to take advantage of. Netscape extensions are featured in Chapter 8, "Netscape and Internet Explorer Extensions."

Often the best way to add color to the page is through graphic images. A few pictures placed strategically on the page can dramatically increase the impact of the page. Your pictures do not have to be sophisticated or high-resolution. Simple is usually best. You should place the images so they focus the reader's attention on the key aspects of the page. For example, placing a small eye-catching graphic at the beginning of a key paragraph. Adding pictures to your documents is featured in Chapter 7, "Adding Multimedia Features with HTML."

The key components of a basic HTML document are headings and paragraphs. Most basic documents also use comments, special characters, and text elements such as quotes or addresses. The next sections discuss the five basic document components:

Headings

Paragraphs

Comments

Special characters

Additional text elements

Creating Headings

Using headings, you can better organize your ideas. The chapters of most nonfiction books use many levels of headings. You will usually find chapter headings, sections headings that pertain to each major topic, and subheadings pertaining to subtopics. Usually, headings are in a bold type and larger than normal font size. The size of the font is often related to the level of the heading. Chapter headings use the largest font size, section headings use a slightly smaller font size, and so on. The boldfaced text at the top of the section is an example of a subtopic heading level.

HTML enables you to create up to six levels of headings, <H1> through <H6>. Like many other tags, heading tags are used in pairs. For example, the begin Level One heading tag <H1> is used with the end Level One heading tag </H1>. HTML headings are displayed in bold type. In general, a Level One heading uses the largest font of heading sizes and a Level Six heading uses the smallest font of heading sizes. Browsers typically insert a space before and after the heading.

> **NOTE**
>
> As the Web publisher, you have no direct control over font size in HTML. The size of the font is determined by configurations set up in the browser displaying the document and heading sizes will be consistent relative to each other and the main text. Most browsers display visible differences only in heading levels one to four. This means a Level Four heading is often displayed in the same font size as Level Five and Six headings.

You can create headings as follows:

```
<H1> A Level One Heading </H1>

<H2> A Level Two Heading </H2>

<H3> A Level Three Heading </H3>

<H4> A Level Four Heading </H4>

<H5> A Level Five Heading </H5>

<H6> A Level Six Heading </H6>
```

Creating Paragraphs

After years of casual or professional writing, some processes of writing seem automatic. You probably don't think about the need to place a period at the end of a sentence, or why we use apostrophes in contractions. Similarly, when you start a new paragraph, you probably add a blank line, indentation, or both to separate the new paragraph from the previous paragraph without giving much thought about why. You add the blank line or indentation because it makes sense and because it is what your grammar teacher told you to do. Blank lines and indentation serve to visually separate the paragraphs and break up the document.

In HTML, the way to visually break up the document into paragraphs is to use the paragraph tag <P>. When a browser sees the paragraph tag, it ends the current line and inserts a blank space before inserting the text or object following the paragraph tag. If you are using a word processor or text editor to create your Web document, keep in mind browsers reduce all ASCII text formatting—including multiple spaces, tabs or blank lines—to a single space.

You can create paragraphs as follows:

```
<P> Insert the paragraph text here. </P>
```

Adding Comments to Your Documents

If you are a programmer or have looked at the printout of a computer program, odds are you have seen comments inserted into the code. Comments are used in computer code to make notes or explanations to anyone who may see the code. Even the original programmer finds the comments useful when changes or additions to the code are necessary, especially if they come up months or years after writing the program. Programmers use comments because having to work through the logic of code every time it has to be changed is a waste of time and resources.

Web publishers can similarly use comments to save time and resources when making changes and additions to HTML documents. You can use comments to track the update history of the document, to make notes about text, links or objects in the document, or to pass on information to anyone who may be reading the source code. Comments are not displayed by the browser with the text and objects on the page and are only viewable if you view the source code for the document.

You can add comments to a document using the open comment tag <!— and the end comment tag —>. Each line of text that you want to be a comment should be individually tagged as a comment. Some comments you might make on your document are:

```
<!— Links on this document last checked July 1995 —>

<!— Don't look at the code too close this document is just for fun —>

<!— Section Four list needs to be updated —>
```

Using Special Characters

Special characters are also called entities. In HTML, there are two types of entities: character entities and numeric entities. Character entities use actual text characters to define the special character, such as " for the double quotation mark symbol. Numeric entities use numbers to define the special character and add a hash mark before the number, such as | for the vertical bar (|) symbol. The numbers used with numeric entities correspond to character positions in the ISO Latin I character set. While lists of the ISO Latin I character set are available on the Web, Table 5.1 includes a short list of the most commonly used special characters and their values.

Table 5.1. Commonly used special characters and associated values.

Entity Value	*Displayed in Browser As*
&amp;	&
&gt;	>
&lt;	<
|	|
&#162;	¢
&#163;	£
&#165;	¥
&#169;	©
&#174;	↔

Using special characters in your Web document is easy. Wherever the special character should appear in the text of your document, you simply type in the value associated with the character. When a browser sees that special character, the browser interprets the character and displays the corresponding symbol if possible. For example, when a browser reads the entity value | it will display the vertical bar symbol.

Typical characters that you must use entity values for include any characters used in HTML markup, which is why you must use the > entity for the greater than symbol and the < entity for the less than symbol when you want them to be displayed with the text in the document. If you use the < or > symbol in text you want displayed, you will confuse the browser and probably get strange results. You should watch out for these and other symbols that may confuse your browser. Whenever you find one, check to see if there is an associated entity value that you can use instead of the special character.

More Text Elements

In addition to headings, paragraphs, and special characters, many Web documents contain other text elements, such as

- Addresses
- Blockquotes
- Preformatted text

Using Addresses

The `<ADDRESS>` tag is used to specify that a section of the document contains an address or signature for the page. Browsers typically display address text in italics with a paragraph break before the begin address tag `<ADDRESS>` and a paragraph break after the end address tag `</ADDRESS>`. No other special formatting is associated with the `<ADDRESS>` tag and an address entered in multiple lines as follows:

```
<ADDRESS>
The Virtual Press
408 Division St.
Shawano, WI
54166
</ADDRESS>
```

Would be displayed in italics as follows:

> *The Virtual Press 408 Division St. Shawano, WI 54166*

Therefore, if you wanted the address to appear on more than one line, you would have to insert the line break tag `<BR>` as follows:

```
<ADDRESS>
The Virtual Press<BR>
408 Division St.<BR>
Shawano, WI<BR>
54166
</ADDRESS>
```

Using Blockquotes

The `<BLOCKQUOTE>` tag is used to specify a section of the document containing a quotation. Browsers typically display `<BLOCKQUOTE>` text in regular type with a paragraph break before the begin blockquote tag `<BLOCKQUOTE>` and a paragraph break after the end blockquote tag `</BLOCKQUOTE>`. To further identify blockquote text from other text, blockquote text is indented from both the left and right margins.

Here is how you can use the `<BLOCKQOUTE>` tag in your documents:

```
<BLOCKQUOTE>Sometimes the dragon wins.<BR>
Other times the dragon retires from the field;<BR>
weary from the battle.</BLOCKQUOTE>
```

Using Preformatted Text

Defining a section of text as preformatted is extremely useful and enables you to use standard ASCII text formatting techniques to format text in your documents. In a section of text declared as preformatted, you can use any of your favorite ASCII spacing tricks, including tabs, multiple tabs, multiple spaces, and multiple blank lines.

The `<PRE>` tag is used in a pair of tags as follows:

```
<PRE> Preformatted text </PRE>
```

Figure 5.1 shows how you could use preformatted text in your documents. The text in the preformatted page is displayed in a monospaced font called Courier New. Listing 5.3 is the code for the page.

Listing 5.3. `pretext.htm`.

```
<HTML>
<HEAD>
<TITLE>Markup Languages</TITLE>
</HEAD>
<BODY>
<PRE>
Markup Languages

SGML                    HTML                    VRML
-------------------     -------------------     -------------------
Standard generalized    Hypertext               Virtual Reality
markup language         markup language         modeling language
-------------------     -------------------     -------------------
Basis language for      Based on SGML           Based on SGML
most other markup
languages

Language Level
-------------------     -------------------     -------------------
Complex language        Basic language          Advanced language
Powerful/Versatile      Simple/Straight forward Great for rendering
                                                3-d images and models

Browser Support
-------------------     -------------------     -------------------
Any SGML browser        Any HTML Browser        Any VRML browser
</PRE>
</BODY>
</HTML>
```

FIGURE 5.1

*Creating a table with
preformatted text.*

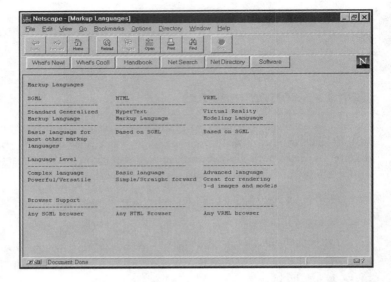

> **CAUTION**
>
> When using the <PRE> tag, keep in mind that monospaced fonts will appear much
> wider than proportional fonts. Proportional fonts use the amount of screen space
> proportional to their size, which means that an *i* uses less screen space than a *w*. In a
> monospaced or nonproportional font, each letter uses the same amount of screen
> space.

The only attribute for the <PRE> tag in HTML 2.0 is the WIDTH attribute. You can use the WIDTH
attribute with the <PRE> tag to specify the maximum number of characters that should appear
on a line. If you do not specify a width, the default is 80 characters. However, as current browsers
do not support the use of the WIDTH attribute, there is no real maximum width or default.

Adding Features to Web Documents

Features you will want to add to your documents are those that increase the visual impact of
the document and those that make the document interactive. Features that add to the visual
impact of the document include using line breaks to create a column of text and horizontal
rules to visually divide the document into sections. To increase the interactive nature of your
document, you can create links to other documents on the Web. You can also create internal
links in your document that can help guide readers to key parts of your publication. You can
also add any of several types of lists to your document, which can add to the visual impact of
the document by clearly organizing material.

Using Line Breaks and Horizontal Rules

The line break tag `<BR>` enables you to break a line without adding a space between the lines. The `<BR>` tag is one of the few tags that has only a begin tag. You can use the simple facility of a line break to format text on your document in many creative ways. Sometimes you don't want a space between lines of text or you want to highlight an example by breaking the line and starting a new line showing the example.

Here is how this could be done:

```
<P>This section will contain:<BR>
An introduction to the document</P>
```

The `<BR>` tag can also be used to format your text into a column or simple list. Not only does text formatted in a column add to the visual impact of the document, it also gets the reader's attention. The following example shows how you could create a simple list:

```
Our on-line publications include:<BR>
<BR>
Books<BR>
Magazines<BR>
Newspapers<BR>
Newsletters<BR>
```

You can use the `<BR>` tag inside other tags without affecting the font or style of the previously declared tag. If you insert `<BR>` into a heading, the text before and after the break will be formatted in the style and font of a heading. All the `<BR>` tag does is start a new line, like the carriage return on a typewriter.

Another way to easily add to the visual impact of the document is to use a horizontal rule. Horizontal rules are shaded lines drawn across the width of the document. The shading of the line makes the line appear to be engraved into the document. You can add a horizontal rule to the document using the `<HR>` tag.

The great thing about `<HR>` tags is you can use them to divide your document visually into sections. However, you should use horizontal rules sparingly. Too many horizontal rules in the document can spoil the effect. Therefore, use the `<HR>` tag to highlight or to help the reader better identify the major sections of the document.

Figure 5.2 depicts a combined example using the `<BR>` and `<HR>` tags. While the figure only shows the outline of the document, you can see how horizontal rules could be used to divide the document into four major sections. The complete HTML code for the outline of the document is shown in Listing 5.4.

Listing 5.4. `hrbrsamp.htm`.

```
<HTML>
<HEAD>
<TITLE>Using Horizontal Rules and Line Breaks</TITLE>
```

continues

Listing 5.4. continued

```
</HEAD>
<BODY>
<P>This section will contain:<BR>
An introduction to the document</P>
<HR>
<P>This section will contain a list of our publications.<BR>
Our on-line publications include:<BR>
<BR>
Books<BR>
Magazines<BR>
Newspapers<BR>
Newsletters<BR>
</P>
<HR>
<P>This section will contain creative works by:<BR>
Writers and poets who want to publish their works on the Web.</P>
<HR>
<P>The final section of the document will contain:<BR>
Contact and copyright information.</P>
</BODY>
</HTML>
```

FIGURE 5.2.

You can break up the document using horizontal rules and line breaks.

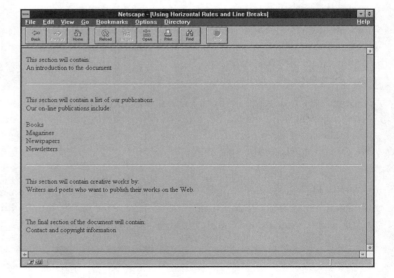

Adding Visual Variety to Your Documents

A Web document that contained only paragraphs and headings would be boring. Often you will want to highlight and emphasize key sections of the text. To do this, you can use a special set of HTML tags called character style tags. Character style tags highlight your text using techniques such as boldface and italics. Unlike heading and paragraph tags that insert white space into the document, character style tags do not insert white space, which makes it possible to use character style tags within other tags to highlight a single word or a group of words.

In HTML, there are two subsets of character style tags: physical styles and logical styles.

Physical Styles

Physical styles tell the browser the precise format to display. In HTML 2.0, four physical styles correspond to bold, italics, underlined, and monospaced type. Additional physical styles are discussed in Chapter 6, "Designing with HTML 3.0." Each physical style has a begin tag and an end tag. The four physical style tags are

```
<B> Bold type </B>
<I> Italics type </I>
<U> Underline </U>
<TT> Typewriter or monospaced type </TT>
```

You could use these tags in an HTML document as follows

```
<P>Physical styles tell the browser the precise format to display.
<B>If you want to display a word or group of words in bold type, you
 use the bold tag just as you see it used in this sentence.</B>
<I>If you want to display a word or group of words in italics type, you
 use the italics tag just as you see it used in this sentence.</I>
<U>If you want to display a word or group of words underlined, you use the
underline tag just as you see it used in this sentence.</U>
<TT>If you want to display a word or group of words in a monospaced or
typewriter type, you use the typewriter tag just as you see it used
in this sentence.</TT></P>
```

You can combine physical style tags with other tags and even with other physical style tags. When combining tags always keep them in parallel order, especially if you are combining style tags. You could, for example, combine the bold and italics style as follows:

```
<I>When combining tags always keep them in parallel order, especially if
you are combining style tags like <B>bold</B> with another style tag.</I>
```

Figure 5.3 shows how the combined example might look in your browser. A browser accessing documents containing physical styles will try to display the text using the strict format you have specified. If it is unable to, it may substitute another style for the one you are using or worse, it may ignore the tag and display the text in the standard style. Consequently, when you want to make sure text will be highlighted, use logical styles. Logical styles are the preferred method of adding highlights to Web documents.

FIGURE 5.3.

Using physical styles.

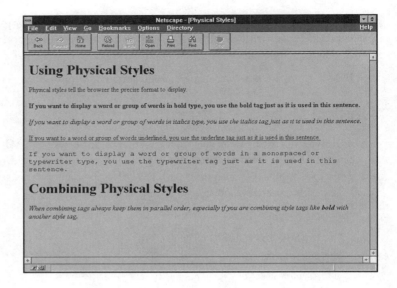

Logical Styles

Unlike physical style tags, logical style tags do not specify a strict format. They tell your browser how the text should be used and let the browser display the text according to a set of configurations specific to the browser. The logical assignment of the style to the browser ensures your text will be highlighted in the document in some way.

HTML 2.0 defines seven logical styles. Each logical style has a begin tag and an end tag. Two specific logical styles are used more than any of the others. The begin emphasis tag <EM> is used to indicate text should be emphasized. Browsers usually display emphasized text in italics. The begin strong emphasis tag <STRONG> is used to indicate text should be strongly emphasized. Browsers usually display strongly emphasized text in bold type. You can use these tags in your document as follows:

```
<P>Logical styles tell the browser how the text should be used.
<EM>If you want to emphasize a word or group of words, you
 use the emphasis tag just as you see it used in this sentence.</EM>
<STRONG>If you want to strongly emphasize a word or group of words, you
 use the italics tag just as you see it used in this sentence.</STRONG></P>
```

FIGURE 5.4.

Using logical styles.

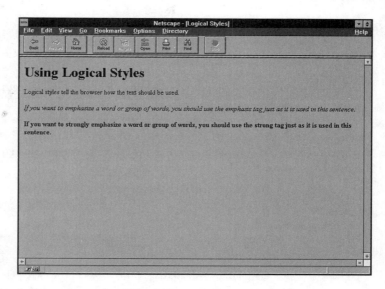

Figure 5.4 shows how the example might look in your browser. The other five logical styles are not uniquely supported by browsers and duplicate styles you can create using other means. Consequently, these styles are rarely used. These five styles are

<CITE>   Indicates the text is a citation. Most browsers display this style in italics. The tag could be used as follows:

```
<CITE>Citation</CITE>
```

<CODE>   Indicates text is computer code or a program sample. Most browsers display this style in a monospaced font such as Courier. The tag could be used as follows:

```
<CODE>Computer Code</CODE>
```

<KBD>   Indicates text that a user would type in on the keyboard. Most browsers display this style in a monospaced font such as Courier. The tag could be used as follows:

```
<KBD>Keyboard Input</KBD>
```

<SAMP>   Indicates a sample of literal characters. Most browsers display this style in a monospaced font such as Courier. The tag could be used as follows:

```
<SAMP>Sample</SAMP>
```

<VAR>   Indicates text is a variable name such as those used in computer programs. Most browsers display this style in italics. The tag could be used as follows:

```
<VAR>Program Variable</VAR>
```

Using Links

The Web without links would not be interactive, so now it is time to put the "hyper" into hypertext. Most Web documents contain hypertext links. Links act as pointers to other resources or files on the Web. Using links, you can connect text, graphic images, and multimedia objects to your documents. The great thing about hypertext linking is that linked text, images, or objects can be located anywhere on the Web. You could add images to your document that don't even reside on your Web server. For example, if you are a fan of the Dilbert comic strip, you could (with United Media's permission) add a link to your document that would display the latest Dilbert comic every day. Here is how you would do it:

```
<P><A HREF="http://www.unitedmedia.com/comics/dilbert/">
<IMG SRC="http://www.unitedmedia.com/comics/dilbert/todays_dilbert.gif"
</A></P>
```

> **NOTE**
>
> The `<IMG SRC>` tag enables you to display an image along with the text of your document. The `<IMG>` tag has three basic attributes and no closing element. The only attribute of the `<IMG>` tag you must use is `SRC`, which specifies the source, or path to the image including the name. Tips and techniques for using the `<IMG SRC>` tag are explored in Chapter 7, "Adding Multimedia Features with HTML."

While the lines of HTML code in the sample code may look like a tangled mess, the mess can be easily untangled. Links tell the browser where to send a request for a particular file. Initially, the browser does not care what type of file it is supposed to retrieve, it just tries to retrieve the file. To get to a file, browsers need to know the location of the resource. The resource's location is specified as a Uniform Resource Locator, commonly called a URL.

The previous example contained two URLs:

`http://www.unitedmedia.com/comics/dilbert/`

and

`http://www.unitedmedia.com/comics/dilbert/todays_dilbert.gif`

The first URL tells the browser to use the hypertext transfer protocol to access a file on the `www.unitedmedia.com` Web server. Here, the file is the base document in the `/comics/dilbert` directory. The second URL tells the browser to use the hypertext transfer protocol to access a file called `todays_dilbert.gif` on the `www.unitedmedia.com` Web server. Here, the file is a graphic image in the `/comics/dilbert` directory. URLs with complete address information such as these enable you to link your documents to files on other Web servers.

> **NOTE**
>
> The base document is typically called `index.html` and can be accessed using the forward slash. Using the slash, you can reference shorter URLs and provide shorter URLs to those who may want to visit your document. As the filename for the base document in a directory can vary depending on the Web server software, here are some of the naming conventions used with popular Web server software:
>
> | | |
> |---|---|
> | MacHTTP | `default.html.` |
> | WinHTTP | `index.htm` |
> | NCSA HTTPD | `index.html` |
> | CERN HTTPD | `Welcome.html` |
> | | `welcome.html` |
> | | `index.html` |

Using the anchor tag, you can create a link. The basic format of a hypertext link is

```
<A HREF="URL">Text or Object reader sees and can click on</A>
```

The opening `<A>` tag contains the address of the files you are linking. The address is not visible in a document unless the mouse pointer is over the anchor. The anchor is the portion of the link that is visible when a browser displays the document. The anchor is positioned between the begin and end anchor tags. To activate a link, you move your mouse pointer over the anchor and click the left mouse button.

The great thing about the anchor portion of the link is the anchor can be textual or graphical. If a line of text is the anchor, the reader can click on the text to activate the link. If an image is the anchor, the reader can click on the image to activate the link. You can also create an anchor that uses both text and an image. More information on using images and linking to images can be found in Chapter 7, "Adding Multimedia Features with HTML."

As Figure 5.5 shows, generally text links will be shown in blue letters and images with links will have a blue border around them. The first link uses text to anchor the link in the document. The reader would click on "The Writer's Gallery" to activate the link. The second link uses an image to anchor the link in the document. The reader would click on the image to activate the link. The third link combines a text and image anchor. The reader could click on either the text or the image to activate the link.

Listing 5.5 contains the HTML code for the document shown in Figure 5.5.

Listing 5.5. `linksamp.htm`.

```
<HTML>
<HEAD>
<TITLE>Using Text &amp; Images to Create Links</TITLE>
</HEAD>
<BODY>
<P><A HREF="http://tvp.com/vpwg.html">The Writer's Gallery</A> a place
for anyone who loves the written word.</P>
<P>
<P><A HREF="http://tvp.com/vpwg.html"><IMG SRC="wpttl1.gif" ></A></P>
<P>
<P><A HREF="http://tvp.com/vpwg.html"><IMG SRC="boom.gif" >
See what the fuss is all about!</A></P>
<P><A HREF="http://tvp.com/vpwg.html"><IMG SRC="raindrops.gif" ></A></P>
</BODY>
</HTML>
```

FIGURE 5.5.

Using text and images to create links.

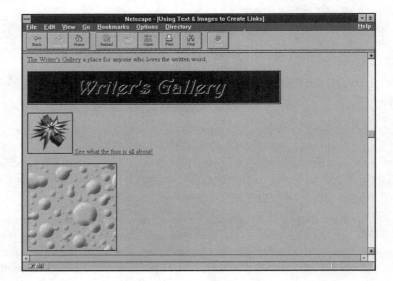

As you can see, hypertext links to text and objects can be the most powerful features on your document. Adding links to your document can be accomplished in three key ways:

- Using relative paths to files in links
- Using direct paths to files in links
- Using links within your documents

Using Relative Paths in Links

You can access local files, files on your local Web server, using a relative file path. URLs with relative file paths generally do not name a protocol or a Web server in the link. This is because when you use a relative path to locate a file, you are locating the file in relation to the current file. Being able to access a file in relation to the current file implies that you have already accessed a file on a particular Web server.

You can use relative file paths in three key ways:

1. A file in the current directory.

   When you click on this link, your browser will expect to find the file `orders.html` in the current directory:

   ```
   <A HREF="orders.html">Orders &amp; Information</A>
   ```

2. A file in a parent directory of the current directory.

   This file is located in the directory above the current directory:

   ```
   <A HREF="../orders.html">Place an order today!</A>
   ```

   This file is located two directories above the current directory:

   ```
   <A HREF="../../orders.html">Place an order today!</A>
   ```

3. A file in a subdirectory of the current directory.

   This file is in the subdirectory called `info`:

   ```
   <A HREF="info/orders.html">Visit our order center.</A>
   ```

TIP

Study the links used throughout the chapter as examples of well-designed links. Good links do not say "Click here." A "click here" link disrupts the flow of the text and the natural thought processes. The interactive nature of the Web is such that you should never have to say "click here." Build hypertext links into the text and by doing so, you'll create documents that flow.

When using links, keep in mind that links are highlighted in the document. Typically, links are shown in underlined blue letters, which makes them stand out from surrounding text.

An example of poorly designed anchor text is

```
<P>To place an order at our on-line order center

<A HREF="info/orders.html">click here</A></P>
```

A better way to create the link is

```
<P><A HREF="info/orders.html">Place an order using our on-line
order center.</A></P>
```

Using Direct Paths in Links

Another way to access files is directly. You do this by specifying the complete path to the file you want to access. While you must specify the protocol to be used for files directly accessed on a nonlocal Web server, you do not have to specify the protocol for files directly accessed on a local Web server.

This means there are two key ways to access files directly:

1. Specify the full path to the file including the transfer protocol.

   The following file could reside on a nonlocal server:

   ```
   <A HREF="http://www.unitedmedia.com/comics/dilbert/index.html">
   Visit Dilbert on the Web</A>
   ```

2. Specify the full path to the file excluding the transfer protocol.

   The following file must reside on a local server:

   ```
   <A HREF="/comics/dilbert/index.html>Visit Dilbert on the Web</A>
   ```

> **TIP**
>
> Designing good links is easy once you know the basics of using relative and direct paths. The key is to keep the anchor text for the link short but descriptive. Usually this text should be three to five words describing the link in a way that is clear to the user. While anchor text can be the key words of a sentence, sometimes you may want the anchor text to include an entire short-but-descriptive sentence. Later sections of this chapter show how you can better organize links using lists and menus.

Using Links Within Documents

Internal document links can provide powerful navigation mechanisms for your readers and are especially useful in long documents. Using internal document links, you can provide ways to quickly jump to key sections of any document. Creating links within documents is a two-part process. First, you specify a link with a keyword using the anchor tag in a form similar to other links you have seen. The only exception to the rules about links covered earlier is that the keyword for the internal document link is preceded by the pound sign(#), as in

```
<A HREF="#keyword">Text or object to use as the anchor</A>
```

The next step is to label the location within the document you want the reader to jump. You do this by labeling the <A NAME> tag with the keyword you selected earlier in the form:

```
<A NAME="keyword">
```

The keyword used in the link and anchor name must match exactly. When a user activates an internal document link, the section of the document associated with the <A NAME> tag will be displayed. If the internal document link is within the current document, the browser will quickly search the document for the <A NAME> tag with the keyword that matches the keyword in the link. When the browser finds the matching <A NAME> tag, the browser will display the corresponding section of the document. If the internal link is within a different document, the browser will load the document and then search for the <A NAME> tag with the keyword that matches the keyword in the link. The location of the keyword relative to the link in the document does not matter. As long as the keyword is within the body of the document, the browser will find it.

You can specify links within the current document as follows:

1. Create a special link with a keyword like this:

   ```
   <A HREF="#keyword">Text or object to use as the Anchor</A>
   ```

2. Label the section of the document the user can jump to as follows:

   ```
   <A NAME="keyword">Text or object to jump to</A>
   ```

Using internal document links, you could create an index for your document such as the one shown in Figure 5.6. If you clicked on the overview link, then your browser would search for the keyword overview. When your browser found the keyword, the section associated with the keyword would be displayed. In the example, the browser would scroll forward and display the overview section of the document. The ellipses show where actual document content would go. Listing 5.6 contains the code for the sample document.

Listing 5.6. `intrlink.htm`.

```
<HTML>
<HEAD>
<TITLE>Web Publishing</TITLE>
</HEAD>
<BODY>
<H1>The HTML Standard</H1>
<H2><A HREF="#overview">Overview</A></H2>
<H2><A HREF="#html_one">HTML 1.0</A></H2>
<H2><A HREF="#html_two">HTML 2.0</A></H2>
<H2><A HREF="#html_three">HTML 3.0</A></H2>
<HR>
<H2><A NAME="#overview">Overview</A></H2>
. . .
<H2><A NAME="#html_one">HTML 1.0</A></H2>
. . .
<H2><A NAME="#html_two">HTML 2.0</A></H2>
. . .
<H2><A NAME="#html_three">HTML 3.0</A></H2>
. . .
</BODY>
</HTML>
```

FIGURE 5.6.

After activating a link, your browser would jump to a section associated with the keyword.

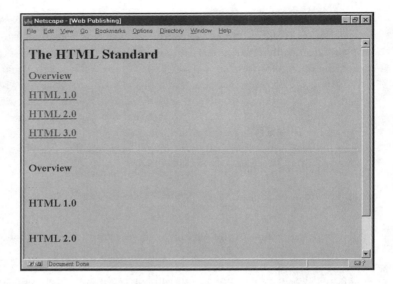

> **NOTE**
>
> In the preceding example code, the <A NAME> tag is placed between a begin and end heading tag. This ensures the <A NAME> tag is directly before the text or object the browser should jump to, which is the preferred way to place the <A NAME> tag in your code. If you place the <A NAME> tag before another HTML tag, you may confuse your browser. Therefore, always place the <A NAME> tag directly before the text or object the browser should jump to.

You can specify internal links to other documents in many ways. Using relative paths and key-words, you can access specific locations in documents on the local Web server. Using direct paths and keywords, you can access specific locations in documents located anywhere on the global Web. The basic format for internal links to other documents is

```
<A HREF="URL#keyword">Text or object reader can click on</A>
```

Relative paths can be used with internal document links in three key ways:

1. An internal link to a file in the current directory can be used.

   When you click on this link, your browser loads the fiction.html document from the current directory, searches the document for the keyword Mystery, and then displays the section of the document corresponding to the keyword:

   ```
   <A HREF="fiction.html#Mystery">Top 100 Mysteries</A>
   ```

   The <A NAME> tag could be defined in the fiction.html document as follows:

   ```
   <H1><A NAME="Mystery">The Top 100 Mysteries Available On-line</A></H1>
   ```

2. An internal link to a file in a parent directory of the current directory can be used.

   When you click on this link, your browser loads the `nonfiction.html` document from the parent directory, searches the document for the keyword `Science` and then displays the section of the document corresponding to the keyword:

   ```
   <A HREF="../nonfiction.html#Science">Science &amp; Technology</A>
   ```

   The `<A NAME>` tag could be used in the `nonfiction.html` document as follows:

   ```
   <H3><A NAME="Science">Resources: Science</A></H3>
   ```

3. An internal link to a file in a subdirectory of the current directory can be used.

   The keyword in this example is `Information`:

   ```
   <A HREF="info/orders.html#Information">Ordering Information</A>
   ```

   The `<A NAME>` tag could be used in the `orders.html` document as follows:

   ```
   <P><A NAME="Information">You can place an order</A> using our on-line
   order form, by sending e-mail to orders@wizard.com, or by sending a check
   or money order to the address below.</P>
   ```

Direct paths can be used with internal links as well. The two key ways you will use internal links with direct paths are

1. Append the internal link to the full file path that includes the transfer protocol, such as

   ```
   <A HREF="http://www.tvp.com/viporder.html#Fantasy">
   Virtual Fantasy E-Books</A>
   ```

   The `<A NAME>` tag could be used in the `viporder.html` document as follows:

   ```
   <H2><A NAME="Fantasy">Virtual Fantasy Imprint</A></H2>
   ```

2. Append the internal link to the full file path that excludes the transfer protocol, such as

   ```
   <A HREF="/home/users/william/index.html#top10">Today's Top 10</A>
   ```

   The `<A NAME>` tag could be specified in the `index.html` document as follows:

   ```
   <P><A NAME="top10">Today's Top 10</A>
   begins with an entry from left field . . .</P>
   ```

CAUTION

Be careful when specifying internal links to someone else's document. Web documents tend to change frequently and a keyword that is specified today may not be there tomorrow.

Using Lists

Lists are one of the most useful tools in your writing and publishing toolkit. Lists can give a clear order to your ideas and add to the visual impact of your document. You can use lists to grab the attention of readers, especially those readers who may be simply browsing or Web surfing your site in their quest to find new and interesting places to visit.

The best lists are designed for a specific purpose. For example, the steps for creating a Web document discussed in this chapter would make a great list:

- Develop a strategy.
- Define the document structure.
- Create the document.
- Add features to the document.
- Proof the document.
- Test the document.
- Publish the finished document.

This type of list is called a bulleted list. Bulleted lists are often used to outline goals, objectives, or tasks that have no specific order. Bulleted lists are also called unordered lists. This list, however, is in a specific order, so a bulleted list is not the best way to present it.

A better way to present the list of steps for creating a Web document would be to number the list:

1. Develop a strategy.
2. Define the document structure.
3. Create the document.
4. Add features to the document.
5. Proof the document.
6. Test the document.
7. Publish the finished document.

This type of list is called a numbered list. Numbered lists are used when tasks must be performed in a specific order. Numbered lists are also called ordered lists.

Lists are also used in the glossary section found in many nonfiction books. A glossary contains a list of keywords and their definitions. You can use glossary lists whenever you want to associate a keyword with a concept or definition. Many glossary lists look something like this:

HTML

> HyperText Markup Language
>
> The HyperText Markup Language is a markup language based on the Standard Generalized Markup Language that enables you to format information in visually appealing ways without sacrificing ease of use and the potential for wide distribution.

SGML

> Standard Generalized Markup Language
>
> The Standard Generalized Markup Language forms the basis for most markup languages and is an advanced language with few limitations.

VRML

> Virtual Reality Modeling Language
>
> Virtual Reality Modeling Language is an advanced markup language based on the standard markup language that enables you to create multidimensional documents.

While the three fundamental types of lists are strongly supported by the HTML standard, the standard defines two additional types of lists designed primarily for programmers. Menu lists can be used to list the contents of program menus. Directory lists can be used to list the contents of directories. Menu lists and directory lists have fallen into disuse and are poorly supported by browsers. If you use a menu or directory list, the chances are very high that your browser will display the list following the rules for another list type. Therefore, it is generally not a good idea to use menu or directory lists.

The next sections offer a close look at how the three primary types of lists are used in HTML.

Bulleted Lists

Bulleted lists are used to outline goals, objectives, or tasks with no specific order. The associated HTML tag for this type of list is <UL>, which is an abbreviation of unordered list. Bulleted list tags are used in pairs and the counterpart of the begin tag <UL> is the end tag </UL>. Items in the list are preceded by the list item tag <LI>. While the <LI> tag can be used with a begin and end tag, the end list tag </LI> is not required.

Listing 5.7 shows how a bulleted list could be added to a sample document.

Listing 5.7. `b-list.htm`.

```
<HTML>
<HEAD>
<TITLE>Creating Web Documents</TITLE>
```

continues

Listing 5.7. continued

```
</HEAD>
<BODY>
<H1>How to Create Web Documents</H1>
<UL>
<LI> Develop a Strategy
<LI> Define the document structure
<LI> Create the document
<LI> Add features to the document
<LI> Proof the document
<LI> Test the document
<LI> Publish the Finished document
</UL>
</BODY>
</HTML>
```

FIGURE 5.7.

Using a bulleted list.

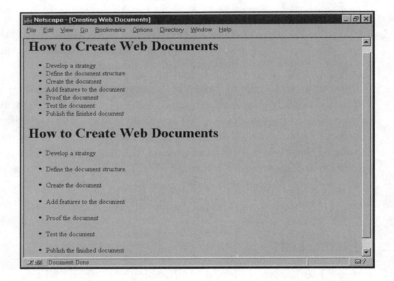

As the first example in Figure 5.7 shows, bulleted lists are generally single-spaced. When your browser sees the begin list tag <LI>, it does two things:

■ Starts a new line
■ Inserts a character called a bullet before the listed item

> **NOTE**
>
> While most browsers display the bullet as a large solid dot, the actual size and shape of the bullet may be different in your browser. Text browsers, such as Lynx, display the

bullet as an asterisk. Other browsers use a different symbol for the bullets at each level of nested lists. Additionally, the Netscape browser uses extensions that enable you to select the shape for the bullet. Netscape extensions are featured in Chapter 8, "Netscape and Internet Explorer Extensions."

Single-spacing of your bulleted list may make the list difficult to read. This is especially true when your list has many items and each list item contains two or more lines of text. If readability is a problem with your list, you can introduce a simple spacing technique such as the one shown in Listing 5.8 that uses the paragraph tag to add white space.

Listing 5.8. `b-list2.htm`.

```
<HTML>
<HEAD>
<TITLE>Creating Web Documents</TITLE>
</HEAD>
<BODY>
<H1>How to Create Web Documents</H1>
<UL>
<LI> Develop a Strategy
<P>
<LI> Define the document structure
<P>
<LI> Create the document
<P>
<LI> Add features to the document
<P>
<LI> Proof the document
<P>
<LI> Test the document
<P>
<LI> Publish the Finished document
</UL>
</BODY>
</HTML>
```

Glossary Lists

Glossary lists are also called definition lists. The associated HTML tag for the list is `<DL>`, which is an abbreviation of definition list. Definition list tags are used in pairs and the counterpart of the begin tag `<DL>` is the end tag `</DL>`. Each item in a definition list contains two elements:

- A keyword called the definition title
- A definition called the definition data

The definition title tag <DT> specifies the glossary term or keyword you are defining. The definition data tag <DD> specifies the definition associated with the glossary term or keyword. You can use more than one definition data tag if the term has multiple definitions. While a begin and end tag are defined for the <DT> and <DD> tags, only the begin tags are normally used.

> **TIP**
>
> A glossary list is generally for words and their definitions, but that does not mean you must use glossary lists for this strict purpose. You can use glossary lists whenever you want to associate a keyword, phrase, or sentence with a concept.

Listing 5.9 illustrates a sample glossary list.

Listing 5.9. `g-list.htm.`

```
<HTML>
<HEAD>
<TITLE>Web Publishing</TITLE>
</HEAD>
<BODY>
<H1>Markup Languages</H1>
<DL>
<DT>HTML
<DD>Hypertext Markup Language
<DD>The hypertext markup language is a markup language based on the
standard generalized markup language that enables you to format
information in visually appealing ways without sacrificing ease of
use and the potential for wide distribution.
<DT>SGML
<DD>Standard Generalized Markup Language
<DD>The standard generalized markup language forms the basis for most
markup languages and is an advanced language with few limitations.
<DT>VRML
<DD>Virtual Reality Modeling Language
<DD>Virtual Reality Modeling Language is an advanced markup language
based on the standard markup language that allows you to create
multidimensional documents.
</DL>
</BODY>
</HTML>
```

As the first example in Figure 5.8 shows, glossary lists are normally formatted with the terms and definitions on separate lines. While the terms are aligned with the left margin, the definitions are indented. Additionally, all aspects of glossary lists are generally single-spaced. While single spacing is good if you want to squeeze the list into a smaller screen space, single spacing makes it difficult to distinguish multiple definitions of a term. Introducing a simple spacing technique such as the one shown in Listing 5.10 may improve the readability of your list.

FIGURE 5.8.

Using a glossary list.

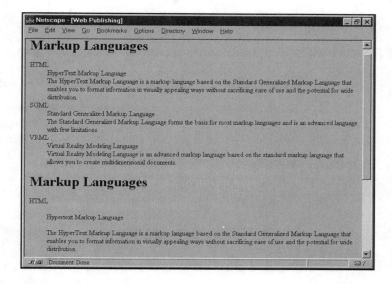

Listing 5.10. `g-list2.htm`.

```
<HTML>
<HEAD>
<TITLE>Web Publishing</TITLE>
</HEAD>
<BODY>
<H1>Markup Languages</H1>
<DL>
<P><DT>HTML</P>
<DD>Hypertext Markup Language
<P><DD>The Hypertext Markup Language is a markup language based on the
Standard Generalized Markup Language that enables you to format
information in visually appealing ways without sacrificing ease of
use and the potential for wide distribution.</P>
<P><DT>SGML</P>
<DD>Standard Generalized Markup Language
<P><DD>The Standard Generalized Markup Language forms the basis for most
markup languages and is an advanced language with few limitations.</P>
<P><DT>VRML</P>
<DD>Virtual Reality Modeling Language
<P><DD>Virtual Reality Modeling Language is an advanced markup language
based on the standard markup language that allows you to create
multidimensional documents.</P>
</DL>
</BODY>
</HTML>
```

Numbered Lists

Numbered lists are also called ordered lists. The associated HTML tag for the list is `<OL>`, which is an abbreviation of ordered list. Ordered list tags are used in pairs and the counterpart of the begin tag `<OL>` is the end tag `</OL>`. Each item in the ordered list is preceded by the list item tag `<LI>`.

Each item in an ordered list is consecutively numbered or lettered. Letters are used only when you nest lists. When a browser sees a begin list tag `<LI>` it does three things:

1. Starts a new line
2. Indents the text of the list item
3. Puts the appropriate number or letter in front of the list item

> **NOTE**
>
> A nested list is a list inside of another list. In HTML, you nest a list by including the entire structure for a list within your current list. For example, you could put bulleted lists within your numbered list structure. The next section contains detailed information on nesting lists.

As you can see from the first example shown in Figure 5.9, numbered lists are single-spaced like other types of lists discussed earlier. You should use numbered lists when tasks must be performed in a particular order or when you want to add specificity to the list. When you number and add a label to a list of resources such as those shown in Figure 5.9, you add specificity to the list. Instead of the list being just another list of resources, the list represents *the* 12 reference works you wish were on your bookshelf. Listing 5.11 is the HTML markup for the document.

Listing 5.11. `n-list.htm.`

```
<HTML>
<HEAD>
<TITLE>The Reference Desk</TITLE>
</HEAD>
<BODY>
<P>12 reference works you wish were on your bookshelf</P>
<OL>
<LI>American English Dictionary
<LI>Bartlett's Familiar Quotations
<LI>Computer Dictionary
<LI>Encyclopedia Britannica
<LI>Global Encyclopedia
<LI>Grammar and Style Guide
<LI>Grolier's Encyclopedia
<LI>Handbook of Poetry Terms
<LI>Hypertext Webster
<LI>Roget's Thesaurus
```

```
<LI>World Factbook
<LI>Worldwide Telephone Codes
</OL>
</BODY>
</HTML>
```

FIGURE 5.9.

Using a numbered list.

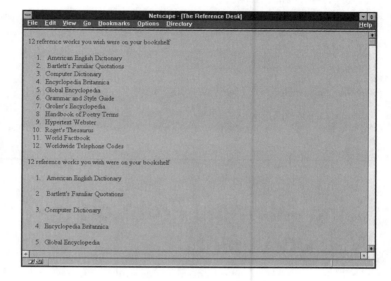

To make the list items more distinct on the page, you could break up the page using a spacing technique. Although you would generally do this with a short numbered list that you wanted to stand out from the surrounding text, Listing 5.12 shows how this could be done by inserting the paragraph tag into the previous example.

Listing 5.12. `nlist2.htm`.

```
<HTML>
<HEAD>
<TITLE>The Reference Desk</TITLE>
</HEAD>
<BODY>
<P>12 reference works you wish were on your bookshelf</P>
<OL>
<LI> American English Dictionary
<P>
<LI> Bartlett's Familiar Quotations
<P>
<LI>Computer Dictionary
<P>
<LI>Encyclopedia Britannica
<P>
```

continues

Listing 5.12. continued

```
<LI>Global Encyclopedia
<P>
<LI>Grammar and Style Guide
<P>
<LI>Grolier's Encyclopedia
<P>
<LI>Handbook of Poetry Terms
<P>
<LI>Hypertext Webster
<P>
<LI>Roget's Thesaurus
<P>
<LI>World Factbook
<P>
<LI>Worldwide Telephone Codes
</OL>
</BODY>
</HTML>
```

Using Alternate Protocols in Web Documents

The Web was designed to be an open-ended multimedia system based on hypertext. However, the hypertext transfer protocol is not the only protocol you can reference in your Web publications. You can reference files using any valid protocol. The format of URLs in hypertext references should follow the URL scheme, as outlined in Chapter 3, "Publishers' Tour of the Web."

The next sections explain how to use these protocols in your Web documents:

- FTP
- Gopher
- Mailto
- NNTP and News
- telnet
- WAIS

Using FTP

Thousands of files are available on FTP sites around the world. Your Web documents can contain links to files that will be retrieved using the File Transfer Protocol. The general form for using a hypertext reference to an FTP file is

```
<A HREF="ftp://host/path"> Anchor text </A>
```

If you specify a directory path instead of the full path to a file, the reader's browser will display a listing of the directory's contents. The following hypertext reference will retrieve a listing of the MS-DOS directory from an FTP server at the University of Florida:

```
<A HREF="ftp://ftp.eng.ufl.edu/pub/msdos">MS-DOS Tools</A>
```

Using Gopher

Gopher information is presented to readers as easy to navigate menus. You can enable readers to access gopher files using a hypertext reference, such as

```
<A HREF="gopher://host/path"> Anchor text </A>
```

The following hypertext reference will retrieve information on the DILS Project from a Gopher server at the University of Toronto:

```
<a href="gopher://gopher.epas.utoronto.ca/11/cch/disciplines/
➡medieval_studies/keefer">DILS Project</A>
```

Using Mailto

You could use a special type of link that starts a create mail session in the reader's browser:

```
<A HREF="mailto:william@tvp.com">
```

This mailto reference tells the reader's browser to open a create mail session that will be sent to `william@tvp.com`. This type of link enhances the interactivity of the page and provides a mechanism for getting feedback from readers. Don't forget to anchor the link to the page with text or graphics that readers can click on. One way to do this is

```
<A HREF="mailto:william@tvp.com">Send e-mail to the publisher</A>
```

Using NNTP and News

In your Web documents, you can reference any of the thousands of newsgroups on the Internet in two key ways: using the reader's local news server or via the Network News Transfer Protocol (NNTP). Referencing newsgroups on a local news server is easy; you just specify the name of the newsgroup in the form:

```
news:newsgroup.name
```

Here you could include a link to the `alt.books.reviews` newsgroup as follows:

```
<A HREF="news:alt.books.reviews"> alt.books.reviews</A>
```

The network news transfer protocol is used to transfer postings to and from a news server. Here's how NNTP could be used to link to the `alt.books.reviews` newsgroup:

```
<A HREF="nntp://news.aloha.com/alt.books.reviews"> alt.books.reviews</A>
```

CAUTION

Generally, to access the news server, the reader must be a known client. While this protocol could be useful to an exclusive group of known users, most readers will be accessing your pages from a remote site and will be unable to use the named news server. Consequently, you should use reference newsgroups available on the reader's local news server using news whenever you want to ensure broader accessibility.

Using Telnet

Using telnet, you can enable readers to access an interactive service on a remote host. In the telnet session, readers can input commands at a command prompt as if they were logged on to the remote host. You can reference telnet in your Web documents as follows:

```
<A HREF="telnet://tvp.com"> Telnet </A>
```

Using WAIS

You can reference indexed databases on wide area information systems using a WAIS URL. To use WAIS, the reader's browser must either be configured to invoke a WAIS client that the reader has installed on their system or be able to act as a WAIS client. You can reference WAIS in your Web documents as follows:

```
<A HREF="wais://tvp.com/wwwdata"> Search our World Wide Web database </A>
```

Summary

Web publishing with HTML is easy. Using the techniques discussed in this chapter, you can create simple yet effective Web documents. The two key sections of your HTML documents are the header section and the body section. You can use the header to provide information about the document to the Web server, but the body section is where your document comes to life. Dozens of HTML tags can be used in the body, and all these tags can add to the visual impact of your documents.

Designing with HTML 3.0

6

by William Robert Stanek

IN THIS CHAPTER

The HTML standard is advancing at an explosive pace. Since 1990, when the World Wide Web initiative began, three major specifications for HTML have been defined. The most powerful and recent specification is HTML 3.0. When completed, the HTML 3.0 specification will open a new chapter in the history of the World Wide Web and clear the way for an entirely new approach to Web publishing. Web publishers will finally have advanced control over the layout of their documents using the simple and easy-to-use facilities of the HyperText Markup Language. HTML 3.0 is so powerful it was originally called HTML+ to show that it is something considerably more than its predecessors.

While the HTML 3.0 specification is still evolving, most of the features specific to HTML 3.0 have already been defined. The goal of this chapter is to be a comprehensive resource for creating advanced publications with HTML 3.0. A growing number of browsers—including NCSA Mosaic, Spyglass Mosaic, Netscape Navigator, Internet Explorer, and the experimental HTML 3.0 browser, Arena—support the most common HTML 3.0 extensions, and Web sites with HTML 3.0 features are everywhere on the World Wide Web. The installed base of the Netscape Navigator and NCSA Mosaic alone mean that up to 15 million Web users already have browsers that can properly display common HTML 3.0 enhancements.

Learning HTML 3.0

To keep pace with the rapidly changing face of Web publishing, you should learn everything you can about the emerging HTML 3.0 standard. HTML v3.0, HTML 3.0, and HTML+ all refer to the level 3 specification for the HTML standard. An objective of the developers of HTML 3.0 is to ensure the HyperText Markup Language continues to be a simple solution for providing platform-independent presentations. Some major features include

> Advanced layout control of text and images
> Banners
> Client-side handling of hot spots in images
> Customized lists
> Horizontal alignment of headers and paragraph text
> Mathematical Equations
> Style sheets
> Tables
> Tables within forms
> Text flow around images

While the standard represents a giant leap forward in HTML publishing, there are some things about the standard that you should know coming out of the gate. HTML 3.0 is fully compatible with previous versions and includes new features. However, HTML 3.0 browsers will deal more strictly with your HTML documents and require you to use the <TITLE> tag.

As HTML 3.0 allows you more control over the layout of text, many clever tricks Web publishers, myself included, use will become unnecessary. While this is good news in general, it will also mean Web publishers will have to carefully reevaluate old documents. Not only will you want to check for inconsistencies, you will also want to use proper HTML 3.0 syntax instead of your quick and dirty workaround.

HTML 3.0 Extensions to Existing Elements

Before you can create a totally awesome HTML 3.0 home page to experiment with, you need to learn what's new in HTML 3.0 and how HTML 3.0 extends the standard. Besides introducing many new elements, HTML 3.0 introduces extensions to existing elements. Some of these extensions are new to HTML 3.0. Other extensions are just used in new ways.

Table 6.1 shows a list of common HTML 3.0 extensions to existing elements. You can use this table as a reference resource.

Table 6.1 Common HTML 3.0 extensions to existing elements.

Platform	Server Software	Web Site to Obtain Software
ALIGN	HTML 2.0/3.0	Specifies the alignment of an element. In HTML 2.0, common values for tags that format images include TOP, BOTTOM, and CENTER. HTML 3.0 adds these common values for tags that format text including: LEFT, RIGHT, CENTER and JUSTIFY. While the values for the ALIGN attribute can be used with most tags that format text, the image alignments CANNOT be used with tags that format text.
CLASS	HTML 3.0	Specifies subclasses for tags. CLASS is commonly used to display a tag in a different style based on the class type. Normally you would define class types and associated formats in a style sheet and reference them in your HTML document. Although style sheets are discussed later in the chapter, you can specify a general class and a specific class as follows: CLASS=general_class.specific_class

continues

Table 6.1 continued

Platform	Server Software	Web Site to Obtain Software
CLEAR	HTML 3.0	Used to make text flow around an image, figure, or table at the margin. Valid values include LEFT, RIGHT and ALL. These values tell the browser to move down until the left, right, or both margins are clear and then start the next tag there.
DINGBAT	HTML 3.0	Inserts standard graphic icons into the document. As these icons are defined in a browser's document type definition, they do not have to be downloaded and this saves time and network bandwidth.
HREF	HTML 2.0/3.0	Specifies a hypertext reference. In HTML 3.0, HREF can now be used with more tags.
ID	HTML 3.0	Labels an element with an identification keyword that can be directly accessed with a hypertext reference. If you activate a hypertext reference containing a keyword that matches the element's ID, the browser will jump to the section of the document containing the ID. The functionality of ID is similar to the NAME attribute for the anchor tag discussed in previous chapters. The only real difference is that you are associating the keyword with an HTML element, such as <P>, instead of a line of text. In HTML 3.0, the ID attribute supersedes the NAME attribute.
LANG	HTML 3.0	Specifies the language to be used for the element. You could use this attribute if you need to set language-specific parameters for punctuation or hyphenation. Valid values associated with this attribute are defined by two standards from the Internet Standards

Platform	Server Software	Web Site to Obtain Software
		Organization. A two-letter language code is defined in ISO 639 and a two-letter country code is defined in ISO 3166.
MD	HTML 3.0	Allows for verification that the document or object the user is retrieving is the same document or object you wanted the user to retrieve. To use the MD attribute in your links, you must specify an encrypted checksum for the associated document or object you are linking. A checksum is a number associated with the document or object that is calculated based on the contents of the file. Any alterations to the file, even if only a single character is changed will result in a different checksum.
NOWRAP	HTML 3.0	Turns off wrapping of lines within an element, such as a paragraph or heading. Although line wrapping is turned off, you can still use the tag to break lines of text at specific locations.
SRC	HTML 2.0/3.0	Specifies the source for a graphic object. In HTML 3.0, SRC can now be used with images and figures.

HTML 3.0 also defines many unique extensions for specific elements. These new and unique extensions combine to ensure the HTML 3.0 standard can be shaped to meet the needs of Web publishers around the world. For example, the <HTML> element has only one optional attribute under HTML 2.0 called VERSION that is used as follows:

```
<HTML VERSION="-//IETF//DTD HTML 2.0//EN">
```

Under HTML 3.0, the <HTML> element now has three optional attributes: VERSION, URN, and ROLE that are used as follows:

```
<HTML VERSION="-//W3O//DTD W3 HTML 3.0//EN" URN=" . . . " ROLE=" . . . ">
```

The VERSION attribute is used to specify the exact version of HTML that the document uses. In the example above, the VERSION attribute specifies that the document conforms to the

150

document type definition for HTML 3.0 as set forth by the World Wide Web Organization (W3O), and further that the document is in the English language.

The URN attribute identifies a universal resource name that is associated with the document. URNs are not formally defined under the HTML 3.0 standard and there are no valid values at this time. Values will be defined at a future date.

The ROLE attribute indicates the function of the document. Some possible functions include home to go to the home page, index, table of contents, and glossary. Actual values will be defined at a future date.

Header Design in HTML 3.0

Although these modifications to the HTML element are minor, the HEAD element is drastically different. HTML 3.0-compliant documents must have a header section. In HTML 2.0, only six tags could be used with the HEAD element: BASE, ISINDEX, LINK, META, NEXTID, and TITLE. HTML 3.0 extends most of these tags and adds RANGE and STYLE.

The following sections look at each of these tags, starting with the <TITLE> tag, which is the most common header tag.

Using <TITLE>

As you've seen in previous chapters, your Web pages can have titles. Titles can only appear within the HEAD element. Titles are typically displayed in a window appropriately called "Document Title" or at the top of the browser's viewing area. The <TITLE> tag identifies the beginning of the document title, and the </TITLE> tag identifies the ending of the document title. The <TITLE> tag does not have any attributes.

In HTML 2.0 and HTML 3.0, each document can have only one title. While the <TITLE> tag was optional in HTML 2.0, it is required in an HTML 3.0-compliant document. The document title could be used as follows:

```
<TITLE>The Virtual Press Home Page</TITLE>
```

Using <BASE>

Both HTML 2.0 and 3.0 enable you to define a base path for all relative links in your document. Using a base path, you can tell the browser to locate files in relation to a specific path that could actually point to a remote server. As HTML 3.0 adds no further functionality to the <BASE> tag, you can use the <BASE> tag in your documents, as described in Chapter 5, "Creating Web Documents With HTML."

Using *<ISINDEX>*

Both HTML 2.0 and 3.0 enable you to use <ISINDEX> queries of your documents. Under HTML 2.0, the process is complex and involves many steps. Users must first access a gateway script that generates an HTML document containing the <ISINDEX> tag. When the user enters information requested by the query, a special URL containing the path to the original script and the information the user typed in is sent back to the gateway script for processing. After processing, the results of the search would be displayed.

Fortunately, HTML 3.0 redefines how <ISINDEX> queries are performed. Although you can still perform <ISINDEX> queries the old way, HTML 3.0 introduces more direct support for <ISINDEX> queries in your documents. It does this using two attributes: HREF and PROMPT.

Using the HREF attribute, you can specify an address to which the query should be sent. The address is generally a URL to a gateway script. If you do not specify an HREF attribute, the default value is the current document. Using the PROMPT attribute, you can specify a string that a browser will use as the prompt for the query.

You could use <ISINDEX> as follows:

```
<ISINDEX HREF="cgiparse.pl" PROMPT="Search the page:">
```

A document containing the example query would be searchable. Anything a user enters after the prompt will be processed by the gateway script `cgiparse.pl`. Gateway scripts are discussed in Chapter 11, "Writing CGI Scripts."

The <ISINDEX> tag could be used in the home page example as follows:

```
<HTML>
<HEAD>
<TITLE>The Virtual Press — A Hot Spot on the Web</TITLE>
<ISINDEX HREF="script.pl" PROMPT="Search our home page:">
</HEAD>
<BODY>
<P> <A HREF="vpbg.html"><IMG SRC="vpttl11.gif" ALT=""></A></P>
<H2><IMG SRC="bboard.gif" ALIGN="BOTTOM" ALT="* ATTN *">
The Original Virtual Press — Hot contests for writers &amp; artists,
job information, electronic publishing information and much more!</H2>
<P><STRONG><A HREF="vphp.html3">Experience the explosive features we've
created especially for HTML 3.0 compliant browsers.</A></STRONG></P>
. . .
</BODY>
</HTML>
```

Using *<LINK>*

Both HTML 2.0 and 3.0 enable you to define special links in the <HEAD> element that define a relationship between the document and other objects. Browsers can use the links you define to provide a standard set of navigation mechanisms between pages at your site with a defined relationship. Your documents can have multiple LINK elements. Using the relationship you define in the header portion of the document, a browser capable of using the LINK element would display a clickable button for each relationship you define. You could, for example, create a relationship for a table of contents of your site or a publication at the site. When a user clicked on the corresponding button, the browser would retrieve the table of contents page and display it.

In both HTML 2.0 and 3.0, the <LINK> tag uses the same attributes as the anchor tag. While you will not use many of these attributes, the four you may use the most are: HREF, REL, REV, and TITLE.

Using References in Links

The HREF attribute is the only required attribute for the <LINK> tag. Using the HREF attribute, you can specify a hypertext reference. You could use a link as follows:

```
<LINK HREF="vphp.html">
```

or

```
<LINK HREF="http://tvp.com/vphp.html">
```

Using Relationships in Links

The value of the REL attribute specifies the relationship that the current document has to the resource referenced by the HREF attribute. HTML 2.0 defines ten relationships for the REL attribute:

```
BOOKMARK
COPYRIGHT
GLOSSARY
HELP
HOME
INDEX
NEXT
PREVIOUS
TOC
UP
```

In HTML 3.0, two additional relationship values are added:

```
BANNER
STYLESHEET
```

The *BOOKMARK* Relationship

The BOOKMARK relationship can be used in HTML 2.0 and 3.0 documents. A link with the BOOKMARK relationship identifies a specific location in a lengthy document. You can create multiple bookmarks for a single document by labeling the bookmark with the TITLE attribute. The reader's browser would display a clickable button for each bookmark you define. The label of the button would correspond to the value of the TITLE attribute. You could use the BOOKMARK attribute in your page as follows:

```
<LINK REL=BOOKMARK TITLE="Writer's Newsgroups" HREF="vpwg.html#wnewsgroups" >
```

The section corresponding to the bookmark in the vpwg.html document could be labeled with an ID attribute. Here, the ID value wnewsgroups is a keyword the browser will search for and jump to:

```
<HTML>
<HEAD>
<TITLE>The Writer's Gallery</TITLE>
</HEAD>
<BODY>
<H1>Writer's Gallery Features</H1>
 . . .
<H2>Books, Magazines &amp; More</H2>
 . . .
<H2>Writer's Gallery Literary Resources</H2>
 . . .
<H2>Writer's Companions</H2>
 . . .
<H2 ID="wnewsgroups>Newsgroups for Writers</H2>
 . . .
<H2>Critique Corner</H2>
 . . .
</BODY>
</HTML>
```

The *COPYRIGHT* Relationship

The COPYRIGHT relationship can be used in HTML 2.0 and 3.0 documents. A link with the COPYRIGHT relationship references a copyright statement for the current document. The reader's browser would display a clickable button providing access to the copyright document. The COPYRIGHT relationship could be used in your page as follows:

```
<LINK REL=COPYRIGHT HREF="copy.html" >
```

The document copy.html could look something like the copyright page for The Virtual Press:

```
<HTML>
<HEAD>
<TITLE>The Virtual Press Copyright & Trademark Information Page.</TITLE>
</HEAD>
<BODY>
```

```
<H2>Copyright Information</H2>
. . .
<HR>
<P> <A HREF="vphp.html">Virtual Press Home Page</A> ¦¦
<A HREF="vpqmenu.html">Quick Access Menu</A></P>
<HR>
<P>This page, and all contents, are Copyright (C) 1994, 1995, 1996
by The Virtual Press, Hawaii, USA. </P>
</BODY>
</HTML>
```

The *GLOSSARY* Relationship

The GLOSSARY relationship can be used in HTML 2.0 and 3.0 documents. This relationship defines a reference to a glossary of terms for the current document. The reader's browser would display a clickable button providing access to the glossary page. The GLOSSARY relationship could be used in your page as follows:

```
<LINK REL=GLOSSARY HREF="glossary.html" >
```

The *HELP* Relationship

The HELP relationship can be used in HTML 2.0 and 3.0 documents. This relationship defines a reference to help documentation for the current document. The reader's browser would display a clickable button providing access to the help page. You could use HELP in your page as follows:

```
<LINK REL=HELP HREF="helppage.html" >
```

The *HOME* Relationship

A link with the HOME relationship is used to reference the home page at your site. You could use the HOME relationship as follows:

```
<LINK REL=HOME HREF="homepage.html" >
```

The *INDEX* Relationship

The INDEX relationship can be used in HTML 2.0 and 3.0 documents. This relationship defines a reference to a keyword or key concept index for the current publication. The reader's browser would display a clickable button providing access to the index. The INDEX relationship could be used in your page as follows:

```
<LINK REL=INDEX HREF="index.html" >
```

The *PREVIOUS, NEXT,* and *UP* Relationships

The PREVIOUS, NEXT, and UP relationships are used as navigation aids to the previous, next, and parent documents, respectively. These relationships can be used in HTML 2.0 and 3.0 documents. If these relationships were used in a Web-published book and you were on page 26 in Chapter 2, the PREVIOUS, NEXT and UP relationships could be referenced as follows:

```
<HTML>
<HEAD>
<TITLE>The Web Book</TITLE>
<!— Current document title is twbch2page26.html —>
<LINK REL=PREVIOUS HREF="twbch2page25.html" >
<LINK REL=NEXT HREF="twbch2page27.html" >
<LINK REL=UP HREF="twbch2index.html" >
</HEAD>
<BODY>
   . . .
</BODY>
</HTML>
```

The *TOC* Relationship

The TOC relationship can be used in HTML 2.0 and 3.0 documents. This relationship defines a reference to a table of contents for the current publication or Web site. The TOC relationship could be used in your page as follows:

```
<LINK REL=TOC HREF="pubtoc.html" >
```

The *BANNER* Relationship

HTML 3.0 adds banners to the list of relationships for the <LINK> tag. Using the BANNER relationship, you can define an area of the document that should always be visible. The content of the banner would come from the document referenced in the HREF attribute.

While using banners is explored in depth later, you could define a banner in a link as follows:

```
<LINK REL=BANNER HREF="the_banner.html" >
```

The *STYLESHEET* Relationship

The developers of HTML 3.0 reached a compromise that allowed additional features to be used in documents yet ensured the standard remained simple, easy to use, and widely portable. The design compromise was to allow for the use of style sheets that provide both the user and the publisher with rich control over document layout. Using style sheets, the presentation can be separated from the content.

One way to define a style sheet is with the `<LINK>` tag. The document referenced in this link is a style sheet for the current document:

```
<LINK REL=STYLESHEET HREF="stylesheet12.dsssl" >
```

Style sheets are discussed later in this chapter.

Reverse Relationships

You can define a REVERSE relationship using the REV attribute. While a normal relationship specifies the relationship the current document has to a specific resource, a reverse relationship specifies the relationship the resource has to the current document. If the current document titled `twbch2.html` has the following relationship defined:

```
<LINK REL=HELP HREF="helppage.html" >
```

and the reader went to the help page, you could specify a REVERSE relationship on this page as follows:

```
<LINK REV=HELP HREF="twbch2.html" >
```

The REVERSE relationship specifies the current document is the help document for `twbch2.html`. Using the preceding link, the readers could return to the page they started on.

Link Titles

You can use the TITLE attribute to specify the title of the document referenced in the link. The reader's browser would display a clickable button labeled with the value of the TITLE attribute. If no title is specified, the default value should be the name of the relationship defined in the link.

You could specify a TITLE attribute in a header link as follows:

```
<LINK REL=BOOKMARK TITLE="Writer's Resources" HREF="vpwg.html#wresources">
```

Using *<META>*

Using the `<META>` tag, you can pass extra or specialized information in the HEAD element of a document. The server retrieving the document would include this information in the response header for the client's use. You can use the `<META>` tag with both HTML 2.0- and 3.0-compliant documents. As HTML 3.0 adds no further functionality to the `<META>` tag, you can use the `<META>` tag in your documents as described in Chapter 5.

Using *<NEXTID>*

The <NEXTID> tag is used by HTML editors to assign an ID value to an element. The <NEXTID> tag can be used in both HTML 2.0 and 3.0-compliant documents. As HTML 3.0 adds no further functionality to the <NEXTID> tag, you can use the <NEXTID> tag in your documents as described in Chapter 5.

Using *<RANGE>*

The <RANGE> tag is new to HTML 3.0 and is used to mark a section of a document. You could mark a section of the document that you wanted to highlight. Perhaps the section matches some search criteria input by the user or is a section you recently updated. The specific type of highlighting for the range you set will be determined by the style sheet associated with the document.

You can specify ranges in the HEAD element using the following three attributes: CLASS, FROM, and UNTIL.

When you assign a class to the range, you are specifying a keyword or key string that will be associated with the range. The FROM and UNTIL attributes tell your browser the start and end points for the range. These start and end points should correspond to elements in the document with a matching ID attribute. You can define multiple range types in a single document. The ranges can even overlap.

A sample range could be:

```
<RANGE CLASS="EDIT" FROM=highlight2 UNTIL=highlight3>
```

or

```
<RANGE CLASS="NEW" FROM=newstuff1 UNTIL=newstuff2>
```

While ranges are defined in the HEAD element of your document, the ID attribute is assigned to tags in the BODY element of your document.

Using *<STYLE>*

The <STYLE> tag is an extremely useful addition to HTML 3.0. Using the <STYLE> tag, you can assign a style sheet to a document. Based on this style sheet, you can make assignments that will be used by a browser to format the document. The style sheet assignments will be used instead of the browser's standard defaults. This provides you with additional control over the rendering of the document.

Style sheets you create will probably be written in the Document Style Semantics and Specification Language (DSSSL). As the style notation DSSSL is very complex and not well-suited to use on the World Wide Web, you will probably use DSSSL Lite. DSSSL Lite is a subset of DSSSL created by James Clark. Using DSSSL or DSSSL Lite, you can map the content tags in the body of your document to style tags that will give you better control over the formatting and style of text. You can control the font style, color, and size associated with any tag. You can also control the indentation of lists, paragraphs, and headings.

The only attribute you can use with the <STYLE> tag is the NOTATION attribute that assigns a style sheet. The style sheet assigned must be a recognized style notation used in the HTML 3.0 document type definition. Currently, there are only two valid style notations: w3-style and dsssl-lite.

These style notations could be used as follows:

```
<STYLE NOTATION="w3-style"> . . . </STYLE>
<STYLE NOTATION="dsssl-lite"> . . . </STYLE>
```

Style assignments you make between the begin and end STYLE tags override the browser's defaults and are based only on a known style sheet referenced in the NOTATION. This is the key difference between a style sheet defined with the <STYLE> tag and one assigned using the <LINK> tag. A style sheet specified in the <STYLE> tag is a reference to a standard style sheet known to the browser, and any style changes are assigned between the open and close STYLE tags. A style sheet specified in a link can be a reference to a style sheet you created and is not included as part of the document.

You could add the <STYLE> tag to your document as follows:

```
<HTML>
<HEAD>
<TITLE>The Web Book</TITLE>
<STYLE NOTATION=dsssl-lite"> . . . </STYLE>
</HEAD>
<BODY>
 . . .
</BODY>
</HTML>
```

Style sheets are fairly new to Web publishing but are powerful enough to warrant close attention. As browsers start to support them, you should start to see dramatic changes in the way textual information is published on the Web. One way to keep pace with changes in Web publishing that may be associated with style sheets is to add the following address to your browser's hot list:

`http://www.w3.org/hypertext/WWW/Style/`

Body Design in HTML 3.0

While the HEAD element has many elements that browser creators have been slow to support, the BODY element has dozens of tags that will be put to immediate use in HTML 3.0 browsers. Some of these tags are so cool many browsers, including NCSA Mosaic, Spyglass Mosaic, Netscape Navigator, and Internet Explorer, already support them. HTML 3.0 adds new functionality to almost every tag previously defined and adds many new elements as well.

The next sections look at each of these tags, starting with the <BODY> tag itself, which has been revised for HTML 3.0.

Using the *<BODY>* Tag

In HTML 3.0, the functionality of the <BODY> tag has been extended. The <BODY> tag now has four attributes:

```
BACKGROUND
CLASS
ID
LANG
```

The *BACKGROUND* Attribute

Most browsers display your text on a gray background. Using the BACKGROUND attribute, you can add images to the background. This feature was originally used with Netscape browser. For a full explanation on using backgrounds, see Chapter 8, "Netscape and Internet Explorer Extensions."

The *CLASS* Attribute

Using the CLASS attribute, you can assign a class to the entire BODY element for use with assignments in a style sheet. As style sheets gain support in Web publishing, you should see this attribute used often.

You can specify a class for all tags within the BODY element as follows:

```
<BODY CLASS="general_class.specific_class">
```

A sample class could be

```
<BODY CLASS="nonfiction.magazine">
```

If your style sheet had a specific style for nonfiction magazines, the text in the BODY element would be displayed in this style.

The *ID* Attribute

The ID attribute is used to label the top of the BODY element with a keyword. By referencing this keyword in a hypertext link, you can create a simple facility to enable the reader to jump to the top of your document. Here's the general form for using the ID attribute with the <BODY> tag:

```
<BODY ID="keyword">
```

The *LANG* Attribute

The LANG attribute enables you to specify the language to be used for the entire BODY element. This is useful if you want to set language-specific parameters for punctuation or hyphenation and apply them to the entire document. The values associated with this attribute are defined in ISO 639 and ISO 3166.

Here is how you could use the LANG attribute with the <BODY> tag:

```
<BODY LANG="en.us">
```

or

```
<BODY LANG="en.uk">
```

While most Web publishers wouldn't need to specify English spoken in the United States as in the first example, you may want to specify English spoken in the United Kingdom as in the second example.

Using Anchor Tags

Both HTML 2.0 and 3.0 enable you to add hypertext links to the body of your documents using the anchor tag <A>. To define a hypertext reference you use the HREF attribute. Links in the BODY element function in almost the same way as links in the HEAD element, and both have many of the same attributes. The key difference between the two is that while HEAD element links have not been supported, BODY element links have been strongly supported, and the Web would not be what it is today without the anchor tag.

While the anchor tag has many attributes in HTML 2.0, only the HREF and NAME attributes are widely used. However, you can specify relationships in anchor tags using the REL and REV attributes discussed earlier. HTML 3.0 adds five attributes to the anchor tag:

```
CLASS
ID
LANG
MD
SHAPE
```

To be useful, these new attributes should be used with the HREF attribute. The next sections explore how the new anchor attributes could be used in your documents.

The *CLASS* Attribute

Using the CLASS attribute, you can assign a class to the anchor tag for use with assignments in a style sheet. The formatting from the style sheet would only be applied to the anchor text in the document.

The *ID* Attribute

The ID attribute for anchor tags supersedes the NAME attribute used in earlier versions of HTML. However, the ID attribute has similar functionality in that it enables you to label a section of the page. When you label the anchor tag with an ID, you are specifying a keyword to be associated with the anchor tag.

Instead of using the HTML 2.0 NAME attribute as follows:

```
<A NAME="keyword">
```

you should use the ID attribute:

```
<A ID="keyword">
```

Most HTML 3.0 tags allow you to specify an associated ID. Therefore, you may or may not need to use the ID attribute in your anchor tags. However, you still specify the keyword for an internal page link as:

```
<A HREF="#keyword">Text or object to use as the anchor</A>
```

or

```
<A HREF="URL#keyword">Text or object to use as the anchor</A>
```

The *LANG* Attribute

The LANG attribute enables you to specify the language to be used for the anchor text. This is useful if you want language-specific parameters for punctuation or hyphenation to apply only to the anchor text.

The *MD* Attribute

The MD attribute enables you to verify that the document or object you intended to link to is the same document or object the link currently specifies. To use the MD attribute in your links, you must specify an encrypted checksum for the document or object you are linking. This checksum will be valid only if the document or object does not change in any way. Any alterations to the document or object, even if only a single character is changed, will invalidate the checksum.

Here is how you could use the MD attribute in the anchor tag:

```
<A MD="checksum"> . . . </A>
```

The specifics of how browsers will handle the MD attribute are still being determined. In theory, the user will be warned that the document or object has changed and will have the opportunity to continue or halt retrieval. If used with all associated links at a site, the MD attribute will put a tremendous burden on the Web publisher. The Web publisher should ensure that the value of the MD attribute in all associated links is updated any time documents or objects at the site change. The Web publisher will also have to periodically check the validity of links to documents or objects not at the site.

The *SHAPE* Attribute

The SHAPE attribute is the most powerful addition to the anchor tag. Using this attribute, you can create an image map with hot areas that can be directly interpreted by the user's browser. A hot area is a part of a graphic image the user can click on. Each hot area can have a specific action tied to it. Previously, image maps could only be used by passing information to a gateway script that interpreted the coordinates and carried out the appropriate action based on the entries in an image map file.

Relying on a gateway script was a drawback. Many Web publishers with accounts through Internet Service Providers do not have access to gateway scripts. Other Web publishers may have server software that is incapable of using gateway scripts. Consequently, one of the hottest areas of Web publishing was not explored as fully as it could be.

Adding images to your Web pages is covered in Chapter 7, "Adding Multimedia Features with HTML." You will learn how to create and design powerful image maps in Chapter 12, "Form and Image Map Creation and Design."

Using Banners

Banners are new in HTML 3.0 and are one of the most useful additions. Using the <BANNER> tag, you can define an area of the document that does not scroll with the rest of the text. This makes it possible for you to add a quick menu, corporate logo, and images that will always be visible. The following attributes are used with the <BANNER> tag in the same way as they are used with other tags described earlier: ID, LANG, and CLASS.

While the `<BANNER>` tag and the `BANNER` attribute for the `<LINK>` element serve a similar purpose, there is a fundamental difference in how the two are used in your documents. The `BANNER` attribute for the `<LINK>` element specifies a document to be used as the banner for the current page in the form:

```
<LINK REL=BANNER HREF="the_banner.html" >
```

The `<BANNER>` tag specifies text or objects that are included in the current document in the form:

```
<BANNER> Text or object to serve as banner </BANNER>
```

Banners are extremely versatile. You can use any valid `BODY` element tag within the banner element. This paves the way for making wide use of banners in Web publications. Yet to avoid confusing your browser, the banner should be the first element in the `BODY` element. Banners are in such high demand by Web publishers that most, if not all, HTML 3.0-compliant browsers should support them.

As creating banners will be a major design issue in your HTML 3.0 publications. The next sections take a look at some related issues.

Banner Design Issues

Soon there will be an explosion of sites using banners. Instead of following the lead of the power houses on the Web, your site can be a leader, and this section shows you how to do it. In fact, banners are something you can design into your pages right now, and here is why: Browsers ignore tags they do not know, and as long as the tags do not include formatting that you are relying on to convey your message, you can use them safely. A browser that cannot interpret the `<BANNER>` tag will simply ignore it and display the elements contained between the open and close `<BANNER>` tags as if the `<BANNER>` tag were not there.

Some of the best sites on the Web feature standardized text and graphic menus on their pages. These menus ensure readers can easily access any page at the site. Using a banner, you can create a menu that will always be readily accessible on your page.

You can also use a banner to ensure your corporate logo, graphic image, or contact information is always visible. Using the corporate logo in a banner helps readers associate the site with the corporation that is providing it. Pictures are worth a thousand words, and using graphic images in a banner can help you convey a point to readers, especially if the graphic relates directly to the text. Providing contact information in a banner is a great way to ensure readers can reach you if they need to and could improve your personal visibility in the Internet community as well.

Banners will also be a boon for advertisers, marketers, and sponsors because banners help keep information in front of readers longer, and exposure for products and services is the key to sales. If your site is open for viewing and use free of charge, why can't you get something in return?

With so many wonderful features you can put in a banner, the question becomes how much is too much. The key to using banners is moderation. While your banner can be an integral part of the page, it should not dominate the page. Consequently, unless the banner is the only item on the page, your banner should be small. A good rule of thumb may be to limit the size of the banner to no more than 25 percent of the browser's window.

You generally do not want the banner to fill the browser's entire viewing area. Consequently, you will want to test your banner in different display modes, especially if you use a large display mode. Display sizes can vary depending on the size of the screen and display modes.

On a Macintosh computer, the number of pixels displayed is related to the size of the monitor you are using. The larger the screen, the more pixels your monitor displays and the larger your viewing area. Mac monitors display roughly 72 pixels per inch. This means if you have a 15-inch monitor, your viewing area will be hundreds of pixels more than if you had a 9-inch monitor. To follow the 25 percent rule, you will want to consider restricting the size of your banner to a maximum of 160 pixels on the vertical.

On a Windows-based computer, the number of pixels displayed is related to the display mode you are using. The larger the display mode, the more pixels your monitor will display. Standard display modes are

> 640×480
> 800×600
> 1024×768
> 1152×900
> 1280×1024

While the most common display modes for Windows-based computers are 640×480 through 1024×768, you will want to test your banner using the 640×480 display mode. This will ensure that all users can enjoy your banner and that it does not fill the browser's viewing area. To follow the 25 percent rule, you will want to consider restricting the size of your banner to a maximum of 160 pixels on the vertical.

UNIX systems, such as SUN SPARCstations, typically don't have problems like other systems because of the large monitors and display modes in use. A typical UNIX system uses a display mode of approximately 1280×1024 or better. However, the user's browser is probably just one of several applications running simultaneously, and the browser window will not normally fill the entire screen. This scenario is especially true in business environments, where UNIX systems are mainly used. Consequently, you will want to limit the vertical size of the banner, and 160 pixels may also be a good benchmark.

Not only will you want to carefully consider the size of the banner, you will also want to consider the size of other elements on the page. If you designed your pages before considering banners, you may have to rethink your page design. Any area of the browser's window occupied by the banner will not be available for your use. Consequently, you will want to look closely at any large graphics, figures, and tables used on your pages and determine if the banner affects the usability of these objects. One way a banner could affect the usability of a large object is to prevent the reader from viewing the entire image on a single screen.

Here are some final notes on designing your banner:

- If the banner is textual, you should minimize the number of lines you use.
- If the banner is graphical, you should restrict the number of images, use small images when possible, and consider presenting multiple images in a side-by-side series when practical.
- If the banner is both graphical and textual, you should restrict the number of images and carefully consider the presentation order of the graphics and text in the banner.

Banner Creation

While creating a banner is as easy as selecting a section of your page to be the banner, you have seen there are many design issues you should first consider. After considering these issues, you will be ready to add banners to your pages. Interactivity is the key to the friendliness and usability of your pages, and the best banners will be highly interactive. If you include text in your banner, the text should contain links.

Here is how a banner using a text menu could be added to the pages I created for The Virtual Press Web site:

```
<HTML>
<HEAD>
<BASE HREF="http://tvp.com/">
<TITLE>The Virtual Press -- A Hot Spot on the Web</TITLE>
</HEAD>
<BODY>
<BANNER>
<P><STRONG>Overview</STRONG> <A HREF="vpbg.html">Background</A> ¦¦
<A HREF="vpfound.html">About the Founder</A> ¦¦
<A HREF="vpqry.html">Query Publisher</A> ¦¦
<A HREF="viporder.html">Orders & More </A> ¦¦
<A HREF="vpcon.html">Hot Contests </A> ¦¦
<A HREF="vpdream1.html"> Sneak Previews</A></P>
<P><STRONG>Features</STRONG> <A HREF="vpjic.html">Job Center</A> ¦¦
<A HREF="vpipc.html">Publishing Center</A> ¦¦
<A HREF="vpwg.html">Writer's Gallery</A> ¦¦
<A HREF="idn.html"> Internet Daily News</A> ¦¦
<A HREF="pin.html">Pulse of the Internet</A></P>
<P><STRONG>Services</STRONG> <A HREF="vpepc.html">Electronic Publishing </A> ¦¦
<A HREF="vpicc.html">Internet Consulting</A> ¦¦
<A HREF="vpwdc.html">Web Design</A> ¦¦
<A HREF="vpadv.html">Advertising &amp; marketing</A> </P>
</BANNER>
 . . . .
</BODY>
</HTML>
```

The key idea I had in mind when creating this banner was to keep it simple, low key, and usable. While the original menu for TVP's home page filled the browser's window, the revised menu for use as a banner is only three lines. To reduce the number of lines, all the text on the menu was streamlined wherever possible. You can use a banner of this type in your pages as well.

> **NOTE**
>
> The Virtual Press Web site promotes the company I founded and our services to businesses. However, the primary attractions at the site are community service areas, including Writer's Gallery, Internet Job Information Center, Internet Publishing Center, and Internet Daily News. As you'll see in the examples throughout this book, the design of the site is fairly basic. Yet with more one million hits in 1995 to the primary site (`http://tvp.com/`) and mirror site (`http://www.tvpress.com/`), the Web site demonstrates something many Web publishers don't understand and that is this: Content and the quality of resources presented are the most important aspects of any good site.

Another useful banner could contain a text menu to the Web site's order center. This type of banner could be created as follows:

```
<HTML>
<HEAD>
<TITLE>The Virtual Press -- A Hot Spot on the Web</TITLE>
</HEAD>
<BODY>
<BANNER>
<P><A HREF="vpdord.html#vfantasy">Virtual Fantasy</A> ¦¦
<A HREF="vpdord.html#vmystery">Virtual Mystery</A> ¦¦
<A HREF="vpdord.html#vscifi">Virtual SciFi</A> ¦¦
<A HREF="vpdord.html#vtruth">Virtual Truth</A></P>
</BANNER>
 . . . .
</BODY>
</HTML>
```

You can also use images to create a banner. Ideally, these images would contain many hot spots for readers to follow. However, you could also use a single image, such as your corporate logo, as the basis of your banner. If you use a single image, the image should be part of a hypertext link that readers could click on. Ideally, the link would take readers to your home page or an overview page. Here is how this type of banner could be added to pages at the TVP Web site:

```
<HTML>
<HEAD>
<TITLE>The Virtual Press -- A Hot Spot on the Web</TITLE>
</HEAD>
<BODY>
<BANNER>
```

```
<P> <A HREF="http://tvp.com/"><IMG SRC="vpttl11.gif" ALT=""></A></P>
</BANNER>
   . . . .
</BODY>
</HTML>
```

Adding HTML 3.0 Highlights to Text Elements

In HTML 3.0, there are many more ways to add highlights to the text of your documents. Some of these highlights are achieved through extensions to HTML 2.0 tags. Other highlights are achieved by introducing entirely new tags.

Using Addresses in HTML 3.0

The <ADDRESS> tag specifies that a section of the document contains an address or signature for the page. Browsers typically display ADDRESS text in italics with a paragraph break before and after the address element. While HTML 2.0 does not specify attributes for the <ADDRESS> tag, HTML 3.0 enables you to use the following attributes:

```
CLASS
CLEAR
ID
LANG
NOWRAP
```

The CLASS and ID attributes are used with the ADDRESS tag as you have seen them used in previous examples. The CLEAR attribute is used primarily when you are aligning text with images and figures. You can use three values with the CLEAR attribute, including LEFT, RIGHT, and ALL. These values tell the browser to move down until the left, right, or both margins are clear and then start the next tag there. In this way, text will flow around an image or figure inserted into the text. (See Chapter 7 for specific tips on combining text and images.)

The NOWRAP attribute prevents the browser from wrapping text associated with the element. However, you can still use the <BR> tag to break lines of text at specific locations. Here is how the CLEAR and NOWRAP attributes could be used in your documents:

```
<ADDRESS CLEAR=ALL NOWRAP>
The Virtual Press
408 Division St.
Shawano, WI
54166
</ADDRESS>
```

Using Blockquotes in HTML 3.0

For the sake of simplicity and ease of manual entry, HTML 3.0 replaces the `<BLOCKQUOTE>` tag with the `<BQ>` tag. Browsers typically display BQ text in regular type with a paragraph break before and after the BQ element. To further identify BQ text from other text, BQ text is indented from both the left and right margins. The `<BQ>` tag serves an identical function as its predecessor with increased functionality because HTML 3.0 adds the following attributes to the tag:

```
CLASS
CLEAR
ID
LANG
NOWRAP
```

HTML 3.0 also specifies a new tag that can be used with the `<BQ>` tag. This tag is called `<CREDIT>`. The `<CREDIT>` tag can be used whenever you want to give someone credit for text or figures you use in your work. You could use the `<BQ>` tag and the `<CREDIT>` tag together as follows:

```
<BQ>Let us now suppose that in the mind of each man there is an aviary
of all sorts of birds—some flocking together apart from the rest,
others in small groups, others solitary, flying anywhere and everywhere.
We may suppose that the birds are kinds of knowledge, and that when we
were children, this receptacle was empty; whenever a man has gotten and
detained in the enclosure a kind of knowledge, he may be said to have
learned or discovered the thing which is the subject of the knowledge:
and this is to know.
<CREDIT>Plato. Dialogues, Theaetetus.</CREDIT>
</BQ>
```

Using Dingbats

Dingbats are a cool addition to HTML 3.0. Using dingbats, you can insert graphic icons into your documents that are defined in a browser's document type definition and do not have to be downloaded. The key reason dingbats were added was because many Web publishers use the same graphic elements and by standardizing these simple graphic elements, downloading time can be saved and ultimately, network bandwidth can be saved as well. HTML 3.0 browsers that support dingbats display a defined graphic icon as if it were a special character.

The HTML 3.0 DTD defines dozens of dingbats that you can use in your documents. These standard ISO/WWW icons are included in the DTD courtesy of Bert Bos and Kevin Hughes. Table 6.2 lists several icons and their uses.

Table 6.2. Common Dingbats.

Dingbat	Use
archive	Icon used to represent an archive server
audio	Icon used to represent an audio sequence

Dingbat	Use
binary.document	Icon used to represent a document containing binary data
binhex.document	Icon used to represent a document containing binhex formatted data
calculator	Icon used to represent a calculator
caution	Icon used to represent a warning or caution
clock	Icon used to represent a clock
compressed.document	Icon used to represent a compressed document
disk.drive	Icon used to represent a removable media drive
diskette	Icon used to represent a floppy disk
display	Icon used to represent a computer screen
document	Icon used to represent an unspecified document type
fax	Icon used to represent a fax machine
filing.cabinet	Icon used to represent a filing cabinet
film	Icon used to represent a video or animation sequence
fixed.disk	Icon used to represent a fixed or hard drive
folder	Icon used to represent a folder or directory
form	Icon used to represent a fill-out form
ftp	Icon used to represent an ftp server
glossary	Icon used to represent a glossary of terms
gopher	Icon used to represent a Gopher server
home	Icon used to represent your home document
image	Icon used to represent a graphic image
index	Icon used to represent a searchable index
mail	Icon used to represent e-mail messages
mail.in	Icon used to represent an in box for mail
mail.out	Icon used to represent an out box for mail
map	Icon used to represent a geographical or schematic map
mouse	Icon used to represent a mouse (pointing device)
next	Icon used to represent the next document
parent	Icon used to represent the parent of current document

continues

170

Table 6.2. continued

Dingbat	Use
previous	Icon used to represent the previous document
printer	Icon used to represent a printer
summary	Icon used to represent a summary
telnet	Icon used to represent a telnet connection
text.document	Icon used to represent a text document that could contain plain text or HTML formatted text
tn3270	Icon used to represent a tn3270 terminal session
toc	Icon used to represent a table of contents
trash	Icon used to represent a waste paper basket
unknown.document	Icon used to represent an unknown document type
uuencoded.document	Icon used to represent unencoded data

Although you will find several tags that enable you to add dingbats in later sections of this chapter, you can insert a dingbat anywhere in your document using the `<!ENTITY>` tag. The `<!ENTITY>` tag enables you to directly specify an element from the document type definition. Using any of the names from Table 6.2, you can easily add any dingbat of your choosing.

The format of an `ENTITY` is:

```
<!ENTITY element_name SDATA "element_name" -- comment -->
```

If you want to add an icon to your page, you only need to know the formal name of the icon. While these are provided in the preceding list, you can also obtain a list from the DTD for HTML 3.0. Let's say you wanted to create a glossary icon. You would simply replace the two occurrences of `element_name` in the previous example and insert the `ENTITY` into your document as follows:

```
<!ENTITY glossary SDATA "glossary" >
```

As you can see from the previous example, comments are not necessary and are only used to provide remarks to someone that may read the markup code for your document. You could add a text.document icon with a comment to your document as follows:

```
<!ENTITY text.document SDATA "text.document" -- plain or html text -->
```

Using Division Tags

Traditional documents are divided into a table of contents, chapters, appendixes, bibliographies, and glossaries. These major sections are generally broken down into subsections corresponding to major topics. In HTML 2.0, there is no way to represent these traditional document sections using formats specific to the section element. HTML 3.0 corrects this shortcoming by enabling you to use the `<DIV>` tag to specify sections of the document.

The following attributes can be used with the `<DIV>` tag:

```
ALIGN
CLASS
ID
LANG
NOWRAP
```

While the ID, LANG, and NOWRAP attributes are used as discussed in previous section, the CLASS and ALIGN attributes have unique uses when associated with the DIV tag. Using the ALIGN attribute with the DIV tag, you can specify the alignment for all paragraphs within a section of your document. The capability to align text in an entire section is a feature in high demand by Web publishers. You can easily apply the alignment to paragraphs of the entire document by inserting the begin division tag `<DIV>` after the start of the BODY element and inserting the end division tag `</DIV>` just before the end of the BODY element.

> **NOTE**
>
> The aligning of text in a division only applies to paragraph text associated with the paragraph tag `<P>` It does not apply to headings and other text you define in the division. This enables you to align headings and other text as necessary without worrying if you are going to conflict with the alignment of the division. Because paragraph text can be aligned based on the ALIGN attribute, I recommend you use the begin and end paragraph tags so you have a clear understanding of what text will be aligned and what text will not be aligned based on the division element.

HTML 3.0 specifies four values for the ALIGN attribute. All paragraphs in this division will be flush left:

```
<DIV ALIGN=LEFT>
. . .
</DIV>
```

All paragraphs in this division will be flush right:

```
<DIV ALIGN=RIGHT>
. . .
</DIV>
```

All paragraphs in this division will be centered on the page:

```
<DIV ALIGN=CENTER>
. . .
</DIV>
```

All paragraphs in this division will be justified with even margins on both sides:

```
<DIV ALIGN=JUSTIFY>
  . . .
</DIV>
```

Using the CLASS attribute with the <DIV> tag, you can divide your document sections into classes. The <DIV> tag used with the CLASS attribute by itself does not create any special formatting. To create specific formatting for a section defined with the CLASS attribute, you must use the <DIV> tag with a style sheet. If you do not use the <DIV> tag with a style sheet dividing your document into major sections with the CLASS attribute will serve only as a pointer to those reading the actual markup code for the document and not those displaying the document using a browser.

Some example classes you could assign are

```
<DIV CLASS=TOC>The text could be associated with a table of contents</DIV>
<DIV CLASS=CHAPTER>The text could be associated with a chapter</DIV>
<DIV CLASS=APPENDIX>The text could be associated with an appendix</DIV>
<DIV CLASS=BIBLIO>The text could be associated with a bibliography</DIV>
<DIV CLASS=GLOSSARY>The text could be associated with a glossary</DIV>
```

You could also further define the class by specifying a general class and a subclass. Here's how you could apply a general class and a subclass to an entire document:

```
<HTML>
<HEAD>
<TITLE>The Web Book: Chapter 1</TITLE>
<STYLE NOTATION=dsssl-lite"> . . . </STYLE>
</HEAD>
<BODY>
<DIV CLASS=NONFICTION.CHAPTER>
The text could be associated with a chapter of a nonfiction book.
</DIV>
</BODY>
</HTML>
```

Here is how you could apply a style sheet you created to the same document:

```
<HTML>
<HEAD>
<TITLE>The Web Book: Chapter 1</TITLE>
<LINK REL=STYLESHEET HREF="your_stylesheet.dsssl" >
</HEAD>
<BODY>
<DIV CLASS=NONFICTION.CHAPTER>
The text could be associated with a chapter of a nonfiction book.
</DIV>
</BODY>
</HTML>
```

Using Header Tags

Headings are an important part of HTML. You can use six levels of headings in your documents (<H1>, <H2>, <H3>, <H4>, <H5>, and <H6>). While HTML 2.0 heading tags have no attributes, HTML 3.0 headings tags can be used with the following attributes:

```
ALIGN
CLASS
CLEAR
DINGBAT
ID
LANG
MD
NOWRAP
SEQNUM
SKIP
SRC
```

As the ALIGN, CLASS, CLEAR, ID, LANG, MD and NOWRAP attributes are used in the same way described in previous sections, this section focuses on the DINGBAT, SEQNUM, SKIP, and SRC attributes. You can easily add a dingbat to your header with the DINGBAT attribute. The dingbat will be inserted in front of the header text. You could use the mail dingbat as follows:

```
<H1 DINGBAT=mail> . . . </H1>
```

By combining the ALIGN and DINGBAT attributes, you could center the heading and the dingbat on the page:

```
<H1 ALIGN=center DINGBAT=mail> . . . </H1>
```

If you do not want to insert a predefined icon before your heading text, you can use the SRC attribute to specify any available image file. This heading will display an image called bang.gif before the heading text:

```
<H1 SRC="bang.gif"> . . . </H1>
```

Also new for headings in HTML 3.0 is the capability to sequence heading levels. Using the SEQNUM attribute, you can numerically order heading levels with section numbers such as Section 1 or Section 1.1. While automated sequencing of headers is another item in high demand by Web publishers, you will want to exercise caution. The sequence number used relates specifically to the heading level you use. Level One headings will be numbered alike, Level Two headings will be numbered alike, and so on.

The style of the section numbering displayed is up to the browser and the style sheet you are using. However, the general form is as follows: The first level header in the document will have a section number of One and could be displayed as Section 1. This number is incremented with each additional Level One heading element in the document. Headings under the Level One heading are numbered as subsections. Lower-level headings under a subheading will have subsection numbers that correspond to the level of the subheading. If this subsection was for a Level Two heading, it could have a section number of 1.1, 2.1, and so on.

Sequence numbers are initialized and incremented automatically. Your browser will insert them based on the style sheet you define. You can specify a starting sequence number for a document using the SEQNUM attribute. The SEQNUM attribute can also be used to specify a specific value for a particular heading. The browser will increment the heading levels starting from the sequence number you have specified. Figure 6.1 shows how sequence numbers for the headings defined in the following code could be displayed.

```
<HTML>
<HEAD>
<TITLE>The Web Book: Chapter 1</TITLE>
<STYLE NOTATION=dsssl-lite"> . . . </STYLE>
</HEAD>
<BODY>
<H1 SEQNUM=1>Web Publishing</H1>
<H2>What is Web Publishing</H2>
<H3>Defining the World Wide Web</H3>
<H3>Defining Web Publishing</H3>
<H3>Brief History of the Internet</H3>
<H3>Brief History of the World Wide Web</H3>
<H2>Why Web Publish</H2>
<H3>Spreading the Word About Your Ideas</H3>
<H3>Powerful Advertising</H3>
<H3>Marketing to Global Audiences</H3>
<H3>Cost-effectiveness of Web publishing</H3>
<H3>Conduct Business</H3>
 . . .
</BODY>
</HTML>
```

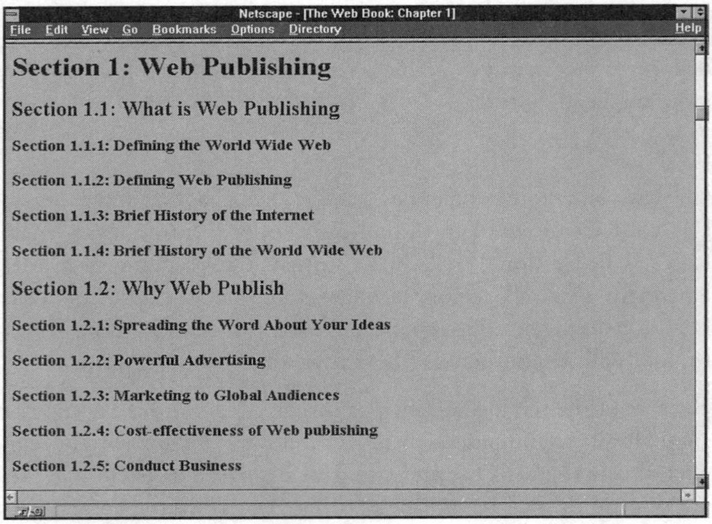

FIGURE 6.1.

Using sequence numbers, you can automatically number headings.

If you want to leave numbers out of the sequence, you can skip them using the SKIP attribute. Figure 6.2 shows the effect SEQNUM and SKIP have on the following sample.

```
<HTML>
<HEAD>
```

```
<TITLE>The Web Book: Chapter 1</TITLE>
<STYLE NOTATION=dsssl-lite"> . . . </STYLE>
</HEAD>
<BODY>
<H1 SEQNUM=2>Web Publishing</H1>
<H2 SKIP=2>Why Web Publish</H2>
<H3>Spreading the Word About Your Ideas</H3>
<H3>Powerful Advertising</H3>
<H3>Marketing to Global Audiences</H3>
<H3>Cost-effectiveness of Web publishing</H3>
<H3>Conduct Business</H3>
<H3>Electronic commerce</H3>
<H2>Features of Web</H2>
<H3>Combining text and images</H3>
<H3>Interactive Documents</H3>
<H3 SKIP=3>Multimedia Documents</H3>
 . . .
</BODY>
</HTML>
```

FIGURE 6.2.

Number sequences can also be skipped.

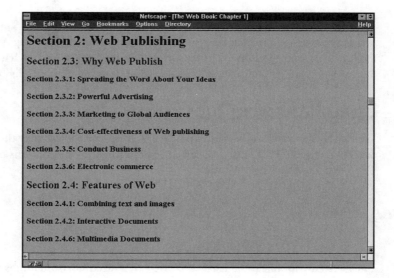

Using Horizontal Rules

Horizontal rules are used to visually divide sections of HTML documents. While HTML 2.0 did not support attributes for the <HR> tag, HTML 3.0 supports the following attributes:

```
CLASS
CLEAR
ID
MD
SRC
```

In HTML 2.0, horizontal rules are standard features used by most Web publishers. Yet some Web publishers wanted to make their documents stand out from others on the Web and used graphical lines instead of horizontal rules. These graphical lines, while visually appealing, had a major drawback in that readers with text-only browsers saw no line break at all. To a reader with a text-only browser, documents with graphical lines had no subdivisions. This was a major problem.

To clear up this problem, HTML 3.0 enables you to specify images to be used with the horizontal rule. Because the image is specified as a part of the <HR> tag, a user with a graphical browser will see a graphical line and a reader with a text-only browser will see a standard horizontal rule. You specify an image to use instead of the horizontal rule using the SRC attribute as follows:

```
<HR SRC="graduated_line.gif">
```

or

```
<HR SRC="your_line.gif">
```

While you can use any image as the source for the horizontal rule tag, you should use an image that creates a graphical line. This ensures you follow the spirit of what the creators of HTML 3.0 intended and also ensures readers see your image as a section divider.

Using Horizontal Tabs

Web publishers demanded it and finally, you have fine control over the horizontal positioning of text. Using the <TAB> tag, you can define tab stops, create columns of text, and much more. The <TAB> tag has four attributes:

```
ALIGN
ID
INDENT
TO
```

The ALIGN attribute can be used to create generalized horizontal tabs that align text after the tab stop. The default value for ALIGN is LEFT, meaning text will be aligned with the left margin. You can also use values of RIGHT for flush right or CENTER to center text on page. Here is how you can use the ALIGN attribute with horizontal tabs in your documents:

```
<P><TAB>The text is flush left by default</P>
<P><TAB ALIGN=LEFT>This text is flush left</P>
<P>This text is normal. <TAB ALIGN=RIGHT>This text is flush right</P>
```

You can also make combined tab alignments:

```
<P><TAB ALIGN=LEFT>The text is flush left <TAB ALIGN=CENTER>This text is
centered <TAB ALIGN=RIGHT>This text is flush right</P>
```

While the ID attribute is used in a different way than in other elements, it serves the same purpose as a label. The key difference is that the ID attribute is used to label a tab stop at a particular location, such as

```
<P>Tab stops in <TAB ID=TAB1>HTML are similar to tab stops in
<TAB ID=TAB2>your word processor.</P>
```

When the line above is displayed, your browser will set two tab stops. One tab stop will be at the H in HTML and the other will be at the y in your. It is important to note that only the displayed text is used as the determinant for the location of the tab stop. Any tags you may have inserted into the line will not be used to determine the location of the tab stop. So, you may want to rewrite your line or paragraph of text without formatting elements so you can easily count the character position of the tab stop.

> **TIP**
>
> While the keyword for your tab can be any word, you should use a keyword that fits the situation logically and helps you to remember the value assigned to the ID attribute creates a tab stop. For this reason, I use the keyword TAB in the examples in this section.

Once you have defined tab stops in a document, you can use the tab stops later in the document. You do this by assigning the keyword value of the tab stop to the TO attribute, as follows:

```
<P>1 <TAB TO=TAB1>2 <TAB TO=TAB2>3</P>
```

In the preceding example, the 2 would be aligned with the *H* in HTML and the 3 would be aligned with the *y* in your. While you can obtain precise positioning using labeled tab stops, the problem is you must introduce a line of text into the document that contains your tab stops. If the line you use as your model for tab stops is short, you may not be able to include all the tab stops you want. Therefore, the line of text you use a model for tab stops should be the first long line of text that occurs naturally in the document prior to the location where you need to use horizontal tabs.

The following line would be a bad choice to use as the model for your tab stops because it is too short:

```
<P>This <TAB ID=TAB1>is <TAB ID=TAB2>bad.</P>
<P>The following <TAB ID=TAB1>line <TAB ID=TAB2> is a <TAB ID=TAB3>better
line to use because it will stretch across the screen and can be used as
a good model sentence for your tab stops.</P>
```

Most of the time, you will want to limit your tab stops to the first 65 characters in a line. This will ensure readers using a different display mode or monitor size from yours will see your text formatted as you intended. You will also want to ensure that your tab stops have a unique name within the scope of the current document.

You can manually specify the horizontal position to move using the INDENT attribute. As this is a manual specification, using the INDENT attribute with the TO attribute serves no useful purpose. Values for the INDENT attribute are specified in en units. An *en* is a unit used by typesetters that is equal to half the point size of the associated text. If the reader is displaying your page in a 12-point font size, an en unit for the page would be roughly six points in size. Keep in mind that one point is roughly equal to 1/72 of an inch, but that can vary depending on the actual font used. This means six points is approximately 1/12 of an inch. Therefore, for every whole digit increment in en units, the tab position for this reader will move 1/12 of an inch. Sound like rocket science? Well, maybe it is. However, the developers of HTML 3.0 needed a generic unit based on the font the reader was actually using and the en filled this need quite well.

The key point to remember when it comes to the INDENT attribute is that the size of the en unit is dependent on the size of the font the reader is using to display the text element with horizontal tabs. If you carefully consider the font sizes readers may be using to display these text elements, you will be well on your way to creating universally usable documents.

TIP

The average user displays paragraph text in an 8 to 12 point font. If you use this to define a general size for your tab positions in en units, one en unit approximates 1/9 inch to 1/6 inch.

The average user displays a level One heading in a 16 to 20 point font. If you use this to define a general size for your tab positions in en units, one en unit approximates 2/9 inch to 5/18 inch.

TIP

Here is how you could use the INDENT attribute for the <TAB> tag:

```
<P>1 <TAB IDENT=12>2 <TAB IDENT=24>3</P>
```

If the preceding text is displayed in a 12-point font, the horizontal position of the 2 will be approximately 1 inch from the left margin and the horizontal position of the 3 will be approximately 2 inches from the left margin.

Using Line Breaks

You use the <BR> tag to insert a line break into the text of your document. In HTML 2.0, the <BR> tag had no associated attributes. HTML 3.0 adds to the functionality of line breaks by enabling you to use the following attributes:

```
CLASS
CLEAR
ID
LANG
```

While these attributes are used as described in previous sections, you can create a line break with a keyword ID as follows:

```
<BR ID=keyword>
```

Using Admonishments

Notes, cautions, and warnings are extremely useful parts of many computer books. Finally, you can include these admonishments in your Web documents using the <NOTE> tag as follows:

```
<NOTE> Insert note, tip or caution. </NOTE>
```

HTML 3.0 browsers should display notes in a distinctive manner that sets them off from the rest of the document text. The following attributes can be used with the <NOTE> tag:

```
CLASS
CLEAR
ID
LANG
MD
SRC
```

Based on the value of the CLASS attribute, the reader's browser may insert an associated dingbat in the left margin, such as a warning sign. You can specify whether the admonishment you are providing is a note, caution, or warning as follows:

```
<NOTE CLASS=note>
<NOTE CLASS=caution>
<NOTE CLASS=warning>
```

Using Paragraphs

The paragraph tag <P> is another tag that has been greatly enhanced in HTML 3.0. While HTML 2.0 does not specify attributes for paragraph tags, HTML 3.0 specifies the following attributes:

```
ALIGN
CLASS
CLEAR
ID
LANG
NOWRAP
```

All these attributes are used as described in previous sections. The most useful addition to the paragraph tag is the ALIGN attribute. By default, the <P> tag allows you to you align text with the left margin, but using the ALIGN attribute you can align with the right margin, center, and justify paragraph text as well. While the standard does not require the use of the end paragraph tag </P>, you may want to use this tag so you can clearly discern where your paragraphs start and end. Here is how you could use the ALIGN attribute:

```
<P ALIGN=RIGHT> This paragraph is aligned with the right margin. </P>
<P ALIGN=CENTER> This paragraph is centered. </P>
<P ALIGN=JUSTIFY> This paragraph is justified. </P>
```

The NOWRAP attribute tells the browser not to wrap lines of text in the associated paragraph. This is useful in a few instances, but should always be used with the <BR> tag. In this way, you can force paragraph text to break where you want it to break without worrying if the text will wrap.

Using Preformatted Text

A section of text is declared as preformatted with the <PRE> tag. Preformatted text can contain ASCII spacing tricks, including tabs, multiple tabs, multiple spaces, and multiple blank lines. Both HTML 2.0 and 3.0 enable you to use the WIDTH attribute with the <PRE> tag to specify the maximum number of characters that should appear on a line. The default width is 80 characters if you do not specify one.

HTML 3.0 adds the following attributes to the <PRE> tag:

```
CLASS
CLEAR
ID
LANG
```

Until recently, the <PRE> tag was used widely to format text into columns and to obtain precise formatting for sections of document text. The problem with using the <PRE> tag to ensure correct formatting is that browsers typically display preformatted text in a monospaced typewriter font such as Courier and monospaced fonts are not as appealing as other fonts.

As HTML 3.0 has addressed many shortcomings of its predecessors, most of the time you will not need to use preformatted text elements in your documents. However, the <PRE> tag can be a time-saver and a quick solution to a presentation problem you face. The <PRE> tag is most useful for any text originally formatted as plain text, such as an e-mail message or newsgroup posting. Using the <PRE> tag, you will not have to reformat, and you will save time.

Using Footnotes

Footnotes are a major part of many forms of writing and in HTML 3.0 you can finally create a fully footnoted document. The way you create a footnote is not as straightforward as with other information tags. Primarily, this is because footnotes are defined as an interactive part of your document that should be rendered by browsers as popup text. Allowing footnotes to pop up at the click of a button will create a wonderful new element in HTML 3.0 documents and should open the door for many additional uses of popup text.

The textual portion of your footnotes are defined with a pair of tags as follows:

```
<FN> A footnote. </FN>
```

Ideally, your footnote text will be defined at the bottom of your document. This will enable a reader with a browser that does not support footnotes to view the document as you intended. Simple footnotes could be defined at the bottom of your document as follows:

```
<FN>1. Renaissance - Time of the great revival of art, learning and
literature in Europe from the early 14th century to the 17th century.</FN>
<FN>2. Medieval - Pertaining to or characteristic of the Middle Ages</FN>
<FN>3. Middle Ages - Time in European history between classical antiquity
and the Renaissance from the late 5th century to about 1350.</FN>
```

You can use the following attributes with footnotes:

> CLASS
> ID
> LANG

While the CLASS and LANG attributes add functionality to the <FN> tag as described in previous sections, it is the ID attribute that allows footnotes to be an interactive part of your document. You do this by assigning keyword values to the ID attribute that match keywords defined in hypertext links. The hypertext link should be an internal page link defined as follows:

```
<A HREF="#footnote_keyword"> . . . </A>
```

Here's how you could use links to footnotes in a document:

```
<HTML>
<HEAD>
<TITLE>Great Literature in History</TITLE>
</HEAD>
<BODY>
<P>Imagine for a moment what it would be like to live in the
<A HREF="#footnote1">Renaissance</A> to be a part of the great
yearning for knowledge. What would your daily routine be? What would
be the most prevalent thought in your mind? Now take a step backward
in time and walk with <A HREF="#footnote2">Medieval</A> man. What
would it be like to live in the <A HREF="#footnote3">Middle Ages</A>?
Great theories begin with a question and if you want answers, you may
to look to <A HREF="http://www.clas.ufl.edu:80/english/exemplaria/">
Exemplaria</A> the Journal for Medieval and Renaissance theories.</P>
<P> . . . </P>
<HR>
<FN ID=footnote1>Renaissance - Time of the great revival of art,
learning and literature in Europe from the early 14th century to the
17th century.</FN>
<FN ID=footnote2>Medieval - Pertaining to or characteristic of the
Middle Ages</FN>
```

182

```
<FN ID=footnote3>Middle Ages - Time in European history between
classical antiquity and the Renaissance from the late 5th century
to about 1350.</FN>
</BODY>
</HTML>
```

If your browser is capable of displaying popup text, the footnote text will appear in a popup window. If your browser supports footnotes but is not capable of displaying popup text, the browser will simply display the section of the document containing the footnote text. To distinguish the word or phrase you footnoted from the associated text, you may want to add additional highlights to the footnote section. Here's how you could add emphasis text to highlight this section:

```
<FN ID=footnote1><EM>Renaissance</EM> - Time of the great revival of art,
learning and literature in Europe from the early 14th century to the
17th century.</FN>
<FN ID=footnote2><EM>Medieval</EM> - Pertaining to or characteristic of
the Middle Ages</FN>
<FN ID=footnote3><EM>Middle Ages</EM> - Time in European history between
classical antiquity and the Renaissance from the late 5th century
to about 1350.</FN>
```

Information Tags in HTML 3.0

Many new information tags can be used in HTML 3.0. Unlike heading and paragraph tags that insert white space into the document, information tags do not insert white space, which makes it possible to use information tags within other tags to highlight a single word or a group of words. As you read this section, keep in mind that many of these elements will be used primarily by indexers that catalog pages at Web sites. The fact that there are so many information tags introduced for indexers says a lot about the growth of Web indexing facilities and their popularity—millions of Web users search through indexed databases to find sites of interest.

Using Abbreviations

You can specify abbreviations in your HTML 3.0 documents using the `<ABBREV>` tag. The `<ABBREV>` tag has no attributes and is used as follows:

```
<ABBREV> An abbreviation. </ABBREV>
```

You can use the abbreviation element any time you use abbreviations in your documents, such as

```
<P><ABBREV>Subs</ABBREV> should be sent to the editorial department.</P>
```

Using Acronyms

HTML 3.0 enables you to specify acronyms in your text using the `<ACRONYM>` tag. The `<ACRONYM>` tag has no attributes and is used as follows:

```
<ACRONYM> An acronym. </ACRONYM>
```

You can use the acronym element any time you use acronyms in your documents, such as

```
<P>Visit <ACRONYM>NASA</ACRONYM> on the Web today!</P>
```

Using Author

You can specify the author of the document or sections of the document using the `<AU>` tag. This new tag under HTML 3.0 has no attributes and is used as follows:

```
<AU> Author's name </AU>
```

You can use the author element any time you specify the author in your documents, such as

```
<P>Written by <AU>William R. Stanek</AU></P>
```

Using Definitions

HTML 3.0 enables you to specify that you are defining the word highlighted by the `<DFN>` tag. The `<DFN>` tag has no attributes and is used as follows:

```
<DFN> A term being defined. </DFN>
```

You can use the definition element any time you define a word in your document, such as

```
<P><DFN>Standard Generalized Markup Language</DFN> is a generalized
markup language that forms the basis for most markup languages and
is an advanced language with few limitations.</P>
```

Using Delete

Revision is a part of writing. Many word processors enable you to mark sections of text that you have revised. While you wouldn't want to show revisions in most forms of writing, there are times when you may want to be explicit about how the document has been revised. Typically, text that has been deleted since a previous version will be displayed with a line drawn through the text, such as

~~This text has been deleted from this version of the document.~~

HTML 3.0 enables you to mark sections of text that have been deleted since a previous version of the document using the `<DEL>` tag. The `<DEL>` tag has no attributes and is used as follows:

```
<DEL> Text that was deleted. </DEL>
```

Browsers should display the deleted text in a strikethrough font similar to the preceding example showing text with a line drawn through it. You can use the `<DEL>` tag in your documents as follows:

```
<P><DEL>The second example shows</DEL>The first example shows . . . </P>
```

Your browser may display the example as follows:

~~The second example shows~~The first example shows . . .

Using Insert

Another way to show revisions to your documents is to use the `<INS>` tag. Inserted text should be displayed by HTML 3.0 browsers in an underline font and is used as follows:

```
<INS> Text inserted in this revision of the document. </INS>
```

You can use the `<INS>` tag in your documents as follows:

```
<P>The example proves <INS>beyond a reasonable doubt</INS> that . . . </P>
```

Using Language

You can use the `<LANG>` tag to designate text that is in another language. The `<LANG>` tag is used just like the `LANG` attribute described in previous sections. However, no special formatting is associated with the `<LANG>` tag. Therefore, you would use this tag in your Web documents when you want to specify text in another language without using any special formatting.

Text in another language could be specified as follows:

```
<P>Lesson four <LANG>Po doroge</LANG>
```

Using Person

With HTML 3.0, you can denote the name of a person used in your documents using the `<PERSON>` tag. The `<PERSON>` tag has no attributes and is used as follows:

```
<PERSON> A person's name. </PERSON>
```

You can use the person element any time you use the name of a person in your documents, such as

```
<P><PERSON>Isaac Asimov's</PERSON> Foundation Trilogy is terrific!</P>
```

Using Quotations

To identify short quotations in HTML 3.0, you use the quotation tag `<Q>`. Short quotations are displayed by your browser in quotations marks. You can use a language-specific style for quotation marks by setting a value for the `LANG` attribute as follows:

```
<Q LANG=de> Short quotation in German </Q>
```

Adding Visual Variety to Your Documents in HTML 3.0

HTML 3.0 enables you to add more variety to the textual portions of your page using strikethrough, big, small, superscript, and subscript text. While the associated tags highlight your text, they do not insert white space into the document. This makes it possible to use character style tags within other tags to highlight a single word or a group of words.

Often when you are creating a document, you want some text to be larger than the surrounding text. The only way to do this in HTML 2.0 was to use a header tag, which is not how header tags are intended to be used and could cause problems with older browsers, like Lynx. In HTML 3.0, Web publishers no longer have this problem. Text highlighted with <BIG> will be displayed in a larger font than normal paragraph text on the page:

```
<BIG> Large text </BIG>
```

Just as you sometimes want sections of large text, you sometimes want sections of small text. As the Web publisher, you may want to use small text in copyright notices, disclaimers, or other legal notes in your documents. Text highlighted with <SMALL> will be displayed in a smaller font than normal paragraph text on the page:

```
<SMALL> Small text </SMALL>
```

A basic addition to HTML 3.0 is strikethrough text. Strikethrough text should be displayed by browsers with a line through it. You can define strikethrough text as follows:

```
<S> Strikethrough text </S>
```

Another useful addition to HTML 3.0 are subscripts and superscripts. Subscript text should be displayed by browsers in a subscript font and is defined using the begin and end <SUB> tag. Superscript text should be displayed by browsers in a superscript font and is defined using the begin and end <SUP> tag. Both subscript and superscript text can be used with the ALIGN attribute to align the script text accordingly with mathematical equations. You can use subscripts and superscripts as follows:

```
<SUB> Subscript text </SUB>
<SUP> Superscript text </SUP>
```

Creating Lists in HTML 3.0

HTML 3.0 enables you to create more powerful and better organized lists. The three primary types of lists (ordered, unordered, and definition) are fully supported by the standard. However, menu and directory lists are not fully supported and have been deprecated, as very few browsers display menu and directory lists in a unique way.

> **NOTE**
>
> HTML elements that have been deprecated are included in the standard for backward compatibility, yet publishers are urged not to use them as the developers of HTML have expressed earnest disapproval of these elements.

Using List Headers

One of the most useful additions to lists in HTML 3.0 are list headers. In HTML 2.0, the only way to create headers for a list was to use the header tag. This was not how header tags are intended to be used and could cause problems with older browsers. In HTML 3.0, Web publishers no longer have this problem and can use the <LH> tag to add headers to lists.

The pair of tags associated with list headers are used as follows:

```
<LH> List Heading </LH>
```

You can insert a list heading wherever it makes sense in your lists. For example, if you use nested lists, each nested list could have its own header.

Using Ordered Lists

Web publishers use ordered lists whenever tasks must be performed in a particular order or when they want to add specificity to the list. The <OL> tag designates the start of the ordered list and the end tag </OL> designates the end of the list. Each item in the ordered list is preceded by the list item tag <LI>.

In HTML 3.0, seven attributes can be used with the <OL> tag:

```
CLASS
CLEAR
COMPACT
CONTINUE
ID
LANG
SEQNUM
```

The CLASS, CLEAR, ID, and LANG attributes are used as described in previous sections. While the COMPACT attribute was specified in the HTML 2.0 standard, few browsers displayed lists in a compact manner. The intended use of the COMPACT attribute is to squeeze the list into a smaller screen space. HTML 3.0 browsers will do this by using less spacing between list items and possibly using a smaller font for the list.

You can use the CONTINUE attribute to continue a previously defined ordered list. This is useful because the numbering will continue in sequence from the last list item previously defined. Here's how this could be done:

```
<OL>
<LH> Steps for creating a Web document
<LI> Develop a Strategy
<LI> Define the document structure
</OL>
<OL CONTINUE>
<LI> Create the document
<LI> Add features to the document
<LI> Proof the document
</OL>
<OL CONTINUE>
<LI> Test the document
<LI> Publish the Finished document
</OL>
```

You will find the CONTINUE attribute is very useful when you want to insert comments or explanations into your list. For example, you could introduce a six-item list, insert the first three items, explain the items in detail to the reader, continue the numbering of the list for the last three items, then explain those items in detail to the reader.

To start a list at a specific sequence number, you can use the SEQNUM attribute. This list will be numbered from 25 to 27:

```
<OL SEQNUM=25>
<LI> Item 25
<LI> Item 26
<LI> Item 27
</OL>
```

Using Unordered Lists

Web publishers use unordered lists to outline goals, objectives, or tasks with no specific order. Unordered lists are also called bulleted lists because an icon called a bullet usually precedes items in the list. The <UL> tag designates the start of the unordered list and the end tag </UL> designates the end of the list. Each item in the unordered list is preceded by the list item tag <LI>.

In HTML 3.0, ten attributes can be used with the <UL> tag:

> CLASS
>
> CLEAR
>
> COMPACT
>
> DINGBAT
>
> ID
>
> LANG

MD
PLAIN
SRC
WRAP

The CLASS, CLEAR, COMPACT, ID, LANG, and MD attributes are used as described in previous sections. While the SRC attribute can be used to specify a bullet you created, the DINGBAT attribute can be used to specify a browser-supported dingbat to use as the bullet. Valid names for dingbats are listed in Table 6.2. You can define a dingbat for the list as follows:

```
<UL DINGBAT=film>
<LI> Item 1
<LI> Item 2
<LI> Item 3
</UL>
```

While bullets can add to the impact of the list, sometimes you don't want a bullet to be used in your list. Then, use the PLAIN attribute and no bullet will be displayed with your list, such as

```
<UL PLAIN>
<LI> Item 1
<LI> Item 2
<LI> Item 3
</UL>
```

The WRAP attribute is also useful. Using WRAP, you can create lists in multiple columns. You can arrange columns vertically or horizontally using the values vert or horiz, respectively. However, you have no control over the number of columns; that is controlled by the reader's browser.

Using Definition Lists

Web publishers use definition lists when they want to specify word definitions in a glossary and to associate a keyword or phrase with a concept. The <DL> tag designates the start of the definition list and the end tag </DL> designates the end of the list. The definition title tag <DT> specifies the term you are defining and the definition data tag <DD> specifies the definition associated with the term.

In HTML 3.0, five attributes can be used with the <DL> tag:

CLASS
CLEAR
COMPACT
ID
LANG

These attributes are used as previously discussed.

Making the Transition to HTML 3.0

Consider carefully how you will transition to HTML 3.0. In theory, an HTML 2.0 browser could read your HTML 3.0 document. The browser should simply ignore the additional elements and tag extensions you have used. Obviously, the more advanced your document is, the more elements the older browser will ignore and the less likely that your document will look anything like you intended.

Distinguishing Your HTML Documents

The refined draft of the specification suggests that you use the extension .html3 or .ht3 to distinguish HTML 3.0 documents from documents using earlier version of HTML during the transition period. The draft also recommends that you identify your document as an HTML 3.0 document using the following declaration:

```
<!doctype HTML public "-//W3O//DTD W3 HTML 3.0//EN">
```

The declaration states this an HTML 3.0 document conforming to the document type definition for HTML 3.0 as set forth by the World Wide Web Organization (W3O) and further that the document is in the English language. If this declaration is added to the list of elements for a correctly formatted HTML 3.0 document, a template for a basic HTML 3.0 document would look like this:

```
<!doctype HTML public "-//W3O//DTD W3 HTML 3.0//EN">
<HTML>
<HEAD>
<TITLE></TITLE>
</HEAD>
<BODY>
</BODY>
</HTML>
```

> **NOTE**
>
> Some HTML 2.0-compliant browsers can, and potentially all HTML 3.0-compliant browsers will, infer HEAD, BODY, and HTML elements. Consequently, a minimal HTML document could consist of only a document title and conform to the HTML 3.0 standard. Still, the best Web publishers will continue to use the HTML, HEAD, and BODY elements to give their documents clear organization and to ensure compatibility.

You should also consider how HTML 3.0 browsers will treat your old documents. To ensure there are no problems, you should add the following line to documents that are strictly formatted for HTML 2.0:

```
<!doctype HTML public "-//IETF//DTD HTML 2.0//EN">
```

The declaration states this is an HTML 2.0 document conforming to the document type definition for HTML 2.0 as set forth by the Internet Engineering Task Force (IETF), and further that the document is in the English language. If this declaration is added to the list of suggested elements for a correctly formatted HTML 2.0 document, a template for the most basic HTML 2.0 document would look like this:

```
<!doctype HTML public "-//IETF//DTD HTML 2.0//EN">
<HTML>
<HEAD>
<TITLE></TITLE>
</HEAD>
<BODY>
</BODY>
</HTML>
```

Creating Navigation Mechanisms for Old and New Browsers

As you transition to HTML 3.0, you will want to ensure that your site is accessible no matter what type of browser a user has. One way to do this is to create several sets of pages. One set of pages would be for users with HTML 2.0-compliant browsers. Another set of pages would be for users with HTML 3.0-compliant browsers. However, if you create several sets of pages, the question becomes how you can make sure the right users are accessing the right pages.

The simplest way to ensure accessibility and compatibility is to create an alternate path from your home page. Alternate paths are currently used to provide readers with text-only browsers with pages specifically formatted for a text-only environment, and the same technique could be used for users with advanced browsers compliant with HTML 3.0. Keeping in mind that HTML 3.0 is backward-compatible with HTML 2.0, your home page should be formatted according to the HTML 2.0 standard or use formatting techniques that, if ignored, wouldn't materially alter the layout of your page.

Here's a home page that uses an alternate path:

```
<HTML>
<HEAD>
<TITLE>The Virtual Press -- A Hot Spot on the Web</TITLE>
</HEAD>
<BODY>
<P> <A HREF="vpbg.html"><IMG SRC="vpttl11.gif" ALT=""></A></P>
<H2><IMG SRC="bboard.gif" ALIGN="BOTTOM" ALT="* ATTN *">
The Original Virtual Press — Hot contests for writers &amp; artists,
job information, electronic publishing information and much more!</H2>
<P><STRONG><A HREF="vphp.html3">Experience the explosive features we've
created especially for HTML 3.0 compliant browsers.</A></STRONG></P>
. . .
</BODY>
</HTML>
```

While providing an alternate path is a simple solution to the problem of document formats, it is not the only solution. Using the Common Gateway Interface discussed in Chapter 11, "Writing CGI Scripts," you could provide documents to readers based on the type of browser they are using. In this way, readers see only documents formatted specifically for their browser.

Summary

Although the HTML 3.0 specification is evolving, support for HTML 3.0 is growing phenomenally. Primarily this is because HTML 3.0 is rich in features and provides many useful extensions to the HTML standard. These features and extensions provide you with more control over the layout of your documents. You can align headers and paragraph text, create customized lists, use alternate languages, and create advanced links in your documents. You can also use advanced design techniques such as style sheets and banners.

Consider carefully how you will make the transition to HTML 3.0. You should ensure you provide navigation mechanisms for old and new browsers. You should also distinguish your HTML 3.0 documents from your HTML 2.0 documents.

Adding Multimedia Features with HTML

7

by William Robert Stanek

IN THIS CHAPTER

194

Multimedia is the driving force behind the phenomenal popularity of the World Wide Web. By adding graphics, sound, and video, you can create visually stunning, highly interactive, and dynamic pages that will entice readers to visit your page time after time. This chapter is filled with insider tips and techniques for incorporating multimedia into your publications.

Enhancing Your Web Publication with Images

Images are the key to unleashing the power of your Web publications. Everywhere you look on the Web, you will find images. Web publishers use images to enhance their pages and get the reader's attention. You can use thumbnail icons to create highlights and navigation mechanisms. You can use computer-designed images as logos, page titles, illustrations, and maps to the hot features at your site. You can use digitized photos to convey your message in a way more powerful than text alone. These photos can help sell your products and services and can even show the rest of the world what your part of the world looks like.

Adding images to your Web pages is easy and can be accomplished using either external images or inline images. Readers access external images by activating a hypertext link to the image, such as

```
<P><A HREF="67chevy.gif">67 Chevy</A> fire-engine red.</P>
```

When a reader clicks on the link, the image is downloaded to the reader's computer. If an image viewer is available and configured for use in the reader's browser, the image is displayed. If an image viewer is not available, the image will be stored on the reader's hard disk for later viewing.

While adding external images to your Web publications is as easy as providing a link to the image, it does require forethought and a fundamental understanding of image formats and related concepts. Browsers know which image viewer to launch based on the file type extension (`.jpeg`, `.gif`, and so forth) of the external image reference in your document. When a reader accesses a link to a GIF image, the browser checks a configuration table to see which application should display the image, which is why your Web files should always be named with the appropriate extension. If the file is in GIF format, name it with a `.gif` extension. If the file is in JPEG format, name it with a `.jpeg` or `.jpg` extension.

Unlike external images that are not displayed directly, inline images can be viewed directly. When a reader with a graphics-capable browser accesses your page, the images can be automatically loaded with the text on the page. You can add inline images to your publications using the `<IMG>` tag. In HTML 2.0, the `<IMG>` tag has four attributes:

```
SRC
ALT
ALIGN
```

ISMAP

The most important attribute for the `<IMG>` tag is `SRC`. The `SRC` attribute specifies the path to the image. This path is in the form of an URL that can be a relative path such as:

`<IMG SRC="67chevy.gif">`

or a full path such as:

`<IMG SRC="http://tvp.com/usr/images/gifs/67chevy.gif">`

The `ALT` attribute for the `<IMG>` tag specifies alternate text to display in place of the image. Readers with a text-only browser will see the alternate text instead of the image. If you do not specify alternate text, readers with a text-only browser will see a note that marks the location of the image on the page, such as [IMAGE].

The `ALIGN` attribute specifies the alignment of the image in relation to a line of text. By default the bottom of the image is aligned with the text, but you can specify this explicitly using a value of `ALIGN=BOTTOM`. You can align the top of the image with the text using a value of `ALIGN=TOP`. You can align the middle of the image with the text using a value of `ALIGN=MIDDLE`.

The `ISMAP` attribute specifies that the image is an image map. You can use image maps to create graphical menus with clickable hot areas. (See Chapter 12, "Form and Image Map Creation and Design," for more information.)

Browsers handle inline images in many different ways. Some browsers load all text and associated images before displaying any part of your document. Some browsers display text and graphics as they read in your document. Other browsers load and display the textual portions of the page, leaving placeholders where the images will go and then retrieve the images one by one. A few advanced browsers let the reader select options for displaying the components of the page.

While individual browsers handle inline images in many different ways, all graphics-capable browsers provide readers with a mechanism for turning off the automatic image-loading feature of the browser. This nice feature for readers means more work for Web publishers. Before you add inline images, there are many concepts you should consider. The most important matters you should think about are when and how to use images in your publications.

When and How To Use Images

As you've seen, adding images to your publications is easy, yet this ease of use makes for easy abuse as well. Your inline images should supplement text, enhance the document, but rarely replace text on the page. One of the most important choices you as the Web publisher have to make is when and how to use images. You can use images in your publications in dozens of ways. Yet before you add an image to the publication, you should ask yourself three questions:

■ Why are you using the image?

■ Will the image add to the impact of the page?

■ Will the image help the reader?

Creating images, even simple images, for use in Web documents is an art form that is largely misunderstood even by professionals. You will find many Web documents with images that are horribly designed and actually lessen the impact of the documents they are in. Many more Web documents have images designed by the skilled hands of graphic designers that fail to create the desired impact because they are over-designed. A common and mistaken philosophy for many of these poorly designed documents is that bigger and more is better. Bigger and more is not better.

When you create images, use a design and style that fit the purpose of the document. Often simple low-resolution images will work just as well as advanced high-resolution images. Nothing gets the reader's attention faster than well-designed and well-placed images. You should use images in your Web documents when they

■ Accent the page

■ Highlight key ideas

■ Serve a specific purpose

Images can highlight the textual portions of the page. Graphic titles and logos can be eye-opening introductions for your publications. Small images can accent key ideas or concepts. Illustrations, figures, and pictures can support key points discussed in the publication.

Images that serve a specific purpose are the most useful. By putting an image tag inside a hypertext link, you can create images that act as links to other documents. If you use a series of images, you can create a simple menu to key pages at your site. Sometimes images can even be the only element on the page. If the image contains hot areas that are mapped to specific pages at your site, a single image can act as your site's menu. In this way, the image could act as the doorway to key areas at the site.

Other questions you should ask yourself when adding images to your page include

■ How large is the image file and how long will it take the average user to download?

■ How many images are there already on the page and does the image fit in with the images on the page?

These questions have more consequence than you may think. The more features you add to the page, the longer it will take for the page to load into the reader's browser. If you add too many features, the reader may get impatient and choose another site to visit. Consequently, for large images you may want to consider using a small image called a thumbnail that links to the large image, or even a simple text link to the image. Also, as you will see later in the discussion of color maps, some images just aren't compatible with each other and cause conflicts that can dramatically affect the way readers see your page.

The best Web publications are user-friendly and highly interactive. You can add images to your pages to make them more friendly and more interactive. To do this, you should design your pages with three types of users in mind:

> Users with text-only browsers
> Users with graphics-capable browsers
> Users with advanced browsers

Image Tips for Text-Only Browsers

Providing ways for readers who cannot or choose not to view images to enjoy your site is a key concept in the design of your documents. Users with text-only browsers and users who have turned off the automatic image-loading feature of their browser will not be able to see your images. Consequently, for these users you will want to provide alternate features in addition to your images.

Sometimes you will want to include alternate text that the reader can see in place of your images. You do this using the ALT attribute of the <IMG> tag, such as

```
<IMG SRC="67chevy.gif" ALT="Car">
```

By specifying alternate text, readers see the text instead of the "[IMAGE]" note telling them an image is on the page. Browsers typically display alternate text for images in brackets. However, telling the reader that a picture of a car is on the page may not enhance the reader's perception of the page. Again, you should add features to increase the impact of the page. A better way to provide information about images is to use several descriptive words that help the reader see the image in their mind's eye. Here, a better use of the ALT attribute is

```
<IMG SRC="67chevy.gif" ALT="My fire-engine red 67 Chevy">
```

If telling the reader what the image contains doesn't enhance the page, you can remove the reference to the image using an empty ALT assignment as follows:

```
<IMG SRC="67chevy.gif" ALT="">
```

Often images are essential to the understanding of concepts explored in your documents. While readers with text-only browsers cannot view your inline images, you may want to make key images available both as inline and external images. For example, if you are comparing the hot new design of your latest product to a competitor's product, a digitized photo can support your claims and help you sell the product. While users with text-only browsers cannot display inline images, they probably can display external images using an image viewer to display the picture.

Image Tips for Graphics-Capable Browsers

As you have seen, there are lots of uses for images in your publications, and readers with graphics-capable browsers will want to see them all. However, you should not add all the features discussed earlier to a single page. Share the wealth and sprinkle these features throughout your site. Before you add images to your documents, you will want to consider three things:

- Sizing your images
- Placing images in your documents
- Design concepts for images

Sizing Your Images

The physical size of your images in terms of bytes is extremely important. Every inline image you include must be loaded when the page is accessed and a 15KB image will take a lot longer to download than a 3KB image. However, slow-loading graphics aren't necessarily large graphics; they could be high-resolution graphics or graphics with many colors. A very large four-color image at low resolution will download faster than a small 256-color image at high resolution.

A good rule to follow when adding images to your Web pages is my 14-second rule. The 14-second rule has the average user in mind. Currently, the average user accessing the Web has a 14,400-bps modem. If you analyze this statistically, use the median so extremes won't have a large effect on the outcome. The current trend is toward 14,400 bps, with many Web users accessing at 9600 bps and an increasing number accessing at 28,800 bps. The philosophy at the heart of the rule is that if it takes longer than 14 seconds under the best of conditions to download all objects in your document, you may want to restructure your document so it downloads in 14 seconds or less.

Fourteen seconds is really the average (median) value in a frustration window that weighs poor performance and slow access speeds at one end, and the top performance and access speeds at the other end. Don't use the rule as an absolute. Use it as a reality check to help you develop user-friendly pages. This is the basic precept of the rule—make sure your pages are user-friendly by valuing the user's time. After you have browsed the Web for a while, you will discover there is nothing more frustrating than waiting for thousands of bytes of graphics to load, and undoubtedly you will wish more Web publishers followed this rule.

NOTE

To test this rule, make sure the automatic image-loading feature of your Web browser is turned on, then try loading one of your Web documents. Use a modem speed of 14,400 bps. If under optimal conditions it takes more than 14 seconds to fully load all text and graphics—assuming no other time delaying features are adversely affecting the download—look at the document and see what is slowing the load time. Consider modifying the offending element. Note that your Web documents will load faster for you because of your proximity to the site. If it takes you 14 seconds to download the document, it will probably take users at disparate sites a lot longer.

One way to avoid putting byte-hogging graphics on a page is to use thumbnail images. Thumbnail images are a great way to link to large images and other resources. The notion of a thumbnail describes how these resources are included in your documents. You use a small image to lead to something bigger, such as a large image or another resource. Here is how you could use a thumbnail to lead to a large external image:

```
<A HREF="chevylarge.gif" ><IMG SRC="chevysmall.gif"></A>
```

To avoid using an external viewer, you could link the thumbnail image to an HTML document that features the large version of the image, such as

```
<A HREF="http://tvp.com/hotcars.html"><IMG SRC="chevysmall.gif"></A>
```

The HTML code for the `hotcars` document could look like this:

```
<HTML>
<HEAD>
<TITLE>Hot Cars</TITLE>
</HEAD>
<BODY>
<P><IMG SRC="chevy.gif"></P>
<P><IMG SRC="fordconvert.gif"></P>
<P><IMG SRC="mustang.gif"></P>
</BODY>
</HTML>
```

Placing Images in Your Documents

The way you place objects on the page is as important as the colors and sizes you choose for your images, especially when you are aligning text and images. One way to align text and images is the ALIGN attribute of the <IMG> tag.

As discussed earlier, the ALIGN attribute has three values: BOTTOM, TOP and MIDDLE. These values align text and images in ways contrary to what you may think when you see the values. For example, the MIDDLE value does not align the middle of the image with the middle of the text. The MIDDLE value aligns the middle of the image with the bottom of the text, which produces a slightly off-center effect. The TOP value does not precisely align the top of the image with the tallest elements in the associated text. The TOP value generally aligns the text and the image along an imaginary line slightly above the text. Similarly, the BOTTOM value does not align the bottom of the image with the lowest element in the text. The BOTTOM value generally aligns the image and text along a base line such as the ones used on lined paper. While text elements such as an *h* are aligned along the base line, text elements such as a *g* extend below the base line.

One reason the BOTTOM value is the default for the ALIGN attribute is because text does not wrap around images. This means if you align a long line of text with the top of the image, part of your text will be aligned with the top of the image and the remainder of the text will be displayed below the image. Consequently, you should only use the TOP and MIDDLE alignment values to align a single short line of text with an image.

However, using the default value for the ALIGN attribute, you can use this formatting method to your advantage to align an image with a paragraph of text. To do this, the image must appear at the beginning of the paragraph. In this way, the first line of text will be aligned with the bottom of the image and the next line of text will start on a new line immediately below the image. Using this technique, you could add a fancy first letter to a story, such as

```
<P><IMG SRC="lettero.gif" ALT="O">nce upon a time in a
far off land . . . </P>
```

Designing Highlights with Images

Add images to highlight your pages and to showcase your ideas. Most pages on the Web use images to introduce the page. These images range from simple text on a colorful background to eye-popping 3-D images. Both types of images are fine when used for the right reasons. The image you use to introduce your documents should fit in with your publishing style, the subject matter you discuss in the document, and the content of related documents. When starting out, simple is usually best.

While your style of publishing will be different from that of other Web publishers, you should generally follow a unified design within pages of the same publication. One of the key areas you will want to focus on is the color scheme for images used in your documents, which is an area of Web publishing that is all too often overlooked. As you look at the colors you plan to use in your images, key in on the colors used in backgrounds and in text. These are the colors you will want to limit.

You could follow a similar color scheme for all the images at your site. In this way, your pages will have a familiar look to readers. You could also follow a color scheme for pages associated with a certain publication or key areas at your site. In this way, each publication at your site will have a familiar look to readers, and they will have a visual cue when they enter a new area. The key concept here is to look at the colors you plan to use in a particular document's images and ask yourself if they work well together and if the colors help the reader. Here is an example of colors that don't work well together: A title page that features a logo with a green background and blue text, header titles with a white background and red text, and other images on the page with gray backgrounds and yellow text.

You may also want to use consistent sizing of key images from page to page. This concept goes back to giving your pages a familiar feel and look. For example, you could make the graphical titles for your pages 150×350 pixels and the graphical subtitles for your pages 75×350 pixels. In this way, your titles and subtitles will be positioned in the same location on the screen.

Figure 7.1 shows how the concepts of introducing your document with an image, using a color scheme, and using consistent sizing could be used in your Web documents. Here is the HTML code for the document:

```
<HTML>
<HEAD>
<BASE HREF="http://tvp.com/">
<TITLE>The Virtual Press Home Page</TITLE>
</HEAD>
<BODY>
<P><IMG SRC="vpttl11.gif" ALT="Corporate Background"></P>
<P>Virtual Press Incorporated offers businesses practical and realistic
advice concerning the Internet and the World-Wide Web.  Our mission is to
provide global solutions for the world's electronic publishing needs
through consulting, full-service electronic publishing and community
service.</P>
<P><IMG SRC="wgttl.gif" ALT=""></P>
<P><A HREF="vpwg.html">The Writer's Gallery</A> is a community service
area for writers and readers.  The goal of the Writer's Gallery is to
promote writing and reading!</P>
<P><IMG SRC="ipcttl.gif" ALT=""></P>
<P><A HREF="vpipc.html">The Internet Publishing Information Center</A>
is a community service area for writers and publishers.  The goal of
the IPC is to support and promote electronic publishing and electronic
publishing issues.</P>
</BODY>
</HTML>
```

FIGURE 7.1.

Introducing your documents with images.

Another way to design highlights for the same document would be to use the images as a graphical menu. Figure 7.2 shows the graphical menu for the redesigned document. This technique provides quick access to the key areas at your Web site. In the following markup, note how the image is anchored to the document using hypertext references:

```
<HTML>
<HEAD>
<TITLE>The Virtual Press Home Page</TITLE>
</HEAD>
<BODY>
<P><A HREF="vpbg.html"><IMG SRC="vpttl11.gif"
ALT="Corporate Background"></A></P>
<P><A HREF="vpwg.html"><IMG SRC="wgttl.gif"
ALT="Writer's Gallery"></A></P>
<P><A HREF="vpipc.html"><IMG SRC="ipcttl.gif"
ALT="Internet Publishing Center"></A></P>
<P><A HREF="vpjic.html"><IMG SRC="jicttl.gif"
ALT="Job Information Center"></A></P>
</BODY>
</HTML>
```

FIGURE 7.2.

Designing a graphical menu.

If you use graphical menus in your publications, provide a text-based way for readers to access the menu. You may be surprised to find that text-based alternatives to graphical menus will help all the readers who visit your site, especially those who are impatient and don't want to wait for your images to load. An interesting outcome of placing an image inside a hypertext reference is that whenever the associated alternate text is displayed, it will be clickable anchor text. This provides readers using text-only browsers with a way to access other pages at your site. It also helps readers with graphics-capable browsers who may have switched off automatic image loading as well as those readers with a browser that displays alternative text while the image is downloading.

Figure 7.3 shows how the alternate text used in the previous example is displayed in browser. As you can see, the alternate text forms a simple menu that readers can use to access key areas at the site. Without the alternate text, the reader using this browser would be lost.

FIGURE 7.3.

Provide alternate text for your graphical menus.

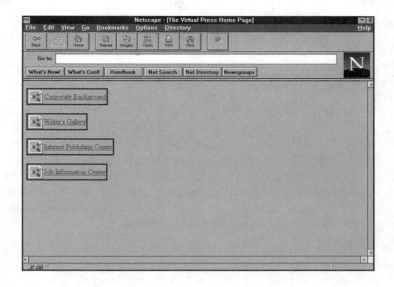

Graphical menus aren't the only way you can provide readers with navigation mechanisms. Many Web publishers use a standard set of small icons to provide readers with access to pages at their site. The most common navigation icons are variations of the left, right, up, and down arrows. The left arrow is generally used to provide quick access to the previous page. The right arrow is generally used to provide quick access to the next page. The up arrow is generally used to provide quick access to the home or top-level page. The down arrow is generally used to provide quick access to the next level page.

Image Tips for Advanced Browsers

HTML 3.0 offers many advanced ways to use images in your documents. Not only do you have more precise control over the way images are placed in documents, you can precisely control the layout of images aligned with text and organize them into columns. You can resize images to fit measurements you specify. Using a special type of image called a figure, you can also define overlays for images.

Using Images in HTML 3.0

The <IMG> tag has been significantly updated in HTML 3.0 and now includes the following attributes:

```
ALIGN
ALT
CLASS
HEIGHT
```

```
ID
ISMAP
LANG
MD
SRC
UNITS
WIDTH
```

While the ALT, CLASS, ID, ISMAP, LANG, MD and SRC attributes are used as described previously, the other attributes can be used in unique or more powerful ways. The ALIGN attribute has been updated to include five values: ALIGN=TOP, ALIGN=MIDDLE, ALIGN=BOTTOM, ALIGN=LEFT, and ALIGN=RIGHT. While the TOP, MIDDLE, and BOTTOM values are used as described in previous sections, the LEFT and RIGHT values can be used to align an image and a paragraph of associated text into columns. The LEFT value puts the image in the left margin and wraps the text around the right-hand side of the image. The RIGHT value puts the image in the right margin and wraps the text around the left-hand side of the image.

By aligning text and images into columns using ALIGN=LEFT or ALIGN=RIGHT, you can create documents with rich layout and styles that merge the image into the text of the document in ways more powerful than previously possible. To get the text to wrap around only the left or right side of the image, you would place the <IMG> tag as the first element in a short paragraph of text as shown in this code example:

```
<H2>Recent Release</H2>
<P><IMG SRC="wpttl.gif" ALT=""></P>
<P><IMG SRC="wpwrld2.gif" ALT="" ALIGN=LEFT>
Unraveling Paths: Dreamers &amp; Mystics is the exciting continuation
of the . . . </P>
```

FIGURE 7.4.

*Aligning text and images
into columns using
HTML 3.0.*

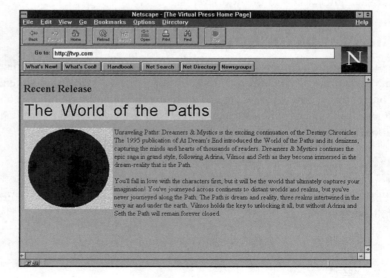

As you can see in Figure 7.4, the image is in the left column and the paragraph text is in the right column. Keep in mind that any subsequent text will be aligned with the image until the left margin is clear. In Figure 7.4, the second paragraph of text is aligned with the image.

Images and text are aligned with minimal spacing. This spacing sometimes makes the text difficult to read. One way to increase the spacing and make the image more useful is to include the image in a hypertext reference as shown in Figure 7.5. The image shown has a border around it that clearly separates it from the associated text and is also clickable.

As Figure 7.5 shows, you can get the text to wrap around two or three sides of the image using `ALIGN=LEFT` or `ALIGN=RIGHT`. To do this, you would insert a line of text before the image tag. Your browser should display complete lines of text before inserting the image. However, if you follow this approach, you would want to preview the document using a standard (13-inch) screen size on a Macintosh system or a standard (640×480) video mode on a DOS/Windows system. Here is how you could use this technique:

```
<H2>Recent Release</H2>
<P><IMG SRC="wpttl.gif" ALT=""></P>
<P> Unraveling Paths: Dreamers &amp; Mystics is the exciting
<A HREF="http://tvp.com/vpdest1.html">
<IMG SRC="wpwrld2.gif" ALT="" ALIGN=RIGHT>
continuation</A> of the . . . </P>
```

FIGURE 7.5.

Merging the image into the text.

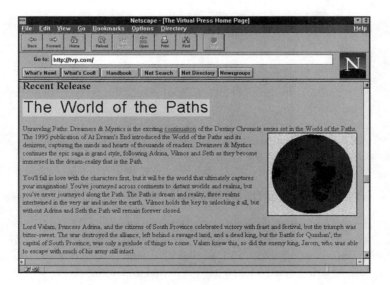

Another useful tag you can use when aligning images and text is the `<BR>` tag. Using the `<BR>` tag and the `clear` attribute, you can insert a clean break into the column of text associated with the image. The text before the `<BR>` tag will be aligned with the image in a column. The text after the `<BR>` tag will be inserted after the margin is clear. If the image is aligned with the left margin, you should use a value of `CLEAR=LEFT` with the `<BR>` tag. If the image is aligned with the right margin, you should use a value of `CLEAR=RIGHT` with the `<BR>` tag.

The <BR> tag can be inserted into the previous example as follows:

```
<H2>Recent Release</H2>
<P><IMG SRC="wpttl.gif" ALT=""></P>
<P> Unraveling Paths: Dreamers &amp; Mystics is the exciting
<A HREF="http://tvp.com/vpdest1.html"><IMG SRC="wpwrld2.gif" ALT="" ALIGN=RIGHT>
continuation</A> of the Destiny Chronicles. The 1995 publication
of At Dream's End introduced the World of the Paths and its denizens,
capturing the minds and hearts of thousands of readers.
<BR CLEAR=RIGHT>
Dreamers &amp; Mystics continues  the epic saga in grand style, following
Adrina, Vilmos and Seth as they become immersed in the dream-reality
that is the Path.</P>
```

The WIDTH, HEIGHT, and UNITS attributes can also be used to create better Web publications. Generally these three attributes are used together to resize an image according to the values you assign. By default, the numeric value you associate with the width and height for an image is a number of pixels. However, using the UNITS attribute you can change the implied default UNITS=PIXELS to UNITS=EN. An en is a unit used by typesetters that is equal to half the point size of the associated text. Thus using the WIDTH, HEIGHT, and optionally the UNITS attributes, you shrink or enlarge an image.

The original size of the global map of the World of the Paths shown in the previous examples is 200×190. By defining a new width and height, the image can be shrunk:

```
<IMG SRC="wpwrld2.gif" ALT="" WIDTH=150 HEIGHT=140>
```

or enlarged:

```
<IMG SRC="wpwrld2.gif" ALT="" WIDTH=275 HEIGHT=190>
```

The capability to shrink or enlarge images on the fly is extremely useful. You can create a menu of images that are consistently sized without having to create new files containing the resized images. You can then reuse the same images later in the document at their original size or sized to suit your needs without having to load new image files. This is convenient for you and reduces the download time of your document.

Using Figures in HTML 3.0

Figures are one of the most useful additions to HTML 3.0. While you can use figures in the same way you use images, figures are intended to offer Web publishers rich control over the placement of advanced images that can include captions, credits, and overlays. Figures are defined using a begin figure tag <FIG> and an end figure tag </FIG>.

Using a begin and an end tag enables the FIG element to be more versatile than the IMG element. A direct result of this is that Web publishers can now add HTML markup to text that will be aligned in a column alongside the figure. You can use the following attributes with the <FIGURE> tag:

```
ALIGN
CLASS
CLEAR
HEIGHT
ID
IMAGEMAP
LANG
MD
NOFLOW
SRC
UNITS
WIDTH
```

As the CLASS, HEIGHT, ID, LANG, MD, SRC, UNITS, and WIDTH attributes are used as described previously, primarily in Chapter 6, "Designing with HTML 3.0," this section focuses on the unique attributes and design concepts related to using figures in your Web publications. The normal values for the ALIGN attribute have been expanded to provide precise control over the placement of figures in your documents. Valid values for the ALIGN attribute include

```
BLEEDLEFT
BLEEDRIGHT
CENTER
JUSTIFY
LEFT
RIGHT
```

The BLEEDLEFT and BLEEDRIGHT values give you more screen area to work with. A value of ALIGN=BLEEDLEFT enables you to place the figure as close to the left border as possible. This differs from the ALIGN=LEFT value that places the figure indented from the left margin. A value of ALIGN=BLEEDRIGHT enables you to place the figure as close to the right border as possible. This differs from the ALIGN=RIGHT value that places the figure indented from the right margin.

Being able to place an image flush with the right or left border is often important when you are trying to squeeze additional information into a column adjacent to the figure. For example, you want to place two figures side by side. When combined, these figures approach 640 pixels in width and when you align the figures in the margin, there is not enough room to align them side by side. You know that the average user has a 640×480 display and are concerned that if you resize the images using the WIDTH and HEIGHT attributes, the figures may not be readable. To solve the problem, you can use ALIGN=BLEEDLEFT in the first figure and ALIGN=BLEEDRIGHT in the second figure to align the figures side by side, such as

```
<FIG SRC="power_logo.gif" ALIGN=BLEEDLEFT></FIG>
<FIG SRC="power_menu.gif" ALIGN=BLEEDRIGHT></FIG>
```

The CENTER and JUSTIFY values for the ALIGN attribute are also useful. Using ALIGN=CENTER, you can center a figure between the left and right margin. Using ALIGN=JUSTIFY, you can automatically resize the figure to fill the space between the left and right margins.

CAUTION

When you center or justify a figure in your document, you cannot align text or other objects in a column beside the figure. Also, you should not use the JUSTIFY attribute with the WIDTH and HEIGHT attributes.

Justified figures appear to be tailored to the reader's display mode or screen size. However, you should test the readability or usability of the resized figure in popular display modes or screen sizes if possible. The automated resizing of a figure may produce an extremely poor-quality or grainy image. This may be especially true in two cases. When a small figure, such as one 300×200 pixels, is enlarged to several magnifications to fill a screen with a display mode such as 1024×768, the figure may be grainy and your text may have rough edges. When a large figure, such as 800×600, is reduced several magnifications for a small screen, such as a 9-inch Macintosh screen, elements of the figure may be difficult to distinguish.

The CLEAR and the NOFLOW attributes for figures serve a similar purpose. You can use the CLEAR attribute to ensure that elements following the FIG element are not aligned in a column alongside a figure. There are three valid values: LEFT, RIGHT, and ALL. These values tell the browser to move down until the left, right, or both margins are clear and then start the next element there. The NOFLOW attribute turns off text flow around the figure. This is useful so you do not have to use the CLEAR attribute with an element that follows the figure.

The IMAGEMAP attribute specifies that the figure has an image map associated with it. You can use the image map to create a graphical menu with clickable hot areas. (See Chapter 12, "Form and Image Map Creation and Design," for more information.)

HTML 3.0 maximizes the functionality of figures by enabling you to use three new tags: <CAPTION>, <CREDIT>, and <OVERLAY>.

The <CAPTION> tag enables you to add a caption to a figure. HTML 3.0 defines a begin and an end tag for captions. You can align the caption above the figure using ALIGN=TOP or below the figure using ALIGN=BOTTOM. The precise placement of the caption above or below the figure is controlled by the alignment value of the figure itself. Your caption will be centered above the figure if the figure is centered, or appropriately aligned with respect to the left or right margin for other values. You can also place the caption to the left or right of the figure using ALIGN=LEFT or ALIGN=RIGHT respectively. You cannot place a caption to the left or right of a figure that is centered or justified.

TIP

To enhance your captions, you can use the highlighting techniques discussed in previous chapters. Some of the tags you may want to use include <B>, <I>, <EM>, and <STRONG>.

The <CREDIT> tag enables you to add a credit to a figure. HTML 3.0 defines a begin and an end tag for credits. The credit will appear below the figure and has only one valid attribute: NOWRAP. If you use the NOWRAP attribute, credit text will be displayed in a single line that will not wrap if it extends beyond the visible area of the browser's window. You can also use highlighting techniques with credits.

Specifying a figure with caption and credit text is easy. The following code defines a figure called `file_diagram.jpeg`:

```
<FIG SRC="file_diagram.jpeg" WIDTH=300 HEIGHT=200 ALIGN=CENTER>
<CAPTION ALIGN=TOP>File Organization Using Directory Trees</CAPTION>
<CREDIT NOWRAP>William R. Stanek, Publisher TVP. August, 1995</CREDIT>
</FIG>
```

While the capability to add captions and credits to your figures is useful, the capability to add overlays to your figures is powerful. Normally when files and objects are downloaded to your system, they are cached. Cached files and objects do not have to be downloaded when they are subsequently referenced in your documents. Using overlays, you can take advantage of the caching mechanism used by most browsers and eliminate the necessity to download a new figure file every time you make a change to the base figure. This provides you with a way to dramatically reduce the download time for documents using complex images.

Overlays can be used with figures in many ways. If the overlay is transparent, the overlay's elements will be merged with the existing figure. If the overlay is nontransparent, the overlay's elements will overwrite sections of the figure. You can define and use multiple overlays for the same figure. A browser displaying a figure with multiple overlays will overlay them in sequence so that elements from the last overlay loaded will take precedence.

You define overlays with the <OVERLAY> tag using the following attributes:

```
HEIGHT
IMAGEMAP
SRC
UNITS
WIDTH
X
Y
```

The HEIGHT, WIDTH, and UNITS attributes for overlays can be used to resize the overlay. The SRC attribute is used to specify the image file that will be used as an overlay. You can also update your previously defined image map based on the additions your overlay incorporates into the figure. You do this using the IMAGEMAP attribute.

When placing overlays onto a figure, keep in mind the upper-left corner of the overlay will generally be positioned over the upper-left corner of the figure. The upper-left corner of a figure has an X,Y coordinate of 0,0. By specifying the X,Y coordinates for the overlay, you can precisely position the overlay on the figure. A figure that is 300×200 will have the following coordinates for its four corners:

Upper-left corner: 0,0
Upper-right corner: 300,0
Lower-left corner: 0,200
Lower-right corner: 300,200

You could add a 300×200 overlay to the bottom of this figure as follows:

```
<FIG SRC="file_diagram.gif" WIDTH=300 HEIGHT=200 ALIGN=CENTER>
<OVERLAY SRC="file_update1.gif X=0 Y=180>
</FIG>
```

You could add overlays to the top and bottom of the same figure as follows:

```
<FIG SRC="file_diagram.gif" WIDTH=300 HEIGHT=200 ALIGN=CENTER>
<OVERLAY SRC="file_update2.gif X=0 Y=0 WIDTH=300 HEIGHT=12>
<OVERLAY SRC="file_update1.gif X=0 Y=180>
</FIG>
```

Image Formats

Dozens of image formats are in use. Each computer platform has its own popular format and usually several popular formats. Drawing and design applications have their own proprietary formats. Some formats have become de facto standards because of their tremendous popularity. Other formats are so specialized only a small group of users benefit from them. Maneuvering through this maze of formats could be a nightmare if you tried to create images for specific groups of users because just when you thought you had the right formats available for the right group of users, another group of users would come along. Fortunately, only two image formats are in wide use on the Web: GIF and JPEG.

Using GIF

The graphics interchange format developed by CompuServe Information Service is the most widely supported and used image format in the world. All graphics-capable browsers support GIF as do most drawing, design, and image processing programs. As you might expect, GIF is the favorite format for Web publishers.

Three variations of the GIF format are in use. The original specification, GIF87a, has been around since 1987. Because of its many advantages over other formats, GIF87a quickly became a de facto standard. Creators of drawing programs quickly discovered how easy it is to write a program that decodes and displays GIF images. GIF images are compressed to 20 to 25 percent of their original size with no loss in image quality using a compression algorithm called LZW. Smaller images require less disk space to store, use less network bandwidth, and download quicker. Additionally, because the LZW algorithm can be quickly decoded, images display almost immediately after downloading.

The next update to the format was the GIF89a specification. GIF89a added some useful features, including transparent GIFs. Using transparent GIFs, you can create images that seem to float on the page because they have a transparent background. (See the section on transparent GIFs later in this chapter, "GIFs with Transparent Backgrounds," for more information.)

All browsers support both the GIF87a and GIF89a formats, which is great news for Web publishers. The only drawback is that you can only use 256 colors in a single image. While this limitation is restricting, it is actually good in most instances. Most images use only a few colors. This is especially true for icons, bullets, or other small features used to accent the page. Most computer systems can only display 256 colors. If you only use 256 colors, the computer will not have to dither the image to create the illusion of additional colors. An image with fewer colors that does not have to be dithered will be displayed quicker, will use less disk space, and will also download quicker.

Recently there has been a lot of controversy over the LZW compression used by GIF images. This compression technology is patented to the Unisys Corporation and in January 1995, Unisys announced that developers using the GIF format in their applications may have to pay a licensing fee. A licensing fee for GIF images could potentially apply to millions of software applications, including your favorite browser. As you might imagine, software developers around the world were in an uproar for months following the announcement. Some developers were so outraged, they removed support for GIF images from their applications. Other developers went in search of alternatives.

One alternative software developers looked to is GIF24. GIF24 has wide support from the Internet user community as well as from CompuServe Information Service. Unlike the original GIF specifications that support only 256 colors, GIF24 supports true 24-bit color, which enables you to use more than 16 million colors. One drawback to using 24-bit color is that most computers currently support only 256 colors. Before a 24-bit image can be displayed on an 8-bit screen, it must be dithered, which requires processing time and may also distort the image.

GIF24 uses a compression technique called PNG, and as there should never be a licensing fee associated with PNG, software developers are gladly turning to GIF24. In the coming months you should start to see drawing, design, and image processing programs that support GIF24.

Using JPEG

JPEG is a standard for still-image compression that was developed by the Joint Photographic Expert Group. The goal of the JPEG members was to create a standard for storage and transmission of photograph-quality images. JPEG supports true 24-bit color.

True 24-bit color means that each pixel displayed on the screen has 24 bits of information associated with it. As there are over 300,000 pixels on an average-size screen, you can imagine how quickly true-color images can eat up your hard disk space. Fortunately, JPEG is a compression standard that uses powerful compression algorithms to dramatically reduce the disk space requirements for the image. Some images can be reduced to a twentieth of their original size.

Compressing an image into such a small size has its drawbacks. The first drawback is that JPEG compression is lossy, meaning that some information in the image is lost in the compression. Depending on how the image is compressed, this loss of information may or may not be perceivable. Another drawback to compressing the image into a small space is that it generally takes longer to decode the image for viewing. However, the actual time period for the decoding depends on the user's system and the amount of compression.

As you consider using JPEG compression for your images, you should consider carefully the types of images that you will compress. While JPEG enables you to use brilliant colors and provides quality support for complex images and digitized photographs, JPEG was not designed to be used for simple images with few colors. JPEG compression may distort simple images, especially if the image has few colors or large areas of the same color. Also, JPEG compression is not as effective as GIF in reducing the size of simple images. A simple image compressed with JPEG compression will be much larger than the same image compressed using GIF.

Because of the drawbacks to JPEG compression, JPEG was not widely supported until recently. One of the issues driving the growth of JPEG use is the controversy surrounding the GIF compression algorithm LZW. The controversy caused many software developers to take another look at JPEG. Most popular browsers, including NCSA Mosaic, Internet Explorer, and Netscape Navigator, will let you use inline JPEG images.

TIP

A great place to learn more about JPEG is the JPEG FAQ. You can find the JPEG FAQ on the Web at the following location:

`http://www.cis.ohio-state.edu/hypertext/faq/usenet/jpeg-faq/top.html`

Creating Your Own Images

You can create images using drawing, design, and image processing programs. While commercial drawing tools, such as CorelDRAW! 6, are powerful and fully featured, shareware drawing tools, such as Paint Shop Pro, provide general-purpose image creation solutions. (To find sources of shareware and freeware image tools on the Internet, see the multimedia section of Chapter 10, "HTML Toolkit: Browsers, Editors, and Converters.")

Using image tools, you can create a simple graphical title or logo in a few minutes. You can use image tools to alter existing images to meet your publishing needs and to convert these images from other formats to the GIF or JPEG formats for use as inline images. While you can easily create and modify images, you can dramatically improve the quality and friendliness of your images through

■ Proper use of color maps

■ Interlacing GIFs when necessary

■ Using GIFs with transparent backgrounds when necessary

Using Color Maps

Color maps are one of the biggest problem areas in image design. All images have color palettes associated with them that define a set of colors for the image. Each color displayed on the screen is loaded into a color map that tracks colors displayed on the screen at any one time. A computer with an 8-bit display uses a color map that can hold 256 color values. A computer with a 24-bit display uses a color map that can hold 16.7 million color values.

Some computer systems reserve a subset of values in the color map for the standard display. Windows systems reserve 20 values in the color map to display standard colors. In addition to reserved colors, any colors currently displayed on the screen will be allocated in the color map. This means if your browser display takes up only part of the screen and other applications are running, the combined set of colors displayed on the screen by all the applications running will be allocated in the color map.

Although you can create 24-bit images with 16.7 million colors, most computers display only 8-bit images with 256 colors. This means when you create an image that uses 16 million colors, most computers displaying the image will have to dither the image to create the illusion that there are extra colors in the image when in fact only 256 colors are displayed.

The distortion of the image caused by the dithering is often the least of your problems. Only 256 colors can be displayed at once on an 8-bit color display. This means there will be a conflict in the color map if the first image uses all 256 colors and the next image displayed on the screen at the same time uses additional colors. These additional colors will be mapped to the closest color value in the current color map, which can produce strange results. Your brilliant red will be mapped to orange, or even green, if that is the closest color value available in the current color map.

Some browsers try to solve the color mapping problem by limiting the number of colors any single image can use. This enables you to display more inline images on the screen at once. However, the cost of this tradeoff is high. If your images use 256 colors and the browser restricts each image to a maximum of 50 colors, the images will have to be dithered to 50 colors each. The result is often a large reduction in the quality of your image.

The best way to ensure your documents have no color map problem is to use a common color map for all images in a particular document. If you are creating original images, most drawing programs will let you select a palette of 256 colors to work with. You can add colors or change color definitions in the palette by removing or altering existing color definitions in the palette. After you are done working with the palette, you should save it, if possible, for future reference and use with your images.

While using a single color palette is easy if you are creating original images, it is not easy if you are incorporating existing images into your documents. One way to overcome this problem is to use an image processing toolkit that can merge the color palettes used in multiple images to a common color palette. A useful image processing toolkit is the UNIX toolkit Netpbm. (See the multimedia section of Chapter 10 to learn more about Netpbm.)

Unfortunately, mapping multiple images to a single color palette is only useful when the images either contain few colors or already use a similar set of colors. This is because the image processing tool merging the color palettes will generally merge the colors using a best-guess algorithm that tries to analyze how multiple colors that are close in value can best be merged into a single color value. Sometimes the tool guesses right and there is no distortion of your images. Other times the tool guesses wrong and your image is distorted. Ultimately, if your images contain few colors in the first place or use similar maps, there is little reason to merge the color maps. For simple images like these, you may want to preview your document using multiple browsers and worry about a conflict in the color map only when you find one.

Another way to fix the color mapping problem is to reorganize your document so that images with conflicting color maps cannot be displayed on the screen simultaneously. This solution to a color mapping problem is simple and fast.

Finally, a great way to avoid potential color map problems is to limit your use of colors in the images you create. For example, if you use a particular shade of red in one image, use the same shade of red in other images. In a palette of 16.7 million colors, there are probably 50 shades of red that are so close in hue that it is difficult to tell them apart. You can also track the values associated with colors in a table. When you are designing additional images for a particular document and want to use consistent colors, having color values at hand can be invaluable.

Interlacing GIFs

An advanced feature you can incorporate into your GIF images is interlacing. Interlaced GIFs are displayed in four stages. As if you were zooming in on something from far away, during each stage, the image gets progressively more detailed until the image is finished loading. This is accomplished by separating the lines of pixels in the image into four groups of lines that are interlaced and displayed in stages. Your television and possibly your monitor display images in this manner.

Many experienced Web publishers do not understand the value of interlacing images. Interlaced images are timesavers to readers and are especially useful when you use large images in your documents. As the image loads in stages, readers can decide when they have seen enough of the image. Based on what they've seen, they may continue reading the document, they may make another selection, or they may wait to see the image finish loading. Readers value their time and if you value their time as well, your documents will be friendly and well-perceived.

Older versions of browsers may not display GIFs in stages. Whether the image is a noninterlaced GIF or an interlaced GIF, these browsers wait until the entire image is downloaded and then display the GIF. While not all browsers display interlaced GIFs in stages, all browsers can display interlaced GIFs.

Creating an interlaced GIF is as easy as using the Save As feature of your image editor and selecting interlaced GIF for the format. Unfortunately, many commercial drawing applications are designed for users who create images in traditional mediums and do not support the interlaced format. Therefore, the best image tools for creating interlaced GIFs are those designed with Web publishers in mind. On the Internet, you can find dozens of such programs. Some of the popular ones are LView Pro, PhotoShop Pro and xv. (See the multimedia section of Chapter 10 to learn more about these programs.)

GIFs with Transparent Backgrounds

Using a GIF with a transparent background, you can create an image that appears to float on the page. This is extremely useful when you want to create a fancy title, logo, icon, or image that does not use a solid colored or rectangular background. With the proper tools, creating a GIF with a transparent background is easy. First, you will need to save your GIF in GIF89a format or convert your existing image and save it in GIF89a format. You will also have to assign a color to the image's transparency index.

The color value assigned to the transparency index indicates which color from the image's color map should be transparent. When a browser displays an image with a transparent background, it changes all occurrences of the color value in the transparency index to the color value for the background of the document. The best images to convert to GIF89a format are those with a single background color. This is important because you can only assign one color value to the transparency index, and if your image has several background colors, only one color will be transparent. Figure 7.6 shows the difference between an image with a normal background and one with a transparent background.

You should also ensure that your background color appears nowhere else in the image. Any part of your image that uses the color value specified in the transparency index will be displayed in the background color for the page. To avoid this problem, you should ensure your images have a unique background color. When you are creating new images, this is easy. You simply select a color you do not plan to use in the image.

FIGURE 7.6.

Images with transparent backgrounds appear to float on the page.

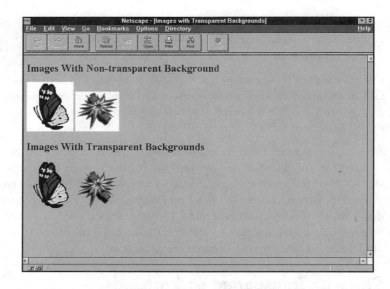

While some Web publishers will tell you to select an outrageous color for your background such as hot pink, you should never use a color that you do not want the world to see if for some reason your image is not displayed with a transparent background. Not all browsers can display your image with a transparent background and if you use an outrageous color, someone somewhere will see your image with that hot pink background. Instead of using an outrageous color, you should use a neutral color such as the gray background used by most browsers. The RGB color value for the background color used by most browsers is 190, 190, 190. Using this color value will ensure your images do not look ridiculous if the transparent background is not displayed and will also make your GIFs appear to have transparent backgrounds on browsers that do not support transparent GIFs.

Once you have made sure your image has an appropriate background color, you are ready to begin. First, you will need to know the color value of your background color. You will use the background color value to specify the color that should be transparent. You can obtain this color value in your favorite drawing tool either by examining the color palette or using a feature of the tool that enables you to see RGB color values. In drawing tools designed for Web publishers such as xv, this is as easy as moving the mouse pointer to the background color and writing down the color value displayed. In PaintShop Pro, you will need to select the Eyedropper tool and move the mouse pointer to the background color. In LView Pro, you will need to select Background Color from the Options menu and choose the appropriate color.

To turn on the transparent features of GIF89a, you will need a drawing application that supports transparent GIFs or a GIF converter. As most graphic artists need to create images with transparent backgrounds at one time or another, most drawing applications support transparent images. However, you will find creating GIFs is easiest with programs developed with Web publishers in mind. Most of these programs are GIF converters, such as transgif.pl for UNIX X Windows systems, Transparency for Macintosh systems, and giftrans or giftool for DOS/Windows systems. (See the multimedia section of Chapter 10 to learn more about these programs.)

Using Giftrans

On a DOS/Windows system, you can use giftrans to create a GIF with a transparent background. From the DOS prompt, type:

```
giftrans -tN -o transparent.gif original.gif
```

You would substitute the index value for your background color in place of the N as follows:

```
giftrans -t45 -o transparent.gif original.gif
```

To find the corresponding index value for your RGB color value, you can list the index by typing:

```
giftrans -l orginal.gif
```

Using Giftool

On a DOS/Windows system, you can also use giftool to create a GIF with a transparent background. From the DOS prompt, type:

```
giftool -rgb ###,###,### -o transparent.gif original.gif
```

You would substitute the actual RGB color value for your background color in place of the number symbols as follows:

```
giftool -rgb 190,190,190 -o transparent.gif original.gif
```

Using transgif.pl

On a UNIX system, you can use transgif.pl to create a GIF with a transparent background. From the shell command line prompt type:

```
transgif.pl -rgb ###,###,### original.gif > transparent.gif
```

You would substitute the actual RGB color value for your background color in place of the number symbols as follows:

```
transgif.pl -rgb 224,224,224 original.gif > transparent.gif
```

Using Transparency

Creating images with transparent backgrounds on a Macintosh is easy. Using Transparency for the Macintosh, you simply follow these steps:

1. Load the image you want to convert.
2. Click and hold the mouse when the pointer is over the background.
3. Choose the color you want to be transparent on the pop-up menu that appears.
4. Save the image in GIF89a format.

Finding Image Resources on the Internet

On the Internet, you can find dozens of image archives. Some of the best sites have hundreds of images you can preview and download if you like. Here's a list of some popular image archives:

NASA's image archive
```
http://hypatia.gsfc.nasa.gov/Images
```
Smithsonian's image archive
```
gopher://bramble.er.usgs.gov/1ftp%3aphoto1.si.edu%40/
```
Sunet's image archive
```
ftp://ftp.sunet.se/pub/pictures
```
Sunsite's image archive
```
ftp://sunsite.unc.edu/pub/multimedia/pictures/
```
University of Arizona's image archive
```
gopher://dizzy.library.arizona.edu:70/1
```
University of Indiana's image archive
```
gopher://enif.astro.indiana.edu:70/11/images
```
Washington University's image archive
```
http://wuarchive.wustl.edu/multimedia/images/
```
or
```
http://wuarchive.wustl.edu/graphics/
```

Icons come in handy when you need a small image to add a splash of color or to highlight a paragraph of text. You can also find icon archives on the Internet. Here is a list of some popular icon archives:

CERN's icon list
```
http://www.w3.org/hypertext/WWW/Icons
```
University of Kansas icon list
```
http://titania.math.ukans.edu:80/icons/
```
NCSA and UIUC's icon list

```
http://www.ncsa.uiuc.edu/General/Icons/
```

Yahoo's icon list

```
http://www.yahoo.com/Computers/World_Wide_Web/Programming/Icons
```

Many Web publishers would say that the Planet Earth home page maintains the definitive page for image resources. From the Planet Earth image page, you can find links to just about every imaginable type of image, including

Space Images
NASA Images
Earth Images and Maps
Travel Images
Medical Images
Image Archives
Icon Archives
Flag Archives

You can find the Planet Earth home page at

```
http://www.nosc.mil/planet_earth/images.html
```

A cool site if you are looking for pictures of animals is the Electronic Zoo. The Electronic Zoo/ NetVet image collection contains links to GIF and JPEG images of just about every animal you can think of. You can find the Electronic Zoo at

```
http://netvet.wustl.edu/pix.htm
```

Kodak's digital image page is a great place to go to learn more about digital images and preview samples. You can find Kodak's digital image page at

```
http://www.kodak.com/digitalImaging/digitalImaging.shtml
```

To stay current with image concepts and resources, you may want to participate or lurk in the newsgroups related to images. Here are some newsgroups you may be interested in:

```
alt.binaries.pictures
alt.binaries.pictures.cartoons
alt.binaries.pictures.fractals
alt.binaries.pictures.misc
alt.binaries.pictures.utilities
```

Enhancing Your Web Publication with Sound

Many Web publishers are experimenting with sound in their publications. These publishers have found that Web users everywhere are fascinated with sound and often visit sites solely to obtain sound clips. You can include many types of sound in your publications. You can use digitized voice messages to provide greetings, installation instructions, and author introductions. You can include music to let readers listen to the latest songs, to add sound tracks to your publications, and simply to entertain. You can add digitized sound effects to your publications to heighten the mood or drama of your publication. You could add simple tones as warnings and audible cues.

Technologies revolving around sound are growing at an explosive pace on the Web. You may be surprised to find that you can include internal and external sound clips in your publications. A few months ago, it would have been impossible to add a sound track to your publications. Now, not only can you include a sound track for your publications, but you can include multiple sound tracks for publications that play on cue when the part of the page containing the sound clip is displayed in the browser's viewing area. The potential uses of internal sound files are phenomenal and will take Web publishing to a new high. (To learn more about internal sound, see Chapter 8, "Netscape and Internet Explorer Extensions.")

While support for internal sound files is just beginning, support for external sound files is widespread. Readers can access external sound files by activating a hypertext link to the sound file, such as

```
<P>The storm swept through the valley and the <A HREF="rainstorm.wav">
sound of thunder</A> echoed across the darkened land.</P>
```

When a reader clicks on the link, the sound file is downloaded to their computer. If a sound player is available and configured for use in the reader's browser, the sound file is played. If a sound player is not available, the sound file will be stored on the reader's hard disk for later playing.

Many browser packages are bundled with a sound player, especially commercial browser packages. The Netscape Navigator package includes a sound player called NAPLAYER. NAPLAYER can play most popular sound formats including: AU, SND, AIFF, and AIFF-C.

Browsers know which sound player to launch based on the file type extension (`.au`, `.aiff`, `.wav` and so forth) of the external sound file referenced in your document. When a reader accesses a link to a WAV file, the browser checks a configuration table to see which application should play the sound file, which is why your Web files should always be named with the appropriate extension. If the file is in WAV format, name it with a `.wav` extension. If the file is in AIFF format, name it with an `.aiff` extension.

When and How To Use Sound

One of the most important choices you as the Web publisher have to make is to decide when and how to use sound. You can use sound in your publications in many ways and especially to enhance and supplement the text and images on the page. While adding sound to your documents is easy using links to external sound files, there are many concepts to consider before adding sound.

Most computer systems come equipped with all the necessary equipment to create sound files. This equipment includes a sound card with an analog-to-digital converter, an audio tool, and a microphone. If your computer does not have this equipment, you can purchase a sound kit, such as the Sound Blaster Pro kit from Creative Labs. The first step in making a recording is generally to plug a microphone into the sound input jack on your computer. Using a microphone to make recordings is an analog-to-digital process, which is widely supported by computers. However, if you want to record a digital audio source such as music from a compact disk or digital audio tape, you will probably need to convert the digital recording to an analog recording before you can record the music on your computer.

As strange as having to convert a digital signal to an analog signal so you can record it in digital format may seem, the conversion is necessary because most computers and sound cards do not support digital inputs. If you want to make a true digital-to-digital recording, you should obtain specialized equipment. Fortunately, however, most of the time you will not need specialized equipment. Most CD and DAT players have an internal analog-to-digital converter that is used to output analog sound on a standard output jack. Using an extension cord that connects the output jack of the CD or DAT player to the input jack of the computer, you can make recordings. Keep in mind that the conversion process from digital to analog back to digital may degrade the audio signal.

Digitized voice can be used to personalize your Web publications. You can provide a prerecorded greeting from your CEO or marketing specialist, or from the author of the latest work you are featuring. Not only can digitized voice add a personal touch to your publication, it also has many practical uses. You can use a sound file to provide commentary on the document's subject matter, which can give readers wonderful insight into the author's thoughts. Before you can add the digitized voice file to your page, you must create the sound file. You can create digitized voice files using a microphone and the audio tool that came with your computer.

You can also use your microphone and audio tool to create or record sound effects. Useful sound effects include doors slamming, horns honking, and jet engines roaring. If you want to add the splosh-splash sounds of a spring rain storm to your publication, you can record the sounds using a standard tape recorder, then later digitize the sounds. To do this you could connect the output of your tape recorder to the input of your computer's sound card or simply press play on the recorder and use your computer's microphone and audio tool to record the sounds.

The key to linking sound files to your documents is to do it in an unobtrusive way. While you do not want to say "Click here to access a sound file," you want to let the reader know the format and size of the sound file. One way to do this would be to simply insert the information within the link as follows:

```
<P>The storm swept through the valley and the <A HREF="rainstorm.wav">
sound of thunder (760KB WAV)</A> echoed across the darkened land.</P>
```

or after the link as follows:

```
<P><A HREF="rainstorm.wav">Greetings from our CEO!</A>(150KB AU)</P>
```

You will want to consider very carefully the sampling rate for your recordings and may be surprised to learn that sound files gobble up 150KB to 10MB of hard disk space per minute. A voice-quality recording sampled at 8Khz uses approximately 150KB per minute. Voice-quality recordings, also referred to as 8-bit mono recordings, are useful for all general-purpose recordings, to include recordings of digitized voice, sound effects, and simple tones. A high-fidelity recording sampled at 44.1Khz uses approximately 10MB per minute. High-fidelity recordings, also referred to as 16-bit stereo recordings, are useful whenever you want to make stereo recordings to include recordings of music from compact disk or digital audio tape.

The primary difference between a mono recording and a stereo recording is the number of audio channels used. Mono recordings use only one audio channel. Stereo recordings use two audio channels. When mono recordings are played back on a system equipped for stereo playback, the same channel is directed to the left and right speakers. When stereo recordings are played back on a system equipped for stereo playback, the one channel is directed to the left speaker and the other channel is directed to the right speaker. While a growing number of computer users can play stereo sound files, the average user does not. The average computer user can play only 8-bit mono sound.

While 8Khz and 44.1Khz are the most commonly used sampling rates, several other rates are used. One rate you may see is 22.05Khz, which is one-half the 44.1Khz sampling rate. Many Web publishers use this rate to record one channel or the mono equivalent of a stereo recording. This is useful because it cuts in half the size of the resulting file. Instead of using 10MB per minute, the 22.05Khz sound file uses 5MB per minute.

Another sampling rate you may see is 22Khz for stereo sound files and 11Khz for mono sound files. Because the sound is sampled at a lower rate, the resulting files use less disk space. You may see this sample rate used on Macintosh computers with System 7 and on Windows systems.

Don't forget, you can create sound clips using an audio tool. Most computer systems come with an audio tool capable of recording sound from the computer's standard input. Using an audio converter, you can convert to and from the popular sound formats discussed in the next section. (To find sources of shareware and freeware audio tools on the Internet, see the multimedia section of Chapter 10.)

Sound Formats

When adding sound files to your publication, you should try to keep the length of the recording to a minimum. The smaller the file, the quicker the reader can download and play back the file. While you have already seen one way to reduce the size of the file, another way to reduce the file size is to use an audio format that compresses the sound file. One such format is MPEG, developed by the Moving Pictures Expert Group.

Using MPEG Sound

MPEG is the world standard in audio and video compression. Just as JPEG images and other graphic images can be compressed, so can digital audio and video. MPEG is a technical standard for compression and not a compression algorithm. Manufacturers who follow the MPEG standard develop or obtain a proprietary compression algorithm to achieve what the standard defines. A compression algorithm is a program that uses an advanced mathematical formula to squeeze audio and video into smaller disk spaces. Using MPEG, you can compress a 10MB sound file into 1MB or even 1/2MB of disk space.

When you compress files, there is a tradeoff between compression and the quality of the file when it is decompressed for playback. The higher the compression ratio, the more information that is squeezed out of the recording and the lower the quality of the playback. For MPEG audio you may want to use a compression ratio of 7:1 to 12:1. MPEG audio players are available for most computer systems, including Amiga, DOS/Windows, Mac, and UNIX. You can use MPEG audio to produce high-quality stereo sound sampled at 44.1KHz and because the files are compressed, the resulting files will be small compared to other stereo formats.

The sound format you use will depend on your publishing needs and the projected needs of your readers. Each computer platform has its own sound format. In fact, most computer platforms have several formats, which makes it difficult to adapt sound for use on different systems. This is why industry standards, such as MPEG, are so important.

Using AU Sound

While MPEG audio is used widely, there are other more prevalent sound formats in use. Some of these formats are so popular they seem to be industry standards. Sun Microsystem's audio format AU is one of these formats.

Sun's audio format is also called the μ-law format. AU formatted sound files are saved with the .au extension. The AU format originated on Sun work stations and in the UNIX environment. Although the AU format is not a quality format, it enjoys wide usage because it is widely supported. Audio players are available for just about every computer platform, including Amiga, Atari, DOS/Windows, Mac, and UNIX. AU sound files with a sample rate of 8Khz are the most common and offer fair sound quality that is a close equivalent to that of a telephone receiver.

Using AIFF and AIFF-C Sound

Two audio formats are associated with Apple's Audio Interchange File Format. AIFF is a basic format that supports high-quality stereo sound. AIFF-C is an advanced format that enables you to compress audio files up to a ratio of 6:1. Using these formats, you can create sound files sampled at a variety of rates. The most popular sampling rates are 16-bit stereo at 44.1Khz and 8-bit mono at 8Khz.

On most systems, AIFF files are saved with the `.aiff` extension and AIFF-C files are saved with the `.aifc` extension. Because DOS/Windows systems limit extensions to three letters, both AIFF and AIFF-C files are saved on DOS/Windows systems with the `.aif` extension. As these formats were originally developed by Apple, they are primarily used on Macintosh systems. Most audio players that support AIFF also support AIFF-C and audio players are available for just about every computer platform, including Amiga, DOS/Windows, Mac, and UNIX.

Using WAV Sound

Microsoft's Waveform audio format is another popular format. WAV-formatted sound files are saved with the `.wav` extension. The proprietary WAV format originated on Windows systems and is capable of producing high-quality sound. Using WAV, you can create sound files sampled at a variety of rates. The most popular sampling rates are 16-bit stereo at 44.1Khz and 8-bit mono at 8Khz. Audio players are available for just about every computer platform, including Amiga, DOS/Windows, Mac, and UNIX.

Using SND Sound

A basic format that is used in various ways on different systems is the SND format. On some UNIX systems, audio files saved with the `.snd` extension are actually AU sound files. DOS/Windows systems use a basic sound format that is saved with the `.snd` extension as well. Macintosh systems also use a basic sound format that is saved with the `.snd` extension. On System 7 for Macintosh, popular sampling rates for SND formatted sound files are 22Khz for stereo sound and 11Khz for mono sound.

Using MIDI and MOD Sound

Other popular formats include the Musical Instrument Digital Interface (MIDI) format and digital music files in module format. MIDI sound files are not sampled like other sound files and contain instructions for how and when to play electronic synthesizers. Using MIDI, you can create very advanced soundtracks that use a very small amount of disk space. To play back MIDI sound files, you need a MIDI player.

Modules or MODs refer to a group of sound formats. MOD files are not sampled and contain sets of digital music samples and sequencing information for those samples. There are more than 100 MOD formats. The three most popular of these formats are MOD, S3M, and MTM. Although MODs originated on the Amiga, popular MOD formats can be played on any computer system when using a compatible audio player.

Summing It All Up

The popular audio formats and summary information for each format are shown in Table 7.1. As you have seen, audio players are available for a variety of sound formats on most computer platforms. However, if you want to ensure that a particular group of users can play your sound file, you should use a sound format that originated on their system.

Table 7.1. Popular Audio Formats.

Format	Extension	MIME Type	Common Sample Rates	Compression
AIFF	.aif/.aiff	audio/x-aiff	44.1Khz, 16-bit stereo	None
			8Khz, 8-bit mono	None
AIFF-C	.aif/.aifc	audio/x-aiff	44.1Khz, 16-bit stereo	6:1
			8Khz, 8-bit mono	6:1
AU/µ-law	.au	audio/basic	8Khz, 8-bit mono	None
MPEG	.mp2	audio/mpeg	44.1Khz, 16-bit stereo	20:1
SND	.snd	audio/basic	22Khz, stereo	None
			11Khz, mono	None
WAV	.wav	audio/x-wav	44.1Khz, 16-bit stereo	None
			8Khz, 8-bit mono	None

Finding Sound Resources on the Internet

One of the best places on the Web to find sound resources is Yahoo. At Yahoo, you can find links to hundreds of resources related to sound. The following links take you to some of Yahoo's most popular sound pages:

Yahoo's multimedia sound page

`http://www.yahoo.com/Computers_and_Internet/Multimedia/Sound/`

Yahoo's MIDI sound page

`http://www.yahoo.com/Entertainment/Music/Genres/Computer_Generated/MIDI/`
`Sounds/`

Yahoo's MOD music page

`http://www.yahoo.com/Computers_and_Internet/Multimedia/Sound/`
`MOD_Music_Format/`

Another great place to find resources related to sound is the World Wide Web Virtual Library. The WWW Virtual Library maintains an audio index and a music department. You can find these areas at

Audio index at the WWW Virtual Library

`http://www.comlab.ox.ac.uk/archive/audio.html`

Music Department of the World Wide Web Virtual Library

`http://syy.oulu.fi/music.html`

If you are looking for sound archives, this popular archive contains lots of Sun AU sounds and a large collection of Ren & Stimpy sounds:

```
ftp://ftp.ee.lbl.gov/sounds/
```

Another good sound archive can be found at Sunsite. While Sunsite maintains a multimedia archive, the best stuff is in these sound directories:

AU sounds
```
http://sunsite.unc.edu/pub/multimedia/sun-sounds
```
WAV sounds
```
http://sunsite.unc.edu/pub/multimedia/pc-sounds
```
Music
```
http://sunsite.unc.edu/pub/multimedia/music
```

To stay current with audio concepts and resources, you may want to participate or lurk in the newsgroups related to sound. Here are some newsgroups you may be interested in:

```
alt.binaries.sounds.misc
alt.binaries.sounds.midi
alt.binaries.sounds.mods
alt.binaries.sounds.movies
alt.binaries.sounds.music
alt.binaries.sounds.tv
alt.binaries.sounds.utilities
```

Enhancing Your Web Publication with Video

Video is another explosive medium that Web publishers are experimenting with. Web users are just as fascinated with video as they are with sound and often seek out sites solely to find video clips. There are two basic types of video: digitized motion video and animation. The ways to create animation and video are closely related. This is because animation is a series of still images and video is a series of moving images on film that must be broken down into still image frames before it can be processed.

The idea of computer-generated animation is very simple. You draw a series of still images and play them back in near real time as if they were motion video. You can create many special effects using animation, like bouncing a ball across the screen, creating a spinning globe, or even making a tiny sun rise and set.

The applications for animation in your Web publications are limited only by your imagination. Thanks to recent innovations, you can include internal and external animation sequences in your Web publications. As the focus of this section is on general rules for creating and using animation and video, you should refer to Chapter 14, "Dynamic Documents with

Client Pull/Server Push," for specifics on creating internal animation for your Web publications.

Generally, digitized motion video refers to video recorded on a video camera that is subsequently digitized for playback on a computer. Although early video productions were nothing more than digitized home videos, these productions attracted tremendous interest from multimedia enthusiasts and Internet users around the world. The applications for using digitized video in your Web publications are limitless.

Another major advance in Web publishing is that you can now include internal and external video clips in your Web publications. Thanks to the development team at Microsoft, not only can you create publications with a digitized video sequence, but you can also control how the video will be played back and when. (See Chapter 8, "Netscape and Internet Explorer Extensions," to learn more about using Internet video clips in your publications.)

While support for internal video and animation sequences is only a recent possibility, there is strong support for external video and animation sequences. Readers can access external video and animation sequences by activating a hypertext link to the video file, such as

```
<P>If you've never been to Niagara Falls, this is the
<A HREF="niagara_falls.mov">video</A> for you.</P>
```

When a reader clicks on the link, the video file is downloaded to his or her computer. If a video player is available and configured for use in the reader's browser, the video file is played. If a video player is not available, the video file will be stored on the reader's hard disk for later playing. Browsers know which video player to launch based on the file type extension (`.avi`, `.mov`, `.mpeg`, and so forth) of the external sound file referenced in your document. Consequently, you should always name your video files with an appropriate extension.

You should also let readers know the format and size of the sound file. One way to do this would be to simply insert the information into the text of your publication as follows:

```
<P>Preview our newest Microsoft AVI movie <A HREF="cool_waves.avi">
Cool Waves (4.5MB)<A/>.</P>
```

Before you add video or animation to your publications, there are many concepts you should consider. The most important matters you should think about are when and how to use video and animation in your publications.

When and How To Use Video

Adding video to your publications is more complicated than other mediums. Primarily this is because video production merges concepts for still images, adds motion, and uses audio. Thus when creating video, you need to understand multimedia concepts related to still images, moving images—which are basically a series of still images that change in time—and audio. However, as you have seen in previous sections, adding multimedia to your publications is easy if you know the standards and related concepts.

Video signals are broadcast using a broadcast standard. NTSC is the broadcast standard in North America and Japan. PAL is the broadcast standard for most of Europe. While there are other broadcast standards, such as SECAM used in France and variations of PAL used in some European countries, NTSC and PAL are the broadcast standards in widest use.

When you create or incorporate a video sequence into your publication, you will probably use your local broadcast standard. However, you will want to consider where the audience for your publication is located. If you are in North America and your primary audience is in Europe, you will want to create a PAL version of your video sequence. Having to switch between broadcast standards can cause problems and affect the quality of the playback. To avoid problems, you should use video equipment that supports both NTSC and PAL. However, specialized video equipment to convert your video sequence to other broadcast standards is available. There are also programs that enable you to display digitized PAL on an NTSC monitor and vice versa.

The key differences between PAL and NTSC are in the number of horizontal and vertical scan lines used and how the images are interlaced for playback. NTSC-PAL and PAL-NTSC software converters take advantage of how the variance in horizontal and vertical scan lines affect screen size. Most of these converters simply convert the horizontal and vertical scan lines to a pixel size for the screen on which to display your images. The result is a screen of slightly different proportions from what you are used to and the ability to play back video recorded using a broadcast standard other than your local standard.

The NTSC standard specifies that broadcast-quality video should be displayed at 60 fields per second. The images are interlaced, with the odd and even horizontal lines alternating during each pass. This means that actually only 30 distinct frames are displayed each second. When you create real-time video or animation sequences for your publications, you will also use the rate of 30 frames per second. If you are digitizing video sequences, you will have to capture 30 video frames to create one second of motion video. If you are creating an animation sequence, you will use a series of 30 still images to create one second of animation.

Many Web publishers create video sequences by capturing them one frame at a time. The primary reason for this is that video digitizing equipment until recently was priced out of reach for most small publishers. Thanks to recent advances in technology, the prices for video digitizing equipment are falling fast. If you plan to create your own video sequences, you will want to check current pricing and may be surprised at how affordable the equipment is.

Creating 30 frames for a single second of motion video is a lot of work, which is why most digital video sequences are less than a minute in duration. In fact, a one-minute video sequence uses 1800 frames, and here's where you want to go back and review the concepts covered earlier. Each video frame can eat up lots of disk space, depending on the pixel bit depth and size of the image. A full-screen (640×480) 24-bit video frame will use as much as 1MB of disk space. Multiply that by 1800 and you will find that each minute of motion video can gobble up as much as 1.8GB of disk space. To top it off, that's 1.8GB of disk space without audio. Add another 10MB per minute for stereo sound sampled at 44.1Khz.

Because video sequences can get so large, many techniques are used to reduce the resulting file size. The primary technique used is compression. When compressing video sequences, you generally select a compression ratio and a quality setting. A compression ratio is the ratio at which video and accompanying audio, if any, is compressed. Some video formats let you compress files as much as 200:1. A 200:1 compression ratio means that your video sequence will be squeezed into a space approximately 1/200th of its original size. While such a large compression ratio seems attractive, you cannot squeeze that much information out of a file without losing information that directly affects the quality of the playback.

The quality setting that is often used with compression is a reality check describing the tradeoff you want to make between the resulting file size and its quality during playback. A general range for quality setting is from 1 to 100. The higher the quality setting, the larger the resulting file will be and the better its playback quality. Quality settings can be confusing because a quality setting of 75 does not mean the resulting file will have 75 percent of the information. The compression ratio describes how much information to squeeze out of the file. The quality setting is used to keep the ratio of compression realistic when compared to your need for a quality playback.

Generally, your goal should be to select the highest compression ratio and lowest quality setting that provides playback quality you feel is acceptable. Try several combinations of compression ratios and quality settings. You should never use a quality factor of 100 and will probably not notice any loss of playback quality using a quality factor of 90.

Although compression is the major technique used to reduce the size of your video files and thus decrease the download time as well, compression alone is often not enough. Many video producers limit the width and height of the video to save disk space and increase playback speed as well. A common size providing good playback speed with an acceptably sized playback window is 160×120. A video recorded at 160×120 will be 16 times smaller than a video recorded at 640×480.

You can save disk space and reduce the download time in other ways as well. For the audio portion of the recording, you could use 8-bit mono instead of 16-bit stereo; 8-bit mono sound saves disk space and generally provides a fair quality playback. For the video format, you could use an 8-bit pixel depth instead of a 24-bit pixel depth. While the 16.7 million colors offered by true 24-bit color can be used to create sharp, high-quality videos, most computers can only display 256 colors anyway. A video recorded in 256 colors will be at least three times smaller than a video recorded in 16.7 million colors.

Video Formats

Although video technology is fairly new, it is advancing at an explosive pace. Video formats are also advancing. Autodesk's original flick format, FLI, was widely used to create animation sequences but is being replaced by the updated flick format, FLC. Because animation and digitized video sequences both display a series of still images that change in time, many Web publishers use popular video formats to create animation sequences.

The most popular video formats are MPEG and QuickTime. MPEG offers advanced compression technology and quality playback. Apple's QuickTime format is a close second to MPEG that offers quality playback and basic compression techniques. Another format working its way into the mainstream is Microsoft's AVI format. The AVI format offers features similar to those of QuickTime. The MPEG, QuickTime, and AVI formats offer quality solutions for video production and editing. As a result, the video format you use will most likely depend on the computer platform you prefer to work with and the video format that originated on that platform. The popular video formats and summary information for each format are shown in Table 7.2.

Table 7.2. Popular video formats.

Format	Extension	MIME Type	Compression
AVI	`.avi`	video/x-msvideo	Yes
MPEG-1	`.mpeg, .mpg, .mpe`	video/mpeg	Yes
MPEG-2	`.mpeg, .mpg, .mpe`	video/mpeg	Yes
QuickTime	`.mov, .qt`	video/quicktime	Yes

The MPEG format is the world standard in video, yet it enjoys the most usage on UNIX systems. If you plan to use a UNIX platform, you will probably want to use MPEG. The QuickTime format was originally developed by Apple. If you plan to use a Macintosh, you will probably want to use QuickTime. The AVI format was originally developed by Microsoft. If you plan to use a Windows-based system, you will probably want to use AVI. While this is true most often, let's explore these formats to help you make a more educated choice of video format for your publications.

Using the AVI Format

With the large installed base of Windows systems, it should come as no surprise that Microsoft's AVI format is gaining widespread popularity. AVI-formatted video files are saved with the `.avi` extension. The AVI format is also referred to as the Video for Windows format. Video for Windows is a video production software package sold by Microsoft. The software package includes a suite of tools for creating and editing video sequences. The main tools are VidCap, VidEdit, Media Player, BitEdit, PalEdit, and WaveEdit.

Using VidCap, you can capture video in real time or step through the frames individually. The key to using VidCap in real time is to ensure your computer is fast enough to process a video frame and save it to disk before the next frame enters the capture hardware. If the processing time exceeds the time it takes for the next frame to enter the capture hardware, you will need to use the step-frame capture mode.

VidCap will process the audio input with the frames as well. In real-time mode, the software captures the audio as it is played. In step-frame mode, the software captures the video frame and audio associated with the frame separately. VidCap will accept NTSC and PAL video sources as inputs.

Using VidEdit, you can create and edit audio and video sequences. VidEdit displays video and audio segments as separate entities that you can edit in a variety of ways. You can cut out video frames and edit them individually with or without their associated audio segment. You can also cut audio segments for editing and paste them into the video sequence in any order. In this way, you can create an entire new sound track for a video segment. With VidEdit, you can save video files in AVI format using a variety of compression algorithms.

VidEdit plays FLC, FLI, DIB, and AVI video formats. You can use the Video for Windows Converter to convert Apple QuickTime to the AVI format. You can also edit your WAV files associated with a video sequence separately using WaveEdit.

Media Player enables you to play your video and audio sequences separately or together. Media Player will play videos in AVI format and audio in WAV format. You can obtain run-time versions of the Media Player free.

BitEdit is a handy drawing tool that enables you to easily touch up your video files. Yet because BitEdit supports over a dozen popular image formats including GIF, you can use BitEdit to convert still images into AVI animation.

PalEdit is a handy editor for color palettes that enables you to perform many necessary tasks for color mapping. You can modify any color in a particular palette, modify the entire palette, reduce the number of colors in a palette, and even copy colors from one palette to another.

> **TIP**
>
> If you are looking for information on the AVI format, visit Microsoft at
> `http://www.microsoft.com/`

MPEG Format

The MPEG format is the industry standard for video. The MPEG standard has several progressive levels, yet only two of these levels have been implemented. While MPEG Level 1 became the world standard in video several years ago, MPEG Level 2 was implemented in 1995. MPEG video files are saved with the `.mpeg`, `.mpg`, or `.mpe` extension.

> **TIP**
>
> The best place on the Web to find information on MPEG is the Moving Pictures Expert Group Frequently Asked Questions page. At the MPEG FAQ page, you can find tools, detailed information on the MPEG standard, and information on making MPEG videos. The URL for the MPEG FAQ is
>
> `http://www.crs4.it/HTML/LUIGI/MPEG/mpegfaq.html`
>
> An alternate source for the MPEG FAQ is here:
>
> `http://www.lib.ox.ac.uk/internet/news/faq/by_category.mpeg-faq.html`
>
> Another great site for technical information on MPEG is the MPEG resource list from the University of Minnesota's graphics and visualization lab. The list contains detailed examples of how MPEG video can be created and then converted to and from popular formats. You can find the MPEG resource list on the Web at
>
> `http://www.arc.umn.edu/GVL/Software/mpeg.html`

Using MPEG Level 1

MPEG Level 1 is the first and most versatile standard implemented by the Moving Pictures Expert Group. MPEG Level 1 video is played at roughly 30 frames per second. Although there are tricks to make the image window larger, MPEG-1 is usually displayed at a resolution of 352×240 pixels or less. MPEG Level 1 can be compressed using either software or hardware encoders. Most Web publishers use MPEG-1 software encoders. The advantage to MPEG-1 software encoders is that they are a very inexpensive alternative for creating video sequences. In fact, you can find free MPEG-1 software encoders on the Internet.

MPEG-l software encoders are inexpensive and friendly, and MPEG-1 hardware encoders are fast and efficient. The time savings offered by MPEG-1 hardware encoders is often a selling point in itself, especially if you plan to create multiple video sequences or are on a tight time schedule. Keep in mind that generally, when you are creating a video sequence, you will experiment with many different compression and quality settings until you find the optimal setting. Each time you use a different setting you must compress the file and test the playback quality. The efficiency of MPEG-1 hardware encoders is another selling point. A more efficient compression routine can generally create more compact and higher quality video files.

While the MPEG-1 standard is not associated with a single compression algorithm, MPEG-1 compression algorithms are generally more advanced than the algorithms used by AVI or QuickTime. Using MPEG-1 compression, you can compress video sequences up to 100:1. Many Web publishers use MPEG-1 compression because there is generally no noticeable quality loss at compression ratios of 7:1 to 12:1. Even with compression ratios of up to 20:1, there is often little noticeable quality loss.

MPEG-1 players are available for all computer systems, including Amiga, Atari, Macintosh, DOS/Windows, and UNIX. While early MPEG video players did not support audio tracks, most current MPEG players support 16-bit stereo at sample rates up to 44.1Khz.

Using MPEG Level 2

MPEG Level 2 is a high-quality video standard implemented by the Moving Pictures Expert Group in 1995. MPEG Level 2 video finally offers Web publishers true full-screen playback capability. Using MPEG-2, you can play 30 video frames per second at a resolution of 720×480 pixels.

While the MPEG-2 standard is not associated with a single compression algorithm, MPEG-2 compression algorithms are the most advanced video compression algorithms in use today. Using MPEG-2 compression, you can compress video sequences up to 200:1. Yet, the really good news for Web publishers is that there is generally no noticeable quality loss at compression rates at high as 30:1.

The drawback to using MPEG-2 compression is that you need an MPEG-2 video encoder chip to compress the video sequence and an MPEG-2 decoder chip to decompress the video sequence. This means in order to play back your recording, users will need a video board with an MPEG-2 decoder chip. Although you can purchase video processing equipment with MPEG-2 encoder and decoder chips for around $2500, it will be some time before standard computer video boards include MPEG-2 decoder chips.

QuickTime Format

Apple's QuickTime format is one of the most popular formats on the Internet. QuickTime video files are usually saved with the `.mov` or `.qt` extension. Macintosh systems have special software and hardware facilities for handling multimedia, and the QuickTime format takes full advantage of these facilities by separating video data into a resource fork and a data fork. The resource fork contains information necessary for system resources like the Macintosh's multimedia hardware. The data fork contains the actual bits and bytes.

To play QuickTime videos on other systems, the two data forks must be merged into a single data fork. The process of merging the data forks is called "flattening," and if someone ever tells you to flatten your QuickTime video, this is what they are talking about. While the process may sound complicated, there are tools you can use to flatten QuickTime videos. These tools enable you to flatten QuickTime videos at the press of a button.

Apple includes QuickTime players with current versions of System 7. If you own a Macintosh and do not have a QuickTime player, you can obtain one for free at the Apple QuickTime site highlighted in the resource section below. You can also find free QuickTime players for Windows and UNIX X Windows systems.

Finding Video Resources on the Internet

Dozens of sites on the Web have video archives. The problem is that most of these sites are on servers maintained by universities and sometimes when a site gets too popular, the site closes. To stay current with the changes, you may want to visit the multimedia section at Yahoo:

`http://www.yahoo.com/Computers_and_Internet/Multimedia/Video/`

If you own a Macintosh, you will want to visit this page at Yahoo:

`http://www.yahoo.com/Computers_and_Internet/Software/Macintosh/Multimedia/`

One of the most popular movie archives on the Internet is the MPEG Movie Archive. At the MPEG Movie Archive, you can find nearly a hundred MPEG movies. The archive contains several categories of movies, including Super Models, Animation, Movies & TV, Music, Racing, Space, and a miscellaneous category. Recently the site closed down because it became too popular, but the developers of the site say the site is back permanently. You can find the archive at the main site or at one of the mirror sites:

Main site
`http://www.eeb.ele.tue.nl/mpeg/index.html`
Mirror site
`http://ftp.luth.se/pub/misc/anim/`
Mirror site
`http://www.wit.com`

Rob's Multimedia Lab, sponsored by the Association for Computing Machinery at the University of Illinois, Urbana/Champaign campus, is a comprehensive resource for all things related to multimedia. The front door to the site contains dozens of links, but you can also go straight to the good stuff, which includes an image archive, a sound archive, and an MPEG movie archive:

Image archive
`http://www.acm.uiuc.edu:80/rml/Gifs/`
Sound archive
`http://www.acm.uiuc.edu:80/rml/Sounds/`

MPEG movie archive
`http://www.acm.uiuc.edu:80/rml/Mpeg/`

Summary

Everywhere you look on the Web, you will find Web publications that use multimedia. Web publishers use images, sound, and video to enhance their pages and to attract readers. You can use multimedia to convey your message in a way more powerful than text alone. Multimedia can help sell your products and services. It can even show the rest of the world what your part of the world looks like.

You can use images to add highlights, navigation mechanisms, logos, page titles, illustrations, and maps to the hot features at your site. Although there are many image formats, the primary image formats in use on the Web are JPEG and GIF. Images are a basic medium for your publications, but you can also use sound and video. Both mediums offer Web publishers a powerful way to express their ideas and reach readers. In fact, many Web users seek out sites that feature sound and video.

Netscape and Internet Explorer Extensions

by
Ro

Two of the hottest HTML browsers on the Web are the Netscape Navigator and the Internet Explorer. Both support many powerful HTML 3.0 elements and feature their own unique extensions. The Netscape Navigator debuted in late 1994 and by early 1995 was already a driving force on the World Wide Web. The phenomenal popularity of the Netscape Navigator is due in large part to its support for HTML 3.0 elements and unique extensions to the standard. Netscape extensions are so popular that several browsers produced by other companies support the extensions, including Microsoft's Internet Explorer.

The Internet Explorer debuted in August 1995 and is an upstart that may take the Web community by storm. Not only does Internet Explorer support Netscape and HTML 3.0 extensions, it also features unique extensions that are bound to become quick favorites for Web publishers. These features are so hot that within weeks after the debut of Internet Explorer, several browser creators either announced plans to support the extensions or had already incorporated the extensions into their browsers. One of the supporters of Internet Explorer's extensions is the browser that started it all, the NCSA Mosaic browser.

This chapter discusses how you can incorporate Netscape and Internet Explorer extensions into your documents as well as important design issues that you as the Web publisher should focus on.

Layout Extras

Netscape Version 1.0 introduced many terrific extensions for document layout. These extras include

- Center
- Blink
- Image Extensions
- Line Break Extensions
- Horizontal Rule Extensions

Centering Text and Graphics

The <CENTER> tag is a Netscape 1.0 innovation that is fully supported by Netscape and Internet Explorer. Using the <CENTER> tag, you can center any objects defined between the begin and end <CENTER> tags. The <CENTER> tag is useful for centering sections of your page that can include text and objects. Here is how you can use the <CENTER> tag:

```
<CENTER>
<IMG SRC="centered.gif" ALT="Welcome!">
<P>This text is centered.</P>
</CENTER>
```

Because the <CENTER> tag is a Netscape-unique enhancement, many Web publishers use paragraph or header alignment to center text. All HTML 3.0-compliant browsers can take advantage of aligned paragraphs and headers. Both Netscape and Internet Explorer accept an alignment value of CENTER, which is used as follows:

```
<P ALIGN=CENTER>A better way to align paragraphs of text.</P>
```

or

```
<H1 ALIGN=CENTER>A better way to align headers</H1>
```

Netscape 2.0 also supports HTML 3.0 division elements. Using the <DIV> tag with a value of ALIGN=CENTER, you can center all text and graphics defined within the division. In this way, users with Netscape 2.0- or HTML 3.0-compliant can take advantage of this feature. Here is how you can use the <DIV> tag:

```
<DIV ALIGN=CENTER>
<IMG SRC="centered.gif" ALT="Welcome!">
<P>This text is centered.</P>
</DIV>
```

	HTML 3.0	*Netscape 1.0*	*Netscape 2.0*	*IE 1.0*	*IE 2.0*
<CENTER>	no	yes	yes	yes	yes
<DIV>	yes	no	yes	no	no
<P ALIGN=CENTER>	yes	yes	yes	yes	yes

Using <BLINK>

Netscape 1.0 introduced blinking text, and it has been a subject of controversy ever since. Imagine, for a moment, an entire paragraph or worse, an entire page blinking on and off while you are trying to read it. Text blinking on and off is like a tiny neon sign on your page that attracts the reader's eyes. Sometimes blinking text is good. You draw the reader's attention temporarily to a key area of the page. Other times blinking text is bad. You distract the readers while they are trying to read the text on the page. The controversy surrounding the <BLINK> tag may be the reason Internet Explorer does not support this feature.

The key to using blinking text is to confine it to a small area of your page and to ensure it only affects a few key words. To do this, you can insert the <BLINK> tag within a paragraph of text as follows:

```
<P>This application is so <BLINK>hot</BLINK> that it has been featured in 12
different magazines.</P>
```

	HTML 3.0	*Netscape 1.0*	*Netscape 2.0*	*IE 1.0*	*IE 2.0*
<BLINK>	no	yes	yes	no	no

Image Extensions

Netscape 1.0 introduced many enhancements for images. While some of these enhancements have been included in the draft for HTML 3.0, most of the enhancements remain unique to Netscape. Both Netscape Navigator and Internet Explorer support the options for aligning text and images discussed in Chapter 7, "Adding Multimedia Features with HTML." These alignment options include

```
ALIGN=TOP
ALIGN=BOTTOM
ALIGN=MIDDLE
ALIGN=LEFT
ALIGN=RIGHT
```

In addition to the HTML 2.0 and 3.0 alignments values, Netscape recognized the deficiencies in how images were aligned with text. To correct these shortcomings, Netscape introduced the following unique extensions:

```
ALIGN=TEXTTOP
ALIGN=ABSMIDDLE
ALIGN=ABSBOTTOM
ALIGN=BASELINE
```

The Netscape image alignment values behave exactly as their names imply they should. The value of TEXTTOP aligns the top of the image with the top of the tallest element in the line of text associated with the image. The value of ABSMIDDLE aligns the center of the image with the center of the line of text associated with the image. The value of ABSBOTTOM aligns the bottom of the image with the bottom of the line of text associated with the image. The value of BASELINE aligns the base of the image with the baseline of the text associated with the image, which is exactly how the value of BOTTOM handles text and image alignment. The Internet Explorer does not recognize these alignment values.

> **NOTE**
>
> Keep in mind other browsers will ignore the Netscape-unique alignment values and display your images with the default alignment value of BOTTOM. Consequently, you should use the Netscape alignment values only on pages that will be displayed by the Netscape browser or when the alignment of the image and text is not critical.

Netscape 1.0 also introduced the HEIGHT and WIDTH attributes for resizing images. These attributes were incorporated into the HTML 3.0 draft specification. Other Netscape innovations for images include

```
BORDER
HSPACE
VSPACE
```

These attributes are fully supported by Netscape and Internet Explorer. The BORDER attribute specifies the pixel size of the border to be drawn around an image. Here is how you can add an image with a border five pixels wide surrounding it:

```
<IMG SRC="../graphics/windows.jpeg" BORDER=5>
```

Borders are visible if the image is anchored to the page as a hypertext link and invisible if the image is not anchored to the page. You can use the BORDER attribute to add white space around images that are not links and to build a picture frame around images that are links. While both techniques enhance the impact of the image, you can also remove the border around linked images by specifying the value of BORDER=0.

The attributes HSPACE and VSPACE are used to increase the amount of white space surrounding the image. HSPACE increases the pixel size of the horizontal margins surround the image. VSPACE increases the pixel size of the vertical margins surrounding the image. These attributes are used to put white space between multiple images or text. If you use the HSPACE or VSPACE attributes, the image will not have a visible border even if it is a hypertext link. You can use these attributes as follows:

```
<IMG SRC="sunset.gif" HSPACE=12 VSPACE=6>
```

The final Netscape enhancement for the <IMG> tag is the LOWSRC attribute. A LOWSRC image is a timesaver that reduces the wait time and makes it possible for other elements on the page to be displayed before a high-resolution image is displayed. On the first pass through the document, Netscape loads the image specified by the LOWSRC attribute. Once all other images in the document are loaded, the image specified by the SRC attribute is loaded. The Internet Explorer and other browsers that do not support the LOWSRC attribute load the image specified by the SRC attribute. The LOWSRC attribute should be used with the SRC attribute as follows:

```
<IMG SRC="powerpicture.jpeg" LOWSRC="picture.gif">
```

TIP

Try to keep your low-resolution image small in terms of byte size. A 2KB low-resolution image will load many times quicker than your 25KB high-resolution image. Netscape fades in the high-resolution image over the low-resolution image. The best low-resolution images act as place holders and are the same size as the high-resolution image. In this way, the text on the page doesn't shift when the high-resolution image is displayed. You can use the WIDTH and HEIGHT attributes to ensure the images are the same size.

	HTML 3.0	*Netscape 1.0*	*Netscape 2.0*	*IE 1.0*	*IE 2.0*
ALIGN=ABSBOTTOM	no	yes	yes	no	no
ALIGN=ABSMIDDLE	no	yes	yes	no	no
ALIGN=BASELINE	no	yes	yes	no	no
ALIGN=BOTTOM	yes	yes	yes	yes	yes
ALIGN=LEFT	yes	yes	yes	yes	yes
ALIGN=MIDDLE	yes	yes	yes	yes	yes
ALIGN=RIGHT	yes	yes	yes	yes	yes
ALIGN=TEXTTOP	no	yes	yes	no	no
ALIGN=TOP	yes	yes	yes	yes	yes
BORDER	yes	yes	yes	yes	yes
HEIGHT	yes	yes	yes	yes	yes
HSPACE	yes	yes	yes	yes	yes
LOWSRC	no	yes	yes	no	no
VSPACE	yes	yes	yes	yes	yes
WIDTH	yes	yes	yes	yes	yes

Line Break Extensions

Netscape 1.0 introduced the CLEAR attribute for line breaks. The CLEAR attribute is extremely useful when you want to clear the left, right, or both margins after placing an image on the page. The CLEAR attribute has been incorporated into HTML 3.0 and both Netscape and Internet Explorer support the following values of

```
<BR CLEAR=LEFT>
<BR CLEAR=RIGHT>
<BR CLEAR=ALL>
```

Besides creating more useful ways to break up text and images, Netscape 1.0 added a way to ensure text stayed together. The <NOBR> tag ensures a line of text is displayed as a single line with no line breaks. While the <NOBR> tag is useful to ensure text is formatted as you want it to be, keep in mind that users may have to scroll their browser window to finish reading the line of text. To minimize the amount of scrolling readers may have to do, Netscape introduced a way you could define where a line of text defined with <NOBR> could break if necessary. Using the <WBR> tag, you can insert soft word break into the line of text and the browser will break the line of text at the point you inserted the <WBR> tag, if necessary.

Here's how you can use <NOBR> and <WBR>:

```
<NOBR>I don't want this line of text to break no matter what</NOBR>

<NOBR>This line of text can break<WBR> in two places<WBR> if necessary.
</NOBR>
```

	HTML 3.0	Netscape 1.0	Netscape 2.0	IE 1.0	IE 2.0
`<BR CLEAR=ALL>`	yes	yes	yes	yes	yes
`<BR CLEAR=LEFT>`	yes	yes	yes	yes	yes
`<BR CLEAR=RIGHT>`	yes	yes	yes	yes	yes
`<NOBR>`	no	yes	yes	yes	yes
`<WBR>`	no	yes	yes	yes	yes

Horizontal Rule Extensions

Horizontal rules become helpful design tools with Netscape and Internet Explorer. You can use the SIZE attribute to make the separation of topics and subtopics on your pages more distinct. The size of a horizontal rule is defined in terms of pixels, such as

```
<HR SIZE=5>
```

To separate topics and subtopics visually, you could use one size value for main topics and another size value for each level of subtopics. You should experiment with rule sizes in your publications. While a size of five pixels is usually sufficient to separate main topics, a size of two pixels is usually sufficient for subtopics.

While horizontal rules normally appear engraved on the page, you can define rules without shading using the NOSHADE attribute. Other unique attributes for horizontal rules include ALIGN and WIDTH. These attributes are best used with each other. Using the ALIGN attribute, you can align a horizontal rule with the left margin, right margin, or center of the page with the values ALIGN=RIGHT, ALIGN=LEFT, and ALIGN=CENTER, respectively. Using the WIDTH attribute, you can define the length of the horizontal rule in pixels or as the percentage of the browser's window width:

```
<HR WIDTH=10>
<HR WIDTH=5%>
```

By combining the two attributes, you can create some powerful effects, such as the one shown in Figure 8.1. The code for the example is shown in Listing 8.1.

Listing 8.1. `fancyhr.htm`.

```
<HTML>
<HEAD>
<TITLE>Fancy Horizontal Rules</TITLE>
</HEAD>
<BODY>
<HR ALIGN=CENTER SIZE=2 WIDTH=65>
<HR ALIGN=CENTER SIZE=3 WIDTH=75>
<HR ALIGN=CENTER SIZE=4 WIDTH=85>
<HR ALIGN=CENTER SIZE=5 WIDTH=95>
<HR ALIGN=CENTER SIZE=4 WIDTH=105>
```

continues

Listing 8.1. continued

```
<HR ALIGN=CENTER SIZE=3 WIDTH=115>
<HR ALIGN=CENTER SIZE=2 WIDTH=125>
<H1 ALIGN=CENTER>Welcome!</H1>
<HR ALIGN=CENTER SIZE=2 WIDTH=125>
<HR ALIGN=CENTER SIZE=3 WIDTH=115>
<HR ALIGN=CENTER SIZE=4 WIDTH=105>
<HR ALIGN=CENTER SIZE=5 WIDTH=95>
<HR ALIGN=CENTER SIZE=4 WIDTH=85>
<HR ALIGN=CENTER SIZE=3 WIDTH=75>
<HR ALIGN=CENTER SIZE=2 WIDTH=65>
</BODY>
</HTML>
```

FIGURE 8.1.

Using fancy horizontal rules.

> **NOTE**
>
> Keep in mind other browsers will ignore the Netscape sizing and alignment values for horizontal rules. These browsers will display the multiple horizontal rules in the example as ordinary horizontal rules. Therefore, it is best to use multiple horizontal rules only on pages that will be displayed by a Netscape-capable browser.

	HTML 3.0	Netscape 1.0	Netscape 2.0	IE 1.0	IE 2.0
SIZE	no	yes	yes	yes	yes
ALIGN=LEFT	no	yes	yes	yes	yes
ALIGN=RIGHT	no	yes	yes	yes	yes

	HTML 3.0	Netscape 1.0	Netscape 2.0	IE 1.0	IE 2.0
ALIGN=CENTER	no	yes	yes	yes	yes
WIDTH	no	yes	yes	yes	yes

Font Enhancements

Both the Netscape Navigator and the Internet Explorer support many useful font enhancements. The next sections explore them one by one.

Defining Font Size

In the HTML specification, there is no way to define a specific font size to use. Primarily this is because the font size is controlled by configurations in the user's browser and the user is the one who selects the font size she would like to use for viewing Web documents. Using various heading levels, Web publishers had some control over font size in graphical browsers. Generally, a Level One heading could be used to create text 8 to 10 point sizes larger than regular text on the page, a Level Two heading could be used to create text 6 to 8-point sizes larger than regular text on the page, and so on. However, this still didn't give Web publishers accurate control over font sizes, especially if the publisher wanted to change font size in the middle of a line of text.

Netscape corrected this shortcoming by allowing Web publishers to define a base font size and later change the font size relative to the base font. Both Netscape and Internet Explorer support the <BASEFONT> and <FONT> tags. You can define the size for the base font using values between 1 and 7. A value of 1 is used for the smallest text. A value of 7 is used for the largest text. The default value for the base font is 3, which corresponds to the size of standard text on the page.

While a begin and end <BASEFONT> tag is specified, you don't need to use both tags. If the end tag is omitted, the basefont setting applies to all text following the begin tag. If the end tag </BASEFONT> is in your document, the basefont setting only applies to text within the begin and end <BASEFONT> tags.

The <BASEFONT> tag is generally used with the <FONT> tag. Using the <FONT> tag, you can define a font size for associated text in two ways: relative to the base font size or directly, using a specific value. You can set the font to a specific size using values between 1 and 7, such as

```
<FONT SIZE=4><P>This line of text is larger than normal</P></FONT>
```

To define the font size relative to the basefont, you can precede the size value by + or − to indicate a relative change to the basefont size. In the following example, the basefont size is set to 5 and two relative font sizes are used to adjust the size of the text:

```
<BASEFONT SIZE=5>
<P>Text is displayed in font size 5.
<FONT SIZE=-2><P>Text is displayed in font size 3.</FONT>
<FONT SIZE=+2><P>Text is displayed in font size 7.</FONT>
```

Being able to adjust the font size is very handy. A small font size is useful for disclaimers or copyright notices you want to place on the page but do not want to eat up page space. A large font size is useful when you want to draw attention to specific keywords or paragraphs of text. You can adjust the font size to create a large first letter for keywords or the first word in a paragraph. As shown in Figure 8.2, you can also create word art by adjusting the font size within words or sentences. Listing 8.2 contains the code for the word art example.

Listing 8.2. `relfonts.htm`.

```
<HTML>
<HEAD>
<TITLE>Using Relative Font Sizes</TITLE>
</HEAD>
<BODY>
<BASEFONT SIZE=3>
<CENTER>
<H1>
<FONT SIZE=-2>T</FONT>
<FONT SIZE=-1>H</FONT>
<FONT SIZE=+0>E</FONT>
<FONT SIZE=+1>H</FONT>
<FONT SIZE=+2>O</FONT>
<FONT SIZE=+3>T</FONT>
<FONT SIZE=+4>T</FONT>
<FONT SIZE=+4>E</FONT>
<FONT SIZE=+3>S</FONT>
<FONT SIZE=+2>T</FONT>
<FONT SIZE=+1>P</FONT>
<FONT SIZE=+0>A</FONT>
<FONT SIZE=-1>G</FONT>
<FONT SIZE=-2>E</FONT>
</H1>
<H1>
<FONT SIZE=+4>N</FONT>
<FONT SIZE=+3>E</FONT>
<FONT SIZE=+2>T</FONT>
<FONT SIZE=+1>S</FONT>
<FONT SIZE=+1>C</FONT>
<FONT SIZE=+2>A</FONT>
<FONT SIZE=+3>P</FONT>
<FONT SIZE=+4>E</FONT>
</H1>
<H1>
<FONT SIZE=+1>E</FONT>
<FONT SIZE=+2>N</FONT>
<FONT SIZE=+3>H</FONT>
<FONT SIZE=+4>A</FONT>
<FONT SIZE=+4>N</FONT>
<FONT SIZE=+3>C</FONT>
<FONT SIZE=+2>E</FONT>
<FONT SIZE=+1>D</FONT>
</H1>
</CENTER>
</BODY>
</HTML>
```

FIGURE 8.2.

Creating word art with relative fonts.

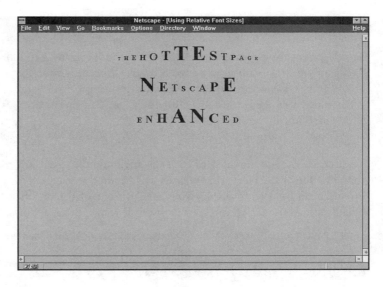

	HTML 3.0	Netscape 1.0	Netscape 2.0	IE 1.0	IE 2.0
`<BASEFONT>`	no	yes	yes	yes	yes
`<FONT SIZE=n>`	no	yes	yes	yes	yes

Defining Font Type

The type of font used to display the text on your page is normally set in the user's browser. This gave the user control over the font face. The problem is that often you as the publisher want to use a certain font face for headings, such as the highly readable Arial, and another font face for paragraph text, such as Century Schoolbook. Or you want to use a decorative font, such as Augsburger Initials, to create a fancy first letter for the first letter of a paragraph. The Internet Explorer 1.0 solves this problem by putting relative control over font type into the publisher's hands.

Using the Internet Explorer FACE attribute for the <FONT> tag, you can assign a font type for the associated text. If the font type is available on the user's system, the specified font will be used to display your text. If the font type is not available on the user's system, the default font as set in the user's browser is used to display your text. When you specify a font face, you must use the full name as follows:

```
<FONT FACE="Lucida Blackletter">
```

TIP

A key concept in using fonts in your Web publications is to limit the number of font styles you use on any single page. To be consistent, you should also limit the number of fonts you use throughout the publication. A good rule of thumb is to use no more than three different fonts styles on any page. You should also try to use the same fonts throughout the publication.

To increase the functionality of the FACE attribute, the extension enables you to specify more than one font face. Here, the browser will attempt to use each font face in turn until it finds one that can be used to display your text. If none of the specified font faces is available, the default font is used. You can specify multiple font types as follows:

```
<FONT FACE="Arial Narrow","Lucida Handwriting","Times New Roman">
```

CREATING TEXT APPEAL

The fonts you use define the way text looks in your documents. Fonts have many different characteristics and are classified in three key ways: by family, proportionally as monospace or proportional, and stylistically as Serif or Sans Serif.

Normal, bold, and italic type form a basic font family. A font family is simply a group of related fonts. Some font families include variations such as normal type, bold type, italic type, and bold italic type. These different font types add emphasis and carry meanings. Italics can convey a sense of nostalgia. Bold type seems to be shouting at you.

Most typewriters use monospace type. In monospace type, each alphabetic or numeric character takes up the same space. A monospaced *l* takes as much space as a monospaced *w*. Monospace type is easy to read and great for tired eyes. Another kind of type is proportional type. With proportional type, each alphabetic or numeric character takes up only the space it needs. Today, most fonts are proportional. Using proportional type, you can add visual variety to your text.

Serifs are the stylistic flourishes, like cross strokes or curves, added to the end of the strokes in a character. Sans is a French word that means without. Thus, Sans Serif fonts do not have stylistic flourishes. For a classical or traditional look, you should use Serif fonts. Serif fonts are the primary fonts used in books, magazines, and newspapers because they are easier to read. Sans Serif fonts have a more contemporary look and are often used for book or magazine titles, captions, and headings. You may want to use a Sans Serif font for headings and a Serif font for normal text.

	HTML 3.0	Netscape 1.0	Netscape 2.0	IE 1.0	IE 2.0
`<FONT FACE=fontname>`	no	no	no	yes	yes

Defining Font Colors

Until recently, the color of the font used in your documents was either black by default or set by the users to a specific color if their browser supported a color option. The Internet Explorer 1.0 introduced a way for Web publishers to control font color anywhere in the text of the document. Using the COLOR attribute for the <FONT> tag, you can set the color in one of two ways:

1. With a predefined color name, such as

   `<FONT COLOR="RED">`

2. With a hexadecimal value to represent the red, green, and blue content of the color. The basic form of the value is preceded by a number sign:

   `<FONT COLOR=#rrggbb>`

   And would be used as follows:

   `<FONT COLOR=#00FF00>`

Using a predefined color name is the easiest option. You simply select a color name from a list of accepted color names. The currently defined color names are

Aqua
Black
Blue
Gray
Green
Lime
Maroon
Navy
Olive
Purple
Red
Silver
Teal
White
Yellow

Basic color combinations using hexadecimal values are shown in Table 8.1. Hexadecimal color values are different from the decimal color values you may be used to seeing. While decimal values allow for 256 colors using the values 0 to 255, hexadecimal values allow for 256 colors using the base 16 numbering system from 00 to FF. The decimal value 0 in hexadecimal is 00.

250

The decimal value 255 in hexadecimal is FF. By combining values or slightly altering values to create darker or lighter shades, you can create a rainbow of colors.

Table 8.1. Using hexadecimal color values.

Color	Hexadecimal Values
Black	00 00 00
Blue	00 00 FF
Brown	99 66 33
Cream	FF FB F0
Cyan	00 FF FF
Dark Blue	00 00 80
Dark Gray	80 80 80
Dark Green	00 80 00
Dark Purple	80 00 80
Dark Red	80 00 00
Dark Yellow	80 80 00
Grass Green	C0 DC C0
Green	00 FF 00
Light Gray	C0 C0 C0
Medium Gray	A0 A0 A4
Purple	FF 00 FF
Red	FF 00 00
Sky Blue	A6 CA F0
White	FF FF FF
Yellow	00 FF FF

USING COLORFUL TEXT

While the capability to assign font colors is extremely useful, the use of color in publications has always caused problems. Some color combinations just don't go together—for example, purple, green, and hot pink text all on the same Web page. Don't use color in your publication because you can, rather use color as a design technique to enhance your page.

When using colorful text in Web publications, you should follow three general rules:

1. Use basic colors for text whenever possible, like black, gray, red, yellow, green, blue, and white.

2. Ensure your font colors are readable on the background you have chosen.

3. Limit the number of colors you use on any single page, and if practical, follow the same color scheme throughout your publication. Four colors are usually sufficient.

	HTML 3.0	*Netscape 1.0*	*Netscape 2.0*	*IE 1.0*	*IE 2.0*
`<FONT COLOR=name>`	no	no	no	yes	yes
`<FONT COLOR=#rrggbb>`	no	no	no	yes	yes

Defining Document Backgrounds

Most browsers display all text on a slate gray background. Netscape Navigator 1.0 introduced extensions for the `<BODY>` tag that enable you to add images and color to the background. Other Netscape extensions enable you to specify the color of normal text and links. Both Netscape and Internet Explorer support these `<BODY>` tag extensions.

With the BACKGROUND attribute, you can specify an image to be used as the background for the document. The image is tiled or repeated to fill the background area. You can use tiling to create design effects using small images. The best image formats to use for background images are GIF and JPEG, which are fully supported by Netscape and Internet Explorer. Here is how you can specify a background image:

```
<BODY BACKGROUND="concrete.gif">
```

TIP

You can use the BGCOLOR attribute with the BACKGROUND attribute to specify a color to use when the background image cannot be displayed. If the background image cannot be displayed for any reason, such as the user has turned off the auto load image feature of their browser, the background color you specified will be displayed. Additionally, if you do not specify a background color and the background you specified cannot be displayed, the browser will not use your color assignments for text and links. This is a fail-safe that ensures you didn't specify text and link colors that would conflict with the standard gray background.

252

Using the BGCOLOR attribute, you can specify a color for the background. The background color can be expressed as a hexadecimal value or a color name. However, only the Internet Explorer supports color names. Here is how you can specify a background color for your documents:

```
<BODY BGCOLOR="#00FF00">
<BODY BGCOLOR="BLUE">
```

CAUTION

Browsers ignore tags, attributes, or assignments they do not support. Until the Netscape Navigator or HTML 3.0 supports color names, I recommend that you do not use color names for backgrounds. Instead of the color name, use the hexadecimal value for the color. This will avoid conflicts when Netscape or other browsers ignore the color name assignments.

Black text on a black background is unreadable. When you use background images or colors, you will normally need to specify the color for text and links to ensure the text and links are readable. To assign colors to text and links, Netscape introduced four additional attributes for the <BODY> tag:

TEXT="#rrggbb"	Specifies the color for normal text
LINK="#rrggbb"	Specifies the color for links that are unvisited
ALINK="#rrggbb"	Specifies the color for active links
VLINK="#rrggbb"	Specifies the color for visited links

Using Internet Explorer, you can specify a color name instead of a hexadecimal value. Color name values could be used in a <BODY> tag as follows:

```
<BODY BGCOLOR="BLUE" TEXT="WHITE" LINK="YELLOW"
➥ALINK="LIGHT GRAY" VLINK="DARK GRAY">
```

Using the Internet Explorer 2.0 extension for background properties, you can create background patterns that do not scroll. Nonscrolling background patterns are called watermarks. Watermarks are much more effective than the traditional scrolling backgrounds. To create a watermark, you specify a background image and set the BGPROPERTIES attribute as follows:

```
<BODY BACKGROUND="dazzle.gif" BGPROPERTIES=FIXED>
```

	HTML 3.0	*Netscape 1.0*	*Netscape 2.0*	*IE 1.0*	*IE 2.0*
ALINK=#rrggbb	yes	yes	yes	yes	yes
ALINK=name	no	no	no	yes	yes
BACKGROUND=image.gif	yes	yes	yes	yes	yes
BGCOLOR=#rrggbb	yes	yes	yes	yes	yes
BGCOLOR=name	no	no	no	yes	yes

	HTML 3.0	Netscape 1.0	Netscape 2.0	IE 1.0	IE 2.0
BGPROPERTIES=FIXED	no	no	no	yes	yes
LINK=#rrggbb	yes	yes	yes	yes	yes
LINK=name	no	no	no	yes	yes
TEXT=#rrggbb	yes	yes	yes	yes	yes
TEXT=name	no	no	no	yes	yes
VLINK=#rrggbb	yes	yes	yes	yes	yes
VLINK=name	no	no	no	yes	yes

List Enhancements

Both Netscape and Internet Explorer support several useful extensions for lists. Using the TYPE attribute, you define the shape of bullet to use for unordered lists and the style of lettering or numbering to use for ordered lists. For unordered lists, you can use these values with the unordered list tag:

<UL TYPE=CIRCLE>	Use an open circle for the bullet
<UL TYPE=SQUARE>	Use a square for the bullet
<UL TYPE=DISC>	Use a solid circle for the bullet, which is the default

The default values used for ordered lists are numerals. When you nest ordered lists, the numerals change to an appropriate level for outlines. You can override this sequencing with the TYPE attribute as follows:

<OL TYPE=A>	Use capital letters for the ordered list elements
<OL TYPE=a>	Use lowercase letters for the ordered list elements
<OL TYPE=I>	Use Roman numerals for the ordered list elements
<OL TYPE=i>	Use lowercase Roman numerals for the ordered list elements
<OL TYPE=1>	Use numerals for the ordered list elements, which is the default

You can set items in an ordered list to start at specific value using the START attribute. You assign a numeric value to the START attribute even if you are using letters or roman numerals to sequence your ordered list. This code specifies that the list will start with the capital letter D:

```
<OL TYPE=A START=4>
```

NOTE

The START attribute corresponds to the SEQNUM attribute in HTML 3.0. As support for HTML 3.0 becomes more widespread, you will want to consider using the SEQNUM attribute instead of the START attribute.

	HTML 3.0	Netscape 1.0	Netscape 2.0	IE 1.0	IE 2.0
`<UL TYPE=name>`	no	yes	yes	yes	yes
`<OL TYPE=x>`	no	yes	yes	yes	yes
`<OL START=n>`	no	yes	yes	yes	yes

Using Dynamic Sources to Create Inline Motion Video

Internet Explorer 2.0 takes the prize for developing one of the most innovative enhancements to the HTML specification. Using Internet Explorer's dynamic sources, you can incorporate motion video directly into your publication. Although the Internet Explorer currently supports motion video only in Microsoft's AVI format, direct browser support for inline video is a major step toward true multimedia Web publications.

The development team at Microsoft considered very carefully how to incorporate video into publications and devised a way to incorporate video into existing pages without altering the way users without the Internet Explorer browser see the page. This key concept for dynamic sources avoids leaving a gaping hole in the document where the video should be. To do this, the developers decided to extend the image tag and add an attribute called DYNSRC, which enables you to specify an SRC image and a DYNSRC video. While users with an Internet Explorer-capable browser see the video, users without an Internet Explorer-capable browser see the image.

The value you assign to the DYNSRC attribute is the URL to your video, such as

```
<IMG SRC="SUNSET.GIF" DYNSRC="SUNSET.AVI">
```

You can combine the WIDTH and HEIGHT attributes to ensure the video and the image use the same space on the screen. Here is how you do this:

```
<IMG SRC="SUNSET.GIF" DYNSRC="SUNSET.AVI" WIDTH=50 HEIGHT=50>
```

You can add the ALIGN attribute to position the video on the page or to align text into a column beside the video. Here is how you could right align the video:

```
<IMG SRC="SUNSET.GIF" DYNSRC="SUNSET.AVI" WIDTH=50 HEIGHT=50 ALIGN=RIGHT>
```

To allow more control over the video, the following attributes for the `<IMG>` tag were also introduced:

```
CONTROLS
LOOP
LOOPDELAY
START
```

	HTML 3.0	Netscape 1.0	Netscape 2.0	IE 1.0	IE 2.0
`<IMG DYNSRC=VIDEO.AVI>`	no	no	no	no	yes

Controls for the Video

By default, user controls for the video are not displayed. To add a basic set of user controls below the video frame, you use the CONTROLS attribute. The basic controls include play, stop, fast forward, and reverse. While there is only one set of controls at this time, Microsoft has plans to offer more control over the style and functionality of the controls.

Here's how you use the CONTROLS attribute with the DYNSRC attribute:

```
<IMG SRC="NYCITY.JPEG" DYNSRC="NYCITY.AVI" WIDTH=45 HEIGHT=45 CONTROLS>
```

Looping the Video

Inline videos normally play only once. You can change this default using the LOOP attribute. The LOOP attribute is used to specify the number of times the video plays. You can set the loop to a specific value, such as LOOP=3. If you want the video to continue to loop as long as the reader is on the page, you can set the value to LOOP=INFINITE or LOOP=-1.

Using the LOOPDELAY attribute, you can specify how long the video waits before looping. As the loop delay is expressed in milliseconds, the following video clip will play once, then wait two seconds before playing the video the second time:

```
<IMG SRC="INDY500.JPEG" DYNSRC="INDY500.AVI" LOOP=2 LOOPDELAY=2000>
```

Starting the Video

The START attribute enables you to set the video so it will play automatically. This is done in two key ways. Either the video will play automatically when the file is fully opened, or the video will play automatically when the user moves the mouse over the video. The values you use to do this are

```
START=FILEOPEN
START=MOUSEOVER
```

Internet Explorer creates an interesting way to use these values by enabling you to combine them. The following video will start when the file is completely downloaded and whenever the user moves the mouse cursor over the video:

```
<IMG SRC="SURFSUP.JPEG" DYNSRC="SURFSUP.AVI" START="FILEOPEN,MOUSEOVER">
```

Creating Documents with Sound Tracks

As you saw in Chapter 7, "Adding Multimedia Features with HTML," sound is a powerful enhancement to any document. Internet Explorer 2.0 introduces another innovation for Web publications by enabling you to create documents with soundtracks. Internet Explorer 2.0 directly supports audio files in Microsoft's WAV format, Sun Microsystem's AU format, or in the MIDI format. You add a soundtrack to a document using the `<BGSOUND>` tag.

The `<BGSOUND>` tag has the following attributes:

```
SRC
LOOP
LOOPDELAY
```

The source audio file you specify with the SRC attribute will start playing when it is fully down-loaded. By default, the sound file will play only once. You can change this default using the LOOP attribute. The LOOP attribute specifies the number of times the audio file plays. You can set the loop to a specific value, such as LOOP=5. If you want the soundtrack to continue to loop as long as the reader is on the page, you can set the value to LOOP=INFINITE or LOOP=-1. To set a delay time between loops you can use the LOOPDELAY attribute. The following soundtrack will play three times:

```
<BGSOUND SRC="../SOUNDS/WAVES.AU" LOOP=3>
```

> **NOTE**
>
> If you are testing a sound that you do not want to loop, you can choose Refresh from the View menu to play the sound again.

	HTML 3.0	Netscape 1.0	Netscape 2.0	IE 1.0	IE 2.0
`<BGSOUND>`	no	no	no	no	yes

Using Scrolling Marquees

Scrolling marquees are moving banners that scroll across the screen. Using this feature of Internet Explorer 2.0, you can provide readers with real-time information like stock reports, sports scores, and late-breaking news. You can also animate advertisements and any other type of information you want to provide at the site.

The tag you use to create a scrolling marquee is called MARQUEE. The begin marquee tag, `<MARQUEE>`, marks the beginning of text you want to scroll. The end marquee tag, `</MARQUEE>`, marks the ending of text you want to scroll. If you specify text within a `<MARQUEE>` tag pair with no attributes, the text will scroll continuously from the right to the left:

```
<MARQUEE>This text will scroll from right to left by default</MARQUEE>
```

Marquees are animated billboards in cyberspace. While marquees can be located anywhere within the body of your HTML document, the key to using marquees is to position them smartly and in an area where they will not be a distraction. The best locations for scrolling marquees are in the top or bottom portion of a document. In this way, the marquee is seen either immediately or when the user is nearly finished reading the page.

The development team at Microsoft did a great job of ensuring scrolling marquees aren't as distracting as blinking text. To do this, they provided a number of controls over how a marquee is animated, sized, positioned, and more importantly, when a marquee ceases to scroll. The attributes that enable you to do this are

```
ALIGN
BEHAVIOR
BGCOLOR
DIRECTION
HEIGHT
HSPACE
LOOP
SCROLLAMOUNT
SCROLLDELAY
VSPACE
WIDTH
```

	HTML 3.0	Netscape 1.0	Netscape 2.0	IE 1.0	IE 2.0
<MARQUEE>	no	no	no	no	yes

Positioning a Marquee

Think of a marquee as an object on the page whose position can be fine-tuned with three alignment attributes. Using the ALIGN attribute, you can specify how text around the marquee will be aligned. Using the HSPACE attribute, you define the amount of horizontal space between the area reserved for the marquee and surrounding text and objects. Using the VSPACE attribute, you define the amount of vertical space between the area reserved for the marquee and surrounding text and objects.

For marquees, the ALIGN attribute has three values that enable you to align text around the marquee with the top, middle, or bottom of the marquee. These values are

```
ALIGN=TOP
ALIGN=MIDDLE
ALIGN=BOTTOM
```

The HSPACE and VSPACE attributes enable you to enhance the impact of the marquee by creating white space around it. You use the HSPACE attribute to add white space to the left and right margins and use the VSPACE attribute to add white space to the top and bottom margins. The value for the HSPACE and VSPACE attributes is defined in pixels. The following marquee has a 10-pixel border all the way around it:

```
<MARQUEE HSPACE=10 VSPACE=10>Sale One Day Only $9.95</MARQUEE>
```

Sizing and Coloring a Marquee

Unless otherwise specified, marquees occupy only a minimum amount of screen space. You can reserve a larger area for the marquee using the WIDTH and HEIGHT attributes. The width of a marquee can be specified as an absolute value in pixels or as a relative percentage of screen width. The height of a marquee can be specified as an absolute value in pixels or as a relative percentage of screen height.

Usually, you will want your marquee to run along the full length of the window. This makes the marquee easier to read and follow. This marquee occupies 25 percent of the screen height and 100 percent of the width:

```
<MARQUEE WIDTH=100% HEIGHT=25%>A full-length marquee is best</MARQUEE>
```

Setting the marquee text off from other text on the page is often important. To clearly differentiate between the area reserved for the marquee and other text, you can use the BGCOLOR attribute. You can combine a background color with a new font color as follows:

```
<MARQUEE BGCOLOR=WHITE><FONT COLOR=BLUE> Marquee Text </FONT></MARQUEE>
```

Animating a Marquee

The way marquees move across the screen can be controlled using five key attributes: BEHAVIOR, DIRECTION, LOOP, SCROLLAMOUNT, and SCROLLDELAY. Normally, marquees scroll in from the right, move all the way across the screen, and go completely off. You can change this behavior using these values for the BEHAVIOR attribute:

```
BEHAVIOR=SCROLL
BEHAVIOR=SLIDE
BEHAVIOR=ALTERNATE
```

While the value BEHAVIOR=SCROLL is the default, the other attributes enable you to animate the marquee in unique ways. A sliding marquee starts completely off one side of the screen, scrolls all the way into position, and then stops. An alternative marquee starts completely off one side of the screen, scrolls in until it touches the far margin, then moves back and forth within the area reserved for the marquee.

Using the DIRECTION attribute, you can change the default value DIRECTION=LEFT to DIRECTION=RIGHT. The following marquee will scroll from the left to the right:

```
<MARQUEE DIRECTION=RIGHT> Check out the new section! </MARQUEE>
```

You can use the LOOP attribute to specify how many times a marquee should loop. While the value you assign to LOOP is normally a positive value, you can use the value LOOP=INFINITE or LOOP=-1 to cause the marquee to loop indefinitely.

Two attributes control how fast a marquee moves across the screen. You use the SCROLLAMOUNT attribute to specify the number of pixels the marquee moves each time it is drawn on the screen. You use the SCROLLDELAY attribute to specify the wait in milliseconds between each successive redraw.

Here's a slow-moving marquee:

```
<MARQUEE WIDTH=75% HEIGHT=10% HSPACE=5 VSPACE=5 BEHAVIOR=ALTERNATE
➥LOOP=INFINITE ALIGN=MIDDLE SCROLLAMOUNT=10 SCROLLDELAY=500>
Slow Marquee </MARQUEE>
```

Here's a fast-moving marquee:

```
<MARQUEE WIDTH=100% HEIGHT=10% BEHAVIOR=SCROLL LOOP=INFINITE ALIGN=MIDDLE
➥CROLLAMOUNT=25 SCROLLDELAY=10> Fast Marquee </MARQUEE>
```

Using Netscape Plug-ins and Embedded Multimedia Objects

The Netscape Navigator 2.0 plug-ins extend the capabilities of the browser and provide native support for new data types. Netscape plug-ins are player or reader modules for software applications that are created specifically for use with the Netscape Navigator. Most plug-ins are designed to be used on a specific platform, such as Windows 95 or Macintosh. However, some plug-ins, like those programmed in Java, can be platform-independent. You can find Netscape plug-ins for Macromedia Director, Apple QuickTime movies, Adobe Acrobat PDF documents, Microsoft Video For Windows, and Java.

Although plug-ins for the Netscape Navigator are created primarily by third-party vendors, they provide features which, when merged with the baseline features, are indistinguishable to the user. This means the end-user can use a plug-in without having to worry about why or how the plug-in is activated and what happens when the plug-in is activated. The way you incorporate files for use with plug-ins is with the <EMBED> tag.

Netscape designed the specification for plug-ins with three things in mind:

1. Plug-ins should be seamless for users.
2. Plug-ins should offer plug-in writers maximum flexibility.
3. Plug-ins should be fully functional across platforms.

	HTML 3.0	*Netscape 1.0*	*Netscape 2.0*	*IE 1.0*	*IE 2.0*
`<EMBED>`	no	no	yes	no	yes

Seamless Incorporation

Plug-ins are seamless because they are configured like built-in helper applications. If the plug-in is available, it is used without having to open a separate window to display the output. The output of the plug-in is displayed in the current window. If a plug-in is not available, the browser will look in the helper application configuration table to find an application that can be used to display the object inline. The output of the helper application is also displayed in the current window. This design concept enables you to embed any type of object into your Netscape-enhanced documents. For example, if your browser is configured to use Windows Paintbrush to display PCX-formatted images, the following embedded element would start Windows Paintbrush, build the image called TIGER.PCX, and then display the image wherever and however you placed it in the current document:

```
<EMBED SRC="TIGER.PCX">
```

Maximum Flexibility

Plug-ins offer plug-in writers maximum flexibility in that the plug-in writers can define the attributes for the `<EMBED>` tag. These attributes can be used to control how the plug-in behaves. For example, Netscape developers created an AVI plug-in called npavi32.dll to demonstrate the capabilities of plug-ins. The AVI plug-in can be used in full-screen or embedded mode. In full mode, the video player displays in the center of the current window. Users can see the control buttons and manipulate the associated video file on their own. In embedded mode, users can use two attributes to specify the behavior for the inline video: AUTOSTART and LOOP.

The AUTOSTART and LOOP attributes can be set to TRUE or FALSE. When AUTOSTART is set to TRUE, the associated video will play as soon as it is finished downloading. Otherwise, the associated video will play only when the user starts it. The LOOP attribute is used to turn looping on or off. When LOOP is set to TRUE, the video will loop indefinitely. Otherwise, the video will play only once. Here's how you can embed an AVI video in the popular 320×200 display size:

```
<EMBED SRC=SURFSUP.AVI WIDTH=320 HEIGHT=200 AUTOSTART=TRUE LOOP=TRUE>
```

If the end-user has obtained the npavi32.dll plug-in, the video will automatically start when fully loaded and will loop indefinitely. If the end-user does not have the npavi32.dll plug-in but has configured a helper application to handle AVI files, the appropriate player will be called to play the video.

Full Functionality

The August 1995 specification for plug-ins looked closely at the functionality of plug-ins. The <EMBED> tag can be used in any HTML document. The values you pass to plug-ins are platform-independent, meaning an attribute that is valid for a Windows 95 version of a plug-in should be valid for a Macintosh version of the plug-in. Regardless of platform, plug-ins can be used in one of three modes:

- Embedded
- Full-screen
- Hidden

In embedded mode, the output of the plug-in is placed in the current window. This means embedded objects are a part of a larger HTML document and can be used just like GIF and JPEG images. Embedded plug-ins can be used with inline video, animation, graphic objects, and anything else you want to display within the current window. A key concept with embedded plug-ins is that they can be highly interactive. For example, if the plug-in allows for it, you could use all the controls for dynamic sources and apply them to your embedded object.

You can use embedded objects like any other type of object on the page. Here's how you can link an embedded image to another document:

```
<A HREF="background.html"><EMBED SRC="BIO.BMP"></A>
```

In full-screen mode, the output of the plug-in fills the browser's inner window but leaves the user controls in place. This means users have full access to Netscape's pulldown menus, toolbar, directory buttons, and URL window. Full-screen plug-ins can be used with any type of object including, video, animation, and graphic objects. The Adobe Acrobat plug-in uses the full-screen mode. Using the Acrobat plug-in, you can access PDF documents. The following line of code would use the Acrobat plug-in if available to display the associated PDF document:

```
<EMBED SRC="AFILE.PDF">
```

In hidden mode, the output of the plug-in is not seen on the screen. Hidden plug-ins can be used with any files that users do not have to see to experience, like an audio file. Hidden plug-ins can also be used to perform background functions, like decrypting or decompressing files for display.

The specification also looked at how plug-ins interact with other plug-ins and the browser itself. Plug-ins can direct output to other plug-ins. This output can be used to display files and open new windows. Plug-ins also have full access to the capabilities of the browser, including the capability to use URLs. This means files displayed with plug-ins can use hypertext references and retrieve other files as necessary.

Document Design Using Unique Extensions

Designing documents with unique extensions enables you to provide advanced enhancements to your Web documents. The enhancements are the driving force behind the widespread popularity of the Netscape Navigator and the Internet Explorer. More than 15 million Web users have the Netscape Navigator or a Netscape-capable browser. The Netscape Navigator Version 1.0 supports some HTML 3.0 features and unique extensions to HTML, including blink, center, backgrounds, font enhancements, image enhancements, and tables. In fall 1995, beta testing of the Netscape Navigator Version 2.0 was nearly completed. Netscape Navigator 2.0 introduces more unique extensions to the HTML standard, including frames and embedding multimedia objects.

Internet Explorer debuted in August 1995. Version 1.0 of the Internet Explorer supports all extensions that the Netscape Navigator 1.0 supports except for blinking text tables and the following unique extensions: true font color, font type, and client-side image maps. Within one month after the debut of Internet Explorer Version 1.0, Microsoft released Internet Explorer Version 2.0. Internet Explorer 2.0 adds support for tables and introduced unique extensions for inline video, inline sound, and scrolling marquees. In the first few months of the debut of the Internet Explorer, millions of Web users downloaded the Internet Explorer.

The mix of old and new versions of Netscape and Internet Explorer, with their varying support for key enhancements to the HTML standard, introduces serious compatibility problems for Web publishers. To get around these problems, many Web publishers create their home page using HTML 2.0 and enable users to branch off to text-only, graphics-enhanced, and Netscape-enhanced pages. This requires the publisher to create three different versions of every page at the Web site. A Web site of 100 pages becomes a Web site of 300 pages. A Web site of 1,000 pages becomes a Web site of 3,000 pages. What happens if you want to enhance your site for Netscape 2.0 frames and Internet Explorer? Do you now create five different versions of every page at the Web site? Do you see the problem here?

The basic solution many Web publishers have adopted is just that, a basic solution. It works today. But in the increasingly complex world of Web publishing, the basic solution of alternate paths through the Web site quickly becomes tedious. Web publishers who understand how the pieces of the HTML standard and enhancements to the standard fit together have adopted more practical solutions.

One solution is to build pages with features for everyone who visits the site, using tags that will not make the page useless to any single group of users. For example, if you use image tags and define alternate text to display instead of the image, you do not need text-only pages. If you use the Netscape <CENTER> tag, a browser that does not support the <CENTER> tag will merely display the elements left-aligned and not centered. However, if you include HTML 3.0 tables in your document and do not include formatting within the table for browsers that do not support tables, the information in the table will be useless to certain users.

The introduction of Netscape frames created another solution for Web publishers who want to feature unique enhancements in their Web pages. While it means you have to create two versions of key pages, it is better than having to create three, four, or five versions of all your Web pages. In the NOFRAME area of the page, you add elements for browsers that are not Netscape 2.0-compliant. In the FRAME SRC element, you reference a Netscape 2.0-enhanced page. Browsers that are not Netscape 2.0-compliant will use the NOFRAME area. Browsers that are Netscape 2.0 complaint will use the page referenced in the FRAME SRC element. For more information on frames see Chapter 9, "Designing Tables and Frames."

Another solution for Web publishers who want to feature unique enhancements in their Web pages is to create documents on the fly based on the type of the user's browser. While this is an advanced solution, it is the best long-term solution available to Web publishers. (See Chapter 11, "Writing CGI Scripts," for more information on creating gateway scripts.)

Summary

The Netscape Navigator and the Internet Explorer offer many enhancements to the HTML specification. You can use these enhancements to dramatically improve the impact of your documents. Layout extras provide better control over the positioning of text and objects. Font enhancements enable you to select font type, color, and relative size. Body tag extensions enable you to use background images and colors. Dynamic Sources provides you with a way to add inline motion video. Using background sounds, you can create documents with soundtracks. Using scrolling marquees, you can create moving billboards. Finally, plug-ins and embedded multimedia objects enable you to extend the capabilities of browsers in a way that is seamless, highly flexible, and fully functional across platforms.

Designing Tables and Frames

9

*by William
Robert Stanek*

IN THIS CHAPTER

Tables are one of the most sought-after features in the HTML 3.0 specification and until recently, the Netscape Navigator was the only mainstream browser to support this feature. Yet the Netscape Navigator did much more than merely support HTML 3.0 tables, it helped pioneer the use of tables in Web publishing. In recognition of this, the current table model used in HTML 3.0 provides backwards compatibility with Netscape's table definition.

With frames, Netscape took one of the most powerful features of popular publishing applications and incorporated them into HTML in grand style. Frames enable you to create documents with multiple windows and in doing so, open the door for an entirely new way to Web publish. Each frame is a mini-page within your Web publication. You can add scroll bars to a frame, enable users to manipulate the size of the frame, and add frames for permanent headers, footers, and menu bars. Hypertext references within frames can contain pointers to any window defined on the page or can be used to launch an entirely new full-sized window. You can even create frames within frames.

This chapter shows you how to design tables and frame-enhanced documents.

> **NOTE**
>
> Learning the most current information on HTML tables and publishing pages that are current with the times is extremely important. The table model has changed drastically since the original implementation. Consequently, this section describes tables as defined in the current draft of the HTML 3.0 specification. If you use tables as outlined in this section, your tables should be fully compliant with HTML 3.0 and backward-compatible with Netscape and Internet Explorer. The next major upgrade to the Netscape Navigator and Internet Explorer should fully support the current table model and display your tables precisely as outlined here. However, Netscape Navigator and Internet Explorer versions 2.0 and older can only use attributes defined in their DTDs. Basically, this means your fully HTML 3.0-compliant tables will look best in a fully HTML 3.0-compliant browser. If you are concerned about the display of your tables in older browsers, use the checklist at the end of each section to help you select supported attributes.

Table Design

No doubt you've seen tables in publications, like those used throughout *Web Publishing Un-leashed*, and may have used tables in your own documents as well. In general, tables have a caption and one or more rows of data organized into columns. The columns of data contain individual cells. Each individual cell is either a header or a data set. While a table can have several levels of headings, all headings serve to identify the data sets contained in the body of the table. Some tables also have footers. Footers are used to make annotations within the table. Thus, tables have three basic parts: header, body, and footer.

After breaking tables into their component parts, the developers of the table model looked at how the data within a table should be displayed by browsers. This was a major area of concern. Web publishers have no direct control over the size of the window used to display a table, which means table data defined in absolute terms, such as pixels or characters, could easily get obscured or clipped. To avoid this, the developers made it possible to define column width in relative terms as well as absolute terms.

Defining a table in relative terms enables you to specify a size that is a percentage of the current window size. The browser displaying the table will size the table accordingly using the currently defined font. The default size for a table is the current window size. Thus, if you do not specify a width for your table, the WIDTH attribute is set to 100 percent. However, as Figure 9.1 shows, tables created using the default sizing will only use as much space as they need.

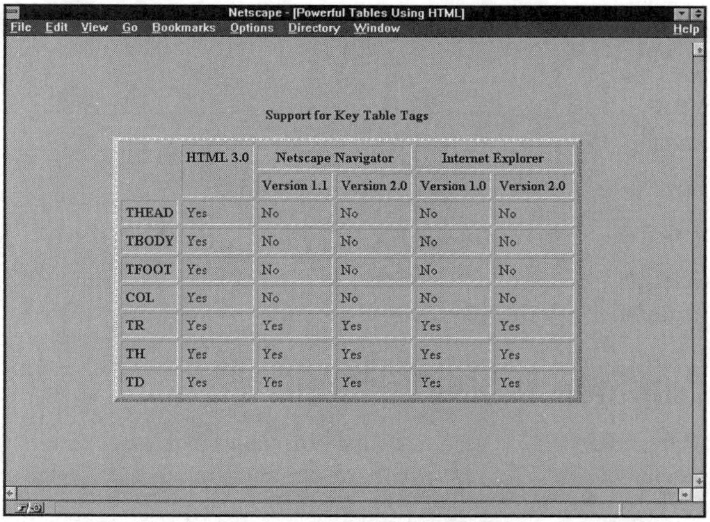

FIGURE 9.1.

Tables are powerful additions to your documents.

Netscape - [Powerful Tables Using HTML]

File Edit View Go Bookmarks Options Directory Window   Help

Support for Key Table Tags

	HTML 3.0	Netscape Navigator		Internet Explorer	
		Version 1.1	Version 2.0	Version 1.0	Version 2.0
THEAD	Yes	No	No	No	No
TBODY	Yes	No	No	No	No
TFOOT	Yes	No	No	No	No
COL	Yes	No	No	No	No
TR	Yes	Yes	Yes	Yes	Yes
TH	Yes	Yes	Yes	Yes	Yes
TD	Yes	Yes	Yes	Yes	Yes

Another item the developers of the table model considered is network speed versus table size. Under the original implementation, the entire table had to be downloaded before any part of the table could be displayed. On a slow network or if your table is large, the wait could be rather long and sometimes longer than a Web user is willing to wait. To alleviate this problem, the current table model allows for incremental downloading of tables if you specify the number of columns and their widths in the begin table tag <TABLE>.

The table model is dynamic in other ways as well. You can

- Add images and figures for your table by defining the image or figure within a cell of your current table
- Add lists to your table by defining the list within a cell of your current table

■ Build forms within your table by defining the form within a cell of your current table

■ Create tables within your table by defining the new table within a cell of your current table

You define the header, body, and footer of an HTML table within the begin and end TABLE tag. Just as some of these parts are optional in traditional tables, they are also optional in HTML tables. The only mandatory part of a table is the table body. Each table you create can have one header section, one or more body sections, and one footer section. The most basic components of any table are the columns and rows that make up the table. You specify the basic components of a table as follows:

```
<TABLE>
<THEAD>
Header Information
<TBODY>
Data Set 1
<TBODY>
Data Set 2
<TBODY>
. . .
<TBODY>
Data Set N
<TFOOT>
Footer Information
</TABLE>
```

The following sections look at each of the basic parts and components for tables in turn, beginning with their common attributes.

Common Table Attributes

Many attributes are used to define how tables look on the page and whether the table should be incrementally loaded. Attributes common to most table elements include the following:

CLASS	Specifies a subclass for a tag. CLASS is normally used to display a tag in a different style based on a class type you've specified in a style sheet.
DIR	Specifies the direction for text layout. While English text is read from left to right, some Asian languages are read from right to left. Using DIR with the LANG attribute, you can specify the text layout as left to right by setting a value of DIR=LTR or right to left by setting a value of DIR=RTL.
ID	Labels an element with a keyword. If you activate a hypertext reference containing a keyword that matches the element's ID, the browser will jump to the section of the document containing the ID.
LANG	Specifies the language to be used for the element. You can use this attribute with the optional DIR attribute if the language is read from right to left instead of left to right.

UNITS   Specifies the type of unit for all numeric values in the associated tag. The implied default is UNITS=PIXELS. You can also specify en units with UNITS=EN.

	HTML 3.0	*Netscape 1.0*	*Netscape 2.0*	*IE 1.0*	*IE 2.0*
CLASS	yes	no	no	no	no
DIR	yes	no	no	no	no
ID	yes	no	no	no	no
LANG	yes	no	no	no	no
UNITS	yes	no	no	no	no

The *<TABLE>* Tag

The table model has advanced significantly since the first draft of HTML 3.0. In many ways, the current model is more flexible and more powerful. This flexibility and power stems largely from the control you have over the way tables are used in your documents. Using the many attributes of the <TABLE> tag, you can define precisely where and how tables are displayed on the page. To specify a table, you use the begin and end TABLE tags.

Valid attributes for the begin table tag <TABLE> include

    CLASS

    DIR

    ID

    LANG

    UNITS

    BORDER

    CELLPADDING

    CELLSPACING

    COLS

    FLOAT

    FRAME

    RULES

    WIDTH

While the ID, CLASS, DIR, LANG, and UNITS attributes are used as described earlier, the other attributes have unique uses when applied to the <TABLE> tag.

	HTML 3.0	Netscape 1.0	Netscape 2.0	IE 1.0	IE 2.0
BORDER	yes	yes	yes	yes	yes
CELLPADDING	yes	yes	yes	yes	yes
CELLSPACING	yes	yes	yes	yes	yes
COLS	yes	no	no	no	no
FLOAT	yes	no	no	no	no
FRAME	yes	no	no	no	no
RULES	yes	no	no	no	no
WIDTH	yes	yes	yes	yes	yes

BORDER and FRAME

Creating the border for a table in HTML 3.0 is generally a two-part process. You use the BORDER attribute to specify the width for framing around the table. You use the FRAME attribute to specify the style of the frame around the table. By default, tables do not have a frame.

You specify the type of framing for a table with these values:

FRAME=NONE	No frame around the table, the default.
FRAME=TOP	Put a frame only on the top of the table.
FRAME=BOTTOM	Put a frame only on the bottom of the table.
FRAME=TOPBOT	Put a frame on the top and bottom of the table.
FRAME=SIDES	Put a frame on the left and right side of the table.
FRAME=ALL	Put a frame on all four sides of the table.
FRAME=BORDER	Put a frame on all four sides of the table, which is the same as the value ALL.

While the values FRAME=BORDER and FRAME=ALL mean the same thing, they are used for different purposes. For backwards compatibility, if you insert the attribute BORDER into the <TABLE> tag without a value, such as <TABLE BORDER>, an HTML 3.0-compliant browser will assume you want the table to have a border on all four sides. The browser makes a substitution using the value FRAME=BORDER and interprets <TABLE BORDER> as <TABLE FRAME=BORDER BORDER=implied>.

Similarly, if you specify <TABLE BORDER=0>, as was possible under Netscape's table model, an HTML 3.0-compliant browser will assume you want the table to be displayed without a border. The browser interprets <TABLE BORDER=0> as <TABLE FRAME=NONE BORDER=0>. You can use the value FRAME=NONE as a design technique to remove extra white space around the table.

CELLPADDING and CELLSPACING

In terms of the readability of your table, CELLPADDING and CELLSPACING are the most important attributes you will define for the table. CELLPADDING is used to specify the spacing within data cells. CELLSPACING is used to specify the spacing between data cells. You specify padding and spacing in the current unit, normally pixels.

COLS

The COLS attribute is used to specify the number of columns in a table. The column number can be used by your browser to display the table incrementally as it is received. If you do not specify the number of columns, the browser will read all table data before displaying any portion of the table.

You can specify a table with four columns as follows:

```
<TABLE COLS=4>
```

FLOAT

Text in your documents can flow around tables. By default tables are aligned with the left margin and text will flow around the right side of the table. You can also align tables with the right margin, which will cause text to flow around the left side of the table. You set the alignment of your table using the FLOAT attribute. Values associated with the FLOAT attribute identify where the table floats on the page.

The developers of the table model chose the word float so as not to conflict with the ALIGN attribute used for other purposes in the table model. The two values for the FLOAT attribute are

```
FLOAT=LEFT
FLOAT=RIGHT
```

RULES

The RULES attribute is used to specify the type of horizontal and vertical lines to display within a table. By default, tables have no horizontal or vertical ruling lines separating columns and rows. As ruling lines serve to visually separate the parts of the table, you can increase the impact of the table by including some type of ruling.

The values for the RULES attribute are

RULES=NONE	No horizontal or vertical rules separating rows and columns.
RULES=BASIC	Separate the header, body, and footer elements with a horizontal rule.
RULES=ROWS	Separate all rows in the table with horizontal rules; some browsers may add a thicker line to the header, body, and footer elements.

272

| RULES=COLS | Separate all columns in the table with vertical rules and adds horizontal rules between header, body and footer elements. |
| RULES=ALL | Separate all elements in the table with horizontal and vertical rules. Some browsers may add a thicker line to the header, body and footer elements. |

WIDTH

The WIDTH attribute is used to specify the relative or absolute width of a table. The default WIDTH is the current window size. You can specify the width in units or as a percentage of the current window size. Any numeric value is interpreted in the current unit, normally pixels, unless you follow the value by a percent sign to define a relative width.

The size of this table is 25 percent of the current window size:

```
<TABLE WIDTH=25%>
```

Adding a Table Caption

After you specify how you want the basic components of the table to look, you may want to add a caption to the table. Captions provide an explanation or description of the data sets contained in a table. To define a caption, you use the begin and end CAPTION tags as follows:

```
<CAPTION>HTML Design Processes</CAPTION>
```

HTML 3.0 gives you some control over the placement of table captions using the ALIGN attribute. Used with captions, the ALIGN attribute has four values:

ALIGN=TOP	Places the caption above the table.
ALIGN=BOTTOM	Places the caption below the table.
ALIGN=LEFT	Places the caption on the left side of the table.
ALIGN=RIGHT	Places the caption on the right side of the table.

Whether the caption is right-aligned or centered at the position you specify is determined by browser displaying the caption. According to the HTML 3.0 specification, browsers should try to display the caption so it fits as appropriate for the width and height of the table. Other attributes you can use with the begin caption tag <CAPTION> include ID, LANG, CLASS, and DIR.

When adding a table caption, keep in mind the best captions are short and descriptive. One way to make the caption more readable is to use bold type. You can add bold type to a caption placed on the right side of a table as follows:

```
<CAPTION ALIGN=RIGHT><B>HTML Design Processes</B></CAPTION>
```

	HTML 3.0	Netscape 1.0	Netscape 2.0	IE 1.0	IE 2.0
ALIGN=TOP	yes	yes	yes	yes	yes
ALIGN=BOTTOM	yes	yes	yes	yes	yes
ALIGN=LEFT	yes	no	no	no	no
ALIGN=RIGHT	yes	no	no	no	no

Defining Attributes for Columns

Before you define the rows and individual cells that make up a table, you may want to specify general rules for all the columns within the table. You do this using the optional <COL> tag. In addition to the common attributes defined earlier, you can use these attributes with the <COL> tag:

ALIGN

CHAR

CHAROFF

VALIGN

WIDTH

SPAN

	HTML 3.0	Netscape 1.0	Netscape 2.0	IE 1.0	IE 2.0
<COL>	yes	no	no	no	no

Horizontal Alignment of Cells in a Column

You can specify the horizontal alignment of data within a cell using the ALIGN attribute. For the <COL> tag, you can use these alignment values:

ALIGN=LEFT

ALIGN=RIGHT

ALIGN=CENTER

ALIGN=JUSTIFY

ALIGN=CHAR

The default alignment for headings in a table is ALIGN=CENTER. The default alignment for data sets in a table is ALIGN=LEFT. Aligning data in column cells based on a character using the value ALIGN=CHAR is often useful, especially for numeric values containing decimal points. For a column aligned on a character, you must specify what character to align with. You do this using the CHAR attribute. The key to using characters for alignment within cells is to use a unique character. To align a column of cells based on a decimal point, you could use the following:

```
<COL ALIGN=CHAR CHAR=.>
```

With the `CHAROFF` attribute, you can specify an offset for the character you are using for alignment. The offset is a positional value expressed as a percentage of the cell width. An offset of zero aligns your unique character with the left cell wall. The default offset of 50 centers the unique character within the cell. An offset of 100 aligns the unique character with the right cell wall. You should use the `CHAR` and `CHAROFF` attributes only with the `ALIGN` attribute. Here's an offset to partially right align the data points using a percent sign as the unique character:

```
<COL ALIGN=CHAR CHAR=% OFFSET=75>
```

	HTML 3.0	Netscape 1.0	Netscape 2.0	IE 1.0	IE 2.0
ALIGN=LEFT	yes	yes	yes	yes	yes
ALIGN=RIGHT	yes	yes	yes	yes	yes
ALIGN=CENTER	yes	yes	yes	yes	yes
ALIGN=JUSTIFY	yes	no	no	no	no
ALIGN=CHAR	yes	no	no	no	no
CHAR	yes	no	no	no	no
CHAROFF	yes	no	no	no	no

Vertical Alignment of Cells in a Column

You can specify the vertical alignment of data within a cell using the `VALIGN` attribute. For the `<COL>` tag, you can use these alignment values:

```
VALIGN=TOP

VALIGN=MIDDLE

VALIGN=BOTTOM

VALIGN=BASELINE
```

The default alignment for headings and data used in tables is `VALIGN=MIDDLE`. To vertically align the first line of text in all the cells in the same row, you can use the `VALIGN=BASELINE`. While the baseline alignment is useful, keep in mind subsequent lines of text after the first line may not be aligned along a common baseline. Here is how you can align the cells of a column with the bottom of the cell:

```
<COL VALIGN=BOTTOM>
```

	HTML 3.0	Netscape 1.0	Netscape 2.0	IE 1.0	IE 2.0
VALIGN=TOP	yes	yes	yes	yes	yes
VALIGN=MIDDLE	yes	yes	yes	yes	yes
VALIGN=BOTTOM	yes	yes	yes	yes	yes
VALIGN=BASELINE	yes	yes	yes	yes	yes

Applying Attributes to Multiple Columns

Usually, the attributes assigned to a particular <COL> tag apply to one column in a table. So, a four-column table could have up to four <COL> tags to define the attributes for cells associated with each column. Using the SPAN attribute, you can apply assignments in a COL element to two or more columns.

The next example contains a partial definition for a table of five columns. Data within the cells of the first column on the table will be justified and aligned with the top of the cell. Data in the next four columns is defined by the single COL element with the SPAN attribute and will be aligned based on the position of the colon character. Here is the sample code:

```
<TABLE BORDER=5 FLOAT=RIGHT CELLPADDING=5 FRAME=ALL RULES=BASIC COLS=5>
<CAPTION ALIGN=LEFT>HTML Design Processes</CAPTION>
<COL ALIGN=JUSTIFY VALIGN=TOP>
<COL ALIGN=CHAR CHAR=: CHAROFF=25 SPAN=4>
 . . .
</TABLE>
```

Defining a Width for a Column of Cells

Usually, column width is determined by the number of characters in the first heading or data set in the column. You can override this function by specifying a relative or absolute width for the column. You do this with the WIDTH attribute of the <COL> tag. For compatibility with tables representation in other table models and particularly in the SGML CALS model, column width does not follow the same rules for widths used elsewhere in HTML 3.0. You specify absolute widths in the current unit by specifying a value. However, you do not specify the relative column width using the percent sign. Instead, you add an asterisk as the suffix for the value, such as

```
<COL WIDTH=0.25*>
```

While the asterisk character used with widths may seem confusing, it serves as a reminder that the behavior of relative widths for columns is different from other relative widths. The value 0.25 is not a percentage of the cell size and the total of your column widths do not need to add up to 100. Rather, the value 0.25 is a weighted factor pertaining to the allocated widths for other columns. If you assigned 2.0 units of width to all columns in the table, the column with the value 0.25 would have a width approximately 12.25 percent of the table's total width.

Using relative widths in this manner is better than using percentages. It saves you the trouble of trying to ensure all your column widths add up to 100 percent of the table width. It enables you to manipulate an individual column size as necessary. It also enables you to remove or add columns without recomputing percentages for width.

Defining the Main Sections of a Table

The main sections of any table are the head, body, and foot elements. You define these elements with the following tags:

```
<THEAD> Table Header </THEAD>
<TBODY> Table Body </TBODY>
<TFOOT> Table Footer </TFOOT>
```

The only mandatory part of a table is the body element. While all tables must include one or more body elements, a table can only have one header section and one footer section. The table model defines a begin and end tag for the head, body, and foot elements. However, the end tags for these elements can generally be omitted. If the table has only body elements, the begin and end body tags can also be omitted. Thus, the minimum table definition could look like this:

```
<TABLE>
  . . .
</TABLE>
```

You would place row, column, and cell assignments where the ellipses are. As a minimum, each defined element must contain one row of data. Keep in mind, if you use a head or foot element, you will need to use the appropriate start tags to separate the component parts of the table. Ideally, browsers will use the head, body, and footer elements to display tables smartly. If the table extends beyond the current window, the browser may let the reader scroll through the data sets of the body section while the header and footer sections remain on the screen. Alternately, browsers may simply display the header and footer sections with the current page of the table and when the user advances to the next page, the browser would display a header and footer as appropriate.

The `<THEAD>`, `<TBODY>`, and `<TFOOT>` tags can be used with the following common attributes:

> CLASS
>
> DIR
>
> ID
>
> LANG
>
> UNITS

In addition to the common attributes, you can also use these alignment attributes:

> ALIGN
>
> CHAR
>
> CHAROFF
>
> VALIGN

The alignment attributes for header, body, and footer sections are used as described in the previous section. By making assignments in the header, body, or footer, you can override the defaults and column assignments you made with the <COL> tag.

The example below shows how the header, body, and footer sections could be added to a table. Note that the header section for the table has vertical and horizontal alignments that override the assignments made using the <COL> tag. Likewise, the footer for the table has vertical and horizontal alignments that override the assignments made using the <COL> tag. If you use a header or footer in your tables, you will probably want unique alignment for the data within associated cells. Here's the example:

```
<TABLE BORDER=5 FLOAT=RIGHT CELLPADDING=5 FRAME=ALL RULES=BASIC COLS=5>
<CAPTION ALIGN=LEFT>HTML Design Processes</CAPTION>
<COL ALIGN=JUSTIFY VALIGN=TOP>
<COL ALIGN=CHAR CHAR=: CHAROFF=25 SPAN=4>
<THEAD ALIGN=CENTER VALIGN=MIDDLE>
 . . .
<TBODY>
 . . .
<TBODY>
 . . .
<TBODY>
 . . .
<TFOOT ALIGN=LEFT VALIGN=BOTTOM>
</TABLE>
```

	HTML 3.0	Netscape 1.0	Netscape 2.0	IE 1.0	IE 2.0
<THEAD>	yes	no	no	no	no
<TBODY>	yes	no	no	no	no
<TFOOT>	yes	no	no	no	no

Creating Rows

All tables must contain one or more rows of data cells. Rows are defined within the header, body, or footer section of a table. Using the <TR> tag, you can define rows for each section your table contains. Thus, a table with one header, two body, and one footer section would have at least four rows. Only the begin <TR> tag is used in tables.

Table rows tags can be used with the following common attributes:

```
CLASS

DIR

ID

LANG

UNITS
```

Besides the common attributes, you can also use these alignment attributes:

ALIGN

CHAR

CHAROFF

VALIGN

The alignment attributes for table rows are used as described previously. By making assignments in a table row you can override the defaults, column assignments you made with the <COL> tag, and the section assignment you made with the <THEAD>, <TBODY>, or <TFOOT> tags. All table rows consist of one or more data cells. No matter the placement of cells, they can be defined as header cells or data cells.

	HTML 3.0	Netscape 1.0	Netscape 2.0	IE 1.0	IE 2.0
<TR>	yes	yes	yes	yes	yes
<TD>	yes	yes	yes	yes	yes
<TH>	yes	yes	yes	yes	yes

Creating Table Cells for Data and Headers

The assignments you make at the cell level are for the individual data sets or headings. Data cells contain the numbers, facts, and statements to display in the table. Using the <TD> tag, you can define data cells. Heading cells contain headings for sections, columns, and rows. Using the <TH> tag, you can define heading cells. To define cells within a row, you simply insert the cell data into the table after a row assignment as shown in the following example:

```
<TABLE BORDER=5 FLOAT=RIGHT CELLPADDING=5 FRAME=ALL RULES=BASIC COLS=5>
<CAPTION ALIGN=LEFT>HTML Design Processes</CAPTION>
<THEAD ALIGN=CENTER VALIGN=MIDDLE>
<TR><TH>Header Cell 1<TH>Header Cell 2<TH>Header Cell 3
<TH>Header Cell 4<TH>Header Cell 5
<TBODY>
<TR><TD>Body Row 1 Cell 1<TD>Body Row 1 Cell 2<TD>Body Row 1 Cell 3
<TD>Body Row 1 Cell 4<TD>Body Row 1 Cell 5
<TR><TD>Body Row 2 Cell 1<TD>Body Row 2 Cell 2<TD>Body Row 2 Cell 3
<TD>Body Row 2 Cell 4<TD>Body Row 2 Cell 5
</TABLE>
```

The definitions for table cells are extremely dynamic. Table cells use most of the previously defined attributes, including these:

ALIGN

CHAR

CHAROFF

CLASS

DIR

```
ID

LANG

UNITS

VALIGN
```

By making assignments in a table cell you override the defaults, column assignments you made with the `<COL>` tag, the section assignment you made with the `<THEAD>`, `<TBODY>`, or `<TFOOT>` tags, and the row assignment you made with the `<TR>` tag. Using the following additional attributes, you can define cells that span multiple columns and rows, disable automatic wrapping of text and more:

```
AXIS

AXES

BGCOLOR

COLSPAN

ROWSPAN

NOWRAP
```

	HTML 3.0	Netscape 1.0	Netscape 2.0	IE 1.0	IE 2.0
AXIS	yes	no	no	no	no
AXES	yes	no	no	no	no
BGCOLOR	no	no	no	no	yes
COLSPAN	yes	yes	yes	yes	yes
ROWSPAN	yes	yes	yes	yes	yes
NOWRAP	yes	yes	yes	yes	yes

Using the *AXIS* and *AXES* Attributes

The AXIS and AXES attributes are used to label cells. Using the AXIS attribute, you can label one cell with a keyword. Using the AXES attribute, you can label row and header attributes that pertain to the cell. The keyword for the row label is separated from the header label by a comma. Values you assign to the AXIS and AXES attributes are not displayed with the text of your table. Most tables you create will not need these attributes. However, you can use cell labels to represent field names from a database or to aid in converting the table data to other formats.

You could label a cell with these attributes as follows:

```
<TD AXIS="keyword" AXES="row header keyword, column header keyword">
```

Using Color in Table Cells

The Internet Explorer 2.0 enables you to add color to header and data cells using the BGCOLOR attribute. You can add color to a cell with a color name or hexadecimal value as described earlier in this chapter, such as

```
<TH BGCOLOR=#0000FF>
```

or

```
<TD BGCOLOR=#FF00FF>
```

The key to using color in your tables is to use it sparingly. You should test the readability of your text when used with this color. If the text is unreadable, use the <FONT> tag to change the color of the cell's text, such as

```
<TR><TD BGCOLOR=BLUE><FONT COLOR=WHITE>12.5%<TD BGCOLOR=BLUE>
<FONT COLOR=WHITE>15.8%<TD BGCOLOR=BLUE><FONT COLOR=YELLOW>28.3%
```

Creating Cells that Span Rows and Columns

HTML 3.0 gives you advanced control over the placements of cells within your tables. Using the COLSPAN attribute, you can create cells that span two or more columns. Using the ROWSPAN attribute, you can create cells that span two or more rows. By combining the COLSPAN and ROWSPAN attributes, you can create cells that span multiple columns and rows.

You can use the COLSPAN and ROWSPAN attributes with header and data cells. In a header, you can use COLSPAN to create major headings for sections of a table. If you use COLSPAN to span several column headers and define subheadings, you will need to use ROWSPAN in columns with only one level of heading to ensure the headings and cells line up appropriately. Here is an example of using COLSPAN and ROWSPAN in a multicolumn table with subheadings:

```
<TABLE BORDER=5 FRAME=TOPBOT>
<CAPTION ALIGN=LEFT>Developing HTML Publications</CAPTION>
<TR><TH ROWSPAN=2>Project Creation<TH COLSPAN=2>Project Design
<TH ROWSPAN=2>Project Publication
<TR><TH>Preliminary Design<TH>Phase II Design
```

Using *NOWRAP*

The NOWRAP attribute for header and data cells is used to disable the automatic wrapping of text. Lines of text that do not wrap may alter the appearance of your table by creating excessively wide cells. Therefore, you should use the NOWRAP attribute cautiously if at all. If you do use NOWRAP, view your table with a small screen size such as 640×480 for Windows systems or 13-inch for Macintosh systems. Here's how you can add NOWRAP to a data cell:

```
<TR><TH>Precise Calculation<TH>Variance
<TR><TD NOWRAP>12.872653872<TD NOWRAP>0.00000001
```

Combined Table Example

Combining the various table creation and design techniques discussed throughout this section is easy. Figure 9.2 shows how the first section of a table created to show how browser support for table tags and attributes could be turned into an HTML table. The key concepts of using column and row headers, setting alignments for columns and rows, and column and row spanning are used in the example.

FIGURE 9.2 .

Support for table features.

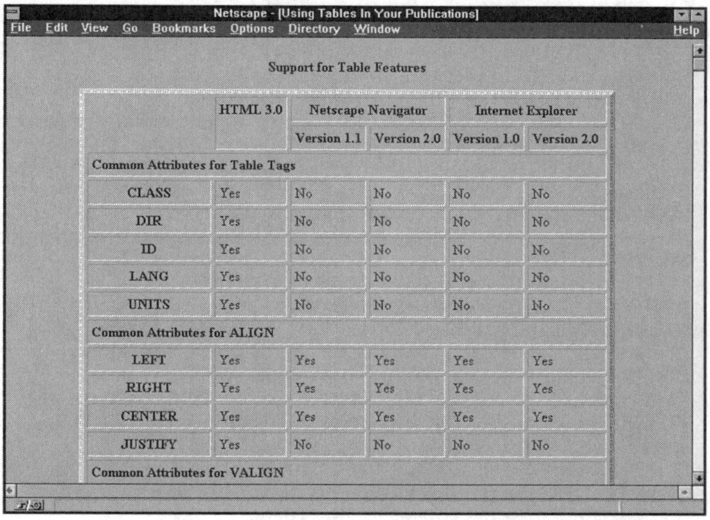

Tables can be a powerful addition to your documents. Use the example as a guideline for creating well-designed tables. The design concepts that went into making the table were simple, but when combined, created a more powerful table. Cell padding and spacing were used to increase the white space in the table and to ensure the data did not touch the cell walls. Headers and subheaders were used for columns. Headers were used for rows. The first letter of the table data was capitalized to enhance the readability of the table. While key table entries were left-aligned, their associated attributes were centered.

Listing 9.1 shows the full code for the example.

Listing 9.1. Using tables in your publications.

```
<HTML>
<HEAD><TITLE>Using Tables In Your Publications</TITLE></HEAD>
<BODY>
<CENTER>
<TABLE BORDER=5 FRAME=ALL CELLPADDING=4 CELLSPACING=4 COLS=6>
<CAPTION ALIGN=TOP><B>Support for Table Features</B></CAPTION>
```

continues

Listing 9.1. continued

```
<THEAD>
<TR><TH ROWSPAN=2><TH ROWSPAN=2 VALIGN=TOP>HTML 3.0
<TH COLSPAN=2 VALIGN=TOP>Netscape Navigator<TH COLSPAN=2 VALIGN=TOP>
Internet Explorer
<TR><TH VALIGN=MIDDLE>Version 1.1<TH VALIGN=MIDDLE>Version 2.0
<TH VALIGN=MIDDLE>Version 1.0<TH VALIGN=MIDDLE>Version 2.0
<TBODY>
<TR><TH ALIGN=LEFT VALIGN=MIDDLE COLSPAN=6>Common Attributes
for Table Tags
<TR><TH>CLASS<TD>Yes<TD>No<TD>No<TD>No<TD>No
<TR><TH>DIR<TD>Yes<TD>No<TD>No<TD>No<TD>No
<TR><TH>ID<TD>Yes<TD>No<TD>No<TD>No<TD>No
<TR><TH>LANG<TD>Yes<TD>No<TD>No<TD>No<TD>No
<TR><TH>UNITS<TD>Yes<TD>No<TD>No<TD>No<TD>No
<TR><TH ALIGN=LEFT VALIGN=MIDDLE COLSPAN=6>Common Attributes for ALIGN
<TR><TH>LEFT<TD>Yes<TD>Yes<TD>Yes<TD>Yes<TD>Yes
<TR><TH>RIGHT<TD>Yes<TD>Yes<TD>Yes<TD>Yes<TD>Yes
<TR><TH>CENTER<TD>Yes<TD>Yes<TD>Yes<TD>Yes<TD>Yes
<TR><TH>JUSTIFY<TD>Yes<TD>No<TD>No<TD>No<TD>No
<TR><TH ALIGN=LEFT VALIGN=MIDDLE COLSPAN=6>Common Attributes for VALIGN
<TR><TH>TOP<TD>Yes<TD>Yes<TD>Yes<TD>Yes<TD>Yes
<TR><TH>MIDDLE<TD>Yes<TD>Yes<TD>Yes<TD>Yes<TD>Yes
<TR><TH>BOTTOM<TD>Yes<TD>Yes<TD>Yes<TD>Yes<TD>Yes
<TR><TH>BASELINE<TD>Yes<TD>Yes<TD>Yes<TD>Yes<TD>Yes
<TR><TH ALIGN=LEFT VALIGN=MIDDLE COLSPAN=6>Attributes For the TABLE Tag
<TR><TH>BORDER<TD>Yes<TD>Yes<TD>Yes<TD>Yes<TD>Yes
<TR><TH>CELLPADDING<TD>Yes<TD>Yes<TD>Yes<TD>Yes<TD>Yes
<TR><TH>CELLSPACING<TD>Yes<TD>Yes<TD>Yes<TD>Yes<TD>Yes
<TR><TH>COLS<TD>Yes<TD>No<TD>No<TD>No<TD>No
<TR><TH>CHAR<TD>Yes<TD>No<TD>No<TD>No<TD>No
<TR><TH>FLOAT<TD>Yes<TD>No<TD>No<TD>No<TD>No
<TR><TH>FRAME<TD>Yes<TD>No<TD>No<TD>No<TD>No
<TR><TH>RULES<TD>Yes<TD>No<TD>No<TD>No<TD>No
<TR><TH>WIDTH<TD>Yes<TD>Yes<TD>Yes<TD>Yes<TD>Yes
<TR><TH ALIGN=LEFT VALIGN=MIDDLE COLSPAN=6>Alignments for the CAPTION Tag
<TR><TH>ALIGN=TOP<TD>Yes<TD>Yes<TD>Yes<TD>Yes<TD>Yes
<TR><TH>ALIGN=BOTTOM<TD>Yes<TD>Yes<TD>Yes<TD>Yes<TD>Yes
<TR><TH>ALIGN=LEFT<TD>Yes<TD>No<TD>No<TD>No<TD>No
<TR><TH>ALIGN=RIGHT<TD>Yes<TD>No<TD>No<TD>No<TD>No
<TR><TH ALIGN=LEFT VALIGN=MIDDLE COLSPAN=6>Specifying Sections,
Columns and Rows
<TR><TH ALIGN=LEFT VALIGN=MIDDLE>THEAD<TD>Yes<TD>No<TD>No<TD>No<TD>No
<TR><TH ALIGN=LEFT VALIGN=MIDDLE>TBODY<TD>Yes<TD>No<TD>No<TD>No<TD>No
<TR><TH ALIGN=LEFT VALIGN=MIDDLE>TFOOT<TD>Yes<TD>No<TD>No<TD>No<TD>No
<TR><TH ALIGN=LEFT VALIGN=MIDDLE>COL<TD>Yes<TD>No<TD>No<TD>No<TD>No
<TR><TH ALIGN=LEFT VALIGN=MIDDLE>TR<TD>Yes<TD>Yes<TD>Yes<TD>Yes<TD>Yes
<TR><TH ALIGN=LEFT VALIGN=MIDDLE>TH<TD>Yes<TD>Yes<TD>Yes<TD>Yes<TD>Yes
<TR><TH ALIGN=LEFT VALIGN=MIDDLE>TD<TD>Yes<TD>Yes<TD>Yes<TD>Yes<TD>Yes
</TABLE>
</CENTER>
</BODY>
</HTML>
```

Frame-Enhancing Your Documents

Frames enable you to create documents with multiple windows. While Netscape Navigator 2.0 is currently the only browser to support frames, this will change quickly. There are plans to incorporate frames into the HTML 3.0 specification and other browsers, like Internet Explorer, plan to support frames in their next major release.

The best thing about frames is that they finally provide a way for Web publishers to easily create unique pages for users with Netscape-enhanced browsers. The two primary tags you will use to create frames are <FRAMESET> and <NOFRAME>. Using the <FRAMESET> tag, you specify a section of a document that will be used by frame-capable browsers. Using the <NOFRAME> tag, you specify a section of a document that will be used by browsers that cannot use frames.

Within the begin and end <FRAMESET> tags, you can only nest FRAME tags. FRAME tags are used to identify the source of the frames for your document. While the source can be any type of document, sources are typically HTML pages. The Virtual Press home page shown in Figure 9.3 uses three window frames. The contents of each mini-window comes from a separately defined HTML document merged into a common window using Netscape frames. As you can see, some of the frames have horizontal and vertical scroll bars. Readers can use these scroll bars to read the additional material contained in the document.

FIGURE 9.3.

The Virtual Press home page frame-enhanced.

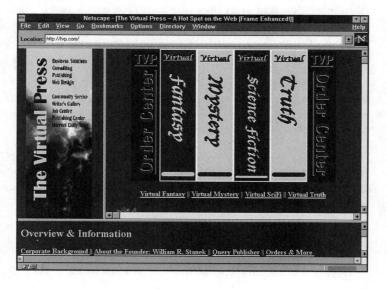

In Figure 9.3, the left-side frame was created from a document containing a title image. The title image is fully animated using client pull/server push and can be clicked on. The right-side frame is the primary frame; as shown here, it contains the contents of a home page created specifically for Netscape-enhanced browsers. The bottom frame contains a text-based menu. When a menu item is clicked on, the contents of the associated document are normally loaded into the main frame.

You do not have to frame-enhance all the pages at your Web site. A key concept in designing publications for frames is to only define frames on the main page readers will use to access the publication. This can be your home page or any top-level page at your site. Using a top-level page reduces the amount of work you must do to frame-enhance your site and enables you to use frames as they were meant to be used.

	HTML 3.0	Netscape 1.0	Netscape 2.0	IE 1.0	IE 2.0
FRAMESET	no	no	yes	no	no
FRAME	no	no	yes	no	no

Dividing a Browser Window into Frames

At first glance, the way you divide a browser window into frames can seem confusing. This is because window frames are organized much like a table is, with each window divided into one or more rows and columns. You count the rows for a window as the number of horizontal frame partitions. You count the columns for a window as the number of vertical frame partitions.

Using the ROWS attribute, you can define the number and size of the rows to display in your browser window. The vertical size of a row is expressed as an absolute or relative value with multiple row assignments separated by a comma. The number of rows is equal to the number of items in the comma separated list.

Using the COLS attribute, you can define the number and size of the columns to display in your browser window. The size of a column is expressed as an absolute or relative value with multiple column assignments separated by a comma. The number of columns is equal to the number of items in the comma separated list.

Column and row size can be defined in three ways:

1. As an absolute value in pixels
2. As a relative value in percentage of window width
3. As a relative value following the CALS table model syntax

While assigning an absolute value in pixels may seem the easiest way to create a column or row of frames, it is never a good idea to define all the rows or columns in terms of pixels. The size of the browser window can vary substantially, depending on the display mode and sizing being used. To avoid filling the window with empty space, the browser will probably override the values you have assigned to ensure all of the window is filled. This can cause a distortion of your row and column assignments. Consequently, you should use fixed pixel values with relative values. The following <FRAMESET> tag defines three rows of frames with fixed pixel sizes:

```
<FRAMESET ROWS="100,300,240">
    . . .
</FRAMESET>
```

Relative values can be expressed as a percentage or on a proportionate scale of the total window size. To use percentages, you assign a value between 1 and 100 and follow it with a percent sign. If the total of all percentages assigned is greater than 100, the values are scaled down to 100. If the total of all percentages assigned is less than 100, the relative sizes are scaled up to 100 and in this way, the relative-sized frames are given the extra space. The following <FRAMESET> tag defines two columns of frames with relative sizes:

```
<FRAMESET COLS="10%,90%">
    . . .
</FRAMESET>
```

To use relative scaling, you use an asterisk with or without a value. An asterisk with no associated value is interpreted as a request to give all remaining space in the row or column to the frame you are creating. An asterisk with a value in front of it is used to scale how much relative space to assign to a frame. A frame with the value 3* would get three times as much relative space as other frames assigned with a relative value. The following <FRAMESET> tag defines two relatively-scaled rows and two fixed-sized rows:

```
<FRAMESET ROWS="3*,*,100,150">
    . . .
</FRAMESET>
```

The way columns and rows of frames are displayed depends on how you make row and column assignments. Each column assignment you make after your row assignments will divide successive rows of frames into columns. Conversely, each row assignment you make after your column assignments will divide successive columns of frames into rows.

In the example that follows, three rows are defined. The first row is divided by two columns of equal size. The other two rows extend across the entire width of the screen. Figure 9.4 shows how the following sample code is displayed:

```
<FRAMESET ROWS="25%,50%,25%">
<FRAMESET COLS="50%,50%>
    . . .
</FRAMESET>
</FRAMESET>
```

FIGURE 9.4.

Creating frames is easiest using percentages.

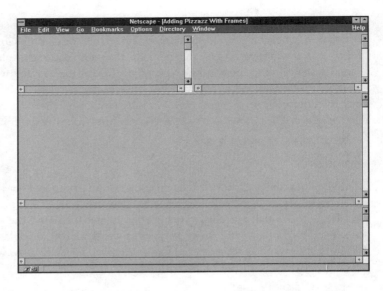

By reversing the order of the column and row assignments, you create an entirely different window. The next example has two columns of equal size. The first column is divided by three rows. The second column extends down the full length of the window. Figure 9.5 shows how this sample code is displayed:

```
<FRAMESET COLS="50%,50%>
<FRAMESET ROWS="25%,50%,25%">
   . . .
</FRAMESET>
</FRAMESET>
```

FIGURE 9.5.

A new window created by reversing column and row frames.

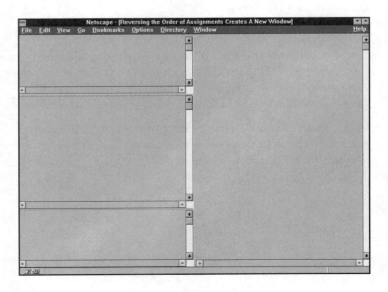

If two <FRAMESET> tags assigned rows for the window previously defined, the second set of row assignments would pertain to the second column.

Creating Individual Frames

The only tag you can use within the begin and end <FRAMESET> tags is the <FRAME> tag. You use the <FRAME> tag to specify the source for the frame and to assign key characteristics of the frame. The source document or object for the frame is specified with the optional SRC attribute. If you do not use the SRC attribute, the frame is displayed as a blank space in the window. As only Netscape-enhanced browsers can use your frames, the source you specify is usually a Netscape-enhanced document.

In the example below, the window is divided into two columns. While the first column is divided into three rows, the second column extends the full length of the windows. The first source assignment fills the frame in the first frame in column one, which is in the upper-left corner. The second source assignment fills the frame in the middle of column one. The third source assignment fills the frame in the bottom column one. The final source assignment fills the large area for column two. Here is the code for the example:

```
<FRAMESET COLS="25%,75%">
<FRAMESET ROWS="25%,25%,50%">
<FRAME SRC="titlepage.htm">
<FRAME SRC="subtitlepage.htm">
<FRAME SRC="menu.htm">
</FRAMESET>
<FRAME SRC="homepage.htm">
</FRAMESET>
```

The way you nest tags within <FRAMESET> tags is extremely important. The first <FRAMESET> tag should enclose all further assignments for frame sets and frames. In the previous example, all elements pertaining to the first column were defined first, then elements pertaining to the second column were defined. You should define elements for rows and columns in the same way.

Other optional attributes for the <FRAME> tag include

> MARGINHEIGHT
>
> MARGINWIDTH
>
> NORESIZE
>
> SCROLLING
>
> NAME

Frame Margins

The MARGINHEIGHT attribute controls the top and bottom margin size for the frame. The minimum margin size is one. If you assign a margin size of less than one, your browser displays the frame with a margin to ensure frame edges do not touch. If you do not assign a margin size, the browser uses a default margin size, which can vary. Consequently, you may want to assign a margin size for the frame's top and bottom margins.

The MARGINWIDTH attribute controls the left and right margin size for the frame. The minimum margin size is also one. You can assign MARGINHEIGHT and MARGINWIDTH as follows:

```
<FRAME SRC="titlepage.htm" MARGINHEIGHT=2 and MARGINWIDTH=2>
```

User Adjustment of Frames

Users can adjust frames in two key ways: with scroll bars and by resizing the frame. In general, users will want to be able to manipulate your frames, especially if they are using a screen size other than the one you created the publication for. However, you can turn these features on or off using the SCROLLING and NORESIZE attributes.

By default, the browser decides if a window should or should not have scroll bars. If the entire document is visible in the frame, the browser will automatically display the frame without scroll bars. If the entire document is not visible in the frame, the browser will automatically display the frame with scroll bars. The browser will display both horizontal and vertical scroll bars regardless of whether both are needed. The SCROLLING attribute has three values:

```
SCROLLING=AUTO

SCROLLING=YES

SCROLLING=NO
```

You can override the default AUTO value for the SCROLLING attribute by setting SCROLLING=YES or SCROLLING=NO. The value SCROLLING=YES ensures scroll bars are always visible. The value SCROLLING=NO ensures scroll bars are never visible.

By default, the size of all frames can be adjusted by the user. Users adjust frames by moving the cursor over a frame edge, holding down the left mouse button when the resizing icon appears, and dragging the frame edge to a new position. You can turn the resizing feature off using the NORESIZE attribute. Keep in mind, even a single frame that cannot be resized will affect the adjustability of other frames in the window.

Targeting and Naming Frames

The NAME attribute plays a key role in how your frames interact with other frames and windows. By default, hypertext references within a frame are targeted to the frame. This means when you activate a link within a frame, the new document will normally be loaded into the same frame. By naming a frame, you can target it from other frames on the page. To name a frame, you use a keyword that begins with an alphanumeric character, such as

```
<FRAME SRC="homepage.html" NAME="MAIN">
```

By default, all frames are unnamed. Yet once you have assigned a name to a frame, the frame can be targeted by other frames. Usually, these frames are on the same page. For example, your page could have a main section named MAIN and a menu section targeted at the main frame. In this way, when a user clicked on a hypertext reference in the menu, the corresponding document would be loaded into the main frame.

To target a frame, you use Netscape's TARGET attribute for the anchor tag <A>. The value assigned to the TARGET attribute should be the name of the frame you want to target. If you wanted to target the frame called MAIN in the window described earlier, here is how you would do it:

```
<A HREF="subpage.html" TARGET="MAIN">
```

You can assign a base target for all links in a document using the <BASE> tag. In this way, you do not have to insert target information for all links in a document. Keep in mind that a target defined in a link overrides the base target defined. Thus, if you want to target most of the links to a single frame and some links to other frames, you can easily do this. Here is how you can assign the base target to the frame called MAIN:

```
<BASE TARGET="MAIN">
```

An interesting way to use the base target is to target a name you haven't used elsewhere. If the target name is not a frame in the currently defined window, the browser will open a new window in addition to the current window. If the current window has two unnamed frames and one frame named CENTRAL1, this base target would open a new window:

```
<BASE TARGET="WINDOW2">
```

The NAME and TARGET attributes can also be used to establish the current document's relationship to other documents. Currently, four relationships are defined:

_blank	Load this link into a new, unnamed window.
_self	Load this link over yourself.
_parent	Load this link over yourself and reset the window.
_top	Load this link at the top level.

While all these relationships are useful, the most useful relationship is _parent. Using the _parent relationship, you force the browser to reset the window entirely and avoid loading a frame document within the current frame. You will want to use this relationship whenever you have a link that leads to a page containing frame assignments. For example, if lower-level documents reference your home page, you can use the following assignment to avoid getting a frame within a frame:

```
<A HREF="yourhomepage.html" TARGET="_parent">
```

Defining the *NOFRAME* Area

With the <NOFRAME> tag, you can define an area of the document that will be displayed by browsers that are not capable of using frames. The <NOFRAME> tag is used in a pair with the begin tag <NOFRAME> specifying the start of the area for browsers that are not frame-capable and the end tag </NOFRAME> specifying the end of this area. All frame-enhanced pages should contain a fully defined NOFRAME area. This NOFRAME area could simply contain your original page before you frame-enhanced it.

Here is a sample document with a NOFRAME area:

```
<HTML>
<HEAD>
<TITLE>Your Home Page [Frame Enhanced]</TITLE>
</HEAD>
<FRAMESET COLS=25%,75%>
<FRAMESET ROWS="20%,80%">
<FRAME SRC="title.html">
<FRAME SRC="menu.html">
</FRAMESET>
<FRAME SRC="main.html">
</FRAMESET>
<NOFRAME>
<HEAD>
<TITLE>Your Home Page [Non-Frame Enhanced]</TITLE>
</HEAD>
<BODY>
 . . .
</BODY>
</HTML>
```

As you can see from the preceding example, documents with frame assignments are not organized like other documents. In general, they do not need a header or body section. However, you can add a header section to the top of the document to specify the title for the frame-enhanced page. You can also add a header and body section to the NOFRAME area of the document. The header and body sections in the NOFRAME area are used by browsers that cannot use frames. Thus, the second title will be used by browsers that are not frame-capable.

Combined Frame Example

This section gives you an inside look at how I frame-enhanced The Virtual Press Web site. The TVP Web site is organized into six main areas or publications:

- TVP Home Page and Corporate Information Pages
- TVP Business Solutions Pages
- TVP Order Center
- The Writer's Gallery
- Internet Job Information Center
- Internet Publishing Center

When I frame-enhanced the TVP Web site, I made a conscious decision to create frame-enhanced pages for each of these six main areas. Primarily, this is because most of the visitors to the site do not start on the TVP home page. They start on one of the other main areas. If I had only frame-enhanced the home page, thousands of visitors might have missed out on the powerful features I had added for users with frame-capable browsers. Frame-enhancing the six top-level pages also enables me to give each area a unique look and feel.

In the series of examples that follow, you will see how the Internet Job Information Center was frame-enhanced and the design concepts that went into frame-enhancing the Internet's JIC. The top-level page is shown in Figure 9.6. In the code for the top-level page that follows, examine how the frame and no-frame area were defined. You can see the frame area contains nested frame assignments that call other documents. The no-frame area contains the original home page.

FIGURE 9.6.

Internet Job Information Center: frame-enhanced.

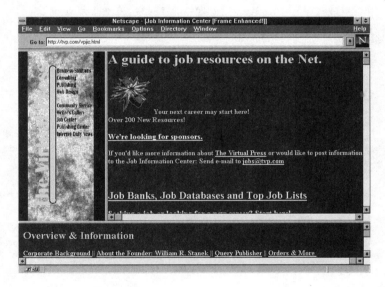

Listing 9.2 shows the markup for the JIC top-level page.

Listing 9.2. A frame-enhanced Web page.

```
<HTML>
<HEAD>
<TITLE>Job Information Center [Frame Enhanced!]</TITLE>
</HEAD>
<FRAMESET ROWS="80%,20%">
<FRAMESET  COLS="25%,75%">
<FRAME SRC="vp.html" NAME="vpside" MARGINWIDTH=0 SCROLLING="no" >
<FRAME SRC="vpjic2.html" NAME="vpmain" MARGINWIDTH=0>
</FRAMESET>
```

continues

Listing 9.2. continued

```
<FRAME SRC="fmenu.html" NAME="vpfooter">
</FRAMESET>
<NOFRAME>
<HEAD>
<TITLE>Job Information Center</TITLE>
</HEAD>
<BODY BGCOLOR="#0000ff" text="#ffff00" link="#fffbf0"
➥vlink="#808000" alink="#ff0000">
<CENTER>
<P><IMG SRC="jicttl.gif" ALT=""></P>
</CENTER>
<P><STRONG><IMG SRC="bboard.gif" ALIGN="BOTTOM" ALT="* ATTN *">
A guide to job resources on the Net.  Your next career may start here!
<BR>Over 200 New Resources!</STRONG>
<P><A HREF="http://tvp.com/"><IMG SRC="netscape.gif"></A></P>
<H3><A HREF="vpspons.html">We're looking for sponsors.</A></H3>
<P>If you'd like more information about <A HREF="vpbg.html">
The Virtual Press</A> or would like to post information to the Job
Information Center:  Send e-mail to <A HREF="mailto:jobs@tvp.com">
jobs@tvp.com</A></P>
<HR SIZE=4>
<H2><A HREF="jresume.html">Job Banks, Job Databases and
Top Job Lists</A></H2>
<H3>Seeking a job or looking for a new career?  Start here!</H3>
<H2><A HREF="jobs.html">Jobs At The Virtual Press</A></H2>
<H3>Part-time &amp; telecommuting jobs at TVP</H3>
<H2><A HREF="jscience.html">Job Opportunities in Science and
Engineering</A></H2>
<H3>A comprehensive resource for finding jobs in science and
engineering</H3>
<H2><A HREF="jintl.html">International Job Opportunities</A></H2>
<H3>Find jobs in Europe, Asia, Africa, Australia</H3>
<H2><A HREF="jacad.html">Job Opportunities in Academia</A></H2>
<H3>Staff, Administrative, Faculty and Research Positions at
Colleges and Universities</H3>
<H2><A HREF="jspecial.html">Specialty and Small Job Databases
and lists</A></H2>
<H3>U.S. Regional Job Databases and Other Small Job Databases.</H3>
<H2><A HREF="jdisab.html">Job Opportunities for Differently
Abled Persons</A></H2>
<H3></H3>
<H2><A HREF="jfedgov.html">US Federal Government and State
Job Opportunities</A></H2>
<H3>Looking for a government or state job?</H3>
<H2><A HREF="jeinfo.html">Essential Information for Job Seekers
and Career Changers</A></H2>
<H3>Great resources if you are looking for help or advice in your
job search or career change!</H3>
<H2><A HREF="jintl.html#world">Newsgroups for Job Hunters Around
the World</A></H2>
<H2><A HREF="jnews.html#us">Newsgroups for U.S. Job Hunters</A></H2>
<H2><A HREF="jnews.html#prof">Newsgroups for Job Hunters by
Profession</A></H2>
<HR SIZE=4>
<H2>Additional Resources To Help Your Job Search</H2>
<P><A HREF="vplink.html#comp">Computer Companies</A> ¦¦
```

```
<A HREF="vplink.html#gov">Government Resources</A> ¦¦
<A HREF="vplink.html#edu">Education Resources</A> ¦¦
<A HREF="vplink.html#www">WWW Information</A></P>
<P><BR>
<HR SIZE=4>
<P>Return to <A HREF="vphp.html">Virtual Press Home Page</A></P>
<H2><A HREF="vpqmenu.html"> Quick Access Menu</A></H2>
<P><STRONG>Use this quick access menu to easily browse our
Web site!</P></STRONG>
<HR>
<P>Questions or comments pertaining to the TVP Web site can be directed
to <A HREF="mailto:webmaster@tvp.com">
<IMG SRC="mail.gif" ALIGN="MIDDLE" ALT="*e-mail*"> webmaster@tvp.com
</A></P>
<P>This page, and all contents, are <A HREF="vpcopy.html">Copyright (C)
1995 by The Virtual Press, Hawaii, USA.</A></P>
</BODY>
</NOFRAME>
</HTML>
```

The window shown in Figure 9.6 is divided into three frames. The first row is divided into two columns. The second row has a single frame that occupies the entire width of the window. Each frame has a document associated with it. The source for the small frame on the left side of the window is a document called vp.html. The source for the large main frame is a document called vpjic2.html. The source for the third frame is a document called fmenu.html. Finally, each frame was named so they could be targeted from other frames on the page. The side frame is called vpside. The main frame is called vpmain. The footer frame is called vpfooter.

Listing 9.3 shows the code for a document called vp.html. This document is used to display a title graphic.

Listing 9.3. Side frame for title graphic.

```
<HTML>
<HEAD>
<TITLE>The Virtual Press</TITLE>
</HEAD>
<BODY BGCOLOR="#000000" text="#ffff00" link="#fffbf0"
➡vlink="#808000" alink="#ff0000">
<CENTER>
<IMG SRC="vpttl.jpg" ALT="" BORDER=0>
</CENTER>
</BODY>
</HTML>
```

The code for the document called vpjic2.html contains the source for the main frame and is a modified version of the original Job Information Center top-level page. The primary modifications were to remove the graphical logo at the top of the page and links to other top-level pages as these are unnecessary. Listing 9.4 shows the code for the main frame.

Listing 9.4. Markup for the main frame.

```
<HTML><HEAD><TITLE>Job Information Center</TITLE></HEAD>
<BODY BGCOLOR="#0000ff" text="#ffff00" link="#fffbf0"
➥vlink="#808000" alink="#ff0000">
<H1>A guide to job resources on the Net.</H1>
<P><IMG SRC="bboard.gif" ALIGN="BOTTOM" ALT="* ATTN *">
Your next career may start here!
<BR>Over 200 New Resources!
<H3><A HREF="vpspons.html">We're looking for sponsors.</A></H3>
<P>If you'd like more information about <A HREF="vpbg.html">The Virtual
Press</A> or would like to post information to the Job Information Center:
Send e-mail to <A HREF="mailto:jobs@tvp.com">jobs@tvp.com</A></P>
<HR SIZE=4>
<H2><A HREF="jresume.html">Job Banks, Job Databases and Top
Job Lists</A></H2>
<H3>Seeking a job or looking for a new career?  Start here!</H3>
<H2><A HREF="jobs.html">Jobs At The Virtual Press</A></H2>
<H3>Part-time &amp; telecommuting jobs at TVP</H3>
<H2><A HREF="jscience.html">Job Opportunities in Science and
Engineering</A></H2>
<H3>A comprehensive resource for finding jobs in science and
engineering</H3>
<H2><A HREF="jintl.html">International Job Opportunities</A></H2>
<H3>Find jobs in Europe, Asia, Africa, Australia</H3>
<H2><A HREF="jacad.html">Job Opportunities in Academia</A></H2>
<H3>Staff, Administrative, Faculty and Research Positions at Colleges
and Universities</H3>
<H2><A HREF="jspecial.html">Specialty and Small Job Databases and
lists</A></H2>
<H3>U.S. Regional Job Databases and Other Small Job Databases.</H3>
<H2><A HREF="jdisab.html">Job Opportunities for Differently Abled
Persons</A></H2>
<H3></H3>
<H2><A HREF="jfedgov.html">US Federal Government and State Job
Opportunities</A></H2>
<H3>Looking for a government or state job?</H3>
<H2><A HREF="jeinfo.html">Essential Information for Job Seekers and
Career Changers</A></H2>
<H3>Great resources if you are looking for help or advice in your job
search or career change!</H3>
<H2><A HREF="jintl.html#world">Newsgroups for Job Hunters Around the
World</A></H2>
<H2><A HREF="jnews.html#us">Newsgroups for U.S. Job Hunters</A></H2>
<H2><A HREF="jnews.html#prof">Newsgroups for Job Hunters by
Profession</A></H2>
<HR SIZE=4>
<H2><A HREF="vpbusres.html">Business Resources</A></H2>
<P>Important business resources on the Internet</P>
<H2><A HREF="vpcomres.html">Computer Companies on the Net and Where to
Find Them</A></H2>
<P>Looking for a technical job with a computer company?<BR>
Start by browsing the company's home site.</P>
<P>The more you learn about the company, its products and personnel,
the better your chances.</P>
<H2><A HREF="vpfinres.html">Important Financial Resources on
the Net</A></H2>
```

```
<P>Looking for the latest stock market information or other
financial information?</P>
<H2><A HREF="vplegres.html">Legal Resources</A></H2>
<P>Need some help with contracts or other legal matters?</P>
<HR SIZE=4>
<P>Questions or comments pertaining to the TVP Web site can be directed
to <A HREF="mailto:webmaster@tvp.com">
<IMG SRC="mail.gif" ALIGN="MIDDLE" ALT="*e-mail*"> webmaster@tvp.com
</A></P>
<P>This page, and all contents, are <A HREF="vpcopy.html">Copyright (C)
by The Virtual Press, Hawaii, USA.</A>
</P>
</BODY>
</HTML>
```

The source for the third frame on the page is `fmenu.html`. While the menu could have used a base target assignment, I did not use one when creating the page. Primarily this is because of the mix of links to top-level pages and supplementary pages. Some links target the main frame called vpmain. Activating one of these links will load the associated document into the main frame. Other links target a parent document. Activating one of these links will cause the parent document to load over the current window. This ensures a top-level document's frame assignments are not loaded into another frame on the page. Listing 9.5 shows the code for the menu document.

Listing 9.5. Markup for the menu frame.

```
<HTML>
<HEAD><TITLE>Frame Menu</TITLE></HEAD>
<BODY BGCOLOR="#0000ff" text="#ffff00" link="#fffbf0"
➥vlink="#808000" alink="#ff0000">
<H2>Overview & Information</H2>
<A HREF="vpbg.html" TARGET="vpmain">Corporate Background </A> ¦¦
<A HREF="vpfound.html" TARGET="vpmain">About the Founder:
William R. Stanek </A> ¦¦
<A HREF="vpqry.html" TARGET="vpmain">Query Publisher</A> ¦¦
<A HREF="viporder.html" TARGET="_parent">Orders & More </A></P>
<H2>Business Solutions</H2>
<P><A HREF="vpepc.html" TARGET="_parent">Electronic Publishing Center</A>
¦¦ <A HREF="vpicc.html" TARGET="_parent">Internet Consulting Center</A> ¦¦
<A HREF="vpwdc.html" TARGET="_parent">Web Design Center</A></P>
<H2>Community Services</H2>
<P><A HREF="idn.html" TARGET="vpmain"> Internet Daily News</A> ¦¦
<A HREF="vpjic.html" TARGET="_parent">Job Information Center</A> ¦¦
<A HREF="vpipc.html" TARGET="_parent">Internet Publishing Center</A> ¦¦
<A HREF="vpwg.html" TARGET="_parent">Writer's Gallery</A></P>
<H2>Hot Topics</H2>
<P><A HREF="vpdream1.html" TARGET="vpmain"> Sneak Previews</A> ¦¦
<A HREF="vpdest1.html" TARGET="vpmain">World of Paths HQ</A> ¦¦
<A HREF="pin.html" TARGET="vpmain">Pulse of the Internet Magazine</A></P>
<H2>Opportunities for Writers & Artists</H2>
<P><A HREF="projint.html" TARGET="vpmain">Project Internet</A> ¦¦
```

continues

Listing 9.5. continued

```
<A HREF="wcontest.html" TARGET="vpmain">Hot Contests </A></P>
<HR SIZE=4>
<H2><A HREF="http://www.tvpress.com/" TARGET="_parent">
Mirror Site</A></H2>
<P>Cybersurf to our mirror site!</P>
<P>Watch for an upcoming contest and the debut of Internet Daily News.</P>
<HR SIZE=4>
<P>The Original Virtual Press -- Fine Publications, Community Service and
Much More Since March, 1994.</P>
<CENTER>
<P><A HREF="vpcopy.html"><IMG SRC="crights.gif" ALT="Copyright (C)
by The Virtual Press, Inc., USA."></A></P>
</CENTER>
</BODY>
</HTML>
```

Summary

Tables and frames are two of the most dynamic elements ever added to the HTML standard. Following the table model specified in HTML 3.0, you can create powerful tables with layout controlled precisely by dozens of useful parameters. Following the frame model specified in Netscape enhancements for the Navigator Version 2.0, you can frame-enhance your Web publication or site. Frames are more than mini-windows within the larger browser window; they are the gateway to an entirely new way to publish on the Web. If you've ever wanted to add power features to your Web publications, table and frame elements provide definite starting points.

PART

Interactive Web Publishing

HTML Toolkit: Browsers, Editors, and Converters

10

by William Robert Stanek

No matter what computer platform you use, this chapter contains the ingredients to make the ultimate HTML publishing toolkit for your system. This chapter gives you the inside scoop on

- Browsers
- Converters
- Editors
- Players

Web Browsers

Following the wild success of the World Wide Web, the number of organizations developing browsers grew explosively. Currently more than 60 organizations have entered the browser development race and are vying for Netscape's coveted position as the leader in browser development. Browsers are available for use on almost any computer operating system, including Amiga, DOS, Macintosh, NeXT, RISC, Windows, Windows 95, Windows NT, and UNIX.

A browser is a software application that enables you to access the World Wide Web. You can think of a browser as your window to the Web. Change your browser and you get a whole new view of the Web. When you use Lynx, your window to the Web has only text. Text-only browsers are the original browsers for the Web. Although it may be hard to believe, several text-only browsers are still being developed.

When you use NCSA Mosaic, your window to the Web has text and graphics. Browsers that enable you to view Web documents containing text and graphics are the second generation of browsers. These browsers are largely responsible for the phenomenal success of the Web.

When you use HotJava, your window has text, graphics, and live animation. Browsers that enable you to view Web documents containing text, graphics, and inline multimedia are the third generation of browsers. These browsers are driving the Web's transition to an extremely visual medium that rivals television for information content and entertainment value.

Although the Web is increasingly commercial, you can still find freeware and shareware browsers. This section provides an overview of most of the commercial, shareware, and freeware browser options available today. While you will probably never use all the browsers listed in this section, as a Web publisher, you should be aware of browser developments.

One reason to keep abreast of browser developments is that somewhere in the myriad of options is the gem that will one day replace Netscape Navigator as top dog. If you've heard about the Netscape Navigator, you may not think this is possible, but keep in mind that until Netscape Navigator came along, a browser called Mosaic was top dog. For nearly two years, Mosaic was the king of browsers; then a team of developers from the company now called Netscape Communications Corporation released the first version of a new browser. This browser, the Navigator, spread like wildfire as Web users learned about its capabilities.

Well, the Netscape Navigator's second anniversary is fast approaching and it may just have to start walking on water to hold its position as the king of the browsers. As I scoured the Net in search of browsers, I was amazed at the number of companies developing browsers superior to anything currently available. Some of these browsers have features that are on most Web surfers' wish lists, including mine.

Accent Multilingual Mosaic

Multiple language support in most browsers is nonexistent. Accent solves this problem by creating a good browser for Windows that is capable of handling multiple languages. As Accent also creates language translation software, you may expect to see an interface between the translation software and browser text soon. Accent has an online help desk that features text in seven languages.

To find out more about Accent Software and download the beta version of Multilingual Mosaic, visit Accent's Web site at

```
http://www.accentsoft.com/
```

Amiga Mosaic

The original browser for the Amiga is Amiga Mosaic. Amiga Mosaic is free for noncommercial use. The team that created Amiga Mosaic and other Amiga Web software have formed Omnipresence Corporation. While Omnipresence still provides access to free versions of Amiga Mosaic, the company has developed a commercial browser for the Amiga called IBrowse.

You can learn more about Amiga Web software and Amiga Mosaic at

```
http://www.omnipresence.com/amosaic/
```

Aficionado Web Surfer

Aficionado Web Surfer is a browser to keep an eye on. Web Surfer is being developed in the United Kingdom by Blackbird Systems, a company created by former members of a couple of prominent Internet software development companies. Web Surfer features support for HTML 3.0, Netscape extensions, and plug-ins. Versions of Web Surfer should soon be available for Macintosh, Windows, Windows 95/NT, and UNIX systems.

To learn more about Web Surfer, visit

```
http://www.blackbird.co.uk/websurfer/
```

ArcWeb

ArcWeb is a graphics-capable browser for Acorn RISC OS computers, with RISC OS 3.1 or later. ArcWeb is a freeware browser being developed by the University of Southampton, Department of Electronics & Computer Science.

You can learn more about ArcWeb at

`http://louis.ecs.soton.ac.uk/~snb94r/arcweb.html`

Arena

Arena was designed as a development tool for the Version 3.0 specification of HTML. HTML 3.0 has some exciting features, including support for mathematical formulas, tables, forms within tables, and additional support for images and lists. You will see and hear more about Arena and HTML Level 3 browsers when the specification is finalized in the coming months. The Arena browser is available for UNIX platforms and is free for noncommercial use.

The Arena FAQ can be found at

`http://www.w3.org/hypertext/WWW/Arena/faq`

You can also visit the Arena home page at

`http://www.w3.org/hypertext/WWW/Arena/`

Cello

Cello is a basic graphics-capable browser developed by Thomas Bruce of the Legal Information Institute at Cornell Law School. One of the key features of Cello is native support for most Internet protocols including: HTTP, FTP, Gopher, News, WAIS, Hytelnet, and telnet. A freeware version of Cello is available for Windows systems.

Although the Cello browser is not being actively developed, you can find information about it at

`http://www.law.cornell.edu/cello/cellotop.html`

Chimera

Chimera is a basic graphics-capable browser for UNIX platforms using X windows. The great thing about Chimera is its simplicity and that it's available for free. You can learn more about Chimera at

`http://www.unlv.edu/chimera/`

Cyberjack

Cyberjack is Delrina Corporation's browser entry. Delrina Corporation is probably best known for the popular communication program WinComm Pro. WinComm PRO 7.0 and later versions include Cyberjack. Cyberjack is an integrated software package that enables you to access the Web, send e-mail, access newsgroups, and even use Internet Relay Chat. As Cyberjack was designed specifically for Windows 95, it features true multitasking and multithreading.

You can learn more about Cyberjack at the Delrina's Cyberjack Web site:

```
http://www.cyberjack.com/
```

Emacs-W3

Emacs-W3 is a good graphics-capable browser that has been ported to just about every computer platform that supports GNU Emacs. These systems include the following:

Amiga
DOS
Linux
NeXT
OS/2
UNIX
VMS
Windows NT/95

This shareware browser supports HTML 2.0 and some HTML 3.0 features, such as style sheets. Emacs-W3 also supports most Internet protocols including secure transfer using HTTPS. You can learn more about Emacs-W3 at

```
http://www.cs.indiana.edu/elisp/w3/docs.html
```

Emissary

The Emissary browser from the company formerly known as Wollongong is a commercial browser that enables you to browse the Web, send e-mail, access newsgroups, and more. Emissary is part of an integrated package for Windows called the Power Desktop. Power Desktop features an HTML editor, Web Browser, Winsock, and dialer. You'll find that Emissary has many nice features, such as macros and smart mail filing.

You download a 30-day evaluation copy of Emissary at the Wollongong Web site:

```
http://www.twg.com/
```

Enhanced Spyglass Mosaic

Enhanced Spyglass Mosaic is a commercial browser that hasn't received as much attention as it should. This quick, light, and feature-rich browser supports most Netscape 1.1 extensions, sound files in AU and AIFF formats, and client-side image maps. Versions of Enhanced Mosaic are available for Macintosh, Windows, Windows 95/NT, and UNIX systems. Multilingual versions of Spyglass Mosaic are becoming available as well.

Spyglass Corporation has an exclusive license for developing enhanced versions of the original Mosaic browser developed at NCSA. Spyglass, in turn, licenses out these enhanced versions of Mosaic to other companies. The core technology for Enhanced Mosaic is inside more than 120 Internet related products, including AB Software's Skyway, Accent Multilingual Browser, Alis Multilingual Browser, CompuServe's Internet in a Box, Corel CD Office Companion, DACOM Internet Starter Kit, Datastorm's PROCOMM PLUS, Microsoft's Internet Explorer, Open Text Internet Anywhere, O'Reilly Mosaic, and Quarterdeck Mosaic.

You can learn more about Enhanced Spyglass Mosaic at

`http://www.spyglass.com/`

You can download a 30-day trial version of Spyglass Mosaic at

`http://www.spyglass.com/products/getspy.html`

Fountain

Fountain is an integrated VRML software package from Caligari. The commercial software package for Windows and Windows 95/NT computers includes a VRML browser designed specifically for viewing fully interactive 3-D environments and a VRML world-building tool.

You can learn more about Fountain and obtain an trial version of the Fountain browser at

`http://www.caligari.com/`

Grail

The Grail Web browser supports most Internet protocols and file formats. Unlike other browsers, Grail can be easily extended to support additional protocols and file formats. Grail is distributed by CNRI and is free for noncommercial purposes. An interesting thing about Grail is that it is written entirely in the Python programming language.

> **NOTE**
>
> Python is a free object-oriented programming language that is available for most UNIX platforms. Python is increasing in popularity partly because of its versatility.

UNIX versions of Grail are available at

`http://monty.cnri.reston.va.us/`

HotJava

The HotJava browser, developed by Sun Microsystems Incorporated, is written entirely in a language called Java. Using Java, you can create platform-independent interactive applications called applets. While the HotJava browser is currently in the testing stages, versions of the browser are available for Windows 95, Windows NT, Sun Solaris, and soon, the Macintosh.

To learn more about HotJava and download an evaluation version, visit Sun Microsystems at

```
http://java.sun.com/
```

I-Comm

I-Comm is a full-featured browser and communications program that does not require a SLIP/PPP connection. The advantage of not needing a SLIP/PPP connection is that your standard UNIX shell account can now be used to view the full graphics capability of the Web. I-Comm is specifically designed for Windows users who access the Internet with a modem and have a standard UNIX shell, VAX, or Freenet account with a service provider.

This commercial browser is available for a 60-day trial period from

```
http://www.best.com/~icomm/
```

IBrowse

IBrowse is a browser for the Amiga. Created by some of the developers of Amiga Mosaic, IBrowse is feature-rich and fast. One of the neatest features is an "Anti Netscape Mode" that warns you if a Web page contains Netscape extensions and/or HTML 3.0 tags. Although IBrowse is under development, the current release should fully support HTML 3.0 and Netscape extensions.

The beta release of IBrowse is available free at

```
http://www.omnipresence.com:80/ibrowse/
```

InterGO

The InterGO browser is a commercial browser that enables you to browse the Web, send e-mail, and access newsgroups. This browser from TeacherSoft, a leading educational organization, has features that should put it on your list of browsers to watch. The browser includes indexed hypertext resources called Research Resource and Cybrarian for finding Web sites containing exactly what you are looking for. The InterGO browser is part of an integrated package that includes an encyclopedia, dictionary, thesaurus, and more than 200 literary works, including the Bill of Rights and *Huckleberry Finn*. InterGO gives you instant access to words and their definitions while surfing the Internet.

Yet the feature that every parent on planet earth will want to learn about is KinderGuard. With KinderGuard, you can block locations containing objectionable materials. As a parent, you assign what amount, if any, of objectionable material your children can be exposed to. KinderGuard can be tailored to individual restrictions for each child in your family and can be used to block nudity, profanity, and violence.

You can visit TeacherSoft on the Web and download a trial version of the InterGO browser at

```
http://www.teachersoft.com/
```

Line Mode Browser

The W3C Line Mode Browser is a text-based Web browser developed for use on UNIX-based computer terminals. The browser can be run as a proxy client in interactive mode and noninteractive mode. You will find that this browser is great for accessing the Web using a shell script or automatic cron job. If you ever need to search the Web and retrieve Web pages for storage or indexing, you should consider using the Line Mode Browser.

You can find more information on the Line Mode Browser and download the browser free from

```
http://www.w3.org/hypertext/WWW/LineMode/Status.html
```

Lynx

Lynx is one of the original text-only browsers. Originally created for users on UNIX and VMS platforms, Lynx is a product of the Distributed Computing Group within Academic Computing Services of the University of Kansas. The browser is free for noncommercial use.

You can find more information on Lynx and download the browser from this page at the University of Kansas Web site:

```
http://kuhttp.cc.ukans.edu/about_lynx/about_lynx.html
```

To address the dire need for users with DOS-based systems to access the Web, Lynx was ported for use on DOS. You can find more information on DOSLynx and download the browser from this page at the University of Kansas Web site:

```
http://kuhttp.cc.ukans.edu/about_doslynx/doslynx.html
```

MacWeb

MacWeb is a good graphics-capable browser for the Macintosh that supports HTML 2.0. Until recently, MacWeb was a freeware product developed by the company formerly known as EINet Galaxy. EINet Galaxy recently joined the dozens of other Internet startups that are playing the name game. You will find that the new company, TradeWave Galaxy, has a more polished and professional image and an improved product line that is quickly moving to the commercial market.

At the TradeWave Galaxy site, you will find trial versions of current MacWeb releases and free versions of older MacWeb releases. The place to look for MacWeb is the MacWeb homepage at

```
http://www.einet.net/EINet/MacWeb/MacWebHome.html
```

Mariner

Mariner is an integrated software package for accessing the Internet. The browser is as an all-in-one solution that lets you quickly and easily integrate and organize Internet resources. With Mariner, you can access e-mail, FTP, Gopher, newsgroups, and the Web. When you are done with your work online, Mariner can organize all the resources you looked at during the session by subject area and will let you work with the resources offline.

Mariner is available for Windows, Windows 95, and Windows NT systems. You can learn more about this commercial software package from NCD at

```
http://www.mariner.ncd.com/
```

Microsoft Internet Explorer

One of the most exciting browsers released in 1995 was Microsoft's Internet Explorer. Internet Explorer supports all Netscape 1.1 extensions and powerful multimedia extensions including background sounds, scrolling marquees, and inline video movies. Internet Explorer also supports the SSL secure transfer protocol and will support the new, more secure, transfer protocol called STT. With the release of the Internet Explorer VR extension that enables full VRML capability, Internet Explorer is definitely the browser to watch in 1996.

The Internet Explorer is available for Macintosh, Windows 95, and Windows NT. International versions of Internet Explorer are available in the following languages: Danish, Dutch, Finnish, French, German, Italian, Japanese, Norwegian, Portuguese (Brazilian), Spanish, and Swedish.

Visit Microsoft's Internet Explorer page at

```
http://www.windows.microsoft.com/windows/ie/iexplorer.html
```

Microsoft Internet Explorer VR

Internet Explorer VR is an add-on module for one of the hottest Web browsers available today. You will find that Internet Explorer VR set-up is quick and easy. Internet Explorer supports Microsoft's live VRML format, which enables you to create animated VRML documents and much more. If you have the Internet Explorer browser or are considering using Internet Explorer, Internet Explorer VR is a must try add-on.

You can learn more about Internet Explorer VR at Microsoft's Web site:

```
http://www.windows.microsoft.com/windows/ie/iexplorer.html
```

MidasWWW

MidasWWW is a Motif X Windows browser for UNIX and VMS platforms. If you are familiar with Motif applications, MidasWWW has a polished Motif look and feel. The browser is fully compatible with the Motif Style Guide and has extensive online help.

You can learn more about this browser and download a free copy from this page at W3O:

```
http://www.w3.org/hypertext/WWW/MidasWWW/Announce1.html
```

MMM

MMM is a WWW browser written in the Caml programming language using the CamlTk4 library. The alpha release of this free Web browser is available for UNIX platforms. Java isn't the only programming language being used to create applets, and the neat thing about this browser is that it can use applets written in Caml. For additional security, you can also use PGP-signed applets that require the user to have PGP and ensure the applet has not been modified in any way.

Visit INRIA's site in France to learn more about MMM and Caml:

```
http://pauillac.inria.fr/~rouaix/mmm/
```

NCSA Mosaic

NCSA Mosaic was developed at the National Center for Supercomputing Applications at the University of Illinois in Urbana-Champaign. NCSA Mosaic is the original graphics-capable browser. As the only browser that can claim it started an Internet revolution, the venerable NCSA Mosaic is the most reliable browser you will ever find. Versions of NCSA Mosaic are available for Macintosh, Windows, and UNIX systems running X Windows. There is no charge for noncommercial use of any versions of NCSA Mosaic. Some versions of NCSA Mosaic support Netscape and Internet Explorer extensions. For example, the Windows version supports background sounds and documents with sound tracks.

To visit NCSA's Mosaic site on the Web, use the URL:

```
http://www.ncsa.uiuc.edu/SDG/Software/Mosaic
```

or

```
http://www.ncsa.uiuc.edu/SDG/Software/Mosaic/NCSAMosaicHome.html
```

Netscape Navigator

The Netscape Navigator is the most widely used Web browser. Versions of Netscape Navigator are available for Macintosh, Windows, and UNIX X Windows systems. Driven by Netscape's rise as a commercial corporation worth hundreds of millions of dollars, all Netscape's products are shifting to a commercial model. However, you can still download beta versions of the Netscape Navigator. The most stable beta version of the Netscape Navigator is Version 1.2. Consequently, if you have problems with beta version 2.0 or higher, you may want to use Netscape Navigator Version 1.2.

For more information on Netscape Navigator, visit Netscape corporation's Web site at

```
http://www.netscape.com/
```

Netshark

Netshark is an enhanced graphics-capable browser that supports HTML 2.0, Netscape 1.0 extensions, and Internet Explorer extensions. While Netshark does not integrate news and mail, it does let you access FTP, telnet, and Gopher resources, as well as HTTP resources. Netshark is fast and reliable. The key features of Netshark that make it a browser to watch is its support for inline QuickTime videos, multiple hot lists, and documents with sound tracks. NetShark plays AIFF and AU sound files as they are being downloaded. Versions of Netshark are available for Macintosh, Windows, and Windows 95/NT.

You can learn more about Netshark and download a trial version at

```
http://netshark.inter.net/netshark/
```

Netsurfer

Netsurfer is an enhanced browser developed for NEXTSTEP computers that supports most Netscape extensions. This multithreaded graphics-capable browser provides integrated access to Web, Gopher, and FTP resources. Netsurfer provides a simple, icon-based index for saving and retrieving frequently accessed Internet resources. Using drag and drop, you can quickly access and retrieve files from anywhere on the Net. Netsurfer is the first Web browser to support multiple video playback integrated directly inside Web pages. Not only can you play multiple videos at the same time, you can drag and drop videos while they are still playing.

Netsurfer Version 1.1 is available for all NEXTSTEP platforms, including Intel based PC's, NeXT computers, Hewlett-Packard PA-RISC, and Sun Sparc work stations. You can learn more about Netsurfer and obtain a trial version at

```
http://software.thoughtport.com/Netsurfer.html
```

OLIAS

OLIAS is an integrated browser for displaying both SGML and HTML documents. This browser, available from HalSoft, is a good browser if you want to access both SGML and HTML documents. Versions of OLIAS are available for UNIX systems. You can learn more about OLIAS at

```
http://www.hal.com/products/sw/olias/index.html
```

OmniWeb

OmniWeb is an enhanced browser for NEXTSTEP computers. If you tried older versions of OmniWeb and were disappointed, you should give Version 2.0 serious second thoughts. Version 2.0 of OmniWeb is a complete rewrite of the original browser. This new version features full support for Netscape 2.0 features, including frames and client-side image maps.

You can read more about OmniWeb and download the free version at

```
http://www.omnigroup.com/Software/OmniWeb/
```

PowerBrowser

PowerBrowser is everything you would expect in a browser created by database giant Oracle. The PowerBrowser software package includes a local database called Blaze. Blaze lets you store and manage large amounts of data efficiently. The browser also supports some extensions to the HTML standard, including backgrounds, tables, and Java. The beta version of Oracle PowerBrowser for Windows 95 is freely available for evaluation.

To learn more about PowerBrowser and download the free beta, visit Oracle on the Web at

```
http://www.oracle.com/
```

Pythia

Pythia is an integrated Web publishing system designed to support sophisticated commercial and institutional use. The Pythia browser is the only browser that features direct support for RDBMS and GIS database access. With Pythia, you get all the benefits of Netscape 1.0 extensions and Internet Explorer 2.0 extensions, and full support for HTML 3.0 elements, including style sheets, tables, backgrounds, and inline multimedia. Pythia features full support for document sound tracks in the WAV format and inline video in the three most popular formats: MPEG, AVI, and QuickTime. Versions of Pythia are available for Windows and Windows95/NT systems.

If these features aren't enough to put Pythia on your list of browsers to watch, here's another good reason: Pythia supports vector graphics using a screen coordinate system. You can use the proprietary <GRAPHIC> tag to create powerful vector graphics within your images. Attributes for the <GRAPHIC> tag include:

PEN (style, thickness, red, green, blue) creates lines drawn with a graphic pen. The values for the PEN attribute are specified as numeric values.

BRUSH (style, red, green, blue) creates lines drawn with a brush. The values for the BRUSH attribute are specified as numeric values.

MOVETO (X,Y) moves the current drawing position to a new location.

LINETO (X,Y) draws a line from the current position to a new location.

RECTTO (X,Y) draws a rectangle from the current position to a new location.

ELLIPSE (X,Y) draws an ellipse from the current position to a new location.

Pythia image tag extensions enable you to precisely position images on the page. You can even layer images and text. The new <IMG> tag attributes for precise image positioning are X, which takes a value equal to the x coordinate for the image on the current window and Y, which takes a value equal to the y coordinate for the image on the current window.

Another useful <IMG> tag extension called ISBACKDROP enables you to specify that an image defined with the SRC attribute should be displayed on all subsequent HTML documents in the current session. This can be useful technique for full-screen backdrop images that will not have to be reloaded.

The Pythia tag that enables live queries of SQL databases is the <QUERY> tag. Queries can be returned in a variety of formats, including reports, tables, bar charts, line charts, pie charts, and even pick lists that drive subsequent queries.

Many Web publishers will also like Pythia's <MARGIN> tag. With the <MARGIN> tag, you can define temporary margins to precisely layout text. Although you can specify all four margin positions, you only need to specify the margins you want to change. Attributes for the tag include the following:

LEFT—The value for this attribute is the width of the left margin in pixels.

RIGHT—The value for this attribute is the width of the right margin in pixels.

TOP—The value for this attribute is the width of the top margin in pixels.

BOTTOM—The value for this attribute is the width of the bottom margin in pixels.

RESET—Used to reset the margins to their original settings. This attribute is not used with other attributes.

To learn more about the Pythia browser and download the free beta version, visit

```
http://pythia.com/
```

WebExplorer

WebExplorer is a browser written exclusively for OS/2 WARP. The browser supports some Netscape extensions and HTML 3.0 elements, including backgrounds and tables. You can learn more about WebExplorer and download the latest version at

```
http://www.phoenix.net/~vccubed/os2apps.html
```

Quarterdeck Mosaic

Quarterdeck Mosaic is an enhanced version of the original Mosaic that was built for speed and ease of use. The browser features advanced mechanisms for managing Web resources and using built-in features, you can make annotations pertaining to these resources. The software also includes a unique Connect and Play mechanism that enables users who do not have an Internet Service Provider to set up an account with one of several commercial ISPs. Quarterdeck Mosaic is currently available only for Windows systems.

Quarterdeck Mosaic is one of the only integrated HTML/VRML browsers available today. Visit Quarterdeck's Web site to get a trial version:

```
http://www.qdeck.com/
```

Secure NCSA Mosaic

Secure NCSA Mosaic is a Web browser with encryption and authentication enhancements. Secure NCSA Mosaic was developed jointly by Enterprise Integration Technologies, RSA Data Security Incorporated, and the National Center for Supercomputing Applications. Versions of this powerful browser are available for Windows, Windows 95/NT, and UNIX platforms.

To learn how Secure NCSA Mosaic protects documents and your transactions, visit Commerce Net's site at

```
http://www.commerce.net/software/SMosaic/
```

Sesame Navigator

0The Sesame Navigator from Ubique adds an interesting twist to Web surfing called Virtual Places. Virtual Places is a client-server architecture that introduces a human presence into Web publications and live interaction. Using the Sesame Navigator at a site enhanced with the Doors Server, you can see an image of other people visiting the site and interact with them. These images appear as portraits or thumbnail images overlaid on the Web page. As a Web publisher, you can see images of users visiting your site, offer assistance, and receive immediate feedback.

Another neat feature of Sesame Navigator is its integrated audio capability that enables users with audio-equipped computers to have voice conversations and teleconferences live online while the participants browse the Web. Text conversations can be used on computers not equipped for audio. If this technology takes off—and it should, considering America Online's recent acquisition of Ubique—you won't have to imagine what it would be like to invite a friend who lives 2,000 miles away to come surf the Web with you, you will be able to do it live. This is because Sesame enables groups of users to Web surf together using a guided tour function. Using this guided tour function, you can give a multimedia presentation to a group of users no matter what their location.

> **NOTE**
>
> Multiparty conferences with Sesame require that all participants be connected to the Internet's MBONE. The MBONE is the Internet's multicast backbone, and if you haven't heard about it, you are missing a key part of the future. Still, if you don't have MBONE access, don't worry—text conferences require no special connectivity and you can still invite friends on a Web surfing safari.

Versions of Sesame Navigator are currently available for

- Sun Sparcstation running SunOS 4.1.3 or later revisions
- Sun Sparcstation running Solaris 2.3 or later revisions
- Hewlett-Packard workstations running HP-UX 9.X
- Silicon Graphics Indy (SGI) running IRIX 5.2

Windows and Macintosh versions of Sesame Navigator should be released soon. To learn more about Sesame Navigator, visit Ubique at

```
http://www.ubique.com/products/sesame_ds.html
```

> **NOTE**
>
> While Sesame Navigator should definitely be on your list of browsers to watch, the chances are good that the browser may change names in the near future. So if you start hearing about a browser that enables you to invite friends to surf the Web with you, you'll know where the new browser got its start—at an Internet upstart called Ubique.

SlipKnot

If your Internet Service Provider uses a UNIX-based system yet charges an exorbitant rate for a SLIP/PPP connection or, as in the case of most freenets, does not offer SLIP/PPP access, you should check out SlipKnot. SlipKnot is a graphics-capable browser that does not require a SLIP, PPP, or TCP/IP connection to the Internet. SlipKnot was designed for users with Windows systems that access the Internet using a UNIX shell account. A nice feature of SlipKnot is that it lets you switch back and forth between your UNIX terminal window and the browser window.

SlipKnot, like many other browsers, allows you to try before you buy. For a timed-trial version of SlipKnot, visit the SlipKnot home page:

```
http://plaza.interport.net/slipknot/slipknot.html
```

Spry AIR Mosaic

Spry AIR Mosaic is an enhanced browser for Windows and Windows 95 systems. While the browser is generally sold as part of an integrated Internet access solution, trial versions of the browser are available. Spry Corporation is a division of CompuServe. Spry's products include Internet in a Box, Internet in a Box for Kids, Internet Office, and Mosaic in a Box. Mosaic in a Box is a one-disk solution for obtaining access to the World Wide Web. You don't even have to find a local Internet service provider first. When you start the installation process, the software is loaded onto your system and a CompuServe account is set up for you. Because CompuServe offers direct access to the World Wide Web, this is an easy way to get online fast.

For more information on AIR Mosaic, visit Spry's Web site at

```
http://www.spry.com/products.html
```

SuperHighway Access

Frontier Technologies' SuperHighway Access 2 for Windows is a fully integrated software package for accessing the Internet. The package provides everything you need to access the Web, e-mail, FTP, newsgroups, and telnet. A key feature of the browser is the Internet Organizer that helps you easily organize your favorite resources.

You can learn more about SuperHighway Access at Frontier Technologies' Web site:

```
http://www.FrontierTech.Com/
```

SurfIt!

SurfIt! is a browser written entirely in Tcl script code. The browser supports HTML 3.0 and most Netscape 1.0 extensions. Versions of SurfIt! are available for UNIX systems. You will find that SurfIt! is a neat browser to take a look at because it can download and execute applets written in Tcl/Tk.

Visit the SurfIt! home page to learn more about Tcl/Tk applets and the SurfIt! browser:

```
http://pastime.anu.edu.au/SurfIt/
```

WebSpace Navigator

Template Graphics Software produces one of the best VRML browsers available today called the WebSpace Navigator. You will find that the WebSpace Navigator has many unique features and a very friendly interface. Interestingly enough, WebSpace is a native Open Inventor application and as the VRML 1.0 specification is based on SGI's Open Inventor language, WebSpace is the most reliable browser for correctly rendering VRML world files.

WebSpace also supports live VRML scenes that are animated using VRML engines. Development versions of WebSpace are available for OS/2, PowerMac, PowerPC, Windows, Windows 95/NT, HP UX, and Digital UNIX. To learn more about WebSpace, visit Template Graphics Software's Web site at

`http://www.sd.tgs.com/`

WebSurfer

WebSurfer is an enhanced browser developed by NetManage. This browser is optimized for high performance on LANs using multiple connections. WebSurfer has many user-definable parameters that enable you to customize the browser's look and feel. Versions of WebSurfer are available for Windows and Windows 95/NT systems.

Visit the WebSurfer home page at

`http://www.netmanage.com/netmanage/apps/websurfer.html`

HTML Converters

Although the task of creating HTML code is fairly complex, some helper applications called *converters* try to automate the task. HTML converters convert your favorite document formats into HTML-formatted documents and vice versa. With a converter, you can transform a Word 7.0 document into an HTML document at the touch of a button. Converters are especially useful when you are converting simple documents and are less useful when you are converting documents with complex layouts.

You can find HTML converters for every major word processor and document design application, including BibTeX, DECwrite, FrameMaker, Interleaf, LaTeX, MS Word, PageMaker, PowerPoint, QuarkXPress, Scribe, and WordPerfect. HTML converters are available to convert specific formats, such as ASCII, RTF, MIF, Postscript, and UNIX MAN pages. There are even converters to convert source code from popular programming languages to HTML. You can convert your favorite programs to HTML if they are in these languages: C, C++, FORTRAN, Lisp, or Pascal.

The definitive site on the Web to learn more about HTML converters and download dozens of converters is the W3O. Their section on HTML converters is the best you'll find on the

316

Web. You should visit this page at the W3O:

http://www.w3.org/hypertext/WWW/Tools/Filters.html

HTML Editors

HTML editors enable you to easily create documents in HTML format. Most editors have features akin to your favorite word processor, such as menu bars, pulldown menus, macros, and quick keys. The job of the editor is to help you place HTML tags in your document. While you will find HTML editors are useful tools, the task of creating HTML documents can be quite complex depending on the type of document you are creating, and the more complexity you add to a task, the more difficult it is to automate. HTML editors are available for many different operating systems, including Macintosh, Windows, and UNIX.

Some HTML editors are template utilities. HTML templates enable you to add the functionality of an HTML editor to your favorite word processor. This enables you to use the familiar features of your word processor to add HTML formatting to your documents.

ANT_HTML

ANT_HTML is a template utility for creating HTML documents that works with Microsoft Word 6.0 and later versions for Macintosh, Windows, and Windows 95/NT. Adding the template called ANT_HTML.DOT is as easy as putting the template in the appropriate directory. Using the template is as easy as opening a new file using the template.

The latest versions of ANT_HTML 2.2 support any and all HTML tags. You select these tags from one of three ANT_HTML toolbars: the basic toolbar supports HTML 2.0, an extended toolbar supports Netscape 1.0 extensions, and a special toolbar can be customized for any tags you choose. ANT_HTML includes utilities for converting special characters to their character or numeric value, converting file formats, and printing HTML documents without the HTML markup.

You can learn more about ANT_HTML at

http://mcia.com/ant/

EasyHelp/Web

EasyHelp/Web from Eon Solutions is a template utility for creating HTML documents and Windows Help files. Versions of EasyHelp/Web are available for Word 2.0 and Word 6.0. While current versions of EasyHelp/Web only support HTML 2.0, an upcoming version should support Netscape extensions and HTML 3.0. You can download full working copies of the software by visiting Eon Solutions at

http://www.u-net.com/eon/

HotDog and HotDog Pro

HotDog is an excellent HTML editor from Sausage Software. HotDog fully supports Netscape extensions and HTML 3.0. While HotDog is a basic editor, HotDog Pro is definitely a power tool. Versions of this commercial editor are available for Macintosh, Windows, Windows 95/NT, and UNIX systems.

You can download a trial version of HotDog at Sausage Software's Web site:

```
http://www.sausage.com/
```

HoTMetaL and HoTMetaL Pro

HoTMetaL and HoTMetaL Pro are undoubtedly the top HTML editors available. HoTMetaL is a freeware version of the more powerful and commercial HoTMetaL Pro. Current versions of these editors from SoftQuad support Netscape extensions and all HTML 3.0 elements. You will find that HoTMetaL Pro has all the features of your favorite word processor, including a spell checker and a grammar checker. Both HoTMetaL and HoTMetaL Pro are available for Macintosh, Windows, Windows 95/NT, and UNIX systems.

The HoTMetaL Pro package includes an image editor called MetalWorks. MetalWorks was specifically designed to meet the needs of Web publishers. With MetalWorks, you can quickly and easily create image maps, transparent GIFs, embossed images, and much more.

To learn more about HoTMetaL Pro, visit SoftQuad at

```
http://www.sq.com/products/hotmetal/hothome.htm
```

To obtain the current version of HoTMetaL, visit

```
http://www.sq.com/products/hotmetal/hm-ftp.htm
```

HTML Author

HTML Author is another good template utility for Microsoft Word. Current versions of HTML Author fully support the HTML 2.0 specification. The beta version of HTML Author is free for evaluation purposes and can be obtained at

```
http://www.salford.ac.uk/docs/depts/iti/staff/gsc/htmlauth/summary.html
```

HTML Writer

If you are looking for a stand-alone HTML editor, HTML Writer may be the editor you are looking for. This terrific editor supports HTML 2.0 and features document style sheets that enable you to quickly create HTML documents. But the best thing about HTML Writer is that it is donationware. The author of the program asks that if you like the program, you make a donation to help pay for the cost of developing future versions of the editor.

You can download the Windows version of HTML Writer from

```
http://lal.cs.byu.edu/people/nosack/
```

Internet Assistant

Internet Assistant from Microsoft is another good HTML template utility, especially because beta versions are freely available. Internet Assistant supports the HTML 2.0 specification and will soon support Internet Explorer extensions, Netscape extensions, and most HTML 3.0 elements. Versions of Internet Assistant are available for Word for Windows 95 and Word 6.0 for Windows NT. Although Word 7.0 should include Internet Assistant, you can obtain the free beta version now at

```
http://198.105.232.6:80/msoffice/freestuf/msword/download/ia/ia95/default.htm
```

<Live Markup>PRO

<Live Markup>PRO is an advanced HTML editor for Windows, Windows 95, and Windows NT. The editor is fully WYSIWYG and feature rich. Current versions support HTML 2.0 and Netscape 1.0 extensions.

You can obtain a free trial version of <Live Markup>PRO at

```
http://www.mediatec.com/
```

NaviPress

NaviPress is a terrific Web publishing solution. You will find that NaviPress is fully WYSIWYG (What You See Is What You Get) and very easy to use. In addition to enabling you to create HTML documents, you can also use NaviPress as a top-notch Web browser. NaviPress supports HTML 2.0 and Netscape 1.0 extensions.

Using NaviPress's MiniWeb, you can use NaviPress to organize your Web site. You can also read, change, and save your Web pages while you are online. Versions of NaviPress are available for Macintosh, Windows, Windows 95/NT, and UNIX systems. You can learn more about this commercial Web publishing package at

```
http://www.navisoft.com/products/press/appl.htm
```

Image Tools

Image tools are widely available on the Internet as freeware or shareware. Most of these tools are under constant development by their creators. While the most widely supported platform for image tools is Windows, you can find image tools for just about any system you can think of. As most image tools are specific to a particular system, this section looks at some of the best image tools for each major operating system.

Many of these programs are located in file archives with dozens and sometimes hundreds of other programs. Not only will this section highlight some of the popular tools, but it will also point you in the direction of the Net's software treasure troves.

TIP

The directories where these applications can be found are treasure troves. You will find dozens of multimedia programs for your system. While most archives are quickly becoming fully accessible by HTTP, you will find many sites are available only with FTP. Anonymous FTP sites are directly accessible through your Web browser. All browser packages include support for FTP using an FTP URL in this form:

```
ftp://ftp_server/directory
```

Your browser will log in to the anonymous FTP site using the login-id of anonymous and a password that is your e-mail address.

Amiga

FastView is a great viewer for JPEG and GIF images and as the name implies, it is quite fast. As this tool requires Amiga OS 2.0 or higher, you will want to make sure you aren't running an older version of Amiga OS. Another good Amiga viewer is FastJPEG. FastJPEG will work on a system running Amiga OS 1.3 or higher. This freeware viewer is very user-friendly.

The hot spots on the Net for Amiga freeware and shareware are the Aminet sites. The graphics directory at the Aminet site contains hundreds of image tools that enable you to create everything from simple images to powerful 3-D images and fractals.

You'll find one of the primary Aminet sites at NetNet:

```
http://laslo.netnet.net:80/aminet/
```

The image tools are in this directory:

```
http://laslo.netnet.net:80/aminet/dirs/tree_gfx.html.
```

You can find Aminet mirror sites at these locations:

USA—`http://ftp.wustl.edu/~aminet/` (main Aminet site)

Switzerland—`http://www.eunet.ch/~aminet/` (partial mirror)

United Kingdom—`http://src.doc.ic.ac.uk/public/aminet/info/www/home-src.doc.html` (complete mirror)

Germany—`http://www.germany.aminet.org/aminet/` (complete mirror)

Germany—`ftp://epix.rrze.unierlangen.de/public/pub/amiga/aminet/aminet.html` (Partial mirror)

Germany—`http://www.leo.org/archiv/amiga/` (Partial mirror)

Germany—`http://www.unihamburg.de/World/Playground/aminet/` `aminet_homepage.html` (complete mirror)

Macintosh

GraphicConverter is possibly the most versatile and powerful shareware image tool for the Macintosh. This program can convert almost 100 image formats and has many useful features for manipulating images. With GraphicConverter you can convert all images on an entire directory from one format to another at the touch of a button. You can download GraphicConverter using this URL:

`http://hyperarchive.lcs.mit.edu/HyperArchive/Archive/gst/grf/`
`➡graphic-converter-231.hqx`

If you have problems getting this version of graphic converter, look in the base graphics directory for the latest version:

`http://hyperarchive.lcs.mit.edu/HyperArchive/Archive/gst/grf/`

GraphicConverter requires System 7 and QuickTime to be installed, so if you have an older system, try GIFConverter. GIFConverter will display fewer image formats but is still a good choice. The creator of GIFConverter has set up a home page dedicated to this useful utility at

`http://www.kamit.com/gifconverter.html`

You can download GraphicConverter directly using this URL:

`http://hyperarchive.lcs.mit.edu/HyperArchive/Archive/gst/grf/gif-converter-237.hqx`

A good image viewer for the Mac is JPEGView and as the name implies, JPEGView excels at displaying JPEG images. You will find that JPEGView is a handy program to have for viewing common image formats like BMP, GIF, JPEG, PICT, and TIFF. You can download JPEGView using this URL:

`http://hyperarchive.lcs.mit.edu/HyperArchive/Archive/gst/grf/jpeg-view-331.hqx`

A good shareware paint program for the Mac is Matt Paint. While the program was modeled after the original MacPaint, it is greatly enhanced. Matt Paint has many nice features for creating and manipulating images. You will find the program is also very user-friendly. You'll find the source for Matt Paint here:

`http://hyperarchive.lcs.mit.edu/HyperArchive/Archive/gst/grf/matt-paint-194.hqx`

A good Macintosh utility for creating transparent GIFs is Transparency. Not only is this freeware utility easy to use, it is also quick solution for creating images with greater impact. To obtain the source for Transparency, use this URL:

`http://hyperarchive.lcs.mit.edu/HyperArchive/Archive/gst/grf/transparency-10.hqx`

As you can probably see from the URLs in this section, the location of the Macintosh treasure trove on the Web is

`http://hyperarchive.lcs.mit.edu/HyperArchive/Archive/gst/`

This archive, known as the info-mac archive, has hundreds of Macintosh tools. You will find everything you need here to rev up your Mac, including image tools, video tools, and sound tools. To ensure you can get access to this busy archive, you can visit any of the following mirror sites:

Australia—`ftp://ftp.ausom.net.au/pub/mirrors/info-mac/` (complete mirror)

Austria—`http://www.univie.ac.at/ftp/systems/mac/info-mac/` (complete mirror)

Belgium—`ftp://ftp.linkline.be/mirror/info-mac/` (complete mirror; only accessible from Europe)

Canada—`ftp://ftp.agt.net/pub/info-mac/` (complete mirror)

Canada—`ftp://ftp.ucs.ubc.ca/pub/mac/info-mac/` (complete mirror)

Finland—`ftp://ftp.funet.fi/pub/mac/info-mac/` (complete mirror)

France—`ftp://ftp.francenet.fr/pub/miroirs/info-mac/` (complete mirror)

France—`ftp://ftp.ibp.fr/pub/mac/info-mac/` (complete mirror)

Germany—`ftp://ftp.informatik.rwth-aachen.de/pub/info-mac/` (complete mirror)

Germany—`ftp://ftp.rrzn.uni-hannover.de/pub/info-mac/` (complete mirror)

Hong Kong—`ftp://ftp.hk.super.net/pub/mirror/info-mac/` (complete mirror)

Israel—`ftp://ftp.technion.ac.il/pub/unsupported/mac/info-mac/` (complete mirror)

Italy—`ftp://cnuce-arch.cnr.it/pub/info-mac/` (partial mirror)

Japan—`ftp://ftp.ims.ac.jp/pub/mac/info-mac/` (complete mirror)

Japan—`ftp://ftp.lab.kdd.co.jp/info-mac/` (complete mirror)

Japan—`http://www.osaka-u.ac.jp/export/info-mac/` (complete mirror)

Japan—`http://www.chem.sci.osaka-u.ac.jp/mirror.html` (complete mirror)

Japan—`http://www.riken.go.jp/archives/info-mac/` (complete mirror)

Korea—`ftp://hwarang.postech.ac.kr/pub/mac/info-mac/` (complete mirror)

Korea—`http://centaur.postech.ac.kr/network/ftpserv.html` (complete mirror)

Netherlands—`ftp://ftp.euro.net/Mac/info-mac/` (complete mirror)

Netherlands—`ftp://ftp.fenk.wau.nl/pub/mac/info-mac/` (complete mirror)

Netherlands—`http://ftp.fenk.wau.nl/pub/mac/info-mac/` (complete mirror)

Norway—`ftp://ftp.bitcon.no/pub/micro/mac/info-mac/` (complete mirror)

Singapore—`ftp://ftp.nus.sg/pub/mac/` (complete mirror)

Singapore—`http://www.nus.sg/NUShome.html` (complete mirror)

Spain—`ftp://ftp.urv.es/pub/mirror/info-mac/` (complete mirror)

Sweden—`ftp://ftp.sunet.se/pub/mac/info-mac/` (complete mirror)

Sweden—`http://ftp.sunet.se/pub/mac/info-mac/` (complete mirror)

Taiwan—`ftp://nctuccca.edu.tw/Macintosh/info-mac/` (complete mirror)

Taiwan—`http://nctuccca.edu.tw/cgi-bin/ftpls/` (complete mirror)

Turkey—`ftp://ftp.bups.bilkent.edu.tr/pub/info-mac/` (complete mirror)

Turkey—`http://www.bups.bilkent.edu.tr/Documentation/bups.html` (complete mirror)

UK —`ftp://src.doc.ic.ac.uk/packages/info-mac/` (complete mirror)

UK —`http://src.doc.ic.ac.uk/packages/info-mac/` (complete mirror)

USA—`ftp://ftp.amug.org/pub/mirrors/info-mac/` (complete mirror)

USA—`http://www.amug.org/index.html` (complete mirror)

USA—`ftp://mirror.apple.com/mirrors/Info-Mac.Archive/` (complete mirror)

USA—`http://mirror.apple.com/` (complete mirror)

USA—`http://ici.proper.com/mac/files/` (complete mirror)

USA—`ftp://tornado.rfx.com/pub/info-mac/` (complete mirror)

USA—`ftp://fiesta.tsc.udel.edu/pub/mirrors/info-mac/` (complete mirror)

USA—`http://www.tsc.udel.edu/info-mac.html` (complete mirror)

USA—`ftp://ftp.hawaii.edu/mirrors/info-mac/` (complete mirror)

USA—`ftp://uiarchive.cso.uiuc.edu/pub/systems/mac/info-mac/` (complete mirror)

USA—`http://uiarchive.cso.uiuc.edu/` (complete mirror)

Windows

As you might imagine, there is a flood of good programs for Windows systems. ACDSee is a fast and easy-to-use image viewer for Windows. The viewer features online help and support for BMP, GIF, JPEG, PCX, Photo-CD, PNG, TGA, and TIFF image formats. To learn more about this shareware viewer, visit the ACDSee home page at

`http://vvv.com/acd/acdsee.html`

Alchemy Mindworks' Graphic Workshop is a good shareware program for viewing, editing, and converting image formats. The program is available for DOS, Windows, and Windows 95 systems and has many features that make it a good choice for a basic image creation and viewing solution. The program also can automatically decode UUENCODED images.

To get a trial version of Graphic Workshop, Visit Alchemy's home page at

`http://www.north.net/alchemy/alchemy.html`

If you are looking for a freeware image solution, GraphX may be your number one choice. GraphX is an excellent freeware program for viewing, editing, and converting image formats. The program will enable you to view and convert images in BMP, Fax G3/G4, GIF, JPEG, PCX, PNG, SunRaster, TARGA, TIFF, and XWD formats. GraphX enables you to create thumbnail catalogs of images and has many advanced features for manipulating images. Another nice feature of GraphX is that it automatically decodes UUENCODED images and enables you to UUENCODE images after you are done manipulating them.

To download this freeware viewer, visit the GraphX home page at

`http://www.group42.com/graphx.htm`

WebImage is an image viewing, editing, and conversion tool designed to meet the needs of Web publishers. With WebImage, you can easily create transparent GIFs, create image map files in NCSA and CERN image map formats, and optimize images to reduce their file size. Versions of this viewer are available for Windows and Windows 95 systems.

You can obtain a trial version of WebImage at

`http://www.group42.com/`

LView Pro is an excellent image tool for most popular PC formats, as well as JPEG and GIF. With it, you can edit and convert file formats and create transparent GIFs. Versions of LView Pro are available for Windows and Windows 95/NT systems. You can learn more about this shareware image tool and download the current version at

`http://world.std.com/~mmedia/lviewp.html`

JASC's Paint Shop Pro is the complete image creation and manipulation solution. Not only is Paint Shop Pro one of the friendliest image tools available, it has many advanced features, such as photo retouching, image enhancement, and batch conversion. This image tool supports more than 30 image formats and enables you to convert images to and from any of these formats.

Trial versions of Paint Shop Pro for Windows are available at JASC's Web site:

`http://www.jasc.com/index.html`

Hamrick Software's VuePrint is an excellent program for viewing and printing images. The best thing about this shareware image tool is that once you pay the shareware fee, you can download upgraded versions of the program as they are released every quarter. Versions of VuePrint are available for Windows and Windows 95/NT systems.

To obtain VuePrint, visit Hamrick Software's home page at

`http://www.primenet.com/~hamrick/.`

The definitive place on the Net for DOS, Windows, Windows 95, Windows NT, and OS/2 applications is the SimTel archive from Coast to Coast Software Repository. One of the primary sites containing this archive is Oakland's SimTel site. This archive contains hundreds of applications for PCs. Oakland's Web site dedicated to the archive is located at

```
http://www.acs.oakland.edu/oak/.
```

The definitive source for MS-DOS applications and utilities is

```
http://www.acs.oakland.edu/oak/SimTel/SimTel-msdos.html
```

The definitive source for Windows applications and utilities is

```
http://www.acs.oakland.edu/oak/SimTel/SimTel-win3.html
```

The definitive source for OS/2 and OS/2 Warp applications and utilities is

```
http://www.acs.oakland.edu/oak/SimTel/SimTel-os2.html
```

A growing archive for Windows 95 applications and utilities is

```
http://www.acs.oakland.edu/oak/SimTel/SimTel-win95.html
```

A growing archive for Windows NT applications and utilities is

```
http://www.acs.oakland.edu/oak/SimTel/SimTel-nt.html
```

You will find that all these directories are mirrored at various SimTel archive sites, including

```
ftp://uiarchive.cso.uiuc.edu/pub/systems/pc/simtel/
```

and

```
ftp://ftp.wit.com/microsoft/
```

UNIX

UNIX image tools primarily run under the X Windows environment. One of the best all-around viewers for X Windows is ImageMagick. It handles JPEG, GIF, and other image formats quite nicely. ImageMagick also gives you the capability to convert image formats. This directory has several good X Windows viewers:

```
ftp://ftp.x.org/contrib/applications
```

The FTP site listed here is the site for the X Consortium's UNIX X Windows archive. The archive contains hundreds of applications and utilities for the UNIX X Windows environment. As the X Consortium is currently compiling a list of mirror sites, you may want to visit the main directory at the archive to check on the status of mirrors for this extremely busy site:

```
ftp://ftp.x.org/
```

A mirror site of X Consortium's archive is at

```
ftp://uiarchive.cso.uiuc.edu/pub/X11/contrib/
```

For Linux, a good viewer is zgv. This Linux viewer works with VGA and SVGA monitors. The most current version of zgv is at

```
http://sunsite.unc.edu/pub/Linux/apps/graphics/viewers.
```

The Linux base directory is a treasure trove of resources for Linux. You can find mirror sites for this archive at the following addresses:

```
ftp://uiarchive.cso.uiuc.edu/pub/systems/linux/sunsite
ftp://ftp.linux.org/pub/mirrors/sunsite/
ftp://ftp.uni-paderborn.de/pub/Mirrors/sunsite.unc.edu/
ftp://ftp.cs.cuhk.hk/pub/Linux/
ftp://ftp.dungeon.com/pub/linux/sunsite-mirror/
ftp://ftp.dfv.rwth-aachen.de/pub/linux/sunsite/
ftp://ftp.maths.warwick.ac.uk/mirrors/linux/sunsite.unc-mirror/
ftp://ftp.rus.uni-stuttgart.de/pub/unix/systems/linux/MIRROR.sunsite/
ftp://ftp.uni-erlangen.de/pub/Linux/MIRROR.sunsite/
ftp://ftp.uni-paderborn.de/pub/linux/sunsite/
ftp://ftp.gwdg.de/pub/linux/mirrors/sunsite/
ftp://ftp.tu-graz.ac.at/pub/Linux/
ftp://pub.vse.cz/pub/386-unix/linux/
ftp://dcs.muni.cz/pub/UNIX/linux/
ftp://ftp.univ-angers.fr/pub/linux/
ftp://ftp.tu-dresden.de/pub/Linux/sunsite/
ftp://ftp.germany.eu.net/pub/os/Linux/Mirror.SunSITE/
ftp://ftp.nus.sg/pub/unix/Linux/
ftp://ftp.uni-tuebingen.de/pub/linux/Mirror.sunsite/
ftp://ftp.cnr.it/pub/Linux/
ftp://ftp.kfki.hu/pub/linux/
ftp://cnuce-arch.cnr.it/pub/Linux/
ftp://ftp.orst.edu/pub/mirrors/sunsite.unc.edu/linux/
ftp://ftp.nectec.or.th/pub/mirrors/linux/
ftp://ftp.switch.ch/mirror/linux/
ftp://src.doc.ic.ac.uk/packages/linux/sunsite.unc-mirror/
ftp://ftp.cc.gatech.edu/pub/linux/
ftp://ftp.engr.uark.edu/pub/linux/sunsite/
ftp://ftp.wit.com/systems/unix/linux/
ftp://ftp.infomagic.com/pub/mirrors/linux/sunsite/
ftp://ftp.rge.com/pub/linux/sunsite/
ftp://ftp.spin.ad.jp/pub/linux/sunsite.unc.edu/
```

```
ftp://ftp.metu.edu.tr/pub/linux/sunsite/
ftp://ftp.cps.cmich.edu/pub/linux/sunsite/
ftp://ftp.io.org/pub/systems/linux
```

Sound Tools

Hundreds of sound tools are available on the Internet. This section highlights a few of the best available as freeware or shareware. Two basic types of sound tools are used to play sound files. A *player* is a general-purpose sound tool that enables you to play sound files. While sound files must be in a format readable by the player, most players can read and play several sound formats. Players are great for the average sound file. A *tracker* is a sound tool specifically designed to play digital music modules (mods). Trackers usually have much wider support for sound formats and advanced features.

The next sections look at the top players and trackers available for each of the major systems.

> **NOTE**
>
> You can use the same hot spots listed in the image section to find dozens of sounds tools for your system. All you have to do is visit the archive dedicated to your system and look for an appropriately named directory, such as sound or snd.

Amiga

Two popular Amiga players are DeliTracker and EaglePlayer. DeliTracker is a good player if you have Amiga OS 2.0 or higher. It plays more than 80 different mod (digital music) formats, including the popular MTM and S3M formats.

EaglePlayer is a good player for the Amiga. It plays more than 100 different mod formats and supports DOS/Windows sound formats. There is also a PC version of the program. Two versions of EaglePlayer are available: a commercial version and a limited shareware version.

One of the hottest trackers for Amiga is Protracker. It is based on the original Soundtracker interface and has been greatly improved over the years. As the name implies, Protracker isn't for the novice. It expects you to know a lot about creating sound. The best thing about Protracker is that it is freeware.

Amiga sound tools are available from the many aminet FTP sites around the world, but these sites are often busy. Not to worry, one of the fastest aminet FTP sites in the United States also has a Web site. You should search the following aminet directory for popular Amiga sound tools:

```
http://laslo.netnet.net:80/aminet/dirs/tree_mus.html
```

> **TIP**
>
> Remember, if you can't access this Aminet site for any reason, you can use a mirror site. Here's how you could access the `/dirs/tree_mus` directory at another archive:
>
> `http://ftp.wustl.edu/~aminet/dirs/tree_mus.html`
>
> or
>
> `http://www.germany.aminet.org/aminet/dirs/tree_mus.html`

Macintosh

For the Macintosh, the two most popular players are Player Pro and Sound Trecker. Player Pro and Sound Trecker are hot players that support digital music mod and Mac formats. Player Pro and Sound Trecker are the most popular for good reason. They are continually upgraded and have good interfaces. Player Pro is fully PowerMac-native. Sound Trecker is comparable to Player Pro and has many advanced features, good menus, and upgrade modules that should enable full PowerMac capabilities.

A good player and sound converter for the Mac is SoundApp. The great thing about SoundApp is its wide support for other popular sound formats. It will play and convert AU, AIFF, SND, WAV and many popular mod formats. SoundApp can also use the advanced features of PowerMac, and it is freeware.

You can search the info-mac archive to find these and other sound applications for the Macintosh. Here's the URL for the info-mac archive at WUSTL:

`http://wuarchive.wustl.edu/systems/mac/info-mac/_Graphic_and_Sound_Tool/`

> **TIP**
>
> Remember, if you can't access this info-mac site for any reason, you can use a mirror site. Here's how you could access the `/dirs/tree_mus` directory at another archive:
>
> `ftp://ftp.ibp.fr/pub/mac/info-mac/_Graphic_and_Sound_Tool/`
>
> Or, if you have problems accessing the directory, try a base directory, such as:
>
> `http://wuarchive.wustl.edu/systems/mac/`

If you are looking for an audio-on-demand solution that provides instant playback, you will want to join the thousands of Web users who are racing to get RealAudio equipped. RealAudio is an integrated system with client and server software for creating high-fidelity sound files that can playback as they are being downloaded to your system. The RealAudio Player for the Mac offers you full control of RealAudio files with a VCR-like interface that provides many features of your CD player, such as the ability to jump to any part of an audio program. You may be surprised to find that something of this quality is offered as freeware and that you can download it to your system simply by visiting

```
http://www.realaudio.com/products/player.html
```

To create RealAudio files, you will need the RealAudio Encoder. The encoder enables you to compress digital audio files in common formats such as Windows WAV and Macintosh AIFF and converts them to RealAudio (RA) format. Once you create a RealAudio file using the encoder, you can play the audio with the RealAudio Player. The encoder is also free and can be downloaded from

```
http://www.realaudio.com/products/encoder.html
```

Windows

MIDAS is a good sound player for Microsoft Windows. It plays most popular mod formats, including S3M, and will also play WAV files. As MIDAS supports 16-bit stereo sound at common mixing rates, this player will give you quality playback. If you are looking for a Windows sound player, you should put the freeware MIDAS player on your list.

A good sound tool for playing and editing sounds files is WHAM. Not only does WHAM enable you to play and edit sound files, you can also convert sound formats from one format to another. WHAM also features support for many popular sound formats. You can find WHAM and other sound tools for windows at the SimTel archive:

```
http://www.acs.oakland.edu/oak/SimTel/win3/sound.html.
```

If you need MS-DOS sound tools, look at

```
http://www.acs.oakland.edu/oak/SimTel/msdos/sound.html
```

If you need OS/2 or OS/2 Warp sound tools, check out

```
http://www.acs.oakland.edu/oak/SimTel/os2/multimedia.html
```

For Windows 95 sound tools, go to

```
http://www.acs.oakland.edu/oak/SimTel/win95/multimed.html
```

For Windows NT sound tools, look here:

```
http://www.acs.oakland.edu/oak/SimTel/nt/multimedia.html
```

NOTE

Directory names and files sometimes change. If you have any problems accessing these files directly, use the base directory to the SimTel archive:

```
http://www.acs.oakland.edu/oak/
```

If you read about RealAudio in the Macintosh sound tools section, don't worry; versions of the RealAudio player and encoder are available for Windows systems as well. You can read more about RealAudio and obtain these tools at the addresses listed earlier.

UNIX

One of the best digital music players for UNIX and Linux systems is Tracker. This sound player supports the popular Protracker player formats and has player modules that will run on most UNIX and Linux systems. If you are looking for a sound editor and converter for your UNIX system, SOX may be your application of choice. SOX is easy to use and can convert many popular sound formats, including AIFF, AU, and WAV.

A good place to find Linux sound tools is

```
ftp://sunsite.unc.edu/pub/Linux/apps/sound/players
```

While RealAudio players and encoders are not available for UNIX systems, the RealAudio server is UNIX-based. This means if you want to server RealAudio files to users who visit your site, you must have a UNIX Web server and obtain the RealAudio server software. Unlike the player and encoder software, which are provided free, the RealAudio server software is a commercial product.

Video Tools

Video is more proprietary than other types of multimedia and as a result, there are fewer video formats. Most video tools write files in their native formats and include the capability to convert other formats to the native format. The three main video formats are AVI, MOV, and MPEG.

All three video formats are excellent formats that offer the capability to include stereo sound tracks with the video. Because of this, your format of choice will most likely depend on the type of system you prefer to work with. Video tools and concepts are rapidly changing. Keeping your video tools current with the times is extremely important, more so than any other form of multimedia.

The AVI format is also called the Video for Windows format. As you might imagine, Microsoft's video format is very popular and widely used. Video for Windows players are available for use on Windows, Windows 95, and Windows NT systems.

The MPEG format is the industry standard for video. MPEG players for MPEG Level 1 are available for all computer systems, making MPEG a true cross-platform video solution. While early MPEG players did not support audio tracks, current MPEG players support CD-quality audio.

The MOV format is also called the QuickTime format. QuickTime is Apple Computer's proprietary video format. Apple has worked hard to ensure their format is portable and playable on other systems. QuickTime players are freely available for Macintosh, Windows, and UNIX X Windows systems.

Macintosh

For the Macintosh, there are many good video tools available. Although Apple includes a QuickTime player with System 7.5 and later versions, you can find the most current version of Apple's QuickTime player at Apple's Web site:

`http://quicktime.apple.com/`

The most popular video tool for Macintosh is called Sparkle. Sparkle is a true gem. With Sparkle, you can play and/or convert AVI, MOV, and MPEG videos, which could make Sparkle your all in one video solution for the Macintosh.

If you are in search of the ultimate QuickTime play, try the latest version of BijouPlay. BijouPlay supports QuickTime 2.0 format, AppleScript, AppleGuide, Drag & Drop, text tracks, and multiple movie playback. If you want to make text tracks in movies try DesktopText, a QuickTime Text movie maker.

A key concept in converting Apple MOV videos to other formats is flattening. When you flatten a MOV video, you merge the data and hardware control streams into a single stream of data that can be used on other systems. A useful tool for flattening MOV videos is flatmoov.

If you really want to get into creating videos for Mac users, try Avid Video shop. Avid Video shop is a good tool for editing video files and creating nice special effects, such as

> Filter Effect plug-ins
> Audio Reverse
> Fade In
> Fade Out
> Transition Effect plug-ins
> Clock Wipe
> Corner Swing In
> Corner Swing Out
> Cross-Mosaic
> Cross-Spin
> Drop
> Explode
> Fan Wipe
> Iris Polygon
> Iris Round
> Iris Stars
> Peel
> Spin In

Spin Out
Tumble In
Tumble Out

You can find all these Mac video utilities, an MPEG player, an AVI converter, and many other useful utilities at the info-mac archive. Here's the path to the video utilities at WUSTL:

```
http://wuarchive.wustl.edu/systems/mac/info-mac/gst/mov/
```

You can also find lots of good information on the QuickTime format and Macintosh video utilities at

```
http://www.astro.nwu.edu/lentz/mac/qt/home-qt.html
```

A recent development for the Macintosh and QuickTime is the QuickTime VR format. Apple's QuickTime VR player enables you to see 3-D graphics and live VR scenes. To use QuickTime VR, you will need the QuickTime 2.0 extensions and the QuickTime VR player, which you can get at

```
http://qtvr.quicktime.apple.com/InMac.htm
```

Once you get the player, you will want to configure your browser to use it. You do this by setting the QuickTime VR player as a valid helper application in your Web browser for your MOV videos.

Windows

As discussed in Chapter 7, "Adding Multimedia Features with HTML," Microsoft Video For Windows players are widely available. If you don't have a runtime version of Media Player, you should visit Microsoft at

```
http://www.microsoft.com/
```

To play other video formats on your system you will need a different video player, such as Apple's QuickTime for Windows player. The QuickTime for Windows player allows you to play MOV videos that have been flattened. By flattening the video, the data and hardware control streams are merged into a single stream readable on your Windows system. You can read more about the QuickTime for Windows player at Apple's Web site:

```
http://www.support.apple.com/pub/apple_sw_updates/US/DOS%20%26%20Windows/QuickTime/
➥QuickTime_For_Windows_2.0.3.txt
```

You can download the QuickTime for Windows Player using this URL:

```
http://www.support.apple.com/pub/apple_sw_updates/US/DOS%20%26%20Windows/QuickTime/
➥QuickTime_For_Windows_2.0.3.exe.
```

If you want to leap into QuickTime VR, you should visit Apple's QuickTime VR site on the Web. To use QuickTime VR, you will need to download the current version of QuickTime and the QuickTime VR player. Versions of the QuickTime VR player are freely available for Windows and Windows 95 systems. You can download QuickTime and QuickTime VR from Apple's QuickTime VR site at

```
http://qtvr.quicktime.apple.com/InWin.htm
```

Once you get the player, you will want to configure your browser to use it. You do this by setting the QuickTime VR player as a valid helper application in your Web browser for your MOV videos.

One of the best MPEG players for Windows systems is XingMPEG. This video player supports MPEG Level 1 and has a lot of nice features. The XingMPEG Player offers an easy-to-use alternative to Microsoft's Media Player and will also enable you to play back Video CDs, Karaoke CDs, and CD-i Movies. Visit Xing Technologies at

```
http://www.xingtech.com/xingmpeg/index.html
```

Xing Technologies also makes a high-quality software MPEG encoder for Windows systems. XingMPEG Encoder is fully compliant with MPEG Level 1. Using XingMPEG Encoder, you can also use AVI videos and WAV audio files to create extremely compact MPEG videos.

For Windows systems, there is a terrific all-in-one solution for playing videos in AVI, MOV, and MPEG formats, and it's called NET TOOB. NET TOOB was developed by Duplexx Software in cooperation with CompCore Multimedia. The most recent upgrade to NET TOOB added a real time audio and video playback capability. This shareware viewer is available for Windows and Windows 95 systems at

```
http://www.duplexx.com/
```

UNIX

The MPEG video format is king on UNIX systems. One of the most popular MPEG players for UNIX X Windows systems is mpeg_play. Versions of mpeg_play are available for most UNIX systems, including SunOS 4.1.3, Solaris 2.3, HPUX 9.0.3, Ultrix 4.4, OSF, IRIX v4, IRIX v5, and Linux. You can find mpeg_play on the Web at two sites:

```
http://www-plateau.cs.berkeley.edu/mpeg/mpeg_play.html
```

```
http://www.geom.umn.edu/docs/mpeg_play/mpeg_play.html
```

To create MPEG videos on your UNIX system, you will need a program called a ppmtoyuv splitter and a software encoder. A ppmtoyuv splitter separates your video into Y, U, and V segments that you can feed to the MPEG encoder. The most popular ppmtoyuv splitter is ppmtoyuvsplit. This splitter is part of the Netpbm toolkit. The Netpbm toolkit contains more than 50 UNIX utilities for manipulating images and video. If you have an image format conversion need, chances are very good Netpbm can solve your problem. You can find Netpbm at three places:

```
ftp://ftp.cs.ubc.ca/ftp/archive/netpbm

ftp://ikaros.fysik4.kth.se/pub/netpbm

ftp://wuarchive.wustl.edu/graphics/graphics/
```

The University of Minnesota's graphic and video library archive has a good MPEG encoder called . The archive also has a collection of video creation and player tools, called movie-tools. The movie-tools collection contains six useful utilities:

- sgifade—Generates transitions between two images
- smart_vfr—A video frame utility for the Abekas A60
- tontsc—Scales images to fit video standards for NTSC, PAL, and others.
- rleto3D—Displays RLE videos in stereo on SGI
- rletoD1—Converts RLE images to D1
- texttorle—Creates video-ready images from text

You can find these and other utilities at these sites:

```
ftp://ftp.arc.umn.edu/pub/GVL/

http://www.arc.umn.edu/html/gvl-software/gvl-software.html

http://www.arc.umn.edu/GVL/manual.html
```

Another great place to find MPEG utilities is the University of California Berkeley Web site. Berkeley's Plateau Multimedia Research Group maintains a terrific Web site to learn about developments in MPEG. An archive called Berkeley MPEG Tools contains an MPEG player called mpeg_play, an MPEG encoder called mpeg_encode, and three video analysis tools—mpeg_stat, mpeg_blocks, and mpeg_bits. You can visit the Plateau Multimedia Research Group and download the latest version of the Berkeley MPEG tools at

```
http://www-plateau.cs.berkeley.edu/mpeg/index.html
```

If you are interested in cutting-edge MPEG players, you won't want to miss the MPEG-2 player developed by the MPEG Software Simulation Group. You can find this player at

```
ftp://ftp.netcom.com/pub/cf/cfogg/mpeg2/
```

Summary

By now, you should have everything you need to create the ultimate Web publishing toolkit. If you don't, visit the sites listed in this chapter and get the tools you need to be a power publisher. Your toolkit should include the following:

- At least three Web browsers so you can test your Web documents using multiple windows to the Web
- HTML converters to convert existing documents to HTML format

- An HTML editor or template utility to help you get a quick start
- One or more image editors, players, and converters
- One or more sound editors, players, and converters
- One or more video editors, players, and converters

Writing CGI Scripts

11

*by William
Robert Stanek*

IN THIS CHAPTER

336

Using CGI scripts, you can create powerful, personalized, and professional Web publications that readers can really interact with. CGI scripts are external programs that act as a gateway between the Web server and other applications. You can use CGI scripts to process input from readers and thus open a two-way communication channel with your readers. Reader input can be data from fill-out forms, keywords for a database query, or values that describe the reader's browser and connection.

Your CGI scripts can use this input to add entries to an index, to search databases, to create customized documents on-the-fly and much more. Yet the most wonderful thing about CGI scripts is that they hide their complexities from users. If you've used a fill-out form or an image map on the Web, you've used a gateway script and probably didn't even know it. This is because everything seems to happen automatically. You enter data, click a mouse button, and a moment later a result is displayed. Learning what actually happens between the click of the mouse button and the display of the result is what this chapter is all about. This chapter explains what you need to know about CGI scripts—what they are, how to use them and why to use them.

What Are CGI Scripts?

CGI scripts are external programs that run on the Web server. You can use CGI scripts to create highly interactive Web publications. The standard that defines how external programs are used on Web servers and how they interact with other applications is the common gateway interface. The three keywords used in the name of the standard—common, gateway, and interface—describe how the standard works:

> By specifying a common way for scripts to be accessed, CGI enables anyone, no matter their platform, to pass information to a CGI script.

> By defining the link or gateway between the script, the server, and other applications, CGI makes it possible for external programs to accept generalized input and pass information to other applications.

> By describing the interface or the way external programs can be accessed by users, CGI reduces the complex process of interfacing with external programs to a few basic procedures.

The developers of CGI worked these key concepts into the CGI standard to create a powerful and extendable advanced feature for Web publishers that shields readers of your publications from its complexities. The reader must only click on an area of an image map or submit their fill-out form after completing it. Everything after the click of the mouse button seems to happen automatically and the reader doesn't have to worry about the how or why, only that it works. As a Web publisher, understanding how CGI scripts work is essential, especially if you want to take advantage of the ways CGI can be used to create powerful Web publications.

While the reader only sees the result of their submission or query, many things are happening behind the scenes. Here is a summary of what is taking place:

1. The reader's browser passes the input to the Web server.
2. The server in turn passes the input to a CGI script.
3. The CGI script processes the input, passes it off to another application if necessary, and sends the output to the Web server.
4. The Web server passes the output back to the reader's browser. The output from a CGI script can be anything from the results of a database search to a completely new document generated based on the reader's input.

On UNIX systems, CGI scripts are located in a directory called `cgi-bin` in the `usr` file system and CGI utilities are located in a directory called `cgi-src` in the `usr` file system. On other systems, your Web server documentation will explain what directories CGI scripts and utilities should be placed in.

Choosing a Programming Language for Your CGI Scripts

CGI scripts are also called *gateway scripts*. The term *script* comes from the UNIX environment, where shell scripts abound, but gateway scripts don't have to be in the format of a script. You can write gateway scripts in almost any computer language that produces an executable file. The most common languages for scripts are

Bourne Shell
C Shell
C/C++
Perl
Python
Tcl
Visual Basic

Two up and coming scripting languages are

JavaScript
VBScript

The best programming language to write your script in is one that is usable on your Web server and meets your needs. Preferably, the language should already be available on the Web server and you should be proficient or at least have some knowledge of the language as well. Keep in mind, most user input is in the form of text that must be manipulated in some way, which makes support for text strings and their manipulation critically important.

The easiest way to determine if a language is available is to ask the Webmaster or system administrator responsible for the server. As most Web servers operate on UNIX systems, you may be able to use the following UNIX commands to check on the availability of a particular language:

```
which
```

```
whereis
```

Both which and whereis are usable on UNIX systems. You would type which or whereis at the shell prompt and follow the command by a keyword you want to search on, such as the name of the programming language you want to use. To see if your UNIX server supports Perl, you could type either

```
which perl
```

or

```
whereis perl
```

As Perl, C/C++, and UNIX shell are the most popular languages for scripts, the sections that follow will look briefly at these languages, with emphasis on why and when to use them. Each section contains a checklist for features and systems supported, which can be interpreted as follows:

Operating System Support—The operating systems the language can be used on

Programming Level—The difficulty of the language to use and learn

Complexity of Processing—The complexity of the tasks you can process with the language

Text-Handling Capabilities—The ability of the language to manipulate text and strings

The sections on common scripting languages are followed by close-ups on the newest scripting languages: JavaScript and VBScript. Both JavaScript and VBScript are hot topics on the Net right now. If you want to be on the cutting edge of Internet technologies, these are languages you want to keep both eyes on.

Using UNIX Shell

The UNIX operating system is in wide use in business, education, and research sectors. There are almost as many variations of the UNIX operating system as there are platforms that use it. You will even find that platforms produced by the same manufacturer use different variants of the UNIX operating system. For example, DEC has variants for the Dec-Alpha, Decstation, and Dec OSF.

What these operating systems have in common is the core environment they are based on. Most UNIX operating systems are based on Berkeley UNIX (BSD), AT&T System V, or a combination of BSD and System V. Both BSD and System V support three shell scripting languages:

> Bourne shell
> C shell
> Korn shell

TIP

You can quickly identify the shell scripting language used by examining the first line of a script. Bourne shell scripts generally have this first line:

```
#!/bin/sh
```

C shell scripts generally have a blank first line or the following:

```
#!/bin/csh
```

Korn shell scripts generally have this first line:

```
#!/bin/ksh
```

All UNIX shells are interpreted languages, which means the scripts you create do not have to be compiled. Bourne shell is the most basic shell. C shell is an advanced shell with many features of the C programming language. Because Bourne shell uses a completely different syntax than C shell, scripts written in Bourne are not compatible with scripts written in C. If you create a script in Bourne shell and later want to use C shell to interpret the script, you must rewrite the script for C shell.

Many programmers often want to merge the simplicity of Bourne shell with the advanced features of C shell, and this is where Korn shell comes in handy. Korn shell has the same functionality as the Bourne shell and incorporates many features of the C shell. Therefore, any shells you've written in Bourne shell can be interpreted directly by the Korn interpreter. This saves time rewriting a script when you later find you want to use a feature supported by Korn. While the Korn shell is gaining popularity, Bourne and C shell are the two most widely used UNIX shells.

Some differences in Bourne, C, and Korn shell are only visible if you are at the shell prompt and using a particular shell. You can change your current shell any time from the shell prompt by typing:

> `/bin/sh` to change to Bourne shell
> `/bin/csh` to change to C shell
> `/bin/ksh` to change to Korn shell

Usually, you will see visible differences between the various shells immediately. For example, the default command prompt for Bourne shell is the dollar sign and the default command prompt for C shell is usually your host name and user id followed by a colon. Beyond this, C shell supports a history function, aliasing of commands, and many other controls that the Bourne shell does not. However, to the CGI programmer, these differences are generally not important. Your primary concerns should be the features the shell directly supports and how scripts behave when executed.

For this reason, Bourne shell is the hands-on favorite. Bourne shell is the smallest of the shells and the most efficient. Consequently, a Bourne shell script will generally execute faster and use fewer system resources. When you want more advanced features, such as arrays, you will want to use Korn shell. Korn shell has more overhead than Bourne shell and requires slightly more system resources. When you want to make advanced function calls or assignments, you will want to use C shell. Because C shell is larger than Bourne and Korn shell, scripts written in C shell generally have higher overhead and use more system resources.

While UNIX shells have good built-in facilities for handing text, such as sed, awk, and grep, they are not as powerful or extensible as traditional programming languages. You should consider using shell scripts when you want to perform simple tasks and moderately advanced text or file manipulation.

> Operating System Support: UNIX
> Programming Level: Basic
> Complexity of Processing: Basic
> Text-handling capabilities: Moderately Advanced

Using C/C++

When you want your scripts to perform complex tasks, you call in the big guns. Two of the most advanced languages used in CGI scripts are C and C++. C is the most popular programming language in use today. C++ is the object-oriented successor to C. Both C and C++ are advanced programming languages that require you to compile your scripts before you can use them. A major advantage of C and C++ is that they enjoy widespread use, and versions are available for virtually every operating system you can think of.

The primary time to use C is when your scripts must execute swiftly and use minimum system resources. C was developed more than 20 years ago and has been gaining popularity ever since. CGI programmers use C because compiled C programs are very small—tiny compared to programs with similar functionality programmed in another language. Small programs use minimal system resources and execute quickly. However, C is a very complex language with difficult-to-use facilities for manipulating text. Therefore, if you are not proficient in C, you should be wary of using C to perform advanced processing of text strings.

The primary time to use C++ is when certain functions of your scripts will be reused and when development costs are a major concern for the long term. C++ is an object-oriented language that enables you to use libraries of functions. These functions form the core of your CGI scripts and can be reused in other CGI scripts. For example, you can use one function to sort the user's input, another function to search a database using the input, and another function to display the output as an HTML document. However, C++ is an object-oriented language that is very different from other languages. If you have not used an object-oriented language before, are not familiar with C, and plan to use C++ for your CGI scripts, you should be prepared for a steep learning curve.

> Operating System Support: UNIX, DOS, Windows, MAC and others
> Programming Level: Advanced
> Complexity of Processing: Advanced
> Text-handling capabilities: Difficult to use

Using Perl

If you want to be on the inside track of CGI programming, you should learn and use Perl. The Practical Extraction and Report Language combines elements of C and UNIX shell features like awk, sed, and grep to create a powerful language for processing text strings and generating reports. Because most of the processing done by CGI scripts involves text manipulation, Perl is rapidly becoming the most widely used language for CGI scripts. Like C and C++, a major advantage of Perl is its widespread use. Versions of Perl are available for virtually every operating system you can think of. You can use Perl to

- Easily manipulate files, text, and processes
- Extract text strings and manipulate them in complex ways
- Quickly and easily search files, databases, and indexes
- Print advanced reports based on the data extracted

Perl, like Bourne and C shell, is an interpreted language. However, Perl does not have the limitations of most interpreted languages. You can use Perl to manipulate extremely large amounts of data and using sophisticated pattern-matching techniques, you can quickly scan files. Perl strings are not limited in size. The entire contents of a file can be used as a single string. Perl's syntax is similar to C's. Many basic Perl constructs, like if, for, and while statements, are used just as you use them in C.

TIP

Like UNIX shell scripts, a script written in Perl will usually specify the path to the source routines in the first line. Therefore, the first line of a Perl script should specify the path to where Perl is installed on the system. This path is usually:

```
#!/usr/local/perl
```

or

```
#!/usr/local/bin/perl
```

Perl is surprisingly easy to learn and use, especially if you know the basics of C or UNIX shell. Perl scripts will generally be faster than UNIX shell scripts and slightly slower than compiled C/C++ scripts. You should use Perl whenever you have large amounts of text to manipulate.

> Operating System Support: UNIX, DOS, Windows, MAC and others
> Programming Level: Advanced
> Complexity of Processing: Advanced
> Text-handling capabilities: Easy to use

Using JavaScript

JavaScript is a new scripting language based on the Java programming language developed by Sun Microsystems. This powerful up-and-coming scripting language is being developed by Netscape Communications Corporation, and as you may have guessed, the Netscape Navigator 2.0 fully supports JavaScript.

Netscape Navigator 2.0 interprets JavaScript programs embedded directly in an HTML page and just like Java applets, these programs are fully interactive. JavaScript can recognize and respond to mouse clicks, form input, and page navigation. This means your pages can "intelligently" react to user input. The JavaScript language resembles the Java programming language—with a few important exceptions, as you can see from the comparisons in the following lists.

JavaScript is

- An interpreted language
- Object-based: lacks classes and inheritance
- Code embedded in HTML
- Loose typing with variable data types not declared
- Object references are checked at runtime
- Secure: cannot write to hard disk

Java is

- Compiled to bytecode before execution on client
- Object-oriented: uses classes with inheritance
- Applet code separate from HTML
- Strong typing with variable data declared
- Object references must exist at compile time
- Secure: cannot write to hard disk

JavaScript is designed to complement the Java language and has some terrific features for Web publishers. You could create a JavaScript program that passes parameters to a Java applet. This would enable you to use the JavaScript program as an easy-to-use front-end for your Java applets.

Further, because a Web publisher is not required to know about or learn classes to use JavaScript and to pass parameters to a Java applet, JavaScript provides a simple solution for publishers who want to use the features of the Java language but don't want to learn how to program in Java.

This powerful up-and-coming scripting language is further discussed in Chapter 12, "Form and Image Map Creation and Design." Look for the section called "Client-Side Scripting Languages" in Chapter 12. To learn more, you can also visit Netscape's JavaScript page:

```
http://home.netscape.com/eng/mozilla/Gold/handbook/javascript/index.html
```

Using VBScript

With VBScript, Microsoft proves once again that it understands the tools developers need. Visual Basic Script is a subset of Visual Basic and is used to create highly interactive documents on the Web. Similar to JavaScript, programs written in VBScript are embedded in the body of your HTML documents.

Visual Basic Script also enables dynamic use of OLE scripting management. The Object Linking and Embedding of scripts will enable Web publishers to dynamically embed VBScript runtime environments. Basically, this allows you to use VBScripts as plug-in modules. You could, for example, embed a VBScript program in your Web document that called other VBScript programs to use as plug-ins. The exact plug-in called could be dynamically allocated based on user input. As Microsoft is working with Internet standards groups to define an OLE scripting standard, we should see this development soon.

Pre-release versions of VBScript are or will soon be available for Windows (Win32 and Win16) and PowerMacintosh systems. Microsoft is also working with third-party vendors to provide UNIX versions of VBScript for Sun, HP, Digital and IBM platforms. Visual Basic Script is packaged as a compiler and associated runtime libraries.

Surprisingly, Microsoft plans to license VBScript to industry companies and corporations free of charge, but it is not surprising that Microsoft plans to provide commercial development tools for VB Script. Currently, pre-release versions of Visual Basic Script are available for evaluation by developers. You can learn more about VBScript at Microsoft's Web site:

```
http://www.microsoft.com/
```

Why Use CGI Scripts?

At this point, you may be worried about having to program. You may also be wondering why you would want to use gateway scripts at all. These are valid concerns. Learning a programming language isn't easy, but as you will see later, you may never have to program at all. Dozens of ready-to-use CGI scripts are freely available on the Web. Often you can use these existing programs to meet your needs.

The primary reason to use CGI scripts is to automate what would otherwise be a manual and probably time-consuming process. Using CGI scripts benefits the reader and you. The reader gets simplicity, automated responses to input, easy ways to make submissions, and fast ways to conduct searches. Gateway scripts enable you to automatically process orders, queries, and much more. Common uses for CGI programs include

- To track visitors to Web pages and post continually updated numbers to the Web page as it is accessed
- To process input, typically search strings, and output a document containing the results of the search
- To validate user identification and password information and grant readers access to restricted areas of the Web site
- To process input from image maps and direct the reader to associated documents
- To generate documents based on the type of browser the reader is using
- To add the reader's feedback or survey responses to a database or index

How CGI Scripts Work

Gateway scripts are used to process input submitted by readers of your Web publications. Input is usually in the form of environment variables passed to the gateway script by the Web server. Environment variables describe the information being passed, such as the version of CGI used on the server, the type of data, the size of the data, and other important information. Gateway scripts can also receive input as command-line arguments and standard input. To execute a CGI script, the script must exist on the server you are referencing. You must also have a server that is both capable of executing gateway scripts and configured to handle the type of script you plan to use.

Readers pass information to a CGI script by activating a link containing a reference to the script. The gateway script processes the input and formats the results as output the Web server can use. The Web server takes the results and passes them back to the reader's browser. The browser displays the output for the reader.

The output from a gateway script begins with a header containing a directive to the server. Currently there are three valid server directives: Content-type, Location, and Status. The header can consist of a directive in the format of an HTTP header followed by a blank line. The blank link separates the header from the data you are passing back to the browser. Output containing Location and Status directives usually are a single line. This is because the directive contained on the Location or Status line is all that is needed by the server, and when there is no subsequent data, you do not need to insert a blank line. The server interprets the output, sets environment variables, and passes the output to the client.

Thus, any transaction between a client and server has many parts. These parts can be broken down into eight steps as follows:

1. Client passes input to a server.
2. Server sets environment variables pertaining to input.
3. Server passes input as variables to the named CGI script.
4. Server passes command line input or standard input stream to CGI script if present.
5. Script processes input.
6. Script returns output to the server. This output always contains a qualified header and sometimes contains a body if additional data is present.
7. Server sets environment variables pertaining to output.
8. Server passes output to client.

Input to CGI Scripts

When a user activates a link to a gateway script, input is sent to the server. The server formats this data into environment variables and checks to see if additional data was submitted via the command line or the standard input stream.

Environment Variables

Input to CGI scripts is generally in the form of environment variables. The environment variables passed to gateway scripts are associated with the browser requesting information from the server, the server processing the request, and the data passed in the request. Environment variables are case-sensitive and are generally used as described in this section. While some environment variables are system specific, many environment variables are standard. The standard variables are shown in Table 11.1.

As later examples show, environment variables are set automatically whenever reader input is passed to a server. The primary reason to learn about these variables is to better understand how input is passed to CGI scripts, yet you should also learn about these variables so you know how to take advantage of them when necessary.

Table 11.1. Standard environment variables.

Variable	Purpose
AUTH_TYPE	Specifies the authentication method and is used to validate a user's access.
CONTENT_LENGTH	Used to provide a way of tracking the length of the data string as a numeric value.

continues

Table 11.1. Continued

Variable	*Purpose*
CONTENT_TYPE	Indicates the MIME type of data.
GATEWAY_INTERFACE	Indicates the version of the CGI standard the server is using.
HTTP_ACCEPT	Indicates the MIME content types the browser will accept, as passed to the gateway script via the server.
HTTP_USER_AGENT	Indicates the type of browser used to send the request, as passed to the gateway script via the server.
PATH_INFO	Identifies the extra information included in the URL after the identification of the CGI script.
PATH_TRANSLATED	Set by the server based on the PATH_INFO variable. The server translates the PATH_INFO variable into this variable.
QUERY_STRING	Set to the query string (if the URL contains a query string).
REMOTE_ADDR	Identifies the Internet Protocol address of the remote computer making the request.
REMOTE_HOST	Identifies the name of the machine making the request.
REMOTE_IDENT	Identifies the machine making the request.
REMOTE_USER	Identifies the user name as authenticated by the user.
REQUEST_METHOD	Indicates the method by which the request was made.
SCRIPT_NAME	Identifies the virtual path to the script being executed.
SERVER_NAME	Identifies the server by its host name, alias, or IP address.
SERVER_PORT	Identifies the port number the server received the request on.
SERVER_PROTOCOL	Indicates the protocol of the request sent to the server.
SERVER_SOFTWARE	Identifies the Web server software.

AUTH_TYPE

The AUTH_TYPE variable is used to provide access control to protected areas of the Web server and can be used only on servers that support user authentication. If an area of the Web site has no access control, the AUTH_TYPE variable has no value associated with it. If an area of the Web site has access control, the AUTH_TYPE variable is set to a specific value that identifies the authentication scheme being used. Otherwise, the variable has no value associated with it. A simple challenge-response authorization mechanism is implemented under current versions of HTTP.

Using this mechanism, the server can challenge a client's request and the client can respond. This is done by the server setting a value for the AUTH_TYPE variable and the client supplying a matching value. The next step is to authenticate the user. Using the basic authentication scheme, the user's browser must supply authentication information that uniquely identifies the user. This information includes a user ID and password.

Under the current implementation of HTTP, HTTP 1.0, the basic authentication scheme is the most commonly used authentication method. To specify this method, the AUTH_TYPE variable is set as follows:

```
AUTH_TYPE = Basic
```

CONTENT_LENGTH

The CONTENT_LENGTH variable is used to provide a way of tracking the length of the data string. This lets the client and server know how much data to read on the standard input stream. The value of the variable corresponds to the number of characters in the data passed with the request. If no data is being passed, the variable has no value.

As long as the characters are represented as octets, the value of the CONTENT_LENGTH variable will equate to the precise number of characters passed as standard input or standard output. Thus, if 25 characters are passed and they are represented as octets, the CONTENT_LENGTH variable will have the following value:

```
CONTENT_LENGTH = 25
```

CONTENT_TYPE

The CONTENT_TYPE variable indicates the MIME type of data. MIME typing is a feature of HTTP 1.0 and is not available on servers using HTTP 0.9. The variable is set only when attached data is passed using the standard input or output stream. The value assigned to the variable identifies the MIME type and subtype as follows:

```
CONTENT_TYPE = type/subtype
```

MIME types are broken down into basic type categories. Each data type category has a primary subtype associated with it. The basic MIME types and their descriptions are shown in Table 11.2.

Table 11.2. Basic MIME types.

Type	Description
application	Binary data that can be executed or used with another application
audio	A sound file that requires an output device to preview
image	A picture that requires an output device to preview
message	An encapsulated mail message

continues

Table 11.2. continued

Type	Description
multipart	Data consisting of multiple parts and possibly many data types
text	Textual data that can be represented in any character set or formatting language
video	A video file that requires an output device to preview
x-world	Experimental data type for world files

MIME subtypes are defined as primary data types, additionally defined data types, and extended data types. The primary subtype is the primary type of data adopted for use as MIME Content-Types. Additionally defined data types are additional subtypes that have been officially adopted as MIME Content-Types. Extended data types are experimental subtypes that have not been officially adopted as MIME Content-Types. You can easily identify extended subtypes because they begin with the letter x followed by a hyphen. Table 11.3 lists common MIME types and their descriptions.

Table 11.3. Common MIME types.

Type/Subtype	Description
application/mac-binhex40	Macintosh binary-formatted data
application/msword	Microsoft word document
application/octet-stream	Binary data that can be executed or used with another application
application/pdf	ACROBAT PDF document
application/postscript	PostScript-formatted data
application/rtf	Rich Text Format (RTF) document
application/x-compress	Data that has been compressed using UNIX compress
application/x-dvi	Device-independent file
application/x-gzip	Data that has been compressed using UNIX gzip
application/x-latex	LaTeX document
application/x-tar	Data that has been archived using UNIX tar
application/x-zip-compressed	Data that has been compressed using PKZIP
audio/basic	Audio in a nondescript format
audio/x-aiff	Audio in Apple AIFF format
audio/x-wav	Audio in Microsoft WAV format
image/gif	An image in GIF format
image/jpeg	An image in JPEG format

Type/Subtype	*Description*
image/tiff	An image in TIFF format
image/x-portable-bitmap	Portable bitmap
image/x-portable-graymap	Portable graymap
image/x-portable-pixmap	Portable pixmap
image/x-xbitmap	X-bitmap
image/x-xpixmap	X-pixmap
message/external-body	Message with external data source
message/partial	A fragmented or partial message
message/rfc822	RFC-822-compliant message
multipart/alternative	Data with alternative formats
multipart/digest	Multipart message digest
multipart/mixed	A multipart message with data in multiple formats
multipart/parallel	Multipart data with parts that should be viewed simultaneously
text/html	HTML-formatted text
text/plain	Plain text with no HTML formatting included
video/mpeg	Video in the MPEG format
video/quicktime	Video in the Apple QuickTime format
video/x-msvideo	Video in the Microsoft AVI format
x-world/x-vrml	VRML world file

Some MIME Content-Types can be used with additional parameters. These Content-Types include: text/plain, text/html, and all multipart message data. The charset parameter is used with the text/plain type to identify the character set used for the data. The version parameter is used with the text/html type to identify the version of HTML used. The boundary parameter is used with multipart data to identify the boundary string that separates message parts.

The charset parameter for the text/plain type is optional. If a charset is not specified, the default value charset=us-ascii is assumed. Other values for charset include any character set approved by the International Standards Organization. These character sets are defined by ISO-8859-1 to ISO-8859-9 and are specified as follows:

```
CONTENT_TYPE = text/plain; charset=iso-8859-1
```

The version parameter for the text/html type is optional. If this parameter is set, the browser reading the data will interpret the data if the browser supports the version of HTML specified. The following document conforms to the HTML 3.0 specification:

```
CONTENT_TYPE = text/html; version=3.0
```

The boundary parameter for multipart message types is required. The boundary value is set to a string of 1 to 70 characters. While the string cannot end in a space, the string can contain any valid letter or number and can include spaces and a limited set of special characters. The boundary parameters are unique strings that are defined as follows:

```
CONTENT_TYPE = multipart/mixed; boundary=boundary_string
```

GATEWAY_INTERFACE

The GATEWAY_INTERFACE variable indicates the version of the CGI specification the server is using. The value assigned to the variable identifies the name and version of the specification used as follows:

```
GATEWAY_INTERFACE = name/version
```

The current version of the CGI specification is 1.1. A server conforming to this version would set the GATEWAY_INTERFACE variable as follows:

```
GATEWAY_INTERFACE = CGI/1.1
```

HTTP_ACCEPT

The HTTP_ACCEPT variable defines the types of data the client will accept. The acceptable values are expressed as a type/subtype pair. Each type/subtype pair is separated by commas, as in type/subtype, type/subtype. Most clients accept dozens of MIME types. The following identifies all the MIME Content-Types accepted by this client:

```
HTTP_ACCEPT = application/msword, application/octet-stream,
application/postscript, application/rtf, application/x-zip-compressed,
audio/basic, audio/x-aiff, audio/x-wav, image/gif, image/jpeg, image/tiff,
image/x-portable-bitmap, message/external-body, message/partial,
message/rfc822, multipart/alternative,
multipart/digest, multipart/mixed, multipart/parallel, text/html,
text/plain, video/mpeg, video/quicktime, video/x-msvideo
```

HTTP_USER_AGENT

The HTTP_USER_AGENT variable identifies the type of browser used to send the request. The acceptable values are expressed as *software type*/*version* or *library*/*version*. The following HTTP_USER_AGENT variable identifies the Netscape Navigator Version 2.0:

```
HTTP_USER_AGENT = Mozilla/2.0
```

As you can see, Netscape uses the alias Mozilla to identify itself. The primary types of clients that set this variable are browsers, Web spiders, and robots. While this is a useful parameter for identifying the type of client used to access a script, keep in mind that not all clients set this variable.

Here's a list of software type values used by popular browsers:

Arena
Enhanced NCSA Mosaic
Lynx
MacWeb
Mozilla
NCSA Mosaic
NetCruiser
WebExplorer
WinMosaic

These values are used by Web spiders:

Lycos
MOMSpider
WebCrawler

PATH_INFO

The PATH_INFO variable specifies extra path information and can be used to send additional information to a gateway script. The extra path information follows the URL to the gateway script referenced. Generally, this information is a virtual or relative path to a resource that the server must interpret. If the URL to the CGI script is specified in your document as

```
/usr/cgi-bin/formparse.pl/home.html
```

the PATH_INFO variable would be set as follows:

```
PATH_INFO = /home.html
```

PATH_TRANSLATED

Servers translate the PATH_INFO variable into the PATH_TRANSLATED variable. It does this by inserting the default Web document's directory path in front of the extra path information. For example, if the PATH_INFO variable was set to home.html and the default directory was /usr/documents/pubs, the PATH_TRANSLATED variable would be set as follows:

```
PATH_TRANSLATED = /usr/documents/pubs/home.html
```

QUERY_STRING

The QUERY_STRING specifies an URL-encoded search string. This variable is set when the GET method is used for submitting a fill-out form or when an ISINDEX query is used to search a document. The query string is separated from the URL by a question mark. All the information following the question mark separating the URL from the query string is data submitted by the user, such as

`/usr/cgi-bin/formparse.pl?string`

When the query string is URL-encoded, the browser encodes key parts of the string. The plus sign is used in a placeholder between words and is substituted in place of spaces, such as:

`/usr/cgi-bin/formparse.pl?word1+word2+word3`

Equal signs separate keys assigned by the publisher from values entered by the user. In the following example, `response` is the key assigned by the publisher and the value entered by the user is `never`:

`/usr/cgi-bin/formparse.pl?response=never`

Ampersand symbols separate sets of keys and values. In the following example, `response` is the first key assigned by the publisher and the value entered by the user is `sometimes`. The second key assigned by the publisher is `reason` and the value entered by the user is `"I am not really sure"`. Here is the example:

`/usr/cgi-bin/formparse.pl?response=sometimes&reason=I+am+not+really+sure`

Finally, the percent sign is used to identify escaped characters. Following the percent sign is an escape code for a special character expressed as a hexadecimal value. Here is how the previous query string could be rewritten using the escape code for an apostrophe:

`/usr/cgi-bin/formparse.pl?response=sometimes&reason=I%27m+not+really+sure`

REMOTE_ADDR

The `REMOTE_ADDR` variable is set to the Internet Protocol address of the remote computer making the request. The IP address is a numeric identifier for a networked computer. The `REMOTE_ADDR` variable is associated with the host computer making the request for the client and could be used as follows:

`REMOTE_ADDR = 205.1.20.11`

REMOTE_HOST

The `REMOTE_HOST` variable specifies the name of the host computer making a request. This variable is set only if the server can figure out this information using a reverse lookup procedure. If this variable is set, the full domain and host name are used as follows:

`REMOTE_HOST = www.tvp.com`

REMOTE_IDENT

The `REMOTE_IDENT` variable identifies the remote user making a request. The variable is set only if the server and the remote machine making the request support the identification protocol. Further, information on the remote user is not always available and should not be relied upon when it is available. If the variable is set, the associated value is a fully expressed name that contains the domain information as well, such as

```
REMOTE_IDENT = william.www.tvp.com
```

REMOTE_USER

The `REMOTE_USER` variable is the user name as authenticated by the user, and as such is the only variable you should rely upon to identify a user. As with other types of user authentication, this variable is set only if the server supports user authentication and the gateway script is protected. If the variable is set, the associated value is the user's identification as sent by the client to the server, such as

```
REMOTE_USER = william
```

REQUEST_METHOD

The `REQUEST_METHOD` specifies the method by which the request was made. For HTTP 1.0, the methods could be any of the following:

```
GET
HEAD
POST
PUT
DELETE
LINK
UNLINK
```

The GET, HEAD, and POST methods are the most commonly used request methods. Both GET and POST are used to submit forms. The HEAD method could be specified as follows:

```
REQUEST_METHOD = HEAD
```

SCRIPT_NAME

The `SCRIPT_NAME` variable specifies the virtual path to the script being executed. This is useful if the script generates an HTML document that references the script. If the URL specified in your HTML document is

```
http://tvp.com/cgi-bin/formparse.pl
```

the SCRIPT_NAME variable is set as follows:

```
SCRIPT_NAME = /cgi-bin/formparse.pl
```

SERVER_NAME

The SERVER_NAME variable identifies the server by its host name, alias, or IP address. This variable is always set and could be specified as follows:

```
SERVER_NAME = tvp.com
```

SERVER_PORT

The SERVER_PORT variable specifies the port number the server received the request on. This information can be interpreted from the URL to the script if necessary. However, most servers use the default port of 80 for HTTP requests. If the URL specified in your HTML document is

```
http://www.ncsa.edu:8080/cgi-bin/formparse.pl
```

the SERVER_PORT variable is set as follows:

```
SERVER_PORT = 8080
```

SERVER_PROTOCOL

The SERVER_PROTOCOL variable identifies the protocol used to send the request. The value assigned to the variable identifies the name and version of the protocol used. The format is *name/version*, such as HTTP/1.0. The variable is set as follows:

```
SERVER_PROTOCOL = HTTP/0.9
```

SERVER_SOFTWARE

The SERVER_SOFTWARE variable identifies the name and version of the server software. The format for values assigned to the variable is *name/version*, such as CERN/2.17. The variable is set as follows:

```
SERVER_SOFTWARE = NCSA/1.4
```

CGI Command Line

In UNIX environments, users can pass information or execute shell scripts from an area known as the command line. Information typed on the command line is usually passed as input to an interpreter that uses the input to carry out an action. As it pertains to Web publishing, the command line is usually used to perform an ISINDEX query. An ISINDEX query is a simple way to add interactive searches to your documents.

While ISINDEX queries are useful, your server must support them. Performing an ISINDEX query under HTML 2.0 is a seven-step process:

1. The user clicks on a link to a gateway script and client relays this to server. A link to a gateway script for searching could be specified as follows:

   ```
   <A HREF"/cgi-bin/search.pl">Document Search</A>
   ```

2. Server passes input to gateway script.

3. As no arguments are passed to the script, the script generates an HTML document containing the <ISINDEX> tag. The <ISINDEX> tag under HTML 2.0 has no attributes and is used in the HEAD element as follows:

   ```
   <HTML>
   <HEAD>
   <TITLE> Searchable Document </TITLE>
   <ISINDEX>
   </HEAD>
   ```

4. The user is prompted to enter a search string and enters the information accordingly.

5. The search string is passed back to the original script as a URL-encoded search string.

6. The script uses the search string to perform an action, such as generating a document containing the results of the search.

7. Server sends results to client.

HTML 3.0 streamlines the query process and makes it easier to perform queries on indexes. Performing an ISINDEX query under HTML 3.0 is a five-step process:

1. The user accesses a document containing an ISINDEX query. Under HTML 3.0, the <ISINDEX> tag has two attributes: HREF and PROMPT. You can use the HREF attribute to specify a gateway script for searching that overrides the server's default URL. You can use the PROMPT attribute to override the default prompt that the user will see. These attributes are used as follows:

   ```
   <HTML>
   <HEAD>
   <TITLE> Searchable Document </TITLE>
   <ISINDEX HREF="address.db"
   PROMPT="What address would you like to search for?">
   </HEAD>
   ```

2. Following the prompt, the user enters a search string and client relays this to server.

3. Server sends search string to the script as a URL-encoded search string.

4. The script uses the search string to perform an action, such as generating a document containing the results of the search.

5. Server sends results to client.

While ISINDEX queries are an easy solution for searching documents, they are not the best solution. Most Web publishers prefer to provide fully indexed document searching or form-based document searching to readers. You can learn more about indexing documents in Chapter 13, "Search Engines and Indexed Databases." You can learn more about forms in Chapter 12.

Some server software will enable you to use command-line arguments in other ways using the exec command. With the exec command, you can directly execute a gateway script that will perform a specific action, such as returning a value to be substituted into your document. The interesting thing about using the exec command is that even if readers view the HTML source code, they see only the output value. This remains true even if they download the source to their computer. The reason for this is that the command is executed explicitly whenever it is encountered.

The exec command tells the server to execute a command or script. The argument to execute is enclosed in double quotation marks. The output of the script is substituted in the current position before the document is passed to the client. The following HTML code contains a command-line argument that executes a script called daily_access:

```
<P>This page has been accessed

<!—#exec cmd="/usr/cgi-bin/daily_access" —>

times today.</P>
```

> **NOTE**
>
> While the exec command is conveniently hidden in a comment tag, it executes nonetheless and will display the results. In order for you to use this nifty trick, your Web server must support it. If you aren't sure if the server supports the exec command, ask your Webmaster.

The daily_access script is a simple script that adds one to a count every time a page is accessed on a particular date. Thus, the 25th visitor of the day would see the following:

```
This page has been accessed 25 times today.
```

CGI Standard Input

Most input sent to a Web server is used to set environment variables, yet not all input fits neatly into an environment variable. When a user submits actual data to be processed by a gateway script, this data is received as a URL-encoded search string or via the standard input stream.

The server knows how to process actual data by the method used to submit the data.

Sending data as standard input is the most direct way to send data. The server simply tells the gateway script how many 8-bit sets of data to read from standard input. The script opens the standard input stream and reads the specified amount of data. While long URL-encoded search strings may get truncated, data sent on the standard input stream will not get truncated. Consequently, the standard input stream is the preferred way to pass data.

Clarifying CGI Input

You can identify a submission method when you create your fill-out forms. Under HTTP 1.0, there are two submission methods for forms:

1. The HTTP GET method uses URL-encoded search strings. When a server receives an URL-encoded search string, the server assigns the value of the search string to the QUERY_STRING variable.

2. The HTTP POST method uses the standard input streams. When a server receives data by the standard input stream, the server assigns the value associated with the length of the input stream to the CONTENT_LENGTH variable.

Let's create a sample Web document containing a form with three key fields: NAME, ADDRESS, and PHONE_NUMBER. Assume the URL to the script is http://www.tvp.com/cgi-bin/survey.pl and the user responds as follows:

```
Sandy Brown
12 Sunny Lane WhoVille, USA
987-654-3210
```

Identical information submitted using the GET and POST methods is treated differently by the server. When the GET method is used, the server sets the following environment variables then passes the input to the survey.pl script:

```
PATH=/bin:/usr/bin:/usr/etc:/usr/ucb
SERVER_SOFTWARE = CERN/3.0
SERVER_NAME = www.tvp.com
GATEWAY_INTERFACE = CGI/1.1
SERVER_PROTOCOL = HTTP/1.0
SERVER_PORT=80
REQUEST_METHOD = GET
HTTP_ACCEPT = text/plain, text/html, application/rtf, application/postscript,
audio/basic, audio/x-aiff, image/gif, image/jpeg, image/tiff, video/mpeg
PATH_INFO =
PATH_TRANSLATED =
SCRIPT_NAME = /cgi-bin/survey.pl
QUERY_STRING = NAME=Sandy+Brown&ADDRESS=12+Sunny+Lane+WhoVille,+USA
&PHONE_NUMBER=987-654-3210
REMOTE_HOST =
REMOTE_ADDR =
REMOTE_USER =
AUTH_TYPE =
CONTENT_TYPE =
```

```
CONTENT_LENGTH =
```

When the POST method is used, the server sets the following environment variables, then passes the input to the survey.pl script:

```
PATH=/bin:/usr/bin:/usr/etc:/usr/ucb
SERVER_SOFTWARE = CERN/3.0
SERVER_NAME = www.tvp.com
GATEWAY_INTERFACE = CGI/1.1
SERVER_PROTOCOL = HTTP/1.0
SERVER_PORT=80
REQUEST_METHOD = POST
HTTP_ACCEPT = text/plain, text/html, application/rtf, application/postscript,
audio/basic, audio/x-aiff, image/gif, image/jpeg, image/tiff, video/mpeg
PATH_INFO =
PATH_TRANSLATED =
SCRIPT_NAME = /cgi-bin/survey.pl
QUERY_STRING =
REMOTE_HOST =
REMOTE_ADDR =
REMOTE_USER =
AUTH_TYPE =
CONTENT_TYPE = application/x-www-form-urlencoded
CONTENT_LENGTH = 81
```

The following POST-submitted data is passed to the gateway script via the standard input stream:

```
NAME=Sandy+Brown&ADDRESS=12+Sunny+Lane+WhoVille,+USA&PHONE_NUMBER=987-654-3210
```

Output from CGI Scripts

After the script has completed processing the input, the script should return output to the server. The server will then return the output to the client. Generally, this output is in the form of an HTTP response that includes a header, followed by a blank line and a body. While the CGI header output is strictly formatted, the body of the output is formatted in the manner you specify in the header. For example, the body can contain an HTML document for the client to display.

CGI Headers

CGI headers contain directives to the server. Currently there are three valid server directives:

- Content-type
- Location
- Status

A single header can contain one or all of the server directives. Your CGI script would output these directives to the server. While the header is followed by a blank line that separates the header from the body, the output does not have to contain a body.

Content-Types Used in CGI Headers

The Content-Type field in a CGI header identifies the MIME type of data you are sending back to the client. Usually the data output from a script is a fully formatted document, such as an HTML document. You could specify this in the header as follows:

```
Content-Type: text/html
```

Locations Used in CGI Headers

The output of your script doesn't have to be a document created within the script. You can reference any document on the Web using the Location field. The Location field is used to reference a file by URL. Servers process location references either directly or indirectly depending on the location of the file. If the server can find the file locally, it will pass the file to the client. Otherwise, the server will redirect the URL to the client and the client will have to retrieve the file. You can specify a location in a script as follows:

```
Location: http://www.tvpress.com/
```

> **NOTE**
>
> Some older browsers don't support automatic redirection. Consequently, you may want to consider adding an HTML-formatted message body to the output. This message body will only be displayed if a browser cannot use the location URL.

Status Used in CGI Headers

The Status field is used to pass a status line to the server for forwarding to the client. Status codes are expressed as a three-digit code followed by a string that generally explains what has occurred. The first digit of a status code shows the general status as follows:

1XX	Not yet allocated
2XX	Success
3XX	Redirection
4XX	Client error
5XX	Server error

While many status codes are used by servers, the status codes you pass to a client via your CGI script are usually client error codes. For example, the script could not find a file and instead of returning nothing, you specify that the script output an error code. Here is a list of the client error codes you may want to use:

Status: 401 Unauthorized Authentication has failed. User is not allowed to access the file and should try again.

Status: 403 Forbidden. The request is not acceptable. User is not permitted to access file.

Status: 404 Not found. The specified resource could not be found.

Status: 405 Method not allowed. The submission method used is not allowed.

Clarifying CGI Output

Creating the output from a CGI script is easier than it may seem. All you have to do is format the output into a header and body using your favorite programming language. This section contains two examples. The first example is in the Perl programming language. The second example is in the UNIX Bourne shell.

If you wanted the script to output a simple HTML document using Perl, here is how you could do it:

```
#!/usr/bin/perl
#Create header with extra line space
print "Content-Type: text/html\n\n";
#Add body in HTML format
print <<"MAIN";
<HTML><HEAD><TITLE>Output from Script</TITLE></HEAD>
<BODY>
<H1>Top 10 Reasons for Using CGI</H1>
<P>10. Customer feedback.</P>
<P>9. Obtaining questionnaire and survey responses.</P>
<P>8. Tracking visitor count.</P>
<P>7. Automating searches.</P>
<P>6. Creating easy database interfaces.</P>
<P>5. Building gateways to other protocols.</P>
<P>4. HTML 2.0 Image maps.</P>
<P>3. User Authentication.</P>
<P>2. On-line order processing.</P>
<P>1. Generating documents on the fly.</P>
</BODY>
MAIN
```

If you wanted the script to output a simple HTML document in Bourne shell, here's how you could do it:

```
#!/bin/sh
#Create header with extra line space
echo "Content-Type: text/html"
#Add body in HTML format
cat << MAIN
<HTML><HEAD><TITLE>Output from Script</TITLE></HEAD>
<BODY>
<H1>Top 10 Reasons for Using CGI</H1>
<P>10. Customer feedback.</P>
<P>9. Obtaining questionnaire and survey responses.</P>
<P>8. Tracking visitor count.</P>
```

```
<P>7. Automating searches.</P>
<P>6. Creating easy database interfaces.</P>
<P>5. Building gateways to other protocols.</P>
<P>4. HTML 2.0 Image maps.</P>
<P>3. User Authentication.</P>
<P>2. On-line order processing.</P>
<P>1. Generating documents on the fly.</P>
</BODY>
MAIN
```

The server processing the output sets environment variables, creates an HTTP header, then sends the data on to the client. Here is how the HTTP header might look coming from a CERN Web Server:

```
HTTP/1.0 302 Found
MIME-Version: 1.0
Server: CERN/3.0
Date: Monday, 4-Mar-96 23:59:59 HST
Content-Type: text/html
Content-Length: 485

<HTML><HEAD><TITLE>Output from Script</TITLE></HEAD>
<BODY>
<H1>Top 10 Reasons for Using CGI</H1>
<P>10. Customer feedback.</P>
<P>9. Obtaining questionnaire and survey responses.</P>
<P>8. Tracking visitor count.</P>
<P>7. Automating searches.</P>
<P>6. Creating easy database interfaces.</P>
<P>5. Building gateways to other protocols.</P>
<P>4. HTML 2.0 Image maps.</P>
<P>3. User Authentication.</P>
<P>2. On-line order processing.</P>
<P>1. Generating documents on the fly.</P>
</BODY>
```

Summary

The common gateway interface opens the door for adding advanced features to your Web publications. This workhorse running quietly in the background enables fill-out forms, database queries, index searches, and creation of documents on the fly. You will use CGI whenever you want to open a two-way communication channel with the reader. While CGI enhancement is a click of the mouse button away for most readers, CGI enhancement means extra work for Web publishers. However, the exponential payoff associated with CGI enhancing your Web publications makes the extra effort truly worthwhile.

Form and Image Map Creation and Design

12

by William Robert Stanek

IN THIS CHAPTER

In previous chapters, you learned how to create wonderful Web publications that include multimedia and sizzling features for the Netscape Navigator, the Internet Explorer, and HTML 3.0 browsers. Yet now that you've created the beginnings of a wonderful publication, how do you get feedback, comments, and praise from visitors that will make all your hard work worthwhile? The answer is easy; add a fill-out form to an appropriate place in your Web publication and invite the reader to participate.

HTML 2.0 introduced forms and Web publishing has never been the same. Forms are the primary way to add interactivity and two-way communication to your Web publications. They provide friendly interfaces for inputting data, searching databases, and accessing indexes. To submit a fill-out form as input to a CGI script, the user only has to click on the submit button. Your forms can contain pulldown menus, pushbuttons, text, and graphics.

Image maps are graphical menus that contain hot spots. Each hot spot is an area the user can click on to go to an associated page. Image maps are as simple or complex as you make them. A single image map could be a menu for 5 or 25 Web pages. The choice is yours.

In this chapter you will learn all about forms and image maps—what they are, how to use them, and much more.

What Forms Are and Why You Want to Use Them

In our daily lives we see forms all the time. The forms you fill out at the doctor's office. The credit card bills that require you to fill in the dollar amount in tiny boxes, subtly reminding you to make sure to include all the zeros that go along with the digit you are sure cannot be right. The surveys and questionnaires you receive in the mail. The juicy compatibility polls in a magazine that you fill out at the checkout counter.

Although you may not think of these items as forms, all of them require you to fill in information or make selections from groups of numbered or lettered items. When you submit a printed form, someone on the receiving end has to file these forms away. In an increasingly computerized world, this usually means entering the information into a database or spreadsheet. Major companies hire dozens of people for the specific task of entering the thousands of forms that flood the company every day into the company database. This is a huge expense and a tremendous burden on the company.

Now imagine a virtual office where thousands of forms are entered into the company database every day without a single worker. The forms are processed efficiently, almost instantly, and the customer can get feedback within seconds of submitting a form. The cost for what otherwise would be a mammoth undertaking is a few hours—the time it takes you to design a fill-out form and build a CGI script to process the information.

Using forms, you open a two-way communication channel between you and visitors to your Web publications. Visitors can send comments directly to you. You can create CGI scripts to process the input automatically. In this way, readers can get immediate results. You can e-mail the input to your e-mail address. This way, you can respond to readers' questions and comments easily and personally. You can also set up a script to process the input, give results to the reader, and send yourself e-mail.

While the scripting part of the process runs in the background, the fill-out form is what the reader sees up close and personal. Readers can interact with forms by entering information in spaces provided, by making selections from pulldown menus, by activating pushbuttons, and by submitting the data for instant processing. Figure 12.1 shows a simple form with areas for text entry. Even this simple form is a powerful tool for inviting reader participation.

FIGURE 12.1.

Even simple forms are useful for inviting reader participation.

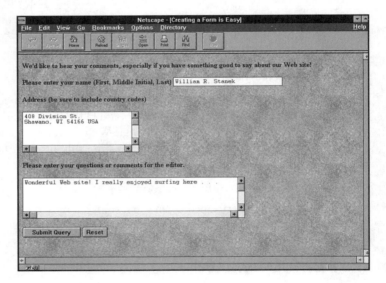

Form Design

While creating a form is easy, designing a good form is not always easy. Some publishers use generic all-purpose forms that fail because the form wasn't designed with a specific purpose in mind. The key to designing forms is to use them for a specific purpose. When you want to get feedback from readers, you create a form for reader feedback. When you want to take orders online, you create a form for submitting online orders.

Designing forms that are useful to readers and to you as the publisher should be your primary goal. A form that is useful to readers will be used. A form that is useful to you as the publisher makes your job easier. The key to creating forms that are useful to readers and you as the publisher is also in form design. As we go through the steps for designing forms, keep the following guidelines in mind:

1. A form that is useful to the reader is
   - Friendly
   - Well-organized
   - Sized correctly

2. A form that is useful to you as the publisher does the following:
   - Uses uniquely named and easily identifiable keywords for fields
   - Allows for brevity of processing and quick indexing whenever possible
   - Provides subtle guidance to the reader on the amount of input you are looking for

The *<FORM>* Tag

All elements of your forms are enclosed by the begin form tag <FORM> and end form tag </FORM>. Within these tags you can include almost any valid HTML tag, such as paragraph and heading tags. Although multiple forms can be on a single Web page, you cannot create subforms within a form. Primarily this is because the form must be submitted to be processed in a specific manner. The way forms are submitted is based on

The method used to submit the form

The action to be performed when the form is submitted

The optional type of encoding to be performed on the form

The *METHOD* Attribute

The METHOD attribute specifies the method for submitting the form. Currently, there are two acceptable values:

```
METHOD=GET
METHOD=POST
```

As discussed briefly in the previous chapter, the preferred submission method is POST. When you use POST, the data is sent as a separate input stream via the server to your gateway script. This enables the server to pass the information directly to the gateway script without assigning variables or arguments. The value of the CONTENT_LENGTH environment variable tells the CGI script how much data to read from the standard input stream. Using this method, there is no limit on the amount of data that can be passed to the server.

The default submission method is GET. Data submitted using GET is appended to the script URL. The script URL and the data are passed to the server as a single URL-encoded input. The server receiving the input assigns the data being passed to two variables. The script URL is assigned to the environment variable SCRIPT_NAME. The data is assigned to the environment variable QUERRY_STRING.

Assigning the data to variables on a UNIX system means passing the data through the UNIX shell. The number of characters you can send to UNIX shell in a single input is severely limited. Some servers restrict the length of this type of input to 255 characters. This means only a limited amount of data can be appended to a URL before truncation occurs. When truncation occurs, you lose data and losing data is a bad thing. Consequently, if you use GET, you should always ensure the length of data input is small.

The *ACTION* Attribute

The ACTION attribute specifies the action to be performed when a form is submitted. As a form without an ACTION attribute will not be processed in any way, your forms should always include this attribute. You can define an action for your forms as the URL to a gateway script to be executed or as an actual action.

By specifying the URL to a gateway script, you can direct input to the script for processing. The URL provides a relative or an absolute path to the script. Scripts defined with relative URLs are located on your local server. Scripts defined with absolute URLs can be located on a remote or local server. Most CGI scripts are located in the cgi-bin directory. You could access a script in a cgi-bin directory as follows:

```
ACTION="http://tvp.com/cgi-bin/your_script"
```

An ACTION could be inserted in the <FORM> tag as follows:

```
<FORM METHOD="POST" ACTION="http://tvp.com/cgi-bin/datasort.pl">
 . . .
</FORM>
```

You can also use the ACTION attribute to specify an actual action to be performed. The only action currently supported is mailto that enables you to mail the contents of a form to anyone. Most current browser and server software support the mailto value. You can use the mailto value as follows:

```
<FORM METHOD="POST" ACTION="mailto:publisher@tvp.com">
 . . .
</FORM>
```

A form created using the previous example would be sent to publisher@tvp.com. The mail to value provides you with a simple solution for using forms that does not need to be directed to a CGI script to be processed. This is great news for Web publishers who don't have access to CGI. As the contents of the form are mailed directly to an intended recipient, the data can be processed offline as necessary. You should consider using the `mailto` value for forms that don't need immediate processing and when you don't have access to CGI but would like to use forms in your Web publications.

The *ENCTYPE* Attribute

The `ENCTYPE` attribute specifies the MIME content type for encoding the form data. The client encodes the data before passing it to the server. Data from fill-out forms is not encoded to prevent the data from being read. Data from fill-out forms is encoded to ensure input fields can be easily matched to key values. By default, the data is `x-www-form-encoded`. This encoding is also called URL encoding and was discussed in the previous chapter. If you do not specify an encoding type, the default value is used automatically.

While in theory you can use any valid MIME type, such as text/plain, most forms on the Web use the default encoding, `x-www-form-encoded`. This is to prevent problems you would experience when trying to manipulate data that has not been encoded in some way. You can use the `ENCTYPE` attribute in your forms as follows:

```
<FORM METHOD="POST" ACTION="cgi-bin/query.pl" ENCTYPE="x-www-form-encoded">
 . . .
</FORM>
```

Adding Content to the Form

The elements designed specifically for use within forms are what make fill-out forms useful and interactive. When adding content to your forms, keep in mind the simple rules outlined earlier in this chapter. Well-designed forms are friendly, well-organized, and sized correctly. With this in mind, you should always provide descriptions along with form fields. As with print forms, the descriptions for fields should be brief. This makes the form easier to read.

Here is a wordy field description:

> *You should enter your full name in the adjacent text window using your first name, middle initial, and last name as appropriate.*

Here is a better field description:

> *Please enter your name (First, Middle Initial, Last).*

Input fields should be correctly sized to ensure they are usable. A good field size ensures all key information entered by the user is visible in the input area. For a telephone number, you could define an input field twelve characters in length. This would allow customers to enter their phone number and area code. If a reader puts parentheses around the area code, the length of the input field should be stretched to fourteen characters. If the reader lives in another country, the length of the input field should be stretched to at least sixteen characters.

The form itself should be correctly sized and well-organized to ensure readers will take the time to fill it out. A good form balances the number of fields against the length of the fields. This means a form that requires lengthy input from readers should have few fields and a form that requires the reader to make many selections but requires limited actual input could have many fields.

Three key elements are used to add content to forms. These elements are:

INPUT   Used to define input fields
SELECT   Used to create selection menus
TEXTAREA Used to define a multiple-line text-input window

Adding Input Fields

Using the INPUT element, you can add check boxes, radio buttons, images text windows, and other elements to your forms. You define an INPUT element by labeling it with a TYPE and a NAME. The input TYPE determines how the input field looks on the screen. The NAME attribute labels the field with a keyword you can use in your CGI scripts. All input fields should have a NAME attribute and a TYPE attribute. The basic format of the INPUT element is as follows:

```
<INPUT TYPE="type of field" NAME="input field name">
```

Input fields and associated data are sent to a CGI script as keyword and value pairs. The method used to submit the form determines the way the data is submitted to the CGI script. Let's look at two examples of the data flow from a form to a script. Both forms have three input fields and the user submits the forms with the following values:

```
answer1 = Monday night football
answer2 = Chicago Bears
answer3 = Super bowl bound
```

The first example uses the GET method:

```
<FORM METHOD="GET" ACTION="cgi-bin/query.pl">
<INPUT TYPE="text" NAME="answer1">
<INPUT TYPE="text" NAME="answer2">
<INPUT TYPE="text" NAME="answer3">
</FORM>
```

When the GET method is used, the server sets the following environment variables, then passes the input to the query.pl script:

```
PATH=/bin:/usr/bin:/usr/etc:/usr/ucb
SERVER_SOFTWARE = NCSA/1.3
SERVER_NAME = www.tvpress.com
GATEWAY_INTERFACE = CGI/1.1
SERVER_PROTOCOL = HTTP/1.0
SERVER_PORT= 80
REQUEST_METHOD = GET
HTTP_ACCEPT = application/octet-stream, application/postscript,
```

```
application/rtf, application/x-compress, application/x-dvi,
application/x-gzip, application/x-zip-compressed, audio/basic, audio/x-aiff,
audio/x-wav, image/gif, image/jpeg, image/tiff, image/x-portable-bitmap,
message/external-body, message/partial, message/rfc822, multipart/alternative,
multipart/digest, multipart/mixed, multipart/parallel, text/html, text/plain,
video/mpeg, video/quicktime, video/x-msvideo
PATH_INFO =
PATH_TRANSLATED =
SCRIPT_NAME = /cgi-bin/query.pl
QUERY_STRING = answer1=Monday+night+football&answer2=Chicago+Bears&
answer3=Super+bowl+bound
REMOTE_HOST =
REMOTE_ADDR =
REMOTE_USER =
AUTH_TYPE =
CONTENT_TYPE =
CONTENT_LENGTH =
```

The second example uses the POST method:

```
<FORM METHOD="POST" ACTION="cgi-bin/query.pl">
<INPUT TYPE="text" NAME="answer1">
<INPUT TYPE="text" NAME="answer2">
<INPUT TYPE="text" NAME="answer3">
</FORM>
```

When the POST method is used, the server sets the following environment variables, then passes the input to the query.pl script:

```
PATH=/bin:/usr/bin:/usr/etc:/usr/ucb
SERVER_SOFTWARE = NCSA/1.3
SERVER_NAME = www.tvpress.com
GATEWAY_INTERFACE = CGI/1.1
SERVER_PROTOCOL = HTTP/1.0
SERVER_PORT= 80
REQUEST_METHOD = POST
HTTP_ACCEPT = application/octet-stream, application/postscript,
application/rtf, application/x-compress, application/x-dvi,
application/x-gzip, application/x-zip-compressed, audio/basic, audio/x-aiff,
audio/x-wav, image/gif, image/jpeg, image/tiff, image/x-portable-bitmap,
message/external-body, message/partial, message/rfc822, multipart/alternative,
multipart/digest, multipart/mixed, multipart/parallel, text/html, text/plain,
video/mpeg, video/quicktime, video/x-msvideo
PATH_INFO =
PATH_TRANSLATED =
SCRIPT_NAME = /cgi-bin/query.pl
QUERY_STRING =
REMOTE_HOST =
REMOTE_ADDR =
REMOTE_USER =
AUTH_TYPE =
CONTENT_TYPE = application/x-www-form-urlencoded
CONTENT_LENGTH = 75
```

The following data is passed to the query.pl script using the standard input stream:

```
answer1=Monday+night+football&answer2=Chicago+Bears&answer3=Super+bowl+bound
```

The TYPE attribute has eight values. Many attributes can be associated with each of these input types. While forms will let you try to associate just about any attribute with any type, certain attributes should be used with certain types. Knowing this will save you a lot of time when you create forms. The next sections describe the useful attributes for each of the following input types:

TEXT	A one-line text field of a width defined in the form
CHECKBOX	Creates one or more boxes that can be checked by a user
HIDDEN	A field that is not displayed to the user but is sent to your script
IMAGE	An image that can be clicked on to submit the form
PASSWORD	A text field where all data entered is seen as the * character
RADIO	Creates one or more radio buttons that can be turned on or off by a user
RESET	Creates a button that clears the form when clicked
SUBMIT	Creates a button that submits the form when clicked

Using *TEXT* Fields

The TEXT type enables you to define a basic input field for text. TEXT fields are displayed on a single line. Four attributes can be used with TEXT fields:

MAXLENGTH	The maximum allowable length of the field. Beware, if this attribute is not set, there is no limit.
NAME	The keyword associated with the input field.
SIZE	The width of the input field, expressed as the number of characters for the text area.
VALUE	An initial value for the field that will be displayed in the text area. The user can add to this information and if necessary delete the information to enter new information.

Here is how you can use TEXT input fields in your forms:

```
<INPUT TYPE="TEXT" NAME="answer1" SIZE="60">
```

In the example, the SIZE attribute defines the visible area for the TEXT field on the screen to be 60 characters wide. Because it does not specify the maximum length of the field, the text will scroll, enabling the user to enter more than 60 characters. To limit the input to a specific value, you should use the MAXLENGTH attribute, such as:

```
<INPUT TYPE="TEXT" NAME="answer1" SIZE="60" MAXLENGTH="60">
```

Using Check Boxes and Radio Buttons

The CHECKBOX input field creates boxes that can be checked by a user. The RADIO input field creates circular buttons that can be checked by a user. Some browsers display selected check boxes and radio buttons using text—an x for a check box and a round bullet for a radio button. Other browsers display check boxes and radio buttons as graphical push buttons with a 3-D flare. These input fields have four attributes:

CHECKED   The check box or radio button is automatically checked when viewed. The best use of this attribute is for default options that can be unchecked, if necessary.

DISABLED   The user cannot manipulate the check box or radio button. You will probably want to use this attribute only for testing your forms.

NAME   The keyword associated with the input field.

VALUE   The value to assign of the user activates the check box of the radio button.

While the primary difference between a check box and a radio button may seem to be their shape, there is a fundamental difference in the way they behave. Check boxes enable users to make multiple selections. Radio buttons, on the other hand, enable users to make only one selection.

When creating check boxes and radio buttons, carefully consider how you will use them. You will want to use radio buttons with a single associated keyword value when the user should make only one selection, such as a choice of A, B, or C. You will want to use check boxes with multiple associated keyword values when the user can make multiple selections, such as a choice of all or any of A through E.

Figure 12.2 depicts how check boxes and radio buttons can be used in a form. While the check box groups will accept multiple responses, the radio button groups will only accept a single response. Listing 12.1 shows the code for the form.

Listing 12.1. Sample form using check boxes and radio buttons.

```
<FORM METHOD="POST" ACTION="/cgi-bin/survey.pl">
<H1>Optimism Survey</H1>
<P>1. Do you consider yourself to be an optimist or a pessimist?
<P><INPUT  TYPE="checkbox" NAME="optimist"  VALUE="yes" >Optimist</P>
<P><INPUT  TYPE="checkbox" NAME="optimist"  VALUE="no" >Pessimism</P>
<P>2. Is a rainy Sunday?
<P><INPUT  TYPE="checkbox" NAME="rainyday"  VALUE="A" >Soothing
<INPUT  TYPE="checkbox" NAME="rainyday"  VALUE="B" >Restful
<P><INPUT  TYPE="checkbox" NAME="rainyday"  VALUE="C" >Dreary
<INPUT  TYPE="checkbox" NAME="rainyday"  VALUE="D" >Dreadful
<P>3. Is a partially filled glass of water
<P><INPUT  TYPE="radio" NAME="glass"  VALUE="A" >Half Empty
<INPUT  TYPE="radio" NAME="glass"  VALUE="B" >Half Full
<P>4. What do you think about Monday Mornings?
<P><INPUT  TYPE="radio" NAME="mondays"  VALUE="A" >First day of a great week
<INPUT  TYPE="radio" NAME="mondays"  VALUE="B" >First day back to work
<P><INPUT  TYPE="radio" NAME="mondays"  VALUE="C" >Four days to go till Friday
<INPUT  TYPE="radio" NAME="mondays"  VALUE="D" >Five days till freedom
</FORM>
```

FIGURE 12.2.

A survey using check boxes.

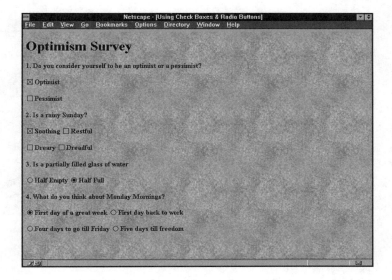

Hidden Fields in Forms

The HIDDEN input field is not displayed and is only useful to provide essential input to your script. Hidden elements have two attributes:

NAME   The keyword associated with the input field

VALUE   The value of the field

Use HIDDEN fields when you want the same script to serve more than one purpose. The Web publisher using this HIDDEN input field has several publications that may be subscribed to:

```
<INPUT  TYPE="hidden" NAME="subscription"  VALUE="magazine-NewsDay">
```

The publisher uses the HIDDEN field to track the publication to which the customer is subscribing. This is done by setting a unique value for the subscription input field in the form. As all subscriptions require the same information from customers, the publisher uses a single CGI script to process subscriptions from multiple sources. Listing 12.2 is the outline of a Perl script that could be used to process the subscription information.

Listing 12.2. Partial Perl script for processing subscriptions.

```perl
#!/usr/bin/perl
#Check the method used to submit the form
$METHOD = $ENV{'REQUEST_METHOD'};
#Tell script where to look for POST submitted input
if  ( $METHOD eq 'POST' )
{
read(stdin, $SINPUT, $ENV{'CONTENT_LENGTH'});
```

continues

Listing 12.2. continued

```
}
else
#Tell script where to look for POST submitted input
if  ( $METHOD eq 'GET' )
{
$SINPUT = $ENV{'QUERY_STRING'};
}
else
#Tell script to exit if neither POST or GET are used
{
exit( 1 );
}
#Process URL-encoded input into key words and value pairs
foreach $SINPUT (split(/&/))
{
$SARRAY[$i] =~ s/\+/ /g;
($input_name, $value) = split(/=/,$SARRAY[$i],2);
$input_name =~ s/%(..)/pack("c",hex($1))/ge;
$value =~ s/%(..)/pack("c",hex($1))/ge;
$SARRAY{$input_name} = $value;
}
#Set the output file for the subscription information
if ($SARRAY{'subscription'} eq 'magazine-NewsDay')
{
$DATAOUTFILE = "news.db"
}
else
if ($SARRAY{'subscription'} eq 'magazine-WebTimes')
{
$DATAOUTFILE = "webtimes.db"
}
else
{
$DATAOUTFILE = "running.db"
}
#The rest of the script would process the customer's subscription information,
#such as name, address, and payment method.
```

Using *PASSWORD* Fields

To enable users to enter password information without revealing the password to onlookers, you can use the PASSWORD input field. All text entered in a PASSWORD field is seen as asterisks. The asterisks are used only to mask the characters and do not affect how the text is passed to your gateway script. By combining this element with a TEXT input field for the user's login ID, you can pass this information to a script that would validate the user's access to protected areas of your Web site.

This element has four attributes:

MAXLENGTH	The maximum allowable length of the field. Beware, if this attribute is not set, there is no limit.
NAME	The keyword associated with the input field.
SIZE	The width of the input field, expressed as the number of characters for the text area.
VALUE	An initial value for the field that will be displayed in the text area. The user can add to this information and if necessary delete the information to enter new information.

Here is a sample PASSWORD element:

```
<INPUT  TYPE="password" NAME="net_password" SIZE=12 MAXLENGTH=12 >
```

Using *RESET* and *SUBMIT*

Two extremely useful input types are RESET and SUBMIT. Usually these features for forms are displayed as graphical push buttons. A reset button clears the form when selected. A submit button submits the form when selected. By default the reset buttons are labeled with the value of RESET and submit buttons are labeled with the value SUBMIT. You change the label for these buttons using the VALUE attribute, such as

```
<INPUT TYPE="reset" VALUE="Clear Form">

<INPUT TYPE="submit" NAME="button1" VALUE="Submit Form">
```

Another useful attribute for the submit button is the NAME attribute. Using the NAME attribute, you can track which SUBMIT button a user pressed. This provides another way of tracking the precise form used to submit input. Using this feature of the name attribute, you can create a down and dirty menu for your site.

The following example uses a CGI script to process the input and direct the user to a new page. When a user clicks on a button, the input is passed to the named script for processing. Fig-ure 12.3 shows the example created using this code:

```
<FORM METHOD="GET"  ACTION="../cgi-bin/quick-menu">
<INPUT  TYPE="SUBMIT"  NAME="BUTTON1"  VALUE="TVP Home Page">
<INPUT  TYPE="SUBMIT"  NAME="BUTTON2"  VALUE="BackGround">
<INPUT  TYPE="SUBMIT"  NAME="BUTTON3"  VALUE="What's New">
<INPUT  TYPE="SUBMIT"  NAME="BUTTON4"  VALUE="Book Info">
<INPUT  TYPE="SUBMIT"  NAME="BUTTON5"  VALUE="Instant Orders">
<INPUT  TYPE="SUBMIT"  NAME="BUTTON8"  VALUE="Resources">
<INPUT  TYPE="HIDDEN"  NAME="MENU"  VALUE="MENU1">
</Form>
```

FIGURE 12.3.

A quick menu using a form.

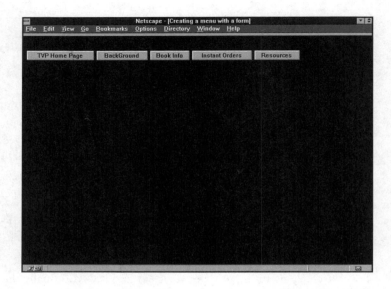

This example uses multiple forms to create a menu. An ACTION attribute is defined for each form. When a user clicks on a button, the browser carries out the assigned action. As the actions can all be processed by the client, no CGI script is involved. Figure 12.4 shows the example created using the following code:

```
<FORM METHOD="GET"  ACTION="vphp.html">
<INPUT  TYPE="SUBMIT"  NAME="BUTTON1"  VALUE="TVP Home Page">
</Form>
<FORM METHOD="GET"  ACTION="vpbg.html">
<INPUT  TYPE="SUBMIT"  NAME="BUTTON2"  VALUE="BackGround"
</Form>
<FORM METHOD="GET"  ACTION="new.html">
<INPUT  TYPE="SUBMIT"  NAME="BUTTON3"  VALUE="What's New">
</Form>
<FORM METHOD="GET"  ACTION="books.html">
<INPUT  TYPE="SUBMIT"  NAME="BUTTON4"  VALUE="Book Info">
</Form>
<FORM METHOD="GET"  ACTION="orders.html">
<INPUT  TYPE="SUBMIT"  NAME="BUTTON5"  VALUE="Instant Orders">
</Form>
<FORM METHOD="GET"  ACTION="resources.html">
<INPUT  TYPE="SUBMIT"  NAME="BUTTON8"  VALUE="Resources">
</Form>
```

### Chapter 12

FIGURE 12.4.

A quick menu using multiple forms processed by client.

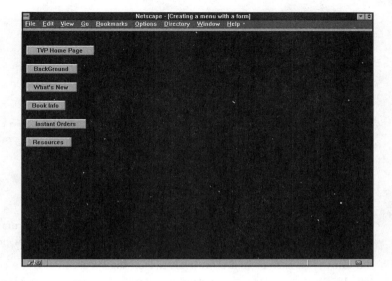

An alternative to the default style of the submission button is to define a fancy button the user can click on to submit the form. You do this with the IMAGE input field. Image elements have three attributes:

ALIGN	Used to align the image with text in the same line. Valid values are TOP, MIDDLE, and BOTTOM.
NAME	The keyword associated with the input field.
SRC	The image to be displayed.

Here is a sample image element:

```
<FORM METHOD="POST" ACTION="/cgi-bin/clickit.pl">
<INPUT  TYPE="image" NAME="pubform"  SRC="fancybutton.gif" ALIGN="MIDDLE">
</FORM>
```

NOTE

You do not need a SUBMIT type in the INPUT field containing the IMAGE type declaration. Here, the IMAGE type is used in place of the SUBMIT type, and if you click on the image, the form will be automatically submitted.

Adding Selection Menus

Beyond input fields for forms, you can also use selection fields. The SELECT element is used to create two types of selection menus for your forms. An on-screen menu has selections that are completely visible on the screen. A pulldown menu has selection elements that are hidden until the reader activates the menu.

The SELECT element has a begin and an end tag associated with it. You use the NAME attribute to specify a keyword for the selection menu. Using the SIZE attribute, you can specify the number of selection elements to display on the screen, such as:

```
<SELECT SIZE=1 NAME="Menu1"> . . . </SELECT>
<SELECT SIZE=7 NAME="Menu2"> . . . </SELECT>
```

By default, the user can only select one option from the menu. The first selection menu has a one-line window with a pulldown menu. The second selection menu is an on-screen menu with seven displayed items and a scroll bar for accessing additional elements.

To allow the user to make multiple selections, you can use the MULTIPLE attribute. The MULTIPLE attribute lets users select as many options as they want. Most browsers enable you to make multiple selections by holding down the control button on the keyboard and clicking with the left mouse button when the pointer is over the additional item you want to select. Here is how you could use this attribute:

```
<SELECT SIZE=7 NAME="books" MULTIPLE> . . . </SELECT>
```

You define selections for the menu using the OPTION element. This element has two basic formats:

```
<OPTION>Item 1
<OPTION SELECTED>Item 2
```

The first menu item can be selected by a user. The second menu item is selected by default. Users can unselect the default option by clicking on it if they want to.

Figure 12.5 shows several types of selection menus. The first example shows an on-screen menu as it first appears on screen. The second example shows an on-screen menu. This menu accepts multiple selections. On-screen menus occupy more space. You should consider using on-screen menus when the user can make multiple selections and pulldown menus when the user can only make one selection. The final example shows a menu with part of the selections displayed and part of the selections hidden. The scroll bar can be used to access additional items. Listing 12.3 contains the HTML for the form.

Listing 12.3. Creating a selection menu in a form.

```
<HTML>
<HEAD>
<TITLE>Favorite Reading</TITLE>
</HEAD>
<BODY>
<FORM METHOD="POST" ACTION="/cgi-bin/books.pl">
<P><B>What types of print publications do you read regularly?</B></P>
<SELECT NAME="publications" SIZE=7 MULTIPLE>
<OPTION>Books
<OPTION>Magazines
<OPTION>Professional journals
<OPTION>Newspapers
<OPTION>Reference works
<OPTION>Comic Books
<OPTION>None
</SELECT>
<P><B>What type of nonfiction do you enjoy reading?</B></P>
<SELECT SIZE=1 NAME="nonfiction">
<OPTION>Autobiography
<OPTION>Biography
<OPTION>Computers/Internet
<OPTION>Cooking
<OPTION>Health/Medicine
<OPTION>How-To
<OPTION>Money/Finance
<OPTION>New age
<OPTION>Parenting
<OPTION>Reference
<OPTION>Self-Help
<OPTION>Sports
<OPTION>Travel
</SELECT>
<P><B>What type of novel do you prefer to read?</B></P>
<SELECT NAME="Fiction" SIZE=3>
<OPTION>Adventure
<OPTION>Fantasy
<OPTION>Horror
<OPTION>Humor
<OPTION>Mystery
<OPTION>Romance
<OPTION>Science fiction
<OPTION>Suspense
<OPTION>Western
</SELECT>
<INPUT TYPE="reset" VALUE="Clear Form">
<INPUT TYPE="submit" NAME="button1" VALUE="Submit Form">
</FORM>
</BODY>
</HTML>
```

FIGURE 12.5.

Using selection menus.

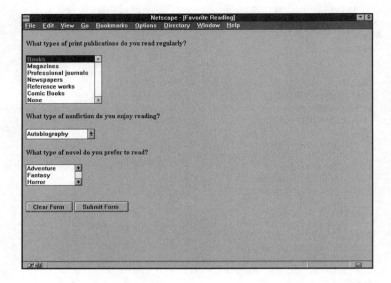

Selection elements and associated data are sent to a CGI script as keyword and value pairs. As with other elements, the method used to submit the form determines the way the data is submitted to the CGI script. To see exactly how this works with selection menus and options, let's follow the data flow from the user's browser to the CGI script. The user selected the following options from the previous form in Figure 12.5:

publications	Books, Magazines, Newspapers
nonfiction	Computers/Internet
fiction	Adventure

The form uses the POST method to submit data to the books.pl script. The client passes the data to the server. The server sets the following environment variables before passing the data to the script:

```
PATH=/bin:/usr/bin:/usr/etc:/usr/ucb
SERVER_SOFTWARE = CERN/3.0
SERVER_NAME = www.tvp.com
GATEWAY_INTERFACE = CGI/1.1
SERVER_PROTOCOL = HTTP/1.0
SERVER_PORT= 80
REQUEST_METHOD = POST
HTTP_ACCEPT = application/octet-stream, application/postscript,
application/rtf, application/x-compress, application/x-dvi,
application/x-gzip, application/x-zip-compressed, audio/basic, audio/x-aiff,
audio/x-wav, image/gif, image/jpeg, image/tiff, image/x-portable-bitmap,
message/external-body, message/partial, message/rfc822, multipart/alternative,
multipart/digest, multipart/mixed, multipart/parallel, text/html, text/plain,
video/mpeg, video/quicktime, video/x-msvideo
PATH_INFO =
PATH_TRANSLATED =
```

```
SCRIPT_NAME = /cgi-bin/books.pl
QUERY_STRING =
REMOTE_HOST =
REMOTE_ADDR =
REMOTE_USER =
AUTH_TYPE =
CONTENT_TYPE = application/x-www-form-urlencoded
CONTENT_LENGTH = 88
```

The following data is passed to the `books.pl` script using the standard input stream:

```
publications=Books,Magazines,Newspapers&nonfiction=Computers/Internet&
fiction=Adventure
```

Adding Text Windows

The final element you can use with your forms is the TEXTAREA element. This element has more functionality than the text field used with the INPUT element because it enables you to define text windows of any size to display on the screen. Text windows can be used to input large amounts of data. Although the size of the window is defined in rows and columns, you have no real control over how much data the user can enter into the window. This is because text windows have vertical and horizontal scroll bars that enable the user to scroll left to right as well as up and down.

Text windows are defined with a pair of tags. Any text between the begin and end TEXTAREA tags is used as the initial input to the text window. Default text provided for a text window is displayed exactly as entered. While the user can erase any default input if necessary, initial input should be used primarily to save the user time. TEXTAREA has three attributes:

NAME   The key word associated with the input field

ROWS   The height of the text window in number of lines

COLS   The width of the text window in number of characters

Here is how you could define a text window 8 rows tall and 60 characters wide:

```
<TEXTAREA NAME="Publisher_Query" ROWS=8 COLS=60></TEXTAREA>
```

Here's a sample form containing two text areas:

```
<FORM METHOD="POST" ACTION="/cgi-bin/job.pl">
<P>Describe your current job.</P>
<TEXTAREA NAME="JobDescription" ROWS=10 COLS=60></TEXTAREA>
<P>What would your dream job be like?</P>
<TEXTAREA NAME="DreamJob" ROWS=10 COLS=60></TEXTAREA>
<INPUT TYPE="reset">
<INPUT TYPE="submit" VALUE="Submit Form">
</FORM>
```

Extensions for Forms

The handling of input from forms is being improved all the time. HTML 3.0 introduces improvements for script handling. Other improvements come from browsers, such as Netscape, that introduce an entirely new way to handle scripts.

HTML 3.0 Script Handling

The up and coming HTML 3.0 specification includes many dramatic improvements for forms. These improvements, when implemented, will forever change the way forms are used in Web publishing. However, many Web publishers wanted HTML 3.0 to be able to creatively manipulate form elements based on user input. The problem is that making calculations, setting values, and determining fields based on input is inherently complex, and creating markup to cover most of the scenarios would be difficult. Therefore, the authors of HTML 3.0 decided to extend the standard using a simple attribute for forms that enables you to associate the form with a script that will be downloaded and interpreted by the browser. The SCRIPT attribute of the FORM element specifies the URL path to the script the browser will download. The SCRIPT attribute is used as follows:

```
<FORM METHOD="POST" ACTION="/cgi-bin/query.pl" SCRIPT="update_form">
```

While client-side handling of scripts for forms enables Web publishers to create powerful forms that adapt and change based on user input, the HTML 3.0 specification does not require support for scripts. Further, the specification does not define how scripts are to be used with forms. This means the browser interpreting the form will determine the type of scripting language used. Client-side scripts for forms will be restricted in what they can do to ensure they cannot do anything that will harm the user's computer.

Other improvements for forms that HTML 3.0 will introduce are

> A new method to enter records into a database
> The capability to group related fields into frames
> Labels for fields
> Nested forms

Of all these new features, the most eagerly awaited is the ability to nest forms. Yes, at long last, under HTML 3.0, Web publishers will be able to nest forms.

Client-Side Scripting Languages

Some browsers like the Netscape Navigator have implemented client-side scripts in an entirely different way. For example, Netscape client-side scripts are based on the Java language and are not restricted to use with forms. Like Java, the Netscape scripting language is extremely versatile and platform-independent. You can include Netscape scripts in any part of your HTML publications without regard to the type of computer that will access the document. Additionally, as Netscape scripts are embedded within comment tags, they do not affect the way other browsers treat your documents.

The Netscape scripting language is called JavaScript. To specify live scripts, you use the Netscape <SCRIPT> tag. The primary attribute for the <SCRIPT> tag is the LANGUAGE attribute, which specifies the scripting language to use to interpret a script within a document. You can specify the Netscape scripting language in your documents as follows:

```
<SCRIPT LANGUAGE="JavaScript">
```

As JavaScript is based on Java, which is in turn based on C/C++, the JavaScript language is surprisingly easy to learn and use. Anyone who knows the basics of C, C++, Java, or Perl will feel right at home with JavaScript. While the initial implementation of JavaScript is admittedly simplistic, it does enable you to perform most of the functions you would otherwise use a server-side script for. If you're interested in learning more about the Netscape scripting language, visit Netscape at

```
http://home.netscape.com/
```

What Image Maps Are and Why You Want to Use Them

If you've browsed the Web, you've probably seen image maps. Image maps are high-power graphical menus. There is no better way to create easy, graphic-based ways for users to browse information at your Web site. Using an image map, you can create a graphic image with multiple hot spots. Each hot spot is a specific part of an image that the user can click on to access other documents and objects.

The wonderful thing about images is that you can pack the equivalent of hundreds of words into tiny symbols within your image map. Image maps are friendly and compulsively usable. Besides being friendly and usable, image maps enable you to pack a lot into a relatively small amount of space. Some image maps in use on the Web lead to dozens of pages, meaning virtually everything on the image is a doorway to something new.

Don't worry about having to write a script to interpret the image map. Scripts for interpreting image maps are included with most server software. NCSA Web servers use a program called imagemap. CERN Web servers use a program called htimap to define image maps. Most image map programs follow either the NCSA or the CERN method for defining image maps, or a derivative of these methods. This is true even with Windows and Macintosh Web servers.

Image Map Design

Under HTML 2.0, gateway scripts are used to process the input from image maps. When a user clicks on the image, the x, y coordinates are sent to the gateway script. The gateway script interprets these coordinates and uses a separately defined map file to determine the action to take. The map file contains a set of coordinates that define the hot areas. The coordinates are the horizontal and vertical locations of hot areas within the image.

The coordinates for image maps are determined slightly different from what you may be used to. The upper-left corner of the image is at coordinate (0,0). As you move outward to the right in a straight line, the x coordinates grow larger. As you move downward in a straight line, the y coordinates grow larger. Figure 12.6 shows an enlarged view of an image that would make a good image map. Coordinates have been placed on the image to show some of the end points you might want to use to create this image map.

FIGURE 12.6.

Enlarged view of an image map.

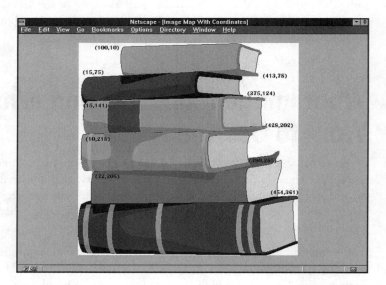

The process of creating an image map with defined hot areas is easier than you think. Under HTML 2.0, image maps are defined by adding the ISMAP attribute to an <IMG> tag. Image maps are used with the anchor tag <A>, which defines the gateway script to call when the user clicks on the image, as follows:

```
<A HREF="/cgi-bin/htimap"> <IMG SRC="power_map.jpeg" ISMAP></A>
```

You can also use image maps with HTML 3.0 figures. Use the IMAGEMAP attribute to specify that a figure is an image map. The value assigned to the IMAGEMAP attribute is the script that will process the input. Here is how you could create an HTML 3.0 image map:

```
<FIG SRC="power_map.jpeg" IMAGEMAP="/cgi-bin/htimap">
```

Hot areas for image maps are defined in terms of three geometric shapes:

- circle
- rectangle
- polygon

While almost any picture can be turned into an image map, the best images to use for image mapping have sections that include basic geometric patterns. Circular and rectangular areas are the easiest to define within images. Yet when you need to, you can define complex shapes using polygons. The polygon shape allows for an object with three or more sides and is defined by end points; almost any shape could be defined. For example, you could define the shape of a house with a garage as a polygon.

TIP

The key to using image maps in your documents is to remember the rules about images that were discussed in Chapter 7, "Adding Multimedia Features With HTML." The usefulness of images is not determined by their size or use of thousands of colors. The best images are simple and serve a specific purpose. Most image maps in use on the Web are between 20KB and 40KB in size. Often you will find that if you limit colors and bit depth and use appropriate compression, you can dramatically reduce the file size of your image map. This is especially true if you create a JPEG image and use a low quality setting to determine the amount of compression.

Image map files for the NCSA imagemap script can include the following shapes and values:

`default URL`	The default action to take when a point not specified is selected.
`circle URL x1,y1 x2,y2`	An action to take when a user clicks on an area defined by the center point of the circle and a point on the circumference.
`rectangle URL x1,y1 x2,y2`	The action to take when a user clicks on an area defined by two opposing coordinates.
`polygon URL x1,y1 x2,y2 ... xn,yn`	The action to take when a user clicks on an area defined by the end points of a polygon.

A map file for use with NCSA imagemap could look like this:

```
circle  ../home.html     10,20 25,20
circle  previous.html    30,20 35,20
circle  next.html        50,20 55,20
circle  ../help.html     70,20 75,20
```

```
rectangle book1.html    10,40 30,20
rectangle book2.html    30,40 50,20
rectangle book3.html    50,40 70,20
rectangle book4.html    70,40 90,20
polygon orders.html    15,50 5,25 25, 25
default http://www.mcp.com/
```

Image map files for the CERN htimap script can include the following shapes and values:

default *URL*	The default action to take when a point not specified is selected
circle *(x,y)* radius *x URL*	An action to take when a user clicks on an area defined by the center point of the circle and a point on the circumference
rectangle *(x1,y1)* *(x2,y2)* *URL*	The action to take when a user clicks on an area defined by two opposing coordinates
polygon *(x1,y1)* *(x2,y2)* ...*(xn, yn)* *URL*	The action to take when a user clicks on an area defined by the end points of a polygon

A map file for use with CERN htimap could look like this:

```
circle  (10,20) radius 15     ../home.html
circle  (30,20) radius 15     previous.html
circle  (50,20) radius 15     next.html
circle  (70,20) radius 15     ../help.html
rectangle (10,40) (30,20)     book1.html
rectangle (30,40) (50,20)     book2.html
rectangle (50,40) (70,20)     book3.html
rectangle (70,40) (90,20)     book4.html
polygon (15,50) (5,25) (25, 25)    orders.html
default                       http://www.mcp.com/
```

Extensions for Image Maps

Until recently, many Web publishers who did not have access to CGI scripts could only dream of using image maps. Now there are two solutions that enable browsers to interpret image maps locally. Although HTML 3.0 introduces what will become the standard for client-side image maps, many browsers have implemented Spyglass Corporation's method for handling image maps.

HTML 3.0 Client-Side Image Maps

The HTML 3.0 specification introduces client-side handling of image maps and eliminates problems for Web publishers who don't have access to CGI. With client-side handling of image maps, all processing of the user input is handled by the browser. This means that when a user clicks on an image map, the browser interprets the map locally and performs the appropriate action. Not only is client-side handling of image maps several times faster than relying on a server to process the input, but it makes sense as the Web transitions toward an extremely efficient client-server environment.

With HTML 3.0, you create client-side image maps using figures. While it may seem strange to use only figures for client-side image mapping, keep in mind that figures are meant to be used for large or complex graphics and images are meant to be used with small or simple graphics. To define hot areas with HTML 3.0 figures, you use the SHAPE attribute of the anchor tag <A>.

As each anchor element is used to define a single action, you have to define one anchor tag for each action associated with the image map. You can also specify a default action if the user clicks on an area of the image you have not defined an action for. There are four acceptable values:

Default
: Used to specify the default action for the image map. If the user clicks on an area not defined, the browser performs the default action specified in an associated HREF attribute.

  You can specify a default action as follows:

  `<A SHAPE="default" HREF="URL"> . . . </A>`

Circle
: Used to specify a circle by defining a center point with coordinates x,y and a radius r. If a user clicks on the area defined by this circle, the browser performs the action specified in the associated HREF attribute.

  The basic form for an action associated with this value is:

  `<A SHAPE="circle x, y, r" HREF="URL"> . . . </A>`

Rect
: Used to specify a four-sided object by defining the upper-left corner with coordinates x,y, width w, and height h. If a user clicks on the area defined as this rectangle, the browser performs the action specified in the associated HREF attribute.

  The basic form for an action associated with this value is:

  `<A SHAPE="rect x, y, w, h" HREF="URL"> . . . </A>`

Polygon
: Used to specify an object with three or more sides defined by specifying the end points through a series of x,y coordinates. If a user clicks on the area defined as this polygon, the browser performs the action specified in the associated HREF attribute.

  The basic form for an action associated with this value is:

  `<A SHAPE="polygon x1, y1, x2, y2, . . . xn, yn" HREF="URL"> . . . </A>`

Creating a client-side image map is in many ways easier than creating a server-side image map. With client-side image maps, you don't have to worry about server support for image maps, trying to figure out what script to use, and building a map file. You merely define the image map to go along with your figure. Here is how you could define an image map using HTML 3.0:

```
<FIG SRC="company_map.gif">
<A SHAPE="rect 0,0 25,25" HREF="background.html" ></A>
<A SHAPE="rect 30,0 55,25" HREF="orders.html" ></A>
<A SHAPE="rect 60,0 75,25" HREF="promo.html" ></A>
<A SHAPE="circle 10,50 5" HREF="new.html" ></A>
<A SHAPE="circle 30,50 5" HREF="cool.html" ></A>
<A SHAPE="circle 50,50 5" HREF="rec_releases.html" ></A>
<A SHAPE="default" HREF="site_help.html" ></A>
</FIG>
```

One reason HTML 3.0 requires you to define actions for image maps separately is that doing so makes it easy to define a text-based menu to go along with your graphical menu. Providing a text-based way to access information helps users who do not have an HTML 3.0-compliant browser, those who may still be using a text-only browser, and those who may have turned off the automatic graphic loading capability of their browser. To add a text-based menu in a column beside or beneath a figure, you simply insert the appropriate formatting and text within the figure element.

Here is how a text-based menu could be added to the previously defined image map:

```
<FIG SRC="company_map.gif">
<H1>Browse Our Site</H1>
<P><A HREF="background.html" SHAPE="rect 0,0 25,25">Corp. Background</A>
<P><A HREF="orders.html" SHAPE="rect 30,0 55,25">Orders &amp; Information</A>
<P><A HREF="promo.html" SHAPE="rect 60,0 75,25">Press Releases</A>
<P><A HREF="new.html" SHAPE="circle 10,50 5">What's New</A>
<P><A HREF="cool.html" SHAPE="circle 30,50 5">What's Cool</A>
<P><A HREF="rec_releases.html" SHAPE="circle 50,50 5">Recent Releases</A>
<P><A HREF="site_help.html" SHAPE="default">Help</A>
</FIG>
```

More Extensions for Image Maps

Netscape, Internet Explorer, and Spyglass Mosaic browsers support Spyglass Corporation's extensions for the client-side handling of image maps. With this nonstandard extension, you define a client-side image map using the HTML 2.0 image tag. This extension uses several new tags to create client-side image maps.

The USEMAP attribute was added to the anchor tag <A> to specify the name of the image map to use with the image. Using this attribute, you can specify a separate map file that the client will download to interpret the image map or a locally defined image map. To use a map file, you specify the URL path to the file, which should be an HTML document, such as:

```
<IMG SRC="logo.gif" USEMAP="map.html">
```

A single map file can contain definitions for multiple image maps. This is done using internal document links such as:

```
<IMG SRC="logo.gif" USEMAP="map.html#map2">
```

Using internal document links, you can also specify that the map is in the current document. To keep things simple, this is the preferred method to use. You can specify an image map in the current document as follows:

```
<IMG SRC="banner.gif" USEMAP="#my_map">
```

Spyglass extensions for image maps follow an interesting implementation that enables older browsers to continue to support image maps as they have in the past and new browsers to use the client-side image map definition. To do this, you create a map file following the method discussed in the section on designing image maps, then create a client-side map definition or map file. When both map files are defined, you add a hypertext reference to the alternate image map program and add the ISMAP attribute to the `<IMG>` tag as follows:

```
<A HREF="/cgi-bin/htimap"><IMG SRC="banner.gif" USEMAP="#my_map" ISMAP></A>
```

If you cannot use server-side image maps or don't want to create two types of image maps, you can create a default document that will be accessed if the user's browser does not support client-side image maps. Here is how you would do it:

```
<A HREF="default.html"><IMG SRC="banner.gif" USEMAP="#my_map" ISMAP></A>
```

To define the actions for the image map, you use two new tags: `<MAP>` and `<AREA>`. With the begin and end MAP tags, you define the hot areas within the image. The only attribute for the `<MAP>` tag is the mandatory NAME attribute, which is used to name the image map. You can name a map as follows:

```
<MAP NAME="map1"> . . . </MAP>
```

The `<AREA>` tag is used to define the actions for the image map and has four attributes: SHAPE, COORDS, HREF, and NOHREF. The SHAPE attribute is used to specify the general shape of a hot area within the image. The COORDS attribute is used to specify the coordinates of the hot area. The HREF attribute is used to specify the action to perform when a user clicks on a defined hot area. The NOHREF attribute is used to specify that no action should be taken when a user clicks on the associated hot area.

The shape, location, and action for a hot area are defined as follows:

Circle   Specifies a circular-shaped hot area. The COORDS attribute is used to define a center point with coordinates x,y and a radius r. If a user clicks on the area defined by this circle, the browser performs the action specified in the associated HREF attribute.

The basic form for an action associated with this value is:

```
<AREA SHAPE="circle" COORDS="x, y, r" HREF="URL">
```

Rect   Specifies a rectangular-shaped hot area. The COORDS attribute is used to define two opposing end points of the rectangle with coordinates x1, y1 and x2, y2. If a user clicks on the area defined as this rectangle, the browser performs the action specified in the associated HREF attribute.

The basic form for an action associated with this value is:

```
<AREA SHAPE="rect" COORDS="x1,y1, x2, y2" HREF="URL">
```

Area   Used to specify an object with three or more sides. The COORDS attribute is used to define the end points as a series of x, y coordinates. If a user clicks on the area defined as this polygon, the browser performs the action specified in the associated HREF attribute.

The basic form for an action associated with this value is:

```
<AREA SHAPE="area" COORDS="x1, y1, x2, y2, . . . xn, yn"
HREF="URL">
```

If you specify that the map definition is in the current document, this information can appear anywhere in the document. Listing 12.4 is a sample HTML document containing an image map and map definition.

Listing 12.4. Using client-side image maps.

```
<HTML>
<HEAD>
<TITLE>Image Map</TITLE>
</HEAD>
<BODY BGCOLOR=#ffffff>
<CENTER>
<A HREF="/cgi-bin/htimap"><IMG SRC="bookstack.gif" USEMAP="#bookmap" ISMAP></A>
</CENTER>
<MAP NAME="bookmap">
<AREA SHAPE="circle" COORDS="5, 5, 10" HREF="../base.html">
<AREA SHAPE="rect" COORDS="25, 25, 50, 50" HREF="main.html">
<AREA SHAPE="area" COORDS="50, 5, 60, 30, 55,15" HREF="URL">
</MAP>
</BODY>
</HTML>
```

Summary

Forms and image maps are two advanced features that are sure crowd pleasers. Forms add interactivity and provide friendly interfaces for inputting data, searching databases, and accessing indexes. Designing forms that are useful to readers and to you as the publisher should be your primary goal. Image maps serve as graphical menus that users can click on to access parts of your Web site. Although there is no better way to create easy, graphic-based ways for users to browse your Web site, you should carefully design your image maps so they are useful and aren't byte-hogs.

Search Engines and Indexed Databases

13

by William Robert Stanek

The hypertext facilities of the World Wide Web put the world's most powerful search engines at your fingertips. Search engines are the gateways to the vast storehouses and databases available on the Web. Thousands of Web search engines are used every day and if you've browsed the Web, you know online searches are easy to perform. You simply enter keywords, press Enter, and the search engine takes over.

A search engine is an application specifically designed and optimized for searching databases. Search engines can race through megabytes of information in nanoseconds. They achieve this terrific speed and efficiency thanks to an application called an indexer. An indexer is an application specifically designed and optimized for indexing files. Using the index built by the indexer, the search engine can jump almost immediately to sections of the database containing the information you are looking for. Thus, creating an indexed database of documents at your Web site requires two applications: a search engine and an indexer. The search engine and indexer are normally a part of a larger application, such as a Wide Area Information Server WAIS.

The trick to creating Web documents that provide access to a search engine is knowing how to integrate the capabilities of the search engine using the existing structure of hypertext and CGI. This chapter unlocks the mysteries of search engines and indexed databases.

What Are Indexers and How Are They Used?

The index for Web Publishing Unleashed is an invaluable resource for quickly finding information in this book. Using the index, you can quickly find the topic or subtopic you want to learn more about. You do this by following an alphabetical listing of keywords selected by the flesh and blood indexer who combed WPU in search of the gems you would be interested in.

The indexer used the text of the entire book to create an alphabetical list of keywords and related concepts. The alphabetical listing is broken down into categories and subcategories. The first categories are broad and divided based on the letters *A* to *Z*. Next, the broad categories are subdivided based on keywords. The keyword categories are sometimes further divided based on related concepts. For quick reference, a page number is associated with keywords and their related concepts. You've probably noticed that articles, such as *a*, *an*, and *the*, and prepositions, such as *in*, *with*, and *to*, are never listed in the index. This is because the indexer has a list of hundreds of common words that should be excluded from the index because they occur too often to be helpful.

A computer-coded indexer builds an index in much the same way. The indexer application uses a list of common words to figure out which words to exclude from the index, searches through the list of documents you specified, and finally, builds an index containing the relevant associations between the remaining words within all the specified documents. As most indexers build a full-text index based on your documents, the index is often larger than the size of the original files. For example, if your Web site has 15MB of data in 125 documents, the indexer would create an index slightly larger than 15MB.

Most indexers enable you to add to or subtract from the list of common words. Often you can do this simply by editing an appropriate file or by creating a stop word file. A stop word file contains an alphabetized list of words that the indexer should ignore. However, a personally defined list of stop words may override the indexer's list of words to ignore.

Another type of word list used by indexers is the synonym list. Synonym lists make it easier for readers to search your Web site by helping them find the information they are looking for even if they don't know the exact word to use to get the right response. Each line of a synonym file contains words that can be used interchangeably. A search for any word in the list will be matched to other words in the same line. Instead of getting no results from the search, the reader will get a list of results that match related words.

Let's say a reader wants to learn how forms are processed on the server but doesn't know the right keyword to use to get a relative response. This line from a synonym file could be used to help the reader find what she is looking for:

```
cgi cgi-bin script gateway interface programming
```

Before you use a synonym list, you should think carefully about the words you will use in the list. Synonym lists are used by the indexer program to create an index. Any modifications of the lists will not be used until the database is reindexed. This means any time you change the synonym list you will have to reindex your Web site.

What Are Search Engines and How Are They Used?

Once an index is created, it can be used by a search engine. Hundreds of search engines are used in commercial and proprietary applications. Usually search engines are part of a larger application, such as a database management system. When Web publishers looked for indexing and searching solutions, they looked at the search engines available and found that most of them were not well-suited for use on the World Wide Web. Primarily, this is because these search engines weren't designed to be used on distributed networks.

One solution Web publishers did find is WAIS. The Wide Area Information Server is a database retrieval system that searches indexed databases. The databases contain any type of file, including text, sound, graphics, and even video. The WAIS interface is easy to use and you can perform a search on any topic simply by entering a keyword and pressing Enter. Once you press the Enter key, the WAIS search engine takes over. You can find both commercial and freeware versions of WAIS.

WAIS was developed as a joint project whose founders include Apple Computer, Dow Jones, Thinking Machines, and the Peat Marwick group. In the early days of WAIS, Thinking Machines maintained a free version of WAIS suitably titled freeWAIS. Although this version of WAIS enjoys the widest usage, freeWAIS is now maintained by the Clearinghouse for Networked Information Discovery and Retrieval. CNIDR started handling freeWAIS when the founders of WAIS turned to commercial ventures such as WAIS, Inc.

Today, CNIDR is the primary developer of WAIS technology. The goal of CNIDR is to develop new software for use in networked information discovery and retrieval. Recent developments at CNIDR include an integrated software package called Isite that includes an indexer, search engine, and communication tools to access databases.

You can find more information on CNIDR and download the latest version of freeWAIS at

```
http://cnidr.org/
```

Using a Search Engine

The largest database on the Web, the Lycos Catalog of the Internet, enables you to perform searches precisely as described. Lycos indexes over 90 percent of Internet sites using a powerful indexer called a Web crawler. The Web crawler uses URLs at Web sites to find new information, and thus can index every page at a Web site and even find new Web sites. Lycos combines the Web crawler with a powerful search engine. Using the search engine, Web users can find the information they are looking for in a matter of seconds.

FIGURE 13.1

Lycos search engine.

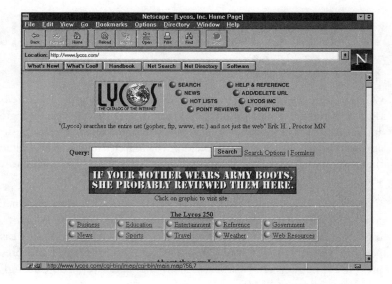

The Lycos search engine is characteristic of the dozens of search engines you will find on the Web that use WAIS or are modeled after WAIS. You can enter a query at Lycos using the simple one-box form shown in Figure 13.1. By default, the Lycos search engine finds all documents matching any keyword you type in the query box. Because the exclusion list for Lycos contains articles, prepositions, and other nonuseful words for searching, you can enter a query just as a complete sentence, such as

> What is WAIS?
>
> Where is WAIS?
>
> How do I use WAIS?

You can enter as many keywords as you want on the query line. As the search is not case-sensitive, the keywords do not have to be capitalized as shown. If you type in two keywords that are not on the exclusion list, the search engine assumes you want to search on both words. This means if you entered:

`WAIS Web`

The search engine would search its index for all documents containing either WAIS or Web. Although you could specify the `or` explicitly in a search, such as `WAIS OR Web`, you generally do not have to. Again, this is because the `OR` is assumed whenever you do not specify otherwise. To search the index only for documents containing both WAIS and Web, you could use the following:

`WAIS AND Web`

Here, the `AND` tells the search engine you are only interested in documents containing the words WAIS and Web. You can combine the basic functions of logical `OR` and logical `AND` in many ways. Since you will often be searching for material on a specific subject, you can use multiple keywords related to the subject to help you get better results on your searches. For example, if you are looking for publishers on the Web, you might try the following keywords:

> book
> fiction
> magazine
> nonfiction
> publisher
> publishing

Often your main topic will reveal dozens or hundreds of relevant sites. As Figure 13.2 shows, a single search on the keyword "WAIS" at Lycos returned 260 matches. The Lycos search engine returns a summary of each document matching the search. The summary is in the form of an abstract for small documents and a combined outline and abstract for long documents. However, most search engines return a two-line summary of the related document that includes the size, type, and title of the document.

FIGURE 13.2.

Results of a Lycos search.

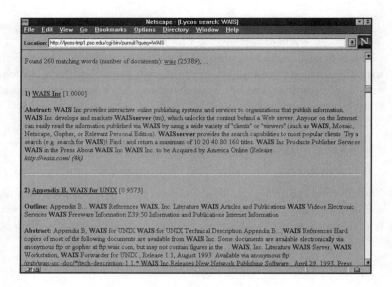

Documents matching your search are weighted with what should be the most relevant documents displayed first and what should be the least relevant documents displayed last. These scores are usually on a 0.0–1.0 scale or a zero to 1,000 scale. The most relevant documents have a high score, with the highest score being 1.0 or 1,000. The criteria used to figure out relevancy aren't the greatest, but do work most of the time. These criteria are

Number of words that match the search string

The proximity of the words to each other in the document

The overall scores based on these two criteria are used to present the matching documents in order from most relevant to least relevant. Although this method of ranking by relevance is used widely, you can see how it could mislead Web users. This is the primary reason other descriptive features, like a title and summary, are provided with the search results.

Accessing a WAIS Database

Originally, you could only access a WAIS database using a WAIS client. WAIS clients have built-in functions and are used much like other clients. Yet few people want to download a new type of client onto their system and learn how to use it, especially when the client can only be used for the specific purpose of searching a database. If you've ever used a WAIS client, you know they aren't the friendliest clients on the block and this is why Web users prefer to use their browsers, which provide a simple interface to just about every resource on the Internet.

Presently, most Web users access WAIS databases using a simple fill-out form, such as the one shown in Figure 13.1. When a user enters data into the form, the data is passed to the server and directed to a gateway script designed for search and retrieval. The script does five things:

1. Processes the input
2. Passes the input to the search engine
3. Receives the results from the search engine
4. Processes the results
5. Passes the output to the client

As you can see, the gateway script creates the interface between the client browser and WAIS. Creating a gateway script to interface with WAIS is not an extremely complex process. Although you could create such a script using fewer than 100 lines of Perl code, there are dozens of ready-made WAIS gateways already available. Some of these WAIS gateways are simple and involve efficient Perl scripts packed into a few kilobytes of file space. Other WAIS gateways are part of all-in-one software packages that contain an indexer and search engines as part of a WAIS server and a gateway script to create the Web to WAIS interface. The sections that follow discuss five freeware options for WAIS gateways.

Basic WAIS Gateways

Three ready-made solutions for processing the information from WAIS searches are

> wais.pl
> son-of-wais.pl
> kidsofwais.pl

WAIS.PL

The very first WAIS gateway, a Perl script called wais.pl, is a quick-and-dirty solution for accessing WAIS. The wais.pl script was created by Tony Sanders and is included with the NCSA Web server software. You can obtain wais.pl from NCSA's FTP server at

`ftp://ftp.ncsa.uiuc.edu/Web/httpd/Unix/ncsa_httpd/cgi/wais.tar.Z`

SON-OF-WAIS.PL

Although you'll find that wais.pl is used widely on the Web, it is slowly being replaced by its offspring: son-of-wais.pl and kidofwais.pl. The son-of-wais.pl script is the second evolution of wais.pl. This Perl script created by Eric Morgan beats its generic parent hands down because it is more advanced than the original and more robust. You can obtain son-of-wais.pl from NCSU at

`http://dewey.lib.ncsu.edu/staff/morgan/son-of-wais.html.`

KIDOFWAIS.PL

The third evolution of WAIS.PL is a script called kidofwais.pl. This script, created by Michael Grady, is a somewhat advanced WAIS gateway programmed entirely in Perl. The features of kidsofwais.pl include debugging, multiple formatting options, table titles, and more. You can obtain kidsofwais.pl from UIUC at

`http://www.cso.uiuc.edu/grady.html.`

The results of a search on the word "computer" using the kidofwais.pl script is shown in Figure 13.3. Many Web publishers prefer the clean output of kidofwais.pl. As you can see, matches are generally displayed on a single line of a bulleted list. Each item on the list is displayed in ranked relevance order with the scores omitted. The title, size, and type of matching documents form the basis of each list item.

FIGURE 13.3.

Search results using the kidofwais.pl script.

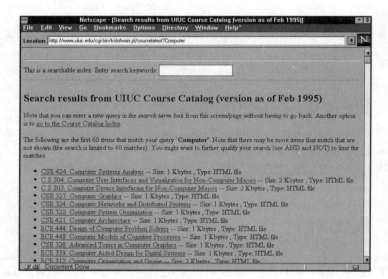

Advanced WAIS Gateways

Two advanced and powerful solutions for your WAIS needs are

> SFgate
> WWWWAIS.C

SFgate

Created by Miao-Jane Lin and Ulrich Pfeifer, SFgate is one of the most advanced freeware WAIS gateways. Unlike other gateways discussed so far, SFgate uses a group of shell scripts to create a smooth and feature-rich interface to your WAIS server. This WAIS gateway is several orders of magnitude larger than other WAIS gateways and uses more than 500KB of disk space. In the days of 2GB hard drives, 500KB of disk space is negligible, but when you compare this to the kidofwais.pl script that is only 24KB in size, you can easily see that SFgate is certainly a more involved gateway. Fortunately, the SFgate distribution includes an installation routine and good documentation.

SFgate provides you with advanced control over the search options. Not only can you search on a keyword, but you can also tell SFgate the specific areas of the indexed database to search. You can search by document type, title, author, date, and contents. You can also tell SFgate precisely how to format the search results. Increased flexibility in the search parameters and output style produces more meaningful results. You can learn more about SFgate and download the latest version at

```
http://ls6-www.informatik.uni-dortmund.de/SFgate/SFgate.html
```

WWWWAIS.C

The wwwwais.c gateway is proof positive that you can pack a lot of power into a small C script. Created by Kevin Hughes of EIT and packed into 54KB of C code, wwwwais.c is arguably the most powerful freeware WAIS gateway. EIT uses the wwwwais.c gateway to search the databases at its Web site. Figure 13.4 shows the results from a wwwwais.c search using EIT's wwwwais.c gateway.

As you can see, the output from wwwwais.c is similar to other WAIS gateways discussed previously. Matches are generally displayed in a numbered list. Each item on the list is displayed in ranked relevance order. The title, size, type and ranked score of the matching documents form the basis of each list item. You can download the latest version of this WAIS gateway at

```
http://www.eit.com/software/wwwwais/
```

FIGURE 13.4.

Using wwwwais.c.

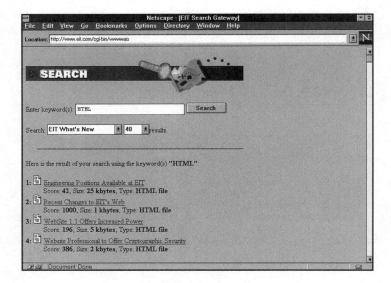

How WAIS Gateways Work

The best way to see how a WAIS gateway really works is to examine the actual code for a script. Ideally, the script should be slightly advanced, yet not too advanced so that it's interworkings cannot be easily studied. As the son-of-wais script is slightly advanced and does not have much clutter and housekeeping, you should study the code for son-of-wais.pl shown in Listing 13.1.

If you go through the code line by line, you will see the first part of the script begins with an overview of changes Eric Morgan made to wais.pl. This section also contains contact information. Because documentation makes it easier to use and maintain a script, good programmers always add documentation to a script.

After the overview, configuration variables are assigned. As these variables are unique to your Web server, you will need to update these variables accordingly. Follow the inline documentation to update the paths to where your data is stored on the server and be sure to update the contact and title information. One variable that you should pay particular attention to is the one that sets the location of the search engine to be used to perform the search. In the script, the variable is $waisq. Using waisq and waissearch to perform access WAIS databases is discussed later in this chapter.

In the next section, the output to waisq is created. The brevity of this section of the code surprises most beginning Web programmers. Yet, keep in mind that waisq is the actual script performing the search against your WAIS database.

In the final section of the script, the output is created. While the actual code for the search fills only a handful of lines, massaging the output and creating the textual portion of the output fills dozens of lines. You can modify the output message to suit your needs. However, the output page should contain the general information provided in the script, which ensures the reader knows how to use the index if they've had problems. If you follow the script, you can see that brief summaries for documents matching the search are displayed according to their relevancy. Ranked relevancy is described by scores associated with the documents.

Listing 13.1 shows the code for the son-of-wais.pl script.

Listing 13.1. The son-of-wais.pl script.

```
#!/usr/bin/perl
#
# wais.pl -- WAIS search interface
#
# $Id$
#
# Tony Sanders <sanders@bsdi.com>, Nov 1993
#
# Example configuration (in local.conf):
#     map topdir wais.pl &do_wais($top, $path, $query, "database", "title")
#
# Modified to present the user "human-readable" titles, better instructions as
```

```
# well as the ability to do repeated searches after receiving results.
#
# by Eric Lease Morgan, NCSU Libraries, April 1994
# eric_morgan@ncsu.edu
# http://www.lib.ncsu.edu/staff/morgan/morgan.html
# To read more about this script try:
# http://www.lib.ncsu.edu/staff/morgan/son-of-wais.html
#
# where is your waiq binary?
$waisq = "/usr/users/temp/wais/freeWAIS-0.202/bin/waisq";

# where are your source files?
$waisd = "/usr/users/temp/gopher/data/.wais";

# what database do you want to search?
$src = "ncsu-libraries-www";

# what is the opening title you want to present to users
$openingTitle = "Search the NCSU Libraries Webbed Information System";

# after searching, what to you want the title to be?
$closingTitle = "Search results of the NCSU Libraries Information System";

# specify the path to add
# this is the same path your subtracted when you waisindexed
$toAdd = "/usr/users/temp/www/httpd/data/";

# specify the leader to subtract
# again, this is the same string you added when you waisindexed
$toSubtract = "http://www.lib.ncsu.edu/";

# who maintains this service?
$maintainer = "<A HREF=http://www.lib.ncsu.edu/staff/morgan/morgan.html>
Eric Lease Morgan</A> (eric_morgan@ncsu.edu)";

# and when was it last modified.
$modified = "April 15, 1994";

# you shouldn't have to edit anything below this line,
except if you want to change the help text

sub extractTitle {
  # get the string
  $theFile = $headline;

  # parse out the file name
  $theFile =~ s/^.*$toSubtract//i;

  # Concatenate the "toAdd" variable with the file name
  $theFile = $toAdd.$theFile;

  # open the file
  open( DATA, $theFile) || die "Can't open $theFile\n";

  # read the file and extract the title
  $linenum = 1;
  $foundtitle = 0;
  $humanTitle = "(No title found in document!) Call $maintainer.";
```

continues

Listing 13.1. continued

```perl
   while ( $line = <DATA>) {
     last if ($linenum > 5);
     $linenum++;
     if ($line =~ s/^.*<title>//i ) {
       chop( $line);
       $line =~ s!</title>.*$!!i;
       $humanTitle = $line;
       $humanTitle =~ s/^\s*//;
       $humanTitle =~ s/\s*$//;
       $foundtitle = 1;
       last;
     }
   }

   # close the file
   close (DATA);

   # return the final results
   return $humanTitle;
   }

sub send_index {
    print "Content-type: text/html\n\n";

    print "<HEAD>\n<TITLE>$openingTitle</TITLE>\n<ISINDEX></HEAD>\n";
    print "<BODY>\n<H2>", $openingTitle, "</H2>\n";

    print "<p>";
    print "This is an index of the information on this server. ";
    print "To use this function, simply enter a query.<P>";
    print "Since this is a WAIS index, you can enter complex queries.
    For example:<P>";
    print "<DT><b>Right-hand truncation</b> (stemming) queries";
    print "<DD>The query 'astro*' will find documents containing the words";
    print " 'astronomy' as well as 'astrophysics'.<P>";
    print "<DT>Boolean '<b>And</b>' queries";
    print "<DD>The query 'red and blue' will find the <B>intersection</b> of
    all";
    print " the documents containing the words 'red', and 'blue'.";
    print "The use of 'and' limits your retrieval.<p>";
    print "<DT>Boolean '<b>Or</b>' queries";
    print "<DD>The query 'red or blue' will find the <B>union</b> of all the";
    print " documents containing the words 'red' and 'blue'.";
    print "The use of 'or' increases your retrieval.<p>";
    print "<DT>Boolean '<b>Not</b>' queries";
    print "<DD>The query 'red not green' will find the all the documents
    containing";
    print " the word 'red', and <b>excluding</b> the documents containing the
    word 'green'.";
    print "The use of 'not' limits your retrieval.<p>";
    print "<DT><b>Nested</b> Boolean queries";
    print "<DD>The query '(red and green) or blue not pink' will find the
    union of all";
    print " the documents containing the words 'red', and 'green'. It will
    then add (union)";
    print " all documents containing the word 'blue'. Finally, it will exclude all
```

```
        documents";
        print " containing the word 'pink'";
        print "<HR>";
        print "This page is maintained by $maintainer, and it was last modified on
        $modified.<p>";
}

sub do_wais {
#       local($top, $path, $query, $src, $title) = @_;

        do { &'send_index; return; } unless defined @ARGV;
        local(@query) = @ARGV;
        local($pquery) = join(" ", @query);

        print "Content-type: text/html\n\n";

        open(WAISQ, "-¦") ¦¦ exec ($waisq, "-c", $waisd,
                                "-f", "-", "-S", "$src.src", "-g", @query);

        print "<HEAD>\n<TITLE>$closingTitle</TITLE>\n<ISINDEX></HEAD>\n";
        print "<BODY>\n<H2>", $closingTitle, "</H2>\n";

        print "Index \`$src\' contains the following\n";
        print "items relevant to \`$pquery\':<P>\n";
        print "<DL>\n";

        local($hits, $score, $headline, $lines, $bytes, $type, $date);
        while (<WAISQ>) {
            /:score\s+(\d+)/ && ($score = $1);
            /:number-of-lines\s+(\d+)/ && ($lines = $1);
            /:number-of-bytes\s+(\d+)/ && ($bytes = $1);
            /:type "(.*)"/ && ($type = $1);
            /:headline "(.*)"/ && ($headline = $1);          # XXX
            /:date "(\d+)"/ && ($date = $1, $hits++, &docdone);
        }
        close(WAISQ);
        print "</DL>\n";
        print "<HR>";
        print "This page is maintained by $maintainer.<P>";

        if ($hits == 0) {
            print "Nothing found.\n";
        }
        print "</BODY>\n";
}

sub docdone {
    if ($headline =~ /Search produced no result/) {
        print "<HR>";
        print $headline, "<P>\n<PRE>";
# the following was &'safeopen
        open(WAISCAT, "$waisd/$src.cat") ¦¦ die "$src.cat: $!";
        while (<WAISCAT>) {
            s#(Catalog for database:)\s+.*#$1 <A HREF="/$top/$src.src">
            ➥$src.src</A>#;
            s#Headline:\s+(.*)#Headline: <A HREF="$1">$1</A>#;
            print;
        }
```

404

Listing 13.1. continued

```
        close(WAISCAT);
        print "\n</PRE>\n";
    } else {
        $title = &extractTitle ($headline);
        print "<DT><A HREF=\"$headline\">$humanTitle</A>\n";
        print "<DD>Score: $score, Lines: $lines, Bytes: $bytes\n";
    }
    $score = $headline = $lines = $bytes = $type = $date = '';
}

eval '&do_wais';
```

How to Create an HTML Document for a WAIS Gateway

Creating an HTML document for your WAIS gateway is easy. All you have to do is create a document with a fill-out form that sends the proper values to your WAIS gateway of choice. Depending on the WAIS gateway you choose this can be a simple one-line form for entering keywords or a complex multiple-line form entering keywords as well as search and retrieval options.

Listing 13.2 is the HTML code for a document using a simple form for use with wwwwais.c.

Listing 13.2. Simple form for use with wwwwais.c

```
<HTML>
<HEAD>
<TITLE>Using WWWWAIS.C</TITLE>
</HEAD>
<BODY>
<CENTER>
<FORM METHOD=GET ACTION="/cgi-bin/wwwwais">
<P><B>Search for:</B>
<INPUT TYPE=TEXT NAME="keywords" SIZE=40>
</FORM>
</CENTER>
</BODY>
</HTML>
```

As the previous form has only one input field, the submit and reset buttons are not necessary. When the user presses return, the form will be automatically submitted to wwwwais.c. The wwwwais.c script passes the value of the "keywords" variable to the WAIS search engine you have installed on your system.

Forms designed for use with the SFgate script can be as simple or complex as you make them. This is because SFgate gives you advanced control over how searches are performed and the way results of formatted. Figure 13.5 shows the search section of an advanced form designed to be used with SFgate. Figure 13.6 shows how users could be allowed to alter your default search and debug parameters.

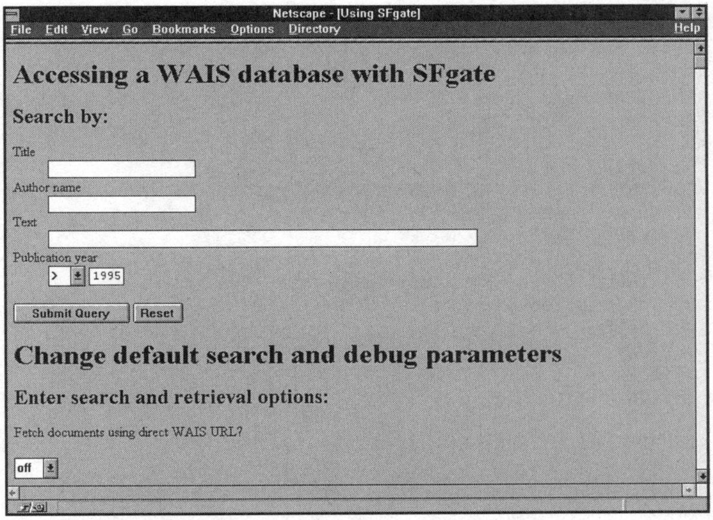

FIGURE 13.5.

Advanced form for use with SFgate.

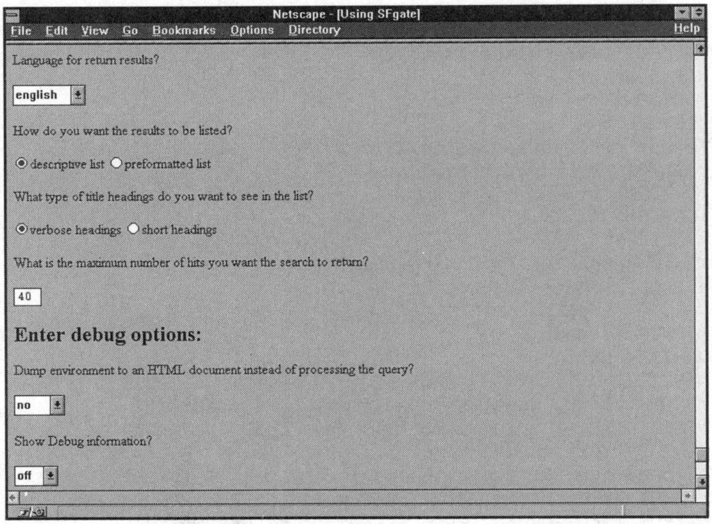

FIGURE 13.6.

Setting additional search and debug parameters.

Listing 13.3 is the HTML code for the document shown in the previous figures.

Listing 13.3. Advanced form with use with SFgate.

```
<HTML>
<HEAD>
<TITLE>Using SFgate</TITLE>
</HEAD>
<BODY>
<H1>Accessing a WAIS database with SFgate</H1>
<FORM METHOD=GET ACTION="/usr/cgi-bin/SFgate">
<INPUT NAME="database" TYPE="hidden" VALUE="www.tvpress.com/site.db">
<H2>Search by:</H2>
<DL>
<DT>Title
<DD><INPUT TYPE=TEXT NAME="ti">
<DT>Author name
<DD><INPUT TYPE=TEXT NAME="au">
<DT>Text
<DD><INPUT TYPE=TEXT NAME="text" SIZE=60>
<DT>Publication year
<DD><SELECT NAME="py_p">
<OPTION> &gt;
<OPTION> =
<OPTION> &lt;
</SELECT>
<INPUT TYPE=TEXT NAME="py" SIZE=4 VALUE="1995">
</DL>
<INPUT TYPE="submit">
<INPUT TYPE="reset">
<H1>Change default search and debug parameters</H1>
<H2>Enter search and retrieval options:</H2>
<P>Fetch documents using direct WAIS URL?</P>
<SELECT NAME="directwais">
<OPTION> off
<OPTION> on
</SELECT>
<P>Use redirection capabilities?</P>
<SELECT NAME="redirect">
<OPTION> off
<OPTION> on
</SELECT>
<P>Language for return results?</P>
<SELECT NAME="language">
<OPTION>english
<OPTION>french
<OPTION>german
</SELECT>
<P>How do you want the results to be listed?</P>
<INPUT TYPE="radio" NAME="listenv" CHECKED VALUE="DL">descriptive list
<INPUT TYPE="radio" NAME="listenv" VALUE="PRE">preformatted list
<P>What type of title headings do you want to see in the list?</P>
<INPUT TYPE="radio" NAME="verbose" CHECKED VALUE="1">verbose headings
<INPUT TYPE="radio" NAME="verbose" VALUE="0">short headings
<P>What is the maximum number of hits you want the search to return?</P>
<INPUT NAME="maxhits" TYPE=TEXT VALUE="40" SIZE=3>
<H2>Enter debug options:</H2>
<P>Dump environment to an HTML document instead of processing the query?</P>
```

```
<SELECT NAME="dmpenv">
<OPTION> no
<OPTION> yes
</SELECT>
<P>Show Debug information?</P>
<SELECT NAME="debug">
<OPTION> off
<OPTION> on
</SELECT>
</FORM>
</BODY>
</HTML>
```

The form used with the SFgate script has many fields. You can assign the NAME attribute to key values that have special meaning to SFgate. The primary search and retrieval parameters are ti, au, text, and py. The title parameter ti enables keyword searches of titles. The author parameter au enables keyword searches of the authors of documents indexed in the database. The text parameter text enables keyword searches of the full text of documents indexed in the database. The publication year parameter py is used to search based on the date the indexed documents were published.

The database variable defines the name of the WAIS database you want to search. Here, this variable is assigned to a hidden input field and in this way, you could use SFgate to search different databases at your Web site. You could even let the user search different databases at your Web site using the same form. You would do this by changing the input field for the database from a hidden field to one the user can manipulate.

Most of the additional search variables are set to default values automatically and do not have to be specified. Yet if you want to provide additional controls to users, you would use these parameters. The debug parameters are used for testing and troubleshooting problems and generally not included in your final search form.

Installing a WAIS Gateway

Installing a WAIS gateway may not be as easy as you think. This section looks at installing basic and advanced WAIS gateways.

Configuring Basic WAIS Gateways

Installing the basic WAIS gateways—wais.pl, son-of-wais.pl, and kidsofwais.pl—is easy. You simply obtain the script, move it to an appropriate directory, such as cgi-bin, and modify the configuration parameters in the beginning of the script. The easiest gateway to configure is wais.pl. Configuring wais.pl involves modifying four lines of code at the beginning of the script:

1. You set the path to the search engine, which is normally waisq if you've installed the freewais server:

   ```
   $waisq = "/usr/local/bin/wais/waisq";
   ```

2. You specify the location of the directory containing your WAIS databases:

```
$waisd = "/usr/local/wais.db/";
```

3. You specify the actual indexed database for the search:

```
$src = "sitedb.src"
```

4. You specify the title for the HTML document used to display the results:

```
$title = "Search Results"
```

If all WAIS gateways were as easy to configure as wais.pl, Web publishers would have no problems creating an interface to WAIS. While configuring son-of-wais.pl and kidofwais.pl is slightly more difficult, the scripts have good step-by-step documentation.

Configuring Advanced WAIS Gateways

Advanced WAIS gateways present more problems to Web publishers because there are more options and variables involved. To install EIT's wwwwais.c, you have to make a minor modification to the source code, compile the source code, move the compiled script to an appropriate directory, and update the configuration file.

Preparing the WWWAIS.C Script

Because the wwwwais.c gateway uses a separate configuration file, you can install the configuration file wherever you would like. For this reason, you must specify the path to the configuration file in the source code. This minor modification is easy to make. You simply edit the source code using your favorite editor. To ensure the configuration file is easy to find if you need to update it later, you may want to place the file in the same directory as the configuration file for your Web server, such as

```
/usr/local/httpd/conf/wwwwais.conf
```

> **NOTE**
>
> Because you specify the full path to the configuration file in the source code, you can name the file anything you want. In the previous example, the configuration file is called `wwwwais.conf`.

Once you've modified the source code, you can compile it using your favorite C compiler, such as gcc. The wwwwais.c script should compile without errors. Now that the program is compiled, you can move it to an appropriate directory on your Web server. Usually this directory is your server's `cgi-bin` directory. After moving the script, make sure the script is executable.

Updating the WWWWAIS.C Configuration File

The wwwwais.c configuration file enables you to set many useful parameters for searching indexed databases and displaying the results. The configuration file contains parameters that can be passed to wwwwais.c. Variables are specified by variable name and associated value. The space between the variable name and value is necessary.

Listing 13.4 is an example of a wwwwais configuration file.

Listing 13.4. Sample wwwwais configuration file.

```
# WWWWAIS configuration file

# If PageTitle is a string, it will be a title only.
# If PageTitle specifies an HTML file, this file will be prepended to
# wwwwais results.
PageTitle "waistitle.html"

# The self-referencing URL for wwwwais.
SelfURL "http://www.tvpress.com/cgi-bin/wwwwais"

# The maximum number of results to return.
MaxHits 40

# How results are sorted. This can be "score", "lines", "bytes",
# "title", or "type".
SortType score

# AddrMask is used to specify the IP addresses of sites authorized access
# to your database
# Only addresses specified here will be allowed to use the gateway.
# These rules apply:
# 1) You can use asterisks in specifying the string, at either
#    ends of the string:
#    "192.100.*", "*100*", "*2.100.2"
# 2) You can make lists of masks:
#    "*192.58.2,*.2", "*.100,*171.128*", ".58.2,*100"
# 3) A mask without asterisks will match EXACTLY:
#    "192.100.58.2"
# 4) Define as "all" to allow all sites.
AddrMask all

# The full path to your waisq program.
WaisqBin /usr/local/bin/waisq
# The full path to your waissearch program.
WaissearchBin /usr/local/bin/waissearch
# The full path to your swish program.
SwishBin /usr/local/bin/swish

# WAIS source file descriptions
# These represent the path to the indexed databases
# For swish sources:
#    SwishSource full_path_to_source/source.swish "description"
SwishSource /usr/local/httpd/wais/index/index.swish "Search our Web"
```

continues

Listing 13.4. continued

```
SourceRules replace "/usr/local/www/" "http://www.tvpress.com/"
# For waisq sources:
#    WaisSource full_path_to_source/source.src "description"
WaisSource /usr/local/httpd/wais/index/index.src "Search our Web"
SourceRules replace "/usr/local/www/" "http://www.tvpress.com/"
WaisSource /usr/local/httpd/wais/index/index.src "Search our Web"
SourceRules replace "/usr/local/www/" "/"
SourceRules prepend "http://www.tvpress.com/cgi-bin/print_hit_bold.pl"
SourceRules append "?$KEYWORDS#first_hit"
# For waissearch sources:
#    WaisSource host.name port source "description"
WaisSource quake.think.com 210 directory-of-servers "WAIS directory of servers"

# Do you want to use icons?
UseIcons yes

# Where are your icons are kept.
IconUrl http://www.tvpress.com/software/wwwwais/icons

# Determining file type based on suffix.
# Suffix matching is not case sensitive is entered in the form:
#    TypeDef .suffix "description" file://url.to.icon.for.this.type/ MIME-type
# You can use $ICONURL in the icon URL to substitute the root icon directory.
# You can define new documents types and their associated icons here
TypeDef .html "HTML file" $ICONURL/text.xbm text/html
TypeDef .txt "text file" $ICONURL/text.xbm text/plain
TypeDef .ps "PostScript file" $ICONURL/image.xbm application/postscript
TypeDef .gif "GIF image" $ICONURL/image.xbm image/gif
TypeDef .src "WAIS index" $ICONURL/index.xbm text/plain
TypeDef .?? "unknown" $ICONURL/unknown.xbm text/plain
```

When you update the configuration file for use on your system, you will want to look closely at every line of the file containing a parameter assignment. As you will need to change almost every parameter assignment, you should be wary of any assignments that you do not change. The most important updates to the configuration file involve specifying the proper paths to essential files on the system. Here's how you should assign these essential values:

SelfURL   The URL path to wwwwais.c.

WaisqBin   The full path to your waisq program.

WaissearchBin The full path to your waissearch program.

SwishBin   The full path to your swish program.

SwishSource   The location of local databases indexed with SWISH and a brief description. If there are multiple SwishSource lines, the user will be prompted to specify the database to search.

WaisSource   Local WAIS databases will be accessed with waisq and remote WAIS databases will be accessed with waissearch. For local WAIS databases, you must specify the location of the database and a brief description. All local databases name should include the .src extension. For remote WAIS databases, you must specify host name, port, database name and a description. All remote database names should not include the `.src` extension.

`SourceRules`	The action to take on the results. Valid actions are

`append`	Information to add after the results
`prepend`	Information to add before the results
`replace`	Replace the local path with a URL path so Web users can access the documents.

`TypeDef`	Enables the script to match filename extensions to MIME types. Any MIME types not configured are assigned to the type unknown.

Passing Additional Parameters to WWWWAIS.C

You can pass additional parameters to wwwwais.c as input from a fill-out form or with environment variables set in a script that calls wwwwais.c. Any additional parameters you reference will override parameters set in your configuration file. The simple form used earlier to pass keywords to wwwwais.c can be easily updated to accommodate these additional parameters. The variables you can set include

`host`	The name of the remote host machine to search with waissearch. The host information should include the domain, such as `host=tvp.com`
`iconurl`	The URL path to icons. The `iconurl` should include the transfer protocol, such as `iconurl=http://tvp.com/icons/`
`isindex`	The keywords to search on.
`keywords`	The keywords to search on.
`maxhits`	The maximum number of matches to return after a search.
`port`	The port number to contact the remote host machine on.
`searchprog`	The search engine to use. This variable can be set to

`searchprog=swish`	A local search using swish
`searchprog=waisq`	A local search using waisq
`searchprog=waissearch`	A remote search using waissearch

`selection`	The indexed database to use as specified by the description set in the configuration file.
`sorttype`	The sorting method for the results. This variable can be set to `sorttype=bytes` Sort by the byte size of the documents

	`sorttype=lines`	Sort by the number of lines
	`sorttype=score`	Sort by score
	`sorttype=title`	Sort by document title
	`sorttype=type`	Sort by document type
`source`	The indexed database to search.	
`sourcedir`	The directory of the indexed database.	
`useicons`	Specifies whether icons based on file type are used. This can be set to	
	`useicons=no`	Do not use icons
	`useicons=yes`	Use icons.
`version`	Provides the version number of your WAIS applications. The default value false can be set to `true` as follows:	
	`version=true`	

You can use either the GET or POST method to submit data from an HTML form to wwwwais.c. You can set variables yourself using hidden fields or allow the users to set these variables using input fields. The wwwwais.c script supports the PATH_INFO variable as well. This means you can add additional parameters to the end of the URL path to wwwwais.c in URL-encoded format. Listing 13.5 shows how you could create a form with additional parameters already added to the URL path:

Listing 13.5. WWWAIS form with additional parameters.

```
<HTML>
<HEAD>
<TITLE>Search our Web site</TITLE>
</HEAD>
<BODY>
<FORM METHOD=GET
ACTION="/cgi-bin/wwwwais/useicons=yes&maxhits=50&sorttype=score">
<P><B>Search for:</B>
<INPUT TYPE=TEXT NAME="keywords" SIZE=40>
</FORM>
</BODY>
</HTML>
```

To set parameters in a script that calls wwwwais.c, you will use environment variables. Any of the variables discussed earlier can be changed into an environment variable that wwwwais.c will recognize by putting www_ before the variable name. As all variable names should be in upper case, Listing 13.6 is a simple csh script to show how you could set variables and call wwwwais.

Listing 13.6. Csh script to set variables for wwwwais.

```
!/bin/csh
#Shell script for setting environment variables for wwwwais
setenv WWWW_USEICONS = yes
setenv WWWW_MAXHITS = 50
setenv WWWW_SORTTYPE = type
#Call wwwwais
/usr/local/cgi-bin/wwwwais
exit
```

Building an Indexed Database

So far this chapter has discussed the basics of indexers, search engines, WAIS and WAIS gateways. After reading the section on accessing a WAIS database, you should understand how WAIS gateways work and how to create an HTML document for a WAIS gateway. The next step is to install a search and retrieval application that includes an indexer and a search engine.

One of the most widely used Wide Area Information Servers is freeWAIS. The freeWAIS server is actually a series of scripts for building and searching an indexed database. An alternative to freewais is SWISH. Developed by the team at EIT Corporation, the Simple Web Indexing System for Humans offers ease of installation and use.

Installing and Configuring freeWAIS

Many versions of freeWAIS are in use on the Internet. The two main variants you may be interested in are the standard freewais package and the freewais-sf package. Standard freewais is the most widely used WAIS system. The freewais-sf package is optimized for use with SFgate.

You can find information on the current version of freewais and obtain the source code at these locations:

```
http://www.eit.com/software/
```
```
http://cnidr.org/
```
```
ftp://ftp.cnidr.org/pub/NIDR.tools/freewais/
```

You can find information on the current version of freewais.sf and obtain the source code at these locations:

```
http://ls6-www.informatik.uni-dortmund.de/SFgate/SFgate.html
```
```
ftp://mirror-site/mirror-dir/SFgate/
```
```
ftp://mirror-site/mirror-dir/freeWAIS-sf-1.2/freeWAIS-sf/
```

After you download the source to your computer from one of the locations listed above and uncompress the source as necessary, you can begin installing and configuring freewais. Both variants of freewais include essentially the same applications. These applications include

    waisserver
    waisq
    waissearch
    waisindex

Using Waisserver

The waisserver program is the primary server program. You only need to run waisserver if you want to be able to search locally available databases. Before you start the waisserver, you will need to know three things:

1. The port you want the waisserver to allow connections on. This port is normally 210. You invoke waisserver with the -p option to set the port number.

2. The directory where your source databases are located. The waisserver program will allow any database in the specified directory to be searched. You invoke waisserver with the -d option to set the directory path to your indexed WAIS databases.

3. How you want errors to be treated. While tracking errors is not mandatory, it is a sound administrative practice. You invoke waisserver with the -e option to specify a log file for tracking errors.

To start waisserver, you should change directories to where waisserver is installed. In the following example, waisserver answers requests on port 210, source databases are in the /usr/local/httpd/wais/sources and errors are logged in /usr/local/httpd/logs/wais.log. To start waisserver using these options, you would type the following all on one line:

```
./waisserver -p 210 -d /usr/local/httpd/wais/sources -e
➡/usr/local/httpd/logs/wais.log &
```

NOTE

The ampersand symbol is used to put waisserver in the background. If you do not put the server process in the background, the server will stop running when you exit. Additionally, to ensure waisserver is started if the host computer is rebooted, you should update the appropriate configuration files. Here's what you could add to the rc.local file on most UNIX systems so that waisserver is started automatically:

```
#Added to start the waisserver process
#waisserver is used to enable searching of the local WAIS databases
/usr/local/httpd/wais/waisserver -p 210 -d /usr/local/httpd/wais/sources -e
➡/usr/local/httpd/logs/wais.log &
```

Using Waisq and Waissearch

The waisq and waissearch programs search WAIS databases for the information you're looking for. The waisq search engine looks in databases on the local host and waissearch looks in databases on remote machines. The waissearch program does things remotely by contacting WAIS servers on different machines, each of which has its own database. In order for waissearch to work properly, you must tell it a host name and a port to connect to. Additionally, the remote host must have a WAIS server of its own running on the port you specified. As your WAIS gateway will call waisq or waissearch for you, you generally do not access these search engines directly.

Using Waisindex

The waisindex program is used to create indexed WAIS databases. When you create an index, you can index all or any portion of the files on the host computer. Generally, files are indexed into a database according to their directory. If you want files to be indexed, you can specify the following:

1. The directory the files to be indexed reside in. You invoke waisindex with the `-d` option to set the directory path to the files you want to index.

2. Whether you want waisindex to recursively index sub directories. You invoke waisindex with the `-r` option to specify that you want sub directories to be indexed.

3. The name of the source database including the file path. Indexed WAIS databases end with the `.src` extension, but are named without the `.src` extension.

4. Whether you want waisindex to index the full contents of the document or just the filename. The default is to index the full contents of the documents. For files indexed with the nocontents flag, only the file names are indexed.

You can specify these additional parameters if you wish:

1. How you want errors to be treated. While tracking errors is not mandatory, it is a sound administrative practice. You invoke waisindex with the `-e` option to specify a log file for tracking errors.

2. The level of detail for logging what waisindex is doing on your system. You invoke waisindex with the `-l` option to specify logging verbosity. The higher the number, the more verbose and detailed the logging will be.

3. The amount of system memory and resources to use during the indexing. You invoke waisindex with the `-m` option to specify the amount of memory and resources to use for indexing. The higher the number, the more system resources will be used.

To run waisindex, you should change directories to where waisindex is installed or specify the full path to the program. In the following example, waisindex is located in the `/usr/local/httpd/wais` directory, the verbosity of the output is small, errors are logged in `/usr/local/`

httpd/logs/waisindex.log, the directory to index is /users/webdocs, the path to the database is /usr/local/httpd/wais/sources, and the name of the database is webdocuments. To run waisindex using these options, you would type the following all on one line:

```
/usr/local/httpd/wais/waisindex -l 1 -d /users/webdocs -e
➥/usr/local/httpd/logs/wais.log -r /usr/local/httpd/wais/sources/webdocuments
```

While you could run waisindex by hand whenever you needed to reindex your site, the best way to handle indexing is to set up a cron job to handle the task. In UNIX environments, cron jobs are run automatically at times you specify. Most systems have multiple cron tables. Jobs in a cron table are run by the owner of the cron tab, which is normally located in the /usr/spool/cron/crontabs directory.

You will usually want to update your indexes daily, especially on a host that is updated often. The best time to run waisindex is when system usage is low. Often, this is in the early morning hours. To add a statement to the root cron table to update your index daily at 1 a.m., you could insert the following lines:

```
# Root Cron
# Entry added to build waisindex
00 01 * * * /usr/local/httpd/wais/waisindex -l 1 -d /users/webdocs -e
➥/usr/local/httpd/logs/wais.log -r /usr/local/httpd/wais/sources/webdocuments
```

Although the previous example assumes you only want to index a single directory and its subdirectories, you can add additional statements to the cron tab to build additional indexed databases. This solution for indexing your site works best on simple document structures. If your host has a complex document structure, there are two solutions:

> Build the index using links.
>
> Build the index using a script.

Building a WAIS Index Using Links

You can add links from your document directories to a base directory that you will index using the -r option to recursively index subdirectories. To do this, you could create a base directory, such as /users/webdocs, add subdirectories to this directory, and link your document directories to the subdirectories. Here's how you would do this on most UNIX systems that enable symbolic links:

```
$ mkdir /users/webdocs
$ cd /users/webdocs
$ mkdir HTML
$ mkdir TEXT
$ mkdir PDF
$ mkdir GIF
$ ln -s /users/webdocs/HTML /usr/local/httpd/docs/html
$ ln -s /users/webdocs/TEXT /home/users/local/text
$ ln -s /users/webdocs/PDF /usr/bin/adobe/acrobat/docs
$ ln -s /users/webdocs/GIF /usr/local/images/samples/gif
```

Now if you ran the command defined earlier, you would index all the appropriate directories you have linked to the /users/webdocs directory. Keep in mind that the actual database would be located in the `/usr/local/httpd/wais/sources` directory and would have the name `webdocuments.src`. The waisindex program adds the `.src` extension to the database name to indicate the file is a source file.

Building a WAIS Index Using a Script

For the most complex document structures, you will want to use a shell script. Using a shell script, you can easily index complex document structures. A script also lets you easily specify the types of files you want to be indexed and the types of files you want to ignore.

The following csh script by Kevin Hughs of EIT indexes documents at your site using waisindex. Documents you don't want to index the contents of, such as GIF images, are specified with the nocontents flag. This flag tells waisindex to index only the filename and not the contents. You can see this in the code from Listing 13.7.

Listing 13.7. Csh script for indexing documents using waisindex.

```
#! /bin/csh

set rootdir = /usr/local/www
#       This is the root directory of the Web tree you want to index.

set index = /usr/local/httpd/wais/sources/index
#       This is the name your WAIS indexes will be built under.
#       Index files will be called index.* in the /usr/local/httpd/wais/sources
#       directory, in this example.

set indexprog = /usr/local/httpd/wais/waisindex
#       The full pathname to your waisindex program.

set nonomatch
cd $rootdir
set num = 0
foreach pathname ('du $rootdir | cut -f2 | tail -r')

        echo "The current pathname is: $pathname"
        if ($num == 0) then
                set exportflag = "-export"
        else
                set exportflag = "-a"
        endif
        $indexprog -l 0 -nopairs -nocat -d $index $exportflag $pathname/*.html
        $indexprog -l 0 -nopairs -nocat -d $index -a $pathname/*.txt
        $indexprog -l 0 -nopairs -nocat -d $index -a $pathname/*.c
        $indexprog -nocontents -l 0 -nopairs -nocat -d $index -a $pathname/*.ps
        $indexprog -nocontents -l 0 -nopairs -nocat -d $index -a $pathname/*.gif
        $indexprog -nocontents -l 0 -nopairs -nocat -d $index -a $pathname/*.au
        $indexprog -nocontents -l 0 -nopairs -nocat -d $index -a $pathname/*.hqx
        $indexprog -nocontents -l 0 -nopairs -nocat -d $index -a $pathname/*.xbm
        $indexprog -nocontents -l 0 -nopairs -nocat -d $index -a $pathname/*.mpg
        $indexprog -nocontents -l 0 -nopairs -nocat -d $index -a $pathname/*.pict
        $indexprog -nocontents -l 0 -nopairs -nocat -d $index -a $pathname/*.tiff
        @ num++
end
echo "$num directories were indexed."
```

The following script for indexing directories based on file type was created by Michael Grady from the University of Illinois Computing & Communications Services Office. This Perl script is based on a csh script written by Kevin Hughes. While both scripts are terrific and get the job done right, the Perl script offers more control over the indexing. Listing 13.8 shows the actual code for the script.

Listing 13.8. Perl script for indexing documents using waisindex.

```
#!/usr/local/bin/perl
# Michael Grady,  Univ. of Illinois Computing & Communications Services Office
# Perl script to index the contents of a www tree. This is derived from a csh
# script that Kevin Hughes of EIT constructed for indexing files.

$rootdir = "/var/info/www/docs";
#       This is the root directory of the Web tree you want to index
$index = "/var/info/www/wais-sources/ccso-main-www";
#       This is the name and location of the index to be created
$indexprog = "/var/info/gopher/src/fw02sf/bin/waisindex";
#       The full pathname of the waisindex program
$url = "http://www.uiuc.edu";
#       The main URL for your Web. No slash at the end!

$numdir = $num = 0;

# Generate a list of directory names, then for each directory, generate an
# array of all the filenames in that directory except for . and .. . Sort this
# list so that if there is an .htaccess file in that directory, it comes near
# the front of the list. We assume that if you've bothered to put special
# access controls into a directory, then maybe you don't want these files
# indexed in a general index. You of course can remove this restriction if you
# want. Then we separate all the files in the directory into two lists: one
# list is those file types for which it is appropriate to index the contents of
# the files, and the second list are those whose file types are such we don't
# want to index the contents, just the filename (gif, for instance). Then
# if there are any files in either of these lists, we call waisindex to index
# them. The first time we index, we do not include the -a flag, so that the
# index replaces the current one. Every subsequent call to waisindex includes
# the -a flag so that we then add to the new index we are building. We include
# the -nopairs option on all waisindex calls, because this saves a lot of
# unused info from being put into the index.

# If this is run by cron, redirect print statements to file (or /dev/null).
# Probably want to add a "-l 0" option to the waisindex call also.
#open (LOGIT, ">>/tmp/waisindex.run");
#select LOGIT;

# Put in the appropriate path on your system to each of the commands
# "du", "cut" and "tail", in case you want to run this from a cronjob and
# these commands are not in the default path. Note that "du" will not follow
# symbolic links out of this "tree".
open (PATHNAMES,"/usr/bin/du $rootdir | /usr/bin/cut -f2 |/usr/bin/tail -r |");
DO_PATH: while ( $pathname = <PATHNAMES>) {
        chop $pathname;

        # The following are "path patterns" that we don't want to
        # follow (subdirectories whose files we do not want to index).
```

```
         # Add or subtract from this list as appropriate. These may
         # be directories you don't want to index at all, or directories
         # for which you want to build their own separate index.
         next DO_PATH if $pathname =~ /uiucnet/i;
         #next DO_PATH if $pathname =~ /demopict/i;
         next DO_PATH if $pathname =~ /images/i;
         next DO_PATH if $pathname =~ /testdir/i;

         print "Current pathname is: $pathname\n";
         $numdir++;
         @contents = @nocontents = ();
         opendir(CURRENT_DIR, "$pathname")
                       ¦¦ die "Can't open directory $pathname: $!\n";
         @allfiles = sort (grep(!/^\.\.?$/, readdir(CURRENT_DIR)));
         closedir(CURRENT_DIR);

         DO_FILE: foreach $file (@allfiles) {
                       # skip directories that contain a .htaccess file
                       # note this is NOT smart enough to be recursive (if a
                       # directory below this does not itself contain an
                       # .htaccess file, it WILL be indexed).
                  next DO_PATH if $file eq '.htaccess';
                       # filetypes for which we want to index contents
                  $file =~ /\.html$/i &&
                     do { push(@contents, "$pathname/$file"); next DO_FILE;};
                  $file =~ /\.te?xt$/i &&
                     do { push(@contents, "$pathname/$file"); next DO_FILE;};
                  $file =~ /\.pdf$/i &&
                     do { push(@contents, "$pathname/$file"); next DO_FILE;};
                  #$file =~ /\.ps$/i &&
                     #do { push(@contents, "$pathname/$file"); next DO_FILE;};

                       # filetypes for which we DON'T want to index contents
                  $file =~ /\.gif$/i &&
                     do { push(@nocontents, "$pathname/$file"); next DO_FILE;};
                  #$file =~ /\.au$/i &&
                     #do { push(@nocontents, "$pathname/$file"); next DO_FILE;};
                  #$file =~ /\.mpg$/i &&
                     #do { push(@nocontents, "$pathname/$file"); next DO_FILE;};
                  #$file =~ /\.hqx$/i &&
                     #do { push(@nocontents, "$pathname/$file"); next DO_FILE;};
         # Comment out the above lines to your liking, depending on what
         # filetypes you are actually interested in indexing.
#        For instance, if the ".mpg" line is commented out, then
#        MPEG files will *not* be indexed into the database (and thus
#        won't be searchable by others).
         } # end DO_FILE loop

         if ($#contents >= 0) {            # Index if any files in list.
                  @waisflags = ("-a", "-nopairs");
                  @waisflags = ("-nopairs") if $num == 0;
                  $num ++;
                  system($indexprog, "-d", $index, @waisflags, "-t", "URL",
                              $rootdir, $url, @contents);
         }
         if ($#nocontents >= 0) {          # Index if any files in list.
                  @waisflags = ("-a", "-nopairs");
                  @waisflags = ("-nopairs") if $num == 0;
```

continues

Listing 13.8. continued

```
                $num ++;
                system($indexprog, "-d", $index, @waisflags, "-t", "URL",
                            $rootdir, $url, "-nocontents", @nocontents);
                # note that "-nocontents" flag must follow any -T or -t option
        }
} # end DO_PATH loop

close(PATHNAMES);
print "Waisindex called $num times.\n";
print "Tried indexing $numdir directories.\n";
# end of script
```

Testing the WAIS Database

Once you have installed freewais, started waisserver, and built an index, you will want to test your new WAIS system. You can do this using waisq. If the database was indexed with the following command:

```
00 01 * * * /usr/local/httpd/wais/waisindex -l 1 -d /users/webdocs -e
/usr/local/httpd/logs/wais.log -r /usr/local/httpd/wais/sources/webdocuments
```

You could invoke waisq as follows to test the database:

```
/usr/local/httpd/wais/waisq -m 40 -c /usr/local/httpd/wais/sources -f -
➥-S webdocuments -g Stanek
```

This command tells waisq to return a maximum of 40 matches and to search the webdocuments source file located in the /usr/local/httpd/wais/sources directory for the keyword Stanek. If all goes well and some documents actually contain the keyword, the server should respond with output similar to the following:

```
Searching webdocuments.src . . . Initializing connection . . . Found 28 items.
```

After this, the server should produce output containing the search word used and the results of the query. Keep in mind that normally, this output will be interpreted by your WAIS gateway. The WAIS gateway will process this output, create a document containing the results and send the document to the client originating the search.

Installing and Configuring SWISH

The Simple Web Indexing System for Humans (SWISH) is an easy-to-use alternative to freewais. SWISH is a good choice if you want to experiment with indexing and search engines. Besides being easy to install, SWISH creates very small indexes as compared to a WAIS index. Using the environment variables PLIMIT and FLIMIT, you can squeeze what otherwise would be a large index into about one-tenth of the file space. As a smaller file is quicker to search, this means SWISH will display results faster than many other search engines. However, there is a trade-off to be made between file size and search results. A smaller file contains less data and the smaller the file size, the less accurate the results of the search.

As SWISH can only search local SWISH databases, you will need to use another indexing system if you need to access remote hosts. Additionally, SWISH works best with small-medium-size databases and if you have a large site with hundreds of megabytes of files to index, you may want to use freeWAIS instead of SWISH. You can find information on the current version of SWISH and obtain the source code from EIT corporation at

```
http://www.eit.com/software/
```

Once you download the source to your computer from the EIT Web site and uncompress the source as necessary, you can begin installing and configuring SWISH. The first step is to change directories to the SWISH source directory and update the `config.h` file. If you've just uncompressed SWISH, you should be able to change directories to `swish/src` or simply `src`. In the `config.h` file, you will need to set parameters for your specific system. This file is also where you update the `PLIMIT` and `FLIMIT` variables that control the size of your index files. Once you set those parameters following the inline documentation, you can compile SWISH. SWISH compiles fine with plain-jane gcc.

Setting Up the SWISH Configuration File

The next step is to edit the SWISH configuration file. This file is usually located in the `src` directory and is used to configure environment variables for search and retrieval results. Once you've updated the configuration file, you can name it anything you want, such as `swish.conf`. Listing 13.9 is a sample configuration file for SWISH.

Listing 13.9. Sample SWISH configuration file.

```
# SWISH configuration file

IndexDir /usr/webdocs
# This is a space-separated list of files and directories you want to index.

IndexFile /usr/local/httpd/swish/sources/index.swish
# This is the name your SWISH indexed database.

IndexAdmin "William Stanek publisher@tvp.com"
IndexDescription "Index of key documents at the Web site"
IndexName "Index of TVP Web site"
IndexPointer "http://tvp.com/cgi-bin/wwwwais/"
# Additional information that can be used to describe the index,
# the WAIS gateway used, and the administrator

FollowSymLinks yes
# If you want to follow symbolic links, put yes. Otherwise, put no.

IndexOnly .html .txt .c .ps .gif .au .hqx .xbm .mpg .pict .tiff
# Only files with these suffixes will be indexed.

IndexVerbose yes
# Put this to show indexing information as swish is working.
```

continues

Listing 13.9. continued

```
NoContents .ps .gif .au .hqx .xbm .mpg .pict .tiff
# Files with these suffixes won't have their contents indexed,
# only their file names.

IgnoreLimit 75 200
# To ignore words that occur too frequently, you will want to
# set this parameter. The numbers say ignore words that occur
# in this percentage of the documents and occur in at least this
# many files. Here, ignore words that occur in 75% of the files
# and occur in over 200 files. If this variable is not set SWISH
# uses a default setting

IgnoreWords SwishDefault
# This variable allows you to set your own stop words.
# To do this, you replace the word SwishDefault with a space
# separate list of stop words. You can use multiple assignments
# if necessary
```

The most important variables in the configuration file are `IndexDir` and `IndexFile`. The `IndexDir` variable enables you to specify the files and directories to index. If you enter multiple directories and filenames, you should be sure to separate them with spaces. You can make more than one `IndexDir` assignment, if necessary. The `IndexFile` variable tells SWISH where to store the index. As SWISH does not add the `.src` extension to the filename, you can name the file anything you want. However, you may want to use an extension of `.swish` so you know the file is a SWISH-indexed database.

Compiling and Running SWISH

Once you've updated the configuration file, you can move the compiled SWISH program, swish, and the configuration file to an appropriate directory, such as

```
/usr/local/httpd/swish/
```

To run SWISH and index the files and directories specified in the configuration file, change directories to where SWISH is located and type the following:

```
./swish -c /usr/local/httpd/swish/swish.conf
```

Based on the settings in the previously defined configuration file, when SWISH finishes indexing your site, the indexed database will be located here:

```
/usr/local/httpd/swish/sources/index.swish
```

Because SWISH lets you specify the full path to the configuration file, you can have different configuration files for different databases. To use SWISH with a gateway, you must ensure the script has been modified to work with SWISH or is SWISH-friendly. To modify a gateway so that it is SWISH-friendly, you may only have to change the path for its search engine from its current setting to the full path to the SWISH executable. An example of a SWISH-friendly gateway is wwwwais.c. The wwwwais.c program enables you to set the path to SWISH executables and sources. Here are the settings that make the program SWISH-friendly:

```
# The full path to your swish program.
SwishBin /usr/local/bin/swish

# WAIS source file descriptions
# These represent the path to the indexed databases
# For swish sources:
#    SwishSource full_path_to_source/source.swish "description"
SwishSource /usr/local/httpd/wais/index/index.swish "Search our Web"
SourceRules replace "/usr/local/www/" "http://www.tvpress.com/"
```

Summary

Building an indexed database and creating Web documents that access the database via a gateway requires a lot of effort on the part of the Web publisher. Yet if you take the process one step at a time, you can join the thousands of Web publishers who have indexed their Web sites and thus provide to Web users the ability to search the site quickly and efficiently. Enabling the interface from a fill-out form in your Web document to an indexed database involves these steps:

1. Obtaining the appropriate software. If you use freeWAIS, the package includes waisserver, waisq, waissearch, and waisindex. These programs will handle searching and indexing. You will also need to select a gateway, such as wwwwais.c.
2. Installing and configuring the software.
3. Building your indexed databases.
4. Creating a fill-out form to submit data to the gateway.
5. Testing the search capabilities of the index.

Dynamic Documents with Client Pull/Server Push

14

by William Robert Stanek

Techniques used in Web publishing are changing all the time. With tour de force entrants like Java and VRML providing readers with extremely dynamic and highly interactive documents, some useful innovations aren't getting the recognition they should. Yet creating documents that come to life before the reader's eyes is not the sole realm of Java and VRML. Using client pull/server push technology, you can make documents that are fully animated and highly interactive and that modify their behavior based on user inputs.

Client pull/server push is the poor man's answer to animation and with pull/push, you can animate text and graphics simply, easily, and efficiently. Sports fans can see the latest scores scroll across the bottom of their screen while they read about yesterday's game. Investors can see the latest stock quotes while they read the financial section. Children can see their favorite cartoon character walk across the screen while they learn about the solar system. And you can do all this using the two simple techniques you will learn about in this chapter.

Creating Dynamic Documents with Client Pull/Server Push

Ever since the first Web user clicked on a link and retrieved a document from a remote host, the Web users that followed have wanted more of the same. Many Web users have asked themselves if you can retrieve information, why can't you get updates to that information and thus create an animated document? The primary reason you couldn't originally create animated documents is because HTTP is designed to be a connectionless and stateless protocol, meaning once you retrieve a file, the connection to the server is broken and the server does not maintain any information about the connection.

Various innovations have come along since then to enable animation and more complex interaction between the user and the publication. Creating documents that come to life before the reader's eyes is what client pull/server push technology is all about. The really good news about pull/push is that you don't need to learn another markup language or have special software, all you need is a bit of ingenuity.

Because client pull/server push is based on established Web standards described in HTML 3.0, all HTML 3.0-compliant browsers and some HTML 2.0-compliant browsers should support it. The Netscape Navigator introduced these innovations with Version 1.1 and other browsers, including the Internet Explorer, have embraced pull/push.

While client pull and server push are similar techniques, the way they behave is very different. Server push is a connection-oriented technique for creating animation and live documents. Client pull is a connectionless technique for creating animation and live documents.

With server push, the server sends data to the client and the client displays the data, leaving the connection open. When the server wants to make an update, it simply sends new data for the browser to display. The connection remains open until the server finishes making updates or until the connection is broken. You can break the connection by accessing a new document or selecting a hypertext link. The mechanism that enables server push is the MIME multipart message format, which makes it possible for a single message to contain multiple sets of data.

With client pull, the server sends data to the client. The data includes a directive to the client that tells the client when and how to update the data. The client displays the data and closes the connection. When it is time to update the data, the client opens a new connection to the server and either retrieves new data or refreshes the current data. Afterward, the client closes the connection and waits until it is time to update the data again. Client pull is enabled using HTTP response headers or HTML markup that behaves similarly.

The key distinction between the two techniques is the way the server handles the connection. Using server push, the connection remains open for an indefinite period, which uses system resources. Using client pull, the connection never remains open, and the client only opens a connection to retrieve new data.

How to Use Client Pull

To use client pull, all you have to do is use an HTTP response header or simulate an HTTP response header that contains a directive to refresh the document after a specified period. HTTP response headers are generally sent by the server to the client with all data. When you send output from a gateway script to a client, you create an HTTP response header. The header is followed by a blank line that separates the header from the body of the message.

Using Simulated Headers to Animate Your Documents

The easiest way to enhance your documents with client pull is to simulate HTTP response headers within your HTML documents. This is done with the <META> tag, which can only be used within the HEAD element of your document. Using the HTTP-EQUIV attribute of the <META> tag, you can simulate an HTTP response header that tells the client to refresh the document after a specified period. The time period to wait before refreshing the document is set with the CONTENT attribute.

You should always use the HTTP-EQUIV and CONTENT attributes together. The following document will reload itself every five seconds:

```
<HTML>
<HEAD>
<META HTTP-EQUIV="Refresh" CONTENT=5>
<TITLE>Using Client Pull to automatically reload a document</TITLE>
</HEAD>
<BODY>
<P> Insert text or graphic here </P>
</BODY>
</HTML>
```

The previous example simulates an HTTP response header that says:

```
Refresh: 5
```

Refresh is a new directive specified in HTML 3.0. The value assigned to this directive tells the client or server to get the document in the specified amount of time. While a self-refreshing document is neat, the real key to client pull animation is creating a document that calls another document. You do this by using the URL attribute of the <META> tag.

CAUTION

You must specify the full URL path to files you call with the <META> tag. If you do not specify the full URL path, the client will not be able to find your file. The full URL path includes the transfer protocol directive, such as

```
http://tvp.com/document.html
```

Pay close attention to how quotes and semicolons are used in the following examples. Quotes and semicolons are potential problem areas; if improperly placed, they will cause your animation not to work.

The following document will call `doc2.html` 30 seconds after it has been downloaded:

```
<HTML>
<HEAD>
<META HTTP-EQUIV="Refresh" CONTENT="30; URL=http://tvp.com/doc2.html">
<TITLE>Using Client Pull to call another document</TITLE>
</HEAD>
<BODY>
<P> Insert text or graphic here </P>
</BODY>
</HTML>
```

The previous example is used to simulate an HTTP response header that says:

```
Refresh: 30; URL=http://tvp.com/doc2.html
```

To keep the animation going, `doc2.html` must contain a fully defined <META> tag that calls another document. If `doc2.html` does not have a fully defined <META> tag, no other document will be called. To create a simple animation that flips back and forth indefinitely, you tell the first document to call the second document and the second document to call the first document. An animation that displays a sunrise, waits 30 seconds before displaying a sunset, then repeats the cycle, could be implemented as follows:

Document 1: `sunrise.html`

```
<HTML>
<HEAD>
<META HTTP-EQUIV="Refresh" CONTENT="30; URL=http://tvp.com/sunset.html">
```

```
<TITLE>Sunrise</TITLE>
</HEAD>
<BODY>
<CENTER>
<IMG SRC="sunrise.jpeg">
</CENTER>
</BODY>
</HTML>
```

Document 2: `sunset.html`

```
<HTML>
<HEAD>
<META HTTP-EQUIV="Refresh" CONTENT="30; URL=http://tvp.com/sunrise.html">
<TITLE>Sunset</TITLE>
</HEAD>
<BODY>
<CENTER>
<IMG SRC="sunset.jpeg">
</CENTER>
</BODY>
</HTML>
```

This animation will continue to run until the user exits the browser window or retrieves another document. As this can become annoying after a while, you should build an escape route into the animation. You can do this by linking the documents to a third document. Here's how you could build a stop mechanism into the animation defined earlier.

Revised Document 1: `sunrise.html`

```
<HTML>
<HEAD>
<META HTTP-EQUIV="Refresh" CONTENT="30; URL=http://tvp.com/sunset.html">
<TITLE>Sunrise</TITLE>
</HEAD>
<BODY>
<CENTER>
<A HREF="stop.html"><IMG SRC="sunrise.jpeg" BORDER=0></A>
</CENTER>
</BODY>
</HTML>
```

Revised Document 2: `sunset.html`

```
<HTML>
<HEAD>
<META HTTP-EQUIV="Refresh" CONTENT="30; URL=http://tvp.com/sunrise.html">
<TITLE>Sunset</TITLE>
</HEAD>
<BODY>
<CENTER>
<A HREF="stop.html"><IMG SRC="sunset.jpeg" BORDER=0></A>
</CENTER>
</BODY>
</HTML>
```

Now when a user clicks on the image of the sunset or sunrise, a third document called stop.html will be loaded. The <IMG> tag attribute BORDER was used to remove the border around the image, which might otherwise be a distracting aspect of your animation. You could easily extend this animation to include a series of images that show everything from the dawn of the new day to the last light of the waning day.

When you take advantage of the fact that most browsers cache or store on the local hard drive several megabytes of data, you can create an animation that is updated in real time. You do this by setting the refresh interval to zero seconds. In this way, the new data will be retrieved when the current data finishes loading and if the data is already cached, this will seem to happen instantly. Are you beginning to see the power and simplicity of this client pull animation?

Client Pull in Action

Creating a client pull animation is easy, and you're probably eager to see how client pull could be implemented in your Web publications. As you have seen, client pull is generally used to refresh the current document or load an entirely new document after a specified period. You can use this feature to turn the pages of a book for the reader, display stock quotes or sports scores, move objects around the screen and much more.

Yet loading a complete document can be problematic, especially if the reader is expected to read your document in the time you set. Therefore, I prefer to create small animation sequences that are used with a larger document. The way I do this is by defining a mini-window for the animation. The mini-window is defined with Netscape frames. A good location for such an animation is a small frame on the left or right side of the browser window.

Here are some things I've done with client pull at The Virtual Press Web site:

Live greeting messages coupled with site navigation tips

Animated logos that rotate back and forth or up and down

Live quotes on writing in the Writer's Gallery

Live tips for publishing in the Internet Publishing Center

Live job hunting tips in the Job Information Center

A multiframe slide show in the Business Solutions section

Let's explore how TVP's logo was animated using Netscape frames and client pull. The first thing I did was to design the framed window. I divided the window into three sections: a large right-aligned frame used for the main text, a left-aligned frame to be used as a sidebar, and a small frame to be used for a menu. Figure 14.1 shows this framed window.

FIGURE 14.1.

The base frame for the document.

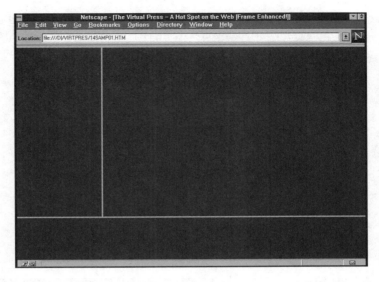

Using Corel Photo-Paint, I created a logo to place in the sidebar. As you can see from Figure 14.2, I designed the image like a bookmark. Next, I sketched out on paper how I wanted to animate the logo. I decided to make the image oscillate back and forth. First the image rotates to the left. Then the image rotates to the center, where it started, before rotating to the right. Finally the image rotates to the center and begins again. With the image rotation feature, I rotated the logo through various stages to give a 3-D rotation effect.

FIGURE 14.2.

The logo to animate.

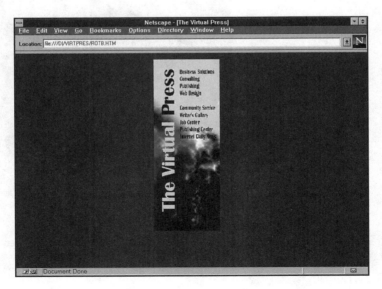

The entire animation sequence is accomplished in eight stages and uses only five images, yet seems quite complex when you watch its behavior in your browser. The code for the rotation documents is presented in sequence. Figures 14.3 through 14.10 illustrate the stages.

Document 1: Starting point. The image is not rotated.

```
<HTML>
<HEAD>
<TITLE>The Virtual Press</TITLE>
<META HTTP-EQUIV="Refresh" CONTENT="1; URL=http://www.tvpress.com/rotb2.html">
</HEAD>
<BODY BGCOLOR="#0000ff">
<CENTER>
<A HREF="bstop.html">
<IMG SRC="vpttlb.gif" ALT="" BORDER=0>
</A>
</CENTER>
</BODY>
</HTML>
```

FIGURE 14.3.

The Virtual Press home page frame and client pull enhanced: Stage 1.

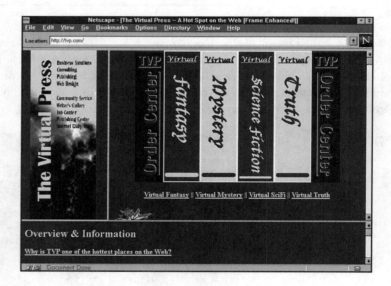

Document 2: Left rotation 1.

```
<HTML>
<HEAD>
<TITLE>The Virtual Press</TITLE>
<META HTTP-EQUIV="Refresh" CONTENT="1; URL=http://www.tvpress.com/rotb3.html">
</HEAD>
<BODY BGCOLOR="#0000ff">
```

```
<CENTER>
<A HREF="bstop.html">
<IMG SRC="vpttlb1.gif" ALT="" BORDER=0>
</A>
</CENTER>
</BODY>
</HTML>
```

FIGURE 14.4.

The Virtual Press home page frame and client pull enhanced: Stage 2.

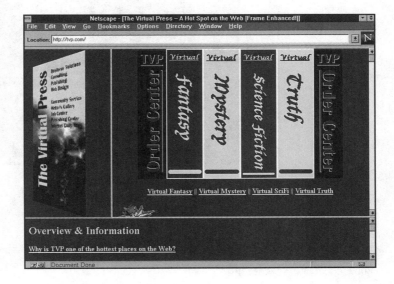

Document 3: Left rotation 2.

```
<HTML>
<HEAD>
<TITLE>The Virtual Press</TITLE>
<META HTTP-EQUIV="Refresh" CONTENT="1; URL=http://www.tvpress.com/rotb4.html">
</HEAD>
<BODY BGCOLOR="#0000ff">
<CENTER>
<A HREF="bstop.html">
<IMG SRC="vpttlb2.gif" ALT="" BORDER=0>
</A>
</CENTER>
</BODY>
</HTML>
```

FIGURE 14.5.

The Virtual Press home page frame and client pull enhanced: Stage 3.

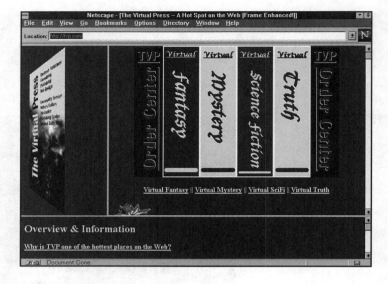

Document 4: Left rotation 1.

```
<HTML>
<HEAD>
<TITLE>The Virtual Press</TITLE>
<META HTTP-EQUIV="Refresh" CONTENT="1; URL=http://www.tvpress.com/rotb5.html">
</HEAD>
<BODY BGCOLOR="#0000ff">
<CENTER>
<A HREF="bstop.html">
<IMG SRC="vpttlb1.gif" ALT="" BORDER=0>
</A>
</CENTER>
</BODY>
</HTML>
```

Document 5: Starting point.

```
<HTML>
<HEAD>
<TITLE>The Virtual Press</TITLE>
<META HTTP-EQUIV="Refresh" CONTENT="1; URL=http://www.tvpress.com/rotb6.html">
</HEAD>
<BODY BGCOLOR="#0000ff">
<CENTER>
<A HREF="bstop.html">
<IMG SRC="vpttlb.gif" ALT="" BORDER=0>
</A>
</CENTER>
</BODY>
</HTML>
```

FIGURE 14.6.

The Virtual Press home page frame and client pull enhanced: Stage 4.

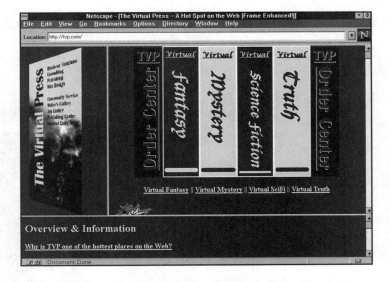

FIGURE 14.7.

The Virtual Press home page frame and client pull enhanced: Stage 5.

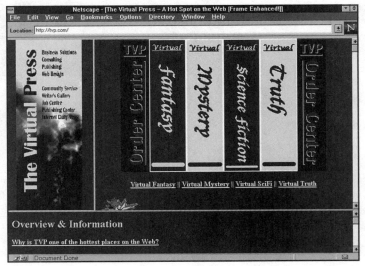

Document 6: Right rotation 1.

```
<HTML>
<HEAD>
<TITLE>The Virtual Press</TITLE>
<META HTTP-EQUIV="Refresh" CONTENT="1; URL=http://www.tvpress.com/rotb7.html">
</HEAD>
<BODY BGCOLOR="#0000ff">
<CENTER>
```

```
<A HREF="bstop.html">
<IMG SRC="vpttlb3.gif" ALT="" BORDER=0>
</A>
</CENTER>
</BODY>
</HTML>
```

FIGURE 14.8.

The Virtual press home page frame and client pull enhanced: Stage 6.

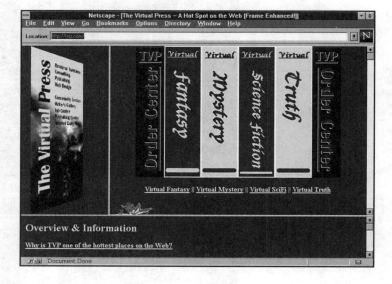

Document 7: Right rotation 2.

```
<HTML>
<HEAD>
<TITLE>The Virtual Press</TITLE>
<META HTTP-EQUIV="Refresh" CONTENT="1; URL=http://www.tvpress.com/rotb8.html">
</HEAD>
<BODY BGCOLOR="#0000ff">
<CENTER>
<A HREF="bstop.html">
<IMG SRC="vpttlb4.gif" ALT="" BORDER=0>
</A>
</CENTER>
</BODY>
</HTML>
```

Document 8: Right rotation 1.

```
<HTML>
<HEAD>
<TITLE>The Virtual Press</TITLE>
<META HTTP-EQUIV="Refresh" CONTENT="1; URL=http://www.tvpress.com/rotb.html">
</HEAD>
<BODY BGCOLOR="#0000ff">
<CENTER>
<A HREF="bstop.html">
```

```
<IMG SRC="vpttlb3.gif" ALT="" BORDER=0>
</A>
</CENTER>
</BODY>
</HTML>
```

FIGURE 14.9.

The Virtual Press home page frame and client pull enhanced: Stage 7.

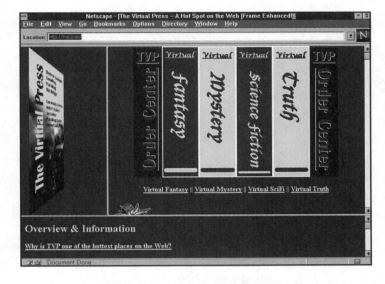

FIGURE 14.10.

The Virtual Press home page frame and client pull enhanced: Stage 8.

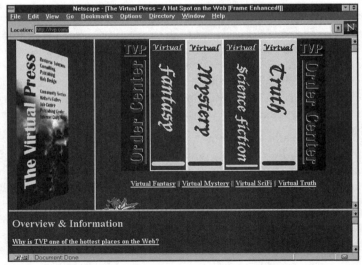

As I knew the animation might cause performance problems on some systems, I included a mechanism for stopping the animation. Each image is clickable and leads to a document called bstop.html. The bstop.html document contains an image of the logo that does not rotate. To enable readers to restart the animation, this image, if clicked on, will take readers back to the first stage of the animation.

Here's the code for the bstop.html document:

```
<HTML>
<HEAD>
<TITLE>The Virtual Press</TITLE>
</HEAD>
<BODY BGCOLOR="#0000ff">
<CENTER>
<A HREF="rotb.html">
<IMG SRC="vpttlb.gif" ALT="" BORDER=0>
</A>
</CENTER>
</BODY>
</HTML>
```

How to Use Server Push

Server push and gateway scripts make perfect combinations. The output of your gateway scripts generally has a defined HTTP header. Using this header, you can create a document that will reload itself or call another document.

Server push is designed to complement client pull and behaves similarly. The key exception again is that server push leaves the connection to the client open. While this uses system resources, it is generally a more efficient way to pass data to a client. Using client pull, the client must contact the server, wait for a reply, establish a connection, retrieve the data, close the connection and repeat the entire process when requesting new data. Using server push, the client contacts the server, waits for a reply, establishes a connection, retrieves the data, and when requesting new data, simply retrieves the data.

Besides giving the server total control over when and how often data is sent, server pull enables users to easily interrupt data updates using the Stop feature of their browser. To create a document that updates itself, you can use the Content-type directive. The Content-Type field in a header identifies the MIME type of data you are sending back to the client. The MIME content type you should use with client pull is

multipart/x-mixed-replace

While most HTTP responses consist of only a single message or document, the multipart message type enables a single response to contain multiple messages or documents. The multipart message type encapsulates other message types within the document you are sending to the client. When you use the MIME type multipart/mixed, you must also specify the boundary string that separates the messages. This string should be unique and not used elsewhere in the text of the message. After the boundary string, you specify the MIME type of the individual message in a header. The header should be followed by a blank line if the message has a body section as well.

The following sample response header for a multipart message contains three messages that are separated by a unique boundary string:

```
Content-type: multipart/mixed;boundary=--YourUniqueBoundaryString

--YourUniqueBoundaryString

Content-type: text/plain

Text for the first message.

--YourUniqueBoundaryString
Content-type: text/plain

Text for the second message.

--YourUniqueBoundaryString

Content-type: text/plain

Text for the third message.

--YourUniqueBoundaryString
```

Some servers have problems processing the multipart message type if you put any spaces after the multipart/mixed assignment. For this reason, do not insert spaces after the semicolon or around the equal sign when you assign the mandatory boundary string.

NOTE

With server push, you use Netscape's experimental multipart/x-mixed-replace message type. This message type tells the client to replace the current data with the new data. This new data will be displayed instead of the current data. The client will finish loading the current document before loading and displaying the new document. Transforming the multipart/mixed message type into a multipart/x-mixed replace message is easy. You simply change the type assignment in the first line as follows:

```
Content-type: multipart/x-mixed-replace;boundary=--YourUniqueBoundaryString

--YourUniqueBoundaryString

Content-type: text/plain

Text for the first message.

--YourUniqueBoundaryString
Content-type: text/plain
```

```
Text for the second message.

--YourUniqueBoundaryString
Content-type: text/plain

Text for the third message.

--YourUniqueBoundaryString
```

Ideally, you would send the client a multipart message as the output from a gateway
script. As the multipart message can contain as many sections as you want, you can use
a for loop or a do-while loop to keep the script running indefinitely. By building
hypertext links into the output documents, you can enable the reader to interact with
your publication. The links could even call other gateway scripts that use server push
animation.

Here's a simple script using server push to display the current time once each second:

```
#!/bin/sh

# Build multipart message using the x-mixed-replace format
# Ensure header is separated from body with space
cat << MAIN
Content-type: multipart/x-mixed-replace;boundary=--YourUniqueBoundaryString

--YourUniqueBoundaryString
MAIN
# Set while to true to loop continuously
while true

do

#Create Document
cat << TIME
Content-type: text/html
<HTML>
<HEAD>
<TITLE>Current Time in Hawaii</TITLE>
</HEAD>
<BODY BGCOLOR="#0000ff" text="#ffff00" link="#fffbf0" vlink="#808000"
➥alink="#ff0000">
<BIG>

date

</BIG>
</BODY>
</HTML>

--YourUniqueBoundaryString
TIME
#wait 1 second before repeating the loop
sleep 1
done
```

> **CAUTION**
>
> While this Bourne shell script works, you should not use UNIX shell scripts with server push if the connection is going to be open indefinitely. The primary reason for this is that shell scripts will not stop running when the user severs the connection and if the script is running on your server, it is using system resources. For this reason, if the server push will open a connection of indefinite duration, you should use a language that handles interrupts well, such as C or Perl.

A neat trick you can do with server push is to have the server update an inline image in the current document. Creating an inline animation is as easy as adding an inline image with a URL to a gateway script that uses server push. While the current document will not get updated, the image will. The following document contains an image that will get updated inline:

```
<HTML>
<HEAD>
<TITLE>Server Push</TITLE>
</HEAD>
<BODY>
<CENTER>
<IMG WIDTH=64 HEIGHT=64 SRC="http://tvp.com/cgi-bin/doit.cgi">
</CENTER>
<P>Only the image in this document will get updated.
<P>The rest of the document will not be updated.
</BODY>
</HTML>
```

Creating a gateway script that uses server push is also easy. All you have to do is create a script that builds a document in multipart message format. The following script in the C programming language called doit.c was created by Rob McCool. The script enables you to animate a series of images. The number of stages for the animation is determined by the variable LASTCHAR. With the LASTCHAR variable, you set the last character of the filename for your images, which are uniquely named and end in an alphabetic letter from lowercase *a* to the value for LASTCHAR. To use this script with images in GIF format, all you have to do is modify the LASTCHAR variable as necessary and compile the script using your favorite compiler.

Listing 14.1 shows the doit.c script.

Listing 14.1. Modified doit.c script.

```
/*
 * doit.c: Quick hack to play a sequence of GIF files.
 *
 * This is a modified version of Rob McCool's original script.
 *
 * This code is released into the public domain.  Do whatever
 * you want with it.
 *
 */
```

continues

Listing 14.1. continued

```c
/* the following lines set up the libraries and variables
 * The most important variables are: HEADER and LASTCHAR
 * With the HEADER variable, you set the HTTP response header.
 * With the LASTCHAR variable, you set the last character of the
 * file name for your images. As this animation has 10 stages,
 * the image names will end in a to j.
 */
#include <sys/types.h>
#include <sys/mman.h>
#include <unistd.h>
#include <fcntl.h>
#include <sys/stat.h>
#include <stdio.h>
#define LASTCHAR 'j'
#define HEADER \
"Content-type: multipart/x-mixed-replace;boundary=YourUniqueBoundaryString\n" \
#define RANDOMSTRING "\n--YourUniqueBoundaryString\n"
#define ENDSTRING "\n--YourUniqueBoundaryString--\n"
#define CTSTRING "Content-type: image/gif\n\n"
int main(int argc, char *argv[])
{
    struct stat fi;
    char fn[32];
    caddr_t fp;
    unsigned char x;
    int fd;
    if(write(STDOUT_FILENO, HEADER, strlen(HEADER)) == -1)
        exit(0);
    if(write(STDOUT_FILENO, RANDOMSTRING, strlen(RANDOMSTRING)) == -1)
        exit(0);
    x = 'a';
    while(1) {
        sleep(1);
        if(write(STDOUT_FILENO, CTSTRING, strlen(CTSTRING)) == -1)
            exit(0);
/* The next line defines the name of the images to use for creating
 * the inline animation. Here, the images are located in the images
 * subdirectory of the current directory which should be cgi-bin.
 * The image files must be named as follows:
 * images/Aa.gif
 * images/Ab.gif
 * images/Ac.gif
 * images/Ad.gif
 * images/Ae.gif
 * images/Af.gif
 * images/Ag.gif
 * images/Ah.gif
 * images/Ai.gif
 * images/Aj.gif
 */
        sprintf(fn, "images/A%c.gif", (char) x);
        if( (fd = open(fn, O_RDONLY)) == -1)
            continue;
        fstat(fd, &fi);
        fp = mmap(NULL, fi.st_size, PROT_READ, MAP_PRIVATE, fd, 0);
        if(fp == (caddr_t) -1)
```

```
        exit(0);
    if(write(STDOUT_FILENO, (void *) fp, fi.st_size) == -1)
        exit(0);
    munmap(fp, fi.st_size);
    close(fd);
    if(write(STDOUT_FILENO, RANDOMSTRING, strlen(RANDOMSTRING)) == -1)
        exit(0);
    if(x == LASTCHAR)
        exit(0);
    else ++x;
```

Summary

Client pull/server push technology enables you to create documents that come to life before the reader's eyes. What is more important, pull/push technology enables you to use the existing structure of HTTP and CGI to create animation sequences using simple techniques. Server push is a connection-oriented technique for creating animation and live documents. Client pull is a connectionless technique for creating animation and live documents. Both techniques have their advantages and disadvantages. With server push, you use more system resources but get better response time. With client pull, you use minimal system resources but may get poor response time. So if you want to liven up your Web publications, why not start with pull/push?

PART

IV

Web Publishing Production Systems

Building and Managing a Web-Based Information System

15

by William Stanek,
Gregory Stenstrom,
Richmond Tuttle,
and Sandra Tuttle

At times it seems the whole of the world has joined the information revolution. Computers are a part of our everyday lives. Globally, most businesses and hundreds of millions of people own or have access to a computer. Most businesses with more than 10 employees have several computers. Often, the computers are connected together in a local area network. Networks can boost productivity, make it easier to communicate without having to leave the desk, and improve the way companies do business.

A growing number of companies have large corporate networks. The company's Wide Area Network may connect hundreds or thousands of computers. A recent trend is to integrate the capabilities of the Internet and the World Wide Web into the corporate information infrastructure; such networks are often called intranets or internets with a small *i*. By using the existing capabilities of the Internet and the Web, companies have found that they can save thousands, hundreds of thousands, and sometimes millions of dollars. Why buy expensive groupware programs at $100–$200 for each license when you can buy Netscape for $29.95? If you represent a nonprofit organization, why pay anything when you can obtain browser and server software for free?

Thousands of savvy business owners and technological people have recognized this tremendous cost savings and set out to merge years, months, or weeks of existing company data into the distributed structure of the Internet. The goal is to save money and improve the bottom line. After all, in the end the bottom line is the only thing that matters. The problem is that very few individuals truly understand how to integrate and manage the large-scale distributed system created by the merger of the company's data with Internet technologies.

Before you make the same mistake, you should take the time to learn exactly what you are getting into and that is exactly what this chapter is all about. The chapter starts by exploring the full benefits of creating a large-scale information structure using Internet tools. Afterward, the chapter discusses how you could build and manage such a structure.

Web Publishing on the Company Network

Web Publishing on the Local Area Network (LAN) or even a Wide Area Network (WAN) is really the practical application of Web publishing to a real-world business problem. The power of the Web is in its diversity. Its handling of hypertext objects enables cross-platform solutions. With network publishing, you easily can set up a mini-Internet within your company. Your mini-Internet can be accessible by the outside world or be exclusive to the company. The choice is absolutely yours.

Before you start, there are some issues you should consider:

- Databases and the paper trial
- Access to the global Internet
- Traditional publishing versus online publishing

Databases and the Paper Trial

A reality in the business world is that most company information is maintained in a database. Databases come in many forms. Often databases are in the form of flat files that are updated by hand. A list of addresses or business contacts in a text document is an example of a flat file. If you maintain flat databases, chances are good that your system administrator has created a program that can extract information from the flat file, such as a person's home address or phone number. While such databases are simple, they are useful and practical, especially in UNIX environments.

More complex company databases are probably maintained on commercial database systems such as Oracle or Sybase. These commercial databases have many advanced uses and once the company builds such a database, it is surely a corporate asset. Where would AT&T be without its database of customer names and addresses?

However, company-wide databases tax resources in both labor costs and real-money terms. Even the best conventional database tools have high learning curves. Yes sometimes you just don't have two to four weeks to train new personnel on the use of the database. And, company-wide databases are growing in size and complexity.

Databases aren't the only part of the company that grows as the company grows. The paper trail of documents—brochures, information packets, policies—also grows with the company. Maintaining an ever-growing paper trail is costly and personnel-intensive. Every time there is a product release, product update, or a press release, documents must be distributed to support personnel and other key personnel within the company. This costs money. Other problems stem from this paper trail. The customer support department may be misinforming customers based on data that is days or weeks old.

To better serve customers, employees need access to the most current information. What employees really need to do this is a meta-index of company resources and documents in a searchable form so information can be retrieved in an instant. A company-wide meta-index of resources and documents would be astronomically expensive using conventional means. Publishing these documents electronically on the Local Area Network or a company-wide Wide Area Network is a nonconventional solution to this problem that will drastically reduce costs and save countless hours.

Extending the functionality of the World Wide Web to the Local Area Network or Wide Area Network to create a large-scale information system within the company is a cost- and time-effective business solution. The facilities of the World Wide Web don't have high learning curves. In fact, there isn't much of a learning curve at all if the facilities and tools are a part of the company's infrastructure.

The only thing network publishing requires is that you install and configure two things:

> Web server communications—a server
>
> Web browser communications—browsers

Through network publishing, you can provide a meta-index of documents, access to company databases, and much more. Using tools discussed in previous chapters, you can automatically convert most existing document formats to the HTML format. The great thing about HTML documents is they are dynamic. Personnel don't have to rummage through a paper trail or learn the commands to interface with the company database. To find a related reference with HTML, all they have to do is click on links. To perform a database search, all they have to do is enter a word or two at a prompt.

Access to the Global Internet

A common misconception about the Web is that to set up a Web server you must be on the Internet. This simply is not true. The company can establish a Web-based information system and does not have to be connected to the Internet to take advantage of Web tools. The Web server doesn't have to be linked to the Internet, and company personnel don't have to be able to access the Internet to make network publishing a reality within the company.

Several books concerning the Web and the Internet specifically—and mistakenly—state that a TCP/IP connection to the Internet is an absolute requirement for setting up a Web server. It's true that an Internet connection would help in obtaining Web server software because server software is widely available on the Internet. However, this software, the installation instructions, and manuals can be downloaded from any Internet account and subsequently loaded onto the company network.

The more correct statement is that if the company wants to use the Internet and take advantage of the World Wide Web that is a part of the Internet, there must be some kind of connection to the Internet. But the company does not have to be connected to the Internet or any part of the Internet to set up a Web server for use within the company.

The Federal government has "private" internets. Some large corporations have "private" internets. You could call these mini-internets or simply internets. The internet with the little *i* is simply a network of networked computers. What these private internets allow on their networks is their business. What you provide on your network is your business.

When you set up a Web server, you tell it the domain—structure—you want it to operate within. You can include or exclude links to the outside world as you see fit. You can even include or exclude divisions within the company. It all depends on how you set up the Web server and the permissions you grant or deny.

Traditional Publishing Versus Online Publishing

No doubt, you've heard the term *paperless office* before. Don't cringe. Although this eventuality isn't outside the realm of possibility, this isn't a lecture on how the Internet and Web publishing can help make the office paperless. The truth is that Web publishing company documents won't eliminate the paper trail, but it can help to dramatically reduce it.

It can help to streamline the update and correction process. It can also help to distribute large amounts of up-to-date information throughout the organization. The decision to create a large-scale information structure using Internet tools ultimately comes down to simple economics:

- Is network publishing affordable?
- Is network publishing cost-saving?
- Is network publishing cost-effective?

Network Publishing Is Affordable

The costs for incorporating Web publishing into an existing network are negligible. Often a network will already have a workstation capable of carrying the additional load as the Web server. The Web server doesn't have to be a dedicated machine. This is especially true for small networks or networks where a limited number of personnel have access to the Web server.

Usually, you won't need a full-time Web server administrator. Existing networks already have, or should have, a system administrator who can handle the additional duties as the Web server administrator. Web servers are very easy to administer once they are set up and running.

Although using an existing workstation is not always a possibility, the good news is that the Web server doesn't have to be a power machine. Web servers serving hundreds of users are running on network-configured 486DX 66MHz computers.

Network Publishing Saves Money

Network publishing the company documents can reduce software licensing costs and other associated costs dramatically. As discussed earlier, Internet tools are inexpensive compared to groupware tools like Lotus Notes that cost $150 for each license. Network publishing documents can save money in other areas as well. Printed documents quickly become outdated. Technical manuals, company policies, and other important documents are expensive to maintain and reprint. With network publishing, there aren't any print costs, and you'll find that maintaining Web documents is easier than maintaining printed documents.

There simply aren't high-learning curves in a point-and-click interface environment. There are even ways to automate the updating of documents. Time savings for easy maintenance and use adds up to big money savings over traditional alternatives. The savings also extend to personnel savings. Your company can realize these personnel savings in fewer hours spent building, searching, and maintaining company documents. Ease-of-use means finding information is less frustrating for workers and a less stressful environment is good for the company and its workers.

Ease-of-use may also mean that new employees can become productive company assets sooner. Using a Web browser, such as Mosaic, a new employee with little training could make retrievals from the company's Oracle database on the first day of the job. To do this, the new employee would access a Web page with a fill-out form or query box like those discussed in Chapter 12, "Form and Image Map Creating and Design." After typing in the information they wanted to retrieve, the employee would simply click on the submit button and soon afterward, the retrieval would display on their screen.

Network Publishing Is Cost Effective

Network publishing is a highly efficient way to ensure that company information is distributed throughout the organization. Putting a document on the company Web can provide instant access for all personnel, several departments, or an individual department. You'll discover that Web documents are easier to maintain, produce, index, and use—which translates directly to cost efficiency.

If cost efficiency is a big consideration for the company (and it should be), consider the case of the company with global offices. These offices are probably already connected via a Wide Area Network or have some kind of dial-up access to the Internet. Despite the ease-of-use of electronic mail, company documents flow back and forth through conventional mail every day. This is because some types of documents aren't suited for posting to e-mail. Posting a 500-page policy manual via e-mail to all company personnel would probably bring the network to a screeching halt. Even if it didn't, the people who should be reading the policy manual wouldn't because of the form of the message.

With network publishing, the policy manual would be an interactive, indexed document that personnel could easily search for references important to the operations of their respective departments. More importantly, the entire huge manual wouldn't have to be mailed and remailed to a dozen global or regional offices. Are you starting to get a better picture of the benefits of building a large-scale information structure using Internet tools?

Building a Large-Scale Information Structure

The definition of a large-scale information structure is often a relative one. For a small company with 25 employees, building a large-scale information structure could mean networking the companies computers so they can access flat files, use e-mail, and share information. For a large company with 10,000 employees and an existing network, the concept could mean using Internet tools to access globally distributed databases and other corporate resources.

Consequently, the method you use to build an information structure using Internet tools largely depends on your situation and needs. Still, the data at the heart of your information structure will generally be in the form of flat files and databases.

Keep this in mind as you explore the next two topics: file-oriented systems and database systems.

File-Oriented Systems

File-oriented environments form the core of most document and information structures. As is often the case, the company's documents are probably scattered about with no real structure. Many important documents are in personal directories on hard drives no one can access and the secretaries spend a lot of time passing floppy disks about the office. Some key documents that could benefit everyone are stored in a location that only one person knows about. A few documents may be in directories or formats that are widely accessible. As the company grows, the value of public directories, files, and exchange of documents becomes increasingly apparent, especially when it is necessary to distribute information to large groups of employees.

The question soon becomes, how do we tap into all the valuable resources employees have created over the years? The answer is to integrate key documents into the company's information structure, but before you begin you should carefully consider how and where you will store files. This is an important decision even in a single-user environment, and critical in a multiuser environment.

Most people do not use a file storage methodology for managing publishing environments. Years of experience working in networked environments shows that it is a rare employee who maintains electronic documents in an organized fashion. Even those computer folks who should know better rarely organize their documents in any fashion except whimsical.

Imagine a file cabinet in your office stuffed with cryptically labeled or unlabeled documents, video tapes, music cassettes, and photos, and you would have an accurate picture of how the majority of users and organizations store their data in computer systems. A common statistic in evaluating large organizations data storage needs is that *more than 90 percent of all documents stored in file cabinets will never be used again,* and so it goes with many computer systems. The 10 percent of documents that you would use again if you could find them are often stored in an electronic labyrinth that only Houdini could help them escape from.

The key to cleaning up this mess is getting organized. The organization of your information is the most important design issue for your information structure. Organize your data into logically named directories that pertain to the departments, projects, and personnel. However, you never want to mix public and private files.

Create clear policies on the types of information that can be placed in public directories and the type of information that has restricted access. Often, you will want to organize information based on need to know. For example, all personnel in a development group may need to access each other's files, but personnel outside the working group should not be able to access the files.

A clear structure for your directories and files becomes increasingly important as your company grows. Hundreds of files in a single directory are difficult to track and maintain. Therefore, you should consider how to structure the subdirectories within primary directories. For example, you could create a directory for each of a working groups projects by category. (See Chapter 26, "Designing and Publishing a Web Site," for a detailed example of creating a logical naming structure for a large-scale information system.)

Database Systems

Databases are at the heart of most information systems and your Web-based information system should be no different. For large publishing systems, a database-driven environment is highly recommended. Issues such as revision control, composition of documents made up of elements produced by multiple authors, text search across multiple production areas, and data retrieval must be addressed in large, multidisciplined environments.

If you plan to use a database system, the key concepts you should consider right now are

- The type of database system to use
- Database storage and retrieval methods

The Type of Database System to Use

Two primary types of databases exist for storing and indexing data, *relational* and *object-oriented*. While relational databases store and retrieve data based on *attribute relationships*, object-oriented databases store and retrieve data based on *object attributes*.

Relational databases index and retrieve data using relationships between attributes. The primary providers of relational databases suitable for integrating in a large-scale Web publishing environment include Oracle, Sybase, and Informix. The best thing about relational databases is that they follow a Structured Query Language, which makes it easier to transfer your data to another database system.

Object-oriented databases index and retrieve data using relationships between objects. Currently, most object-oriented database systems are a part of proprietary document publishing environments. These database systems can also be adapted for Web publishing use. Although object-oriented databases provide powerful capabilities and exciting potential, there is no standard available to move your data from one database system to another.

When you publish on the Web, your audience is potentially a global one. The capability to intelligently thread through a hypertext-based document (whether HTML, SGML, VRML, or some other language) to meet the needs of multiple locales can be a huge business advantage to Web publishers when managed effectively.

Database-driven systems offer the advantage of assigning unique information to a data element, commonly referred to as *attributes*, which permit users to better manage their publishing environment. An attribute of a data element can refer to anything that is useful to the publishing environment, such as a customer's ZIP code, address, or product preferences. An attribute could also refer to a key element of a larger document, such as a Web-published reference guide with attributes that refer to the format the guide is written in (such as SGML), the author, the revision number, whether it is a rough draft or in final form, and so on. This collection of attribute information about the document and its individual components, as well as the information regarding organization and structure, make up the *data model* for a database-driven publishing system.

Figure 15.1 represents one possible example of a relational data model and a simple parent-child relationship. The figure shows the various methods that can be used to retrieve a document (or document element) without having to reference any information contained in the document itself.

FIGURE 15.1.

Simple data model for a database-driven publishing system.

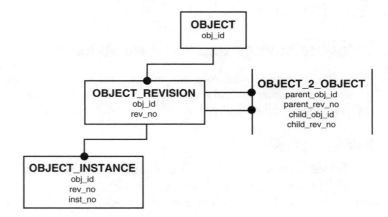

In this example, an object such as a document would have an entry in a database table called OBJECT. The database attribute obj_id is the unique identifier (or primary key) for this piece of information. Every entry in OBJECT that needs to be revision-controlled would then have one or more entries in OBJECT_REVISION (one for each revision of OBJECT). The additional attribute rev_no, combined with obj_id, serves to uniquely identify the entries in this table and is the mechanism that permits retrieval of specific revisions of the element.

If it is necessary to support multiple object formats (for example SGML, PostScript, and soon), then the additional table OBJECT_INSTANCE could be added where each REVISION is related to one or more INSTANCE. Each INSTANCE represents the same data but is stored in a format that may be required for a specific use. This could also be used to store the same SGML data using different DTDs because many companies are required to release information using a standard DTD (such as the J2008 DTD for the auto industry), but prefer to author in their own DTD. Using DTD translation tools (some of which are available on the Web), an automatic process could be developed which, when initiated by the user or some system event, would translate the components to the target DTD and then put them together using the hierarchy represented in the database.

TIP

> Database-driven systems are particularly useful in environments that can take advantage of a "write once, use many times" methodology. For example, technical publishing generally involves maintaining documents associated with a piece of equipment that is constantly being modified. Rewriting an entire maintenance manual every time a piece of equipment is modified would be an expensive proposition for even a single piece of equipment. When considering multiple pieces of equipment spread out across a large region, or even the world, the usefulness of defining a document as multiple elements with specific attributes becomes apparent.

Database Storage and Retrieval Methods

Two primary methods of storing and indexing information in a database-driven publishing system are the *pointer* method and the *blob* method. Both have advantages and disadvantages, and your choice will generally be based on your data retrieval time and storage requirements.

Pointer Method

The pointer method basically refers to a database storage methodology that stores all associated file element information (attributes) in the database, but does not move the actual data into the physical database and instead stores a pointer to the physical location of the file.

This method is useful in managing information across distributed sites on a network. The advantage of this method is that it minimizes the actual physical size of the database and makes it possible for the documents to be updated at remote locations without having to access the central databases. The disadvantage is that distributed data may not always be available, and careful design of the database system is called for to ensure the system is not corrupted.

Blob Method

The blob method basically refers to a database storage methodology that stores the physical file and all associated file element information (attributes) in the database. In a large organization, this type of database can grow quickly from megabytes to gigabytes. Hence, the name of the method.

You will find that the blob method is useful in environments where maximum access and control of data is desired or required. The advantage of this method is that it centralizes all data elements. The disadvantage is that centralized data may not always be available on a network and can become a major chokepoint.

> **TIP**
>
> When considering using a centralized database for your Web publishing system, verify that the query transaction rates you will require for your Web publishing system are supported. The locking and blocking techniques used by various database vendors differ and can specifically effect blob-related operations.

Web Publishing Database Products and Providers

As databases are sure to be an important part of your large-scale information system, you will want to carefully consider your options. This will be true even if you currently use database systems. Although you may unfortunately have to change database systems or write your own gateway to the database, the good news is that the major database vendors have pulled out all the stops to ensure their database systems can take advantage of Internet technologies.

Two vendors stand out from the crowd: Oracle and Sybase.

Oracle WebSystem 1.0

The Oracle WebSystem consists of Web server and client products that provide easy integration with existing databases. Using WebSystem, you can easily develop Web-based data-driven client/server applications that can reliably manage high volumes of data. The Oracle WebSystem family of products includes

- Oracle WebServer
- Oracle WebServer Option
- Oracle PowerBrowser

Oracle WebServer

The Oracle WebServer provides a complete Web publishing and database solution for new Oracle customers. Oracle WebServer combines the power and reliability of Oracle7 Workgroup Server with the capabilities of the Web. The Oracle7 Workgroup Server is used as the database engine for the Web publishing package.

The package also includes the following:

Oracle Web Listener—A high-performance HTTP server

Oracle Web Agent—A gateway program to Oracle7-stored procedures from the World Wide Web

Developer's Toolkit—Enables developers to create complete applications using Oracle-stored procedures and functions

Administration utilities—Enable publisher to administer the Web publishing system

The key selling points of WebSystem are that it

- Supports transaction-based Web applications
- Works with any browser
- Creates dynamic HTML pages in real time
- Creates custom pages "on the fly"
- Delivers a new breed of Web applications
- Enables you to create scripts using the BASIC programming language

Oracle WebServer Option

Oracle WebServer Option is designed for companies that currently use the Oracle7 Enterprise Server and want to take advantage of Web publishing capabilities. Consequently, the package includes everything the basic WebServer package includes except for the Oracle7 Enterprise Server license and software.

Oracle PowerBrowser

Oracle PowerBrowser features a BASIC-programmable Web browser as well as an HTML authoring environment. This powerful browser was discussed briefly in Chapter 10, "HTML Toolkit: Browsers, Editors, and Converters."

Sybase and Silicon Graphics WebFORCE CHALLENGE

The integration of SYBASE software and Silicon Graphics' WebFORCE CHALLENGE servers effectively enables data-rich personalized marketing on the World Wide Web. This integrated solution set enables Web publishers to market to specific user profiles as well as to the general Web audience. Key areas that can be supported include inventory management, customer tracking, marketing, and transaction management.

Inventory Management

Inventory management systems enable Web site providers to manage inventories such as catalogs or corporate marketing materials. The inventory can be dynamically adjusted to respond to the level of interest in an inventory item.

Customer Tracking and Marketing

Customer tracking systems can store information on customers, including their purchase history, access to Web pages, and so on. In addition, systems can be developed to analyze Web user interactions or dynamically modify Web pages to match user preferences.

Transaction Management

These applications manage online purchases, including storing and tracking of purchases, storing customer billing and shipping information, and tracking backorders.

Giving Your Files and Databases a Home

Hopefully, the previous sections got you thinking about how you might organize your data and integrate it into an information system accessible using Internet technology. Now it's time to select a home for the files and databases at the heart of your large-scale system. As you have seen, there are many ways to organize the data. You can create public files and directories and move files into the directories. Using a database with pointers, you can leave the data where it is and access the distributed data using the database. You can also create a centralized database that follows the blob methodology.

What you want to consider now are the following two questions:

1. Can you use current computer resources?
2. Should you give the data a new home?

Creating or enhancing a Web publishing environment should not require trashing your old hardware or software. To the contrary, a properly designed system should integrate older systems and data. Web client and server software is available for almost every platform you can think of. Generally, the best Web software for you is most likely the software that will run under your favorite operating environment.

If you are currently publishing documents using InterLeaf, Framemaker, TeX, WordPerfect or other document formats on a mini, mainframe, or even an old 286, inexpensive filters exist to turn your documents into Web-browsable formats. You may also be surprised to find that a good use of an old computer is to provide services, such as serving files. While you wouldn't want to use an old computer to serve files in a time-critical environment, that old PC will serve files just fine otherwise.

In a perfect world, you'd go to the nearest computer store and buy the latest and greatest computer to store your data on. In a less-than-perfect world, you have to worry about many things. Before you give your files and databases a home, you must decide whether to use computer resources currently available within the company or to purchase new equipment. The issues that can help you make this decision include

- The costs involved
- Friendliness of the interface
- Suitability of existing computer hardware for database operations
- Security
- User training requirements

> **NOTE**
>
> Often, servers and clients used in Web publishing systems will have different needs. As you read through the following sections, think in terms of both your client and server needs.

Cost

Web Publishing systems are available at a wide range of costs. While some systems include a wide range of capabilities at an all-inclusive cost, other systems offer separate system elements at a lower individual cost. The best Web publishing systems are commercial products that cost from $250 to $2000. Typically, the more features the system includes the more it costs, but this isn't always so.

Some readers may think that they are limited to a PC running Microsoft Windows, but this just isn't so. Check out Sun, DEC, SGI, and HP for reasonably priced systems that can significantly boost your capabilities. These systems can also run Windows using emulation software. You can also run Sun Solaris (UNIX), SCO Unix, or Linux (UNIX) on an Intel-based PC. Overall costs are comparable.

You can also find Web publishing systems on the Internet for free. For example, your Web publishing system could consist of a UNIX server running NCSA HTTPD and Windows clients using NCSA Mosaic. Both of NCSA HTTPD and NCSA Mosaic are free as long as you use them within the guidelines specified in the license agreement.

Friendliness of the Interface

Generally, a user-friendly interface increases productivity. As most users and administrators will be accessing the company data remotely from a work station, you will want to ensure your Web publishing system includes clients with GUI interfaces. The days of typing cryptic text on a command line are not gone yet, but Graphical User Interfaces (GUIs) have become the norm on most operating systems.

The most common GUI known to most users is the Microsoft Windows interface. Windows insulates users from the underlying operating system. All mainstream RISC-based hardware vendors have a GUI that overlays the UNIX operating system. Additionally, all mainstream hardware vendors have agreed to support a standard Common Desktop Environment (CDE) to ensure that applications maintain a consistent look and feel across all platforms.

As you can see, various operating systems can be used in your publishing environment. Silicon Graphics produces hardware and software well recognized for superlative multimedia presentations on UNIX workstations. Complex 3-D modeling applications for producing VRML information may reside on a Sun Microsystems, Hewlett Packard, or Digital Equipment Corporation UNIX Workstation. Finally, PC systems running DOS and Windows or Windows NT provide excellent document processing capabilities. The point here is not to advocate any one system over another, but rather to illustrate the wide range of options available to meet your Web publishing needs.

Suitability for Database Operations

If you have a database or plan to build a database, the client/server interface of the database is the lynch pin. While database applications of some sort are available for every operating system on the market, within the context of Web publishing a database suitable for multiple users and multitasking is generally required. Furthermore, clients must be able to access the database using the company-adopted operating systems. If there isn't a client that can access the database you plan to use or adopt and you can't write the gateway interface, you should choose another database system.

Security

Security of the Web publishing system generally refers to capabilities that will prevent unauthorized access to both the system and data associated with the system. For purposes of Web publishing in large multiuser environments, C2-level security is generally preferred whether sensitive data will be used or not.

The requirements for a C2 secure system are defined by the U.S. National Security Agency's National Computer Security Center (NCSC) in the publication *Trusted Computer System Evaluation Criteria*, also known as the *Orange Book*.

Some of the more salient requirements of C2-level security that should be considered by Web Publishers include

- Discretionary Access Control. The owner of a resource (such as a file) must be able to control access to the resource.
- Auditing. System administrators must be able to audit security-related events and the actions of individual users. Access to this audit data must be limited to authorized administrators.

- Object Re-use. The operating system must protect data stored in memory for one process so that it is not reused by other processes. This protection must also extend to the disk, monitor, keyboard, mouse, and any other devices.

- Identification and Authentication. Each user must uniquely identify him/herself. The system must be able to use this unique identification to track the activities of the user.

NOTE

All mainstream commercial UNIX systems (such as Sun Solaris, HPUX, IBM AIX, and DEC OSF) are C2-compliant. Windows 3.1 and 95 are not C2-compliant, but Windows NT is (despite claims to the contrary by Novell).

User Training Requirements

Creating or enhancing a Web publishing environment may require training, depending on the new capabilities incorporated. The applications you would like to use, and their ease-of-use, need to be considered together with the operating system before you make any final choices. While training is a significant cost factor too frequently ignored in systems evaluation, you should also consider the training-related cost-savings Web publishing offers. Instead of spending six weeks learning the ins and outs of the company database, new employees spend three hours learning how to point, click, and submit queries with a Web client.

TIP

Initial cost is deceptive. A $200 publishing package that takes a $50,000 per year technical writer four weeks to master is actually twice as expensive as a $1000 package that only takes a week to learn. Do the math, and show it to your procurement people before they do you any "favors."

A Brief Walk-Through of a Large-Scale Web Publishing System Implementation

This chapter has covered the basic building blocks for creating and managing a large-scale Web publishing environment to support a company-wide information structure. The final steps and associated issues are critical to the successful implementation and maintenance of the system:

- Building the Web publishing system
- Administering the system

Building the Web Publishing System

By now you may know what type of platforms you plan to install server and client software on. If you do, you're ready to begin the installation process. You may be amazed at how easy it is to get the client and server running now that the major decisions as to the platform and software are behind you. Although commercial software is nearly trouble-free and includes automatic installation processes, freeware software is not a bad way to go either.

Most of the Web server and client software packages you'll find on the Internet are compressed. Although the type of compression really depends on the platform for which the software was designed, the installation instructions will usually explain how to uncompress the software. Before uncompressing the software, you should create a new directory and move the file to that directory for unpacking. Uncompress the software, if necessary, and then start the installation process. You may be prompted to enter the domain name you selected earlier or be directed to add the domain name to a system file.

Each type of Web server or client software has different configuration steps. The best source for configuration information is the online documentation at the site from which you obtained the software. Read the documentation thoroughly. If the documentation isn't clear on an area that involves security, you should follow the strictest security option.

Configuring commercial software is a simple process. After starting the installation process, you either select configuration options or make simple adjustments to your system. At some point during this process, you'll be asked to input the domain name you have selected.

For freeware software, you may have to spend some extra time editing configuration files. However, the cost savings is usually worth the extra effort. The seven basic steps of the software installation process are

1. Purchase or download the software.
2. Begin the installation process by compiling the software or selecting installation options after initiating the automatic installation process.
3. Configure the software, or select automatic configuration options.
4. Ensure that all the files are in the locations specified in the documentation and that permissions are set correctly. This is usually an automatic process for commercial and freeware software, but it doesn't hurt to be safe.
5. Start the server software.
6. Start the client software.
7. Test the server and the client.

Administering the System

Someone should be assigned to administer the new Web publishing system. Although the network administrator or system administrator could easily take over the additional responsibilities, administrative duties don't have to be the responsibility of one person. As you'll see, it is sometimes a good idea to share these responsibilities.

There are four general administrative duties:

- Fielding user questions
- Checking logs
- Keeping the system running
- Updating the system

Fielding User Questions

The company should have points of contact for answering user questions. User questions will be either general or technical in nature. General user questions stem most from insufficient training. If the users aren't trained on the use of the system, they won't know how to use the system.

Technical questions are normally directed to the Webmaster, an electronic mail alias providing a point of contact for the system. Users can direct queries or comments to the Webmaster. A mail alias is a generic mail address that can be assigned to a single user or group of users. The Webmaster can be a single person, your system administrator, or many people who answer specific types of questions. The mail address for the Webmaster is typically webmaster@yourcompany.com.

Checking Logs

Checking system logs should be the responsibility of one person. Logs are created on server software, which can include file servers, database servers, and Web servers that support the company information structure. There are different types of logs. The most important log is the server's error log. The error log keeps track of system problems. Another important log is the access log. The access log tracks who accessed what documents.

If the system seems sluggish or is experiencing problems, the first place the administrator should look is in the error log. The error log will tell the administrator what has been going wrong, and repeated entries will provide an excellent time-picture of the problem. The error log also tracks bad links and bad HTML documents. If you search through the log for these problems, you will be able to identify problem documents and erroneous links.

The access log is another good log for the administrator to check periodically. This log tracks who accessed what documents. The accesses to documents can be critically important in tracking down security violators and suspicious system activity. The access log will also come in handy when you want to count the number of accesses to your site or accesses to particular pages at your site.

Keeping the System Running

The most critical administrative duty is keeping the system running. Just as someone is responsible for the operational status of other network systems, someone must be responsible for the operational status of the Web publishing system. While this responsibility will usually rest on one person's shoulders, the scope of the system generally crosses responsibility areas. For example, database administrators generally maintain the databases, and network administrators generally maintain the network.

Updating the System

The Web system's administrator should ensure that the software and tools are kept up-to-date. Most Web software is under constant development. The most recent version will probably run more efficiently and include new features.

The responsibility of publishing, maintaining, and ensuring the accuracy of Web documents should not rest on the shoulders of the Web server administrator. Although network publishing is understandably a cooperative process between the administrator and department personnel, the administrator should be responsible for technical problems and not content. The administrator is there to answer questions and help with the general network publishing process if need be—and not to create documents for every department within the organization.

Large organizations should assign the additional duty of creating and maintaining Web documents to appropriate personnel in each major department that will network publish. Often, the logical choice for this additional duty is the person who was responsible for creating and disseminating these documents under the old mechanism for distribution.

Network Publishing on Your New Web-Based Information System

Network publishing on your new Web-based information system may at times be frustrating. This is especially true when you are first trying to install and configure the system. The important thing to remember is that network publishing can pay off in huge dividends. The time and money savings for network publishing company user and technical manuals alone make network publishing worthwhile. Not only can the documentation be maintained so that it is always up-to-date at a cost less than the original publishing and distribution of the manuals, but employees can search the entire text of manuals in an instant and at the touch of a button.

While network publishing can bring dramatic improvements in the accessibility of information within the company, part of the problem with any project is that people often have unrealistic expectations or mismatched perceptions. The process of setting up your network publishing operation is no exception. The best thing you can do is to remember the following:

> **Building and managing a Web-based information system is a learning process.** This is your first Web-based information system. It should be a learning process. Do not expect all the pieces to fall into place in a day. It simply will not happen. Give yourself and the project a fighting chance. Manage your expectations to help the project become a success and always keep in mind that your expectations may not match the expectations of your superiors. To avoid problems, be sure to keep the communication channels open between you and your superiors.

> **Go one step at a time.** Never let your thoughts about the complexity of the project overwhelm you. Your perceptions about the project play a decisive role in whether you will ever finish the project. Convince yourself you can do this.

> Often, people forget that sometimes you need to take a breather. You cannot possibly try to do everything all at once. Set up your network publishing operation one step at a time. Begin by planning your course of action, and slowly progress from platform selection to installation.

> **Set realistic goals.** One of the first things you should do is make sure that your goals are realistic. Your goals should take into account both the complexities of the project and the possible setbacks. Your goals should be clear and relevant to the problem at hand: setting up a Web-based information system that involves client and server software. As you set goals and milestones for each stage of the project, remember to provide flexibility. Never give yourself deadlines you cannot meet. If possible, give yourself a window for project completion.

> **Adopt a company-wide policy.** When you complete the project, remember to adopt a company-wide policy pertaining to the use and publishing of information on the network. The key is to not only adopt a policy, but to communicate it throughout the organization.

Summary

Building and managing a Web-based information system for the company could be the best career move you ever made. Network publishing is an extremely cost-effective and time-saving way to publishing company documents. As explained in this chapter, there are many issues you should consider before you begin. Weigh those decisions carefully, and make the right decisions for the right reasons.

Designing Web Documents Using Your Favorite Word Processor

16

by William Robert Stanek, Gregory Stenstrom, Richard Tuttle, and Sandra Tuttle

IN THIS CHAPTER

Creating new Web documents can be an exciting process. The right choice of Web publishing tools can make a tremendous difference in producing a professional product. Even with the increasing number of multimedia options available for Web publishing, simple text and text-based media remain at the heart of Web publishing. After all, the markup tags used to create HTML, SGML, and VRML documents are coded with text.

A wide array of options exist for creating new documents and for converting your old document formats to HTML. Aside from a basic knowledge of HTML and the extended options available with various browsers such as Netscape, you should also be aware of the methods available to implement this knowledge. You could certainly learn all of the available HTML tags and all the special extensions of a targeted browser and type them in by hand. But do you really want to continue "roughing it" with nothing but a flat-file text editor and a tattered HTML reference as your only ally? Should you give up the composition capabilities inherent in the document tools you're currently using and switch to a flashy HTML editor such as HoTMetaL Pro?

The good news is that if you're an expert in Word, WordPerfect, InterLeaf, FrameMaker, TeX, or another commercially proven product, you may not have to abandon it. The simple fact is most Web publishers create their Web documents in the comfort of their favorite word processor, and this chapter shows you how you can, too.

Basic Word Processors Versus Advanced Word Processors

Web publishers use many types of word processors to create Web documents. A word processor is really a text editor with fancy features, like spelling and grammar checking. Using a word processor, such as Microsoft Word, you have advanced control over all aspects of the documents. You can easily manipulate and format text. You can create macros to carry out a series of editor functions for you automatically. You can create rich document formats with multiple columns, bullets, headings, and much more. You can also integrate documents from other programs as objects, such as a figure to be printed with the main document.

Interestingly enough, if you asked hard-core Web publishers what type of word processor they use, you'd probably find that while some use commercial word processors, many use basic text editors, like the one built into DOS systems or the UNIX vi editor. Yet if you've ever used the DOS editor or vi, you may be wondering why in the world would anyone prefer such a basic editor over FrameMaker or Microsoft Word?

As it so happens, my favorite text editor for UNIX environments is vi. Primarily this is because the vi editor is a basic part of most UNIX systems and when all else fails, I can be fairly certain I can access documents using vi. Yet it is also because vi has many built-in features that can be accessed using simple key combinations. Once you learn these key combinations, you will find they are actually easier and faster to use than using a mouse to click on a button. For example, the period is the most useful vi editor command. In command mode, you push the period key to repeat the last action you performed. If you use Microsoft Word, you can use the F4 key to repeat the last action as well.

As you learn more and more of these key combinations, you will find that you prefer the key combinations over mouse controls. Why use the mouse to access the edit menu in Microsoft Word and then have to click on Repeat Last Action when all you have to do is push F4? As you can see, even advanced functions of word processors with powerful graphic interfaces are often reduced to basic functions you'd find in a plain-jane text editor. Consequently, your word processor of choice for creating Web publications will probably be the one you know the most about and feel the most comfortable using.

Using Basic Word Processing Features to Create Web Documents

You can use a text-based means to create Web publications no matter the final format. This is true whether you plan to create HTML, SGML, VRML or Java-enhanced documents. The simple fact is that you markup Web documents with text and can type the <P> tag just as fast as you can use the graphical interface of a fancy HTML editor to add the tag to your document. To show you just how easy it is to create Web publications using a word processor, I'm going to give you an inside look at how I create the Web pages for the *Internet Daily News*.

> **NOTE**
>
> *Internet Daily News*, a publication of the company I founded, The Virtual Press, is a project I launched in late 1995 as part of my commitment to provide free community services to Internet users. Currently, the newspaper is being published on a six-month trial to test the long-term feasibility of such a project. This test period will end in June 1996; you can join the 25,000+ Net surfers who visit IDN daily by pointing your browser at
>
> `http://tvp.com/idn/`
>
> The mirror site for the paper is maintained at
>
> `http://www.tvpress.com/idn/`

Columnists for the paper submit their columns several weeks ahead of the publication date. Using a gateway script that filters my e-mail, I organize the columns automatically by issue. The result of this filtering process is a single file containing all the text for a particular issue of the paper. After spell checking, grammar checking, and editing the column text, I am ready to markup the document for publishing. The general steps for getting the text ready for publication include

- Reformatting the text
- Creating a text column
- Prepublishing to test for possible problems

Reformatting the Text

My word processor of choice on my home office PC is Microsoft Word. Figure 16.1 shows the column text before reformatting. As you can see, paragraph returns don't line up, the text has extra spaces—it definitely needs some HTML tags. The only formatting for the columns so far is that column headings are separated from column text with a double space and all extra lines between paragraphs have been removed. This was done during the editing process.

FIGURE 16.1.

The original text before reformatting.

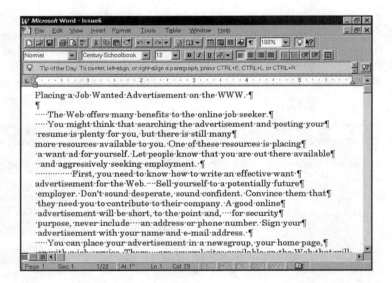

The first step to reformatting the text into a Web-publishable format is to ensure the integrity of paragraphs in the columns are maintained. I ask all writers to use the `<P>` tag to designate the beginning of paragraphs. Sometimes they forget and use the old standard of five spaces to indicate the beginning of a paragraph. Using Word's search and replace mechanism, I search for all occurrences of five spaces and replace them with the `<P>` tag.

Next, I reformat the text into easy-to-read paragraphs. Initially, I replace paragraph markers with tabs. In Microsoft Word, you can do this by entering ^p in the find dialogue box and ^t in the replace dialogue box. Afterward, I replace all occurrences of two tabs with a paragraph marker. This ensures the column headings are separated from the jumbled column text. Then I replace all remaining occurrences of the tab character with a single space and all occurrences of <P> with ^p<P>. This puts a paragraph return between all the paragraphs of text. Next, I delete extra spaces by replacing all occurrences of two spaces with nothing. You can do this simply by entering two spaces in the find dialog box and putting nothing in the replace box. Sometimes it takes two or more complete searches through the document to erase all the extra spaces. The result of this is shown in Figure 16.2.

FIGURE 16.2.

Reformatted text nearly ready for Web publishing.

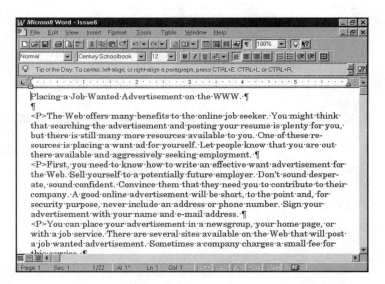

If you're wondering why I delete extra spaces and paragraph returns when HTML browsers will ignore them, keep reading. To make the text more visually appealing and easier to read, the plan is to create a single column of text that uses the screen space to enhance the page.

While all this manipulation of the text may sound like a lot of work, the process only takes about 10 minutes to reformat the entire text of the current issue of the paper. If you've used Word macros before, you probably know that this could easily be automated, which is exactly what I did after plotting out the steps necessary to format the text. Now, one click of a macro button reformats everything for me in about 30 seconds.

Creating a Text Column

To create a single column of text that uses the screen space to enhance the page, I need to add markup tags that break the text into a column. First, I increase the size of the left and right margins to 2 inches, effectively reducing the usable page area to 3 × 11 inches. With Microsoft Word, you can set the page margins using the Page Setup submenu. Then, I save the document as text only with line breaks. Even the most basic word processors generally let you save your document as text only with line breaks. If you're trying this on your computer, close the current document and open the document that you saved in text only format. The format of your document should be similar to the one shown in Figure 16.3.

FIGURE 16.3.

Text-only document saved with line breaks.

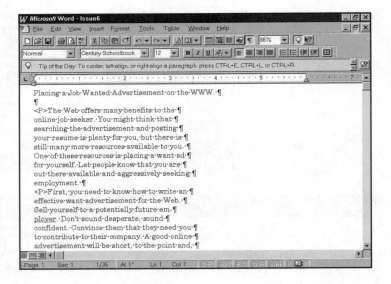

The next step is to replace all occurrences of the paragraph marker with a <BR> tag and the paragraph marker. The <BR> tag inserts a line break into an HTML document. In Microsoft Word, you can do this by entering ^p in the find dialogue box and
^p in the replace dialogue box. The result of this search and replace operation is shown in Figure 16.4.

FIGURE 16.4.

Adding line breaks to the document.

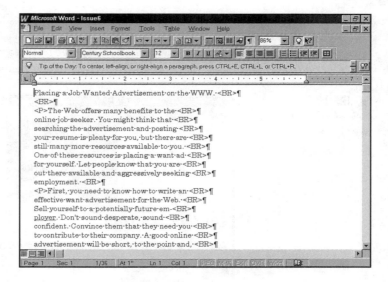

Prepublishing to Test for Possible Problems

At this stage, you should preview the document in an HTML browser. The first step is to save the document as text only with an `.htm` or `.html` extension. Then you should access the file in your favorite browser. Based on what you see, you may want to make minor changes to the text to ensure the column is nicely formatted. This usually means hyphenating large words so they split evenly or moving a word from one line to the next. Figure 16.5 shows how the document is displayed using Microsoft's Internet Explorer.

FIGURE 16.5.

Preview of the document using Internet Explorer.

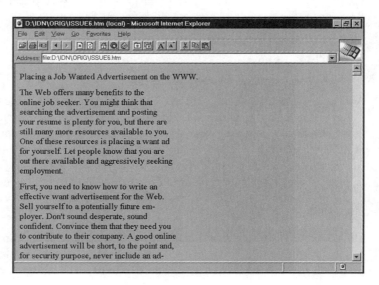

Once the alignment of the column is satisfactory, you can enter any additional HTML markup tags, such as those that add headings, italics, or bold to the text. You can also add any hypertext references to images or other files. What I do is to merge the text into existing templates for the individual *Internet Daily News* columns. The result is shown in Figure 16.6.

FIGURE 16.6.

Finished column for IDN's online job hunt.

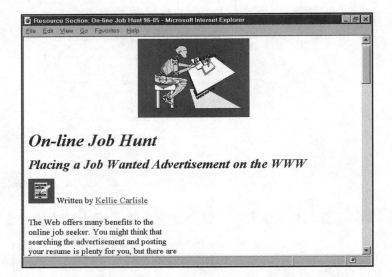

Using HTML Add-ons for Word Processors

Helper applications are the key to publishing on the Web. Chapter 10, "HTML ToolKit: Browsers, Editors, and Converters," discusses the basic types of HTML helper applications:

- HTML converters
- HTML editors
- HTML templates for word processors

Although the task of creating HTML code is fairly complex, some helper applications called *converters* try to automate the task. HTML converters convert your favorite document formats into HTML code and vice versa. At the touch of a button, you could transform a Word for Windows file into an HTML document. Converters are especially useful if you're converting simple documents and are less useful when you're converting documents with complex layouts. (Converting your existing documents created in your word processor is the subject of the next section, titled "Converting Your Word Processor's Document Format to a Web-Usable Format.")

HTML editors have features similar to your favorite word processor and enable you to easily create documents in HTML format. Typically, these editors enable you to select tags from a pulldown menu. The menu has brief descriptions of elements you can add to the document.

The editor places the tags in the document in the proper format, which frees you from having to memorize the format. When creating complex forms, you'll find HTML editors especially useful. But why should you switch to an HTML editor, when you feel right at home in your favorite word processor?

Enter HTML templates. HTML templates could be considered a subset of HTML editors. After all, they enable you to add the functionality of an HTML editor to your favorite word processor. The great thing about templates is that you can use all the word processor's features, which could include checking grammar and spelling. More importantly, you'll be using the familiar features of your word processor to add HTML formatting to your documents.

HTML templates for word processors and text editors are starting to come into widespread use. This is especially true for Microsoft Word. HTML document templates for MS Word 2.0, MS Word 6.0, and Word for Windows 95 are available from a variety of sources.

> ### TIP
>
> A great document template for MS Word 2.0 is CU_HTML, which you can find on the Web at CERN's Web site:
>
> `http://info.cern.ch/hypertext/WWW/Tools/cu_html.html`
>
> Two of the best document templates available for MS Word 6.0 and Word for Windows 95 are Internet Assistant and HTML author. Both templates are freeware and are discussed in Chapter 10.

If you want to add functionality to your word processor and obtain the push-button ease of an HTML editor, I highly recommend using HTML templates. The primary reason for this is that by using an HTML template in your word processor you will be in a familiar environment. You won't have to spend days or weeks learning how to use a new tool. And you won't be frustrated when you try to perform familiar functions only to find the HTML editor doesn't support them.

The primary strength of using mainstream, commercial word processors is that you can keep the environment and functionality you are used to. For example, if you use the Revision Control and Markup features of Word, you can incorporate these capabilities into your Web publishing process.

Other strengths of products in this genre include flexibility and relative immunity to changing standards. Being able to change templates while leaving the core word processing functionality intact is an important cost consideration. Likewise, the HTML standard continues to evolve. Tying yourself to a product too closely coupled with a particular HTML version is not recommended. In an SGML environment, you may need to use multiple DTDs or switch between DTDs. Upgrading your template is certainly preferable to upgrading an entire product suite. You are also protected from waiting for an upgrade while the rest of the world moves forward.

The capability to read an HTML or SGML file and open it in your chosen publishing environment is important when you have multiple authors using different tools. Making this capability a requirement thins the competition considerably. Standards enforcement varies from product to product, depending on the developer's interpretation. It is not uncommon for an HTML 2.0-compliant program to detect errors in documents produced by another such program, and vice versa. The key to protecting yourself from this problem is to select products that are robust enough to ignore or correct "errors."

> **TIP**
>
> Word processors that won't read a noncompliant document and simply reply "Error in file—Cannot open" should be regarded with caution. This is evidence of poor programming; a good program contains fault-tolerant code. Because products are constantly being fixed and upgraded, to find out how robust a product is before you purchase it, check out current reviews on the Web.

Converting Your Word Processor's Document Format to a Web-Usable Format

Being able to convert your word processor's document format to a Web-usable document format saves time, especially if you plan to re-use existing documents. The good news is that commercial word processors such as Word, WordPerfect, InterLeaf, FrameMaker, and TeX can all create documents in a format that can be reformatted for the Web. The bad news is that sometimes you have to convert documents to an intermediate format such as PostScript. Once the file is in the PostScript format, you can integrate it with an Adobe product to create a document in Adobe's Portable Document Format. A growing number of Web published documents are in PDF format.

The PDF is one example of an alternative to HTML. As discussed earlier in this book, HTML is based on a specific SGML Document Type Definition (DTD). Other DTDs are also available, or waiting to be written, to meet your needs. There are many mature SGML products from which to choose. New and improved products for the Web are announced every month. Common Ground is one example of a new environment that provides a balanced suite of tools to create Web documents.

As detailed in Chapter 10, tools for converting your documents to Web publications abound. Converters basically enable you to compose data in one format and convert your data to another format. Various implementations of converter technology have been applied effectively to create Web documents using software products not originally intended for this purpose.

This is not a new concept. When you send a document to a printer, the document is converted into a format the printer understands. For example, when you write a document using Microsoft Word, Word's file format stores not only content, but also formatting commands. When you print the document, a print driver (or Word itself) converts the document's content and formatting commands into a format your printer understands, such as PostScript (PS) or Encapsulated PostScript.

Most word processing programs can also create a print file and store it to disk. The programs and filters associated with this process are similar to the filters used to create Web-formatted documents. Figure 16.7 shows the conversion process.

FIGURE 16.7.

Document conversion from native format to Web format.

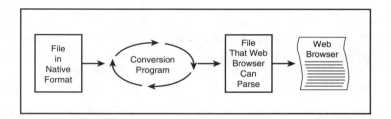

There are many ways to apply filter methods to your Web publishing solution. Theoretically, a Web document can be generated from any formatted document. Programs can be written to search for key characteristics and to replace them with a Web formatting tag. Even a flat text file can be *parsed* in this way by searching for things like line breaks, headings denoted by Roman numerals, single lines of text, and so on. If you have a large cache of consistently formatted documents, you may want to investigate writing a custom conversion program to prepare them for the Web.

However, the mapping between a non-Web document's native formatting and the target Web format (HTML, SGML, and so on) must be consistent. The feasibility of using a custom program diminishes when the original documents have different internal structures.

TIP

Although developing custom software can be an expensive option, this is not always the case. A myriad of inexpensive options for processing documents exists. Developing a program to convert a consistently formatted set of files to a format like HTML is relatively straightforward. In some cases, scripting languages like sed and awk may fulfill your needs. Other options include using the macro capabilities of most commercially available word processors to insert Web tags into your documents.

Microsoft Word's use of *document templates* (DOT files) lends itself well to filter and conversion routines. By following a well-defined template when creating a Word document, and thus maintaining a consistent structure, you can easily convert the Word formatting codes to Web format codes. Methods of converting a Word document to Web format include using macros to replace and insert Web formatted tags prior to saving a document, or running a conversion program on the Word file after saving it.

In either case, this type of conversion involves *post processing,* meaning that you must check the document for accuracy after using the converter. Standard Web-formatting errors are detected only after you edit your document. Having to recheck and possibly reprocess your documents after using a converter is characteristic of all filter-based document technologies.

One way to recheck documents is to simply display them in your Web browser and ensure everything is displayed as it should be. You can also use a program that checks the documents for accuracy, such as Quarterdeck's WebAuthor. Figure 16.8 shows the first window that appears in WebAuthor when you launch it from Word. As you can see, WebAuthor has a specific setting for opening HTML documents created in Microsoft Word.

FIGURE 16.8.

*Quarterdeck WebAuthor
initial window.*

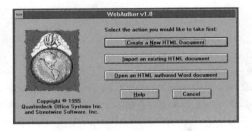

If you select Open an HTML authored Word document, and then select the filename of your document, WebAuthor opens the file. As it opens the file, it checks the consistency of the document to ensure it is properly formatted HTML. While WebAuthor won't catch all errors, it will catch most of the conversion errors. Figure 16.9 depicts the type of errors WebAuthor reports if it finds poorly formatted HTML code.

What WebAuthor has actually flagged as "bad syntax" is the #char notation. Is WebAuthor wrong? Well, the error as reported is somewhat misleading, but still useful if you take into consideration that the error was found while parsing for HTML tags. WebAuthor interpreted the special character # within the <A HREF...</A> as noncompliant. What you need to do is move forward with your work by selecting one of the three options Quarterdeck provides you: remove the tag, edit it and reparse, or exit. Ignoring the "error" is not an option in this case because of the validation criteria built into WebAuthor.

The validation of Web documents after conversion is an essential post-processing activity. This fact can significantly impact costs in converting a large number of documents, even when small discrepancies are found *after* a document has been converted.

FIGURE 16.9.
*QuarterDeck WebAuthor
parse error window.*

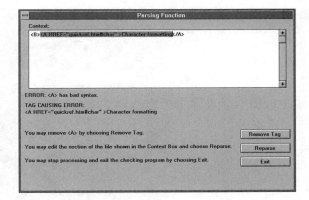

Up to this point, the chapter has covered mostly converters for Microsoft Word. Again, a large number of converters exist to handle the output of almost every word processing environment. Products like InterLeaf, FrameMaker, and other top-end publishing environments either offer HTML filter and conversion programs or access to third-party providers of such programs.

Finally, two notable applications that make conversion from word processor formats to Web-usable formats easier are the Adobe Acrobat and Common Ground product suites.

The Adobe Acrobat suit of products includes a number of programs for creating and displaying portable documents in Adobe's PDF format. Two key programs in this product suite are Adobe Exchange and Adobe Distiller. Adobe Exchange and Adobe Distiller were originally developed to convert PostScript files to electronic hypertext documents; they are now being integrated into Web publishing environments with hypertext PDF files as the target end product. Their ability to more closely approximate a magazine format than HTML or SGML is a strong point that has attracted many mainstream publishers. An example of the Adobe Acrobat Reader format appears in Figure 16.10.

Common Ground is similar in concept to Adobe Acrobat. Common Ground converts your documents to a Digital Paper (DP) format that can be viewed with their browser called MiniViewer on any platform. You can use any publishing suite you want, and keep all the composition capabilities you are used to. The online Common Ground document shown in Figure 16.11 looks exactly like it would if you printed it, but you can include hypertext links in it. The Common Ground MiniViewer is freely distributed, like the Adobe Acrobat reader, and is catching on quickly on the Web.

Both Adobe Acrobat and Common Ground product suites enable you to use your favorite word processor to create documents and then convert them to their portable document format. For example, if you purchased Adobe Acrobat Pro or Adobe Exchange, you could use the Adobe PDFWriter print utility to convert your word processor documents to PDF documents simply by printing them using PDFWriter. In Microsoft Word, this conversion process is as easy as selecting PDFWriter as your printer when you print a document.

FIGURE 16.10.
*Adobe PDF file displayed
in Acrobat Reader.*

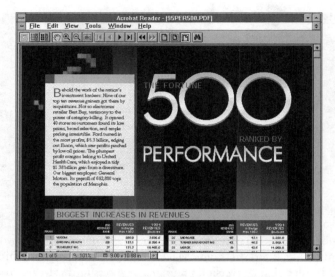

FIGURE 16.11.
*Digital Paper file displayed
in Common Ground.*

NOTE

I like Common Ground's ease-of-use. It works right out of the box and produces browsable documents of exceptional quality. I highly recommended it for publishers who want to get their documents on the Web quickly. Minimal user training is required—I produced my first Common Ground Document one minute after I finished loading (minus links) and was inserting links five minutes later. My only concern was memory requirements (it occasionally locks up my Windows 3.1 system), but I was able to eventually convert even my largest complex documents during stress testing. Impressive.

Summary

Chances are good that your favorite word processor has powerful features that you don't want to abandon. Not only can you save time when you use a familiar word processing environment, but you can also create a better product. The key ways that you can Web-publish using your favorite word processor are

- Use the basic features of your word processor to mark up Web documents
- Use templates for word processors to mark up Web documents
- Convert your word processor's document format to a Web-usable format

Other Document Systems

17

*by William
Robert Stanek,
Gregory Stenstrom,
Richard Tuttle,
and Sandra Tuttle*

IN THIS CHAPTER

As emphasized throughout this book, markup languages are becoming very advanced. You can create powerfully interactive publications with HTML, SGML, and VRML, but generally, the complexity of your documents is restricted by the features of the markup language you use. Currently, no markup language provides you with total control over page layout so you can achieve a Hot Wired-print-edition effect online. This is where document systems come into play. Document systems provide you with total control over the structure of pages, enabling you to create advanced magazine-style documents.

This chapter begins by defining what is meant by document systems. As you will see, the terms associated with document systems are sometimes misleading. Next, the chapter features previews of popular document systems. This is followed by an in-depth review of what is quickly becoming the most popular document system, Common Ground.

Defining Document Systems

Two key categories of document systems are page layout systems and portable document systems. Although the makers of page layout systems and portable document systems try to distinguish themselves from each other, a portable document system is really a page layout system with an extra feature.

The term *page layout system* is used loosely throughout the book to refer to advanced computer applications that enable you to create highly structured pages. One of the best-known page layout systems is FrameMaker. With FrameMaker, you can create highly structured documents that include hypertext links.

A recent trend in document systems is the capability to create portable documents in electronic formats that are complete with hypertext capabilities; such portable documents are the wave of the future. Two of the best applications for creating portable documents are Common Ground and Adobe Acrobat.

While Common Ground and Adobe Acrobat are praised as portable document solutions, the only real difference between them and a traditional page layout system, such as FrameMaker, is the availability of a program called a reader. If you have the Common Ground reader, you can view documents in Common Ground's Digital Paper format. If you have the Adobe Acrobat reader, you can view documents in Adobe Acrobat's Portable Document Format.

Adobe Acrobat

Adobe Acrobat is probably a very familiar document system. Its features were discussed briefly in the previous chapter. Acrobat presents magazine-quality documents to users across multiple platforms using the Portable Document Format. PDF is basically an extension of Encapsulated Postscript format with the ability to use hypertext linking. All you need to view PDF files is the Adobe Acrobat reader, which is currently available for

DOS
Macintosh
SGI
Sun SPARC and HP UNIX platforms
Windows

Adobe Acrobat is a family of products. While the most comprehensive publishing solution is offered by Adobe Acrobat Pro, the best value is Adobe Acrobat Exchange. With a retail price of $150, Adobe Acrobat Exchange represents a substantial cost savings over Acrobat Pro, which retails for nearly $600. Most Web publishers will find that Adobe Acrobat Exchange enables them to do everything they would like to do with Adobe's PDF documents. For that reason, this section focuses on Adobe Acrobat Exchange and an extension of Adobe Acrobat Exchange called Adobe Amber.

Adobe Acrobat Exchange

Adobe Acrobat Exchange enables you to create documents in Adobe's PDF format. Using Exchange, you can view, print, annotate, build navigational links into, and add security controls to PDF files. Adobe Acrobat Exchange includes an extremely useful print utility called Adobe PDFWriter. In your word processor, you can use PDFWriter as your printer of choice, which will create a PDF document. Another reason to purchase Adobe Acrobat Exchange is that you can increase the functionality of applications using free plug-ins available at Adobe's Web site:

`http://www.adobe.com/Acrobat/Plug-Ins/`

Here's a list of some of the free plug-ins.

> **WebLink** enables Acrobat Exchange users to add World Wide Web (URL) links to PDF documents and follow those links to PDF or HTML files anywhere on the Internet.
>
> **SuperCrop** adds a new crop tool to the toolbar that looks and works like the Adobe Photoshop crop tool.
>
> **SuperPrefs** adds new preferences to Acrobat Exchange, such as
>
> - File Open Behavior—Enables you to specify the maximum number of open documents and automatically closes the least recently used document if you try to open more documents than the current limit.
> - Acrobat Always On Top—Makes the Acrobat Exchange window the topmost window at all times.
> - AutoSave Currently Open Docs—Automatically saves open documents when you quit, and the next time you start Acrobat Exchange, the documents will be automatically reopened to the same page and position on-screen.

AutoIndex enables users to set up auto index features.

OLE Server enables Acrobat Exchange to act as an OLE server to view PDF documents embedded in other OLE-capable applications.

Monitor Setup gives users better control over color.

Adobe Amber

Adobe Amber is intended to be an update for owners of Adobe Acrobat Exchange and the free Adobe Acrobat reader. In reality, Amber is an Internet-friendly extension of the reader capabilities of Adobe Acrobat products. Although Amber uses some of the Adobe Exchange plug-ins just described, it also has unique features that make it very Internet-friendly. If you've ever become impatient trying to download a large PDF document and wished there were some way you could preview the document as it was downloading, Amber is what you've been looking for.

By combining the built-in features of Amber with an Amber-friendly Web server, Web users finally can view PDF documents one page at a time as the document is downloaded. The capability that makes Web servers "Amber-friendly" is byteserving, or in other words, the capability to serve a document in byte-sized chunks. The byteserving capability has already been integrated into the Netscape and Open Market server products. Other servers can become Amber-friendly using a CGI script, which Adobe plans to freely distribute.

More good news about Amber is its capability to use URLs within PDF documents. Amber can also be used as a plug-in for the Netscape Navigator 2.0. Currently, Amber is available for free and you can obtain it from

```
http://www.adobe.com/Amber/
```

FrameMaker

FrameMaker is a huge success as the document system of choice of thousands of corporations, educational institutions, and scientific organizations, especially in UNIX environments. Largely, this is because FrameMaker is one of the most advanced document systems available. It is also one of the most expensive document system options; FrameMaker has a retail price of between $900 and $1600 depending on the type of system you are using and the number of licenses purchased. The expense of using FrameMaker as your publishing solution for a distributed networked environment seems astronomical compared to alternatives, primarily because with FrameMaker there is no equivalent reader program and if there were one, you can almost be certain it would not be free.

Without a reader program, FrameMaker is not a portable document solution and is not a good choice for documents you plan to use on the Web—yet there is good news for current users of

FrameMaker or anyone who wants to use this truly powerful document system. Recently, Frame Technology Corporation, the developers of FrameMaker, was acquired by Adobe. This was a move by Adobe to gain a more dominant position in the industry and to increase their foothold in UNIX environments. Because of this acquisition, we may soon see a reader application for FrameMaker or the integration FrameMaker and Adobe products, either of which will make FrameMaker a better choice for your document system.

Until that time, if you are a current user of FrameMaker and want to use your FrameMaker-formatted documents on the Web, you should use a FrameMaker-to-HTML converter. Several FrameMaker-to-HTML conversion products have come on and off the market over the past two years with varying levels of functionality and support. Many of the products were freeware or shareware products that have since faded from the Internet or are in limited use.

An exception is a commercial-grade conversion suite originally developed by CERN and subsequently supported by Harlequin, named WebMaker 2.0. Harlequin's WebMaker 2.0 is an inexpensive Web publishing solution for creating full-featured Web pages from existing FrameMaker documents. It is available for Windows 3.*x* as well as the following UNIX platforms: SUN SunOS 4.1.*x*, SUN Solaris 2.*x*, SGI IRIX 5.2, IBM AIX 3.2, and HP-UX 9.*x*. A Macintosh beta is currently available and a release version should be ready about the same time this book is published.

WebMaker was developed by CERN, the European Laboratory for Particle Physics. CERN developed WebMaker to convert scientific publications written in FrameMaker into HTML format. After WebMaker became available to the public in mid-1994, market demand prompted CERN to select Harlequin to continue the development, supply, and support of WebMaker.

WebMaker 1.4 was a command-line application designed for users running FrameMaker under UNIX. Harlequin has expanded WebMaker's functionality to include graphical user interfaces, as well as a variety of features designed to help make the conversion process easy and effective. The graphical user interface is minimal, but functional enough for a dedicated user.

Basically, the user maps FrameMaker tags to HTML tags through the graphical user interface. Error checking alerts the user to unmapped tags. WebMaker offers very precise control over FrameMaker-to-HTML mapping. In the reviewed version of WebMaker, there are 169 rules pertaining to the formatting of paragraphs. Rules for paragraphs encompass all primary text elements in your documents, including headings, footnotes, and tables.

A sample of a FrameMaker-to-HTML mapping sequence using WebMaker appears in Figures 17.1 and 17.2. Figure 17.1 shows how WebMaker flags undefined rules. Figure 17.2 shows the dialog box you would use to map rules.

FIGURE 17.1.
WebMaker flags undefined rules as errors.

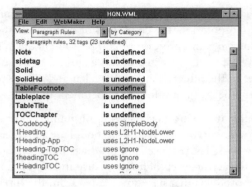

FIGURE 17.2.
Defining the mapping rule for SimpleBody text.

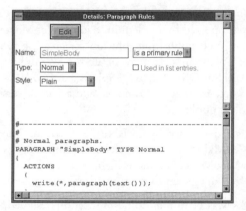

WebMaker 2.1 can be downloaded for evaluation or purchase from the WebMaker pages at Harlequin's WWW site

```
http://www.harlequin.com/webmaker/
```

Using WebMaker, you can

- Convert FrameMaker text to HTML
- Convert FrameMaker tables to HTML 3.0 tables
- Convert all FrameMaker-supported graphic formats to inline GIF format
- Write equations in GIF or HTML 3.0 format
- Customize the conversion process

Although WebMaker 2.0 currently supports only FrameMaker 4, WebMaker 2.1, which will be released by the time this book is published, will work with FrameMaker 5. However, WebMaker 2.1 will not support many new features of FrameMaker 5, such as Import Text by Reference. These new FrameMaker 5 features will be supported in a future release of WebMaker.

TeX

TeX is another document system that enjoys widespread use in corporations, educational institutions, and scientific organizations. One of the most highly regarded features of TeX is its support of advanced mathematical equations. TeX has a highly structured language syntax, which forms the basis of many popular TeX derivatives such as LaTeX. Publishers with TeX conversion requirements should review both TeX-to-LaTeX conversion issues and LaTeX-to-HTML conversion issues before committing to a solution.

LaTeX2HTML is a conversion tool that makes it possible for documents written in LaTeX (or converted from TeX to LaTeX) to be converted into hypertext format using the HTML 2.0 standard. LaTeX2HTML recreates the basic structure of a paper document as a set of interconnected hypertext nodes that can be explored using automatically generated navigation panels. Any defined annotations, such as cross-references, citations, or footnotes, are converted into hypertext links. Special formatting information, such as special font character mappings for mathematical equations, is converted into GIF images that are placed automatically in the hypertext document.

> **NOTE**
>
> The use of imbedded GIF images for converted mathematical equations is required to accurately present the author's intended notations to users. Remember that HTML only parses data, not formatting information.

LaTeX2HTML is being widely used for the preparation of electronic books, documentation, scientific papers, lecture notes, training and coursework material, literate programming tools, bibliographic references, and much more. LaTeX2HTML will run on most UNIX systems, but requires at least Perl Version 4. If you've upgraded to Perl 5, there is a version of LaTeX2HTML compatible with Perl Version 5.

You can get LaTeX2HTML from via ftp from

```
ftp://ftp.tex.ac.uk/pub/archive/support/
```

Common Ground

Common Ground is a family of products for creating portable documents. Common Ground presents magazine-quality documents to users across multiple platforms using the Digital Paper Format. All you need to view DP files is the Common Ground ProViewer or the MiniViewer. The free MiniViewer is currently available for Windows and Macintosh systems. Viewers are also being developed for UNIX platforms.

> **NOTE**
>
> The costs of Adobe Acrobat and Common Ground are competitive. Having used both product suites, I prefer Common Ground's offerings for both ease of document creation and the functionality of its viewers. Both product suites have occasionally "blown up" on me during document conversion. Average-size documents convert without problems in both, and I was also able eventually to create extremely large documents. Product support and online help will play an important part in determining which product you prefer. Therefore, you should visit both the Adobe and Common Ground Software sites on the Web if you are interested in these products.
>
> Adobe's site can be found at
>
> `http://www.adobe.com/`
>
> Common Ground Software's site can be found at
>
> `http://www.commonground.com./`

Common Ground documents can be printed in hard copy form from any system and will look exactly as the author intended. This feature represents a significant advantage over many HTML-based browsers that are still working on printing strategies. Common Ground documents can be distributed as executable (EXE) files on diskettes, CDs, networks, file servers, or by modems or electronic mail. This capability means that many publishers can publish both hard copy and soft copy documents in essentially the same step. It also means that Common Ground documents can be distributed to electronic audiences who are not Web-enabled.

The Common Ground software suite has three parts:

- The Maker
- The ProViewer
- The MiniViewer

The Maker

Common Ground works by taking a document created with any Windows or Macintosh application and converting it into a Digital Paper file. This is done using the application's print capability, with the Common Ground Maker serving as the printer driver. A Common Ground utility called Maker prints your document to a specified disk drive, directory, and filename. The result is a Common Ground document that can be viewed and printed by the Common Ground ProViewer or MiniViewer. If needed, the Maker can combine the document and a MiniViewer into a single executable file, which can be viewed and printed by users even if they do not have Common Ground. The catch is that if you create an executable file on a Windows system, only Windows users will be able to use the file. Similarly, if you create an executable file on a Macintosh system, only Macintosh users will be able to use the file.

### Chapter 17

FIGURE 17.3.

Common Ground Maker window that appears after you select Print.

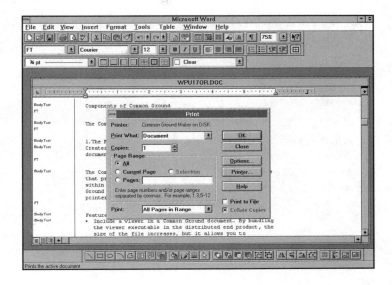

You invoke Maker from an application by selecting the Maker printer driver and executing the Print command. Figure 17.3 shows the Maker's popup Print window.

The Maker has the following features:

- You can include a viewer in a Common Ground document. By bundling the viewer executable in the distributed end product, the size of the file increases, but you can distribute the document to readers who may not have Common Ground. When embedding a viewer, you can choose either the ProViewer, for which you pay a royalty to Common Ground, or the smaller MiniViewer, which can be distributed freely.

- You can select the page size and the page layout and identify specific pages from your document to include in the Common Ground document. Both text and graphics can be included in your Common Ground file.

NOTE

Printing to paper of different sizes can be a problem when distributing page-oriented documents globally. If you have ever tried to print a document prepared for 8.5 × 11-inch paper on A4 paper, you know what I mean. It can be an ordeal. Although many applications enable you to select different paper sizes, the resulting document may not print the way you want it to. Common Ground appears to have anticipated and tested for this problem because I was able to print several test documents on both 8.5 × 11-inch and A4 paper with no problems.

- You can apply JPEG compression to color bitmaps in your document, selecting the quality level you desire (and thus affecting the size of the file).
- If you specify that you wish to view the Common Ground document after creating it, the ProViewer is invoked automatically.

NOTE

Common Ground lists the capability to invoke their product automatically after printing as a feature, but it saves only a click or two of the mouse if you have used the `File Associate` feature in Windows. This capability would be most useful in networked environments where a single copy of Common Ground ProMaker, licensed for multiple users, is mounted on a remote disk and users are not necessarily aware of its location. In such a configuration, this feature would also enable users to associate their DP files with the MiniViewer on their local workstation, rather than with ProMaker.

The ProViewer

The Common Ground ProViewer lets anyone read, search, copy from, and print Common Ground documents. Because the documents contain all their original textual information, you can perform string searches and file search indexing on them. They also contain meta data, which means you can logically group documents or sets of documents. For database-oriented solutions, you can group Common Ground documents readily by class and type to develop comprehensive file retrieval routines.

Figure 17.4 shows a Common Ground brochure in the main window of the ProViewer.

With the ProViewer, you can

- View a Common Ground document and its information.
- Choose one or more Common Ground documents to view, either sequentially or simultaneously. This is a feature not normally available in publishing tools.
- Change the way you look at a document by selecting from multiple viewing options, including Normal View or Single Page View.
- View different parts of a document by using scroll bars, page commands, and a Grabber tool.
- Obtain meta-information about the document that is not included in the textual data.
- Annotate a document with bookmarks, highlights, and "sticky notes," and provide navigation links to move through these annotations.

FIGURE 17.4.

*Common Ground
ProViewer.*

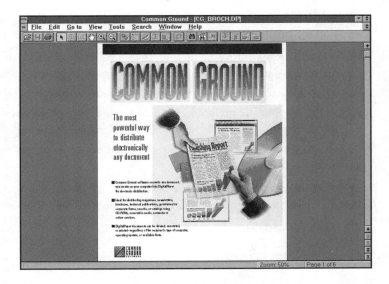

The capability to create annotations and forward them through a production environment is a powerful feature for users who do not have redlining capabilities inherent in their publishing environments. It is particularly useful for moving documents in a common format across organizational boundaries where different publishing tools with different merge or redline-acceptance functionality are used. Common Ground truly lives up to its name in this case.

- Create tables of contents and hypertext links and use these to navigate through documents.
- Select portions of a document and copy them to the Windows clipboard.

The clipboard feature of Common Ground is more useful than the typical Web browser Save (as HTML) or Save as Text feature because formatting data is also included on the clipboard. Since Common Ground maintains the font information with its documents, seamless integration of documents using a common font schema is possible.

■ Print a document from Common Ground to printers enabled in the local environment.

■ Search for text within a document, define collections of Common Ground documents using meta data, and search for text within many document sets.

■ Save the contents of the document in multiple formats.

■ Configure personal preferences to select commonly used commands from a toolbar and view status, page count, and current page on a status bar.

■ View online help that you can use to get information on any command or feature of the ProViewer.

ProViewer includes many useful built-in tools. By exploring how you can use these tools, you can gain a better understanding of Common Ground. These tools include

The Bookmark Tool
The Grabber Tool
The Highlighter Tool
The Hyperlink Tool

In the next section, we explore some of the key features of ProViewer: Navigating with Annotations, Notes, Document Security, Search, and Print.

> **NOTE**
>
> As you read through the following section on ProViewer tools and features, keep in mind that MiniViewer enables you to use most of these as well.

Using the Bookmark Tool

You can use the Bookmark tool to mark a specific location in the document. Once the location is marked, you can return to it at the click of a button. Here's how to use the BookMark tool on a Windows system:

1. Click the Bookmark tool in the toolbar or choose the Bookmark command from the Tools menu.

2. Position the cursor where you want the bookmark to be placed.

3. Click the left mouse button or drag the Bookmark tool to select a region of the document.

4. When the Bookmark Properties dialog box appears, enter a name for the bookmark to override the default name.

5. Click OK. To terminate the Benchmark tool, just select another tool.

Using the Grabber Tool

You can use the Grabber tool to move the current page in any direction. This is useful when the actual page size extends beyond the screen and it is not practical to reduce the zoom level so you can view the entire contents of the page on your screen at one time. To use the Grabber tool on a Windows system, do the following:

1. Choose the Grabber command from the Tools menu or its equivalent icon from the toolbar. When the Grabber tool is active, the mouse cursor changes to a small hand when you move it over the document page.
2. Position the cursor on the page and hold the left mouse button down while moving the mouse. The page moves in the same direction.

When you are finished with the Grabber tool, choose another tool or choose the Pointer command to bring back the normal cursor.

Using the Highlighter Tool

The Highlighter tool can be used like your favorite yellow marker. Using the Highlighter tool, you can highlight key sections of a document. To use the Highlighter tool on a Windows system, do this:

1. Click the Highlighter tool on the toolbar or choose the Highlighter command from the Tools menu.
2. Select an area of the document by holding down the left mouse button and dragging the mouse. To stop highlighting the area, release the left mouse button.

To terminate the Highlighter tool, select another tool.

You can control the highlighting properties of Common Ground by using the Preferences command on the File menu. Choosing this command and clicking the Highlights tab in the Preferences dialog box displays the default properties for highlights.

To change the default color of highlights do the following:

1. Select a highlight in the Navigation Pane by clicking it and choosing the Preferences command from the File menu.
2. Click the Highlights tab to display the defaults for highlights.
   - To change the default color, click the arrow in the Color field to display a drop-down list of colors; select a color. The new color appears when you close the drop-down list.
   - To define a new color, click the Custom Color button and make a selection.
3. Click OK to save the change.

Changing the color affects all highlights that you subsequently create. If you want to change the properties of an existing highlight, use the Annotation Properties command on the Edit menu.

Using the Hyperlink Tool

Using the Hyperlink tool, you can add hypertext links to any document. While Hyperlinks are usually created by the author of a document, they can also be created and used by anyone who wishes to take a nonsequential path through the document. The Common Ground ProViewer displays Hyperlink entries listed one per line in a separate window called the Navigation Pane. Scrollbars appear if the entries do not fit in the Navigation Pane.

Any Hyperlinks you add to a document are saved when you save the document. Closing the document without executing a Save command discards any hyperlinks you added or changed. To display existing hyperlink annotations, choose the Hyperlinks command on the View menu. Figure 17.5 shows the dialog box for creating a hyperlink.

FIGURE 17.5.

Common Ground Hyperlink function.

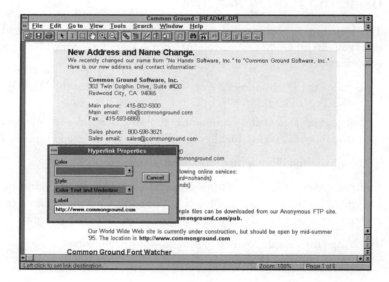

To create a hyperlink:

1. Click the Hyperlink icon on the toolbar or choose the Hyperlink command on the Tools menu. The mouse cursor changes to resemble the icon on the toolbar plus an I-beam. You can change the I-beam to a marquee by clicking the right mouse button.

2. Drag the cursor over the area in the document that you want to be the starting point or source of the hyperlink.

3. Release the mouse button.

The Hyperlink Properties dialog box appears, with the default color displayed in the Color field and a choice of styles in the drop-down list box. If the area you selected contains text, it appears in the Label field.

- To change the color for this hyperlink, click the arrow and select another color.
- To select a style, click the arrow in the Styles field and make a selection from the drop-down list.
- To change the label of this hyperlink, edit the text in the Label field.

4. Move the mouse cursor out of the dialog box. Notice that the cursor now has an arrow in it to indicate that you are to select the destination for the hyperlink.

5. Find the location in the document that you wish to specify as the destination for the link; click the left mouse button to create the link.

6. Repeat this process to create additional hyperlinks.

Using Annotations to Navigate a Document

Common Ground considers any additional markup in a document to be an annotation. Categories of annotations include

- Bookmarks
- Highlights
- Hyperlinks
- Notes
- Table of Contents

You can use annotations to navigate through a Common Ground document. Such annotations are displayed in a side window called the Navigation Pane. The Navigation Pane is placed alongside the primary window that displays the document's contents.

When you select one of the annotations in the hot list, ProViewer moves to the section of the document containing the annotation. ProViewer can also build a list as you navigate through a document and thus "remember" where each previous step led you. This feature is similar to typical Web browser's Go Back capabilities. You can retrace your steps by using the Go Back icon on the toolbar or the Go Back command on the Go To menu.

To navigate via annotations using the Navigation Pane take these steps:

1. Display the desired annotation Navigation Pane by selecting one from the View menu. For example, to view the Bookmarks Navigation Pane, choose the Bookmarks command from the View menu.

2. By double-clicking on an entry, the associated annotation in the document is displayed near the center of the display.

To navigate via annotations using menu commands, use the Next or Previous commands on the Go To menu to traverse the annotations in the document. You can specify the next or previous highlight, hyperlink, note, or other type of annotation. When located, the annotation is positioned near the center of the Document Pane. From there, you can

■ Choose one of the Next commands to search for the next instance of an annotation, starting with the current selection (text, annotation, area, and so forth) or the top of the current page (if nothing is selected).

■ Choose one of the Previous commands to search for the previous instance of an annotation, starting with the current selection (text, annotation, area, and so forth) or the top of the current page (if nothing is selected).

Using Notes

A note is text that the reader creates and "sticks" on the document. It is not an actual part of the document text. Notes are typically created by readers of the document who wish to remember a thought or make a comment about the document. Figure 17.6 shows how notes are displayed in ProViewer.

> **TIP**
>
> As noted earlier, this capability is useful for making notes on a document that will be viewed throughout an organization.

FIGURE 17.6.

Common Ground Notes function.

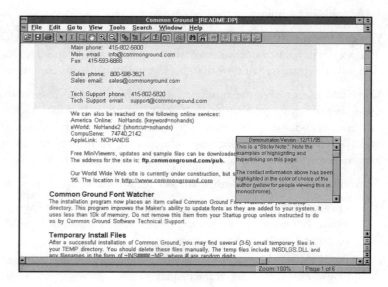

As shown in Figure 17.6, notes are displayed on the document itself within a small window. Note entries are listed one per line. Horizontal and vertical scrollbars appear if needed to let you view the full text of each entry. To display existing note entries, choose the Notes command on the View menu.

To create a note:

1. Click the Notes icon on the toolbar or choose the Notes command on the Tools menu. The mouse cursor changes to a form that resembles the icon on the Toolbar.

2. Drag the cursor to define a rectangular area of the document that is the size of the note you wish to create. (If you single-click with the Notes tool, you create a default-sized note.)

3. Release the mouse button. The Note Properties dialog box appears, with the default text and background colors indicated, and empty edit fields where you enter the label and contents of the note.

4. Enter the note contents by one of the following methods:

   ■ Type the text for the note into the Note window.

   ■ Type the text in the Contents field of the Note Properties dialog box.

   ■ Use the Paste command to bring text into the note from the Windows clipboard.

   ■ Text in notes may be put into the Windows clipboard with the Cut and Copy commands on the Edit menu. Conversely, text in the Windows clipboard may be put into a note using the Paste command on the Edit menu.

5. Select one or both of the remaining options:

   ■ To use your own label instead of the default, type a label in the Label field of the dialog box.

   ■ To display the completed note in icon form on the document, check the Icon box.

6. Press OK. The Note Properties dialog box closes, the note appears on the document, and the label of the note appears in the Notes Navigation Pane as a single-line entry. If it is not the first entry, the note's position in the list of entries corresponds to its relative position in the document.

7. Repeat this process to create additional notes.

Text in notes can be printed by checking an option in the Print dialog box. Notes are printed at the end, after the last document page is printed.

Using Common Ground Security Features

Common Ground provides several desirable security features. Documents can be encrypted, and the ability to copy specific text or graphics can be disabled for proprietary data that you want to share but do not want to allow to be easily copied. The capability to disable printing is also useful when you want to provide sensitive information across a network and maintain positive control over it. Figure 17.7 shows the security settings in a sample document.

FIGURE 17.7.

Common Ground security features.

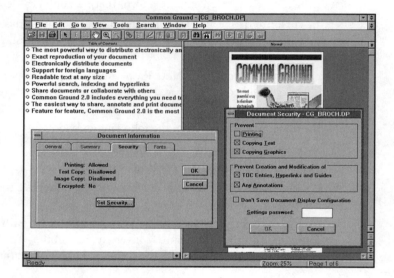

Using Common Ground Search Features

Common Ground provides excellent search capabilities. In addition to making it possible to find a text string in the current document, Common Ground offers the capability to span document sets and subsets using meta-information. Most impressive is the fact that you can search using thesaurus and proximity switches typically found only in top-end search engines.

Because most documents are never used once they are filed, the powerful search engine capabilities provided by Common Ground can help to overcome even the most disorganized electronic filing system, even if it is only minimally configured for meta-data. Figure 17.8 shows the search dialog box. As you can see, there are many terrific options for searching your documents.

FIGURE 17.8.
Common Ground global search features.

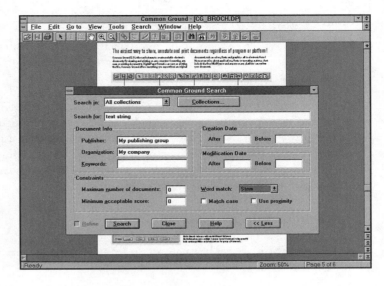

Using Common Ground Print Features

Another powerful Common Ground feature is the capability to carry information about a document's fonts with the document. This feature enables the end-user to print the document using the fonts you intended. This feature is different from being able to print a raster image of a document to a printer. Common Ground actually passes the correct font information to the printer for conversion and output. The feature of being able to store text strings, graphics, and formatting data is important to portability.

The MiniViewer

Using the freely distributable MiniViewer, anyone can read and print Common Ground documents. The MiniViewer provides a limited set of capabilities for viewing a document. The MiniViewer can be used in two modes:

Embedded within a Common Ground document

Stand-alone

Embedded MiniViewer

The embedded MiniViewer can be bundled with a Common Ground document and permits creation of a self-launching document. It is an executable file with an .exe (or Macintosh executable) extension that automatically starts the MiniViewer and displays the document.

With the embedded MiniViewer, you can

- Navigate through a Common Ground document using menu commands, keyboard commands, and scrolling
- Print the document

While the capability to embed the viewer is a nice feature, it is only good for distributing Common Ground documents to specific groups of end-users, such as users who use Microsoft Windows or users who own a Macintosh. I do not recommend using this feature for Web publishing. Digital Paper files can be moved seamlessly across platforms, like HTML files or files in any other standardized format. If you create a DP document that only one group of users can view, you are excluding other groups of users.

Stand-alone MiniViewer

The stand-alone MiniViewer has many of the features of the ProViewer. With the stand-alone MiniViewer, you can

- View and browse multiple Common Ground documents
- Navigate through Common Ground documents using menu commands, keyboard commands, and scrolling
- Display and navigate through annotations and hyperlinks
- Print Common Ground documents
- Obtain online help on any feature of the MiniViewer

Summary

Although makers of page layout systems and portable document systems try to distinguish themselves from each other, a portable document system is really a page layout system with a reader application. FrameMaker is one of the best known page layout systems. With FrameMaker, you can create highly structured documents that include hypertext links.

Common Ground and Adobe Acrobat are two of the best product suites for creating portable documents. Both Common Ground and Adobe Acrobat can be used to create high-quality documents for users across multiple platforms. However, Common Ground documents are in the Digital Paper format and Adobe Acrobat documents are in the Portable Document Format. If you have the free Common Ground MiniViewer, you can view documents in Common Ground's Digital Paper format. If you have the free Adobe Acrobat reader, you can view documents in Adobe Acrobat's Portable Document Format.

Desktop Publishing

18

*by
William
Robert Stanek,
Gregory Stenstrom,
Richmond Tuttle,
and Sandra Tuttle*

IN THIS CHAPTER

The Web is a tool that empowers you to publish to an audience of millions, but you do not have to limit yourself to the electronic byways of the Information Superhighway. If you are an experienced or intermediate-level Web publisher, you will find that you can take the core experience you have gained as a Web publisher and apply it to many more traditional areas of publishing. One of the most logical areas to extend your Web publishing operation to is desktop publishing. Similarly, if you are an experienced or intermediate-level desktop publisher, you will find that you can take the core experience you have gained in desktop publishing and apply it to Web publishing.

This chapter explores the similarities in publishing traditional and nontraditional publications and the ways you can extend your current publishing strategy into new areas using a common desktop publishing environment. The chapter begins with a comparison of traditional and nontraditional publications, then discusses desktop environments. Afterward, the chapter explores the answer to these two important questions:

> If you have published on the Web, how do you make the transition to the desktop?
>
> If you have published on the desktop, how do you make the transition to Web publishing?

Comparing Traditional and Nontraditional Publications

Look at the transformation taking place in the magazine publishing industry alone, and you will quickly see that high-tech is the way business is done. Traditional publishers create their masterpieces using advanced desktop publishing tools. These tools enable them to create documents that would have been impossible to produce 20 years ago. Would it surprise you to learn that many traditional publishers use these same tools to create print publications?

In this book, you have read about the document systems Web publishers use to create electronic documents. Document systems like Adobe Acrobat and Common Ground can be an important part of your publishing environment, especially if you plan to distribute advanced electronic documents. Yet these same document systems are used by traditional publishers to create magazines, newsletters, and much more.

The clear lines between traditional and nontraditional publishing are fading. Both traditional and nontraditional publishers using computer applications, such as document systems, refer to the desktop as the environment on which they design their publications. Often, the only difference in how these publishers actually publish is the form of their end product.

Traditional publishers publish their documents by printing them. Often the printer is a high-quality laser or a special-purpose printer. Nontraditional publishers publish their documents in electronic formats. While the electronic documents will sometimes have a tangible distribution medium, such as floppy disk or CD-ROM, most electronic documents are simply distributed electronically over the Internet or the Web.

Obviously, this is only one example of similarities between traditional and nontraditional publishers. The comparison between print newspapers and electronic newspapers in the next section reveals other similarities. Then we take a brief look at the differences between traditional and nontraditional book publishing. Hopefully, these comparisons will help you better understand how publishing strategies for print publications and electronic publications differ.

Newspapers

Newspapers provide timely information to readers in an inexpensive, portable, and disposable format. People enjoy picking up a newspaper for less cost than an accompanying cup of coffee, flipping directly to the sections they are interested in, doing the crossword puzzle, clipping a cartoon, and generally enjoying a quiet moment. A paper can be carried in a briefcase or large pocket or stuffed under an arm. It can be read anywhere, from the bathroom to an office, with no power required. After the reader is finished, the paper can be recycled, used to wrap up fish, or shredded for packing.

Newspapers are inexpensive for readers and lucrative for publishers because advertisers pay for space. Newspaper publishers receive compensation based on advertising. Advertising costs for space in a newspaper are broken down by the location and size of the ad in the paper. Reliable demographics allow a newspaper to justify advertising costs based on a long history of who reads the front section, the business or sports pages, the leisure and community reports, the comics, the classifieds, and so on. Newspapers also have the benefit of providing a product that changes often to a steady reader base. Most newspapers are published daily or weekly and have large circulations, making the newspaper the most read print media in the world.

Publishers and consumers alike see the promise in electronic newspapers as well. Generally, electronic newspapers are provided freely to readers who access them on the Web. Just as with a print newspaper, Web-published newspapers are profitable because advertisers pay for space. The advertising costs are broken down by the location and size of the ad in the paper as well as the number of readers. Web-published newspapers ensure a steady readership by providing a product that changes often, usually daily or weekly. Publishers have the added benefit of being able to easily publish updates for late-breaking stories. They can even report stories as they unfold.

People who enjoy picking up a traditional print newspaper are just as likely to enjoy the Web-published version of the newspaper. At the click of a button, they can jump directly to the sections they are interested in. They can read stories the publisher could not afford to run in the original edition. They can read additions or updates to stories within seconds after they are published.

Books

Hardcopy book publishers receive compensation based on sales of individual volumes. Whether a good publisher knows the difference between a book that makes money and one that does not has little to do with whether the book is a potential best-seller and more to do with good judgment on the part of the publisher. Book publishers enjoy long-term financial success by considering, before the first page is printed, demographics, perceived needs and desires of readers, and the costs of producing and distributing a book.

Book publishers incur expenses every time they go to press. For each printing, there are associated setup fees beyond the printing and material costs for the publication. When publishers print 5,000 books, they have to then store those books. The books have to be shipped to distributors and retailers. Books that do not sell might be shipped back to the publisher at the publisher's expense.

After considering all expenses and potential demand, publishers estimate the size for the print run. Publishers lose money if they overestimate demand and lose opportunities to make sales if they underestimate demand. All in all, it's a tricky business from which Web publishers can learn many important lessons from.

While many Web-published books are distributed freely, a growing number of Web-published books are available for a fee, and publishers receive compensation based on sales. The way this works is that the reader accesses information about the book or is able to read a few chapters of the book on the Web. If readers like what they see, they can then download the book and pay a shareware fee or order a floppy-published version of the book. This makes it possible for the small publishers to publish book orders as they come in. You have low overhead and only have to maintain sufficient supplies of disks, labels, and mailers in stock to meet the immediate demand.

Immediate demand versus perceived demand is an important concept that too many would-be publishers learn the hard way. The most important lesson you can learn from traditional book publishers is caution. Print books only when it is to your advantage. As you have no expenses, little overhead, and will not incur an opportunity loss by not printing 5,000 copies of your electronic book, it is to your advantage to publish your electronic books only when they are ordered.

Desktop Environments

Throughout this book, we have discussed focusing on your mission. The desktop publishing environment you select should meet your needs for conveying information. In the end, the most important aspect of publishing is empowering consumers to obtain information in a friendly and usable form.

Enabling consumers to obtain information in a friendly and usable form is a critical concept for publishers. How you present information is important for attracting and keeping readers. Successful publishers ensure that their presentations do not overshadow the information they are trying to convey. They do this in part by publishing in the correct medium for the correct reasons.

Web publishing no longer specifically refers to the World Wide Web. Internal corporate webs are evolving to serve special communities in the same way the Web originally served the academic community. Organizations that deal with security issues related to national defense, or even with highly sensitive corporate data, could use internal webs that are superimposed on secure operating systems and databases to make it easy to access and retrieve data.

As we have said, the way you present information is important. Do you need complex tables, inline special symbols for formulas, or special fonts? If elements of composition like these help to convey your information on demand, you may need to consider SGML or LaTeX publishing environments.

Depending on your publishing perspective, HTML may have some limitations. Traditional hardcopy publishing concepts do not translate to HTML in several areas. This is not a case of erroneous development, but of design for a specific purpose. HTML is not a page-description language and therefore does not currently support advanced page layout. Alternatives to HTML may better serve your needs and better provide your readers with information in a format they can use.

Consequently, your desktop environment should be a comfortable marriage of tools that will enable you to publish in formats that serve your needs and meet the needs of your readers. To do this, sometimes it may be necessary to distribute documents in printed form. At other times, for widest dissemination, it may be necessary to distribute documents electronically. This means that both Web publishers and traditional desktop publishers may have to redefine their desktops.

Redefining the Desktop for a Virtual World

The use of hardcopy documents for obtaining information is deeply rooted in our traditional culture. I was recently asked an intriguing question. "Why do I need to make a document anymore? With all this new technology, isn't there a way for me to just provide the information my reader wants?" It is a compelling question for a publisher, and perhaps the idea of producing a "document" is outdated.

The value you provide to readers is what is important in publishing. Providing value to readers should largely influence your decisions on which publishing tools you should use. There are a myriad of options available for bringing information to readers; these options are discussed throughout this book. Serve your readers, meet your needs, and provide useful means for accessing your information.

You also need to consider the perspective of the readers who will be accessing your information. The fact that you have a neat new product may overwhelm your sense of what the reader wants. For example, 200MB of images showing your neat new product will take a long time to download before the user ever has the chance to review the product. The reader will probably never get to the important stuff before moving on. A better way to distribute this level of detail for a new product is in printed form.

Similarly, if you distribute a 500-page policy manual to all corporate employees, you can almost guarantee the manual will not be read. No one wants to wade through hundreds of pages on policies. Yet large corporations, educational institutions, and government organizations create and distribute such manuals all the time. A better way to publish the policy manual is online, where it can be fully indexed and cross-referenced.

Still, publishing does not have to and should not be an all or nothing concept. Sometimes you have to redefine your publishing plans for a virtual world. You may want to and often should publish your documents both in printed form and electronic form.

The desktop has changed in the last few years. Modems are fast enough to access relatively large amounts of data quickly. Computers are powerful enough and efficient enough to display advanced publications and high-resolution graphics. This makes it easy for users to find information they want in a form they find interesting. This ease of access is changing our world.

New acronyms and words for the way we present information are waiting to be coined. Web users no longer read information, they "surf." Every possible variant of names with "hyper," "cyber," and "web" in them have been used to describe the distribution information on the Internet. Providing virtually instant access to information encompasses all aspects of Web publishing. Providing textual and database search forms, contents and index pages, images with alternate text, and logical hierarchical nesting are all excellent ways to ensure that your readers can quickly find what they want when they want it. Still, there comes a time when readers want to hold a book in their hands or thumb through the early morning edition of the newspaper.

Bringing the Web to the Desktop and Vice Versa

As the publisher, you have to decide when it's in your best interest to publish documents electronically and when you need to distribute them in printed form. If you've published on the Web, how do you make the transition to the desktop? And if you've publishing on the desktop, how do you make the transition to Web publishing?

Making the Transition to the Desktop

If you have published on the Web or have a firm understanding of Web publishing, making the transition to desktop publishing is easier than you may think, especially if you follow the sound design concepts discussed in this book and apply them to the desktop. To ease your transition, you should select a document system, such as Common Ground or Adobe Acrobat, and use this document system to create both electronic and print versions of key documents.

Examples of key documents that you may want to make available in both electronic and print forms are

> Brochures
>
> Catalogues
>
> Corporate overview and background summaries
>
> Credentials
>
> Information packets
>
> Company newsletters
>
> Press kits
>
> Resumes

Just as the layout of your electronic documents is important, so is the layout of your print documents. Your print documents should say something about who you are and what you represent. Areas with which you will have trouble are primarily in page design. On the desktop, you have access to many features you don't have in Web publishing. You have precise control over page layout, fonts, and colors.

The key concepts you should reevaluate based on the type of print publication you plan to produce are

> Colors
>
> Fonts
>
> Graphics
>
> Headings
>
> Spacing Techniques

Colors

The use of color in publications has always caused problems. In the early days of desktop publishing, people were discovering color printers. Documents were printed in color combinations you may not even be able to imagine. This was not done because it was a sound design technique, but because the desktop publisher could. You should use color in your print publications judiciously.

The primary reason to use color is to differentiate text elements in charts, tables, or figures. Most of the time, you will find that one color for the main text in a publication is fine. Otherwise, you should limit the number of colors for text to no more than three whenever possible.

Fonts

Fonts come in thousands of styles. Each font style, called a font family, has different type sizes and should include normal, bold, italic, and bold italic fonts. The font you choose for the main text does not have to be the font you chose to use in headings. However, you should limit the number of fonts you use on any single page.

You should also limit the number of fonts you use throughout the publication. A good rule of thumb is to use no more than three different fonts styles on any page and, if possible and practical, use the same fonts throughout the publication.

Graphics

By adding a few graphics to the page, you will dramatically increase the page's impact. The images or features you add to the page do not have to be sophisticated or high resolution. Simple is almost always best. The placement of images and features on the page should be such that they draw the reader's attention to the primary textual portion of the page.

Headings

Headings divide chapters or topics of the publication into sections or subtopics. In traditional publications, headings are used to break up the page for many reasons. A page broken into topics looks more manageable and interesting. Headings help the reader envision the organization of the publication at a glance by identifying the main points. They also help the reader quickly find topics of interest.

Normally, you will find that nonfiction works contain many headings and fiction works relatively few. Fiction works generally break down the publication by chapter or story. Nonfiction works generally break down the subject into topics and subtopics. Breaking down the subject into manageable pieces is critically important, especially for difficult material.

Spacing Techniques

In traditional publications, graphic designers carefully balance the amount of empty space on the page to emphasize material. They do this by using wide margins whenever possible. Open your favorite text book, and you will probably find that the top margin is smaller than the bottom margin.

You may also find that on the left-hand page the left margin is wide and the right margin near the binding is narrow. On the right-hand page the left margin near the binding is narrow and the right margin is wide. Print publications are usually designed this way to make them more visually appealing.

Another common spacing technique is to vary the length of paragraphs. If you use the same paragraph length repeatedly, even the most lively material can seem monotonous. You should use short paragraphs more often and restrict the use of long paragraphs. A short paragraph has less than six lines. A long paragraph is more than ten lines.

Making the Transition to the Web from the Desktop

If you have published on the desktop or have a firm understanding of traditional publishing, making the transition to Web publishing is easier than you may think, especially if you follow the examples in this book and apply the design concepts. To ease your transition for existing documents, you should review Chapter 16, "Designing Web Documents Using Your Favorite Word Processor," and Chapter 17, "Other Document Systems." Based on the discussion in these chapters, you may want to use your word processor or current document system to create both electronic and print versions of new documents or to make existing documents Web-ready.

Examples of documents that are well-suited to Web publishing include

> Advertisements
>
> Books
>
> Brochures
>
> Catalogues
>
> Corporate overview and background summaries
>
> Credentials
>
> Flyers
>
> Information packets
>
> Journals
>
> Magazines
>
> Newsletters
>
> Newspapers
>
> Press Kits
>
> Reference works
>
> Resumes

Summary

As you have seen, there are many similarities between traditional and nontraditional publications. These similarities make it easy to extend your current publishing strategy into new areas. One of the ways you can do this is by using a common desktop publishing environment. Web publishers considering a transition to the desktop should select a document system, such as Common Ground or Adobe Acrobat, and use this document system to create both electronic and print versions of key documents.

Should You Upgrade To SGML?

19

by Steven J.
DeRose

The World Wide Web has brought more attention to SGML than anything else. Most WWW documents (other than bitmapped graphics) are SGML documents that use the HTML DTD. If you're using HTML, you're using SGML, although there's much more to SGML. On the other hand, most Web browsers don't support any other DTDs besides HTML. This means that all the other SGML data in the world can't be browsed easily on the Web. (But take heart! Several solutions are presented in this chapter.)

This chapter begins by telling you how SGML relates to HTML and what's happening with SGML on the Web already. Then you learn about the practical issues: how to decide whether to go with HTML or SGML for your Web data, and how you can take advantage of each one's strengths and avoid their weaknesses.

How HTML and SGML Relate

People often say that HTML is a subset of SGML. This is nearly right, but it's a bit more complicated. Technically, HTML is an *application* of SGML. This means that it's really a DTD, a set of tags and rules for where the tags can go. SGML is a language for composing DTDs that fit various kinds of documents. There are many applications, and therefore many DTDs. (HTML, the DTD for the World Wide Web, is probably the best-known one.)

You already know that a DTD is always designed for some particular type of document: business letters, aircraft manuals, poetry, and so on. An important question to ask when deciding whether to put some data in HTML or another SGML DTD is, "What kind of documents is the HTML DTD meant for?"

Here is a sample of the kinds of tags that exist in HTML. (The new Version 2.1 of HTML is being finalized even as I write, and further improvements are still coming, so this list will improve a bit very soon.) First, HTML has a lot of tags for marking up common kinds of structures. Here's a partial list:

- Headings: `<H1>`, `<H2>`...
- Divisions (the actual big containers like chapters and sections, that *contain* headings and other data): `<DIV>`
- Basic document blocks (paragraphs, block quotations, footnotes, various kinds of lists): `<P>`, `<BQ>`, `<FN>`, `<OL>`, `<UL>`, `<DL>`
- Tables and equations (only in newer browsers): involve many different element types
- Text emphasis: `<EMPH>`, `<STRONG>`
- Hypermedia links: `<A>`, `<IMG>`
- Interactive forms: `<INPUT>`, `<TEXTAREA>`

HTML also includes several element types that express formatting rather than structure. These pose some portability problems, but they can be useful in cases where you simply *must* have a certain layout:

- Font changing, such as for getting bold and italic type: `<B>`, `<I>`
- Various extensions that work only with certain browsers: `<BLINK>`, `<FONT>`, and so on
- Forced line breaks (most used in code samples, "preformatted text," and similar examples): `<BR>`, `<PRE>`
- Drawing rules, boxes, and so on: `<HR>`

From the selection of element types, you can easily see the kinds of documents HTML is best for: fairly simple documents with sections, paragraphs, lists, and the like. In fact, most of the HTML element types are pretty generic; nearly every DTD has paragraphs and lists in it. One place where HTML excels, however, is in linking. Although it only has a couple of element types for links, those element types can use URLs to point to any data anywhere in the world. For more details on HTML, you may want to read *Special Edition: Using HTML*, also from Que.

So, why use other SGML DTDs? The main reason is that not all documents consist of only these basic kinds of elements. Whenever you run across some other kind of element, you have to "cheat" to express it in HTML. A very common example is the Level 6 heading element in HTML (`H6`). Because the first browsers formatted `H6` headings in small caps and there was no text emphasis tag that would give the same effect, people got in the habit of using `H6` to mean "small caps." Of course, some people also use `H6` as a heading, and many people use it both ways.

This works fine—until something changes. Suppose that a browser comes along that enables users to adjust the text styles for different tags, for example. Someone changes `H6` to look like something besides small caps, and everyone who was counting on small caps is surprised. Sometimes this won't matter, but it might; what if the user wants all the headings big and all the text emphasis small? Or what if the user is blind? When his browser runs across an `H6` element, it wouldn't do any good for his browser to put it in large type, so instead maybe its computer-generated voice says "section" and reads the heading loudly; in the same way, maybe such a browser is not supposed to do anything special for small caps.

The most important problem, though, is that you might want to use the tags for something completely different than formatting later. What if a browser is really friendly and makes automatic outlines by grabbing all the headings? Or what if you want to do a search, but only for text in headings? (You might want to do that because if a word occurs in a heading, it's probably more important than if it just occurs in the main text.)

Using a tag because it gets the right formatting effect is always a problem, usually a delayed one; it works fine when you do it, but the "gotcha" comes later. People working with the distant ancestors of SGML made up a name for this: "tag abuse syndrome."

The only thing to do about tag abuse syndrome is to make sure you have the right types of tags available. Few people would use `<H6>` for small caps if there were a more appropriate emphasis element available. That is exactly why SGML is important for the Web; a lot of documents contain elements that don't fit into the HTML set. Here are some kinds of elements for which tags aren't available in HTML:

■ Poetry and drama: STANZA, VERSE, SPEECH, ROLES.

■ Computer manual-speak: COMMAND, RESPONSE, MENUNAME.

■ Bibliographies, card catalogs, and the like: AUTHOR, TITLE, PUBLISHER, EDITION, SUB-JECT-CODE, DATE.

■ Back-of-book indexes: ENTRY, SUBENTRY, PAGEREF.

■ Dictionaries: ENTRY (of many levels), PRONUNCIATION, ETYMOLOGY, DEFINITION, SAMPLE-QUOTATION.

This problem will continue to exist even though later versions of HTML will add many useful new tags—no one can predict all the kinds of documents that people will invent. SGML provides the solution, because when you need a new kind of element, you can create it. You can avoid problems by trying not to force every kind of document into a single mold (just as you don't try to make a single vehicle do the work of a bicycle, car, and Mack truck).

From time to time, as you tag a document, you might feel as if the right tag just isn't available. How often this happens is a good way to tell how well the DTD you're using fits the document you're working with. If the fit is too poor, the time may come to extend the DTD or switch to an entirely different one—though this shouldn't happen very often. It's better to use the right DTD for each job than to force-fit; to be able to do this, users must have software that handles SGML generically rather than forcing data into any one mold.

TIP

Moving data from one DTD to another can sometimes be easy. It helps to have at least a little skill with some programming tool like Perl, as well as SGML. Even so, the job is not always easy. If the two DTDs use similar structures and differ primarily in tag names, it may be as easy as running some global changes to rename tags. If you aren't using much SGML minimization, non-SGML tools like Perl or even a word processor's Search and Replace command may be enough, because all the tags are right there: you can search for a string like <P> and change it to <PARA>—but remember to allow for tags with attributes! On the other hand, if you're using a log of omitted tags or changing to a very different DTD where you have to add or subtract containers, re-order things, and so on, it can be a lot more work.

There are also special tools available to help transform SGML documents in this way. Among them are OmniMark from Software Exoterica, the SGML Hammer from SoftQuad, and Balise from AIS.

What Data Is Already in SGML?

A lot of data is already available in SGML, and a lot of that has already gone onto the Web. Because SGML was adopted first by large organizations (after all, they had the biggest document problems to solve), those organizations have been able to make a lot of data available.

From Commercial Publishers

Many publishers are moving to SGML for all their documents. Some want to preserve their investment so they can reproduce books even after the latest wiz-bang word processor is history. Some want to simplify the data-conversion they do when authors send in their drafts. Some want to support new forms of multimedia delivery, information retrieval, and so on.

One of the earliest success stories for SGML in publishing is the many-volume Oxford English Dictionary (OED). For many decades, the entire OED used rooms full of 3×5 cards. But in the early 1980s, the publishers decided to go electronic. They worked with Waterloo University and developed sophisticated conversion programs to get the whole dictionary into SGML. One of the hardest tasks was teasing apart 25 or so different uses for italics in the scanned text: book titles, foreign words, emphasis, word origins, and so on. This is just a severe case of tag-abuse syndrome (one they couldn't avoid, since they had to work from scanned text, and scanners can't tell you much about distinctions other than font choice). Success in this conversion made it much easier to keep the dictionary up-to-date; it's also resulted in a great electronic edition that can be searched in very sophisticated ways. Because of the up-front tagging work, if you ask for all the words with Latin origins, you don't also get all the places where "Latin" happens to show up as an emphatic word or in a book title.

Another major SGML publishing project is the Chadwyck-Healey *English Poetry Database*. This project is collecting all English poetry from the earliest stages of English up to 1900 and publishing it on a series of CD-ROMs with sophisticated search software. Some of it everyone has read, some of it only an English professor could love—but it's all going to be there, in SGML.

Journal publishers have recently started using SGML to speed up the review and publishing cycle (see Figure 19.1). Platform and format independence make it easier to ship files to the many people involved. The fact that all kinds of software—from authoring to online and paper delivery systems—can now deal with SGML also makes it a good common format for them.

FIGURE. 19.1.

SGML is being used for a variety of sophisticated documents, including technical and scientific journals. Screen shot courtesy of Lightbinders, San Francisco (`http://lbin.com`*).*

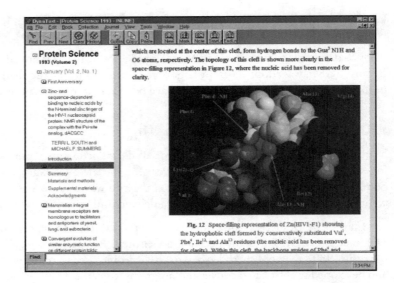

From Computer Vendors

When computer companies started using SGML, SGML won the battle. Now that the publications and documentation departments right inside computer companies are demanding good SGML tools, the need is obvious to those companies. When software companies notice a problem, there's a nice side benefit: They not only notice, but can do something about it, and so new tools are beginning to appear.

Silicon Graphics, Inc. was one of the first companies to move its documentation to SGML, calling its system "IRIS InSight" (see Figure 19.2). SGI makes the high-end graphics workstations that bring us a lot of special effects. Novell moved too, and reportedly saves millions of dollars (and trees) per year by shipping NetWare documentation on CD-ROM rather than paper. Novell used SGML to its advantage in moving to the Web; in only a few days, a single person set up over 110,000 pages of NetWare documentation for Web delivery, using a Web server that can convert SGML portions to HTML on demand. The data is still stored and maintained in generic SGML using its original DTDs, and so is always up-to-date without a complicated conversion and update process.

Sun Microsystems, AutoDesk, Phoenix (of BIOS fame), and many others also use SGML heavily, and there are reports that Microsoft does the same in-house. As one SGML Web publisher put it, a lot of the information you *have to* have is going onto the Web in SGML. IBM started using a predecessor of SGML, called GML, long ago, and may have more data in SGML-like forms than anyone.

FIGURE 19.2.

SGI customers access documentation using the IRIS InSight system.

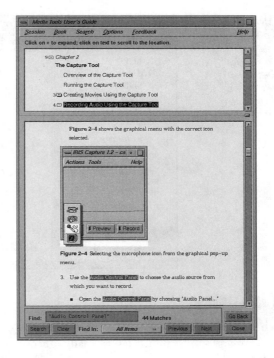

From Libraries and Universities

Libraries already use a standard computer form for card-catalog information, called MARC (MAchine-Readable Catalog). This is not SGML, but the DTD for an SGML equivalent is being worked out right now. SGML is also being used for *finding aids,* which are the equivalent of catalogs for unique items like special collections of archives, personal papers, and manuscripts. The University of California at Berkeley's library is spearheading this work, quietly converting huge numbers of finding aids into SGML and working with many other libraries to refine a DTD. They can (and do) deliver this information easily on any medium, from CD-ROMs to the Web.

Scholars and teachers also have put a lot of information into SGML and are starting to move it to the Web. The Brown University Women Writers' Project is collecting and coding as many English documents as possible from female authors prior to 1950. Several theological tools, such as CDWord, provide access to sacred texts, commentaries, and the like. And the complete works of philosophers as varied as Nietzsche, Wittgenstein, Pierce, and Augustine are in various stages of conversion to SGML.

The Oxford Text Archive and the Rutgers/Princeton Center for Electronic Texts in the Humanities are developing large literary collections in SGML; some parts are already available on the Web. Many individuals also encode and contribute their favorite literature, as part of research or teaching.

FIGURE 19.3.

Berkeley and many other libraries have cooperated to develop the "Encoded Archival Description" DTD to help give easy access to a wide variety of manuscripts and other collections.

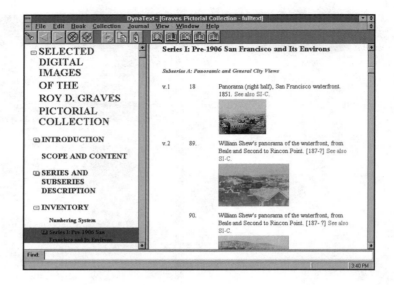

From Industry

High-tech industries moved to SGML very early because of its power for managing large documents. Aircraft and similar industries use many subcontractors; assembling complete manuals using parts from a variety of sources is hard unless you set up some standards. So the aircraft manufacturers and the airlines got together and set up a DTD. The companies that make central-office telephone equipment have done the same.

Not long after these industries went to SGML, the automobile and truck industries did also; companies like Ryder and FreightLiner have improved their speed of repairs and overall reliability using SGML. Other success stories abound in power companies, copier and other office machine companies, and many others.

From Government and the International Community

They say the U.S. Government is the world's biggest publisher, and it's probably true. The Patent Office puts out about 109 megabytes of new patent text per week (not counting figures); the Congressional Record adds a lot, too. Both of these are moving to SGML, though it's a challenge because they must be very careful not to disrupt current practices or delay delivery during the transition.

Internationally, there is much interest in SGML in Europe, and increasing interest in Asia. The International Organization for Standardization (ISO, despite the English word-order), which put SGML together in the first place, uses it for publishing some of its standards.

Why Is This Data in SGML, Not HTML?

Because of all these users, there is a lot of SGML data out there. Why did all these companies choose SGML instead of HTML? Mostly because it's a generic solution; it lets them use tags appropriate to the kinds of documents each one cares about. This means describing the document parts themselves rather than how they should appear on today's output device. This generic approach is why SGML data outlasts the programs that process it, and that can mean huge long-term savings. HTML can do this for a limited number of cases, but not in general. There are other reasons for using SGML:

- *Scalability.* SGML has features, such as entity management, that make it easier to work with large documents. A printed airplane manual often outweighs the plane itself, and the documentation system better not choke.

- *Validation.* SGML's ability to check whether documents really conform to the publisher's rules is important in industry, especially in the current world of liability lawsuits. However, validating a document doesn't ensure it makes sense, any more than spelling correctly ensures it makes sense.

- *Information retrieval.* Big documents are hard to work with, and SGML tagging puts in the "hooks" you need to make search and retrieval software work much better. True containers for big organizing units are especially helpful here, like CHAPTER and SECTION instead of just H1 and H2.

- *Version management.* High-tech manuals and ancient literature share a common problem because they come in many versions; it can make a big difference which one you get. Although not a true version-management system by itself, SGML has features that form a good foundation for one (such as marked sections, attributes, modularity, boilerplating, and so on).

- *Customizable presentations.* This relates to version management, too. Because SGML doesn't predefine formatting and layout, delivery tools can customize the display for each user as needed—show extra hints for novices, hide secret information, and so on. This is what Ted Nelson (he invented the term *hypertext*) calls *stretchtext*: the document should smoothly expand and contract to match the user's interests.

- *Access for print disabled.* Again because SGML gets away from formatting details, it is easy to convert SGML documents for delivery in Braille, via text-to-speech converters, and so on. Several books have been converted this way in record time.

All these advantages apply to paper production, online delivery, and information retrieval. But once you lay out pages for print, most of these advantages disappear; once all the lines and page breaks are set, the page representation takes over, and getting back to the structure is very difficult.

Five Questions to Ask About Your Data

Given all the advantages of generic SGML for big projects, yet all the simplicity of HTML for simple ones, how do you decide which way to go? There are five questions you can ask that will help you choose.

What Functionality Do I Need?

If your documents fit the HTML model and consist mostly of the kinds of elements HTML provides, HTML is probably a good choice. This is especially true if the documents are also small (tens of pages, not thousands). But if you have big documents or documents with special structures or elements, SGML will take you a lot farther.

If you need to do information retrieval, SGML is also better. You can search HTML, but you can't easily pin down just *where* hits are. This is because the HTML tags don't divide data up as finely as you can with full SGML, and HTML doesn't typically tag large units such as sections. (The tags have only been added in the latest revision, and they're still optional.)

Finally, if you need to deliver in more forms than just the Web, you should consider SGML. Tools are available to turn SGML not only into Web pages, but into paper pages, most kinds of word processor files, CD-ROM publications, Braille, and many other forms. This can all be done with HTML in theory, but it's harder in practice.

Do I Need Flexible Data Interchange?

SGML eases data interchange in several ways. Because it helps you avoid using tags for things they don't quite fit, your data is easier to move to other systems, especially if the tags can take advantage of finer distinctions. For example, if you tag book titles, emphasized words, and foreign words as <I> in HTML, you have a problem when you a move to something that can distinguish book titles and emphasis, such as a program to extract and index bibliographies. If you make the finer distinctions, you have a choice later whether to treat the items the same or differently.

Computers are pretty bad at sorting things into meaningful categories when they look the same. You almost need artificial intelligence to decide which italic text is a book title and which is something else. The good news is that computers are really good at the opposite task; if you've already marked up book titles and emphasized words as different things (say, <TI> and <EMPH>), it's no problem at all for a computer to show them both as italic.

Because of this, interchange is much easier down the road if you break things up early and make as many distinctions as practical. On the other hand, each distinction may be a little extra work, so you need to balance long-term flexibility versus how much time and effort you can put in up front. To figure out this balance, be sure to consider just how long you think your data will last (you're safest to at least double your first guess) and how important your data is.

Importance and lifespan don't always go together. Stock quotes are pretty important when they're current, but after a year only a few specialists ever look at them. At the other extreme, some literature that started out on stone tablets thousands of years ago is still important. Where does your data fit?

How Complex Are Your References and Links?

HTML has great strength as a linking system. This is mostly because URLs can point to any data in any format, and browsers provide a very convenient way to get any of that data. URLs (the most commonly available way of identifying information on the Net, though more advanced ways are coming) can get data via all these protocols (Web-speak for "methods") and others.

Protocol	Description
ftp	The data is copied down to your local machine.
http	The data is formatted and shown in the browser itself (or by a helper application for graphics, sound, video, and so on).
e-mail	Communication works like electronic mail.
news	Postings from network newsgroups are retrieved and presented.

HTML does all of this with only a few tags, mainly `<A>` and `<IMG>`. This means that the linking *itself* is not very complex or sophisticated, even though the data that the links point to is. For example, both `<A>` and `<IMG>` are *one-way links*; they live somewhere in document A and point to document B, as shown in Figure 19.4. But if you're in document B, you don't know that document A exists or that it points to you.

FIGURE 19.4.

The HTML <A> tag makes one-way links.

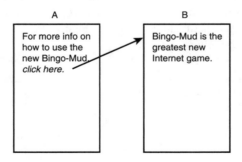

If you click a link and travel from document A to document B, most browsers will remember where you were and provide you with a Back button to return to the same document (though perhaps not to the same *place* in that document). That's an important feature, but not at all the same as also being able to get from document B to document A in the first place—with true *two-way links* you know while in document B that there's a link from document A.

> **NOTE**
>
> It's also hard with HTML links to go from document A to a specific place inside document B because URLs normally point to whole files. HTML does give rudimentary support for getting a whole file *and then* scrolling it to some element with a given "name" (like an SGML ID). This is useful, but doesn't help much with larger SGML documents. With large documents, the problem of having to wait for the whole thing to download (even though you only need a small portion of it) becomes very important.
>
> Link precision will probably improve in the future with conventions for a URL to give not only a file, but an ID or other location within a file, and to use this information to optimize downloading, not just scrolling. In fact, some servers already let you add a suffix to a URL to pick out a certain portion. For example, a server could let you put an SGML ID on as if it were a query, and then just serve up the element with that ID (including all its subelements, of course):
>
> ```
> <a href="http://xyz.org/docs/book.sgm?id=chap4">
> ```

Though you can simulate a *bi-directional* (or two-way) link in HTML, you have to do it by creating two links (one in document A and one in document B). This poses a couple of problems; the most important one is that you have to actually go in and change both document A and document B, so you can't just do this between any two documents you choose. Even if you can get at both documents to insert the links in the first place, it's easy to forget to update one "half" of the link when you update the other. Such links gradually tend to break.

What do other hypermedia systems do about this? The best ones, SGML-based or not, provide a way to create links that live completely outside of documents, in a special area called a *web*. (That name may change now that it's popular as a shorthand for the World Wide Web.) In that case, the picture looks more like Figure 19.5. Many systems provide both methods, not just one or the other.

FIGURE 19.5.

An external web lets you create two-way links.

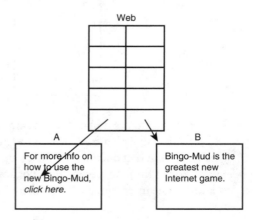

This is a much more powerful system, and you can do it with a number of SGML linking methods, such as HyTime and the TEI guidelines, and some recent systems like Hyper-G. It seems to have originated with the Brown University InterMedia system. Doing links this way has these benefits:

■ Because links live outside the documents, anyone can create them without needing permission to change the documents themselves. You can even link in and out of documents on CD-ROM or other unchangeable media. This is especially important for big data like video, because it's still much more effective to keep local copies on CD-ROM or similar media than to download huge files every time they need to be viewed.

■ Because documents aren't touched every time a link is attached, they can't be accidentally trashed. Most HTML links have this advantage at one end since the destination document needn't be touched. But the only way for HTML to point to a particular place *inside* a destination document is via an ID; so to do that you may have to add one, and in that case HTML loses even this one-ended advantage.

■ Because a set of links is a separate thing, you can collect links into useful groups and ship them, turn them off or on, and so on. Siskel's and Ebert's links to movie-makers' home pages can be in two separate webs, so you can choose to see either or both.

If you don't need this more sophisticated linking, HTML's links may be just fine. Otherwise, you need to go beyond HTML and beyond what current HTML browsers can do. The good news is that such a web can still use URLs and related methods to do the actual references, so you can keep the power HTML gets from them. You can add URL support (or even the <A> and <IMG> tags themselves) to another DTD that packages them up to provide greater capabilities.

> **NOTE**
>
> TEI and HyTime links provide a very good way to express this kind of linking.

What Kind of Maintenance Is Needed?

There are two areas where HTML files run into maintenance problems that SGML can help with:

■ Links tend to break over time.

■ HTML itself changes through improvements such as new tags.

While the URLs and other identifiers that HTML uses for links are very powerful, the most common kind right now, the URL itself, is also fragile. A URL names a specific machine on the Internet, and a specific directory and filename on that machine (technically, this doesn't have to be true, but in practice it almost always is). This method has an obvious maintenance problem: what if the file moves? A URL-based link can break in all these ways:

- The owner moves or renames the file, or any of its containing directories (say, to install a bigger disk with a different name).

- The owner creates a new version of the file in the same place and moves the old one elsewhere. (There's an interesting question about which version old links *should* take you to, but you needn't get into that here.)

- The owner's machine gets a new domain name on the Internet (for example, if someone else trademarks the name the owner had).

- The owner moves to a new company or school and takes all of his data with him.

The Internet Engineering Task Force (IETF) is working hard on *Uniform Resource Names* or *URNs*, which let links specify names instead of specific locations. This is like specifying a paper book by author and title, as opposed to "the fifth book on the third shelf in the living room at 153 Main Street." URNs will make links a lot safer against simple changes like the ones just mentioned.

SGML provides a similar solution for part of the problem already, through names called *Formal Public Identifiers* or *FPIs* for entire documents or other data objects. SGML IDs for particular places *within* documents can be used both in general SGML and in HTML. By using FPIs or URNs to identify documents, you can ignore where documents live. When a document is really needed (such as when the reader clicks a link to it), the name is sent off to a "name server" that looks it up and tells where the nearest copy is. This works a lot like library catalogs and like the Internet routing system used for e-mail and other communications.

NOTE

You can make HTML links a little safer against change by using the new BASE feature. Very often, a document will have many links that go to nearly the same place as the document itself, such as to several different files living in the same directory on the same network server, or in neighboring directories. When this happens, the beginning of the URLs on those links are all the same, such as

```
http://www.abc.com/u/xyz/docs/aug95/review.htm

http://www.abc.com/u/xyz/docs/aug95/recipe.htm
```

Instead of putting the full URL on every link, you can "factor out" the common part and put it on the BASE element in the header. The links all get much shorter, but the bigger plus is that you can update them all in one step if the server or a directory moves.

```
<BASE ID=b1 HREF="http://www.abc.com/u/xyz/docs/aug95/">
..
<A BASE=b1 HREF="review.htm">
...
<A BASE=b1 HREF="recipe.htm">
```

HTML is constantly being improved. While this is a good thing, it also poses compatibility problems. In HTML 1.0, `<P>` was not so much the start of an SGML element as a substitute for the Return key. It was an EMPTY element, so the content of the paragraph was never actually part of the P element, and there was normally no `<P>` tag before the first paragraph in any section. This has been fixed in HTML 2.0, but funny things can happen if you view an old document in a new browser or vice-versa; for example, you might not get a new line for the first paragraph after a heading.

A newer issue is tables. HTML 2.1 adds a way to mark up tables and get good formatting for them; they can even adjust automatically when the reader changes the window-width. But what about tables in earlier documents? Authors often deleted their tables entirely, but when they couldn't, they had to type tables up e-mail style, using HTML's preformatted-text tag (`<PRE>`) and putting in lots of spaces:

```
<PRE>
....China....1400.million
....India.....800.million
....USA.......250.million
....France.....50.million
....Canada.....25.million
</PRE>
```

These will still work in a new browser (because the `<PRE>` tag is still around), but they don't get the advantages or capabilities that the new tables support. They won't rewrap to different window widths, you can't wrap text within a single cell, and so on. So you can end up with awful effects like this:

```
    China     1400
million
    India      800
million
    USA        250
million
    France      50
million
    Canada      25
million
```

To get the new capabilities, you have to go in and actually change the documents. This is one reason it's considered bad form in SGML to use spaces for formatting. SGML helps you avoid this painful updating because you can represent your documents in whatever form makes sense for the documents themselves. That form is much less likely to change than the way you have to express it in one fixed DTD or system.

With SGML, if you need to accommodate software that doesn't handle your markup structures, you can use a "down-translation"—that is, a process that throws away anything that a certain HTML version can't handle. For tables, you can mark them up in any table DTD you want (CALS is the most popular) and use a program as needed to translate them to a simpler form— even the HTML 1.0-formatted kind. Then when table support is common in browsers, you just throw the down-translation program away and deliver the same data without conversion.

This works where "up-translation" won't, because computers are so much better at throwing information away than creating it. Tables are a lot like the earlier example with italics. If your DTD distinguishes book titles and a few (or a thousand!) other kinds of italics, it's easy to write a program to turn all of them into just <I> for HTML-only browsers. The reverse is much harder.

Can I Make Do with HTML?

Given all these trade-offs, here are the main things to think about when making the HTML versus full SGML decision for Web delivery:

> **The form the data is already in**. If your data is already in SGML (or in something conceptually similar, like LaTeX), it's much easier to stick with full SGML and have tags that fit your data naturally. This way you don't have to design a complicated set of correspondences, and whatever data conversion you do will be simpler.

> **The document size and number of authors**. If your documents are small, don't have a lot of internal structure, and don't need to be shared among multiple authors or editors, HTML may be all you need. But a little Web-browsing easily shows the bad things that can happen when people try to break big documents into little pieces—the forest can be lost by dividing it into separate trees.

> **The structures needed for searching**. If you need to do searches that target specific data in your documents, you'll probably need SGML to label that data. Doing without it is like doing a personnel database without having names for the fields; if you searched for people with salaries less than $30,000, you'd get not only that, but all the people who are less than 30,000 years old!

> **The frequency of changes**. If your data is going to change frequently, you're better off in SGML, where you can modularize your documents using marked sections, entities, and other features.

All these things relate to each other, so you often can't answer one question without thinking about the others. One example is that frequent changes to a document matter a lot less if the document is really small and you have complete unshared control over it. But if a document is big and several authors have to cooperate to maintain it, frequency of changes matters a lot.

How to Use HTML Safely

If you choose to put your data in HTML rather than another SGML DTD, there are several things you can do to make a later transition easier. These things are also helpful in the short term because they make your HTML more consistent, portable, and reliable.

> **Make sure your HTML is really valid**. Run it through an SGML parser—such as sgmls, yasp, or sp—or use one of the HTML "lint" programs. (They're called that because they go looking around for unwanted dirt that accumulates in dark pockets of HTML documents.) Weblint is one such program; you can find it at

```
http://www.unipress.com/weblint.
```

Be very careful about quoting attributes. Any attribute value that contains any characters other than letters, digits, periods, and hyphens needs to be quoted (either single or double quotes are fine, but not distinct open/close curly quotes).

TIP

There are a couple of very common HTML errors that you can get away with in some browsers, but that will break others, and will prevent you from using generic SGML tools. The biggest one is failing to quote attributes, as just described. Probably the next biggest is getting comments wrong. These are right:

```
<!— some text of a comment —>
<!— another comment, with two text parts -
   — of which this is the second —>
```

But these are wrong (that is, they're not comments):

```
<!— this comment never ends —!>
<! This is an SGML syntax error !>
<— This is just data to SGML —>
<!— This one -- really -- is not a comment —>
```

Avoid any part of HTML that is labeled "deprecated" in the HTML DTD or its documentation. Deprecated is a polite term standards use to say, "Don't use this, it's dangerous, not recommended for the future, and not even universally supported at present."

Be sure to use the HTML "DIV" containers, not just free-standing headings—especially in larger documents. This makes the structure of your document easier for programs to find and process, and it can also help you find tagging errors.

Avoid colliding with SGML constructs, even if some HTML parsers ignore them. For example, don't depend on an HTML parser failing to know that the string <![starts a marked section, that <? starts a processing instruction, or that <!— starts a comment; always escape such strings, for example, by changing the < to <.

Challenges of Upgrading

If you decide to put your data in an SGML DTD other than HTML, there are a few "gotchas" to watch out for. None are fatal, but you'll want to start out knowing the rules of the game. The issues are briefly summarized here.

Fewer Browsers To Choose From

At this time, only a few networked information browsers can receive and format SGML regardless of the DTD. Most Web browsers have the HTML tag names built right into the program and require a new release to add new ones. This is true even if the new ones don't require any new formatting capabilities; adding a BOOK-TITLE element type won't work, even though you may only want it to mean "show in italics."

The main exception that is already released is a viewer called Panorama, developed by Synex and marketed by SoftQuad. Panorama is an add-on "helper" to existing browsers, like various graphics viewers. This means it does not talk to the network by itself; instead, when a Web browser follows a link and notices that the data coming back claims to be "SGML," it can forward the data to Panorama for display.

If there are Internet-based links in the SGML, Panorama calls the browser back to retrieve them. If the destination is HTML or GIF, it shows up directly in the Web browser. If it's SGML, the browser calls Panorama again.

Another SGML-capable Web browser is a new version of the DynaText SGML delivery system that can view SGML or HTML off a hard disk or CD-ROM, across the Net, out of a database, or from a compiled/indexed form used for big documents. It provides a unified environment for viewing all these data types, as well as graphic and multimedia formats.

Although there aren't many SGML-capable Web browsers, these two are very flexible and give you a lot of control over formatting, style, and other capabilities. Hopefully, more browsers will start to support generic SGML over time.

In the meantime, there are several server-end options available, too. You can always create and maintain documents using full SGML, and then run a conversion program to create HTML from it and put that on the Web. This is especially useful if you have an SGML-based authoring system in use for general publishing or other applications.

There are also Web servers available that can store SGML directly and then translate it to HTML on demand (for example, DynaWeb from Electronic Book Technologies—you can try it out at http://www.ebt.com). This method has the advantage that you can adjust the translation rules any time without rerunning a big conversion process over all your data. It also means the translation can be customized as needed, for example, to adjust to whichever browser is calling in, or even to modify the document by inserting real-time information during translation.

A DTD To Choose or Design

Even if you have all the software you need, with full SGML you'll need to answer a question that never arises with HTML: What DTD should I use? Very good DTDs are already available for a wide range of document types, and you can probably put off DTD-building for as long as you want by using them. This makes the task a lot easier. But even so, you have to think about your documents and then learn at least enough about a few DTDs to make a choice. You may also want to tweak an existing DTD—this is easier than starting from scratch, but still takes skills beyond those needed for tagging.

More Syntax to Learn

If you want to make up your own DTDs, you need to deal with all kinds of declarations, parameter entities, content models, and so on; there's a lot of syntax to learn (tools like Near & Far help a lot). If you use an existing DTD, there is less syntax to worry about, but there's still a little more than with HTML.

SGML provides many ways of saving keystrokes in markup, and many special-purpose constructs you never see used in HTML. Using these constructs in an HTML document will result in errors of one kind or another. For example, if you try to "comment out" a block of HTML with a marked section, its content is still there because typical HTML parsers don't recognize marked sections. In fact, for those parsers, the characters <![IGNORE [and]]> all count as text content!

```
<P>
<![ IGNORE [ This text is not part of the document, really.
   In fact, it's <EMPH>really </EMPH> not there. ]]>
   And the paragraph goes on right here.
</P>
```

In an HTML application that isn't quite following the rules, this might be taken as just a paragraph that starts with some funny punctuation marks (a really bad HTML implementation might instead complain that you used a tag named ![). If you got used to this, you might be surprised when you go to a more generic SGML system and discover that the <![in your document causes some very different effects—this is something you just have to memorize and know. In this case, the first two lines within the paragraph are not part of the content at all, and a browser shouldn't show them to you.

Using a WYSIWYG SGML editor helps a lot, for the same reasons that using MS Word is a lot easier than typing Microsoft's RTF interchange format directly. But even with the best tools, you can be surprised if you're not aware of such restrictions—for example, you might get a "beep" whenever you try to type <![in a paragraph, and not know why.

Benefits of Upgrading

If there's less delivery software to choose from and more to learn, why bother? The reasons are mostly the same ones that influenced big publishers to go with SGML, although which reasons are most important varies from project to project.

Platform Independence

Other SGML DTDs are even better at abstracting formatting than HTML. SGML can be retargeted to anything from a top-line photocomposition system down to text-only browsers like Lynx, Braille composers, and anything in between. SGML itself greatly benefits flexibility. HTML accomplishes this to some extent, but less so because a small and fixed tag set can force authors to think more about display effects and less about describing structure.

Browser Independence

Because generic SGML software (by definition) handles many DTDs, using a new or modified DTD won't faze it. If it works for CALS and TEI, it'll almost certainly work for whatever DTD you choose.

SGML vendors spend a lot of time testing interoperability. A standard demo at trade shows used to be to pass a tape or disk of SGML files from booth to booth throughout the show. Each product had to read the data, do whatever it did with the data (like let you edit or format it), and then write it out to pass on—without trashing it.

The "SGML Open" vendor group gets together regularly online, at shows, and at special meetings to work out agreements on details and make sure SGML documents can move around easily. For example, a popular DTD for tables has a "rotate" attribute to let you lay out tables in either portrait or landscape mode, but doesn't say whether rotation is clockwise or counter-clockwise. The vendors sat down and decided, so now they all do it the same way. Simple agreements like this can save a lot of pain for end users.

> **NOTE**
>
> The central point for finding out about SGML Open activites is http://www.sgmlopen.org. Most companies that support SGML are involved in SGML Open, and you can find links to their home pages from the SGML Open Web site, along with links to other useful SGML information.

If you use an SGML-aware server, you can benefit from greater browser independence—even on the Web. Each Web browser has its own strengths and weaknesses. If you can ship slightly different HTML to each one, you can capitalize on the strengths and avoid the weaknesses. This is easier if your data uses a more precise DTD; clients tell servers who they are, so a server that has enough information can down-translate appropriately for each one.

HTML Revision Independence

Keeping your data in SGML also lets you avoid recoding it each time a new HTML feature arrives. You learned earlier about tables—how you'd have to completely rework them if you started by assuming the browser can't support table markup, and then had to change your data when browsers caught up. The same problem came up when Netscape introduced their FRAME element and a lot of reauthoring had to happen. The same problems can happen with any kind of markup. By keeping your documents in DTDs designed to fit, you can leave them untouched and merely adjust a conversion filter.

Appropriate Tag Usage

The biggest fundamental benefit of going to SGML is that your markup can tell the truth about what components are in your document, even if the document doesn't fit into any pre existing scheme. If the tags you need are there (or, at worst, you can add them yourself), you avoid having to "pun" and use a single tag for a bunch of purposes it may not have been meant for.

> **NOTE**
>
> The question of having the right tag available for the job is very important, so here are a few examples. We've already talked about how sixth-level HTML headings (<H6>) get used to mean small caps, and how italics (<I>) get used to mark many things like emphasis, foreign words, book titles, and so on.
>
> Sometimes preformatted text (<PRE>) gets used for quick-and-dirty tables. Line-break (<BR>) gets used heavily for forcing particular browsers to lay things out a certain way (and usually that way only works well for certain browsers, certain window widths, and so on).
>
> Another big example is equations; since there are not yet HTML elements for doing math, journal publishers and others are stuck turning equations into graphics for Web delivery. This sort of works, but the fine print tends to disappear, and zooming in doesn't help. This is a case where there's dire need for more a more adequate set of tags. And there are already some very good equation DTDs in wide use outside the Web.

Large Document Management

SGML helps you manage the conflict between big documents and slow modems. You can't very well ship a whole manual or a lengthy paper of any kind every time a user wants to see the nth paragraph (even if browsers could handle documents that big, which many can't)—no user would wait for the download to finish. Novell certainly couldn't ship tens of thousand of pages of NetWare manuals every time a user wanted a summary of some installation detail.

The only viable option with documents bigger than several tens to hundreds of pages is to break them up; you can make many smaller documents, say one for each subsection, and a bunch of overview documents that give you access similar to the table of contents in a paper book. This is usually done manually for HTML because HTML documents don't usually contain explicit markup for their larger components. (Some do now that HTML has added the DIV element.) This method works except for these problems:

■ If you are also publishing a paper document, you have to maintain two quite different forms.

■ The document ends up in many pieces that aren't visibly related; only a person can tell whether some link between HTML files A and B means they're part of the same document, or two somehow-related documents. This makes it hard to maintain consistency between all the parts of your original document.

■ If users want to download the whole document for some reason, it's very hard to do. First, they have to find all the pieces, distinguishing "is-part-of" links from "is-related-to" links; then they have to assemble all the parts in the right order and put the larger containing structures in. It's not enough to just pack them end-to-end because some of the connections between lower sections appear only in "header" or "table of contents" documents.

■ Users can't scroll smoothly through the complete document; at best, you can carefully provide Next Portion and Previous Portion buttons on every piece.

Internationalization

A final benefit of other SGML DTDs over HTML is that they have more provisions for international and multilingual documents. HTML prescribes the "Latin 1" character set. Latin 1 includes the characters for most Western European languages, but not Eastern European, Asian, or many other languages. Future revisions will probably support "Unicode," a new standard that includes characters for nearly all modern languages. SGML itself lets each document specify a character set and doesn't particularly care whether characters are one, two, or more bytes wide.

Many DTDs also provide a way to mark that individual elements are in different languages. This can have a big effect on display and searching. For example, it helps a lot if you're searching for the English word "die," to not get the German word "die," which means roughly "the," and is very common.

DTDs that specifically mark language are also very helpful when you want to create multilingual documents or documents that can customize to the reader's language. You can create documents where every paragraph has a subelement for each language, and then set up your software to show only the type the user wants; this automatically customizes the document for the reader's own language:

```
<P>
    <ENGLISH>...</>
    <FRENCH>...</>
    <ITALIAN>...</>
    <GERMAN>...</>
    <SPANISH>...</>
    ...
</P>
```

Summary

SGML is especially strong for large or structured documents, documents where several authors share writing and editing, and documents that have components HTML doesn't provide. A single DTD such as HTML may not provide the types of elements your documents need, in which case you end up using some other type because it gets the desired appearance in the authoring software. This leads to problems down the line. HTML also has only limited support for expressing larger units such as sections, and that makes document management a bit harder.

PART

Multimedia and Beyond

Image, Sound, and Video Formats

Greg
Ric
and

IN THIS CHAPTER

Although Chapter 7, "Adding Multimedia Features with HTML," explores the concepts of adding pictures, sound, and video to your Web documents, this chapter provides a more detailed discussion of multimedia formats. In a way, this chapter picks up where Chapter 7 finishes. It does this by exploring additional multimedia formats available today—even those formats that aren't in widespread use but which may be useful for your Web publishing operation.

As discussed in earlier chapters, publishing for the Web is primarily a matter of using standard formats that other users on your target network can read. While the World Wide Web has settled on several standards that most users are familiar with (GIF, JPEG, AIF, MPEG, and so on), many other alternatives exist that may be more suitable to your needs. Also, many of the standards that you are familiar with provide additional capabilities that are seldom used, but that can enhance your presentation.

Common Standards and Formats

The previous chapters have emphasized that publishing on the Web does not involve magic, but an awareness of the common standards and formats that make electronic distribution of digital data possible. Applications that read nontextual data work much like the Web browsers you are already familiar with. They read, or *parse*, a data stream into individual units or unit sets that are then sent to your computer's processors and peripherals as command parameters. In the case of sound, waveform data is typically parsed and passed to the software and hardware in units. These sound units are then translated into variations in amplitude and frequency that drive sound from a computer's speaker.

This concept is important. Most of the emerging multimedia technology incorporates dynamic processing of incoming data streams so that near real-time playback of digital data is possible. In much the same way that you "see" an HTML document being built on your Web browser display, you can now hear music or see a video while it is being downloaded. Functionality that only permitted the parsing of a static sound or video file is being supplanted by technology that brings us closer to interactive multimedia.

Graphic Standards for Images

If you want to distribute graphical data, it's important that you have a fairly comprehensive understanding of how a graphics file is parsed and disassembled. This knowledge will help you produce Web documents that present graphics to a user more quickly and at the highest resolution practical. Understanding the difference between a raster image and a vector image is also important when distributing graphical data.

Vector and Raster Images

The two main categories of computer graphics are vector images and raster images. Understanding the difference between these two types of images is useful when you're creating and editing digital images.

Vector images are made up of mathematically defined lines and curves. For example, in vector-based applications, a blue circle with a radius of one inch can be located in a specific spot on a page. You can move, resize, or change the color of the circle by performing operations on the mathematical model that defines the image; the program always references the mathematical definition of the shape. Vector-based programs are best for bold graphics, such as logos, that require crisp, clear lines at any size.

Raster images consist of a grid of small squares known as pixels. For example, a raster image of a one-inch blue circle would be made up of a collection of colored pixels that formed the shape of a circle in the specified location on the page. When you edit the circle, you directly edit the pixels in the grid. Raster-based images are best used for working with continuous-tone images, such as photographs or images from painting programs. Because raster images are resolution-dependent, they can appear jagged and lose detail if they are scanned, or if they are created at a low resolution (say, 72 pixels per inch) and then printed at a high resolution.

NOTE

Remember that computer screens are made up of a grid of pixels. Both vector and pixel images are displayed online as pixels. Vector-based products render their shapes into pixels for display.

BMP/DIB Formats

BMP and DIB files are Device-Independent Bitmap files that can exist in two formats: the OS/2 format and the Windows format. Files in either format can be named with either a BMP or DIB extension. OS/2 formats can be used with OS/2's Presentation Manager and are not compressed. Windows BMP or DIB files may be stored using Run Length Encoded (RLE) compression for four- and eight-bit images. Keep in mind that an image with an 8-bit color depth generally requires twice as much file space as an image with a 4-bit color depth. This is because 8 bits of data are used to define each pixel on the screen.

> **NOTE**
>
> Distributing BMP/DIB files across the Web is not recommended, but may be necessary in older, Windows-based internal networks that do not support more advanced graphical formats. BMP graphics files are commonly used in Windows as background "wallpaper." DIB files can be used across platforms, but more effective means of distributing graphical data exist. DIB files translate well across platforms, but support for them in UNIX environments is poor.

CGM Format

Computer Graphic Metafiles (CGMs) are composed of a series of graphic instructions that are portable across multiple hardware platforms. CGMs are often referred to as *vector drawings*.

The CGM format is defined by several different standards organizations, including the International Standards Organization (ISO), the American National Standards Institute (ANSI), the Federal Information Processing Standard (FIPS), and the National Institute of Standards and Technology (NBS). As a result, creating a CGM-compliant graphical file is not a straightforward exercise, and any vendor who produces an application that creates and reads a CGM graphic must also verify the application's compliance with at least one of these standards. There is no independent organization that validates an application's ability to create or read CGM graphics.

> **NOTE**
>
> For publishers providing CGM graphics to the U.S. government, acceptance of a graphics compliance will depend on whatever CGM viewer the government acceptance agent uses. The documentation for a particular standard should describe the conformance test suite that an application must pass.

Moving a CGM file across applications and then viewing it may have surprising and sometimes dismaying results. Lines might appear to float in space or color shadings might seem misplaced. As consolation, remember that a CGM file can be edited and corrected, but check with the end-user before selecting a graphics tool suite. A CGM graphic created by your $100,000 graphics suite could be rejected by an agent using a $99 graphics suite. There is no right or wrong here—only differences of opinion over how the standards should be interpreted.

In spite of its shortcomings, use of CGM as a graphics format is still strongly encouraged because it is a documented international standard, not just a commonly accepted format like JPEG and GIF. More importantly, the CGM format is the only internationally agreed upon vector format.

The only practical way to transmit reusable mechanical drawings is to use a vector format like CGM. Objects such as lines and polygonal shapes are transmitted as such and can be modified individually. A raster image format like JPEG and GIF, on the other hand, provides just an uneditable snapshot of the drawing. The key factor in deciding to use CGM as a graphical standard is reusability and portability.

PS and EPS Formats

PostScript and Encapsulated PostScript are device-independent page description languages for both text and graphics. EPS files can be moved across platforms and will produce identical output on any PostScript printer.

As with the challenges associated with CGM, interpretations of EPS standards may vary. This format also has the decided disadvantage of having no international governing standard for creating EPS-compliant applications.

EPS is not recommended for use on cross-platform environments like the Web, but it generally works well within single-platform architectures such as an all-Intel, PC Windows network.

GIF Format

GIF files were designed to create the smallest possible image files for uploading and downloading from electronic Bulletin Board Services (BBSs). GIF format is raster-based and has achieved acceptance throughout the World Wide Web.

Two common GIF file versions are referred to as versions 87a and 89a. Both versions can use a graphics encoding method referred to as *interlacing*. A Web user who downloads an inline-interlaced GIF image sees the image decoded in four passes and after a single pass may abort the download of the partially displayed image to save time and move on.

GIF format is recommended for distributing raster images because of its wide acceptance and the proliferation of freely available viewers. Further, most available HTML editing and conversion tools support the composition of documents with inline GIF images, so you can see what a final document will look like as you compose it. This is not the case at present with CGM, JPG, and other formats.

JIF/JPG/JPEG Formats

The Joint Photographic Expert Group, acting as an ISO standards group, created the format known as JPEG. The JPEG format originally existed only as a series of required steps to compress an image. No standard was provided for storing the compressed image, and interoperability between applications became a problem. As a result, the JPEG File Interchange Format (JFIF) standard was developed. Originally, this format used the JPG file extension. Although the latest standard calls for the use of JIF as the file extension, the JPG extension persists.

JPEG is "lossy," meaning that the decompressed image isn't quite the same as the one you started with. JPEG achieves much greater compression than is possible with lossless methods. JPEG is designed to exploit the way a person interprets images, notably the fact that small color details aren't perceived as well as small details of light and dark. Thus, JPEG is intended for compressing images that will be looked at by people. If you plan to analyze your images using electro-optical methods, the small errors introduced by JPEG may be a problem, even if they are invisible to the eye.

A useful property of JPEG is that the degree of lossyness can be varied by adjusting compression parameters. This means that the person who creates the image can trade off file size against output image quality.

There are two good reasons to use JPEG in your Web publishing environment:

- To reduce the size of image files
- To store 24-bit-per-pixel color data instead of 8-bit-per-pixel data

NOTE

The fundamental advantage of JPEG is that it stores full color information: 24 bits/pixel (16 million colors). GIF 87a and GIF 89a, the other image formats widely used on the Web, can only store 8 bits/pixel (256 or fewer colors). GIF is well matched to monitors capable of displaying only 256 colors. But many users currently have more capable monitors, and 24-bit JPEG images look much better than 8-bit GIFs on such hardware. (Refer to Chapter 7 for a discussion on the development of a 24-bit variation of GIF.)

Smaller file sizes translate to reduced transmission times across networks and reduced storage space requirements for archiving libraries of images. Because JPEG files have a larger data content, it may take longer to decode and view a JPEG image than to view an image in a simpler format, such as GIF (JPEG 24-bit data versus GIF 8-bit data). Choosing JPEG is essentially the result of a time/space tradeoff: you give up some time in order to store or transmit a high-quality image.

JPEG format is recommended for distributing raster images because of its wide acceptance and the proliferation of freely available viewers.

MAC Format

MAC files are produced by the Macintosh MacPaint program. The MAC format is not commonly used for Web publishing and is not recommended for distributing graphical images.

PCD Format

PCD format is the Kodak Photo CD file format. Usually, these images are created using Kodak Photo CD imaging workstations. PCD format has specialty application value, but it is not recommended for distribution across the Web because of the limited readers available for viewing this type of file.

PCX Format

Originally created for the Zsoft Paintbrush program, large libraries of PCX images can now be found on the Web. PCX format is not recommended for use across the Web. It has the disadvantage of being device-dependent on the resolution mode of the PC monitor. A high-resolution PCX Version 5 graphic created on a 16-million color, 1024×768 monitor generally blows up when an attempt is made to display it on a 256-color, 800×600 monitor.

TIF/TIFF Format

The Tagged Image File Format (TIFF), designed to become a standard format, can save images in an almost infinite number of variations. As a result, no available image application can claim to support all TIF/TIFF file variations, but most support a large number of variations. TIF/TIFF images can be found on the Web, but may create problems for users with incompatible TIF/TIFF image viewers.

TIF/TIFF format is not recommended for distribution on the Web.

TGA/Targa Format

Developed by TrueVision for their Targa and Vista products, TGA/Targa format supports high-resolution 32-bits-per-pixel images, but can create problems in Windows environments (which only support 24 bits per pixel) and graphics applications that cannot step down the image when decoding.

TGA/Targa format is not recommended for distribution on the Web.

WMF Format

The Windows Meta File is not a bitmapped image, but rather a series of graphics instructions. This permits dynamic scaling for applications capable of handling WMF files.

Strangely enough, distributing WMF files across the Web is discouraged, but it is still an alternative to consider. More than 80 percent of the world's computer users use Microsoft Windows, and most non-Windows graphical applications will read or convert WMF graphical files.

> **CAUTION**
>
> Publishers who plan to invest heavily in creating large stores of WMF image files should consider Microsoft's propensity to change direction for whatever reason; they may find themselves sitting on large stores of unsupported data in the future. Again, the advantage of CGM and the use of an internationally accepted standard (not affected by commercial interests) should be given due consideration.

Amiga IFF Format

The Amiga Interchange File Format (IFF) is used to transfer documents to and from Commodore Amiga computers. This format is also supported by a number of paint programs on IBM-compatible computers, including DeluxePaint from Electronic Arts (IFF is the best export format to use with that program). To save files in the HAM version of this format, use the Amiga HAM Export module.

IFF format is not recommended for distribution on the Web.

PIXAR Format

The PIXAR format is designed specifically for exchanging files with PIXAR image computers. PIXAR workstations are designed for high-end graphics applications, such as those used for three-dimensional images and animation.

PIXAR format is not recommended for distribution on the Web.

Raw Format

Raw format is a flexible file format for transferring documents between applications and computer platforms. Raw format consists of a stream of bytes describing the color information in the file. Each pixel is described in binary format, in which 0 equals black and 255 equals white.

You can choose to save an image in an interleaved or noninterleaved format. If you choose the interleaved format, the color values (such as red, green, and blue) are stored sequentially. The choice you make depends on the requirements of the application you plan to use to open the document.

Raw files are not recommended for distribution on the Web.

Scitex CT Format

The Scitex Continuous Tone (CT) format is available for RGB and CMYK color images and grayscale images. Scitex computers are used for high-end image processing and are generally not used in Web applications.

Other Formats

There are other graphic formats available that are not mentioned in this chapter. The key considerations in determining which format is appropriate for your Web publishing needs are conformance to an available standard and portability across platforms.

Graphics Programs

Not surprisingly, graphics are the primary type of multimedia used on the Web. Consequently, you should carefully select a graphics program to create images for your Web publications. Not only should your graphics program be capable of saving images in the format you plan to use, it should also be rich in features that make creating images a joy.

Adobe Photoshop

Adobe Photoshop falls in the category of high-end raster graphic editing/publishing products. Similar products of comparable capability and price include CorelDRAW and PageMaker.

It would be easier to list the failings of a product like Adobe Photoshop than to list all its capabilities. Basically, Adobe Photoshop has more features than an intermediate-to-advanced graphic artist will ever use. One feature of Photoshop that is extremely useful when creating Web graphics is the capability to mask graphical information that is not critical to the message you want to convey. Consider the two images displayed on the Adobe Photoshop display screen inFigure 20.1.

FIGURE 20.1.

Adobe PhotoShop window.

The graphic image `truck.jpg` includes a rectangular photograph with a garden background. This rectangular image is approximately 35,000 bytes in size. The `truck1.jpg` image is a copy of the `truck.jpg` file with the background masked out and is approximately 19,000 bytes in size.

The resultant cropping affects how the images appear and how long it takes to download them in a Web browser. Note the difference in how the graphics appear in the Presentation Mode of Mosaic, as shown in Figure 20.2.

FIGURE 20.2.

Web browser displaying full image and masked image.

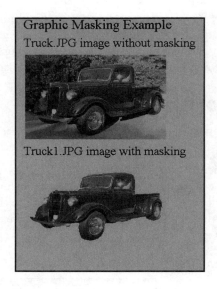

HiJaak PRO

HiJaak PRO is a popular midlevel graphics package with excellent capabilities. It is highly recommended for publishers and individuals with moderate financial resources. Figure 20.3 shows how HiJaak PRO displays the images from the previous example.

With HiJaak PRO you can

- View, edit, and process an image
- Convert a file from one format to another
- Capture a screen
- Organize graphics files

FIGURE 20.3.

HiJaak PRO displaying full image and masked image.

Viewing an Image

HiJaak Pro supports most popular image formats, including BMP, CGM, GIF, JPEG, and TIFF. You can use HiJaak PRO to view an image if the image is stored in any of the dozens of input formats supported by HiJaak PRO. You can view an image before you convert it for verification.

Editing an Image

Upon viewing an image, HiJaak PRO enables you to edit the image by

- Cutting and pasting it to and from the Windows clipboard
- Cropping it
- Changing its size
- Changing fonts (if it's a vector image with text or a DOS text screen capture)
- Rotating it

Working with Colors in an Image

HiJaak PRO offers the following options for manipulating colors in an image:

- Smoothing
- Color reduction method
- Grayscale

- Palette optimization
- Invert colors
- Reveal background color objects
- Reverse black and white
- Halftone screen frequency
- Histogram equalization
- Contrast
- Brightness
- Gamma correction

Converting a File from One Format to Another

HiJaak PRO enables files to be converted to and from any of more than 70 formats. HiJaak PRO can choose a file format for you if you are using one of many popular software applications.

Capturing a Screen

HiJaak PRO supports capture of Windows or DOS screens, which can then be saved in any of HiJaak PRO's supported raster file formats. DOS text-mode screens can also be saved in vector formats.

Organizing Graphics Files

HiJaak PRO enables you to organize graphics files, in any of the formats it supports, through the HiJaak Browser utility.

HiJaak Browser

With HiJaak Browser, you can create thumbnails of your HiJaak PRO-compatible images and place these thumbnails in folders. As Figure 20.4 shows, HiJaak browser can display groups of thumbnail images, thus enabling you to organize and preview groups of graphics files online. With HiJaak PRO, you can also update thumbnails whenever you want or configure HiJaak PRO to update them during computer idle time.

FIGURE 20.4.

HiJaak Browser displaying thumbnail images.

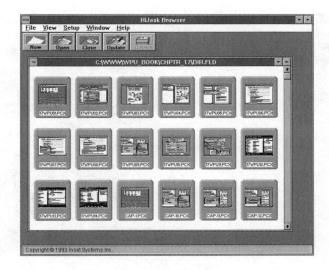

> **NOTE**
>
> HiJaak Browser cannot be used without HiJaak PRO.

Paint Shop Pro (PSP) for Windows

Paint Shop Pro is a popular shareware graphics package with capabilities that approach, and in many cases exceed, midlevel packages that cost hundreds of dollars more. It is strongly recommended for publishers and individuals with limited financial resources and is an excellent companion to mid- and high-level tools.

Figure 20.5 shows the main window of Paint Shop Pro. With Paint Shop Pro you can

- View, edit, and process an image
- Convert a file from one format to another
- Capture a screen

FIGURE 20.5.
Paint Shop Pro displaying full image and masked image.

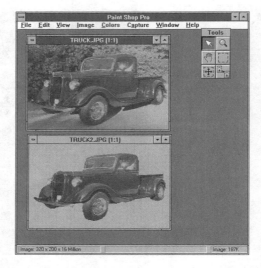

> **NOTE**
>
> The organization and thumbnail capabilities included with products like HiJaak PRO and HiJaak Browser can be added to a low-cost (but capable) Web publishing solution set by complementing PSP with the Graphic Workshop for Windows (GWS) shareware product described in the next section.

With the exception of the HiJaak Browser capabilities described earlier, and a narrower scope of file conversion utilities, PSP is very similar to HiJaak PRO in range of capabilities. The most significant difference in graphics packages such as PSP is vector and metafile handling capabilities. PSP handles only raster images and limited variations of file types like Encapsulated PostScript (EPS). HiJaak PRO and similar packages can translate more complex formats like CGM.

One of the strongest features of PSP is the ease-of-use of the capture capability for on-screen graphics.

Graphic Workshop for Windows

Graphic Workshop for Windows (GWS) is a popular shareware graphics package with excellent capabilities and an outstanding graphical user interface. With a shareware registration fee of $40, it is strongly recommended for publishers and individuals with limited financial resources and is an excellent companion to mid- and high-level tools.

With Graphic Workshop for Windows you can

■ View, edit, and process an image

■ Convert a file from one format to another

■ Capture a screen

■ Organize graphics files

■ Play MPEG video files (without audio tracks)

GWS meets or exceeds many of the capabilities provided by graphics packages costing ten times more. As you can see from Figure 20.6, Graphic WorkShop can also display thumbnails.

FIGURE 20.6.

Graphic Workshop for Windows displaying thumbnails.

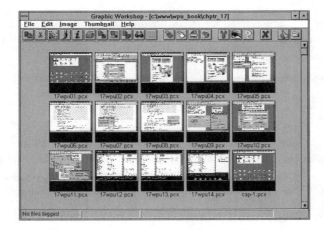

GWS is highly configurable and provides a graphical user interface that is easy to understand and more informative than typical menu-driven interfaces. Figure 20.7 shows the Setup screen provided by GWS, which is a good example of the typical GWS interface.

FIGURE 20.7.

Graphic Workshop for Windows Setup Screen.

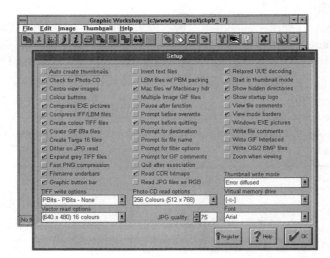

Integrating Sound

Integrating sound into your Web publishing environment is generally as easy as providing a link to an audio file. MPEG is the world standard in audio and video compression. Just as JPEG images and other graphic images can be compressed, so can digital audio and video. When selecting an audio format, always consider the issues of portability and audio quality. An understanding of the components of an audio file, as described in this section, should help you select an appropriate format.

Audio data is characterized by the following parameters, which correspond to settings of the Analog-to-Digital (A/D) converter used when the data was recorded. Generally, the same settings must be used to play the data.

- Sampling rate in samples per second (such as 8000 or 44100)
- Number of bits per sample (such as 8 or 16)
- Number of channels (one for mono, two for stereo, and so on)

Approximate sampling rates are often quoted in hertz (Hz) or kilohertz (KHz), and are also referred to as samples per second (samples/sec). Sampling rates are generally measured per channel, so for two-channel stereo data recorded at 8000 samples per channel, there are actually 16000 samples in a second (counting left and right channels).

Multichannel samples are generally interleaved on a frame-by-frame basis. If there are N channels, the data is a sequence of frames, where each frame contains N samples, one from each channel. For stereo, the left channel usually comes first.

The specification of the number of bits for μ-law samples is somewhat problematic. These samples are logarithmically encoded in 8 bits, but their dynamic range is that of 12-bit linear data. The official definition is specified in the CCITT standard G.711.

There exists another encoding scheme similar to μ-law called A-law, which is used as a European telephony standard. While the μ-law format is widely supported on UNIX workstations, there is little support for the A-law format on UNIX workstations.

You will find that some sampling rates are more popular than others, for various reasons. While some recording hardware is restricted to (approximations of) these rates, some playback hardware has direct support for others. The popularity of divisors of common rates can be explained by the simplicity of the clock frequency dividing circuits that are used as a reference in translating sound.

Samples/sec	Description
5500	One-fourth of the Macintosh sampling rate (rarely seen).
7333	One-third of the Macintosh sampling rate (rarely seen).

Samples/sec	Description
8000	Exactly 8000 samples/sec is a telephony standard that goes together with μ-law (and also A-law) encoding. Some systems use a slightly different rate; in particular, the NeXT workstation uses 8012.8210513, which apparently is the rate used by Telco CODECs.
11000/11025	A quarter of the CD sampling rate, or half the Macintosh sampling rate (perhaps the most popular rate on the Macintosh).
16000	Used by, for example, the G.722 compression standard.
18900	CD-ROM/XA standard.
22000/22050	Half the CD sampling rate, or the Mac rate; the latter is precisely 22254.545454545454 but is usually misquoted as 22000.
32000	Used in digital radio, and other TV work, at least in the UK; also long-playing DAT and Japanese HDTV.
37800	CD-ROM/XA standard for higher quality.
44056	This unusual rate is used by professional audio equipment to fit an integral number of samples in a video frame.
44100	The CD sampling rate. (DAT players recording digitally from CD also use this rate.)
48000	The DAT (Digital Audio Tape) sampling rate for domestic use.

There seems to be a tendency emerging to standardize on only a few sampling rates and encoding styles, even if the file formats differ. Suggested rates and styles are as follows:

Rate (samp/sec)	Mono/Stereo
8000	8-bit μ-law mono
22050	8-bit linear unsigned mono and stereo
44100	16-bit linear signed mono and stereo

Audio Data Summary

For readers who are less concerned with the physics of sound and more concerned with the "bottom line" on audio file formats, I recommend using one of the three "popular rates" mentioned in the preceding table. The size of the audio file created will be proportional to the fidelity you require. For audio that will be used to convey voice-range sound data, the 8000 and 22050 sampling rates are more than adequate. For high-quality recordings associated with music and scientific biological audio, the 44100 rate is recommended.

Audio formats that support these "popular rates" are described in the following sections.

RIFF Waveform Format

RIFF Waveform is the Microsoft Windows WAVE sound format. It is used for Windows system sounds. RIFF Waveform files have the extension WAV. RIFF Waveform sounds may be of either 8-bit or 16-bit resolution.

Creative Voice Format

Creative Voice is the Sound Blaster sound format and has the extension VOC. WHAM can currently only deal with uncompressed VOC files.

Amiga IFF Format

IFF is the standard Amiga 8-bit sound (8SVX) format. IFF files are often given the extension IFF. They can contain only 8-bit sounds.

Sun/NeXT Sound Format

Standard sound format files for the Sun and NeXT workstations traditionally have the extension AU. These files can contain either 8-bit or 16-bit linear or μ-law samples.

AIFF Format

AIFF format was developed by Apple and is also used by Silicon Graphics workstations. The AIFF file structure is based on the Amiga IFF tagged file structure, although it is not the same as the IFF (8SVX) format. AIFF files may be of 8-bit or 16-bit resolution.

Raw 8-Bit Sample Format

Sound files in this format consist of nothing more than the samples that they comprise. In other words, the sound format is raw, as the name implies, and contains no special encoding or compression.

> **NOTE**
>
> I recommend the RIFF (WAV) and NeXT/Sun (AU) formats, as they are the most flexible and have the widest support. Most audio recorders and players support these formats. A close second choice is the AIFF (IFF) format.

Waveform Hold and Modify (WHAM) Shareware Audio Tool

There are many audio product suites available that will meet Web publishing needs. Most commercially available sound boards are provided with bundled audio software, and most sound-enabled hardware operating systems (DOS, Windows, UNIX, and so on) come bundled with audio software.

The Waveform Hold and Modify (WHAM) product is an excellent representative product that meets typical Web publishing requirements. The $20–$30 shareware/freeware donation is one-tenth of the cost of commercially bundled software with comparable functionality.

The WHAM display shown in Figure 20.8 is representative of many audio tools that provide functionality suitable for Web publishing.

FIGURE 20.8.
WHAM display with simple WAV file presentation.

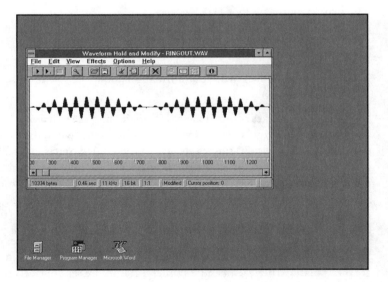

Video Standards

Incorporating video in Web documents is primarily a matter of using links to permit a user to download and view a video file. Primary consideration here is, once again, compliance with standards, but the issue of portability is a much larger factor when considering video. Only several video formats are supported across platforms and are in wide use on the WWW. The reason for this is the reliance of many high-end video formats on hardware boards and peripherals that most computer users don't have.

For the purpose of discussing video and Web publishing within the context of this book, only several formats can be considered to offer portability across platforms and a Web. Video standards and de facto standards suitable for Web publishing are listed in the following sections.

MPEG 1 Standard Format

The Moving Pictures Expert Group (MPEG) is the name of the ISO committee working on a digital color video and audio compression standard. And by no mere coincidence, MPEG is also the name of the standard.

MPEG 1 defines a bit-stream representation for synchronized digital video and audio, compressed to a bandwidth of 1.5 MB/sec. This corresponds to the data retrieval speed from CD-ROM and DAT. A major application of MPEG is the storage of audio-visual information on these media. MPEG is also gaining ground on the Internet as an interchange standard for video clips.

The MPEG 1 standard has three parts:

- Video encoding
- Audio encoding
- "Systems" (which includes information about the synchronization of the audio and video streams)

The video stream takes approximately 1.15mbits, and the remaining bandwidth is used by audio and system data streams. MPEG video encoding starts with a fairly low-resolution video picture (352×240 pixels×30 frames/second in the United States; 352×288×25 frames/second in Europe). RGB pixel information is converted to chrominance/luminance, and a complex, lossy compression algorithm is applied. The algorithm takes the time axis as well as spatial axis into account, so a good compression ratio is achieved when the picture is relatively unchanging.

The compressed data contains three types of frames: I (intra) frames are coded as still images; P (predicted) frames are deltas from the most recent I or P frame; and B (bi-directional) frames are interpolations between I and P frames. I frames are sent once every 10 or 12 frames. Reconstructing a B frame for display requires the preceding and following I and/or P frames, so these are sent out of time order.

Substantial computing power is required to encode MPEG data in real time—perhaps several hundred MIPS to encode 25 frames/second. Decoding is less demanding. The quality of MPEG 1-encoded video is comparable to a VHS video recording. A major reason to use MPEG 1 is that you can use a software encoder to create videos and a software decoder to view videos. As you will see with MPEG 2, this is not always the case.

MPEG 2 Standard Format

In 1995, MPEG 2 became the high-quality standard in video. It offers true full-screen play capability at 720×480 pixels and 30 frames per second (United States). In order to compress MPEG 2 you need an MPEG 2 video encoder chip. To decompress MPEG 2, you need an MPEG 2 video decoder chip.

A few years ago, this type of video processing hardware would have cost as much as $50,000. Today, you can purchase MPEG 2 video production boards for under $2500. The really good news for electronic publishers is the MPEG 2 decoder chip is priced right to become standard equipment on computer video boards. You will undoubtedly see MPEG 2 in action soon.

QuickTime (MOV) Format

QuickTime, or MOV format, is the file format sponsored by Apple Computer for the storage and interchange of sequenced data, with cross-platform support. A QuickTime movie contains time-based data that may represent sound, video, or other time-sequenced information such as financial data or lab results. A movie is constructed of one or more tracks, with each track being a single data stream.

Movie resources are built up from basic units called atoms, which describe the format, size, and content of the movie storage element. One type of container atom is the "movie" atom that defines the time scale, duration, and display characteristics for the entire movie file. It also contains one or more track atoms for the movie.

Media atoms contain information relating to the type of data and information relating to the QuickTime driver that will handle the data. Component-specific information is contained in a media information atom that is used to map media time and media data.

There are many more atom types that define a wide variety of features and functions, including a TEXT media atom that enables displayed text to change with time, and user-defined data atoms called "derived media types." These allow for the custom handling of data by overriding the media handler with a user-supplied driver.

The actual movie data referred to by the movie resources may reside in the same file as the movie resource (a "self-contained" movie), or more commonly, it may reside in another file or on an external device.

DVI Format

DVI is Intel's Digital Video Interactive video compression technology. This format is rarely used on the Web.

Video for Windows (AVI) Format

AVI is Microsoft Windows Video format. This format is gaining widespread popularity and not only because Microsoft's Internet Explorer features direct inline support for it. It is a quality format comparable to Apple's QuickTime format.

Video Tools

Web publishers who intend to produce video files must purchase a video board to process video inputs and will usually receive bundled software with the hardware. Most commercially available video boards accept video/audio format from a number of sources, but typically accept input from VCRs and camcorders. Multimedia editing tools for editing video clips are available to create professional videos.

Video is still an emerging technology on the Web, but it appears that MPEG will eventually become the accepted standard. There are numerous collections of software for parsing and playing video files. The most comprehensive playback product suite that I have found is the NET TOOB Multimedia Viewer from Duplexx Software, Inc. In addition to excellent playback capabilities for static files, Duplexx has stated the ability to play video files while they are being downloaded will be available shortly. Figure 20.9 shows the NET TOOB interface.

FIGURE 20.9.

NET TOOB Multimedia Player interface overview.

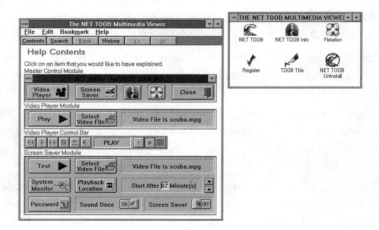

Summary

As you've seen, there are dozens of file formats for graphics, sound, and video. While steering through this maze of options can sometimes be difficult, use the discussion in the chapter to help you select the format that's best for you. Once again, your primary considerations are compliance with standards and the file-size-to-content tradeoff.

Multimedia Presentation Tools

by Mary Jo Fahey

21

The Web is a medium marketers now refer to as the "new fourth mass market medium" because it's lining up as number four after print, radio, and television. At the start of a new medium, Web artists have a unique opportunity to shape the multimedia content with many of the same tools that have been used for print. For example, Photoshop can be used to edit still images, movie frames, and animation stills. Although most text on a Web page is created with a text editor, Photoshop can be used to create text occasionally as a paint graphic that can add unusual typography to a Web page that has limited fonts.

This chapter presents detailed information about the tools a Web artist can use to create images, sound, animation, and video. Tools for both the Macintosh and Windows platforms are included. Although some tools are well-known software programs such as Adobe Photoshop, Adobe Premiere, and Macromedia Director, there are also shareware programs a Web artist can download from software archives on the Web. To locate multimedia software tools on the World Wide Web, look for tips in this chapter that give the URLs or Web addresses where the software can be downloaded.

Web Page Images

To edit images for Web pages, artists need a bit-depth reduction tool that *cannot* be found in all paint software programs. If you work on the Macintosh platform and if you have the budget, buy Photoshop and Debabelizer. Artists who work on the Windows platform should also buy Photoshop, and they can look forward to a Windows release of Debabelizer sometime this year. Windows artists with a smaller budget should look for Haddad Loriero's LView Pro, a shareware tool that is mentioned in this chapter.

Image Editors

Artists who have already learned how to edit images for print graphics are very well prepared for Web graphics. The distinction is primarily in the file size and bit-depth of the images. In print, the objective is to capture a large amount of data and for the Web, the objective is to use minimal data so as to keep file sizes small.

Photoshop (Macintosh and Windows)

Photoshop is a sophisticated tool for creating digital color images. Although the program was originally conceived as a high-end image editor and color separation tool for print, it has become the most popular image editor for digital images created for online media.

Digital artists who are becoming acquainted with Photoshop will discover what print artists have known for several years: Photoshop's extraordinary editing tools provide a means to change color, correct color, invert color, simulate color duotones, simulate 3-D effects with drop shadows, create a color montage, and add motion blurs. Other features include a whole host of plug-in filters as well as tools to create gradients, air brushed effects, color textures, embossing, painting effects, solarization, posterization, reflections, cross fades, and dithering.

Artists who use Photoshop often start with Photoshop's simple editing tools. The Selection Marquee, the Lasso, the Grabber Hand, the Paint Bucket, the Type tool, the Pencil, the Eraser, the Airbrush tool, and the Line tool are based on the early MacPaint tools. Typically, an artist quickly moves on to the Rubber Stamp tool, the Sharpen/Blur tool, and the Dodge/Burn/Sponge tool, then advances to the Channels, Paths, and Layers.

The Layers feature added in Version 3.0 has been very well-received because it offers a significant improvement in the way paint graphics are assembled. The tiny screen elements in paint graphics (called pixels) are difficult to select. As a result, making a change in an image has always been difficult in paint graphics. Layers enable an artist to isolate sections of an image to prevent the intermingling of pixel elements. These independent layers can later be integrated into a single layer when editing is complete.

TIP

The Photoshop newsgroup (`comp.graphics.apps.photoshop`) is a useful resource for Web artists who may need to post general questions about image editing and the Photoshop software. The Netscape browser comes equipped with a Usenet newsgroup reader or "newsreader," which before Netscape was a separate program. Similar to electronic bulletin boards, newsgroups are places readers can post messages for other readers. When a Netscape user subscribes to a newsgroup, Netscape's newsreader stores the name of the newsgroup for quick retrieval.

For a list of all newsgroups and a page that will help you subscribe to a newsgroup of your choice, visit

`http://skye.icr.ac.uk/usenet.htm`

TIP

For additional resources on Photoshop or any other topic, search the Alta Vista search engine at `http://www.altavista.digital.com` or the Yahoo search engine at `http://www.yahoo.com`. Type the word Photoshop in the blank space provided and the search engine will display a list of related links.

For Web publishing, one of the most important image editing concepts to learn is bit-depth reduction. Unlike print, which demands a large amount of color information for optimal image quality, images created for Web pages should be low-resolution 72 ppi images with a low bit-depth. Bit-depth is defined as the number of colors per pixel and a low-numbered bit-depth translates into a small file size, an ideal characteristic for transmission over a modem.

Game developers understand the concept of lowering bit-depth to conserve on file size because smaller files mean faster, smoother movement when images need to be drawn on-screen. In a similar way, images with a small file size load faster on a Web page.

Since Photoshop was not designed as an image editor to be used for creating digital images, the technique for lowering bit-depth is awkward. Conserving on bit-depth is never a concern to artists who work in print because in print, the objective is to produce images with high bit-depth or many colors per pixel. File size is not an issue for an artist who delivers an image to a printer on a SyQuest disk or optical disk. However, when an image is used on a low-bandwidth medium such as the Web, bit-depth is an issue.

In Photoshop, bit-depth is adjusted through the Mode command on a dialog box that is displayed when Indexed Color is selected from the Mode pull-down menu. (See Figure 21.1.) If Indexed Color is already selected, an artist must first switch to RGB mode and then back to Indexed Color to make the dialog box appear.

FIGURE 21.1.
Indexed Color dialog box, Photoshop.

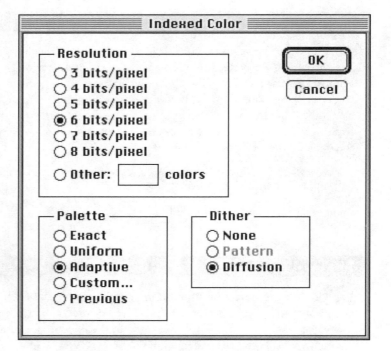

> **TIP**
>
> For best results, always select Adaptive Palette and Diffusion Dithering when you lower the bit-depth of an image. Dithering fools the eye into thinking there are more colors present.

There are no rules governing the selection of a bit-depth number. Through trial and error, an artist can gradually lower the bit-depth to see what is acceptable. Dithering should be selected each time the bit-depth is reduced. If a bit-depth is not right, the image will book patchy and coarse. In such a situation, an Edit/Undo command restores the previous selection. For example, an artist could start by reducing the bit-depth to 7 bits per pixel, look to see if the color is acceptable and try 6 bits per pixel, then 5 bits per pixel, and so on.

Artist Mark Elbert has created several photo montage images on the Web for record company Web sites. He starts by scanning original black-and-white photos, then uses Photoshop to add color. The image in Figure 21.2 is saved as a JPEG file because that file format is small and makes downloading easier.

FIGURE 21.2.

A photo montage image created by Mark Elbert.

Photoshop has a versatile array of selection tools, and the most powerful of these is the Pen tool. Mark uses the Pen tool's bezier curves to select rounded edges when isolating an irregular shape from a complex background. For example, to isolate singer Barbara Gandia in the image shown in Figure 21.3, Mark scanned the photo and used Photoshop's Pen tool. After Barbara's image was selected, Mark deleted the rest of the image and added a logo and a color background, as shown in Figure 21.4. These and other images can be downloaded from

`http://www.echonyc.com/~art/mesh/mesh.html.`

FIGURE 21.3.

Singer Barbara Gandia's image in a scanned group photo prior to image editing.

FIGURE 21.4.

Mark Elbert altered Barbara's image with posterization and saturated colors.

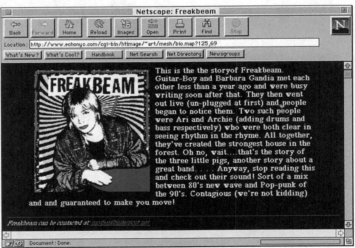

For details on how to add color to the browser background and text, see "Color Backgrounds and Text" in this chapter.

> **TIP**
>
> Elbert recommends keeping the total number of colors in an image to a minimum. This will provide superior results when you try to lower the bit-depth.

BoxTop's Plug-ins for Photoshop

Browsers can load images that have been saved as either GIF or JPEG. The GIF file format, owned by CompuServe, uses a lossless, 8-bit compression scheme called LZW compression. This means data is not thrown away when an artist saves a file as GIF.

Although GIF files may not be as small as JPEG files, more browsers "see" GIF images than JPEG and the file format is versatile for special effects. For example, GIF89a is a popular format to use for silhouettes on a Web page. The GIF89a or the transparent GIF image is a file that has been saved with a transparent background. Typically, an artist assigns a transparent value to the background and the image becomes a silhouette since the browser shows through the image background.

> **TIP**
>
> Since JPEG compression is a "lossy" compression algorithm, data is discarded when the image is saved in this file format. Try to avoid saving a file as a JPEG image more than once because the image will deteriorate.

Interlaced GIF images appear to load in layers on the browser page and the effect makes the image appear to load more quickly. This is an important characteristic in a medium where downloading speed is critical. An interlaced GIF image really doesn't load any faster than a noninterlaced GIF. It simply helps the Web visitor's patience factor.oxTop software has created the PhotoGIF plug-in, a shareware software program that adds the GIF89a and Interlaced GIF to Photoshop's Save As options. In Photoshop Version 3.*x*, the plug-in is added to the File Formats folder inside the Plug-ins folder.

Although the GIF file format is versatile for special effects, there are occasions when an artist will want to use the JPEG file format. JPEG images have smaller file sizes and sometimes have a superior image quality because the format is a 24-bit file format. Because the GIF file format is 8-bit, flesh tones in a GIF image sometimes appear posterized. Posterization is a flattening of brightness values that can make an image look like it has "paint-by-number" quality.

The Progressive JPEG file format has been introduced recently to imitate the interlaced GIF file format. BoxTop's ProJPEG is a plug-in that adds Progressive JPEG to the Save As options in Photoshop.

> **TIP**
>
> BoxTop's Plug-ins may be downloaded from
>
> `http://www.aris.com/boxtop/PhotoGIF/welcome.html`
>
> Also look for BoxTop's new GIF Animation software covered in the animation section of this chapter.

Photoshop has recently had the transparent and interlaced GIF file formats added to the Save As menu. Artists who use earlier versions of Photoshop can have these formats added to the Save As menu by adding BoxTop's PhotoGIF plug-in to the Plug-ins folder. This will cause the GIF89a file format to be added to the Save As menu, as shown in Figure 21.5. The ProJPEG file format, shown on the Save As menu in Figure 21.6, can be added to the Save As menu by adding BoxTop's ProJPEG Plug-in to the Plug-ins folder.

FIGURE 21.5.

The GIF89a option is added to the Save As menu with BoxTop's PhotoGIF plug-in.

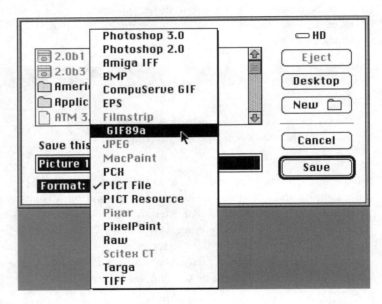

FIGURE 21.6.
*A ProJPEG option is
added to the Save As
menu with BoxTop's
ProJPEG plug-in.*

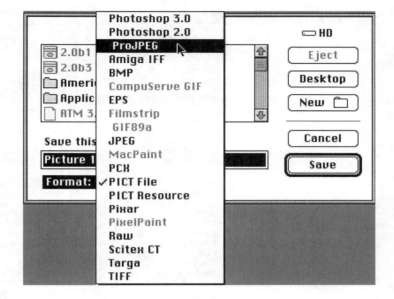

Debabelizer (Macintosh)

David Theurer's Debabelizer from Equilibrium Software is the ultimate color palette manipulation tool for Macintosh Web artists. David worked at Atari for eight years, and he
understands how to optimize color to create small file sizes. Debabelizer can read and write a
large variety of file formats and optimize palettes for cross-platform development. A Super Palette
feature is a palette analysis tool that creates and saves a palette of the best 256 colors in an
8-bit image. This palette can then be used on similar images. Web artists who work on large
numbers of images will appreciate a scripting feature that can be used to batch-process
large numbers of images.

Debabelizer's bit-depth reduction menu includes more information than Photoshop's. In
Figure 21.7, the bit-depth of the yellow sneaker is reduced from 8 bits per pixel to 5 bits per
pixel. The resulting file size is reduced by half. Note that at 5 bits per pixel, as shown in Figure
21.8, the quality of the image has not changed.

FIGURE 21.7.

Debabelizer's bit-depth reduction menu includes more information than Photoshop's.

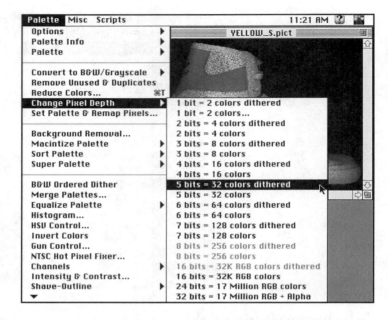

FIGURE 21.8.

At 5 bits per pixel, the quality of the image has not changed.

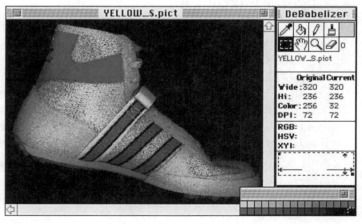

Debabelizer is well-known for the wide variety of file formats that the software can read and write. Note the choices on the Save As menu, shown in Figure 21.9.

Although the bit-depth reduction function in Photoshop and Debabelizer are similar, Debabelizer files are somewhat smaller when the bit-depth is reduced. Figure 21.10 shows the file size of the sneaker image before and after bit-depth reduction.

FIGURE 21.9.

Debabelizer's Save As menu.

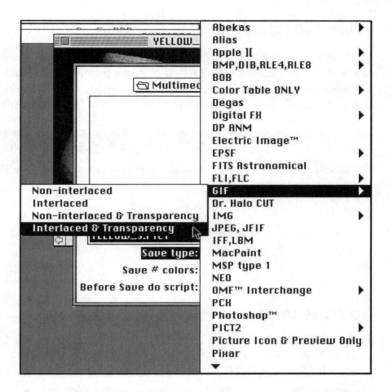

FIGURE 21.10.

File size before and after bit-depth reduction.

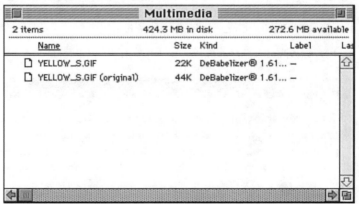

LView Pro (Windows)

Haddad Loriero's LView Pro is a remarkably sophisticated image editor that is available as shareware. Although LView Pro has far fewer features than Debabelizer on the Macintosh, an important feature includes a color depth palette that provides the commands necessary to reduce bit-depth. It will also save images as Transparent GIF, Interlaced GIF, or JPEG.

> **TIP**
>
> Haddad Loriero's LView Pro software can be downloaded from the SimTel Coast-to-Coast Software Repository:
>
> `http://www.coast.net/SimTel/`
>
> You can also find it at the c/net shareware site:
>
> `http://www.shareware.com`

Sources for Stock Photos

Grant Hulburt's Graphics on Call stock photo collection at Pacific Coast Software's Web site is an online source for free-of-rights stock photos (conditions apply). Photos are priced at $6 and his "Shopping Cart" database software on the Web site provides a means to shop online. Figure 21.11 shows the thumbnail images Web visitors browse on site. Photos are digital 640×480, 24-bit JPEG images that are sent to customers electronically via an e-mail attachment. Pacific Coast Software's site is at

`http://www.pacific-coast.com/`

> **TIP**
>
> When you visit Grant Hulbert's Graphics on Call stock photo database, you'll be asked to type in a keyword to browse the database. If you're not sure of a keyword and you want to browse a large number of photos, type comp into the field provided. The database will respond with photos stored as a "compilation."

FIGURE 21.11.
*Grant Hulbert's
Graphics on Call
stock photo Web site.*

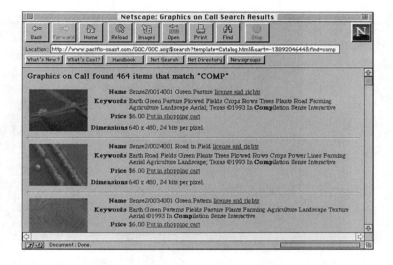

Sound

Just as motion picture "talkie" films represent a turning point in the history of film, the addition of sound to digital still images is a pivotal juncture in the evolution of the Web.

Sound Editors

Sound editors provide tools to edit a sound clip's wave pattern, which is a graphic representation of a digitized sound. Besides simple editing tools such as cut, copy, and paste, sound editors usually include tools to fade or amplify sound. The more powerful editors provide tools to mix sound and save the sound at different rates and sample sizes.

SoundEffects (Macintosh)

Alberto Ricci's SoundEffects is a shareware sound editor that will be available soon as a commercial program called Soundmaker. This powerful editor enables you to edit sound clips with a simple cut, copy, and paste technique. The software, shown in Figure 21.12, has many special effects that are comparable to larger, more expensive programs. It's also a tool for recording sound at a rate and sample size your hardware will allow. Recorded sounds can be mixed, edited, and altered with an easy-to-use interface.

FIGURE 21.12.
*Alberto Ricci's
SoundEffects software.*

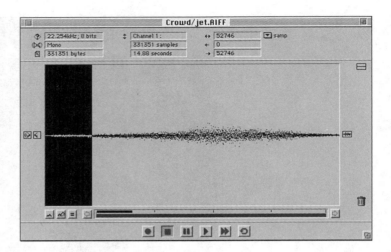

> **TIP**
>
> Alberto Ricci's SoundEffects software can be downloaded from
>
> `http://www.isc.rit.edu/~dmbwml/ftp.html`
>
> Note that shareware is not freeware. Shareware programs all have registration forms to fill out that provide the author's address. Fees typically range from $20 to $30. Every Macintosh Web page artist should be aware of the c/net shareware site at
>
> `http://www.shareware.com`
>
> and the Macintosh software archives at Stanford University:
>
> `ftp://sumex-aim.stanford.edu/info-mac/`

WHAM (Windows)

Andrew Bulhak's WHAM (Waveform Hold and Modify) is a Windows 3.1 shareware application for editing digitized sound. Although it's versatile, it has not been updated for Windows 95 or Windows NT. The software can read AU, AIFF, IFF, VOC, and WAV files and write WAV files, raw eight-bit digitized sound files, and several other formats.

Streaming Sound

Streaming sound or audio-on-demand is an exciting new development that emulates broadcast radio. It's been called "live" sound because there's no waiting for sound to download.

RealAudio (Macintosh and Windows)

RealAudio from Progressive Technology was the first streaming sound client introduced to the Web and also the first audio-on-demand client to be made available as a Netscape plug-in. When a Web visitor clicks on a RealAudio sound link, the sound clip starts playing immediately, as the file is being downloaded.

In order to distribute RealAudio sound, a RealAudio server software program is required. Sound files must also be put through an encoder program called RealAudio Studio. Progressive Technology has announced that future releases of the software will include bandwidth negotiation (for customizing audio quality to your connection speed), multimedia synchronization, and Java integration capabilities.

All the vendors in the field of streaming sound are interested in the broadcast market. Today, the broadcast market is limited by bandwidth, but that limitation is only temporary as telephone companies and cable firms will soon offer homes and businesses a variety of high-bandwidth options for connectivity to the Internet.

In spite of the existing bandwidth limitations, new, digital "media" companies are experimenting with digital sound formats that emulate traditional radio. Pseudo, a new media company in New York City, does a weekly "netcast" or online radio broadcast using RealAudio technology. The live, one-hour radio show is sponsored by Prodigy, *Net Guide Magazine*, and Nynex and is broadcast every Monday through Friday from 10:00 until 11:00 p.m. (Eastern Standard Time). The variety format features multimedia guru/celebrity interviews and live interactivity with cyber- and real-world audiences. Details about Pseudo's online radio broadcast can be found on its home page, shown in Figure 21.13.

FIGURE 21.13.

"Online radio" is described on Pseudo's home page at `http://pseudo.com/`.

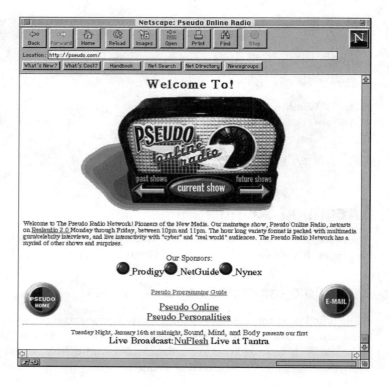

Streaming sound is now available from several vendors for both the Macintosh and Windows platforms. All of the vendors are distributing free players and free encoders and some charge for the server software that is necessary to distribute "sound streams."

Players, otherwise known as client software programs, can be downloaded from a sound vendor's Web site and reside on your hard drive. The entire Internet revolves around client/server software programs and streaming sound is just one example. For example, MCA Records' site contains a recording of Meat Loaf's concert at the Beacon Theater in New York recorded in RealAudio sound. The Web site (see Figure 21.14) describes the concert. In order to listen to the sound, however, Web visitors must first download a RealAudio client program from

`http://www.mca.com/mca_records/meatloaf.html`

After the client program is installed, a click on a sound link launches the RealAudio floating palette shown in Figure 21.15.

FIGURE 21.14.

MCA Records' site contains a recording of Meat Loaf's concert.

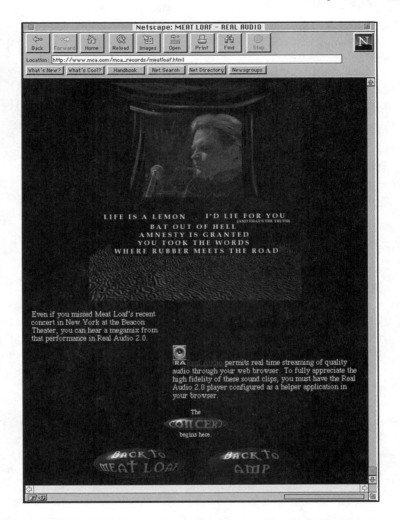

TIP

The RealAudio player, now available in its 2.0 version, is free and so is the encoder that is used to create RealAudio sound. For instructions on how to download the player and the encoder, visit the RealAudio site at

`http://www.realaudio.com`

For a complete list of RealAudio sites, visit

`http://www.realaudio.com/raguide.cgi`

FIGURE 21.15.
The RealAudio client software consists of a floating palette that has buttons to control sound.

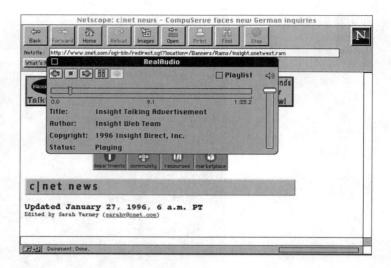

Internet Wave (Windows 3.x, 95, and NT)

Although Progressive Technology was the first to market its RealAudio streaming sound, Vocaltec, the company that makes the popular IPhone or Internet phone application, has introduced IWave or Internet Wave. Vocaltec and IWave are receiving a lot of attention since no server software is required to distribute sound. The sound files may be distributed through an httpd daemon. The player and the encoder are also free.

> **NOTE**
>
> *Daemon* is a UNIX term that refers to the process of waiting for a request. Servers such as the NCSA httpd or the CERN httpd are referred to as daemons because they wait for requests from the Web.

Sound Wire, a large record store on the Web (http://www.soundwire.com/), contains examples of how sound and other multimedia elements can be added to Web pages. (See Figure 21.16.) On the site, Web visitors can browse through a text index of album titles and click on links to view JPEG images of album covers. (See Figure 21.17.) Web sites that offer streaming sound often display an appropriate icon to identify the streaming sound format. For example, in Figure 21.18, the IWave icon is displayed on a Sound Wire Web page. Sound Wire owner Joe Maissel makes use of the IWave icon on other pages. Figure 21.19 shows how Joe has used the icon to flag the songs that are available in the IWave streaming sound format.

FIGURE 21.16.

Sound Wire, a large specialty record shop on the Web.

FIGURE 21.17.

Album cover image from Sound Wire.

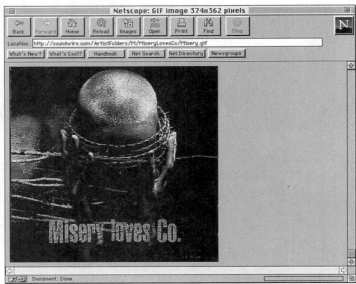

FIGURE 21.18.

*An IWave icon on a Sound
Wire Web page.*

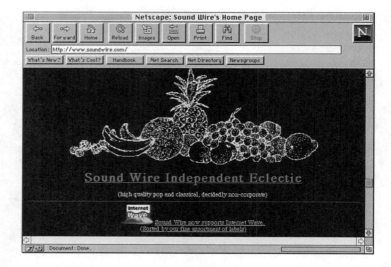

FIGURE 21.19.

*Sound Wire makes use
of the IWave icon in
a sound directory.*

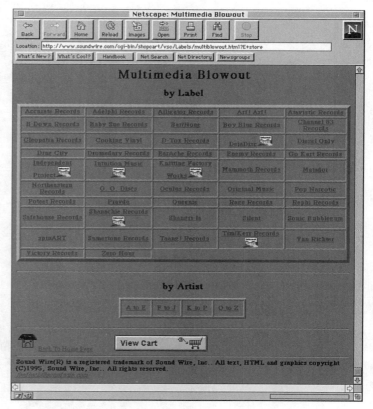

TIP

The IWave player is free, and so is the server software. For instructions on how to download the player, the server software, and the encoder, visit the IWave site at

`http://www.vocaltec.com/iwave.htm`

For a complete list of IWave sites, visit

`http://www.vocaltec.com/sites.htm`

Sound Clips

Although streaming sound is valuable for longer sound formats such as talk radio and full-length songs, sound clips are useful for short, often humorous, sound downloads. For example, the Zima site (`http://www.zima.com`), developed by Modem Media, uses sound clips the way they were once used on radio shows. The creators of this site have invented Duncan, a fictional Generation X character. Humorous soap opera-like installments involve Duncan and the details of his life with his roommates and his dates.

Writer Charles Marelli, the writer who created the Duncan character, weaves sound links into the Duncan dialog, as shown in Figure 21.20. In this soap opera-like installment, if a visitor clicks on the word *fire*, a sound is downloaded and a player application plays the sound. Web visitors who click on the Zima site's Fridge graphic (shown in Figure 21.21) are led to other Web pages containing archived pictures and sounds. For example, the "earwacks" bowl is a link to the sound archive shown in Figure 21.22.

FIGURE 21.20.

The Zima Web site's home page features the Duncan dialog.

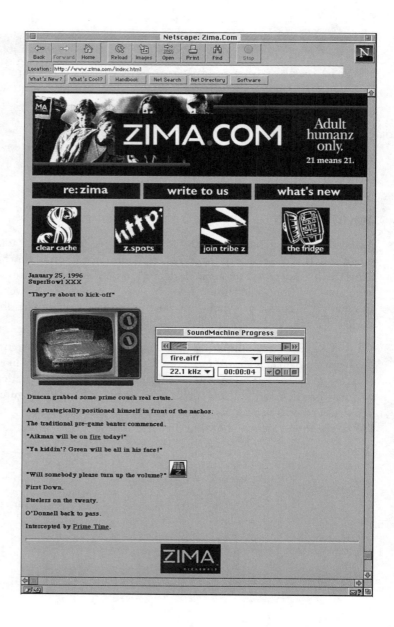

FIGURE 21.21.

"The fridge" on the Zima home page is a link to this humorous graphic that contains archived pictures and sounds.

FIGURE 21.21.

"The fridge" on the Zima home page is a link to this humorous graphic that contains archived pictures and sounds.

FIGURE 21.22.

Zima's "earwacks" directory of sound downloads.

Source for Sound Clips: University Archives

Sound clip libraries can be found at university archives located all over the Web. File formats vary and clips may need to be converted with sound applications for playback on different platforms.

Rob's Multimedia Lab, sponsored by the Association for Computing Machinery at the University of Illinois, maintains an archive of AU sound files. AU is a file format that can be read by Sun Sparc, NeXT workstations, and Macintosh computers.

> **TIP**
>
> Look for Rob's Multimedia Lab at
>
> `http://www.acm.uiuc.edu/rml/`
>
> Also check the following university sites for sound effects:
>
> `http://sunsite.sut.ac.jp/multimed/sounds/sound_effects/`
>
> `http://www.cs.uah.edu/cs/students/sanderso/ssndeff.html`

Source for Sound Clips: Sound Effects CD-ROMs

Bainbridge Records has created four sound effects CD-ROMs that are free-of-rights for non-commercial use. There is a one-time commercial licensing fee of $60 per disk. (Bainbridge Records, P.O. 49628, Los Angeles, California 90049, 1-800-621-8705 FAX: 1-310-440-4496.)

Video

Video on the Web is limited by bandwidth until the telephone and cable companies offer increased bandwidth options at reasonable costs. One such option is a cable modem. As of this writing, cable giants Time Warner and TCI are testing cable modems in Sunnyvale, California and Elmira, New York. Cable modems will connect computers to the Internet at a speed that is 700 times faster than a 14.4 Kbps modem.

Cable modem hardware is expected to cost somewhere in the range of $200–300 and cable firms predict monthly fees to range from $10–30 per month. The connection will require a coaxial cable installation, which is separate from the coaxial cable used for television. In California, this installation charge is a one-time fee of $60.

Although the cable companies have a larger "wire," the system is not symmetrical. Until the cable companies upgrade their cables to accommodate two-way data transmission, Web surfers interested in cable modems will need two modems. They'll stack their telephone modem on top of their cable modem for the time being. Data will be delivered *to the Web surfer's computer* at a speed that is 700 times faster than a 14.4Kbps modem and the data sent *from the Web surfer's computer* will still use the traditional modem connection of 14.4Kbps or 28.8Kbps.

In spite of the obstacles, the development of cable modems heralds a significant turning point in the delivery of high-bandwidth multimedia over the Web. It will enable a flood of elements such as video and sound. In the wake of such aggressive performance, the demand for digital video and sound can be expected to surge.

Video Editors

In the category of digital video editing for Macintosh and Windows, Adobe Premiere has no competitor. Larger, more expensive software programs also require dedicated hardware. Adobe Premiere is a reasonably priced off-the-shelf program that is held in high regard by the computer graphics community.

Adobe Premiere (Macintosh and Windows)

Just as Adobe Photoshop is the most popular image editing tool among Web artists, Adobe Premiere is the most popular video editing tool. Although the Macintosh and the Windows versions are identical, the Macintosh version creates QuickTime movie files and the Windows version creates AVI files. Premiere can be used to edit existing clips or be used in combination with a capture board to digitize video from any video source.

Adobe Premiere gives an artist control over numerous variables. Among these, those that have an impact on file size include the following:

- frame size
- color
- presence or absence of an audio track
- frame rate
- software compression

For movies that will be distributed over the Web, follow these guidelines:

- Use the smallest possible frame size.
- Sacrifice color for black and white whenever possible.
- Eliminate audio if possible.
- Use the lowest possible frame rate and use Premiere to delete frames containing objects that do not move.
- Use Cinepak compression for best results.

To keep a video clip's file size to a minimum, keep the dimensions of the frame within the "postage-stamp" size of 160×120 pixels, as shown in Figure 21.23. Premiere will allow cropping to achieve even smaller frame sizes if desired. Eliminating the audio track is another technique which can be used to keep file size to a minimum. Every time an edited movie gets written to disk, Premiere's output options provide the means to define the movie's characteristics. For example, in Figure 21.24, the Audio check box in the Project Output Options dialog box is left unchecked, so the audio track does not get saved. In addition to selecting output options, a movie editor typically selects a movie compression option. In Figure 21.25, Cinepak is selected as the compressor option in this Adobe premiere dialog box which appears when a movie is output as a QuickTime clip.

FIGURE 21.23.

The 160×120 pixel frame has been nicknamed the "postage-stamp."

FIGURE 21.24.

The Project Output Options dialog box.

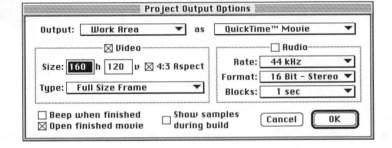

FIGURE 21.25.

The compressor option dialog box.

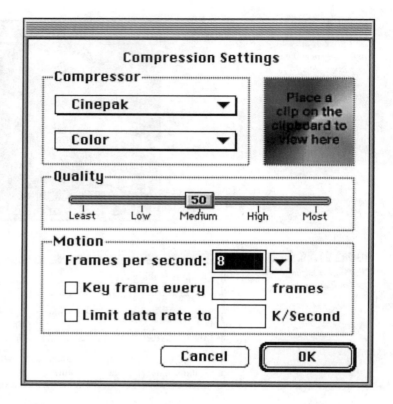

For a Web artist concerned with bandwidth limitations, Premiere's Movie Analysis tool provides a valuable means to understand the variables that determine a video clip's file size. Beginners should consider downloading a few video clips and studying the movie's characteristics with the Movie Analysis tool. (See Figure 21.26.) The tool provides valuable movie statistics such as file size, data rate, frame rate, and the compressor used.

Sony Music and Sound Wire Music are examples of Web sites that offer digital video clip file downloads. Figure 21.27 shows The Spin Doctor's video clip in a QuickTime player window and Sony's list of video clips listing the file size, the number of seconds, the frame rate, and the video file format (http://www.sony.com). Figure 21.28 shows Sound Wire Music's similar list and a Flaming Lips video (http://www.soundwire.com).

FIGURE 21.26.

Adobe Premiere's Movie Analysis tool.

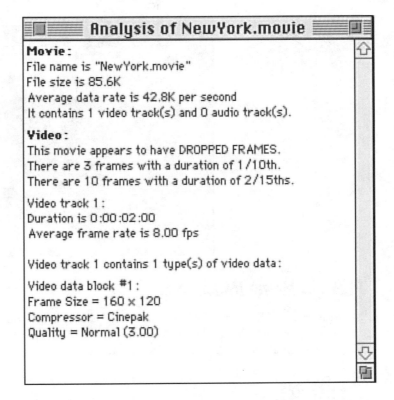

FIGURE 21.27.

The Spin Doctors video clip from the Sony site.

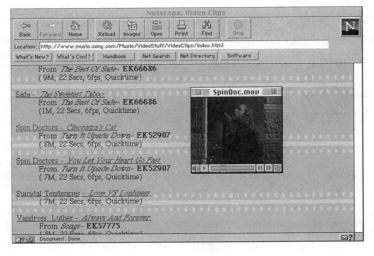

FIGURE 21.28.

The Sound Wire record shop on the Web offers video clips of music videos.

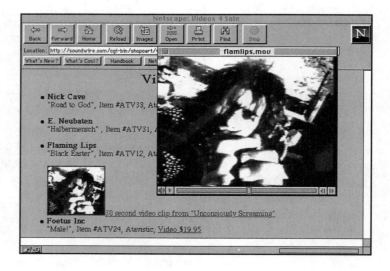

PICTS to Movie (Macintosh)

David Rees's PICTS to Movie is a Macintosh freeware utility that will stitch a QuickTime movie together from PICT files on your hard drive. Just open the software and point to one PICT image or a folder of PICT images. David can be reached at `D.Rees@cs.ucl.ac.uk`.

Animation

Animation on the Web comes in a variety of forms, including cgi or server push animation, GIF animation, Macromedia's Director Shockwave animation, and Java animation. Cgi and Java both require advanced programming skills and aren't covered in this chapter.

GIF Animation

BoxTop's GIF-mation software is a $20 program that saves multi-image GIF file animations instead of QuickTime movies. These multi-image animations can be embedded in an HTML file to play as inline animations in the Netscape browser.

Multiple image GIF files are part of the original GIF89a spec. Netscape has implemented support in their browser to play them when the browser sees the file in an IMG tag. In the multiple-image animation shown in Figure 21.29, Fred Krughoff has created a plug that moves across the screen (`http://www.romdog.com`).

BoxTop Software's GIF-mation software, shown in Figure 21.30, imports Photoshop, PICT, TIFF, JPEG, PCX, BMP, ScitexCT, and PhotoCD files. The software also provides a color reduction feature for cutting imported images down to 256 colors or less. There is also support for creating a "matching global palette" for all images in a multi-image GIF. It opens single and multiple image files directly and saves single or multiple image GIFs. You can download GIF-mation from BoxTop's page at

`http://www.aris.com/boxtop/GIFmation`

FIGURE 21.29.

Multiple-image GIF animation causes the plug to move across the screen.

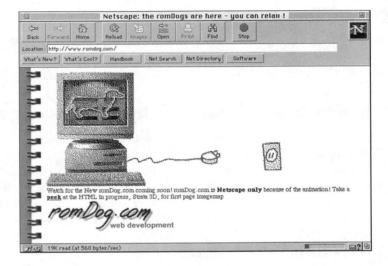

FIGURE 21.30.

GIF-mation software from BoxTop software.

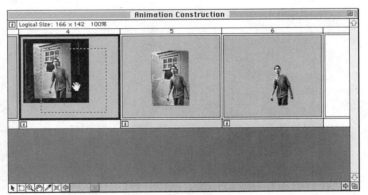

Macromedia's Shockwave

Macromedia has introduced their own "streaming" technology to the Web that provides animation and interactivity in the form of Director movies. The technology, nicknamed "Shockwave," delivers movies to Web viewers on Macintosh and Windows computers and through a Netscape plug-in. The plug-in plays Director movies the same way streaming audio players play sound.

Although file size is not as much an issue with streaming files as it is with movie downloads, artists should always consider file sizes as a courtesy to end-users on the Web who have minimal hardware. Although Macromedia supplies an efficient movie compression tool called Afterburner, these tricks can help keep Shockwave movies to minimum file sizes:

- Colorize one-bit cast members on-stage whenever possible.
- Use Director's tiles to fill a background.
- Keep an eye on cast member size and remap the bit-depth (to a lower bit-depth) whenever possible.
- Use small sound clips and loop sound whenever possible.

Macromedia's Lingo, a Scripting Language

One of the best ways to create compact Director movies is to use Lingo, Macromedia's Hypertalk-like language. Lingo provides almost unlimited interactivity and animation through English-like sentences used to initiate action while the movie is running. The language can also be used to control conditional actions based on viewer responses such as text entry or mouse clicks on objects. Figure 21.31 shows a Shockwave animation created for alt.coffee, an Internet cafe in New York's East Village (`http://www.altdotcoffee.com`).

FIGURE 21.31.

The Shockwave movie, created for alt.coffee, was developed and art directed by Larry Rosenthal and "shocked" by DJ Hacker. It has a minimal file size because the animation is controlled through Lingo scripts.

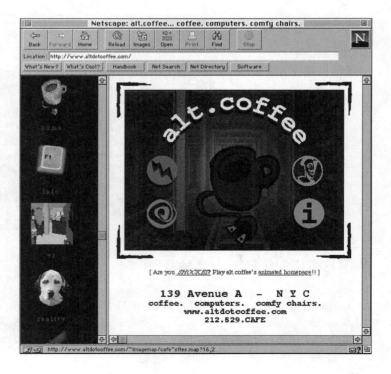

Color Backgrounds and Text

Anyone who tours the Web notices the possibilities for color in the Netscape background and text. What may still be a mystery are the tools that can be used to find a desired shade.

HTML Color and RGB Hex

Tools have evolved to help Web artists find the necessary hexadecimal red-green-blue triple required to add color to the browser background and browser text. The hexadecimal triplet is added to the body background HTML tag, and when the tag gets read by the browser, these elements change color. The tools that help an artist convert familiar RGB data found in Photoshop to the necessary triplet are called color editors.

BBS Color Editors

Robert Liu, who runs the Best Business Solutions (BBS) Web site, has provided an online tool that can be used to convert Photoshop RGB data to the hexadecimal red-green-blue triplet required in the body background HTML tag.

Although BBS provides an on-screen list of colors, they've added special fields to their color editor for Photoshop users. If you're familiar with Photoshop's color palette, you'll be familiar with the RGB data Photoshop displays for each color on the Color Picker dialog box. Photoshop will display RGB data for any shade, the most popular of which are the Pantone shades. When the Input data field is checked and the RGB data is typed into the BBS RGB fields, click the Test it Now button shown in Figure 21.32. The color editor will turn the background color to the selected shade and display the red-green-blue triplet, as shown in Figure 21.33.

The BBS online color editor can be found at

```
http://www.infocom.net/~bbs/cgi-bin/colorEditor.cgi
```

In addition to their online color editor, Best Business Solutions has also created a color editor application for Windows that can be downloaded to your hard drive. Since HTML documents are usually created offline, this is a useful tool to have on hand. Look for the offline color editor at

```
http://www.bbsinc.com/colorEditor_FAQ.html#WIN
```

FIGURE 21.32.
*The Web's BBS
color editor.*

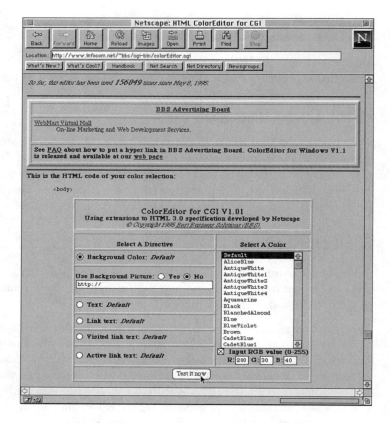

FIGURE 21.33.
*The BBS color editor
returns a tomato-red color
and the hexadecimal triplet
is displayed. Note the
#c81e0a in this figure.*

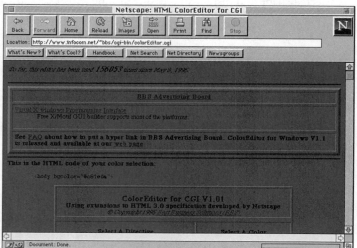

HTML Tools for Assembling Multimedia

The next sections feature some tools from assembling multimedia from Microsoft, Adobe Systems, and Astrobyte.

Microsoft Tools

Microsoft has created what they refer to as a "spectrum" of HTML authoring tools for different users and their needs. The most basic tool is the Microsoft Office Internet Assistants, which add HTML functionality to the Microsoft Office product line. An intermediate-level technology called FrontPage is designed for end-users, business professionals, and Web-site managers who are not programmers. Microsoft's advanced tool is called Internet Studio. It can include programming and interactive multimedia.

Microsoft Office Internet Assistants—Microsoft has added Web authoring tools to the Microsoft Office line by providing "Office Internet Assistants" to be used with applications such as Microsoft Word, Microsoft Excel, and Microsoft PowerPoint. The Office Internet Assistants are designed to create simple, stand-alone HTML pages.

FrontPage—On January 16, 1996, Microsoft acquired Vermeer Technologies, Inc., a pioneer of standards-based Web publishing tools based in Cambridge, Massachusetts. Although FrontPage is designed with the non-programmer in mind, the application is much more sophisticated than the Office Internet Assistants. It includes document management tools, text searches, feedback forms, and threaded discussion forums entirely without programming. The Office Internet Assistant products can be integrated with FrontPage technology because those documents can be incorporated into FrontPage Web documents.

Internet Studio—Microsoft's most sophisticated Web publishing is known as Internet Studio (formerly code-named Blackbird). Although Internet Studio contains drag-and-drop functionality, eliminating the need for any programming, the program can include integrated programming via OLE and a published SDK.

TIP

Microsoft's FrontPage technology and its Internet Studio are tools that add enhancements to Web publishing in the form of style sheets. At the same time Microsoft is introducing products that incorporate style sheets, the W3 Consortium is about to draft its own specification. The W3 Consortium was formed as an international joint initiative to develop common standards and is run by the laboratory for Computer Science at the Massachusetts Institute of Technology. For background information on the "Cascading Style Sheet Specification," see

```
http://www.w3.org/hypertext/WWW/Style/css/draft1.html
```

A Tool from Adobe Systems

PageMill, a Web authoring tool from Adobe Systems, offers Web page artists a word processing-like environment where they can apply styles, place and resize images, and drag and drop parts of a document to another position. PageMill will output an HTML 2.0 document; it also supports some of the commonly used Netscape extensions such as text, link, and background color. Future releases of PageMill will support features from HTML Version 3. Although a Web page artist cannot see HTML tags from within PageMill, HTML tags may be entered directly into a PageMill page using the Raw HTML style.

A QuarkXpress Xtension

BeyondPress is a QuarkXpress Xtension from a company called Astrobyte located in Denver, Colorado. The software converts documents designed for print into a linear online format. It also converts linear articles into HTML pages and images into JPEG or GIF images. Users can create hypertext links in their QuarkXpress documents in the form of references to elements on the same page or other URL addresses. Astrobyte's Web site is at

```
http://www.astrobyte.com
```

Summary

Many of the first multimedia presentation tools for Web artists are adaptations of tools created for print artists. Later this year and next year, a second generation of tools will emerge with Web-specific features. If HTML, text, pics, and Netscape extensions are the Web's first wave of technology, then Java, database engines, and Shockwave are the second. Watch for interfaces that artists can use to create Java applets and database publishing applications.

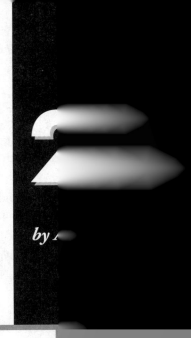

Creating VRML Worlds

by

Virtual Reality Modeling Language (VRML) is a way to describe virtual worlds on the Web, just as HTML describes Web pages. Soon, having a home page on the World Wide Web will not be enough. You'll need your own home world (`home.wrl`) as well! As Java becomes integrated with VRML, you'll also be able to write Java code to animate and enliven your VRML worlds.

This chapter introduces what Virtual Reality Modeling Language is, what it looks like (see Figure 22.1), what you can do with it, and how it works. You get a look at the most exciting developments so far in wedding Java to VRML, from such companies as Dimension X, Paper Software, and WorldMaker; source code for Java/VRML examples is included. At this point, Java APIs for VRML are still being developed, so these examples are right at the cutting edge. Java is discussed in technical detail in Chapter 24, "Writing Java Applets."

FIGURE 22.1.

Aereal Serch is a VRML world by Dennis McKenzie and Adrian Scott with links to other worlds inside the various buildings.

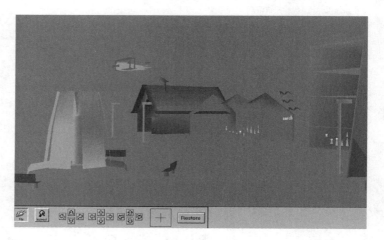

This chapter also discusses designing a VRML site and what kinds of business models could work for VRML creators. Appendix E, "VRML Resource Directory," offers pointers to URLs relating to information, software, examples, and converters.

The goal of virtual reality is to create an immersive experience, so that you feel you are in the middle of a separate virtual world. Virtual reality generally relies upon three-dimensional computerized graphics plus audio. Virtual reality uses a first-person outlook. You are moving about in the virtual world, rather than controlling a computer-generated figure moving around in the world.

Whereas HTML is a markup language, VRML (pronounced "ver-mul") is not. This chapter presents a look at a simple world described in the standard VRML ASCII text representation, including screen shots of what it actually looks like using a VRML browser.

What is a VRML browser? A VRML browser is to VRML what a standard browser like Mosaic or Netscape is to HTML. The VRML browser loads in a virtual world described in VRML, then renders it in three-dimensional graphics and lets you roam through the virtual world. You can select links in the virtual world that can take you to other worlds, or any other URL, such as an HTML page or a GIF image.

Your VRML and standard WWW browsers will communicate, so that when you select a link to an HTML file from a virtual world, your standard WWW browser will load in that URL. Conversely, when you select a link to a VRML file from your standard WWW browser, the WWW browser will recognize the MIME type and pass the URL or VRML file over to your VRML browser. In the future we may see added capabilities in VRML browsers, so that they can render an HTML page without having to switch to the standard WWW browser.

One of the exciting developments in browsers has been the use of VRML plug-ins to other browsers, which Paper Software's WebFX VRML plug-in pioneered. Working as a plug-in, the VRML is displayed in the standard area of the WWW browser where HTML is normally displayed. And in some cases, such as Netscape's browser, there can be multiple VRML worlds showing at one time within an HTML page.

VRML files can be sent using the standard HTTP servers you use for your current HTML Web sites. In the future, we may see new kinds of servers with special capabilities suited to virtual reality applications, or these may be a part of HTTP NG, a future version of HTTP.

So what might your home world look like? You might have a three-dimensional figure of yourself, or even of your living room (real or virtual?!). If you like windsurfing, you might have a windsurfer in some waves, linked to a map of your favorite windsurfing spots. Or you could have an artistic sculpture floating in mid-air.

History of VRML

At the first World Wide Web conference in 1994, Tim Berners-Lee (developer of the World Wide Web concept) and Dave Raggett organized a session known as a "Birds-of-a-Feather" (BOF) session to discuss Virtual Reality and how it could be applied to the Web. Things took off rapidly, with the creation of an e-mail list for discussion of what was then called Virtual Reality Markup Language.

Since VRML isn't an equivalent to SGML or HTML, and because of its graphical nature, the word Markup was later changed to Modeling, though you can still find references to VR Markup Language floating around the Net. Memes are hard to kill.

The initial BOF meeting included several people who were working on 3-D graphical interfaces to the Web. The e-list grew and grew: within a week, there were more than one thousand members on the list. The list moderator is Mark Pesce, one of the prime architects of VRML. Pesce announced the goal of having a draft version of the VRML specification ready for the Fall 1994 WWW Conference.

Rather than reinvent the wheel, the list members wanted to choose an existing technology as a starting point. Several proposals were put together. You can still see these proposals at the VRML

Repository Web Sites. Eventually (try getting agreement among that many people!), the list chose the Open Inventor ASCII File Format developed at Silicon Graphics.

A subset of this format with extensions for WWW hyperlinks came to form VRML's birthday suit. With input from the list members, Gavin Bell of SGI adapted the format for VRML. SGI allowed the format to be used in the open market, and also put a parser into the public domain to help VRML gain momentum.

After the draft specification of VRML 1.0, the list members looked at what changes might be needed. This was around the time I joined the list. We considered the complexity of various enhancements and the desirability of having them available. We decided that text was pretty important. Without a text node, you would have had to create a file describing all of the text letters as polygons. Thus, the AsciiText and FontStyle nodes were introduced. In addition, changes were made to the LevelOfDetail node, and it was renamed LOD.

The three credited authors of the VRML 1.0 specification are Gavin Bell of SGI, Anthony Parisi of Intervista, and Mark Pesce, the list moderator. Other major contributors are Chris Marrin of SGI and Jan Hardenbergh of Oki Advanced Products.

After the VRML 1.0 specification had been published for some months and browser writers and authoring tool developers rushed to complete their VRML software, it became clear that there were some ambiguities in the specification. Thus, a clarification to the 1.0 version was published.

In December of 1995, the first VRML Symposium was held in San Diego. It was the first exclusive VRML gathering and excitement was everywhere. Several large companies not initially involved in VRML had become quite interested and came to the Symposium with their own proposals for how VRML should evolve in the future.

A VRML Consortium will most likely be created very shortly. In the meantime, the www-vrml e-list and a group known as the VRML Architecture Group (http://vag.vrml.org) are involved with leading the analysis of proposals for future versions of VRML.

There are currently proposals for VRML 1.1 and 2.0. Neither has been finalized.

What You Need for VRML

The very minimal setup for experiencing VRML is a computer and VRML browser software. An Internet connection is necessary to download worlds. However, VRML worlds stored on a computer disk can be viewed without an Internet connection. Actually, when I started out creating VRML software, I didn't even have VRML browser software, so I had to use wetware— my imagination—to visualize how my VRML worlds might look.

A basic VRML setup would include a 486/50 computer with 8MB of RAM; VRML browser software such as WebFX, WebSpace, or WorldView; and an Internet connection over a 14.4

Kbps modem. This will give you basic performance; as the first versions of the VRML browsers are CPU-intensive and complicated, uncompressed VRML worlds can take up as much as 500K (which takes a while to transfer over a 14.4 Kbps Internet connection). However, world authors are learning how to create interesting worlds that can be as small as 20K compressed.

Serious VRML creators will want to move towards a UNIX workstation and a T1 connection for improved rendering and Internet bandwidth. However, to create VRML worlds, all that you really need is a text editor and knowledge of the VRML Specification.

There are many VRML browsers available. The most popular ones are WebFX from Paper Software (http://www.paperinc.com), WebSpace from Silicon Graphics (http://webspace.sgi.com) and Template Graphics (http://www.tgs.com/~template), WorldView from Intervista (http://www.intervista.com), and VR Scout from Chaco Communications (http://www.chaco.com).

To go beyond the basic system setup, you can start getting into fancy input and output devices. Head-mounted displays bring virtual worlds closer to your eyes by displaying the worlds on two small screens that are part of glasses you wear. Some HMDs block out the outside world or let you see through the display, so that your virtual world can overlay the real world. Prices on head-mounted display devices have dropped into the $500–$700 price range, so they will become more popular.

Head tracking devices on the HMDs can figure out which direction you are facing and relay this information to the browser to change your orientation.

Using a 3-D mouse, you can move around in the three-dimensional virtual world, just as a standard mouse lets you move around in two dimensions. Another input device is the data glove. However, data gloves are not yet user-friendly, nor are there any great applications for them. In general, 3-D input devices are not yet mature, so that many people will still be happy using keyboard/mouse combinations. Some of the recent input and output devices for virtual reality are the 5th Glove from Fifth Dimension Technologies and the "i-glasses!" HMD with tracking from Virtual I/O. As the VRML browsers develop, expanded support for advanced input and output devices will expand.

Using the Browsers

Once you have downloaded a VRML browser from the Internet (see Appendix E for URLs) and installed the browser, you are ready to get started.

Browsers come with some simple worlds that you can load into the VRML browser to begin with. Once you get familiar with the navigation commands, you can start moving out around the Web. A nice starting point on the Web is Aereal Serch, which is a VRML world with links to many other VRML worlds found at

http://www.virtpark.com/theme/serch/home.wrl.gz

WebFX

In the main navigation mode, you can use a combination of keyboard and mouse to move around. For example, in WebFX from Paper Software (Figure 22.2), the keys in Fly mode resemble the keys in the game Descent: the arrow keys affect the orientation of your head, and A and Z move you forward and backward. In Walk mode, the keys are like the game Doom: the up and down arrow keys move you forward and backward, and the left and right keys turn you left or right. Holding down the Alt key while using the arrow keys lets you pan to the sides. Several browsers feature an Examiner or Model mode, where you can spin around the world rather than moving around inside it. In WebFX, this is accomplished by holding down the right mouse button and moving the mouse. A fun thing to do in WebFX and WebSpace is to "fling" with the mouse: hold down the button and quickly move the mouse and let go of the button while the mouse is moving. This will spin the world around and leave it spinning—very cool!

FIGURE 22.2.

WebFX from
Paper Software.

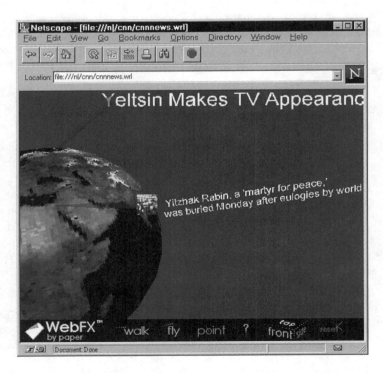

In WebFX, if you tap the right mouse button for a moment, a menu appears that enables you to change the settings or change cameras (move to a different part of the world).

WebSpace

WebSpace from SGI and TGS features a unique user interface for the mouse. Examiner mode, where you spin the world around, is controlled with a trackball-style sphere (which will look familiar to fans of the old Centipede) and a roller that moves you forward into and backward out of the world. In Walk mode (Figure 22.3), you move around with a bar that looks like the handlebars of a tricycle. Somehow, I feel like I'm driving a golf cart. Note that there is a little notch on the right side of the bar; this notch attempts to give an indication of the vertical tilt of your viewpoint. This enables you to see if you are looking up or down while you move around.

FIGURE 22.3.

A VRML world viewed with WebSpace.

WorldView

WorldView from Intervista is geared towards using the mouse for navigation (Figure 22.4). It has three boxes of buttons that correspond to panning, tilting, and flying. You can also choose between Fly and Inspect modes. In Inspect mode, you are spinning around the world itself rather than navigating in it. WorldView defaults to a blue background in worlds. Also, WorldView works as a stand-alone browser, so you can start navigating around VRML space without starting up a standard WWW browser.

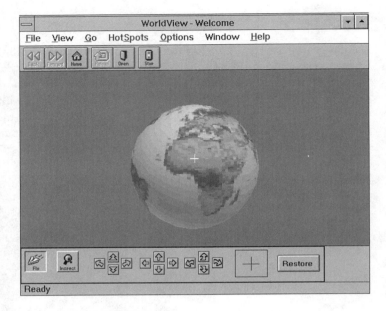

FIGURE 22.4.
A Virtual World viewed with WorldView from Intervista.

Introduction to Creating VRML Worlds

Creating VRML can be challenging at first. It's not nearly as easy as HTML, nor are VRML browsers nearly as forgiving as HTML browsers. There are two ways to get started. First you can use a Web-based VRML authoring tool called Aereal Phonts to create VRML that uses 3-D fonts. You can also get into hand coding some simple VRML worlds.

Aereal Phonts

To give you a feeling for what VRML looks like, Listing 22.1 offers a short VRML world, created with Aereal Phonts, a simple Web-based, publicly accessible VRML authoring tool (http://www.virtpark.com/theme/phonts.html). A dialog box for this world is illustrated in Figure 22.5.

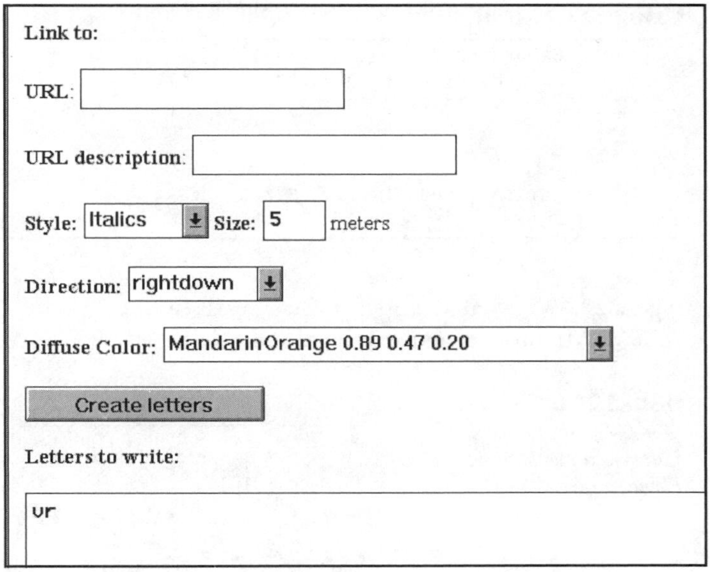

FIGURE 22.5.

Creating a simple VRML world with Aereal Phonts.

Link to:

URL:

URL description:

Style: `Italics` ⬦ Size: `5` meters

Direction: `rightdown` ⬦

Diffuse Color: `Mandarin Orange 0.89 0.47 0.20` ⬦

Create letters

Letters to write:

`vr`

Listing 22.1. The letters "vr" in VRML, created with Aereal Phonts (re-formatted for easy reading).

```
#VRML V1.0 ascii

Separator {
     Material { diffuseColor 0.89 0.47 0.20 }
     Scale { scaleFactor 5 5 5 }
     MatrixTransform { matrix 1 0 0 0 .3 1 0 0 0 1 0 0 0 0 1 }
     Separator {
          Translation { translation .1 .2 0 }
          Separator {
               Rotation { rotation 0 0 -1 -.4 }
               DEF a Cylinder { radius .05 height .45 }
          }
          Translation { translation .2 0 0 }
          Separator {
               Rotation { rotation 0 0 -1 .4 }
               USE a
          }
     }

     Translation { translation .5 0 0 }
     Separator {
          Translation { translation .05 .2 0 }
          Cylinder { radius .05 height .4 }
          Translation { translation .15 .12 0 }
```

continues

Listing 22.1. continued

```
        Separator {
            Rotation { rotation 0 0 -1 1.57 }
            Cylinder { radius .05 height .25 }
        }
    }

    Translation { translation .5 0 0 }
}
```

Figure 22.6 shows an example of what you'll see when you load this world (Listing 22.1) into your VRML browser and spin it around.

FIGURE 22.6.

Wandering in VRML world created with Aereal Phonts.

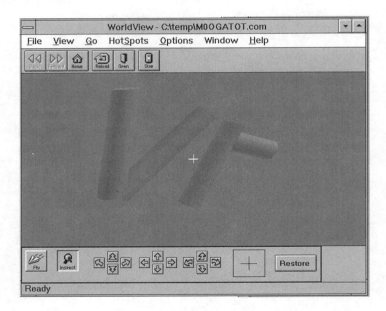

Creating a Simple Home World

The MIME-type for VRML is x-world/x-vrml. If you haven't convinced your Web site administrator to add the VRML MIME-type to your Web server yet, you can set up a simple CGI script that starts out with the following line (in Perl).

```
print "Content-type: x-world/x-vrml\n\n";
```

After that, you can have the script print out the rest of your VRML world.

As shown in Listing 22.1, a VRML world starts off with the first line:

```
#VRML V1.0 ascii
```

Anything after a "#" in a line of a VRML script is considered a comment. For transmission purposes, comments can be stripped out of a VRML file before it is transmitted across a network. If you want anything like a copyright or other information to get to the viewer, you should use an Info node. The Info node lets you put nonrendered information into a VRML file in legal VRML. However, at the current time, none of the HTTP servers have been configured to strip the comments out, so you can be a bit sloppy in the near future!

Each VRML world consists of one node. Typically, that one node will be a Separator node that includes a grouping of various nodes inside it. Nodes can represent shapes like cubes and cones, properties like colors and textures, or groupings. Nodes can also give World Wide Web references, such as hyperlinks or inline worlds, similar to HREFs and inline graphics in HTML. (Shouldn't we call them inspace worlds?) As an example, the Material node is a property node that enables you to assign colors and transparency properties.

For a detailed description of VRML nodes, refer to the VRML Specification, at

`http://www.hyperreal.com/~mpesce/vrml/vrml.tech/vrml10-3.html`

A VRML-enabled HTML version of the Spec is at

`http://www.virtpark.com/theme/vrml/`

Now to make a simple VRML Home World from scratch, by hand, to illustrate how the language works. Figure 22.7 illustrates what it looks like in a VRML browser.

FIGURE 22.7.

Simple, hand-created VRML world.

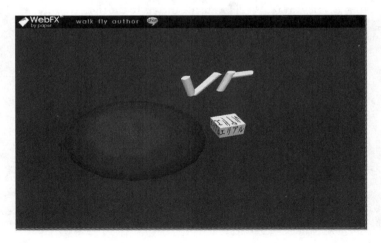

We start off with the VRML header and a Separator node to hold the nodes we will soon add (Listing 22.2).

Listing 22.2. A basic VRML file.

```
#VRML V1.0 ascii
Separator {
}
```

This is a valid VRML file. It will load into your VRML browser, but you won't see anything. Listing 22.3 shows the code to add a blue sphere. We use a Material node to set the color to a blue, and then add a Sphere node with radius 5 meters.

Listing 22.3. A blue sphere in VRML.

```
#VRML V1.0 ascii
Separator {

    # blue sphere
    Material { diffuseColor 0 0 .7 }  # sets the color to blue
    Sphere { radius 5 } # creates the sphere with radius 5 meters
}
```

Now that we have something showing up in the browser, we'll add something with more visual depth to it. Find an image file on your computer or on the Web. Your VRML browser should support JPEG, GIF, and maybe BMP formats. We are going to add a cube that uses the image as a texture. We'll locate it 7 meters to the right (positive x) of the blue sphere by adding in a Translation node (Listing 22.4).

Listing 22.4. A blue sphere and a texture-mapped cube.

```
#VRML V1.0 ascii
Separator {

    # blue sphere
    Material { diffuseColor 0 0 .7 } # sets the color to blue
    Sphere { radius 5 } # creates the sphere with radius 5 meters

    # textured cube
    Translation { translation 7 0 0 } # moves away from the sphere
    Texture2 { filename "image.jpg" } # sets the texture to image.jpg
    Cube { } # creates the cube
}
```

In Listing 22.4, image.jpg refers to the URL or filename of your image file. Now your home world is starting to get somewhere. As the final touch, add in the VRML you created using Aereal Phonts. We do this using the WWWInline node and the URL for the VRML world you created with Aereal Phonts. We'll also use another Translation node to move from the center of the cube to the area above and between the sphere and cube (Listing 22.5).

Listing 22.5. The blue sphere and texture-mapped cube plus the letters "vr" in VRML as a WWWInline.

```
#VRML V1.0 ascii
Separator {

    # blue sphere
    Material { diffuseColor 0 0 .7 } # sets the color to blue
    Sphere { radius 5 } # creates the sphere with radius 5 meters

    # textured cube
    Translation { translation 7 0 0 } # moves away from the sphere
    Texture2 { filename "image.jpg" } # sets the texture to image.jpg
    Cube { } # creates the cube

    # WWWInline the Aereal Phonts world
    Translation { translation -3.5 6 0 } # move above the sphere & cube
    WWWInline { # render the following VRML world inside this world
        name "http://www.virtpark.com/theme/cgi-bin/world/Proteinman.wrl"
    }
}
```

Just replace the "name" URL in the WWWInline node with the URL of your Aereal Phonts world and your simple VRML home world is ready. As you can see in this example, WWWInline is a very powerful feature that taps into the power of the World Wide Web as a whole and differentiates VRML from non-Web attempts at VR.

VRML Site Design

Follow these steps when designing a VRML site at Aereal:

1. Identify goal of site.
2. Identify participants.
3. Create wild ideas for site possibilities, including multiuser interactivity, sound, and behaviors.
4. Consider bandwidth and rendering concerns of participants.
5. Plan range of site configurations.
6. Design overall framework of site.
7. Create actual VRML objects.
8. Integrate into completed site.
9. Perform initial testing and refinement.
10. Conduct testing with amateur users, assessment of site goal feasibility, and refinement.
11. Continue ongoing improvement and redesign of site.

The next sections examine these steps in detail.

Identify Goal of Site

This is the most important step for any Web site. If it's a commercial site, is the goal to build name recognition or actually sell product? For a political site, is the goal to win votes or register voters? Without clear goals, Web sites end up being little more than a show of what technology can do. To have a successful site, you first need to figure out what being successful means to you. VRML sites should be more than fancy 3-D worlds.

Identify Participants

Note that I don't write audience or viewers here. In the immersive experience of virtual reality, everyone at your site is part of your world. Companies have experienced how easy it is to offend Netizens (Net denizens/citizens) with overly commercial pitches. With VRML, the emotions are raised to a higher level. Therefore, you want to know who you're creating this site for. What are their desires, values, attitudes and concerns?

Create Wild Ideas for Site Possibilities

At the beginning, you'll want to create wild ideas without regard for the current limitations of technology. Include plans for multiuser interactivity, sound, and behaviors. What is your world about? What should it feel like to wander around your world? What kind of amusements or information representations would participants like?

Bandwidth and Rendering Concerns

There are two key bottlenecks for networked VRML: bandwidth and rendering speed. Thus, you'll want to think about the technological limitations of your participants. Will they be dialing up from 14.4 Kbps modems? Will they have UNIX graphics workstations or just 486 PCs?

It's important not to limit yourself too much by these considerations at this planning stage because technology is advancing so quickly that concepts of slow and fast are continually changing.

Plan Range of Site Configurations

Based on the previous steps, you should have some idea of what you want from your site. Now you can think about what kind of site configurations you want. Do you want different versions (different file sizes) for participants on different bandwidths? Will there be a version of your world with texture-mapping or more polygons for users with advanced graphics capabilities?

Design Overall Framework of Site

Now is the time to lay out an overall framework or foundation for your site. You can do this on paper, or in a CAD package, or even in VRML. At this step, you're just developing an outline, saying, "The house is here," without creating the whole house. This gives you an idea of what the experience of being in your world will be like, without having to get it fully there.

At this stage, you might use common objects to get a quick draft up. For instance, you might have the file house.wrl lying around in one of your directories. Though eventually you want to have an intricate house in that location, you can use this one as a WWWInline in the meantime.

Another important point at this step is to plan the number of polygons that will be visible from each point in the world. You can plan LOD node levels of detail to kick in at various distances with different polygon counts. The LOD node lets you describe an object with different representations at different distances. Then look at the overlap of the different LOD areas to make sure you don't sock the user's computer with tens of thousands of polygons in parts of your world. This planning will help make rendering quicker and navigation easier for the user. A good starting range is 5,000 to 10,000 maximum polygons visible at one time. (Expect this number to go up over the next couple of years!)

Create Actual VRML Objects

Next you can create the actual VRML objects to populate your world. You can use CAD packages together with file format conversion software, use VRML authoring tools, or even write VRML by hand with a text editor.

Integrate into Completed Site

At this stage you want to collect all of the objects and the framework together to bring your world into virtual existence. As an example, you might have started out designing your framework and objects in a CAD software package. At this stage, you can edit the files after converting them to VRML. You'll insert special VRML features like the hyperlink nodes WWWAnchor and WWWInline, plus the special LOD node giving VRML information on switching between different objects at different distances. You also can run scripts to optimize file sizes at this point.

Initial Testing and Refinement

At this stage, you want to make sure that the basic world works and that it can be accessed through the various combinations of bandwidth and rendering speeds your participants will have. You will also want to check that navigation is easy. Navigation is one of the biggest challenges in the first VRML worlds that have been created. See if you and other people are able to move around in the world and find the links and information you want them to find.

Testing, Assessment, and Refinement

If you're designing a site where you're expecting tens of thousands of accesses daily and you want the site to represent your product, it's worth testing the site out with amateur users. Ad campaigns and film features generally do this, but people rarely think of trying this out with Web sites. The first, simple way of testing is just to e-mail the URL out to a few friends and ask what they think. Depending on who your friends are, this can be a start.

To get a comprehensive look at what people think of your site, gather several VRML-neophytes in a room and set them loose in your world. Observe closely where they go first and when they get a confused look in their eyes. You might even want to videotape the session, so you can review it later. You can get much more feedback on your site this way, more than you'll get from waiting for people to voice or e-mail feedback.

Ongoing Improvement and Redesign of Site

Rather than set your site loose and forget about it, you'll want to update your site with new information and approaches. Together with this, you'll also want to get continued feedback on your site. A standard tool we've used to get feedback on our VRML Web sites is to include a mailto WWWAnchor node with the name field set to `mailto:theme@virtpark.com`.

Authoring Tools and Converters

There are a variety of tools becoming available to ease VRML world development. Trying to create VRML worlds by hand in a text editor can take quite a while and give you a headache as you try to spatially imagine your world. There are two categories of tools: authoring tools and converters.

Authoring tools are software packages that enable you to create worlds described in VRML. The HTML equivalent is software programs like HoTMetaL and HTML Assistant. Hopefully, VRML authoring tools will enable you to develop and test your worlds in 3-D. Most VRML authoring tools are still in very preliminary versions, though you can expect to see an explosion of these tools in the near future. Some that have been announced include Virtual Home Builder from Paragraph, Fountain from Caligari, EZ3D from Radiance, and Aereal Phonts from Aereal. For the latest authoring tool information, the best bet is to check the VRML repository Web sites mentioned in Appendix E.

Converters enable you to create a world using CAD or 3-D modeling software, and then translate a file from the 3-D file format into the VRML format. Converters exist, or are being developed, for formats like DXF, 3DS, OFF, and IV. There are also commercial converter programs, such as Interchange from Syndesis, that convert between several 3-D file formats and support or are planning to support VRML.

There's a problem with converters: they tend to generate huge, inefficient VRML files. In addition, the files may not be true, up-to-spec VRML. There are currently many .wrls out on the Net that are not real VRML.

Optimizing Virtual Reality on the Web

In the beginning of VRML, many worlds took up large amounts of time to transfer on the Internet because their file sizes were so big. Then once you downloaded the file, it took forever to move around in it. If you would like to avoid these problems, you'll want to optimize your VRML for file size, rendering speed and ease of navigation.

File Size

In addition to converters, people have been developing Perl scripts to optimize converted worlds. Typically, running a converter creates a very inefficient, big VRML file. The scripts attempt to trim down the file size to make the world more usable. For example, one technique is to trim the number of decimal places on values. Therefore, you'll want to understand what an optimized script does before using it. If you are creating a medical or architectural world where precision is important, you'll get in trouble if the script you use affects the accuracy of the placement of objects.

Creating efficient and effective VRML worlds is quite different than using a standard CAD package, so I think a niche will develop for VRML-specific authoring tools. In addition, we'll see the CAD and 3-D modeling packages include an "export" capability that enables people to save or convert their files in VRML format.

As part of working with the Interactive Multimedia Festival, James Waldrop developed a script that reduces file size by about 75 percent. One file was reduced from 2.3M down to 570K. Information on the script is located at `http://www.arc.org/vrmltools/datafat.html`. It's important to understand what this script does before you use it, as the special optimizations it performs may or may not be appropriate for your world. The script was developed for a VRML version of the Interactive Media Festival. (See Figure 22.8.)

FIGURE 22.8.

Interactive Multimedia Festival in VRML.

Using this script and gzip compression, James, Mark Meadows, and others with the Interactive Multimedia Festival (http://vrml.arc.org) managed to compress their files by 94 percent! File sizes of 1.4 to 2.3 MB shrunk down to 88K to 126K. The 2.3 MB file represented the first floor of the arts center. The files came from using the 3DS to VRML converter. Some of the techniques they used were

- Turning infinitesimal numbers like 3.9e-09 (which is almost zero) into zero.
- Trimming off long decimal expansions (3.4567890 gets trimmed down to 3.456).
- Getting rid of white space.
- Getting rid of unnecessary normal information (VRML Normal nodes).

The main compression method being used for VRML is Gnu zip, also known as gzip in UNIX. A gzip'd filename will look like home.wrl.gz. Using gzip will compress a VRML file down to about 30 percent of its original size. The HTTP server can transmit the gzip'd file with appropriate MIME type and the VRML browser will uncompress the file after it receives it.

Note that you can also use gzip compression for files that the VRML file refers to. For instance, you might have Texture2 nodes referring to textures in JPEG format or to WWWInlines of other VRML objects. Most VRML browsers that can understand gzip compression can also uncompress gzip versions of textures, WWWInlines, and any other URL referred to in the VRML file.

Rendering Speed

The techniques listed in the preceding section are useful for optimizing transmission time for users with low-speed network connections. The other main area for optimization is in rendering speed. These two concerns, transmission and rendering speeds, are sometimes at cross-purposes, as improving rendering speed can sometimes result in a larger file.

Three important techniques for optimizing rendering time are using cameras, rendering hints, and varying levels of detail. Another concern is when to use texture maps.

Use of Cameras

In designing your HTML-based Web Sites, you've probably found occasion to use anchors within a page, particularly inside a long document. The same kind of capability exists within VRML. Cameras represent viewpoints that the user can start from. If there is no camera in a VRML file, the VRML browser will start you from a default position (0,0,1) and orientation.

If you have cameras in your world, using the PerspectiveCamera or OrthographicCamera nodes, a viewer can start out from various preset viewpoints. If we had the following camera in a file called `sample.wrl`, we could go into the world from that viewpoint by going to the URL `sample.wrl#LongView`. (This feature is not implemented in the many first versions of VRML browsers.)

```
DEF LongView PerspectiveCamera {
    position 100 500 100
    orientation -1 -5 -1 0
    focalDistance 500
}
```

This gets exciting when we use these cameras like stepping stones to hop and skip through a world. In a virtual world without cameras, to get from point A to point B we would need to go along a path of points in between them. That's fine if we have a maxed-out graphics workstation.

But if we're using a computer that can barely render the world, that could take forever. An ergonomic design will give you camera viewpoints with hyperlinks to other camera viewpoints using the WWWAnchor node. Then you can jump from one camera to the next, so that traveling 100 meters takes only a few seconds rather than half an hour.

Rendering Hints

As well as cameras, VRML provides the ShapeHints node to help optimize rendering of polygonal faces. Using the ShapeHints node, VRML enables you to tell the rendering engine in the VRML browser that a group of polygons are solid or have convex faces. It also tells when to generate smooth edges or creased edges when the polygons intersect.

Levels of Detail

If an object is far in the distance or isn't something you're focused on, your eye doesn't give you much detail. If you're wandering around a virtual world, you'll want your limited computing power focused on important objects. One of the ways to accomplish this in VRML is to use the LOD node. The LOD node makes it possible for you to view different representations of an object from different distances. When you are far away from a building, you might just see a huge block. As you get closer, the floors and windows gradually become visible. Then as you zoom in, you can see and hear pigeons hanging around in ledges of the building.

Texture Maps

Texture maps are like wallpaper—they provide a pattern that is draped on an object, which can simulate rough surfaces like mountains, even though the underlying object might have flat surfaces. Texture maps provide a high degree of realism, but they are very computation-intensive. At the same time, they can be less computation-intensive than rendering a very detailed part of an object with many polygons. For fast movement around your virtual world, you might skip texture maps. Here, as in other design considerations, the question is how much value your texture map will add, given the extra computing power it requires. At the same time, texture maps are easy candidates for the preferences section of VRML browsers. Browsers will probably have an option that lets you turn off texture mapping, just as standard WWW browsers let you turn off inline images.

The Future of VRML, Version 2.0 and Beyond

The four main enhancements that are expected for Version 2.0 of Virtual Reality Modeling Language are interactivity, behaviors, 3-D sound, and multiuser capability. The VRML community is currently considering proposals for VRML 2.0. Some of them, such as the Moving Worlds proposal from SGI/Sony/WorldMaker, build on VRML's 1.0 Open Inventor-inspired format. Proposals from Apple, Microsoft, and others depart from it significantly. The next sections examine what these enhancements mean.

Interactivity

In an interactive virtual world, you can open doors, and watch them slowly open. You might move around the furniture in your apartment. Or hit the snooze button on your twitching, ringing alarm clock, after you get pulled out of a dream virtual world back into your home virtual world. Designing this level of interactivity into VRML will be a challenge. It also may increase file sizes significantly.

Behaviors

Version 1.1 of VRML should include some limited capacity for animations. In Version 2.0 and beyond you should be able to create behaviors, so that objects tend to have a minimal life of their own. Besides having some limited movements, such as a windmill turning, we may get objects that affect each other, so that when Don Quixote tries to joust with the windmill, his horse shies away, or else the windmill shreds the tip of his lance.

It could be chaotically exciting. Have you ever seen hypnotist magicians on television? One day I saw one create a whole set of dependent behaviors in a group of hypnotized people and then set them loose. One person was continually creating imaginary sand castles on the stage. Each time he got one theoretically finished, another person would walk through them. Another person seeing this would shout. A person hearing the shout was programmed to put on a tie (on top of other ties he was previously wearing). All in all, total havoc.

Now imagine this wildness going on in your virtual world, with sound floating around, hyperlinks that appear and disappear, and other people wandering around too. Wow!

To get involved in VRML behaviors, check out the VRML behaviors e-list information in Appendix E.

Sound

3-D sound gets very interesting and brings in a whole range of new possibilities. Sound has been a key feature in creating good immersive environments. In fact, people experimenting in VR have found that small improvements in sound improve the immersive experience, as perceived by the user, more than small improvements in graphics quality.

As it applies to VRML worlds, there are all kinds of exciting methods for deploying sound. For example, you could create soundproof rooms for privacy. Then someone might create virtual bugging, where they listen in on conversations in soundproof rooms. Sound transmitted at lower frequencies can be used to simulate vibrations (like earthquakes!). Or imagine various sound encoding and transmittal schemes used in real life. We could end up with virtual cellular phones and radio stations. And the frequency range that you perceive might not be the standard human range. For example, you are in a game where you are a dog. Then only you perceive sound frequencies within a dog's hearing range. And who knows, maybe sound transmitted by human characters would be unintelligible, unless they knew how to speak dog language.

Multiuser

Imagine playing football with a group of people in a virtual world in cyberspace. Or imagine designing a new product with them. For these applications, you need to have a multiuser capability in your virtual world. VRML will hopefully allow support for multiuser worlds in the future. It is currently possible to do some basic multiuser worlds using intensive CGI programming. In the future, we may see a range of server software emerge for adding multiuser functionality to virtual worlds. Some of the issues that need to be tackled include logging of who is currently in the world, including killing off vampires, meaning being able to detect when people have stopped being involved even if they have not explicitly sent a message to the server saying that they are signing off. Also, in some worlds you will want collision detection, to prevent two avatars (bodies in cyberspace) from existing in the same space. In addition, there needs to be a way to hand off avatars to other servers if someone chooses a hyperlink to another world. Other considerations will include how a person's avatar is created, how it is logged and transmitted, and what rules it may need to follow in various worlds.

In addition, copyright issues may become important. If you're Batman, for others to see you as Batman, they will need to download a file or data that is a representation of Batman. They could thus potentially save that file, use it in their own worlds, or modify it as well. These are "bastard worlds," the illegitimate children of other worlds. You might create a corporate VRML site for an automobile manufacturer, when somebody comes along, spraypaints virtual graffiti on the showroom cars, kicks the tires in, and posts the new version on their own Web site.

Other VRML 2.0 Issues

Besides the technical issues, probably the biggest challenge for VRML 2.0 (as Mark Pesce alludes to in an interview later in this chapter) is getting a consensus for what VRML 2.0 should be. At this point, there are a lot of companies, money, and people involved in VRML, each with their own interests. It will be interesting to see how things work out.

Java Meets VRML

Java will most likely drive multiuser interactions and behaviors in VRML 2.0 worlds. It is likely that other languages will be used in VRML 2.0 in addition to Java. This section takes a look at how this may evolve.

How Java Will Interact with VRML

Java can interact with VRML in at least two ways: describing extension nodes and as scripts loaded "inline" to describe the interactions of VRML objects.

The first work combining VRML and Java resulted in Liquid Reality, a VRML toolkit written in Java by Dimension X. In Liquid Reality, if the Liquid Reality browser does not recognize a node, it requests the Java code describing the node from the server that served the file.

In most of the approaches being drafted for VRML 2.0, scripts can be used to animate VRML objects. The Java code can be referenced in a URL attached to the geometry.

Dimension X's Liquid Reality

Using Liquid Reality and extension nodes, you can create worlds with flying birds (Figure 22.9) and bouncing apples (Figure 22.10)!

FIGURE 22.9.

A Liquid Reality VRML world with flying birds, a flowing stream, and a spider that runs away from you when you get close to it.

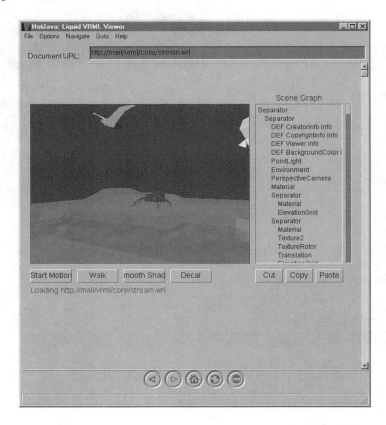

FIGURE 22.10.

A bouncing apple in a Liquid Reality VRML world.

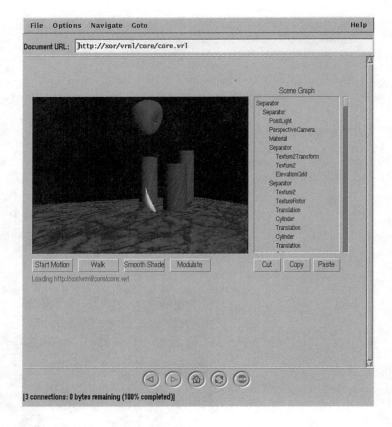

Listing 22.5 is an example of a VRML world that has a rotating object in it, as referenced by the Rotor node.

Listing 22.5. A Liquid Reality Java-extended VRML file containing the extension "Rotor."

```
#VRML V1.0 ascii

Separator {
    DEF BackgroundColor Info { string "0.5 0.5 0.5" }
    DEF Viewer Info { string "walk" }
    DEF ViewerSpeed Info { string "0.3" }

    Clock {}

#   PointLight { location 0 0 10 }
    PerspectiveCamera {
```

```
        position 0 0 8
        orientation 0 1 0 0
    }

    DirectionalLight { direction 1 0 0 }


    Material {
        ambientColor [ 0 0 0 ]
        diffuseColor [0.1 0.5 0.2 ]
#       specularColor [0.8 0.8 0.8]
        shininess 0.25
    }
    Separator {
#       Rotation { rotation 0 1 0 1.57 }
        Sphere { radius 1.1 }
    }

    Translation { translation -3 0 0 }

    Material {
        ambientColor [ 0 0 0 ]
        diffuseColor [ 0.7 0.1 0.1 ]
    }
    Cube { height 1.5 width 1.5 depth 1.5 }

    Translation { translation 6 0 0 }
    Material {
        ambientColor [ 0 0 0 ]
        diffuseColor [ 0.2 0.7 0.8 ]
#       specularColor [1 1 1]
        shininess 0.4
    }

    Separator {
        Rotor { rotation 1 0 0 1 }
        Cone {}
    }
#   Cylinder {}

}
```

Listing 22.6 presents the Java code that describes the Rotor extension node with calls to Liquid Reality's API.

Listing 22.6. Java code for the Liquid Reality Rotor node.

```
// RotorNode.java
//
// Copyright  1995 Dimension X, Inc.
```

continues

Listing 22.6. continued

```
//    Chris Laurel 8-14-95

package ice.scene;

import ice.Matrix4;


//  Rotor {
//     rotation    0 0 1 0       # SFRotation
//     speed       1             # SFFloat
//  }
public class RotorNode extends ModelTransformationNode
{
    static String fieldnames[] = {
        "rotation",
        "speed"
    };
    static NodeField defaults[] = {
        new SFRotation(0, 0, 1, 0),
        new SFFloat(1)
    };

    public SFRotation rotation = new SFRotation((SFRotation) defaults[0], this);
    public SFFloat speed = new SFFloat((SFFloat) defaults[1], this);
    NodeField fields[] = {
        rotation, speed
    };


    public int numFields() { return fields.length; }
    public String fieldName(int n) { return fieldnames[n]; }
    public NodeField getDefault(int n) { return defaults[n]; }
    public NodeField getField(int n) { return fields[n]; }

    public void applyModelTransformation(Action a)
    {
        a.state.rotateModelMatrix(rotation.getAxisX(),
                    rotation.getAxisY(),
                    rotation.getAxisZ(),
                    (float) (rotation.getAngle() +
                        speed.getValue() *
                        a.state.getTime() % (2 * Math.PI)));
    }

}
```

Paper Software

Paper Software is creating a Java API for VRML. The preliminary version is code-named Xpresso, and this section presents a simple example to see the direction it is heading in. Expect it to be different when it is released.

This example is a bouncing ball, with Java code `javaball.java`. It is referenced by putting the line:

```
DEF BALL Sphere {}
```

in the VRML file. Figures 22.11 and 22.12 show the ball in action.

Listing 22.7 shows what the Java code looks like. Notice that `import xpresso` brings in Paper's VRML API. You can see the calls to the API that start with `webfxObject`.

FIGURE 22.11.

A bouncing ball in air created with Paper's Java API.

FIGURE 22.12.

The bouncing ball is now squished on the ground.

Listing 22.7. Java code for the bouncing ball using Paper Software's preliminary API.

```java
// Bring in some Java classes we will need
import java.awt.Graphics;
import java.util.Date;
import java.lang.Math;
import xpresso;

// A Java class that runs in its own thread as an applet
public class javaball extends java.applet.Applet implements Runnable {


    // variables
    Thread  ballThread;
    int     y = 0 ;
    float   fTemp = 0.0f;
    float   fHeight = 0.0f;
    int     object_id = 0 ;
     int     lSession = 0 ;
     int     lObjectID = 0 ;
    float   ff[] = new float[16] ;

    // Create an object to interface with VRML
    xpresso webfxObject = new xpresso() ;

/**********************************************************************
// init method
**********************************************************************/

    public void init()
    {


        // Initialize the VRML interface
        while (lSession == 0)
            lSession = webfxObject.XpressoInit() ;


        // Get pointers to the Ball object
        if (lSession != 0)
        {
            String strCube       = "Ball";
            String strFloor    = "Floor";

            while (lObjectID == 0)
                lObjectID = webfxObject.XpressoGetObject(lSession, 0, strCube) ;

        }


    }

/**********************************************************************
// start method
**********************************************************************/
```

```
    public void start()
    {
        if (ballThread == null)
        {
            ballThread = new Thread(this, "Ball");
            ballThread.start();
        }

    // Initialize to Identity matrix
    ff[0]=    1.0f;
    ff[1]=    0.0f;
    ff[2]=    0.0f;
    ff[3]=    0.0f;
    ff[4]=    0.0f;
    ff[5]=    1.0f;
    ff[6]=    0.0f;
    ff[7]=    0.0f;
    ff[8]=    0.0f;
    ff[9]=    0.0f;
    ff[10]=   1.0f;
    ff[11]=   0.0f;
    ff[12]=   0.0f;
    ff[13]=   0.0f;
    ff[14]=   0.0f;
    ff[15]=   1.0f;


    }

/*********************************************************************
// run method
*********************************************************************/

    public void run()
    {

        while (ballThread != null)
        {

            fHeight = 0.0f;

            // Ball falls down in 20 steps
            for (y = 1; y < 20; y++)
            {
                fTemp   = (float) y ;
                fHeight = fHeight + (1/fTemp);
                ff[13]  = fHeight;

                if (y>0)
                {
                    ff[0]   = 1f;
                    ff[5]   = 1f;
                    ff[10]  = 1f;
                }
```

continues

Listing 22.7. continued

```
                        // Transform this ball to its new location and squoosh factor
                        // then .... render the scene so we see the results
                        if (lObjectID != 0)
                        {

                            webfxObject.XpressoTransformObject(lSession, lObjectID, ff, 2) ;

                             webfxObject.XpressoRenderScene(lSession, 0) ;


                        }

                }


                // Ball bounces up ... in 20 steps
                for (y = 20; y > 0; y—)
                {
                    fTemp   = (float)y;
                    fHeight = fHeight - (1/fTemp);
                    ff[13]  = fHeight ;

                    if (y==1)
                    {
                        ff[0]  = 1.2f;
                        ff[5]  = .8f;
                        ff[10] = 1.2f;
                    }

                    if (y>1)
                    {
                        ff[0]  = 1f;
                        ff[5]  = 1f;
                        ff[10] = 1f;
                    }

                    // Transform this ball to its new location and squoosh factor
                    // then .... render the scene so we see the results
                    if (lObjectID != 0)
                    {
                        webfxObject.XpressoTransformObject(lSession, lObjectID, ff, 2) ;

                         webfxObject.XpressoRenderScene(lSession, 0) ;


                    }

                }

            try {
                ballThread.sleep(5);
```

```
            } catch (InterruptedException e){
            }

        }
    }

/*****************************************************************
// stop method
*****************************************************************/

    public void stop()
    {
        ballThread.stop();
        ballThread = null;
    }

}
```

Java/VRML People

The relationship between Java and VRML is evolving rapidly. To see where things are heading, I interviewed several of the people involved in these cutting-edge efforts.

Dimension X's Karl Jacobs and Scott Fraize

Karl Jacobs is CEO and Scott Fraize is Caffeinated Alchemist of Dimension X. Dimension X (http://www.dnx.com) has developed Ice, a Java API for 3-D, and Liquid Reality, a VRML toolkit for Java based on Ice.

Q: What is Liquid Reality?

> *Karl:* It is a VRML toolkit. It provides everything you need to read in VRML and write out VRML and extend it with Java. It has all the mechanisms to do that on the fly. It's wrapped around Intel's 3DSound, which only took two days to add into Liquid Reality. You just use a Directed Sound node. Here's where you are in space, here's the sound file, and there you are.
>
> Liquid Reality is based on Ice, fully integrated with the toolkit. It differs from other APIs in that Liquid Reality is written in Java, so that it provides hardware independence. It's not as fast as Renderware and Reality Labs [the APIs other PC VRML browsers are written in] yet.
>
> We'll be able to go to 2.0 relatively easily, whereas others will have to redesign. We can update the toolkit without re-releasing, by putting new Java classes up on the servers. Chris just ported Liquid Reality to SGI and Linux over the weekend.

Q: How will Sun's efforts to add 3-D support to Java affect Liquid Reality?

Karl: Sun's 3-D efforts are complementary to Liquid Reality. Rather than "canvas," you'll say, "canvas3d."

Q: Will people need to be able to program in Java to do Java-enabled VRML?

Scott: Right now, you do have to program a bit. However, there's a library of plug-ins and effects, like Rotor node, that you can use.

Q: What business model do you foresee?

Karl: Ice is an API—we want to get it out there quickly and as widely as possible. The idea is that even if you want to put it up on your Web page as a free game, that's fine.

Liquid Reality is a toolkit so you have to pay a fee for updates and so on. The viewer is free. It's the try and buy which seems to be proven on the Internet.

Paper Software's Mike McCue

Mike McCue is the founder and CEO of Paper Software, creators of the WebFX VRML browser. Paper Software is developing a Java API for VRML.

Q: How will world creators author Java-enabled VRML?

Mike: Our goal is that you will write a series of Java scripts that orchestrate behaviors. The behaviors themselves will probably be in DLLs initially. Right now the threading model is too slow for the performance people will want. Java will be an orchestrating mechanism for the overall world.

You kick off a canned behavior that exists native in our DLLs. That's the short term. Longer term, I think there will be a set of Java classes that will give you canned behaviors. As a world author, maybe I'll have a canned behavior that allows a man to run. I see that happening very soon after the first versions come out.

A few months later the canned Java behaviors will come out, and you will be able to drag and drop them onto VRML objects.

Longer term to that, eventually Java itself will become the behaviors' engine, and you'll have some physics such as collision detection, gravity, and elasticity in the browser, but you'll have Java gradually implementing that too.

Q: How would you describe the future of Java and VRML? Will it even be possible to differentiate between Java and VRML?

Mike: Yes, I think it will be possible to differentiate between the two. That's because VRML is a file format and Java is a programming language.

You'll see VRML in OCXs and C++ APIs. There's a life beyond Java for VRML in a big way. I think it will be incorporated into Microsoft Powerpoint and Excel. I think it will be incorporated into your mission-critical applications.

Our goal is to begin with Java but to make sure we don't back ourselves into a corner by relying on it. We want to be language neutral.

On the Internet, Java and JavaScript will be the way to go.

Q: You've mentioned an interest in VRML as a starting point for multidimensional interfaces. What do you mean by that?

Mike: I gradually see the bulk of applications and operating systems today taking more advantage of 3-D space to organize info rather than 2-D windows. I think 3-D represents the next major user interface step. You will run all of these applications in a 3-D environment. It will become a core, centralized part of the operating system.

WorldMaker's Mitra

Mitra is the Chief Technology Officer of WorldMaker (http://earth.path.net/worldmaker), a new company focusing on Java and VRML. He has been doing cutting-edge technology in networking for some time, including previously at Worlds Inc. He is also a member of the VRML Architecture Group.

Q: What are you doing with Java and VRML?

Mitra: WorldMaker's purpose is to build the tools that help put the "reality" in virtual Worlds. Mostly this means building extensions in Java that can be easily integrated by content developers to add functionality to their worlds. Typical functionality includes, for example, multiuser support.

Q: What's your business model for earning revenue?

Mitra: The business model is to do well by helping our customers do well—so that might mean licensing a set of classes to a developer, or charging for online time, or whatever makes sense.

Q: Will VRML and Java be distinguishable from each other in the future?

Mitra: Yes—I believe they will remain distinguishable for the foreseeable future; the equivalent is HTML and Java, where the HTML provides the structure, and Java the functionality. In fact, in 3-D they are likely to remain more distinguishable because the only way for the Java applets to influence the world is by manipulating a VRML scene graph.

Q: How will people use your software to create worlds?

Mitra: Our extensions will map cleanly into the Moving Worlds proposal for VRML 2.0, which I co-authored. Typically, authors will reference one of our files using an EXTERNPROTO declaration, to include a model with geometry and/or behavior. Alternatively, authors can add script files to their worlds that reference our extensions directly.

Mark Pesce

Mark Pesce (http://www.hyperreal.com/~mpesce) is one of the creators of VRML and a member of the VRML Architecture Group. I interviewed him over e-mail about Java and VRML.

Q: What will Java mean to VRML and vice versa?

Mark: Java and VRML are perfect complements. Java is all about how things behave, but says very little about how they appear. VRML is all about appearances, without speaking to how things behave. You could say that VRML is, while Java does.

They need each other.

Q: How will world creators create Java-enabled VRML?

Mark: That's the $64,000 question. We have a number of proposals out there now, including the SGI/Sony/SDSC/WorldMaker "Moving Worlds" proposal. It's certainly one possible methodology. SUN has its own ideas, as does Paper.

Q: What will be the most challenging part of integrating Java and VRML?

Mark: Getting a political agreement on the right way to do it.

Q: Where do you see Java and VRML heading over the next several years?

Mark: Into a closer relationship—one where it becomes difficult to know where VRML ends and Java begins, and vice versa. I expect that when people want to talk about "imaging" Java, they'll use VRML, and when they think of "motivating" VRML, they'll use Java.

Business Models for Virtual Reality on the Web

The constant question among business people is, "How can we make money on the Net?" VRML will open up new business models and possibilities on the Net. These will include shopping worlds, virtual theme parks, marketing efforts, and group communication.

At its crudest, Virtual Reality on the Web can include shopping worlds, three-dimensional stores. Initial attempts will probably focus on the earth-bound metaphors of the shopping mall, as initial HTML Web pages have done. Advanced attempts will dismiss old metaphors and will also take advantage of interactivity to generate excitement about buying a product. Imagine "The Price is Right" TV show in virtual reality. Or an exciting, glamorous auction, where it turns out that all the other bidders are computer-generated automatons!

Virtual theme parks encompass all forms of entertainment models. Users might play in a huge, multiplayer game, represented by avatars (3-D bodies in VR). Or small groups might buy $30 tickets for an hour-long group adventure on a special server that gives them an overwhelming, emotional, high-bandwidth experience. Users might subscribe on a monthly basis to basic games or worlds they can enter and interact in. Smart Internet Service Providers (ISPs) will probably bundle access to these worlds as part of an integrated value strategy.

Probably the first area of business in VRML, as in HTML, will focus on marketing. VRML provides marketers with new kinds of capabilities to appeal to emotions and abstraction. In HTML's text-intensive environment, the standard approach has been to give lots of detail and information. In the world of VRML, marketers and advertisers will instead attempt to create powerful virtual worlds that affect users' feelings and the thoughts they attach to products.

Group communication can develop into an important area for business as VRML develops into the 3-D equivalent of e-mail. With VRML, businesses can have meetings across distances that have the benefits of video conferencing (representing people by avatars), yet in a much lower-bandwidth environment. To develop this capability, avatar software will have to have some basic capabilities to represent personality, such as facial expressions.

Another related possibility is Management by Virtually Wandering Around (MBVWA). Management journals emphasize the benefits of managers wandering around to see what's going on in their factory or organization. That can be difficult if the facility you'd like to visit is in another country. An advanced VRML application could let a manager "virtually wander around" an office in another country. The manager might even be able to see inventory stock and items moving around the factory, through a VRML representation of the factory or a video camera interface.

We can apply this concept to Network Administration. Network administrators are challenged with looking after huge numbers of computers at one time. Network Administration software is starting to use two-dimensional graphics to help network administrators keep a handle on all of the information associated with their computers. Imagine a VRML approach to this, where the user is in the middle of a virtual world populated by computers. When the computers have problems or break down, they start moving towards the user at the center of the world at a speed related to the severity of the computer problem and importance of the particular computer. If the user (network administrator) isn't fixing the computers quickly enough, the computers surround the user. The user can't move until they fix the computers. However, the user could call for help and have a second person come in to help fix the computers. The computers would move towards the user most likely to be able to fix their problems—or in some cases, they might run away from both! The color and shape of the representation of the computers also could be based on other relevant data, such as how long the computer has been down. The same model can be applied to managing telecommunications networks, air traffic control, or strategic defense systems.

Virtual reality has been successfully applied to stock market and portfolio management in the past. With VRML, the use of WWWInline nodes can be used to link in data from many sources. LOD nodes can be used so that as you move closer to the representation of a certain financial instrument or derivative, you get more and more information, plus additional hyperlinks to other sources of information and intelligence.

Another market that may open up through VRML is the video game market. The new game platforms, such as the Sega Saturn, Sony Playstation, and Nintendo Ultra64, are essentially small systems optimized for rendering 3-D worlds. Interfaces to the Internet are being developed for them. Browsers can be developed for these systems, modems can be attached to the game systems, and then the users can go wandering around the Internet through VRML.

In most of the chapter, we've made the assumption that all of the VRML worlds will be transmitted over the Internet. However, that's not necessarily the case. Diskettes and CD-ROMs containing VRML files can be created with a few purposes in mind. They could be a database of commonly used objects like streetlamps, chairs, and tables, that could be accessed by other worlds as inline worlds. Or they could just be static, highly detailed worlds for a person to wander around in. What is really exciting is to distribute background worlds that can be used as inline objects in CGI-dependent interactive adventures. The nice thing about the CD-ROM and diskette distribution model is that consumers are used to paying for these media.

Business is going to fall in love with virtual reality on the Web. This new technology will also raise the playing field, with increased costs required to develop excellent Web sites.

Summary

The explosion of interest in the World Wide Web has been incredible! VRML promises to ramp this exponential growth up to a new level of interactivity and feeling. Java will be the pump to drive motion and interaction in advanced VRML worlds.

As VRML moves into its 2.0 version and Java adds life to it, virtual reality on the Net will become as commonplace as HTML is today. Interactivity, animations, and behaviors will enliven virtual worlds with personality and attitude.

Businesses will take advantage of virtual reality on the Web, starting with marketing efforts and graduating to original content.

Using 3-D Modeling Tools to Create VRML Worlds

23

by Adrian Scott

After taking a look at the overall concept of 3-D modeling, this chapter presents an in-depth example of building a VRML world with Fountain, a VRML modeling package from Caligari. At the end of the chapter, you'll find an overview of various VRML world authoring software and URLs for VRML worlds created using various 3-D modeling packages, such as Fountain, TriSpectives, and Virtual Home Space Builder.

The whole purpose of using 3-D modeling tools in this chapter is to create VRML worlds. The first graphical user interfaces for computers have been built on a 2-D interpretation of "the desktop." The future of user interfaces is in 3-D. However, creating 3-D worlds is a challenge, since most of us are still using the vestiges of a 2-D GUI. We use a 2-D computer monitor and a 2-D mouse. The main way we sample the real world is using scanners or cameras that convert 2-D images into computer format.

This makes creating emotionally rich 3-D worlds a challenge. We have to convert 3-D notions into 2-D to get them into the computer. Hopefully this will change soon. Scanners are starting to be developed for 3-D input—one has a computer arm that you move to map vertex points on an object's surface. Logitech and other companies have developed 3-D computer mice.

In the meantime, we're stuck with a 2-D interface to a 3-D creation. But 3-D/CAD companies have been innovative, so that 3-D authoring can be a lot of fun after some practice.

Introduction to 3-D Modeling

This section takes a quick look at the 3-D coordinate system. A basic knowledge of the 3-D coordinate system can help you understand what the modeling software does, and is particularly helpful if you ever end up editing VRML by hand in a text editor. (However, if you don't understand it, you can still get by!)

Given that there are three dimensions, there are three axes that go with them. We usually call these X, Y, and Z. In VRML, the initial viewpoint is looking from the positive Z to the negative Z (into the screen). The X direction goes from the left (negative) to the right (positive). The Y direction goes from the bottom (negative) to the top (positive). This is what's known as a "right-handed" coordinate system (Figure 23.1). The most important thing to remember is that looking into the screen means looking in the negative Z direction. (Former physics and mathematics students will be used to a different right-handed coordinate system, with positive X going out of the screen, Z going up, and Y going to the right.) Although you have flexibility in what you define as different directions in your world, it is important to follow this convention since the VRML browser's Walk navigation mode is tied to it.

The intersection of the three axes is called the origin, and has the coordinates X=0, Y=0, and Z=0 (0,0,0). The 3-D modeling software will usually start off looking at the origin from the positive Z axis. A useful point to note here is that if you use a world as a WWWInline in a bigger VRML world, the origin of the WWWInline'd world will be at the current point in the bigger VRML world.

FIGURE 23.1

The X, Y, and -Z coordinate axes, and their intersection at the origin (0,0,0). The arrow points in the -Z direction, looking into the screen.

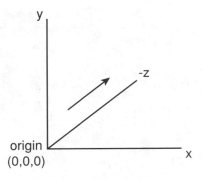

Fountain from Caligari

Fountain is a VRML authoring package from Caligari, based on its Truespace 3-D modeling software. Fountain enables you to create VRML worlds, and you can also create WWWAnchor hyperlinks on objects in the worlds to link to other URLs on the Web.

The next sections take you through a step-by-step example of creating a simple corporate VRML home world in Fountain, pretending we have a client called "Space Age Donut Co." whose motto is "We Dunk for VRML Worlds."

Navigation Modes

Start by running the Fountain program. (You can download Fountain from `http://www.caligari.com`.) It starts out in Web Browsing mode. Note the airplane icon in the center of the bottom of the screen. This indicates that you are in Fly through World navigation mode. (The status line underneath the row of icons gives the names of the icons and keyboard shortcuts.) If you click and hold down your mouse button on the airplane, a menu pops up, with another icon, a pair of feet for Walkthrough World navigation mode. Switch to Walk navigation mode. When you hold down the left mouse button and move the mouse, you walk around. When you hold down the right mouse button and drag the mouse, you levitate up and down.

After you are familiar with navigating around the world, click on the World-Building mode icon in the bottom-left corner of the screen (to the left of the Undo icon). You'll notice the icons change, and now you are ready to start creating VRML. First, start with an empty scene by selecting Scene—New from the File menu at the bottom of the screen.

Primitives and Object Movement

For Space Age Donut's corporate home world, you'll want to include their space-age donut. Start off by selecting the Primitives Panel icon, which brings up a little window that includes a sphere, a cube, and several other shapes. There's a donut shape, called a torus, so click on that (Figure 23.2).

FIGURE 23.2.

Starting off with a torus from the Primitives Panel in Fountain.

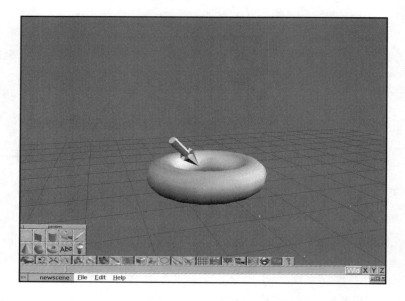

Since you're designing a "space age" object, you might want to point it towards the heavens, to give the impression of movement. Click and hold on the Object Move icon until a little menu pops up. Select the Object Rotate icon from the menu. Now click on the donut, hold down the mouse and move the mouse around until the donut has a little heavenly tilt to it.

Now you can add some fins, as if it were a surfboard. To do this, take one polygon from each side of the donut and extend them. Click on the Point Edit: Faces icon. Now click on a polygon towards the bottom and rear of the donut and pull it down a little. Do the same on the opposite side of the donut (Figure 23.3).

It can be challenging to get both of the fins lined up similarly. You'll probably need to use Object Rotate mode again. Note that you sometimes need to click the arrow icon when you are switching from Object Rotate to Point Edit: Faces mode.

You may have noticed that another little panel popped up when you clicked the Point Edit: Faces icon. The Point Navigation panel defaulted to Point Move mode, which you used to create the fins. You can use the Point Rotation mode to create an exciting front "grill" for the Space Age donut.

First rotate the donut so that the front faces of it are in view. Then return to Point Edit: Faces mode and use Point Move to pull the front face of the donut out a little (just like you did for the fins). Now select Point Rotate from the Point Navigation panel, click on the same face and twist it around 180 degrees, as if it were real dough! Now it's definitely looking like something from the Space Age (Figure 23.4).

FIGURE 23.3.

Adding fins to the Space Age donut.

FIGURE 23.4.

Space Age donut with fins and a front grill.

Adding Color

Next you can add some color to the donut. Select the Paint Face icon with the paintbrush on it. Several panels will pop up, including the Material Color, Shader/Maps, and Shader Attributes panels. In the Material Color panel, you can choose the color you want to use to paint the donut. The Shader Attributes panel enables you to set the Ambient Glow, Shininess, Roughness, and Transparency of the current Material. The transparency settings are the most fun to play with because you can make part of the donut totally see-through, or even just partially see-through.

In Fountain, you can discover very nice colors using the Shader Attributes, but the main one to use is Transparency. At this point in the evolution of VRML, different combinations of shading, attributes, and lighting will look different in different browsers. Therefore, you'll want to keep the colors relatively simple and also test your world in several browsers.

Try choosing colors and applying them to the faces of the object. You can end up with something like Figure 23.5.

FIGURE 23.5.

Painting the faces of the object with varied colors.

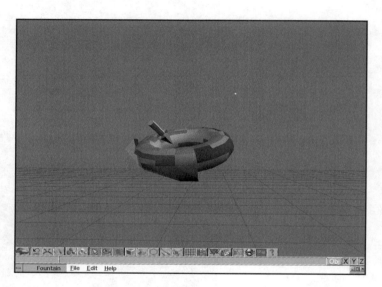

Lettering

Now that you have a central object for Space Age Donut Co.'s corporate home world, you can add in some lettering. Return to the Primitives Panel that you used to create the original torus by clicking on the Primitives Panel icon. When you click with the right button on the letters "abc" in the panel, a menu pops up from which you can choose a font style to use.

Fountain creates lettering using IndexedFaceSet nodes in VRML. This adds very quickly to the file size. The other way is to use an AsciiText node, which barely requires any file space. If you have a lot of text to type in, the best way is to use an AsciiText node. After you have finished creating in Fountain, you can edit the VRML file by hand in a text editor to add the AsciiText node. You would want to use it in combination with Separator, Translation, and maybe Rotation nodes, as in the following code snippet:

```
Separator {
    Translation { translation 5 7 -10 }
    AsciiText { string "hello world" }
}
```

You can type in a FontStyle node as well, to set the style of the AsciiText. The drawback to the AsciiText approach is you don't have control over exactly what the text will look like and exactly how it will appear. You also don't have all the font choices you can have using the IndexedFaceSet approach, which specifies all of the polygons for the letters. So as a general rule, it's good to reserve the IndexedFaceSet approach for special lettering and use the AsciiText approach for regular lettering.

Returning to the example, after you have chosen the font, you can click on the "abc" in the Primitives panel to activate the text mode. Then select a starting point for the text inside the world. Don't worry about getting it in a special position—you can move it around after you type it in. After you have typed in Space Age and moved it into place with Object Move and Object Rotate, you can do the same with "Donut Co." (See Figure 23.6.)

NOTE

In the beta 5 version of Fountain, I've noticed a bug that sometimes prevents the text primitive from working. As a workaround, I've found that you can save the file, exit Fountain, restart Fountain, use the text primitive in the default world, then load your saved file, and the text should work.

FIGURE 23.6.

The letters "Space Age Donut Co." have been typed in and placed.

Now you are ready to have some fun with the text—but first, now is a good time to remember to save your world, so you don't lose it if something goes wrong. Next, select a line of text (Arrow mode). Now select the Sweep mode icon, to the right of the Point Edit: Faces icon. The letters pop out in three dimensions. You can use the left and mouse buttons to change the direction and magnitude of this extrusion, as illustrated in Figure 23.7.

FIGURE 23.7.

Using Sweep mode to give the text a third dimension, depth.

An important consideration when you're using 3-D text is readability. It's easy to get carried away with cool effects while you're creating the text, but end up with an unreadable blob when people are actually navigating in your world. You'll want to consider which direction the text faces. Traditional 3-D text design has been based on 2-D display of the 3-D text on paper or signs, where people are only looking at it from one direction. However, in VRML, people will be experiencing your world from different directions, so authoring must flow from that context.

Another factor that helps readability is the color of the text (Figure 23.8). You must take into account the background color of the world and the color of objects nearby or within view of the text. A fun effect can be to paint the outside of the 3-D text with a half-transparent color and paint the inside with an opaque color.

Now that you have the company's name you can put its logo, "We Dunk for VRML Worlds," underneath the company name and donut. Again, you can use the text primitive from the Primitives Panel, and use Paint Face to color the text.

FIGURE 23.8.

Paint Face mode is used to color the faces of the 3-D text.

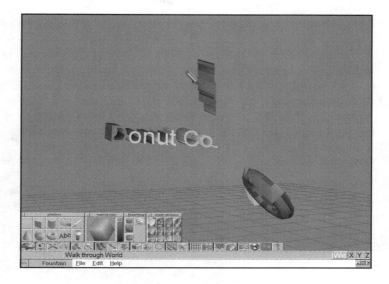

Adding Hyperlinks

Perhaps you'd like to add a way for visitors to the world to contact you and a link to Space Age Donut Co.'s HTML home page. First, select the object you'd like to add the link to, for instance, the donut. Now select Attach a hyperlink URL and type in a URL, for example http:/ /www.aereal.com (Figure 23.9). The link can be to any kind of URL on the Web, not just VRML worlds. This means you can link to HTML pages, sounds, and movies.

FIGURE 23.9.

Attaching a URL to the donut.

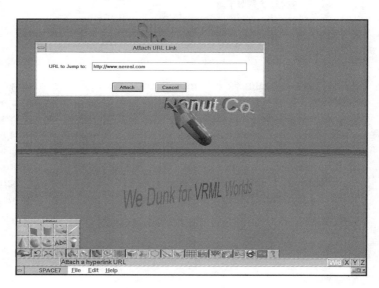

Another option is to include a `mailto:`-style URL, a technique used on the mailbox in Aereal Serch (a VRML world) to let people give feedback on the world. To finish off the world, you can add a simple object (maybe a Sphere from the Primitives panel) with a `mailto:` URL attached to it. Now click on the "car" Browser mode icon in the bottom-left corner to take a look at the finished world in Browser mode, pictured in Figure 23.10.

FIGURE 23.10.

Viewing the finished world in Fountain's Browser mode.

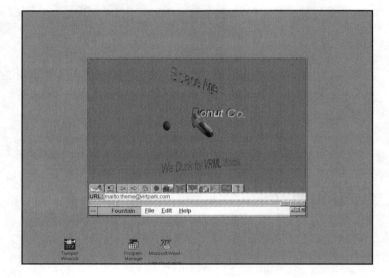

Saving the World

Now is a good time to make sure your VRML world looks good in other VRML browsers. To do so, first you need to save the world! Select Scene—Save from the File menu. After you've typed in a filename, the export VRML menu will pop up, giving you several options.

You can use the default settings most of the time. However, when you're about to put a world up on the Web, you may want to change the settings to minimize the size of the resulting VRML file. Under Options, you can unselect ASCII Formatting and lower Precision to 1 or 2 to save file size. ASCII Formatting makes a VRML file easier to read when you are editing it in a text editor. Precision refers to the number of digits after the decimal place in numbers in the VRML file. If you lower it to 1 or 2, that can lower the file size significantly, making it quicker for people to download your VRML world over the Internet. As an example, contrast the following two snippets of VRML code from Space Age Donut Co.'s VRML Home World, shown in Listings 23.1 and 23.2.

Listing 23.1. Part of Space Age Donut Co.'s VRML Home World saved with ASCII Formatting and Precision set to 3 digits.

```
    DEF LocLight_2 PointLight {
        color 0.800 0.800 0.800
        on TRUE
        location 0.000 0.000 0.000
        intensity 1.000
    }
}
Separator {
    MaterialBinding {
        value PER_FACE_INDEXED
    }
    Material {
        ambientColor [
            0.100 0.100 0.100,
            0.100 0.100 0.100,
            0.100 0.100 0.100,
```

Listing 23.2. Part of Space Age Donut Co.'s VRML Home World saved in Fountain without ASCII Formatting and with Precision set to 1 digit.

```
DEF LocLight_2 PointLight {
color 0.8 0.8 0.8
on TRUE
location 0.0 0.0 0.0
intensity 1.0
 }
 }
Separator {
MaterialBinding {
value PER_FACE_INDEXED
 }
Material {
ambientColor [
 0.1 0.1 0.1,
 0.1 0.1 0.1,
 0.1 0.1 0.1,
```

You can see that the second will take up much less space to store! Now that you've created a VRML home world, here's an interview with a modeler who has more tips on creating exciting works in VRML.

Interview with a VRML Modeler

Cindy Reed is the Technical Director of Yglesias Wallock Divekar, Inc. (http://www.ywd.com), a 3-D design and production firm.

Q: What are you doing with VRML?

Cindy: One half of 3Name3D/YWD is a 3-D database vendor. They make high-quality/lower price point (as compared to most of our competitors) 3-D models for general-purpose use. The other half is a custom modeling and production facility doing, well, whatever a client wants done. I'm involved with the production side. When VRML translators first became available, I got ahold of a few and started playing around with them and familiarizing myself with VRML. It was mostly a spare time, "for my own information" kind of thing, although I kept my employers informed about what I was doing. We talked about pursuing the VRML market for 3-D databases, but we decided that none really existed at the time. About eight months ago, we were approached by a large corporate entity that I can't name, but which you'd recognize, about doing a full-on VRML interface for an online commerce application. My employers had me meet with these clients, and we arranged to do their project. Over the course of about 3 months, I created several extensive VRML worlds, adhering strictly to VRML 1.0 standards while really leaning on 3-D modeling and texturing techniques from the high-end animation world. This project has not yet been made public, but hopefully that will happen over the next few months and we will do more work on it.

Since this project, we have followed the developments in the VRML world very closely. Due to several factors—the tumultuous nature of the VRML spec at the moment and inability to prevent theft of models—3Name3D has decided to adopt a "wait and see" attitude for the moment. However, I've chosen to remain involved and to learn as much as I can about this exciting area of 3-D and our company is still bidding on VRML projects as they come in.

Q: What software do you use? What features are most important to you?

Cindy: For modeling and mapping, I use Alias|Wavefront's Advanced Visualizer. That's kind of major overkill for VRML, but I need it for animation and production work, so I've got it lying around. Since VRML is a sideline to the other work I do, and since I know the modeler very well, it's an economical choice for us. We could also use 3DStudio, or any good 3-D modeler, I just happen to know this one best. I use ObjToVI to translate from Wavefront to Inventor formats, and viToVRML to go from Inventor to VRML. There are single step translators available, but I like the files these two produce when used together. I always do major hacking on all my VRML files, and I use vi—the standard UNIX text editor—for that.

Features that are important to me are good polygonal control in the modeler. I need to be able to precisely place and adjust polygons. Functional polygon reduction tools—yeah, right. And really solid mapping tools. I really try to reduce the number and size of the maps I use, so precise mapping is very important to me. Translators should NEVER MESS WITH THE DATA! I just need the format changed, not my grouping, not my materials, not my indexing, not my precision. And I need a really powerful text editor. I suppose if I was really hardcore I'd use emacs, but there's a limit to how nerdy I can get.

Q: What's on your wish list of software capabilities?

Cindy: It'd be nice if the "VRML authoring" programs were more functional. VRML doesn't require a lot of the features that broadcast animation does, but some of these programs do more to discourage people than anything else.

I'd like to see browsers display the same world more or less the same. Right now, I have to test on too many different browsers and I know that my (totally legal) stuff will look different on all of them and will break many of them.

Mostly, I'd like to see the spec grow up. VRML 2.0 will give us a lot of power and break us out of the "dead world" syndrome we're stuck in now.

Q: What hints or tips would you give to people creating VRML using 3-D modeling software?

Cindy: You need to understand the same old boring 3-D things to do VRML that you do for any other kind of 3-D. It's just a new file format, that's all.

Polygon counts and texture map sizes are more important than behaviors or anything else. I'm really serious about that. I've worked on two big budget VR projects with Onyxes, bunches of really gifted programmers, and tons of money, that were brought to their knees by polygon counts and texture memory.

On a more specific level, some browsers have big problems with polygons that are even close to being coplanar. Also, some browsers don't like interpenetrating polygons.

Use an object-oriented approach to your databases. It's a lot easier to go in and fix things if everything isn't all mushed together. And NAME EVERYTHING!

An Overview of Modeling Software

There is a variety of modeling software available for creating VRML (besides Fountain). Here is a quick look at several of the packages.

ClayWorks

ClayWorks is a DOS 3-D modeler for the PC. You can export your creation in the VRML file format. The user interface is a bit difficult, but the software runs quickly. ClayWorks is available as shareware from

```
http://cent1.lancs.ac.uk/tim/tim.html
```

or

```
ftp://ftp.sdsc.edu/pub/vrml/software/modelers/
```

The software was written by Tim Lewis of Lancaster University.

Distributed Discovery

Distributed Discovery is an object-oriented toolkit that you can use to create VRML based on real-time information feeds and database information. It is commercial software from Visible Decisions, Inc. There are some neat possibilities in Discovery, though they'll probably require VRML 2.0 to be realized. You can find Discovery at

```
http://www.vdi.com/
```

Ez3d Modeler

Ez3d Modeler and Ez3d VR Pro 2.0 are for UNIX machines. The software is easy to use and lets you use advanced features of VRML like WWWInline and WWWAnchor hyperlinking nodes and LOD nodes (level of detail). It has a nice user interface, so users should be able to start creating worlds quickly. Ez3d is available from Radiance Software International at

```
http://www.webcom.com/~radiance/
```

Fountain

Fountain from Caligari enables you both to browse and to build home worlds on the World Wide Web. It can interact with a standard WWW browser to handle links to HTML pages. A new feature lets you create a private home world with links to other worlds, like a 3-D bookmarks list. It's available from

```
http://www.caligari.com/ws/fount.html
```

G Web

G Web is a virtual worlds authoring package for VRML from Virtual Presence Ltd. G Web includes modeling capabilities and the ability to import popular 3D CAD formats. G Web is available for a price for Windows 3.1, Windows NT, Silicon Graphics, and Sparc from

```
http://www.demon.co.uk/presence/
```

PhotoModeler 2.1

PhotoModeler 2.1 is a Windows program for creating 3-D models using photographs of existing objects and scenes, developed by Eos Systems, Inc. It exports in VRML with support for full-surround photograph-derived texture maps. You can find it at

```
http://www.telemark.net/eos/
```

Sony Cyber Passage Conductor

Cyber Passage Conductor is a Windows 95 tool that enables you to add behaviors, sound, and images to VRML 1.0 files. Support for behaviors is via the Sony extensions to VRML, so they are not standard VRML. Behaviors are written in TCL and the authoring tool enables you to drag and drop scripts onto existing VRML objects to build interactive, animated worlds. You will only be able to view the new version with Sony's Cyber Passage Browser. As the VRML 2.0 standard is developed, expect Cyber Passage Conductor to expand to support it. The Japanese site is

`http://vs.sony.co.jp/VS-E/vstop.html`

A U.S. mirror site is at

`http://sonypic.com/vs/index.html`

Sample worlds created with Conductor include a floating airship (`http://sonypic.com/WORLD/ToyWorld/hikousen/main.wrl`), a UFO (`http://sonypic.com/WORLD/ToyWorld/ufo/main.wrl`), a buggy on a winding road with a steep curve (`http://sonypic.com/WORLD/ToyWorld/drive/main.wrl`), and a flying sea gull (`http://sonypic.com/WORLD/ToyWorld/origami/main.wrl`).

Spinner

Spinner is a VRML authoring tool for Microsoft Windows from 3D Web. Spinner lets you import previously developed 3-D objects (in formats such as 3DS, DXF, NFF, and OBJ) that you've created in other modeling or CAD software. In Spinner, you can add VRML specific features to the objects. These include creating multiple levels of detail for each model, arranging the objects in a real-time rendered 3-D scene, adding URL hyperlinks to 3-D objects in the world, and wrapping textures or materials around an object. Spinner is at

`http://www.3dweb.com/`

Strata StudioPro Blitz, Version 1.75

Strata StudioPro Blitz is a full modeling, rendering, and animation system for Macintosh with full support for VRML, QuickDraw 3D, and QuickTime VR. Many Mac enthusiasts have delighted in it. You can find it at

`http://www.strata3d.com:80/tools/studiopro/index.html`

TriSpectives 1.0

TriSpectives is a multifunction 3-D drawing program for Windows 95 which includes VRML support from 3D/Eye. You can do a lot of different things with the software, including adding 3-D objects and scenes into documents from other programs. It includes 1000 objects to get you started. You can use TriSpectives to place 3-D animations in presentations; create professional 3-D illustrations in brochures, flyers, and posters; and design 3-D drawings for your diagrams and reports. A professional version is also available with more advanced features. Look for it at

`http://www.eye.com/`

Virtual Home Space Builder

Virtual Home Space Builder is good for creating cube-like environments, like homes and galleries, and overlaying them with wallpapering, floor textures, and wall hangings. It comes with preset templates and textures to help you get started quickly. It also has a neat icon-based interface. Home Space Builder is from Paragraph and is available for Windows from

`http://www.us.paragraph.com/whatsnew/homespce.htm`

Virtus WalkThrough Pro 2.5

This latest version of Virtus's modeling package includes the capability to export VRML, and supports stereo head-mount displays. You can download a free demo of an old version of the software from their site and use it in conjunction with format conversion software. The site is at

`http://www.virtus.com/vwtpro.html`

WebSpace Author 1.0

WebSpace Author 1.0 from SGI is a nice VRML authoring tool, though it is only available on SGI hardware. It has a nice LOD editor that generates versions of an object with different polygon counts. It also has an integrated publishing facility that trims down the file size and generates a compressed version of the VRML file. WebSpace is at

`http://webspace.sgi.com/WebSpaceAuthor/index.html`

World Builder

World Builder is the "big brother" of Fountain, currently under development by Caligari. It will include advanced modeling tools such as 3D Booleans, organic deformations, numerical modeling, and surface sculpting. In addition, you will be able to do polygon reduction, automatic levels of detail, automatic compression, simple behaviors, simple animations, and transparent publishing across the Web. World Builder is at the Caligari site

`http://www.caligari.com/`

Sample Worlds

To help you get started using modeling packages, here are several URLs for VRML worlds created with Fountain, Home Space Builder, and TriSpectives.

Created with Fountain

You can find some VRML worlds created with Fountain in

```
ftp://ftp.caligari.com/pub/fountain/contrib
```

One world in the directory is Booscary by Robert Saint John, a Halloween scene:

```
ftp://ftp.caligari.com/pub/fountain/contrib/booscary.wrl.
```

Tardis, a scene based on Doctor Who, uses a panoramic view inside of a cylinder, similar to the QuickTime VR concept. This file will only work in Fountain. Its address is

```
ftp://ftp.caligari.com/pub/fountain/contrib/tardis.wrl
```

Created with Virtual Home Space Builder

Virtual Home Space Builder creates visually intensive spaces. They maintain a catalog of VHSB spaces at

```
http://www.paragraph.com/3dsite/catalog/spaces
```

Flying Dutchman is at

```
http://www.paragraph.com/3dsite/vrml/dutchman/church.wrl
```

Andrei Kryukov, a Russion artist, has a gallery of art at

```
http://www.paragraph.com/3dsite/vrml/krukov/krukove.wrl
```

Moritzburg has one at

```
http://www.paragraph.com/3Dsite/vrml/morizbur/morizbur.wrl
```

Eugeni's Personal Arts Gallery is at

```
http://www.paragraph.com/3dsite/vrml/chechet/chechet.wrl
```

Created with TriSpectives

A model of a hammer is at

```
http://www.eye.com/event/hammer.wrl
```

A PMI-3 paintball gun created by Han Wang using TriSpectives is at

```
http://www.eye.com/gallery/pmi3gun.wrl
```

3D/Eye's Virtual Resource Locator is at

```
http://www.eye.com/vrmltour/3deyetxr.wrl.gz
```

Summary

When using 3-D modeling software to create VRML, there are three main concerns to be aware of: colors/lighting, file sizes, and polygon counts.

Color standards in VRML are still being developed, so colors will look different in different browsers. The WebSpace VRML browser uses OpenGL lighting and color implementation that looks very beautiful, though it takes significant processing power to compute all of the lighting. This can make it slow to navigate through the world. Other browsers, like WebFX and WorldView, have a simpler lighting and color implementation for fast speed, but less pretty colors. So make sure to test your worlds out in different browsers.

Many people expect VRML files to take up at least 1MB. That isn't the case. You can create some significant worlds that are as little as 20K using gzip compression. In addition, strategic use of the LOD and WWWInline nodes can streamline the download times necessary to experience your world. WWWInline lets you segment different parts of your world into different files, so that you might have the initial viewpoint within the main VRML file, but have other areas of the world still loading in from separate files as WWWInlines. A person experiencing the world doesn't notice the rest of the world missing, because it has been downloaded by the time they get there.

Polygon counts are a consideration as you start developing more advanced and larger worlds. While using Fountain, you discovered how using Fountain's 3-D text facility can add quickly to the number of polygons and file size. Strategic use of the LOD node is a key way to combat polygon hypergrowth. What matters is the number of polygons that are viewable at one time, as this is what slows down your computer. Since this is an advanced feature of VRML, most modeling software packages are slowly adding LOD support. In the meantime, keep your objects simple, use texture maps rather than many polygons for small details, and test out your world's navigation speed in several browsers on various hardware configurations.

Now that you have the tools and the knowledge, go forth, and grow cyberspace!

Writing Java Applets

24

by John J. Kottler

IN THIS CHAPTER

As exciting as the World Wide Web is, its frequent users are always expecting more from it. Simple presentation of information and form processing capabilities for a Web site are acceptable and the norm, but the Web lacks true interactive communication with a user. As a result, most Web sites are quite dull. A site may have spiffy graphics and loads of good information, but no sites are interactive in real time.

The reasons for this situation are numerous. First, the Web is painfully slow for most users. People accessing the Web at modem speeds have built up a tolerance for slowly painting graphics. When they submit forms for further information, they are accustomed to the time necessary to route this information to a site, have the server perform work based on the information, and return the results. This slowness truly inhibits the idea of real-time interactive communication with the user.

A second reason for the lack of interactive sites is that most Web pages are treated as client/server applications in the very lightest of definitions. Most site developers view client/server technology simply as a client accessing data on the server. In a true client/server relationship, data should be passed back and forth between the client and server machines, but neither machine should do all the work itself. Data-intensive, time-consuming functions should be performed on the server, which is typically a robust machine that has vast access to databases. A local PC can handle the simpler functions. Having the client do some of the processing minimizes the amount of traffic between the user's computer and servers on the Internet, resulting in quicker access. In addition, because the many functions are being performed on a local computer, the speed of the overall Web site appears to be much faster.

Finally, and most importantly, the ability to write interactive applications that run on a user's computer was not widely available until now. But thanks to the work of developers at Sun Microsystems (www.sun.com), there is a new technology that is becoming wildly popular.

Java Break

Sun's Java is the answer to the dilemma regarding how to run truly complex Internet applications on your computer. It solves the mystery of writing a single application that can work on any machine. Because Java applications run on your computer, they are fast and highly interactive. Because the resulting applications are small, they come across the Internet as fast as most graphic files. Because Java was written especially for the Internet and is based on C++, it is extremely powerful and robust.

This chapter takes an introductory look at how to create Java applications. It does not cover every feature of Java or Java programming. It is meant to serve as an introduction for those who want to begin writing their own Internet applications. You learn how to write a basic Java application and some of the necessary, related functions. Coverage of each method and function of the entire Java programming language clearly extends beyond the scope of this book, but there are a couple of good Java books already on the market, such as *Presenting Java* and *Teach Yourself Java in 21 Days*, both from sams.net Publishing. This chapter examines a simple Java application and disseminates each function of it and every line of significant code. Through this process, you will acquire appropriate knowledge to use when writing your own Java applications.

In order to write Java applications, you should have an adequate understanding of C/C++ and the concepts of object-oriented development. Of course, experience with Windows development or a similar graphical user interface helps. This chapter works off this base of knowledge to present Java application development. For more information on C/C++ and object-oriented programming, check out *Teach Yourself C++ in 21 Days* from Sams Publishing.

Understanding Java

If you searched for *Java* on the Internet with a search engine, chances are you would find two types of results. The first would be links to gourmet coffee stands and the second would be links to a new language for the Web. This chapter deals with the latter.

Java has grown from its roots at Sun Microsystems and was developed primarily as a language for creating software for electronic consumer products. Normally, C++ was the language of choice for creating embedded software in such systems, but as the developers worked, they discovered numerous disadvantages with C++. Therefore, they decided to create a language that was extremely similar to C++, but that removed some of the complexity of C++ that often caused more havoc than good for the developer. The result is a language that enables application developers to easily create object-oriented programs that are very secure, portable across different machine and operating system platforms, and dynamic enough to allow for easy expandability. Because C++ is a common development language, there is little need for vast amounts of training like an entirely new language would require; therefore, Java can be more easily adopted.

Applets Work on Any Computer

But what *exactly* is Java? The Java language is a compiler-based language. That is, once a developer has written the Java code, that code must be passed through another program called a *compiler*. The compiler translates the textual code a programmer writes into something the machine understands. In the world of C++ and similar languages, the compiler creates an executable program that can run on a computer. However, that executable program has been compiled for a particular machine and cannot also be run on a different machine. Computers may look similar on the outside or even in the way they work, but the very core of the machine can be drastically different. This difference is why an application written and compiled on a Macintosh cannot run on a Windows PC or a UNIX machine.

Although Java is a compiler-based language like C++, it has been modified so that a single compiled application may work on any type of computer. How is this possible? Java code is compiled into a compact and optimized program called an *applet*. The applet consists of instructions called *bytecodes* that are then fed to a program called a *runtime module*. The runtime module translates the bytecodes into machine instructions for a particular computer.

Sun Microsystems has created a Web browser for Java applications called Hot Java. This browser works like typical Web browsers, but it includes the runtime program that reads Java instructions and translates them into machine instructions. Other browsers such as Netscape Navigator 2.0 also offer a Java runtime module in its browser so that Netscape users can view Java applets as well. The runtime program is the only Java-related program written specifically for each type of computer.

To illustrate how Java works, assume that there is a Java application on a Web page that you want to view with Windows 95 and Netscape. When you view that page with Netscape, Netscape retrieves the Java applet and passes that applet to a Java runtime program that is bundled with Netscape. That runtime program, in this case written specifically for Windows 95, reads the Java applet's instructions and translates them to function appropriately with Windows 95. It's similar to being able to put any brand coffeemaker coffee into any brand coffeemaker.

Object-Oriented Programming

Java, because of its roots with C++, is even more tightly integrated with object-oriented concepts. Object-oriented languages enable developers to create Windows-type applications with less effort than with traditional techniques. Object-oriented languages rely on the concepts of objects, properties, and methods. These concepts can be related to a coffeemaker and the process of making coffee.

Clearly, in this case the coffeemaker is the object you are working with to perform a task. Properties of the coffeemaker might include the color of the plastic and where it is located in your kitchen, things that are attributes of the coffeemaker. Methods are actions that an object can perform. For instance, the Make Coffee button triggers the process of making coffee. There also may be events associated with this coffeemaker. *Events* are the triggers that cause an object do something. For example, if the coffeemaker has a timer built into it and the capability to start coffee at a particular time, the clock triggers the brewing process when the correct time occurs.

With object-oriented technology, a Java applet can react differently according to different types of input. Also, because pieces of the object are treated as components, you can replace components easily. This component approach of object-oriented programming also enables Java to handle multiple things at once, independently of each other. A Java applet can have multiple components working on continuously updating live information from a variety of sources while another component is available to handle user interaction. Each independently running task is referred to as a *thread* in Java. You can think of the thread as a series of events that occur in a line. The lines run parallel to each other, but the threads do not necessarily affect each other.

Secure and Robust

You cannot listen to a coffee commercial without hearing about its robustness, and you should expect no less from computerized Java. When Java applications are compiled, they are heavily scrutinized to avoid possible problems. The language itself removes many of the error-prone functions associated with C++, and Java even does dynamic checking for errors while the applet is running. This checking helps protect the developers from creating errors and forces them to not use ambiguous declarations that a language like C++ would allow. As an example, programs written in languages such as C++ historically had to remember to free resources that they had allocated during execution. A Java application does not need to explicitly release memory; the Java interpreter automatically handles this function for you.

The way Java implements this robustness also indirectly heightens security on the applet. Because Java forces developers to be more structured, there are fewer chances for information to be illegally altered in the applet. Security is also heightened with the use of encryption and compression. Java can squeeze and scramble the contents of its applets to limit the threat of tampering.

What Can You Do with Java?

The capabilities of Java outlined in the preceding sections allow for more dynamic, animated, and interactive Web pages in the future. To make you fully appreciate what these features can offer to the Web and you, the section examines an example of a Java application.

> **TIP**
>
> Earlier, alpha versions of Java applets may not run on newer Web browsers that support Java. To determine whether a Web page is using an older version of Java, examine the HTML source for a Web page. Newer versions of Java use the <APPLET> tag to indicate a Java application; older versions use the <APP> tag.

Netscape offers a daily crossword puzzle at its site. You can access this page by jumping to Netscape (http://www.netscape.com). Then choose to view Java information on Navigator 2.0. A list appears with a few sample Java applications.

One nice feature of Java is that you do not have to explicitly invoke a Java application. Most Web browsers will automatically display the application—in this case, a screen similar to that in Figure 24.1. This crossword puzzle applet is an excellent example of a Java application that is very graphic in nature and requires user interaction. It also stresses the importance of adding instructions or creating clearly intuitive interfaces for Java applets. Each Java applet may behave entirely differently from other Java applets, and the user requires instruction for the first time an applet is used.

FIGURE 24.1.

This crossword puzzle application demonstrates how Java applets allow for enhanced interaction between a user and a Web page.

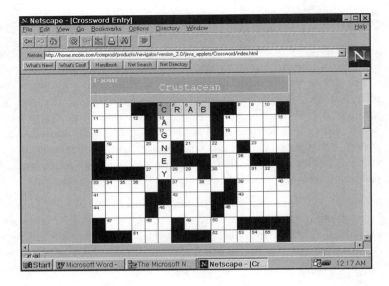

Notice that when you view the crossword puzzle page, the crossword puzzle itself is embedded in the Web page, just like an inline GIF image. From the HTML source code, you can control where the Java application appears, just as you would images.

To work on the crossword puzzle, click any row or column in the puzzle to highlight that row or column. The hint for that row or column is then displayed at the top of the puzzle. To toggle between horizontal row selections and vertical column selections, press the spacebar. When you're ready, you can enter the word you think is the answer into the currently highlighted area. Incorrect letters are then highlighted in red.

As you can see, this Java application is accepting many different types of events from the user: the keyboard for text entry, the space bar for row/column selection, and the mouse for selecting rows or columns in the puzzle. This application also demonstrates how Java can produce very graphical results by drawing the board, highlighting appropriate sections, and adding multicolor text.

Creating a Java Applet

So, now that you have an idea of what a Java applet is and what it can do, how do you write your own specific Java applet? This chapter examines the coding and creation of a single Java applet, which will help you to further understand the technology so that you can create your own custom applets. The applet that this chapter examines is the Marquee applet. At times, you may want scrolling text to appear on your Web page. For instance, if you were designing a Web site that tracked stock prices, you might want to implement the familiar ticker symbol line. The ticker line consists of a solid rectangle in which text and numbers are scrolled. The information in the ticker scrolls off the left side of the ticker line and returns on the right side of the ticker area. This applet is also very similar to the Windows Marquee screen saver, which has been aptly renamed in Windows 95 as Scrolling Marquee. The idea is the same; text you enter is scrolled across the screen until it disappears, and it then scrolls back onto the screen from the opposite side.

Writing this effect in Java ensures that the applet can run on a plethora of operating systems and hardware platforms. The computer that the application is running on must simply have the Java interpreter software installed on it. If the computer is using Netscape Navigator 2.0, Hot Java, or a similar Web browser to view Java applications, then this interpreter is included.

Choosing Java as the development tool also enables you to use graphics for smoother scrolling and have greater font and color control. You can also set the applet to run continuously in the background, which is essential for the effect as well. The text should continuously loop around the marquee area instead of just scrolling once. Java offers support for these requirements.

Parameters for the Marquee Applet

The Marquee applet exists as a Java applet embedded in a Web page. Because it is embedded, it takes on all of the typical attributes of Java applets. It exists within a window as defined by the HTML code and is loaded/unloaded appropriately as the Web page is loaded and unloaded from the Web browser. The applet will also accept additional parameters from the Web page, defining the nature of the applet.

For this applet, the HTML document for a Web page can set several options:

- `text`—This text is scrolled within the applet's window. The default is `Scrolling Marquee`.

- `direction`—The marquee's text may scroll either to the left or to the right. This parameter may be set to `right` to indicate that direction; otherwise, the default is `left`.

- `speed`—The scrolling text may be sped up or slowed down by modifying this value. Speed is measured in milliseconds; therefore, a value of 1000 is equivalent to a one-second delay. The default is one tenth of a second (100 milliseconds).

- `bgcolor`—This parameter indicates what the background color of the applet's window should be. The value must consist of a nine-digit number. The number represents three separate three-digit numbers. These individual numbers represent values between 000 and 255. Each three-digit number represents the amounts of red, blue, and green color, respectively. This parameter is similar to the #00 to #FF values typically found in the HTML `<BODY>` tag for setting colors. Instead of using hexadecimal values, however, this Java applet is expecting decimal numbers. The default is white (255255255).

- `fgcolor`—Just as the background color for the marquee may be determined through HTML, so can the text color. This value expects the same nine-digit color format as explained in the `bgcolor` value. The default is dark blue (000000128).

Assuming that this Java applet is correctly embedded within your Web page, the result may be a screen similar to the one in Figure 24.2.

FIGURE 24.2.

A sample of the Marquee Java applet within the Netscape browser window.

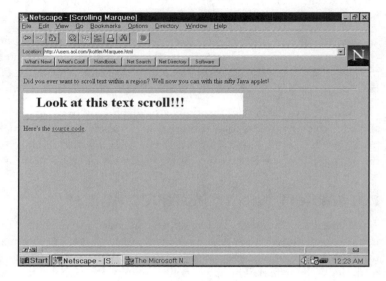

The Marquee Applet's Code

Listing 24.1 shows the complete code listing for the Marquee Java applet.

Listing 24.1. The code for `Marquee.java`.

```
// *******************************
//     Application: MARQUEE.JAVA
// *******************************

import java.awt.*;

public class Marquee extends java.applet.Applet implements Runnable {
  Thread    appThread;
  Font      fFont;
  String    sMsg;
  int       speed=100;
  int       direction=-1;
  int       x=0;
  int       bg_red=255,bg_green=255,bg_blue=255;
  int       fg_red=0,fg_green=0,fg_blue=128;

  // Bunch of setup stuff, read in values from HTML
  public void init() {
    String sParam;

    // Use the Times Roman font, BOLD 32pt.
```

```
      fFont = new java.awt.Font("TimesRoman",Font.BOLD,32);

      // Get the text to scroll from HTML
      sParam = getParameter("text");
      if (sParam==null)
        sMsg="Scrolling Marquee";
      else
        sMsg=sParam;

      // Default is to scroll left, can specify right
      // Set from HTML
      sParam = getParameter("direction");
      if (sParam!=null){
        if (sParam.equalsIgnoreCase("right"))
          direction=1;
      }

      // How fast to scroll
      sParam = getParameter("delay");
      if (sParam!=null)
        speed=Integer.valueOf(sParam).intValue();

      // Find background color for Marquee window
      // Like <BODY> tag's #FFFFFF format, but uses
      // Decimal:
      //    255255255 is white
      //    000000000 is black
      sParam = getParameter("bgcolor");
      if (sParam!=null){
        // Check that the string looks long enough
        if (sParam.length()==9){
          // Get the Red value (0-255)
          bg_red=Integer.valueOf(sParam.substring(0,3)).intValue();
          // Get the Green value (0-255)
          bg_green=Integer.valueOf(sParam.substring(3,6)).intValue();
          // Get the Blue value (0-255)
          bg_blue=Integer.valueOf(sParam.substring(6,9)).intValue();
        }
      }

      // Find foreground color for Marquee text
      // Works same as background above
      sParam = getParameter("fgcolor");
      if (sParam!=null){
        if (sParam.length()==9){
          fg_red=Integer.valueOf(sParam.substring(0,3)).intValue();
          fg_green=Integer.valueOf(sParam.substring(3,6)).intValue();
          fg_blue=Integer.valueOf(sParam.substring(6,9)).intValue();
        }
      }
  }   // End of INIT


// Paint to the applet's Window within Web browser
// "g" represents that window's canvas
public void paint(Graphics g) {
  Dimension       d = size();
  FontMetrics     fm;
```

continues

Listing 24.1. continued

```
    // We have a pointer to the font we want to use from above,
    // now we have to set it.
    g.setFont(fFont);
    fm=g.getFontMetrics();

    // Use rectangle to paint background color
    // drawRect is the border, fillRect is interior
    g.setColor(new java.awt.Color(bg_red,bg_green,bg_blue));
    g.drawRect(0,0,d.width,d.height);
    g.fillRect(0,0,d.width,d.height);

    // Set text color and draw it
    g.setColor(new java.awt.Color(fg_red,fg_green,fg_blue));
    g.drawString(sMsg,x,fFont.getSize());

    // Update text position
    x+=(10*direction);
    // If we're scrolling right and outside window, then wrap
    if (x>d.width-1 && direction==1)
      x=-fm.stringWidth(sMsg);
    // If we're scrolling left and outside window, then wrap
    if (x<-fm.stringWidth(sMsg) && direction==-1)
      x=d.width-1;
  }  // End of PAINT

public void start() {
  // Create a thread to run in background
  appThread = new Thread(this);
  appThread.start();
}

public void stop() {
  appThread.stop();
}

public void run() {
  while (true){   // While applet is running on page...
    repaint();     // update graphics
    try {
      // Pause the thread, which pauses the animation
      Thread.currentThread().sleep(speed);
    }

    // Exception handling for interrupted thread
    catch (InterruptedException e) {
    }
  }
}  // End of RUN
}  // End of MARQUEE Class
```

At first glance, the code certainly appears daunting. However, it is really not as confusing as it may seem at first. The following sections explain each line of this applet.

> **NOTE**
>
> A single comment line for a Java code listing begins with the double forward slash (//).
> Comments may span multiple lines by beginning the comment block with /* and
> ending it with */.

Imported Java

If you are familiar with other languages such as C and C++, you may quickly realize that the
first line of the Java code, `import java.awt.*`, resembles the familiar #include statement in C.
Like the #include statement, Java's import statement allows the application you are writing to
import code from other sources. In this case, Java can retrieve code from other Java classes.

One of the nice features of the import statement is that it can import multiple classes using the
wildcard (*) notation. Because this applet draws results to the applet window, it requires several
classes from the AWT (Abstract Window ToolKit). This toolkit serves as the mediator between
the Java applet and the operating system. Because every computer system uses different operating
systems and supports different hardware, translating graphical user interface (GUI) functions
appropriately is necessary in order for Java to maintain its cross-platform advantage. The AWT
takes requests for drawing information to the screen or managing windows and associated
controls. The Java interpreter translates these requests to draw information correctly onto your
computer's screen, whatever type of computer it may be.

You probably will include the AWT in one way or another in most of your Java applets. The
import statement in Listing 24.1 imports all of the AWT classes. Some of these classes include
support for drawing windows, buttons, graphics such as rectangles and polygons, fonts, and
colors, for instance.

When importing classes, all those related to Java specifically begin with *java.* If you have your
own custom classes, you may reference them as well. A Java applet is built on dozens of classes
that you invoke within your own program. It is important that you include all of the Java
methods that your program will require.

Because the Java language is built on classes, there is a class hierarchy. (For a complete description
of these classes, their properties and methods, and their relationships, see Sun's Java site at
www.javasoft.com.) Therefore, you can specify a particular class to use in your applet instead
of using them all through the * notation. You must separate the levels along the hierarchy with
a period (.). The period is essential to identifying objects and methods and specifying relations
within the Java language. Suppose that you were going to place a button somewhere within
your Java applet. To use the appropriate class to handle the buttons, you would use the following
line:

```
import java.awt.button;
```

Because you usually import many classes into your final Java applet, it is sometimes more convenient to use the wildcard notation (*) to import all classes within the group of classes.

Head of the Class

Whether or not you realize it, you are creating a class when you create an applet. The Java language uses a truly object-oriented approach, and your applet is treated as a leaf on the end of the object-oriented tree. So it should be no surprise that the first thing you must do when creating a Java applet is create its class. The Marquee applet declares itself using the following syntax:

```
public class Marquee extends java.applet.Applet implements Runnable
```

This line creates a Java applet or class with a particular name and options. This example creates the class Marquee, which will become a Java *interface*. An interface is similar to subclassing or inheriting another class with one important difference: interfaces do not inherit all the excess baggage from the superclass. An interface only implements the methods of the class that are specific for the applet.

The `extends java.applet.Applet` code instructs this class to inherit the capabilities of the main Java applet class, which allows this Marquee class to be used as an applet by the Java interpreter. The actual definition of the applet is defined by the methods that you implement within your applet, as you will see in a moment. The `implements Runnable` portion of this line instructs Java to use threads to control this applet.

As mentioned earlier in the chapter, threads are processes that run independently of other processes. They can be thought of as a series of instructions that execute without interfering with each other. This concept is similar to multitasking, which is found in many operating systems. In fact, operating systems use threads for tasks in one fashion or another.

Because you want the text within the marquee window to scroll continuously in the background, you need to implement a thread for this Java applet. You may argue that you do not have to implement a thread to scroll the text. This is true, but if you did not use a thread, the Java interpreter would end up spending all of its time processing this single application. This is not effective when more than one Java applet exists on a page.

Now that the class is defined, any code that exists between the starting brace ({) and the ending brace (}) is implemented in that class. On the first line past the first starting brace, notice that a number of variables are declared. If you have experience with C or C++, you should recognize some familiar data types. Some of the types, such as Font or Thread, are specific Java data types. Also, notice that these variables are defined before any additional methods are introduced to the class. This order causes the variables to have a wider scope. Each of these variables are available to any method within the Marquee class.

The *init* Method

Every Java applet must be initialized. Because Java is an object-oriented language, it is important to remember that there may be multiple instances of a class that you design. For example, you may use this Marquee applet on the main page of your Web site as well as in an additional page deeper in the site. Therefore, you must initialize each instance of this applet if each instance is to contain different data and display different results. The Java interpreter triggers the init method automatically. Typically this triggering occurs after the Java applet is first retrieved from the network. Once the applet is created on the client computer, the applet is started and this is the first function that is executed.

You can use the init method for many different purposes. Often it is used to allocate resource memory, retrieve additional resources from the Internet, retrieve the parameters sent to the applet from the Web page, and set properties of the applet, such as color or position. In the Marquee applet, the init method is used to set the font to be used in the applet and retrieve the parameters passed into the applet from the HTML document for a Web page. The init method is actually a function within the Marquee class and is defined appropriately. It is a simple method that accepts no arguments and returns no value. It is also made public so that other applets or the interpreter may invoke the method.

Getting the Right Font

The first line after the string declaration within the init method uses the Font class from the Java AWT:

```
fFont = new java.awt.Font("TimesRoman",Font.BOLD,32);
```

Because fonts are drawn to the computer screen, each system may handle this function differently. In addition, each system may have different names that identify a Times Roman font face. Therefore, it is up to the AWT to process this request and set up a pointer to the correct font type to use when drawing the text later in the applet. As you can see from the line of code, the new instruction allocates memory for the new font object that is created from the Font class. That memory is assigned to the fFont variable for future reference within the applet.

Parameters

The next four sections of the init method retrieve variables passed in from the HTML document of a Web page. This capability allows Java applets to be more generic. Suppose you want to scroll text to the right on one Web page and to the left on another. You could write two separate applets—one that scrolls text to the left and another that scrolls text to the right—but that would be foolish. Instead, you could pass a parameter from the HTML document for a Web page that determines the direction: left or right. That parameter would then be read by a single Java applet, which would take the appropriate action. This capability to pass information between the Web page and an applet allows for even greater dynamic Web pages when coupled with the JavaScript language. JavaScript can control what parameters to pass to the Java applet based on criteria that you specify. Later in this chapter you learn how to embed Java applets and pass parameters to those applets.

Each parameter that is passed into a Java applet is named, which makes it much easier to parse through the arguments and retrieve the correct ones. The sParam is a temporary string used to hold the results of an argument. The getParameter method retrieves the argument that is specified within the method's parentheses.

```
sParam = getParameter("text");
```

In the preceding line, the "text" parameter is passed in from the HTML for the page. For example, the HTML source for a Web page could include the following tag for a Java applet:

```
<param name=text value="Look at this text scroll!!!">
```

This tag indicates to the Java applet that the "text" parameter is to be set to "Look at this text scroll!!!" Therefore, the getParameter would set the string sParam to "Look at this text scroll!!!"

Testing the Strings

After reading in a parameter, you may want to perform some tests on the data returned. Most Java applets accommodate Web page developers who may neglect to include all of the parameters for the applet. When a parameter is not yet specified in HTML retrieved in the Java applet through the getParameter method, the result of the getParameter method is null.

On the surface, this result appears to be harmless. However, it can prove to be quite disastrous. What if an applet is reading a parameter to be converted to a number to be used in an equation and that parameter is not specified? The applet may encounter an error. Although error handling is built into Java, it is good practice to catch errors before they occur. In the Marquee applet, each parameter is tested to determine whether it was set to null. If so, a default value is substituted.

The second parameter read by the applet specifies the direction in which text is to scroll within the Marquee applet. After the parameter is read and guaranteed not to be set to null, the applet checks the value of the parameter. The default direction for scrolling is to the left; therefore only the "right" condition needs to be considered.

```
if (sParam.equalsIgnoreCase("right"))
```

Your first inclination may be to test the string returned by getParameter using the == notation. Experienced C developers quickly realize that this notation is not suitable for strings. The equivalence test (==) is only appropriate for testing logical equivalence between numbers or Boolean values. Strings must be compared using a dedicated method that is a member of the string class.

Strings defined within Java inherit the string class, which contains many methods. Examples of just a few of these methods are: `length`, `substring`, and `append`. The method for comparing strings is inherited as well. The `equalsIgnoreCase` method tests whether two strings are equivalent. The string `sParam` in the preceding line of code is tested via its `equalsIgnoreCase` method with the data passed into that method (`"right"`). If the result is true, appropriate action is taken to change the direction of the scrolling text. As the method clearly indicates, the strings are compared, but the case of individual letters in those strings is ignored.

Converting Strings to Numbers

One of the requirements for this applet is to be able to specify parameters other than text from within a Web page. These parameters include background and foreground colors to use for the marquee, as well as the speed at which the text scrolls. The actual parameters that are read from the HTML document for a Web page are treated as strings. In the applet, however, these values must be treated as numbers.

Java offers numerous class conversion methods for converting between strings and numbers and vice-versa. In the case of the Marquee applet, several values are to be read in from the Web page and processed as integer values, or more specifically, `int` values.

```
speed=Integer.valueOf(sParam).intValue();
```

You must use the `Integer` class to process a string and convert it appropriately. This class contains the `valueOf` method that converts the string (which `sParam` holds the value for from the Web page) to an `Integer` object format. However, because the Java application requires `int` values and not objects, you must also invoke the `intValue` method. The `intValue` method is invoked for the integer object that is a product of the `valueOf` method. The result is an `int` value that is returned to the `speed` variable.

Substrings and Lengths of Strings

Values are passed from the Web page to the Marquee applet that indicate the colors to use for the background of the window, as well as the text that scrolls within that window. For simplicity, the requirements defined these color numbers to be nine digits in length. Each number actually consists of three separate numbers, each three digits in length, which are concatenated together. These three numbers represent the amount of red, green, and blue to mix respectively to form a color. These individual components may range in value between 000 and 255. This format is similar to the one that the HTML `<BODY>` tag uses to indicate colors; however, the numbers are represented in decimal as opposed to hexadecimal. Table 24.1 shows examples of valid colors for the Marquee applet.

Table 24.1. Example color values for the Marquee Java applet.

000000000	Black
255000000	Red
000255000	Green
000000255	Blue
255255000	Yellow
255128000	Orange
255000255	Purple
255255255	White
128128128	Medium Gray

Because a color number is passed as a nine-character string, this string must be separated into three components, each three characters in length. The easiest approach to this process is to use the substring method. This method retrieves only a particular number of characters from a main string. As with the equalsIgnoreCase method, the substring method comes with any string you create in Java.

The substring method accepts two parameters. The first specifies the starting position within the string from which you would like to begin reading. The second parameter indicates the position immediately after the last character in the string that you would like to read.

```
sParam.substring(0,3)
sParam.substring(3,6)
```

The preceding two lines return two separate pieces of the string sParam. Assume that sParam holds the value 255196000. In this case, sParam.substring(0,3) would return the value 255, and sParam.substring(3,6) returns 196. You may notice that the substring method retrieves the characters starting at and including the first parameter of the method and ending at the character just before the second parameter of the method.

> **NOTE**
>
> You can identify each character of a string by a number in Java methods such as substring or charAt. The numbering of these characters begins at zero and ends at one less than the length of the string.

The substring method returns a particular range of characters from the string between zero and one less than the length of the string. But how do you determine the length of a string? Java strings also inherit another method: length. This method determines the number of characters that a string consists of and returns that number for you to use.

Painting Applets

Any Java applet that draws to the applet window or uses buttons, windows, or other objects that the AWT offers, requires the paint method. This method may be triggered either through your own code or automatically by the Java interpreter. For instance, the interpreter may trigger the method when the Web browser window is resized.

If you are familiar with Graphical User Interface development, you already know the unparalleled importance of the paint method. This method is triggered any time a window is to be repainted. This method has the appropriate source code for drawing graphics or controlling the placement of GUI (Graphical User Interface) objects. In the Marquee applet, this method is the appropriate place for painting the background color of the applet's window and for drawing the text within that window at a particular location.

The paint method, like the init method, is a public method, which means that other applets or the Java runtime module, not just other methods within the Marquee class, can call this method. The paint method does not return a value, but it does accept one argument, the Graphics class. You can think of this class as the canvas that is linked to the Java applet. The Java applet may then paint on this canvas by using methods associated with this class.

In the Marquee applet, this canvas is painted with the appropriate background color, and new text is drawn on the canvas in the correct color at a particular location. On subsequent paint events, which are triggered later in the applet by a thread, the location of this text is updated to give the illusion that it is scrolling. To prevent text streaks, the background must first be painted each time the text is drawn. Painting the background clears the window, which removes the text that was already drawn at the old position, before the text is drawn at the new position.

Setting the Current Font

The applet sets the font to use when drawing the text. Earlier in the init method, the font object was prepared and stored as fFont. The setFont method uses that font class and sets the current font for drawing text on the canvas using that class. At the same time the font metrics—information such as the width and height of the font—are retrieved for use later in the method:

```
g.setFont(fFont);
fm=g.getFontMetrics();
```

> **NOTE**
>
> Remember to use the setFont method to set the current font to draw with on the canvas. A common mistake is to expect that when an instance of the font class is created that it also sets the font for drawing.

After the font object has been initialized, the background of the window is painted to the appropriate colors found earlier by the `init` method. This process involves drawing an opaque rectangle that occupies the entire width and height of the Java applet window. In order to know how big of a rectangle to paint, the applet must be able to determine the size of its own window. Fortunately, Java offers a `Dimension` object that holds information regarding the dimensions of the applet's window after its `size` method is invoked.

Three steps are used to draw the rectangle. First, the current drawing color must be set to the background color specified by the Web page and read by the `init` method. Because this is a custom color, you must create a new object to hold it. The color of the object is determined by using the `Color` method in the AWT class. This method accepts three integer values that represent the amount of red, green, and blue to mix together to create the final color. Only after the new color object has been created may the current drawing color for the canvas be set by the `setColor` method.

```
g.setColor(new java.awt.Color(bg_red,bg_green,bg_blue));
```

The rectangle is then drawn to fill the window, effectively painting the applet's window. AWT supports two methods for drawing rectangles: `drawRect` and `fillRect`. The difference is that `drawRect` draws a transparent rectangle, and `fillRect` draws an opaque rectangle. The border of the rectangle is drawn in the current color when `drawRect` is used, and the solid rectangle is painted with the current color when `fillRect` is used. The Marquee applet uses both methods to explicitly draw the opaque rectangle with a border of the same color. This approach was used so that both the `fillRect` and `drawRect` methods would be demonstrated. It is more efficient to use the `fillRect` by itself and to stretch its coordinates wide enough to compensate for the border typically drawn with `drawRect`. The following is the code for these methods:

```
g.drawRect(0,0,d.width,d.height);
g.fillRect(0,0,d.width,d.height);
```

As you can see, both `drawRect` and `fillRect` expect four parameters. Each parameter specifies the coordinates to use when drawing the rectangle. These coordinates designate the left position, top position, width, and height of the rectangle, respectively.

Writing Text

After the background of the applet window has been painted, the Marquee application is ready to draw text on top of it. As with most drawing methods of the Graphics class, text is drawn using the current color. If the current color is not appropriate, a new color object must be chosen. If the current color was used for drawing text in the Marquee applet, the color would be the same as the background color, effectively not painting text at all. The applet must therefore create a new color to use:

```
g.setColor(new java.awt.Color(fg_red,fg_green,fg_blue));
g.drawString(sMsg,x,fFont.getSize());
```

The current color to use for drawing text is set in the same fashion as the rectangle's drawing color. A new color object is created using the parameters passed in from the Web page to the applet and is assigned as the current color. The `drawString` method then draws a line of text using the current color. This method expects three parameters: the text to display, the horizontal position of the text, and the vertical position of the text. The positions describe where the text is to be drawn, starting at the first character in the text.

Reading Font Information

After the text is drawn to the canvas, the variable representing the horizontal position of the text is updated appropriately for the direction in which it is to scroll. Immediately following this update, two conditionals check to see whether the text has scrolled completely outside of the applet's window. The first condition determines whether the text has scrolled past the right side of the window if it is scrolling to the right. The second condition determines whether the text has scrolled past the left side of the window when it is scrolling left. In both instances, the space that the text occupies when drawn is required. This size is necessary to ensure that the entire length of the text has scrolled beyond the bounds of the window, not just the starting point of the text:

```
if (x>d.width-1 && direction==1) x=-fm.stringWidth(sMsg);
if (x<-fm.stringWidth(sMsg) && direction==-1) x=d.width-1;
```

If the current horizontal position of the text (x) is greater than the width of the window and the text is scrolling to the right, the text should reappear on the left. However, if the horizontal position (x) was merely reset to zero, the effect would not appear correctly. The text would scroll beyond the right side of the window and then reappear in full on the left side of the window. Instead, the text should scroll on from the left, starting with its last character. To accomplish this effect, the horizontal position of the text must be as far to the left as the amount of space that the entire text string occupies. This same theory works for text that scrolls to the left, only the parameters are different.

So how is the amount of space required by the drawn text calculated? Java provides this feature for the applet developer. Earlier in the `paint` event, the `FontMetrics` object was introduced. This object allows the applet to query particular information regarding the font being used. In the Marquee example, the applet must determine how much space text in a particular font requires. The `FontMetrics` class features a method `stringWidth` that performs this calculation. Most fonts consist of individual characters that require different widths, depending on the character. For example, the *W* character may be four times wider than the *I* character. Therefore, for the `stringWidth` to return an accurate measurement for the width of the text, you must pass the text to be measured into the method.

Threads

Earlier in this chapter you were introduced to threads. Threads are vital in operating systems for processing multiple tasks at once. Threads are equally as important in order for the Java interpreter to work with several applets at once. A thread is basically a series of instructions that define the nature of the applet. Typically, threads have a start point and an end point, but these points are not required. For instance, in the Marquee applet, a single thread is used to instruct the application to continuously scroll text. This task is accomplished by constantly forcing the applet window to be repainted. The thread instruction to repaint the window is continuously looped and is started or stopped as determined by the interpreter.

The Java runtime program starts the applet when the Web page that the applet exists on is loaded and stops the applet when the page is unloaded. It is important to notice that the applets are either started or stopped; they are not unloaded from memory. Therefore, they are still available. If an applet uses threads, those threads are still running. For performance, it is important to prepare appropriate `start` and `stop` methods within your Java applet that control the threads within your applet.

The *start* Method

Each time the Marquee applet is started, the `start` method is triggered, which in turn starts a thread that scrolls the text:

```
public void start() {
    appThread = new Thread(this);
    appThread.start();
}
```

These lines of code in the `start` event create the thread object and start it. You may notice the keyword `this` in the line that creates the thread object. Often you may want to refer to the current object within your Java applet, which is accomplished through the use of the `this` keyword. In the case of the preceding `start` method, `this` refers to the current applet.

The *stop* Method

Just as there is a method that your applet may use to control what happens when the applet is started, there is an equivalent method that is triggered when the applet is stopped. As mentioned earlier, it is important to stop running threads when the applet is stopped for performance reasons.

```
public void stop() {
    appThread.stop();
}
```

The `stop` method for the Marquee applet is fairly basic. It is triggered when the applet is stopped and its sole responsibility is to stop execution of the application's thread.

The *run* Method

Because the Marquee applet has `implements Runnable` in its class definition, a `run` method is available that may be used for thread execution. The `run` method constructs the instructions that a thread is to follow. The requirements of the Marquee example indicate that the text should be continuously flowing. Therefore, the first thing that is implemented in the `run` method is an infinite loop. Now you are probably wondering why you would ever want to implement an infinite loop. The fact of the matter is that threads may be interrupted by other threads or by the Java interpreter. When the applet is stopped or closed, this loop is stopped because the thread is halted.

The loop implements two simple tasks: repainting the window to update the scrolling text and causing the thread to pause momentarily for effect. The `repaint` method forces the window of the applet to be redrawn, triggering the `paint` event discussed earlier. The `sleep` method for the current thread delays the thread for a predetermined number of milliseconds. As you can see from Listing 24.2, the `sleep` method belongs to the object `Thread`. To clarify which thread should be stopped (particularly useful with multithreaded applets that use several threads at once), the `currentThread` method is used.

Listing 24.2. The `run` method implements the instructions for a thread in a Java applet.

```
public void run() {
    while (true){
        repaint();
        try {
            Thread.currentThread().sleep(speed);
        }

        catch (InterruptedException e) {
        }
    }
}
```

Exception Handling

Although you should always try to avoid errors, some errors cannot be detected through your code. These types of errors are often referred to as *exceptions*. Java handles these exceptions more elegantly than most languages and allows your code to perform based on the occurrence of an exception. Java cannot do it all for you, however. It will handle exceptions gracefully for you, but in order for your program to do something about an exception, you must specify the portion of code where the error may occur. You must also create code that handles what happens when the exception occurs.

Java uses the keywords try and catch in this process. Each of these keywords is followed by a set of beginning and ending braces ({}) that indicate the block of code to be applied to each keyword. In Listing 24.2, the Marquee applet instructs Java to be wary of exceptions that may occur while the thread is paused. A typical exception that may be raised while a thread is paused is InterruptedException. The fact that a thread was sleeping when another thread interrupted it may cause an error.

The catch keyword indicates the block of code to execute when a particular exception is raised. In the Marquee application, an InterruptedException error may occur. When it does, the catch keyword will trap that error and safely prevent the applet from crashing. Although the applet could have performed some action based on this event, it is not necessary in this case, and therefore no code exists in the catch section of the Marquee applet.

Because you are specifying to the Java interpreter what section of code may raise exceptions, you must also indicate which type of exception to expect. The catch keyword accepts one argument, the type of exception to catch. If you specify a different type of exception than the one actually raised, the block of code following the catch statement may not be executed.

The block of code following the catch statement that handles exceptions is aptly called an *exception handler*. This is one method by which exceptions may be trapped. As with most any language, there is more than one way to accomplish the same thing. Another approach is to use the throws statement, which triggers a specific Java class when an exception is raised.

Compiling Java Applets

Sun Microsystems offers the Java Development Kit (JDK) at its Web site, and it is also available on the CD-ROM that is included with this book.

The JDK includes several binary programs for compiling, disassembling, and debugging Java applets. To compile an applet like the Marquee applet shown in Listing 24.1, you first need to create a new file called Marquee.java and key in the code. I recommend that you create a special subdirectory for your Java applet. In this case, a Marquee subdirectory would suffice. The Marquee.java file that you create should be in this subdirectory as well.

Once you are ready to compile the applet, you must use the JAVAC program that is included with the JDK. Run the JAVAC compiler program from the directory that holds the applet you want to compile.

The result of this compilation is a .class file that you may embed into your HTML documents for Web pages. When you compile the Marquee applet, a Marquee.class file is generated in the current working directory.

Most developers who write applications experience errors. Some experience more errors than others. Because the JAVAC program is a console-based application, the results are pumped to the screen. And if you have more errors than there are lines of text, those error messages will zip by. I recommend that you make a quick batch file to help you compile your Java project. For the Marquee applet, I wrote the simple batch file shown in Listing 24.3 on a Windows 95 PC. It served two purposes: it paused the output of errors so that I could actually read them, and it made invoking the compiler easier because I named it JC.BAT. One word of caution, though; remember to change the name of the applet you are compiling if you plan on using this batch file for additional applets in the future.

Listing 24.3. A DOS batch file for compiling Java applets.

```
@echo off
c:\java\bin\javac Marquee.java > results
type results ¦ more
```

Embedding Java Applets in HTML

Now that you know how to create an applet, how do you use it with your Web page? Java-enabled browsers support the embedding of applets with the <APPLET> tag. One of the greatest advantages to Java applets is that you may place them anywhere on a page, just as you would inline graphics. The <APPLET> tag has a corresponding ending tag, </APPLET>. Between these two tags, you may use additional <PARAM> tags to specify parameters for the Java applet. Listing 24.4 shows a simple HTML document for embedding the Marquee applet.

Listing 24.4. Embedding the Marquee applet.

```
<HTML>
<HEAD>
<TITLE>
Scrolling Marquee
</TITLE>
</HEAD>

<BODY>
Did you ever want to scroll text within a region?
Well now you can with this nifty Java applet!
<HR>

<APPLET CODE="Marquee.class" WIDTH=500 HEIGHT=50>
<param name=text value="Look at this text scroll!!!">
<param name=direction value="left">
<param name=delay value="250">
<param name=bgcolor value="255255255">
<param name=fgcolor value="000000128">
</APPLET>

<HR>
Here's the <A HREF="Marquee.java">source code</A>.
</BODY>

</HTML>
```

The *<APPLET>* Tag

As you can see from Listing 24.4, the Java applet and pertinent information is embedded in the HTML document within the <APPLET> and </APPLET> tags. The <APPLET> tag requires three parameters: CODE, WIDTH, and HEIGHT:

```
<APPLET   CODE = "classname.class"
         WIDTH = width in pixels
        HEIGHT = height in pixels>
```

CODE—This parameter specifies the applet to be embedded on the Web page. In the case of the Marquee example, the code would be "Marquee.class".

WIDTH—This parameter specifies the width of the applet's window in pixels. The Marquee applet reads this information using the size method discussed in the "Painting Applets" section of this chapter.

HEIGHT—Just as WIDTH determines the width of an applet's window, HEIGHT determines its height in pixels.

The *<PARAM>* Tag

By now you are well aware that Java applets accept parameters from the Web page into which they are embedded. Parameters are optional, and default values should always be used for Java applets. However, when parameters are specified by the Web page, they are identified by single <PARAM> tags. Each parameter passed to the Java applet must have its own <PARAM> tag. The <PARAM> tag accepts two parameters of its own: NAME and VALUE:

```
<PARAM  NAME = Java parameter to change
       VALUE = "Java parameter's value">
```

NAME—A Java applet may accept multiple parameters. To indicate which parameter the Web page is changing, the Web page must specify the parameter's name within the <PARAM> tag.

VALUE—Once the parameter to be changed has been identified, the actual value it is to be changed to must be passed from the Web page. The value must be enclosed by quotation marks because it is treated as a string by Java.

What's Next?

Java's increasing popularity is making it a hot technology. In the future, you can expect to see some very innovative uses of this technology to make Web sites truly dynamic and more interactive than ever imaginable. In addition, you can expect to see more Java applets being developed and used as Web authoring tools make the creation of these applications even easier. For now, you have a basic understanding of what Java is and how to go about creating your own brand of Java applets.

PART

VI

IN THIS PART

Putting It All Together

Designing and Publishing a Web Document

25

by William Robert Stanek

IN THIS CHAPTER

Publishing on the World Wide Web may be your ticket to success. Success can be measured in many ways. Your success may be increased sales, attracting new clients, or simply gaining widespread visibility for your ideas. Every success story has a beginning, and in Web publishing, the first step is creating a Web document to tell the world who you are and what you represent.

As the Web publisher, you are responsible for more than the content and quality of the information you provide. You are also responsible for its friendliness and usability. The easiest markup language to create friendly, usable, and informative documents with is the HyperText Markup Language. This chapter takes you through the seven steps necessary to create and publish a Web document. These steps are

1. Develop a strategy.
2. Define the document structure.
3. Create the document.
4. Add features to the document.
5. Proof the document.
6. Test the document.
7. Publish the finished document.

Developing a Strategy

The Web is the ultimate forum for your ideas. By adding sound, graphics, and video, you can create visually stunning, highly interactive, dynamic documents that will entice readers to visit your site time after time. However, you have only a few minutes to convince readers to read your Web publication. If you do not, they are going to go somewhere else for their information needs as quickly and as effortlessly as you can change the channel on your television by remote control. Therefore, you should carefully organize your ideas and develop a specific strategy before creating a Web document.

Creating your Web document can either be a continuous struggle or a logically flowing process. Take the time to organize your ideas. Not only will the payoff be a better product, it will also mean time and resource savings. Your strategy should focus on four areas:

- The purpose of the document
- The scope of the document
- The audience for the document
- The structure of the document

Defining the Purpose of the Document

The purpose of the document is the reason you are creating the document. Are you creating a Web document to tell the world about your latest book? Are you creating a Web document to tell the world about a service you offer? Are you creating a Web document simply because you want to share your ideas or expertise?

If the purpose of a document is to sell a service or a product to Web users, do not hide that purpose, come right out and say it. This ensures readers are informed about what they are reading. Value the readers' time, and they will probably return if they need the product or service later.

If the purpose of the document is to provide an Internet community service, make sure the readers know that, too. You can build tremendous goodwill by simply providing information free. So why not share a bit of your expertise with the world?

Defining the Scope of the Document

Another key concept to keep in mind is scope. Scope is sometimes defined in terms of the focus and size of the project. As you organize your thoughts, determine the subject matter you will discuss and how broadly or narrowly you will cover the subject. Will your document be broadly focused and cover many topics related to computer games? Or will it be narrowly focused and cover very specific topics related to Multi-User Dimensions (MUDs)?

After you determine the focus, you should determine the level of detail for the document's subject matter. You could briefly discuss many topics or discuss a few topics at length. If you decide you want to cover a few specific topics at length, you may want to cover the topics on a single Web document. However, if you want to cover many topics at length, you may want to present your ideas on a series of documents with increasing levels of detail. For example, the initial document is an overview document discussing the popularity of Multi-User Dimensions. From this document readers can access other documents that discuss the features of specific MUDs in detail. From the detailed document, readers can access other documents that cover newsgroups, mailing lists, and Web sites related to a specific MUD and so on. Documents set up in progressive levels of detail is the basic format for a Web site. For more information on setting up a Web site see Chapter 26, "Designing and Publishing a Web Site."

Defining the Audience for the Document

Developing a strategy with your audience in mind is also essential to your success, yet determining the group you want the work to reach is not always easy. On the Web you can reach an extremely diverse global audience and words written in your native language may be read by people from dozens of countries. A document that specifically focuses on resources for U.S. writers may exclude or alienate writers from dozens of other countries. A document written in Spanish may be read by native speakers from the many Spanish-speaking countries in the world or by the millions of people who speak Spanish as a second language.

> **TIP**
>
> While English is the dominant language used on the Web, it is not the only language in use on the Web. Many European Web publishers create documents in several languages and because of this, millions of people who otherwise couldn't read the document can. If you are proficient in a second language, you may want to consider publishing your ideas in both your native and secondary language. You have nothing to lose and everything to gain by ensuring your publication can reach the largest audience possible.

As you consider the potential audience for your ideas, products, or services, focus on specifics of who, what, why, and how:

- Who are you trying to reach?
- What will this group of people be interested in?
- Why would they want to buy your product or service?
- How will you reach them?

Tell yourself you are writing a document for anyone interested in extreme sports who is between the age of 16 and 35. Readers will be interested in your service because you are the only such service featuring excursions in the Australian outback and the mountains of New Zealand. You will reach readers by featuring a virtual tour and offering a 2-for-1 discount that is only available to Web surfers. Got the idea?

Defining the Document Structure

Before you start creating the actual markup for the document, you should carefully consider how you will organize the document. Getting organized is extremely important. Not only will it save you time, it will help you create a better document. The quality of your document is what will convince readers your document is worth reading.

You can write out the initial structure for your document as an outline or simply as notes you scratch down during a brainstorming session. While you write down your ideas, focus on the purpose, scope and audience you defined earlier. Key areas of the document you want to concentrate on are

The introductory section—Introduce the document and provide readers with a brief overview of what is ahead.

The main features—Showcase the content of your site.

The hook—Give readers a reason to come back to your site.

The final section—Close the document in style.

After you develop the basic concept for the document, you may want to try to improve your ideas through freethinking, brainstorming, or storyboarding. These and other techniques for unleashing your creativity and better organizing your publications are explored in depth in Chapter 7, "Organizing and Information," of *Electronic Publishing Unleashed*, also published by Sams.

Creating the Document

Creating the document is the next step. You can use the knowledge you gain as you create your first document as a stepping stone to more advanced projects. With this in mind, you can create your first document for fun or business, but should try to keep the document simple. If you are unsure of the type of document you want to create, try creating a document that involves something you are interested in or revolves around a subject that you have expertise in. For example, I'm a bookworm. I could spend hours in the local library just wandering the aisles looking for books on any of a hundred topics. One of the first Web documents I created relates directly to my interest in reading and writing. I called this document the Writer's Gallery and as Figure 25.1 shows, I designated it as "A place for anyone who loves the written word."

> **NOTE**
>
> The examples in this chapter show how the Writer's Gallery looked in the early stages of development. You can visit the current incarnation of the Writer's Gallery on the Web at `http://tvp.com/vpwg.html`.

FIGURE 25.1.

The Writer's Gallery: A document on the Web.

> **TIP**
>
> One of the easiest ways to create Web documents is to create the file using your favorite word processor or text editor. Using a tool you are familiar with eases the transition to HTML publishing by letting you start with a tool you know. If you create a file using a word processor, you will want to save the file as plain ASCII text with an extension that designates the file as an HTML document. On a DOS/Windows system, you will want to save the file as ASCII text with the .htm extension. On an Amiga, Macintosh, or UNIX system, you will want to save the file as ASCII text with the .html extension. In Figure 25.1, the file named CH8SAMP1.HTM resides in the VIRTPRES directory on my D hard drive.

When you create a Web document, you can load it into your browser at any time for viewing. Previewing the document in your browser periodically as you create it is a great way to check format and content. With most browsers, you can load a file from your local hard drive simply by selecting "Open File" from a pull-down menu.

As you create your Web document, you will want to use the strategy and structure you developed. My strategy for the Writer's Gallery was to create a document for anyone who was as interested in the written word as I was. While I was not trying to sell a service to the people who read the document, I wanted to make the document an interesting place to visit, and I planned to freely share my knowledge of Web resources related to writing. Readers would be interested in the Writer's Gallery because it provided a resource for many different areas related to the written word. The primary audience I focused on was writers, but I made sure the document would also interest readers and anyone who might be looking for writing resources.

Adding Features to the Document

After you create the basic outline of the document, you can add features to the document. The key features you will want to add to the document are those that add to its visual impact and those that make the document interactive.

Introducing the Document

The primary way to increase the visual impact of your document is to use images. You can use images to enhance all aspects of your document. As Figure 25.1 shows, the first section of the Writer's Gallery document uses a graphical logo to introduce the document. This section also provides an overview of what readers can expect to find at the site.

The overview gives Web surfers who are interested in writing a reason to continue reading the document. The organization of this part of the document is critically important. Here is where you want to establish the purpose of the document and grab the reader's attention.

The HTML code for this section of the document includes a relative link to the Critique Corner:

```
<P ALIGN=CENTER><IMG SRC="vpttl11.gif" ALT="The Virtual Press Present's">
</P>
<P ALIGN=CENTER><IMG SRC="wgttl.gif" ALT="The Writer's Gallery"></P>
<H2>A place for anyone who loves the written word!</H2>
<P>Do you have short stories, poetry or articles that are so wonderful
you feel compelled to share them  with the world?  Why not post it to the
<A HREF="#CCorner">Critique Corner</A>?</P>
<P><IMG SRC="boom.gif" ALIGN="BOTTOM" ALT="* ATTN *">
Put a bookmark here.  Come back and visit!</P>
<HR SIZE=4>
```

Creating the Main Features of the Document

While the most obvious features that can add to the visual impact of the document are images, other features that can add to the visual impact of the document include using line breaks to create a column of text and horizontal rules to visually divide the document into sections. You can also add any of several types of lists to your document, which can add to the visual impact of the document by clearly organizing material.

The more useful your document is, the more powerful it is. The key to increasing the usefulness of your document and its impact on readers is interactivity. To increase the interactive nature of your document, you can create links to other documents on the Web. Interactivity was added to the Writer's Gallery page using three interactive lists.

The first list included in the page is a glossary list. This is shown in Figure 25.2. A glossary list is used to relate the key terms with related phrases. Adding interactivity to your glossary list is easy, and you can include links wherever the links make sense. In the following example, links are anchored to the keyword text and to words in one of the definitions:

```
<H2>Books, Magazines &amp; More</H2>
<DL>
<P><DT> <A HREF="gopher://rsl.ox.ac.uk/11/lib-corn/hunter">
ALEX Catalogue of Electronic Texts</A></P>
<DD>The ALEX catalogue of electronic texts is a comprehensive list of
books, magazines and periodicals available for reading on-line.
<P><DT> <A HREF="http://www.yahoo.com/Entertainment/Books/">
Book links at Yahoo</A></P>
<DD>Yahoo maintains a list of books available on the Web. If you haven't
 visited Yahoo before and are interested in book resources on the Web,
this is a great place to start.
<P><DT> <A HREF="http://white.nosc.mil/books.html">Books and
Libraries</A></P>
<DD>On the Web, there are many virtual libraries. These libraries
 feature collections of creative works available for on-line viewing.
<P><DD>One of these virtual libraries is the
<A HREF="http://eryx.syr.edu/Main.html">ERIC Virtual Library</A>,
which is an educational resource.</P>
```

FIGURE 25.2.

More interactive lists.

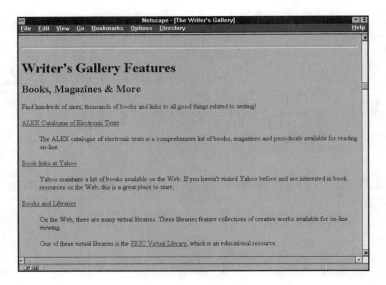

The second list included in the page is the bulleted list shown in Figure 25.3. A bulleted list was used because the items have no specific order. Here's the code for the bulleted list:

```
<H2>Writer's Gallery Literary Resources</H2>
<UL>
<LI> <A HREF="http://chronicle.merit.edu">Academe This Week</A>
<P>
<LI> <a href="http://auden.fac.utexas.edu/~daniel/amlit/amlit.html">
American Literature E-texts</A> from Hawthorne to Melville -
University of Texas
<P>
<LI> <A HREF="http://rs6.loc.gov/amhome.html">American Memory</A>
Collection on Americana at Library of Congress
<P>
<LI> <A HREF="http://www.umn.edu/nlhome/m059/mh/britper.html">
British Periodicals from the Early Nineteenth Century</A>
a resource from the University of Minnesota.
<P>
<LI>The <a href="gopher://gopher.epas.utoronto.ca/11/cch/disciplines
➥/medieval_studies/keefer">DILS Project</A> includes studies of 10th
Century England and much more.
<P>
<LI> <A HREF="http://www.clas.ufl.edu:80/english/exemplaria/">
Exemplaria</A> is a journal for Medieval and Renaissance theories.
<P>
<LI>An excellent <A HREF="http://info.desy.de/gna/interpedia/greek_myth
➥/greek_myth.html">Greek Mythology</A> resource on-line.
<P>
<LI> <A HREF="http://edziza.arts.ubc.ca/0c:/english/emlshome.htm">
Journal of 16th and 17th century English literature</A> is a terrific
resource from the University of British Columbia.
<P>
<LI> <A HREF="http://www.georgetown.edu/labyrinth/labyrinth-home.html">
Labyrinth</A> is a topnotch collection of Medieval resources from
```

```
Georgetown University.
<P>
<LI> <A HREF="http://coombs.anu.edu.au/~andrea/LiteraryLinks.html">
Literary Links from Keats to Shakespeare to Wordsworth</A>
<P>
<LI> <A HREF="http://gopher.well.sf.ca.us:70/1/Publications">Literary
Sites on the Internet</A>
<P>
<LI> <A HREF="http://www.artsci.wustl.edu/~jntolva/">Renaissance Studies
and E-texts</A> - University of Washington
</UL>
</BODY>
</HTML>
```

FIGURE 25.3.

Using a linked bulleted list.

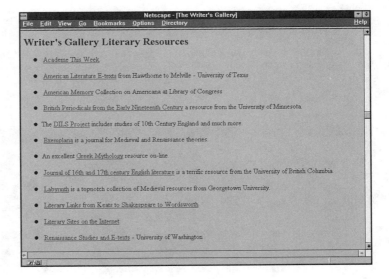

As you can see from Figure 25.4, the final list is a numbered list. Instead of providing a simple list of resources, you can include links that let readers jump to the resources in your list. The HTML code for the numbered list follows:

```
<H2>Writer's Companions</H2>
<P>12 reference works you wish were on your bookshelf</P>
<OL>
<LI> <A HREF="gopher://uts.mcc.ac.uk/77/gopherservices/enquire.english">
American English Dictionary</A>
<P>
<LI> <A HREF="http://www.columbia.edu/~svl2/bartlett/">
Bartlett's Familiar Quotations </A>
<P>
<LI> <A HREF="http://wombat.doc.ic.ac.uk/">Computer Dictionary</A>
<P>
<LI> <A HREF="http://www.eb.com/">Encyclopedia Britannica</A>
<P>
<LI> <A HREF="http://www.halcyon.com/jensen/encyclopedia/">
Global Encyclopedia</A>
<P>
```

```
<LI> <A HREF="http://www.library.upenn.edu/grammar.html">
Grammar and Style Guide</A>
<P>
<LI> <A HREF="http://gagme.wwa.com/~boba/grolier.html">
Grolier's Encyclopedia</A>
<P>
<LI> <A HREF="http://www.cc.emory.edu/ENGLISH/Handbook/Handbook.html">
Handbook of Poetry Terms</A>
<P>
<LI> <A HREF="http://c.gp.cs.cmu.edu:5103/prog/webster">
Hypertext Webster</A>
<P>
<LI> <A HREF="gopher://odie.niaid.nih.gov:70/77/.thesaurus/index">
Roget's Thesaurus</A>
<P>
<LI> <A HREF="http://www.ic.gov/94fact/fb94toc/fb94toc.html">
World Factbook (1994)</A>
<P>
<LI> <A HREF="http://www.digital.com/gnn/wic/refbook.10.html">
Worldwide Telephone Codes</A>
</OL>
</BODY>
</HTML>
```

FIGURE 25.4.

Numbered list to important resources.

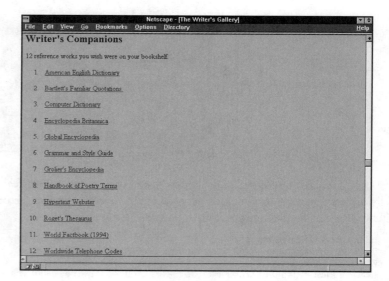

Creating Additional Pages

All your information doesn't have to be on a single page. As Figure 25.5 shows, you can provide a link to other pages containing additional resources. The header "Newsgroups for Writers" contains links that will take readers to a document called wnewsgroups.html.

In your first document, these additional areas don't have to contain dozens of resources or even be finished. However, if the area is under construction, tell readers the area is under construction. To do this, you can use an inline image such as a warning sign. As most pages on the Web are "under construction," meaning they are constantly changing and growing, you should remove the warning signs when these areas have useful content.

> **CAUTION**
>
> The construction areas shown in Figure 25.5 are meant as examples only. Normally, you would not include links to multiple pages that are under construction. Pages that are under construction are frustrating for readers. If a linked section of your document has bare-bones content, warn the reader before they access the section as you see in this example. Often it is best to wait until you have useful content for the page and then add a link to the page.

FIGURE 25.5.

All your information doesn't have to be on a single page.

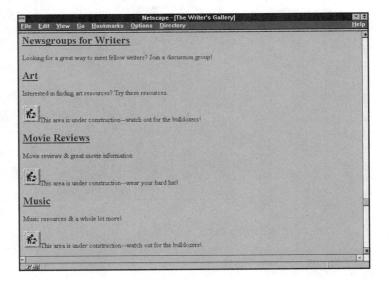

The HTML code for this section of the page follows:

```
<H2><A HREF="wnewgroups.html">Newsgroups for Writers</A></H2>
<P>Looking for a great way to meet fellow writers?
Join a discussion group!</P>
<H2><A HREF="vpwart.html">Art</A></H2>
<P>Interested in finding art resources? Try these resources.</P>
<P><IMG SRC="constr.gif">This area is under construction—watch out
for the bulldozers!</P>
<H2><A HREF="vpwart.html">Movie Reviews</A></H2>
<P>Movie reviews & great movie information</P>
<P><IMG SRC="constr.gif">This area is under construction—wear
```

```
your hard hat!</P>
<H2><A HREF="vpwart.html">Music</A></H2>
<P>Music resources & a whole lot more!</P>
<P><IMG SRC="constr.gif">This area is under construction—watch out
for the bulldozers!</P>
```

Bringing Visitors Back

A key attraction for Web surfers is growth potential. Web surfers like to visit sites that are changing and growing. Add a section to your document that gives readers a reason to return to the site. The Writer's Gallery also has a section that is sure to change over time, called Critique Corner, which is shown in Figure 25.6.

FIGURE 25.6.

Include a section of the document that will grow to give readers a reason to return to the site.

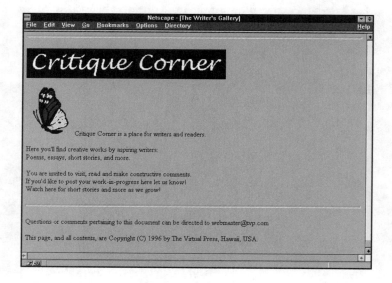

Here's the code for this section of the page:

```
<HR>
<H2><IMG SRC="ccorner.gif" ALT=""></H2>
<P><A NAME="CCorner"><P><IMG SRC="bfly.gif" ALT="">
Critique Corner is a place for writers and readers.</P>
<P>Here you'll find creative works by aspiring writers:<BR>
Poems, essays, short stories, and more.</P>
<P>You are invited to visit, read and make constructive comments.<BR>
If you'd like to post your work-in-progress here let us know!<BR>
Watch here for short stories and more as we grow!</P>
```

Finishing the Document

In addition to providing readers with another area to explore in the future, the final section of the document shown in Figure 25.6 provides contact and copyright information. Well-designed documents provide a point of contact for questions, technical or otherwise, about the document. Typically, the point of contact for technical questions is called the Webmaster, which is an electronic mail alias. A mail alias is a generic mail address that you can assign to an individual or group who will receive mail directed to the Webmaster. The mail address for the Webmaster is typically `webmaster@`*`yourcompany`*`.com`.

If you cannot use a mail alias, your site can still have a Webmaster. In this case, you could use the following:

```
<P>This page was webmastered by william@tvp.com.</P>
```

You could also use a special type of link that starts a create mail session in the reader's browser:

```
<A HREF="mailto:william@tvp.com">
```

The mailto reference above tells the reader's browser to open a create mail session that will be sent to `william@tvp.com`. This type of link enhances the interactivity of the page and provides a mechanism for getting feedback from readers. Don't forget to anchor the link to the page with text or graphics that readers can click on. One way to do this is

```
<P>Questions or comments pertaining to the site can be directed to
<A HREF="mailto:webmaster@tvp.com">webmaster@tvp.com</A></P>
```

The final section of your document should also contain copyright information. Adding a copyright notice to the document tells the world that the document is an intellectual property and as such is protected under U.S. and international copyright laws.

Here's how the copyright and contact information was added to the Writer's Gallery page:

```
<HR>
<P>Questions or comments pertaining to this document can be directed
to webmaster@tvp.com</P>
<P>This page, and all contents, are Copyright  1996 by
The Virtual Press, Hawaii, USA.</A></P>
```

The Complete Document

As you have seen, your Web document can have many features and still be fairly basic. You should create a document that has enough features to attract visitors but isn't so complex that you never get it ready for publishing. You can always include places that are sure to grow and will bring visitors back.

The complete HTML code for the Writer's Gallery document is shown in Listing 25.1.

Listing 25.1. The Writer's Gallery Web page.

```
<HTML>
<HEAD>
<TITLE>The Writer's Gallery</TITLE>
</HEAD>
<BODY>
<P ALIGN=CENTER><IMG SRC="vpttl11.gif" ALT="The Virtual Press Present's">
</P>
<P ALIGN=CENTER><IMG SRC="wgttl.gif" ALT="The Writer's Gallery"></P>
<H2>A place for anyone who loves the written word!</H2>
<P>Do you have short stories, poetry or articles that are so wonderful
you feel compelled to share them  with the world?  Why not post it to the
<A HREF="#CCorner">Critique Corner</A>?</P>
<P><IMG SRC="boom.gif" ALIGN="BOTTOM" ALT="* ATTN *">
Put a bookmark here.  Come back and visit!</P>
<HR>
<H1>Writer's Gallery Features</H1>
<H2>Books, Magazines &amp; More</H2>
<P>Find hundreds of zines, thousands of books and links to all
good things related to writing!</P>
<DL>
<P><DT> <A HREF="gopher://rsl.ox.ac.uk/11/lib-corn/hunter">
ALEX Catalogue of Electronic Texts</A></P>
<DD>The ALEX catalogue of electronic texts is a comprehensive list of
books, magazines and periodicals available for reading on-line.
<P><DT> <A HREF="http://www.yahoo.com/Entertainment/Books/">
Book links at Yahoo</A></P>
<DD>Yahoo maintains a list of books available on the Web. If you haven't
 visited Yahoo before and are interested in book resources on the Web,
this is a great place to start.
<P><DT> <A HREF="http://white.nosc.mil/books.html">
Books and Libraries</A></P>
<DD>On the Web, there are many virtual libraries. These libraries
feature collections of creative works available for on-line viewing.
<P>
<DD>One of these virtual libraries is the
<A HREF="http://eryx.syr.edu/Main.html">ERIC Virtual Library</A>,
which is an educational resource.
</DL>
<H2>Writer's Gallery Literary Resources</H2>
<P>If you need a literary reference on the Web, this is a great
place to start.</P>
<UL>
<LI> <A HREF="http://chronicle.merit.edu">Academe This Week</A>
<P>
<LI> <a href="http://auden.fac.utexas.edu/~daniel/amlit/amlit.html">
American Literature E-texts</A> from Hawthorne to Melville -
University of Texas
<P>
<LI> <A HREF="http://rs6.loc.gov/amhome.html">American Memory</A>
Collection on Americana at Library of Congress
<P>
<LI> <A HREF="http://www.umn.edu/nlhome/m059/mh/britper.html">
British Periodicals from the Early Nineteenth Century</A>
a resource from the University of Minnesota.
<P>
```

```
<LI>The <a href="gopher://gopher.epas.utoronto.ca/11/cch/disciplines
➥/medieval_studies/keefer">DILS Project</A> includes studies of
10th Century England and much more.
<P>
<LI> <A HREF="http://www.clas.ufl.edu:80/english/exemplaria/">
Exemplaria</A> is a journal for Medieval and Renaissance theories.
<P>
<LI>An excellent <A HREF="http://info.desy.de/gna/interpedia/greek_myth
➥/greek_myth.html">Greek Mythology</A> resource on-line.
<P>
<LI> <A HREF="http://edziza.arts.ubc.ca/0c:/english/emlshome.htm">
Journal of 16th and 17th century English literature</A> is a terrific
resource from the University of British Columbia.
<P>
<LI> <A HREF="http://www.georgetown.edu/labyrinth/labyrinth-home.html">
Labyrinth</A> is a topnotch collection of Medieval resources
from Georgetown University.
<P>
<LI> <A HREF="http://coombs.anu.edu.au/~andrea/LiteraryLinks.html">
Literary Links from Keats to Shakespeare to Wordsworth</A>
<P>
<LI> <A HREF="http://gopher.well.sf.ca.us:70/1/Publications">
Literary Sites on the Internet</A>
<P>
<LI> <A HREF="http://www.artsci.wustl.edu/~jntolva/">Renaissance Studies
and E-texts</A> - University of Washington
</UL>
<H2>Writer's Companions</H2>
<P>12 reference works you wish were on your bookshelf.</P>
<OL>
<LI> <A HREF="gopher://uts.mcc.ac.uk/77/gopherservices/enquire.english">
American English Dictionary</A>
<P>
<LI> <A HREF="http://www.columbia.edu/~svl2/bartlett/">
Bartlett's Familiar Quotations </A>
<P>
<LI> <A HREF="http://wombat.doc.ic.ac.uk/">Computer Dictionary</A>
<P>
<LI> <A HREF="http://www.eb.com/">Encyclopedia Britannica</A>
<P>
<LI> <A HREF="http://www.halcyon.com/jensen/encyclopedia/">
Global Encyclopedia</A>
<P>
<LI> <A HREF="http://www.library.upenn.edu/grammar.html">
Grammar and Style Guide</A>
<P>
<LI> <A HREF="http://gagme.wwa.com/~boba/grolier.html">
Grolier's Encyclopedia</A>
<P>
<LI> <A HREF="http://www.cc.emory.edu/ENGLISH/Handbook/Handbook.html">
Handbook of Poetry Terms</A>
<P>
<LI> <A HREF="http://c.gp.cs.cmu.edu:5103/prog/webster">
Hypertext Webster</A>
<P>
<LI> <A HREF="gopher://odie.niaid.nih.gov:70/77/.thesaurus/index">
Roget's Thesaurus</A>
<P>
<LI> <A HREF="http://www.ic.gov/94fact/fb94toc/fb94toc.html">
```

continues

Listing 25.1. continued

```
World Factbook (1994)</A>
<P>
<LI> <A HREF="http://www.digital.com/gnn/wic/refbook.10.html">
Worldwide Telephone Codes</A>
</OL>
<H2><A HREF="wnewgroups.html">Newsgroups for Writers</A></H2>
<P>Looking for a great way to meet fellow writers?
Join a discussion group!</P>
<H2><A HREF="vpwart.html">Art</A></H2>
<P>Interested in finding art resources? Try these resources.</P>
<P><IMG SRC="constr.gif">This area is under construction—watch out
for the bulldozers!</P>
<H2><A HREF="vpwart.html">Movie Reviews</A></H2>
<P>Movie reviews & great movie information</P>
<P><IMG SRC="constr.gif">This area is under construction—wear
your hard hat!</P>
<H2><A HREF="vpwart.html">Music</A></H2>
<P>Music resources & a whole lot more!</P>
<P><IMG SRC="constr.gif">This area is under construction—watch out
for the bulldozers!</P>
<HR>
<H2><IMG SRC="ccorner.gif" ALT=""></H2>
<P><A NAME="CCorner"><P><IMG SRC="bfly.gif" ALT="">
Critique Corner is a place for writers and readers.</P>
<P>Here you'll find creative works by aspiring writers:<BR>
Poems, essays, short stories, and more.</P>
<P>You are invited to visit, read and make constructive comments.<BR>
If you'd like to post your work-in-progress here let us know!<BR>
Watch here for short stories and more as we grow!</P>
<HR>
<P>Questions or comments pertaining to this document can be directed
to webmaster@tvp.com</P>
<P>This page, and all contents, are Copyright  1996 by
The Virtual Press, Hawaii, USA.</A></P>
</BODY>
</HTML>
```

Proofing Your Web Document

Proofing is the most neglected aspect of Web publishing. Time and time again I see Web documents with multiple typos and formatting inconsistencies—even at major sites. Documents with glaring typos and inconsistencies reflect poorly on you and your Web publishing practices.

Proofing is neglected in Web publishing primarily because of the ease with which ideas and words can be published electronically. You can create a document in your word processor or editor and publish it on the Web within minutes after you've finished—seconds if you are quick enough. You do not have to spend hours checking spelling and grammar and generally poring over every punctuation mark on the document, worrying if you have missed something glaringly obvious that is going to cost you a fortune to reprint 10,000 copies. If you make a mistake, you just open the file, correct the mistake, and republish your masterpiece on the Web for the world to see. Right?

Wrong. The quality of your work is a direct reflection on you. Thousands, and possibly millions, of people around the world are going to see your published document. Isn't it worth a few hours of your time to ensure days, weeks, or months of hard work gets the credibility it deserves?

Here are a few tips to help you better proof your Web documents:

- Use spelling and grammar checkers to find the tedious errors—the typos or grammar mistakes you made because you were hurrying to meet a deadline, worn out from long hours at the keyboard, or otherwise.

- Never rely solely on spelling and grammar checkers to find the critical errors; load the document in your browser and read it several times, noting typos or inconsistencies you need to correct.

- For long documents or lengthy projects, reading the document three times, looking for specific problems each time, is often helpful. The first time you proofread, focus on the look of the document and if you find formatting inconsistencies, missing or misplaced items, correct them. The second time you proofread, check the logic and flow of ideas and words. The third time you proof, scrutinize all the text on the document, checking syntax, spelling, capitalization, and punctuation.

- Always check images, figures, and charts on your document. Not only do you want to ensure they are consistent with your textual references, but you also want to check any text that may be included in the graphics. You should even check images you believe do not contain text. You might be surprised to find text and greatly relieved when you find and fix a typo you otherwise would have missed.

Some typos and inconsistencies slip by—the dragon wins every once in a while. But if you find an error after you have already published your document, correct it.

Testing Your Web Document

Testing all aspects of your Web document before you publish is crucial. At this stage in your Web publishing operation, you will want to focus on the accuracy of your links and HTML markup. However, as you add features like images and multimedia, you should test these features as well.

Testing Your Links

The easiest way to test links is to load the document in your browser and click on the links one at a time. You will want to ensure that all internal document links access the appropriate section that corresponds to the keyword you have designated. One key thing to watch out for are multiple sections of the document labeled with the same keyword that can produce strange results. If you know that a section of your publication is labeled with a certain keyword and the browser jumps to a different section of the document, check the keyword label in the section the browser displays. You probably mislabeled the keyword.

You will also want to ensure all document links to other documents are valid and access the appropriate document. If you cannot access a document that you are sure should be available, check the syntax of your links. Did you specify the protocol correctly? Did you use the correct filename extension? Did you forget the tilde (~) symbol?

NOTE

In UNIX, the tilde symbol is used to specify the home directory of a user whose system name follows the tilde. Using the tilde symbol in a URL, you can refer to the Web documents in the user's home directory as follows:

```
http://www.aloha.com/~william/vphp.html
```

The Web server servicing this request would know to look in my home directory for the file called `vphp.html`. While Web documents are typically in a directory called `public_html` under the user's directory, Web servers know that when you use a tilde in a URL, you are referring to the directory containing the user's Web documents. The process of inferring a directory using the tilde is called *mapping*.

Troubleshooting Problems in Your Document

You've created a wonderful document, but for some reason it just doesn't look right. Troubleshooting problems in your document can be difficult, especially because you created the code and have a mental picture of what you meant to type in your mind's eye. This section contains tips to help you solve common problems. Most problems with your document can be directly attributed to errors in the structure of the document's markup code. Syntax is critically important in HTML. The four most common syntax problems involve:

1. The tag enclosure set < >
2. Pairing of HTML tags
3. The double-quotation marks " "
4. Nesting of tags

Troubleshooting: This Tag Format Goes On and On

Wait a minute you say, how come half the text of the document looks like a heading? A tag format that goes on longer than it should is usually caused by one of the following:

■ An improperly formed end tag, meaning one of your tags is missing the < or the > character

■ A missing end tag

■ A mismatched pair of HTML tags

A closing tag that is missing the < or the > symbol will not be properly interpreted by your browser. As a result, the format will not end until the browser finds a matching end tag. This can cause a section of the text to be displayed in the wrong format. If this element is a header, all text between the associated header opening tag and a matching closing tag will be displayed as a heading. If this element is anchor text, all text between the start of the anchor text and a matching closing tag will be displayed as underlined anchor text.

A missing end tag and a mismatched pair of tags will cause a problem similar to the one described above. Sometimes these problems are difficult to trace because you check the document where the problem ends and find nothing wrong. Don't look where the problem ends, look where the problem begins. After loading the HTML code for the document in your editor or word processor, go through the code to the section of the document where the begin tag associated with the problem is located and trace the problem forward from there. Tracing the problem forward instead of backward is especially useful when the document contains multiple format problems.

The section of the Writer's Gallery document shown in the following code contains a format error. As shown in Figure 25.7, the missing end anchor tag for the second anchor defined causes all text until the next valid end anchor tag to be displayed as underlined anchor text:

FIGURE 25.7.

Troubleshooting formatting problems.

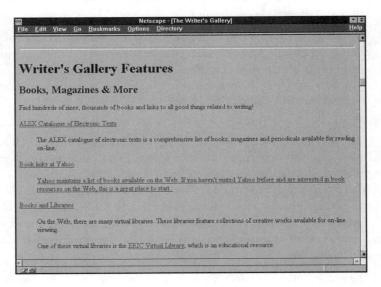

```
<H2>Books, Magazines &amp; More</H2>
<DL>
<P><DT> <A HREF="gopher://rsl.ox.ac.uk/11/lib-corn/hunter">
ALEX Catalogue of Electronic Texts</A></P>
<DD>The ALEX catalogue of electronic texts is a comprehensive list of
books, magazines and periodicals available for reading on-line.
<P><DT> <A HREF="http://www.yahoo.com/Entertainment/Books/">
Book links at Yahoo</P>
```

```
<DD>Yahoo maintains a list of books available on the Web. If you haven't
 visited Yahoo before and are interested in book resources on the Web,
this is a great place to start.
<P><DT> <A HREF="http://white.nosc.mil/books.html">Books and
Libraries</A></P>
```

The easiest way to fix this problem is to go to the section of the code where the second begin anchor tag was defined and trace the problem forward. You would look specifically for a missing, mismatched, or improperly formed end tag.

Troubleshooting: There's Text Missing from the Document

Wait a minute, you say, how come half the document is missing? Missing text or objects can usually be traced to those pesky double quotation marks and to misclosed tags that contain URLs. If your document has a " inside a tag, the closing " must be present to avoid potential problems. A tag with a missing double quotation mark may not be properly interpreted by older browsers, and this can produce strange results. If the tag missing the double quotation mark is an anchor tag, all text from the first double quotation mark to the next double quotation mark—no matter where it is located in the text—could be interpreted by your browser as part of an address URL. Address URLs are not displayed on the screen unless you move your mouse pointer to the associated anchor text.

Another problem that may cause missing text is a misclosed tag containing an URL. If a tag containing an URL is not closed properly, your browser could interpret any text following the tag up to the next properly closed tag as part of the URL. This problem is especially difficult to track because while the text following the image will not be displayed, the image with the misclosed tag will often be displayed.

Missing text is also difficult to trace because the problem may seem sporadic. Some browsers, primarily older browsers, display the page with missing text. Others browsers, primarily newer browsers, display the page with no problems. This can make tracking down the source of the problem difficult. Again, don't look where the problem ends, look where the problem begins. After loading the HTML code in your editor or word processor, look at tags that occur before the missing section of text. This should either be the first tag you find with a double quotation mark or URL as you work your way down from the top of the document, or a tag with a double quotation mark that displayed correctly on the document and occurs immediately before the missing section.

The section of the Writer's Gallery document shown in the next section of code contains a format error. As Figure 25.8 shows, the misclosed <IMG> tag for the image called boom.gif causes the text following the image not to be displayed:

```
<H2>A place for anyone who loves the written word!</H2>
<P>Do you have short stories, poetry or articles that are so wonderful
you feel compelled to share them  with the world?  Why not post it to the
<A HREF="#CCorner">Critique Corner</A>?</P>
<P><IMG SRC="boom.gif" ALIGN="BOTTOM" ALT="* ATTN *"
```

```
Put a bookmark here.  Come back and visit!</P>
<HR>
<H1>Writer's Gallery Features</H1>
<H2>Books, Magazines &amp; More</H2>
<P>Find hundreds of zines, thousands of books and links to all
good things related to writing!</P>
<DL>
<P><DT> <A HREF="gopher://rsl.ox.ac.uk/11/lib-corn/hunter">
ALEX Catalogue of Electronic Texts</A></P>
```

FIGURE 25.8.

Troubleshooting: tracking down missing text.

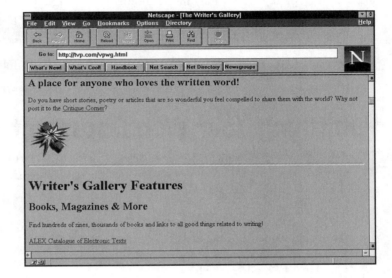

NOTE

The quotes must also be the standard ASCII double quotation marks. Some word processors have so-called smart quotes, where the opening quotes look different from closing quotes. If your word processor has this feature, disable it. Smart quotes are not standard ASCII and will not work in your HTML documents.

Troubleshooting: The Format I Want Just Won't Display

Wait a minute, you say, everything looks okay, I've fixed all the bugs, but my browser still won't display the third sentence in bold face. This problem can usually be traced to your browser or to the code. You may want to check your browser's compatibility with character styles. Your browser must be capable of displaying the physical style you have selected. Additionally, when displaying logical styles, the browser ultimately makes the decision about what style to display your text in. A quick way to check to see if you have a compatibility problem or a code problem is to display your document using a different browser. This browser should preferably be one that you know supports the specific style you are trying to use. If the compatible browser won't display the text the way you want, check the code.

The problem in the code could be related to invalid nesting of tags. After loading the HTML code in your editor or word processor, check the section of the document associated with the formatting and ensure all tags are used in parallel fashion. While you can place the begin and end tags for an element fully inside another pair of tags, the tags may not overlap. The emphasis tags overlap with the strong emphasis tags and will cause problems:

```
<EM>Thank you for visiting<STRONG>The Virtual Press</EM></STRONG>
```

The right way to use these tags is to use them in parallel fashion as follows:

```
<EM>Thank you for visiting<STRONG>The Virtual Press</STRONG></EM>
```

Publishing Your Web Document

To publish your Web document, you need access to a Web server. Once you have access to a Web server either through an Internet Service Provider or your own Web server, you are ready to publish your finished document.

Publishing a single Web document is as easy as

> Checking the name of the file
> Moving your file to an appropriate directory
> Checking the mode of the file

Checking the Name of the File

When moving files between different types of platforms, you will want to check the filename to ensure it is appropriate for the system you are moving the file to. Some systems restrict the length of filenames. Other systems are case-sensitive, meaning a file with a name in uppercase letters becomes a different file if saved in lowercase letters.

When moving from a DOS/Windows system to a UNIX or Macintosh system, watch out for these potential problems:

1. While DOS filenames must be only eight characters long with a three-character extension, some systems do not recognize files with an .htm extension as an HTML document. Therefore, after moving your file to the UNIX or Mac system, change the .htm extension to .html. For example, change home.htm to home.html. This will ensure the UNIX or Mac Web Server will recognize your file as an HTML document.

2. While your filename may have appeared in all uppercase letters on the DOS system, the filename on the UNIX system will likely be in lowercase letters. UNIX systems are case sensitive and you must reference filenames in the appropriate case in your links.

When moving from a Macintosh or UNIX system to a DOS/Windows system, be aware of these differences:

1. Before moving your file to a DOS/Windows machine, the file must be renamed to conform to DOS naming conventions. DOS filenames must be only eight characters long with a three-character extension. If, for example, your file was called `my_home_document.html`, you could change the name to `homedocument.htm`.

2. Watch out for wildcard characters in filenames. While on a Macintosh or UNIX system you can use wildcard characters when naming files, you cannot use wildcard characters on a DOS machine.

Moving Your File

The first step in publishing your document is to move your file to a directory designated for Web documents. While this directory may reside on the Web server, typically it is mapped to a subdirectory in your home directory called `public_html`. If you are using a Web server someone else has installed, contact the server administrator to find out where to put your documents.

> **TIP**
>
> A mapped directory contains pointers to directories where the actual files reside. Web servers usually map directories to a subdirectory in a user's home directory that you can point to using the tilde followed by the user's system name. Setting up a Web server to map requests is easy. On most servers, your service provider or system administrator can enable this feature by setting a variable called `UserDir` to the subdirectory that will be mapped to users' home directories, such as:
>
> `UserDir          public_html`
>
> If this variable is set as shown, requests to `http://www.`*`your_provider`*`.com/~`*`you`* would be mapped to the subdirectory called `public_html` in your account and a Web document called `home.html` could be accessed with the following URL:
>
> `http://www.your_provider.com/~you/home.html`

Moving your files to the Web server or to an Internet account from your home or office system is easy. The two most common methods to transfer the files are: File Transfer Protocol (FTP) and modem transfer.

Using FTP

FTP is a quick and easy way to transfer files, especially if you are transferring files between UNIX systems. The best way to transfer files using FTP is to initiate a binary file transfer. In this way, you do not have to worry about which files are binary and which files aren't.

To start a binary transfer, you could type the following at the shell command prompt:

```
ftp hostname
bin
```

You can transfer multiple files between systems using the mget and mput commands. You use mget to retrieve multiple files from the host you are connected to using FTP, and mput to send multiple files to the host you are connected to using FTP. When you are transferring multiple files between systems, another useful FTP command to know is prompt. Without toggling the prompt to the off position, your system will prompt you before sending or retrieving each file. Here's how you could toggle the prompt to the off position if it was on, retrieve all files that start with music, and then quit:

```
ftp aloha.com
bin
prompt
cd /users/music/fun_stuff
mget music*
quit
```

Modem Transfer

Many modem transfer protocols could be used to transfer files. Some popular transfer protocols are

> ASCII
> Kermit
> Super-Kermit
> Xmodem
> Xmodem CRC
> Xmodem 1K
> Ymodem
> Ymodem batch or Ymodem-G
> Zmodem

While these transfer protocols are popular, the most popular transfer protocol is the Zmodem transfer protocol. The reason for Zmodem's popularity is its ease-of-use and reliability. You can initiate a Zmodem transfer within your communication's program while connected to the Internet, and there are only two commands you'll ever have to learn:

```
rz     Receive via Zmodem transfer protocol.
sz     Send via Zmodem transfer protocol.
```

From your Internet account, you can type sz or rz at the shell prompt. If you type sz or rz and then press Enter, you will get a brief summary of how to use the commands. The most basic format is as follows, where filename is the name of the file to transfer:

```
rz filename
```

> **NOTE**
>
> If you own a Macintosh and are transferring files to a different computer platform, you should transfer your files as regular binary files. Other computer platforms cannot read Macintosh binary files and your files will be unreadable in this format.

Checking the Mode of the File

On some systems, files have strictly defined permissions that can be granted or denied to users. These permissions include the ability to read, write, and execute the file. Permissions are generally set by changing the mode attributed to the file. Make sure that files have the appropriately restricted mode for Web access, such as 705 on a UNIX system, which means that the file is readable, writeable, and executable by you, but only readable and executable by others.

> **NOTE**
>
> The command to change the mode of a file on a UNIX system is chmod. The chmod command can be used to set permissions for you, your associated group, and others. You can grant or deny permission to read, write, and execute the file. Permissions are generally set using a three-digit number that equates to the permissions you are setting.
>
> The first digit sets the permissions for you, the owner of the file. The second digit sets the permissions for the group of users you are associated with on the UNIX system. The third digit sets the permissions for anyone else who might use the file. Read permissions are set by adding one to the digit count. Write permissions are set by adding four to the digit count. Execute permissions are set by adding two to the digit count.
>
> A file with the mode of 000 has no permissions. If we changed the mode to 754, the file would be readable, writeable, and executable by you; readable and executable by anyone in your group; and readable by anyone else.

Summary

Creating and publishing your first Web document is easy if you follow the steps outlined in this chapter. Although your first document will be basic, developing a strategy can save you time and help you better organize your material. A good strategy focuses on the purpose, audience, scope, and structure of the document.

You can add to the visual impact of your document by adding features. While images are powerful features to express your ideas and enhance your document, other features you can add are horizontal rules, line breaks, links, and lists. Once the document is finished, you should proof your work and test the features you have added to the document so you can proudly publish your document on the Web for the world to see.

Designing and Publishing a Web Site

26

by William Robert Stanek

Creating and publishing your first Web page was only a starting point. The key to establishing a Web presence and building a name for yourself in cyberspace is to create a killer Web site that will stop Web surfers in their tracks. To do this, you must learn the basics of organizing, creating, and publishing a Web site where you can feature a collection of dozens or hundreds of pages. Following the steps outlined in this chapter, you can become one of the thousands of individuals successfully publishing in cyberspace.

The difference between a successful site and an unsuccessful site is attention to detail, good content, and good organization. Many books on the Internet and Web publishing discuss theories, cover key subjects, show basic examples, but rarely follow a practical hands-on approach to Web publishing. Books without practical hands-on examples can leave you wondering where to start, how to start, and what to do when you do finally manage to start. This chapter follows a hands-on approach for creating a Web site. Through practical, step-by-step examples, you learn how to create, organize, and publish your own Web site. The chapter goes on to tell you how you can publicize your site, which is a critical yet all too often neglected part of Web publishing. If you don't tell people your site exists, no one will know and no one will visit.

Here are the eight steps for creating, publishing, and publicizing your Web site:

1. Define the Web site.
2. Learn Web site design concepts.
3. Create the Web site's content.
4. Learn about advanced linking of pages and publications.
5. Add rooms to your Web home.
6. Proof and test your Web site.
7. Publish your Web site.
8. Publicize your Web site.

Defining Your Web Site

You build a Web site one step at a time, and the first step is simply defining what you want to publish on the Web. The basic components of a Web site are the pages you link together. These pages can contain text, graphics, and multimedia. The type of information you can publish on the Web is limited only by your imagination.

You can create a site that has many features, such as community services, product samples, and product information. For example, the Web site I created for The Virtual Press has the following features:

- Community service areas for writers, publishers, and job seekers
- Corporate background and history

- Information on products and services
- Online ordering center
- Personal information and résumé
- Product samples
- Web publications

Your Web site can be a commercial venture or simply an adventure. There are no strict rules that say you must either publish for fun or for profit. Your site can be for profit and still provide the Internet community with a useful resource containing information about you, your company, your products, and your services. Your site can be strictly informational with no sales information whatsoever, providing the Internet community with a fabulous free resource. Your intentions could be to show the world you are the definitive expert in a particular subject area, which may ultimately sell yourself, your ideas, or your company to consumers.

You should carefully consider what you want to publish on the Web. You can start by creating a list of your creative projects, the plans for your business, your favorite hobbies, and your areas of interest or expertise. You can use this list to help you decide areas you may want to Web publish in.

Web Site Design Concepts

Competing in a global marketplace requires planning from day one. Before you start building your Web site, you must establish objectives and define what you hope to gain from your Web presence. Establishing an identity for yourself and your company in cyberspace does not come easily. You must use your skills and ideas to sell yourself and your company to the world.

To establish a presence on tomorrow's Web, you must adopt a vision for success focused on global outreach. At the heart of this vision should be a strategy similar to the one you developed in the previous chapter. This strategy should focus on

- The goals of the site
- The audience for the site or key areas within the site
- The scope of the site's content

You must create a friendly Web site that continues to grow and change. Yet it won't be the size of your site that sells your ideas and products. It will be your vision and ability to find your place in the world community. Two major design concepts you will want to consider immediately are

- The general organization of your information
- The organization of your site's directories and files

Getting Organized

Whether you are thinking on a grand scale or a small scale, the organization of your information is the most important design issue in setting up a Web site. Carefully consider how you will organize your site. The power of Web publishing is that you can seamlessly integrate complex presentations. Behind those complex presentations are dozens, possibly hundreds, of individual pages that can contain text, images, and multimedia. The result can either be an unfriendly place to visit and a nightmare to maintain or, if organized properly, a friendly place to visit and a joy to maintain.

As the Web publisher, you are breathing life into an information infrastructure that may be seen by thousands, possibly millions, of users around the world. Once this information infrastructure is in place, you should not haphazardly delete, rename, or rearrange this structure. If you delete, rename, or rearrange your site, not only will you frustrate users, but all links that were leading visitors to your site may become invalid.

> **NOTE**
>
> Your address URLs are the only thing leading visitors to your site. Readers save lists of their favorite places in their browser using a bookmark or hotlist feature. Some users may have published your link as a favorite site on their home page. Many readers also find new places to visit through the lists published by Web databases, and if your pages are in new locations, the reader may not be able to find your site.

Organizing Your Site's Directories and Files

Your site's directory and file structure can play a key role in helping you organize your ideas. Carefully consider how the outside world will regard the structure of your site. You can organize different types of information into directories. You can organize your site into directories that pertain to the projects or publications featured at the site. You can also organize the files within your directories into a logically named structure.

Directory Organization

The base directory of the site should pertain to the overall site or to the organization sponsoring the site. The best way to set up the base directory is to use an index or default page that pertains to the site as a whole. This default page will serve as your home page and will most likely be the first page visitors to your site see. The address URL for your base directory is usually something like this:

```
http://www.your_company.com/
```

or

```
http://www.your_service_provider.com/~you
```

In both of the preceding cases, a browser accessing the URL would display the default page for your site. As the default page is usually named index.html, this means you will want to install a document called index.html in the appropriate directory on the Web server. If you are using an ISP's Web server with a virtual domain or an account with Web publishing privileges, this directory is normally called public_html and is located under your user directory.

> **NOTE**
>
> If the public_html directory was not created by your service provider, you can easily create it. On a UNIX or DOS-based system, type the command:
>
> ```
> mkdir public_html
> ```
>
> The command shown above will make a directory called public_html for you. Before you type the command, you should ensure you are in your user directory. One way to do this on a UNIX system is to type the command cd on a line by itself as follows:
>
> ```
> cd
> ```

Subdirectory Organization

A clear structure for your directories and files becomes increasingly important as your site grows. Hundreds of files in a single directory are difficult to track and maintain. Therefore, you should consider a subdirectory structure at an early stage in your Web site creation. Subdirectories at the site should be logically organized and could pertain to projects, publications, or departments within a company. For example, you could create a directory for each of your projects by category and develop the following structure:

Base directory	Contains pages that pertain to your company. Base refers to the default path to your documents, such as /usr/httpd/docs.
BOOK directory	Contains pages that pertain to your book-length projects
BUS directory	Contains pages that pertain to business services you plan to provide

Each subdirectory would be located under your base directory and could have its own default page associated with it. To access the default page within the BOOK directory, a user could use these URLs:

```
http://www.your_company.com/BOOK/
```

or

```
http://www.your_service_provider.com/~you/BOOK/
```

To access a page called `projects.html` within the `BOOK` directory, a user could use these URLs:

```
http://www.your_company.com/BOOK/projects.html
```

or

```
http://www.your_service_provider.com/~you/BOOK/projects.html
```

File Organization

Just as it is important to logically name directories, you should also logically name your files. Each file that pertains to a particular presentation could use an element of the project's name to relate it to the project. This is true even if you plan to put individual projects in their own directories and especially important when you plan to publish multiple projects that are closely related. A book publisher that planned to publish extracts of her books on the Web would not want to name the parts of the first book:

```
page1.html
page2.html
page3.html
```

or

```
chapter1.html
chapter2.html
chapter3.html
```

A better naming scheme is to relate the parts of the project to the project itself, which will avoid confusion when publishing additional projects and make the site easier to maintain. Imagine a site with a dozen books that has identical names for the pages of the publications. What happens when the new employee you've hired moves pages 12 to 27 for your third book into the directory reserved for your first book?

To relate the parts of the project to the whole, you could prepend an abbreviation for the project or part of the project's title to the file names. For example, the *Web Publishing Unleashed* title could be abbreviated as WPU. You could then prepend the abbreviation to the component parts of the project as follows:

```
wpuch1index.html
wpuch1pg1.html
wpuch1pg2.html
wpuch1pg3.html
wpuch1title.gif
```

Creating the Web Site's Content

A Web site is much more than pages linked together. It is your home on the Web and as such it should contain doorways that reduce communications barriers and help spread your ideas to a global audience. The first doorway you will want to establish on the Web is the front door to your Web site, your home page. As the first thing most visitors to your site will see, your home page should be friendly and inviting.

Creating a friendly and inviting home page involves much more than hanging up a virtual welcome mat. It involves creating a well-organized page that reflects who you are and what you plan to do on the Web. The page should follow a sound design that provides an overview of what is available at the site. You can present an overview of content in many ways, but the best way to organize the overview is to make it a sneak preview of what visitors to the site can expect to find.

Your sneak preview can tell the world that you are dull and unimaginative, such as a home page organized like the table of contents you would find in a print publication. A home page organized in such a pure linear fashion may seem a logical way to go, but generally this design has only first-time visitors in mind. While you want to attract new visitors, you also want to attract repeat visitors. If McDonald's attracted only one-time customers, they would have never sold billions of hamburgers. The key in business, even if that business is not-for-profit, is to build a customer base, and you cannot build a customer base if your customers only visit your site once. Therefore, your sneak preview should tell the world this is a place to add to their hot list.

Designing a site with content for first-time and repeat visitors is extremely important in creating an inviting place to visit. Yet you also want your house on the Web to be a friendly place to visit. The friendliest sites on the Web are considerate of your time and present information in the right level of detail based on your location within the site. There are many houses on the Web that I visit. Some sites I visit often because they are friendly, useful, or entertaining. Other sites I visit once and only once because they are unfriendly and do not respect my time or anyone else's. These are the sites with the 50,000-byte graphics doing the greeting instead of the Web publisher. Anyone can create monstrous graphics and pitch them at the world, but it takes practice and skill to obtain a working balance between efficacy and grandeur.

The design of your site does not stop at your home page. The best sites on the Web have many special areas or mini-sites within the site. These mini-sites can be the star attractions with features that constantly change and grow. My house on the Web at tvp.com is no exception. The design of the site has changed many times, but the features were always designed with first-time and repeat visitors in mind.

In addition to the community service area developed in Chapter 25, "Designing and Publishing a Web Document," some areas you may want to add to your first Web site are

- A home page
- Business background page highlighting your products and services
- Personal background page highlighting your achievements and telling the world who you are

Through step-by-step examples, the remainder of this chapter builds these pages. You can use similar pages to form the basis of your Web site and save hours of work.

Advanced Linking of Pages and Publications

This section explores advanced techniques for linking the pages of your site. Page linking is extremely important. The more navigation mechanisms you provide within the site, the easier it will be for visitors to find their way around.

Your site should follow a flowing design with multiple routes through the information infrastructure you have created. Readers should be able to advance from overview pages to more detailed pages within your site. They should also be able to go back to your home page and start a new search from any level within the site.

Realize from the start that the structure of the Web is such that readers can enter your site at any level and you will have a head start on many Web publishers. I don't know how many times I have come across a Web page that gives me no indication of where the page is within the information infrastructure at the site. The worst of these pages become dead-end streets with no way to return to the site's home page and no way to access any other information at the site. Finding a dead-end street on the Web is frustrating to say the least, but the reason the dead-end street exists is that its creators lacked foresight. They either thought that all visitors would access the site starting from the front door, or they just never stopped to think about the consequences of creating such a page.

The key to building a friendly and inviting home page is good linking. The following sections show you how to

- Create links in your home page
- Link with image and text menus
- Use links to keep visitors informed
- Link contact and copyright information

Linking Your Home Page

When I created The Virtual Press (TVP) site, I considered the navigation mechanisms I would provide to readers very carefully. The first thing visitors to the home page (Figure 26.1) see is an image featuring TVP's motto. The simple image serves a dual role. It introduces TVP and is a clickable image linked to the corporate background and information page. The remainder of the section provides a brief overview of what new visitors can expect to find at the site and includes a link to a page that explains our user-friendly features. Your home page should also contain an initial section that provides a quick overview of the site.

FIGURE 26.1.

The Virtual Press Web site begins with a home page.

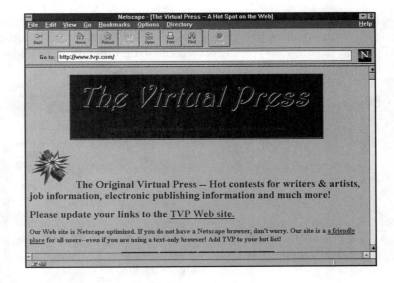

Here is the HTML markup for this section of the page:

```
<P ALIGN=CENTER> <A HREF="vpbg.html"><IMG SRC="vpttl11.gif" ALT=""></A></P>
<H2><IMG SRC="bboard.gif" ALIGN="BOTTOM" ALT="* ATTN *">
The Original Virtual Press -- Hot contests for writers &amp; artists,
job information, electronic publishing information and much more!</H2>
<H2>Please update your links to the
<A HREF="http://tvp.com/">TVP Web site.</A></H2>
<P><STRONG>Our Web site is Netscape optimized.  If you do not have a
Netscape browser, don't worry.  Our site is a <A HREF="vpintro.html">
a friendly place</A> for all users—even if you are using a text-only browser!
Add TVP to your hot list!</STRONG></P>
```

> **NOTE**
>
> Note the naming convention used for the files. I use the abbreviation vp to denote Virtual Press. In the links, you will see vpbg.html, vpttl11.gif, and vpintro.html. The naming scheme gives my Web projects clear organization and association with a specific project. At 2 a.m. on a Saturday, you may appreciate this when you accidentally move your pages to the wrong directory and you won't be asking yourself later, "Did the prompt say 'overwrite' and did I really answer yes?"

Linking with Images and Text Menus

The next section of the home page contains the eye-catching front door to TVP's order center shown in Figure 26.2. Each book between the bookends is a clickable image that will take the reader to a key section of TVP's order center. While these graphics appear large on the screen, they are not byte hogs. Under the images, a mini text menu provides readers with an alternate route to the order center. A text menu ensures that readers with a text-only browser can easily navigate the site. It also provides easy access to the order center for readers who may have turned off the graphics-loading capability of their browser.

FIGURE 26.2.

Graphical links to The Virtual Press order center.

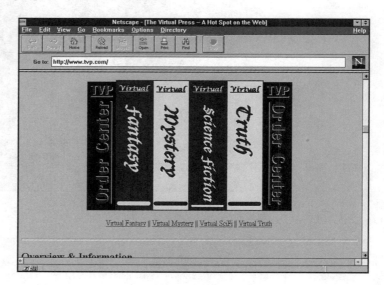

Although I could have designed a visually stunning image to replace the text-based menu shown in Figure 26.3, I decided not to do this. Minimizing loading time whenever possible is an important concept in Web page design, especially when you consider most Web users have a 14,400-bps modem. So, I use a text-based menu as the primary navigation mechanism to the key areas of the site. If your site has many attractions, you will want to consider using a text-based menu as the primary navigation mechanism.

Here is the code for this section of the page:

```
<P ALIGN=CENTER><IMG SRC="vorder1.gif" ALT=""><A HREF="vpdord.html#vfantasy">
<IMG SRC="vf.gif" ALT=""></A><A HREF="vpdord.html#vmystery">
<IMG SRC="vm.gif" ALT=""></A><A HREF="vpdord.html#vscifi">
<IMG SRC="vsf.gif" ALT=""></A><A HREF="vpdord.html#vtruth">
<IMG SRC="vt.gif" ALT=""></A><IMG SRC="vorder2.gif" ALT=""></P>
<P ALIGN=CENTER><A HREF="vpdord.html#vfantasy">Virtual Fantasy</A> ||
<A HREF="vpdord.html#vmystery">Virtual Mystery</A> ||
<A HREF="vpdord.html#vscifi">Virtual SciFi</A> ||
<A HREF="vpdord.html#vtruth">Virtual Truth</A></P>
<HR SIZE=4>
<H2>Overview & Information</H2>
<P><A HREF="vpbg.html">Corporate Background </A> ||
<A HREF="vpfound.html">About the Founder: William R. Stanek </A> ||
<A HREF="vpqry.html">Query Publisher</A> ||
<A HREF="viporder.html">Orders & More </A></P>
<H2>Business Solutions</H2>
```

```
<P><A HREF="vpepc.html">Electronic Publishing Center</A> ¦¦
<A HREF="vpicc.html">Internet Consulting Center</A> ¦¦
<A HREF="vpwdc.html">Web Design Center</A></P>
<H2>Community Services</H2>
<P><A HREF="idn.html"> Internet Daily News</A> ¦¦
<A HREF="vpjic.html">Job Information Center</A> ¦¦
<A HREF="vpipc.html">Net Publishing Information Center</A>  ¦¦
<A HREF="vpwg.html">Writer's Gallery</A></P>
<H2>Hot Topics</H2>
<P><A HREF="vpdream1.html"> Sneak Previews</A> ¦¦
<A HREF="vpdest1.html">World of Paths HQ</A> ¦¦
<A HREF="pin.html">Pulse of the Internet Magazine</A></P>
<H2>Opportunities for Writers & Artists</H2>
<P><A HREF="projint.html">Project Internet</A> ¦¦
<A HREF="vpcon.html">Hot Contests </A></P>
<HR>
```

FIGURE 26.3.

Using a text-based menu for key areas at the Web site.

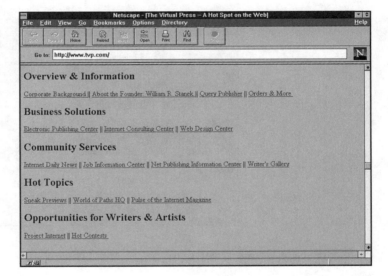

This section of the page uses relative links to other pages at the site. The links in the order center images are internal page links that specify a keyword using the format discussed in the previous chapter, such as:

```
<A HREF="vpdord.html#vmystery">
```

When a reader activates this link, the browser will load the page called vpdord.html, search for the keyword vmystery, and display the corresponding section when the keyword is found.

Using Links to Keep Visitors Informed

Informing visitors of upcoming events at the site is extremely important. I use the section of the page depicted in Figure 26.4 to tell readers that the site is growing. For large or complex Web sites, you may want to have a "What's New" page. A "What's New" page is a great way to inform visitors of recent changes. Repeat visitors to your site will appreciate the effort because a "What's New" page makes it easier for them to use your Web site efficiently. You will help them find new information faster, and ultimately, they'll return the favor by revisiting your friendly Web site.

FIGURE 26.4.

Upcoming projects at the TVP Web site.

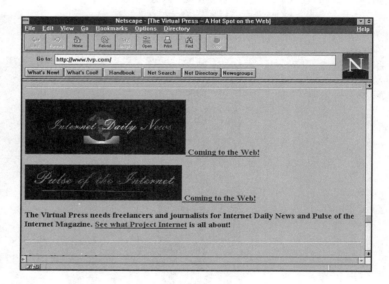

The HTML code for this section of the page is as follows:

```
<HR>
<H3><A HREF="http://tvp.com/idn.html">
<IMG SRC="idnttl4.gif" ALT=""> Coming to the Web!</A></H3>
<H3> <A HREF="http://tvp.com/pin.html">
<IMG SRC="pinttl3.gif" ALT=""> Coming to the Web!</A></H3>
<H3>The Virtual Press needs freelancers and journalists for
Internet Daily News and Pulse of the Internet Magazine.
<A HREF="http://tvp.com/projint.html">See what Project Internet</A>
is all about!</H3>
<HR>
```

Linking Contact and Copyright Information

The final section of the page, shown in Figure 26.5, provides contact and copyright information. You should always provide a point of contact for questions, technical or otherwise, about the site. You should also provide a copyright notice to the pages of your site to tell the world that the site is an intellectual property and as such protected under U.S. and international copyright laws. Instead of displaying complete copyright information on every page, you may want to create a link to a copyright page.

FIGURE 26.5.

Always provide contact and copyright information.

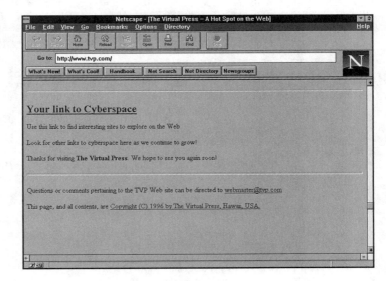

Here is the HTML code for the final section of the home page:

```
<HR>
<H2><A HREF="http://tvp.com/vplink.html">Your link to Cyberspace</A></H2>
<P>Use this link to find interesting sites to explore on the Web<P>
<P> Look for other links to cyberspace here as we continue to grow!</P>
<P> Thanks for visiting <STRONG>The Virtual Press</STRONG>. We hope to
see you again soon!</P>
<HR SIZE=4>
<P>Questions or comments pertaining to the TVP Web site can be directed
to <A HREF="mailto:webmaster@tvp.com"> webmaster@tvp.com</A></P>
<P>This page, and all contents, are <A HREF="vpcopy.html">
Copyright (C) 1996 by The Virtual Press, Hawaii, USA.</A></P>
```

The Completely Linked Home Page

This section contains the complete code for the home page used in the examples. You can use this to help you design and create the front door to your Web site.

Listing 26.1 shows the complete HTML code for the home page.

Listing 26.1. The front door to the Web site.

```
<HTML>
<HEAD>
<TITLE>The Virtual Press -- A Hot Spot on the Web</TITLE>
```

continues

Listing 26.1. continued

```
</HEAD>
<BODY>
<P ALIGN=CENTER><A HREF="vpbg.html"><IMG SRC="vpttl11.gif" ALT=""></A></P>
<H2><IMG SRC="bboard.gif" ALIGN="BOTTOM" ALT="* ATTN *">
The Original Virtual Press -- Hot contests for writers &amp; artists,
job information, electronic publishing information and much more!</H2>
<H2>Please update your links to the
<A HREF="http://tvp.com/">TVP Web site.</A></H2>
<P><STRONG>Our Web site is Netscape optimized.  If you do not have a
Netscape browser, don't worry.  Our site is a <A HREF="vpintro.html">
a friendly place</A> for all users--even if you are using a text-only browser!
Add TVP to your hot list!</STRONG></P>
<P ALIGN=CENTER><IMG SRC="vorder1.gif" ALT=""><A HREF="vpdord.html#vfantasy">
<IMG SRC="vf.gif" ALT=""></A><A HREF="vpdord.html#vmystery">
<IMG SRC="vm.gif" ALT=""></A><A HREF="vpdord.html#vscifi">
<IMG SRC="vsf.gif" ALT=""></A><A HREF="vpdord.html#vtruth">
<IMG SRC="vt.gif" ALT=""></A><IMG SRC="vorder2.gif" ALT=""></P>
<P ALIGN=CENTER><A HREF="vpdord.html#vfantasy">Virtual Fantasy</A> ||
<A HREF="vpdord.html#vmystery">Virtual Mystery</A> ||
<A HREF="vpdord.html#vscifi">Virtual SciFi</A> ||
<A HREF="vpdord.html#vtruth">Virtual Truth</A></P>
<HR SIZE=4>
<H2>Overview & Information</H2>
<P><A HREF="vpbg.html">Corporate Background </A> ||
<A HREF="vpfound.html">About the Founder: William R. Stanek </A> ||
<A HREF="vpqry.html">Query Publisher</A> ||
<A HREF="viporder.html">Orders & More </A></P>
<H2>Business Solutions</H2>
<P><A HREF="vpepc.html">Electronic Publishing Center</A> ||
<A HREF="vpicc.html">Internet Consulting Center</A> ||
<A HREF="vpwdc.html">Web Design Center</A></P>
<H2>Community Services</H2>
<P><A HREF="idn.html"> Internet Daily News</A> ||
<A HREF="vpjic.html">Job Information Center</A> ||
<A HREF="vpipc.html">Net Publishing Information Center</A>   ||
<A HREF="vpwg.html">Writer's Gallery</A></P>
<H2>Hot Topics</H2>
<P><A HREF="vpdream1.html"> Sneak Previews</A> ||
<A HREF="vpdest1.html">World of Paths HQ</A> ||
<A HREF="pin.html">Pulse of the Internet Magazine</A></P>
<H2>Opportunities for Writers & Artists</H2>
<P><A HREF="projint.html">Project Internet</A> ||
<A HREF="vpcon.html">Hot Contests </A></P>
<HR>
<H3><A HREF="http://tvp.com/idn.html">
<IMG SRC="idnttl4.gif" ALT=""> Coming to the Web!</A></H3>
<H3> <A HREF="http://tvp.com/pin.html">
<IMG SRC="pinttl3.gif" ALT=""> Coming to the Web!</A></H3>
<H3>The Virtual Press needs freelancers and journalists for
Internet Daily News and Pulse of the Internet Magazine.
<A HREF="http://tvp.com/projint.html">See what Project Internet</A>
is all about!</H3>
<HR>
<H2><A HREF="http://tvp.com/vplink.html">Your link to Cyberspace</A></H2>
<P>Use this link to find interesting sites to explore on the Web<P>
```

```
<P> Look for other links to cyberspace here as we continue to grow!</P>
<P> Thanks for visiting <STRONG>The Virtual Press</STRONG>. We hope to
see you again soon!</P>
<HR SIZE=4>
<P>Questions or comments pertaining to the TVP Web site can be directed
to <A HREF="mailto:webmaster@tvp.com"> webmaster@tvp.com</A></P>
<P>This page, and all contents, are <A HREF="vpcopy.html">
Copyright (C) 1996 by The Virtual Press, Hawaii, USA.</A></P>
</BODY>
</HTML>
```

Adding Rooms to Your Web Home

Your home on the Web should have many rooms. Filling those rooms with wonderful content is not always easy, especially when you have to choose which room to fill first. A new site should build its rooms a little at a time. You should start by building a solid framework for the site that tells the world who you are and what you plan to do. Show visitors you are dedicated to the development of a wonderful resource, and they will return to see how your site is progressing even if it is in the early stages of development.

This section shows you how to build two more rooms for your site:

- Business-oriented background page
- Personal background page

Your Business Background Page

All Web publishers—from well-known national or international companies to individual business people—should take the time to tell the world a bit about their businesses. Too many sites on the Web offer products or services to the world and forget to tell the world who they are and what they represent. Your business background page provides an essential background on what your site represents to the Internet community. This page can provide the background and history of your business. It can also provide an overview of products and services you currently offer or plan to offer.

Your business background page could be broken down into four parts:

- Overview
- The selling points
- Product and service summary
- Additional and closing information

Building the Overview Section

Your background page could begin with an overview that summarizes the background of your company or your business efforts in a few paragraphs. The summary should point out the key points about your business and could focus on your business's

>   Mission
>   Goals
>   Objectives

Figure 26.6 shows the overview section on TVP's background page. The summary is short and points out the corporate mission, goals, and objectives. Your summary should also be short and to the point.

FIGURE 26.6.

A background page could begin with an overview.

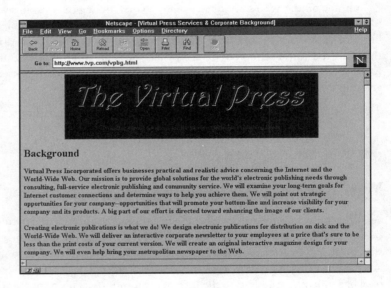

Here is the HTML code for this section of the page:

```
<P ALIGN=CENTER><A HREF="vphp.html"><IMG SRC="vpttl11.gif" ALT=""></A></P>
<H2>Background</H2>
<P>Virtual Press Incorporated offers . . . </P>
<P>Creating electronic publications is . . . </P>
<HR SIZE=4>
```

Building in the Selling Points

Showing the world you are serious about business can be the purpose of the next section of your page. The design and content of the page tells the reader a great deal about who you are. You want to show the world you are a professional. You also want to show the world you are serious about business. If you are presenting a service to readers, you want to demonstrate why they should use your company and not one of the other companies they could jump to at the click of their mouse button. One way to do this is to show that you know your subject area and have studied the market.

The Virtual Press provides services to Internet-smart consumers and businesses. The purpose of Figure 26.7 and Figure 26.8 is to demonstrate that we have studied the market.

FIGURE 26.7.

Show the world you mean business and are a professional.

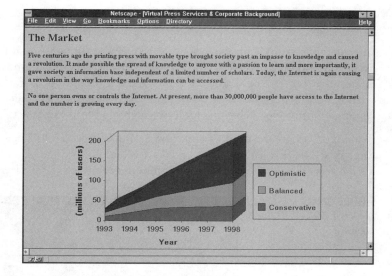

FIGURE 26.8.

Demonstrate your expertise and business savvy.

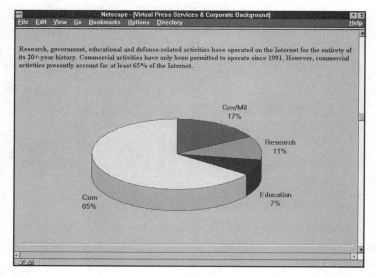

Here's the HTML code for this section of the page:

```
<H2>The Market</H2>
<P>No one person owns or controls the Internet . . . </P>
<P ALIGN=CENTER><IMG SRC="netusers.gif" ALT=""></P>
<P>Research, government, educational and . . . </P>
<P ALIGN=CENTER><IMG SRC="netacty.gif" ALT=""></P>
<HR SIZE=4>
```

Building a Product and Service Summary

After demonstrating your expertise and business savvy, you should provide readers with a list of your products or services. Ideally, your list will contain links to pages with detailed information that readers could access if they wanted more information. However, if you are just starting out, this can be an excellent place to tell readers what they can expect to see in the coming months. No Web site is built overnight and readers know this.

Figure 26.9 shows the product and service summary for TVP. The summary is presented as three lists. The first list pertains to books TVP publishes. The second list pertains to services TVP offers. The third list pertains to community service areas TVP maintains.

FIGURE 26.9.

A product and service summary.

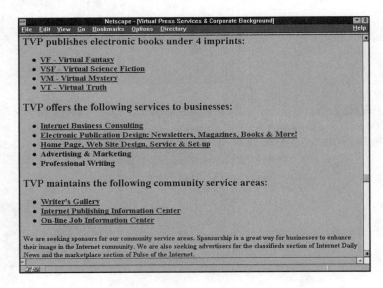

Here is the HTML code for this section of the page:

```
<H2>TVP publishes electronic books under 4 imprints:</H2>
<H3>
<UL>
<LI><A HREF="vpdord.html#vfantasy">VF - Virtual Fantasy</A>
```

```
<LI><A HREF="vpdord.html#vscifi">VSF - Virtual Science Fiction</A>
<LI><A HREF="vpdord.html#vmystery">VM - Virtual Mystery</A>
<LI><A HREF="vpdord.html#vtruth">VT - Virtual Truth</A>
</UL>
</H3>
<H2>TVP offers the following services to businesses:</H2>
<H3>
<UL>
<LI><A HREF="vpicc.html" >Internet Business Consulting</A>
<LI><A HREF="vpepc.html" >Electronic Publication Design:
Newsletters, Magazines, Books & More!</A>
<LI><A HREF="vpwdc.html" >Home Page, Web Site Design, Service & Set-up</A>
<LI>Advertising & Marketing
<LI>Professional Writing
</UL>
</H3>
<H2>TVP maintains the following community service areas:</H2>
<H3>
<UL>
<LI><A HREF="vpwg.html" >Writer's Gallery</A>
<LI><A HREF="vpipc.html" >Internet Publishing Information Center</A>
<LI><A HREF="vpjic.html" >On-line Job Information Center</A>
</UL>
</H3>
<P>Currently, we are seeking sponsors for our community service areas . . .  </P>
<HR SIZE=4>
```

> **NOTE**
>
> The header tag <H3> is used creatively in this example. I use the header tag to add white space and to separate the parts of the list from the list titles. While this is not proper form, it meets my presentation needs. Most browsers will display the lists as I intended. However, a few browsers, including Lynx, will not add the additional white space. If you use similar tricks to meet your presentation needs, ensure that several major browsers display the effect you are trying to create. The true solution for this dilemma is HTML 3.0. HTML 3.0 enables you to add list headers to listings and will add the extra white space.

Adding Information and Finishing the Page

The way you complete the page is as important as how you start the page. Don't create a dead-end for readers. At the very least, provide them with a way to easily return to your home page. Finish your background page with address and contact information similar to what is shown in Figure 26.10.

FIGURE 26.10.
*Always include a way to
return to your home page.*

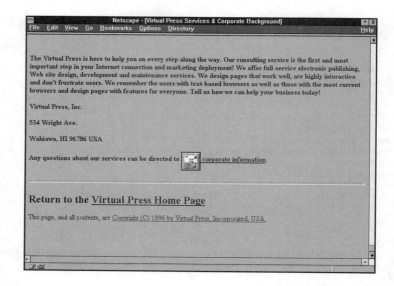

The HTML code for the final section of the page follows:

```
<HR SIZE=4>
<P>The Virtual Press is here to . . . <P>
<P>Virtual Press, Inc.</P>
<P> 534 Wright Ave.</P>
<P> Wahiawa, HI 96786 USA</P>
<P>Any questions about our services can be directed to
<A HREF="mailto:corpinfo@tvp.com" ><IMG SRC="mail.gif" ALT="">
corporate information</A>.</P>
<HR SIZE=4>
<H2>Return to the <A HREF="vphp.html" >Virtual Press Home Page</A></H2>
<P>
<P>This page, and all contents, are <A HREF="vpcopy.html">
Copyright (C) 1996 by Virtual Press, Incorporated, USA.</A></P>
```

The Complete Business Background Example

This section contains the code for the business background page used in the examples. Use the page to help create your own background page, and by doing so you will add another room to the framework of your Web site.

Listing 26.2 shows the HTML code for the business background page.

Listing 26.2. The business background page.

```
<HTML>
<HEAD>
<TITLE>Virtual Press Services & Corporate Background</TITLE>
</HEAD>
<BODY>
```

```
<P ALIGN=CENTER><A HREF="vphp.html"><IMG SRC="vpttl11.gif" ALT=""></A></P>
<H2>Background</H2>
<P>Virtual Press Incorporated offers . . . </P>
<P>Creating electronic publications is . . . </P>
<HR SIZE=4>
<H2>The Market</H2>
<P>No one person owns or controls the Internet . . . </P>
<P ALIGN=CENTER><IMG SRC="netusers.gif" ALT=""></P>
<P>Research, government, educational and . . . </P>
<P ALIGN=CENTER><IMG SRC="netacty.gif" ALT=""></P>
<HR SIZE=4>
<H2>TVP publishes electronic books under 4 imprints:</H2>
<H3>
<UL>
<LI><A HREF="vpdord.html#vfantasy">VF - Virtual Fantasy</A>
<LI><A HREF="vpdord.html#vscifi">VSF - Virtual Science Fiction</A>
<LI><A HREF="vpdord.html#vmystery">VM - Virtual Mystery</A>
<LI><A HREF="vpdord.html#vtruth">VT - Virtual Truth</A>
</UL>
</H3>
<H2>TVP offers the following services to businesses:</H2>
<H3>
<UL>
<LI><A HREF="vpicc.html" >Internet Business Consulting</A>
<LI><A HREF="vpepc.html" >Electronic Publication Design:
Newsletters, Magazines, Books & More!</A>
<LI><A HREF="vpwdc.html" >Home Page, Web Site Design, Service & Set-up</A>
<LI>Advertising & Marketing
<LI>Professional Writing
</UL>
</H3>
<H2>TVP maintains the following community service areas:</H2>
<H3>
<UL>
<LI><A HREF="vpwg.html" >Writer's Gallery</A>
<LI><A HREF="vpipc.html" >Internet Publishing Information Center</A>
<LI><A HREF="vpjic.html" >On-line Job Information Center</A>
</UL>
</H3>
<P>Currently, we are seeking sponsors for our community
service areas . . .   </P>
<HR SIZE=4>
<P>The Virtual Press is here to . . . <P>
<P>Virtual Press, Inc.</P>
<P> 534 Wright Ave.</P>
<P> Wahiawa, HI 96786 USA</P>
<P>Any questions about our services can be directed to
<A HREF="mailto:corpinfo@tvp.com" ><IMG SRC="mail.gif" ALT="">
corporate information</A>.</P>
<HR SIZE=4>
<H2>Return to the <A HREF="vphp.html" >Virtual Press Home Page</A></H2>
<P>
<P>This page, and all contents, are <A HREF="vpcopy.html">
Copyright (C) 1996 by Virtual Press, Incorporated, USA.</A></P>
</BODY>
</HTML>
```

Your Personal Background Page

Just as Web publishers sometimes neglect to tell the world about the background of their business, they also sometimes neglect to tell the world about themselves. Telling the world about yourself is extremely important, especially if you are offering a service or product to Internet users. Again, I am amazed at the number of sites on the Web that offer services or products to Internet users and then fail to provide adequate credentials.

Why should anyone listen to your advice on rebuilding classic cars? Perhaps they should because you have been an auto mechanic for 20 years, rebuilt hundreds of cars, and won dozens of awards. Well, no one will know this unless you tell them. The mechanic's background page could show a picture or contain a link to a picture of every award-winning car featured at the site.

> **NOTE**
>
> As you develop the page, keep in mind that a reader who visits your business background page may not visit your personal background page and vice versa. Consequently, you will probably want to build some overlap into the material you cover on both pages.

Your background page could contain four main sections:

- Personal background summary
- Plans, goals, and objectives
- Credentials
- Additional and closing information

Building In Your Personal Background Summary

Your background page should begin with a summary of your personal and professional life. Often it is best to keep the section short, usually three to five paragraphs will do. Project a positive image by touching on the high points of your life and career, not the low points.

This is the place where you can bring down the barriers between you and the reader. You can do this by adding a few tidbits of personal information that let the reader know the world isn't so large after all. You, the publisher, have a family, interests, and hobbies to match your ambitions and dreams.

Figure 26.11 shows the first section of my personal background page. To ensure the page is as interactive as possible, I worked the key links to other pages at the site into the summary. I also provided a link with a mailto reference so readers can easily send me an e-mail message. Try to work links into your list as well; the more interactive your page is, the better.

FIGURE 26.11.

Show the world your personal side.

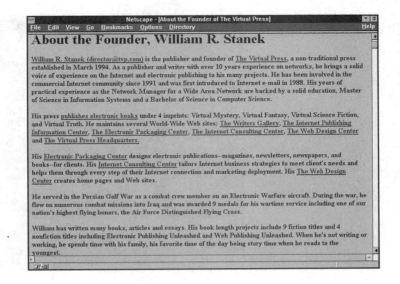

The HTML code for this section of the page follows:

```
<H1>About the Founder, William R. Stanek</H1>
<P><A HREF="mailto:director@tvp.com">William R. Stanek
(director@tvp.com) </A> is the publisher and founder of
<A HREF="vphp.html">The Virtual Press</A>,
a non-traditional press . . . </P>
<P>His press <A HREF="vpbg.html">publishes electronic books</A>
under 4 imprints:  Virtual Mystery, Virtual Fantasy,
Virtual Science Fiction, and Virtual Truth.  He maintains several
World-Wide Web sites:  <A HREF="vpwg.html">The Writers Gallery</A>,
<A HREF="vpipc.html">The Internet Publishing Information Center</A>,
<A HREF="vpepc.html">The Electronic Packaging Center</A>,
<A HREF="vpicc.html">The Internet Consulting Center</A>,
<A HREF="vpwdc.html">The Web Design Center</A> and
<A HREF="vphp.html">The Virtual Press Headquarters.</A></P>
<P>His <A HREF="vpepc.html">Electronic Packaging Center</A> designs
electronic publications—magazines, newsletters, newspapers, and books
--for clients.  His <A HREF="vpicc.html">Internet Consulting Center</A>
tailors Internet business strategies to meet client's needs and helps them
through every step of their Internet connection and marketing deployment.
His <A HREF="vpwdc.html">The Web Design Center</A> creates home pages
and Web sites.</P>
<P>He served in . . . </P>
<P>William has written . . . </P>
<HR>
```

Building in Your Plans, Goals, and Objectives

After you tell the world about yourself, tell the world about your plans, goals, and objectives for the Web site. These plans should be an overview and only provide as much or as little information as you feel comfortable providing. Figure 26.12 shows this section of the background page.

FIGURE 26.12.

Tell the world a bit about your plans.

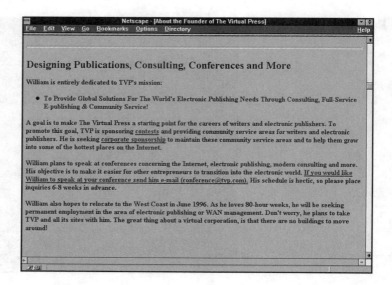

Here is the HTML code for this section of the page:

```
<H2>Designing Publications, Consulting, Conferences and More</H2>
<P>William is entirely dedicated to TVP's mission:
<UL>
<LI>To Provide Global Solutions For The World's Electronic Publishing
Needs Through Consulting, Full-Service E-publishing & Community Service!
</UL>
<P>A goal is to make The Virtual Press a starting point for the careers
 of writers and electronic publishers.  To promote this goal, TVP is
sponsoring <A HREF="vpcon.html">contests</A> and providing community
service areas for writers and electronic publishers.  He is seeking
<A HREF="vpspons.html">corporate sponsorship</A> to maintain these
community service areas and to help them grow into some of the hottest
places on the Internet.</P>
<P>William plans to speak at conferences concerning the Internet,
electronic publishing, modern consulting and more.  His objective is
to make it easier for other entrepreneurs to transition into the
electronic world.   <A HREF="mailto:conference@tvp.com">If you would like
William to speak at your conference send him e-mail (conference@tvp.com).
</A> His schedule is hectic, so please place inquiries 6-8 weeks in
advance.</P>
<P>William also hopes . . . </P>
```

Building In Your Credentials

After telling the world about your plans, back those plans up with your credentials. Here you should publish an electronic version of your resume or simply an outline of the milestones in your professional career. A great way to present your resume is as a series of bulleted lists, such as those shown in Figure 26.13.

FIGURE 26.13.

Add your credentials with a Web version of your resume.

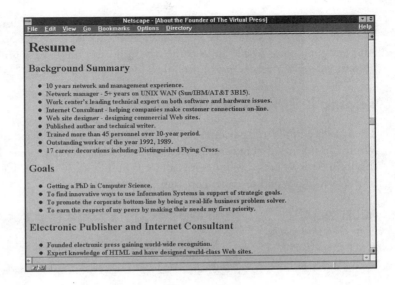

The HTML code for this section of the page follows:

```
<H1>Resume</H1>
<H2>Background Summary</H2>
<UL>
<LI>10 years network and management experience.
<LI>Network manager - 5+ years on UNIX WAN (Sun/IBM/AT&T 3B15).
<LI>Work center's leading technical expert on both software and
hardware issues.
<LI>Internet Consultant - helping companies make customer connections
on-line.
<LI>Web site designer - designing commercial Web sites.
<LI>Published author and technical writer.
<LI>Trained more than 45 personnel over 10-year period.
<LI>Outstanding worker of the year 1992, 1989.
<LI>17 career decorations including Distinguished Flying Cross.
</UL>
<H2>Goals</H2>
<UL>
<LI>Getting a PhD in Computer Science.
<LI>To find innovative ways to use Information Systems in support of
strategic goals.
<LI>To promote the corporate bottom-line by being a real-life business
problem solver.
<LI>To earn the respect of my peers by making their needs my first
priority.
</UL>
<H2>Electronic Publisher and Internet Consultant</H2>
<UL>
...
</UL>
```

Whenever possible, work links into your resume section as well. If you worked for IBM, then add a link to IBM's home page in the section of your resume that outlines your job at IBM. Another good place to add links is the education section of your resume. My alma mater is Hawaii Pacific University, and I proudly added the links to HPU's home page.

Adding Information and Finishing the Page

The final section of the personal background page features contact and address information. While this information may be on your business background page, it is a good idea to include this information here as well. As you can see from Figure 26.14, the page ends with a link back to the home page and provides copyright information as well.

FIGURE 26.14.

Finish the page with links and contact information.

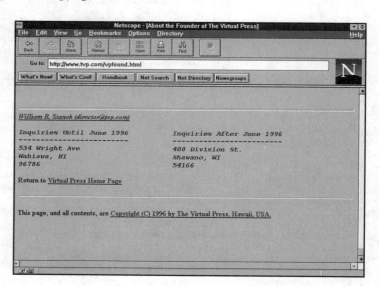

The code for this section of the page follows:

```
<HR>
<P ALIGN=CENTER> <A HREF="vpbg.html"><IMG SRC="vpttl15.gif" ALT=""></A></P>
<ADDRESS>
<A HREF="mailto:director@tvp.com">William R. Stanek (director@tvp.com)</A>
<PRE>
Inquiries Until June 1996        Inquiries After June 1996
------------------------         ------------------------
534 Wright Ave                   408 Division St.
Wahiawa, HI                      Shawano, WI
96786                            54166
</PRE>
</ADDRESS>
<P>Return to <A HREF="vphp.html">Virtual Press Home Page</A></P>
<HR>
```

```
<P>This page, and all contents, are <A HREF="vpcopy.html">Copyright
(C) 1996 by The Virtual Press, Hawaii, USA.</A></P>
</BODY>
</HTML>
```

> **NOTE**
>
> Many Web publishers use the `<ADDRESS>` tag as a way of signing the page. Text within the begin and end `ADDRESS` tags is usually displayed in italics. As shown in the example, addresses are usually preceded with a horizontal rule and are often one of the last elements on the page.

The Complete Personal Background Example

This section contains the code for the personal background page used in the examples. You can use this to help you create your own background page, and thus add another room to the framework of your Web site.

Listing 26.3 shows the HTML code for the personal background page.

Listing 26.3. The personal background page.

```
<HTML>
<HEAD>
<TITLE>About the Founder of The Virtual Press</TITLE>
</HEAD>
<BODY>
<H1>About the Founder, William R. Stanek</H1>
<P><A HREF="mailto:director@tvp.com">William R. Stanek
(director@tvp.com) </A> is the publisher and founder of
<A HREF="vphp.html">The Virtual Press</A>,
a non-traditional press . . . </P>
<P>His press <A HREF="vpbg.html">publishes electronic books</A>
under 4 imprints:  Virtual Mystery, Virtual Fantasy,
Virtual Science Fiction, and Virtual Truth.  He maintains several
World-Wide Web sites:  <A HREF="vpwg.html">The Writers Gallery</A>,
<A HREF="vpipc.html">The Internet Publishing Information Center</A>,
<A HREF="vpepc.html">The Electronic Packaging Center</A>,
<A HREF="vpicc.html">The Internet Consulting Center</A>,
<A HREF="vpwdc.html">The Web Design Center</A> and
<A HREF="vphp.html">The Virtual Press Headquarters.</A></P>
<P>His <A HREF="vpepc.html">Electronic Packaging Center</A> designs
electronic publications--magazines, newsletters, newspapers, and books
--for clients.  His <A HREF="vpicc.html">Internet Consulting Center</A>
tailors Internet business strategies to meet client's needs and helps them
through every step of their Internet connection and marketing deployment.
His <A HREF="vpwdc.html">The Web Design Center</A> creates home pages
and Web sites.</P>
<P>He served in . . . </P>
<P>William has written . . . </P>
```

continues

Listing 26.3. continued

```
<HR>
<H2>Designing Publications, Consulting, Conferences and More</H2>
<P>William is entirely dedicated to TVP's mission:
<UL>
<LI>To Provide Global Solutions For The World's Electronic Publishing
Needs Through Consulting, Full-Service E-publishing & Community Service!
</UL>
<P>A goal is to make The Virtual Press a starting point for the careers
 of writers and electronic publishers.  To promote this goal, TVP is
sponsoring <A HREF="vpcon.html">contests</A> and providing community
service areas for writers and electronic publishers.  He is seeking
<A HREF="vpspons.html">corporate sponsorship</A> to maintain these
community service areas and to help them grow into some of the hottest
places on the Internet.</P>
<P>William plans to speak at conferences concerning the Internet,
electronic publishing, modern consulting and more.  His objective is
to make it easier for other entrepreneurs to transition into the
electronic world.   <A HREF="mailto:conference@tvp.com">If you would like
William to speak at your conference send him e-mail (conference@tvp.com).
</A> His schedule is hectic, so please place inquiries 6-8 weeks in
advance.</P>
<P>William also hopes . . . </P>
<P>While relocating will mean . . . </P>
<H1>Resume</H1>
<H2>Background Summary</H2>
<UL>
<LI>10 years network and management experience.
<LI>Network manager - 5+ years on UNIX WAN (Sun/IBM/AT&T 3B15).
<LI>Work center's leading technical expert on both software and
hardware issues.
<LI>Internet Consultant - helping companies make customer connections
on-line.
<LI>Web site designer - designing commercial Web sites.
<LI>Published author and technical writer.
<LI>Trained more than 45 personnel over 10-year period.
<LI>Prior military with top security clearance.
<LI>Outstanding worker of the year 1992, 19826.
<LI>17 career decorations including Distinguished Flying Cross.
</UL>
<H2>Goals</H2>
<UL>
<LI>Getting a PhD in Computer Science.
<LI>To find innovative ways to use Information Systems in support of
strategic goals.
<LI>To promote the corporate bottom-line by being a real-life business
problem solver.
<LI>To earn the respect of my peers by making their needs my first
priority.
</UL>
<H2>Electronic Publisher and Internet Consultant</H2>
<UL>
...
</UL>
<H2>Computer Management Experience</H2>
<H3>Automatic Data Processing Manager (ADP)/Network Manager</H3>
<UL>
...
```

```
</UL>
<H3>Senior UNIX WAN/LAN System Administrator</H3>
<UL>
...
</UL>
<H3>PC Manager</H3>
<UL>
...
</UL>
<H2>Training Experience</H2>
<UL>
...
</UL>
<H2>General Experience</H2>
<UL>
...
</UL>
<H2>Education</H2>
<UL>
...
</UL>
<H2>Foreign Language Skills</H2>
<UL>
...
</UL>
<HR>
<P ALIGN=CENTER> <A HREF="vpbg.html"><IMG SRC="vpttl15.gif" ALT=""></A></P>
<ADDRESS>
<A HREF="mailto:director@tvp.com">William R. Stanek (director@tvp.com)</A>
<PRE>
Inquiries Until June 1996          Inquiries After June 1996
----------------------             ----------------------
534 Wright Ave                      408 Division St.
Wahiawa, HI                         Shawano, WI
96786                               54166
</PRE>
</ADDRESS>
<P>Return to <A HREF="vphp.html">Virtual Press Home Page</A></P>
<HR>
<P>This page, and all contents, are <A HREF="vpcopy.html">Copyright
(C) 1996 by The Virtual Press, Hawaii, USA.</A></P>
</BODY>
</HTML>
```

Proofing and Testing the Web Site

Now that you have several finished pages and the makings of a wonderful site, you will want to test the site before you publish it. The easiest way to test your Web site is to check the accuracy of your information one page at a time. Follow the advice on proofing and testing your pages discussed in Chapter 25, "Designing and Publishing a Web Document."

> **TIP**
>
> Browsers can change your window to the Web and different browsers may display your page in different ways. Always test features at your site with multiple browsers. I typically use three different browsers to test pages: Lynx, Air Mosaic, and Netscape Navigator. Lynx is a text-only browser, and I use it to test features for readers with a text-only browser. Air Mosaic is a graphics-capable browser, and I use it to test images and features for the average reader. Netscape Navigator is an advanced browser that supports its own unique extensions and some HTML 3.0 extensions. I use Netscape Navigator to test advanced and Netscape-specific features at the site.

Publishing Your Web Site

The moment of truth has arrived and you are finally ready to publish the Web site. To publish your Web site, all you need to do is to move your pages to the appropriate directory either on the Web server or within the public HTML directory of your account. Always contact the server administrator if you are not sure where to put your files.

While publishing your new site, you may encounter problems that you did not encounter when publishing your first page. Sometimes you just can't access your pages. The first thing you should do is to make sure all files are where they should be. Most of the time, HTML pages and associated files must be in very specific directories in order for the files to be accessed, such as the `public_html` directory. If your files are in the proper directory and you still can't access them, check the following:

- File and directory permissions
- File extensions
- Index files

File and Directory Permissions

All operating systems flag files and directories with permissions. The permissions on files and directories are very important. This is especially true on UNIX systems where the default file permissions are set according to an involved permission set. If you are having problems accessing the file, check permissions on both the file and the directory the file is in.

NOTE

On a UNIX system, a directory must be executable by the user to be readable. Typically you will want permissions on your public UNIX directories and files set so users can access your files but cannot write to the directory. The command you would use to put your files and directories in this mode is

```
chmod 705 filename
chmod 705 directory_name
Or
chmod 755 filename
chmod 755 directory_name
```

NOTE

On a DOS or Windows system, valid modes for files and directories include

```
System
Hidden
Read-only
Executable.
```

If you are having problems accessing files and directories make sure the files are at least readable by the user. Your files and directories should not be hidden.

File Extensions

The file extension you use should match the file type and format. Web servers may use the extension to determine what type of file you are trying to access. Web browsers may use the extension to determine what type of file you are retrieving and the action to take on the file. If you use a UNIX, Macintosh, or Amiga server, your HTML pages should have the extension .html. While your UNIX, Macintosh, or Amiga server may be configured to recognize the extension of .htm as a valid HTML document, it is often easiest to avoid a potential hassle and use the extension .html. If you use a Windows-based server, your HTML pages should have the extension .htm.

Index Files

Most Web server software wants directories with HTML documents to have an index file. Servers will generally display the index when a user specifies a directory name instead of a filename and if the index file doesn't exist, you may experience problems. The index file is sometimes called index.html, but not always. On a Macintosh server running MacHTTP or WebStar, each folder should have an index file called default.html.

Publicizing Your Web Site

You've published your Web site. You have a wonderful Web site or at least a start on what will become a wonderful Web site. Now you have to tell the world about it. In fact, you *must* tell the world about it. On the Internet there are no road maps and unless you tell people you've created a new site, no one is going to find out. Thankfully, dozens of Web sites specialize in spreading the word about Web resources. These sites maintain databases that Web users can search or meander through using links to specific categories.

The good news is you can register your site with most of these sites for free. All you have to do is to tell the site where they can find you and what to expect.

In the past year over a dozen new databases have appeared on the Web and soon dozens more will be available. Tracking down all these databases individually to ensure maximum exposure to the millions of Web users is difficult and time-consuming to say the least. Instead of spending an entire day registering your site, one solution would be to register your site only at the major databases, but then the question becomes which major databases. Here is a list of the major databases and the URL to their submission page:

Apollo: `http://apollo.co.uk/`

EINet Galaxy: `http://galaxy.einet.net/cgi-bin/annotate`

GNN: `http://www.gnn.com/gnn/wn/whats-new-form.html`

Harvest: `http://harvest.cs.colorado.edu/Harvest/brokers/register-with-CU-gatherers.html"`

HomeCom Global Village: `http://www.homecom.com/global/gc_entry.html`

InfoSeek: `http://www.infoseek.com/doc/FAQ/_How_do_I_get_my_web_page_inde.html`

Jump Station: `http://js.stir.ac.uk/jsbin/submit`

Lycos: `http://lycos.cs.cmu.edu/lycos-register.html`

New Rider's WWW Yellow Pages: `http://www.mcp.com/newriders/wwwyp/submit.html`

Nikos: `http://www.rns.com/www_index/new_site.html`

Open Text: `http://opentext.uunet.ca:8080/omw-submit.html`

Starting Point: `http://www.stpt.com/util/submit.html`

Web Crawler: `http://webcrawler.com/WebCrawler/SubmitURLS.html`

What's New Too: `http://newtoo.manifest.com/WhatsNewToo/submit.html`

Whole Internet Catalog: `http://gnn.com/gnn/forms/comments.html"`

World Wide Web Worm: `http://www.cs.colorado.edu/home/mcbryan/WWWadd.html`

World Wide Web Yellow Pages: `http://www.yellow.com/`

Yahoo: `http://www.yahoo.com/bin/add`

Another solution for registering your site with a database is to use a site that acts as a pointer to the databases. Pointer sites provide a way of automating the registration process and using the fill-out form provided at the site, you can submit information to multiple databases at the touch of a button. Currently, there are two primary pointer sites: Scott Banister's Submit-It page and HomeCom's Pointers to Pointers page.

The Submit-It page is shown in Figure 26.15. A great thing about the Submit-It page is that all the database sites you see listed at the top of Figure 26.14 are automatically selected to receive your submission. You can tell the site is selected by the X in the box associated with the database. If you don't want to register with a certain site, you would click on the box to unselect the site and the X would disappear.

Once you complete the online form partially depicted in Figure 26.16, you can automatically register your site with more than a dozen Web databases. The key information you enter into this form includes your name, business address, e-mail address, site URL, site title, and a brief description of your site.

FIGURE 26.15.

Use Submit-It to register your site with more than a dozen databases.

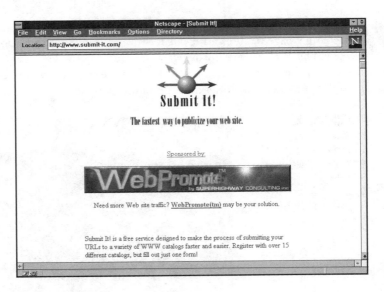

The Pointers to Pointers page is shown in Figure 26.17. The organization of this page is very different from the organization of the Submit-It page. Dozens of large, small, and specialized databases are listed in a comprehensive list. Some databases are presented with a checkbox that you must select individually to place an automated submission. Other databases, particularly the specialized databases, are provided only as links that you must visit individually to submit your information.

FIGURE 26.16.

A fill-out form at Submit-It makes submission easy.

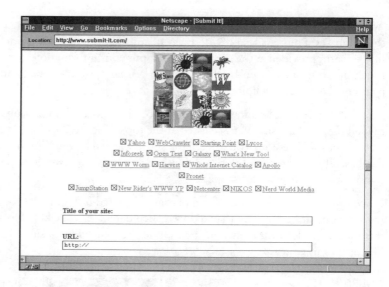

HomeCom's page features a fill-out form for automatic submission to databases you have selected. This form is partially depicted in Figure 26.18. The key information you enter into this form includes your name, business address, e-mail address, phone number, fax number, site URL, site title, and a brief description of your site.

FIGURE 26.17.

Use Pointers to Pointers to register your site with large, small, and specialized databases.

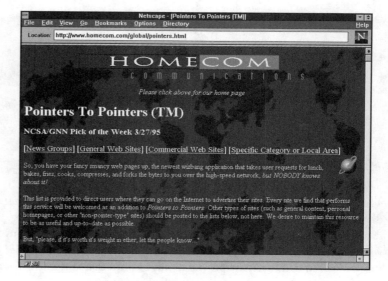

FIGURE 26.18.

The Pointers to Pointers submission form.

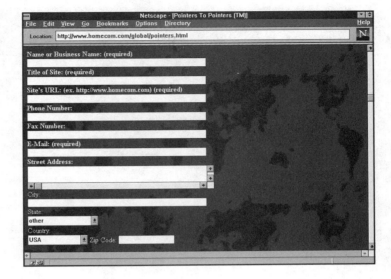

Summary

Creating, publishing, and publicizing your first Web site is easy if you follow the eight steps outlined in this chapter. If you follow the advice the examples present, your first Web site could have as many as four pages. These include your home page, business background page, personal background page, and the community service page developed in the previous chapter. Creating a Web site involves much more than creating pages; it involves developing a strategy and focusing on sound design concepts.

To attract visitors, your pages must be friendly and inviting. One way to ensure your pages are friendly is to design them with both first-time and repeat visitors in mind. You should also ensure there are no dead-ends at your site. Dead-ends are frustrating and can easily be avoided by following a sound page design that includes adequate linking. You can use links to create image and text menus, to keep visitors informed, and to provide a feedback mechanism for readers. You can also use links to ensure that all your pages lead somewhere, even if it is only back to your home page.

Designing and Publishing a Multimedia Presentation

27

by Mary Jo Fahey

IN THIS CHAPTER

Artists who are beginning to learn how to design Web pages should consider studying conventional design principles in order to understand where they should improvise on a Web page. If you are a beginner, either look for books and articles on graphic design, or borrow graphic design ideas from print. Although the Web represents an opportunity to stray from some established ideas, you'll discover many well-designed Web pages still conform to traditional graphic design principles.

Magazines are a good source of graphic design ideas. Look carefully at type, color, textures, shadows, letter spacing, paragraph spacing, space between text and graphics, space between text and rules, and the total amount of white space. Start a file and collect images that you like. Consider buying one or more subscriptions to famous graphic design publications such as *Print Magazine, Communication Arts, HOW Magazine,* or *Step-by-Step Graphics.* In large cities, you'll find these publications at newsstands. Also, consider buying the design award issues published by these magazines.

As you study conventional graphic design, you'll begin to see the design principles that professional graphic designers follow. Without art training, it may be difficult to "see" these principles at first. For example, many graphic designers position elements on an invisible page grid. The invisible grid is a subtle alignment tool for designers to follow. By positioning elements along an axis, there's a balance and a symmetry created that has an important impact on the subconscious mind.

The Web itself is also a source of pages a new Web page artist can study. For example, the Netscape browser has buttons labeled "What's New" and "What's Cool" that branch to lists of new and visually interesting Web pages. Yale's Center for Advanced Instructional Media has a WWW Style manual at `http://info.med.yale.edu/caim/C_HOME.HTML`. The online publication offers an excellent guide to interface design.

Develop a Concept

Developing and refining a concept before your project begins helps you to develop a focus. As your focus becomes clear, the design process will become easier and easier.

The taxi driver interview covered in this chapter did not require the kind of planning that is necessary for business presentations. The taxi driver interview, shown in Figure 27.1, is a humorous multimedia addition to the launch of www.1996.com, an interactive zine created and art-directed by Bill Murphy of the Webology Group. (See Figure 27.2.)

Other types of multimedia presentations might involve a decision concerning the amount of information to present. With complex business issues, this requires a lot of effort. If more than one person is involved in the design or decision-making process, more than one meeting might be necessary to create a clear idea of what the presentation should contain.

FIGURE 27.1.

Taxi driver interview, www.1996.com.

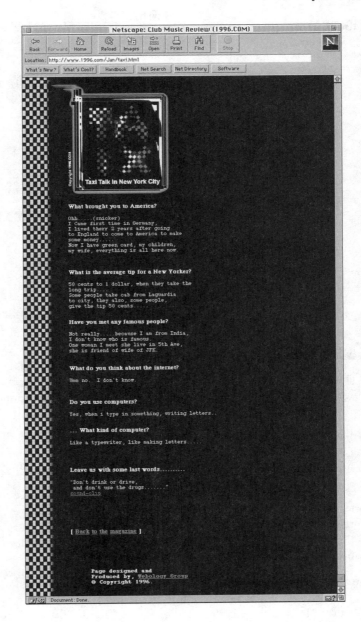

FIGURE 27.2.

*Home page for
www.1996.com, an
interactive zine.*

Technology

Technology often affects the presentation content. For example, of the elements one might expect to see in a multimedia presentation on the Web, sound and video often need to be limited because the Web is a low-bandwidth medium.

Bill Murphy decided the interview would be too long to distribute in a sound file on the Web. Alternatively, he used text to display most of the interview, and he digitized a few sound clips from an analog tape he used during his interview with the taxi driver.

Recent developments in sound technology provide Web page artists with the capability to offer "streaming" sound or clips with a longer duration. Vocaltec, the company that introduced Internet Phone to the Web, has recently introduced IWave, a streaming sound format that is the least complex of the streaming sound options because it does not require special server software. (See Figure 27.3.)

Streaming sound clips do not need to be downloaded. Bill added these as an option for Web visitors who have downloaded streaming sound players to their computer hard drives. (See Chapter 21, "Multimedia Presentation Tools," for details on where to find streaming sound players.)

FIGURE 27.3.
Vocaltec's IWave Web page.

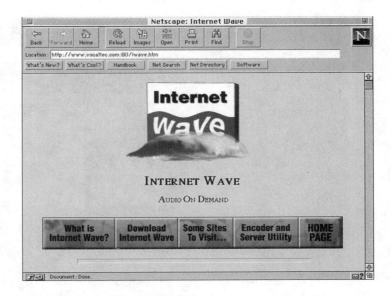

TIP

At the beginning of the planning process, be sure to survey the recent technological developments that might affect the quality of your presentation. Just as streaming sound has been introduced to the Web, so has streaming video and streaming animation.

End-User Hardware and Software

End-user hardware will have an impact on your plan. Companies that sell software or hardware know that the IBM PC/compatible market is approximately eight times as large as the Macintosh Market. Although many companies strive to create a Windows and a Macintosh version of their product, there are gaps. Try to select software that will play on both platforms. Van Halen's Web page, shown in Figure 27.4, offers a variety of sound file formats—including AIFF, AU, and WAV—for Web visitors with different computer platforms.

When you're planning your multimedia presentation, consider the player(s) and hardware end-users will need. For example, Macintosh multimedia artists take sound and sound hardware for granted since these elements have always been built into the Macintosh. Sound components have only become a standard on IBM-compatible hardware for the past two years.

FIGURE 27.4.
Van Halen's Web page.

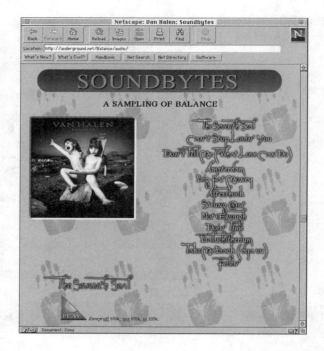

Try to estimate whether your audience has the appropriate hardware to play your multimedia presentations. For example, many large companies make the Web available to employees, but most firms prefer to buy "silent" computers for employees—computers without sound cards.

Consider building a "Help" page on your site with links to various sources of multimedia players on the Web. Figure 27.5 shows IUMA's help page, which guides Web visitors to the appropriate players that they'll need to play sound and video on the IUMA Web site. Useful links include Macromedia's Shock wave plug-in and the streaming sound vendors such as Vocaltec, Xing, and RealAudio. (See Chapter 21 for URLs to the Macintosh and IBM shareware archives on the Web.)

FIGURE 27.5.

IUMA's help page.

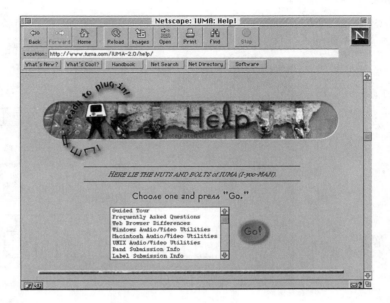

Plan the Navigation

Navigation through a two-dimensional Web site is accomplished with links. When 3-D becomes more widespread, navigation will change and VRML browsers will help Web visitors travel through 3-D space.

> **NOTE**
>
> VRML is an acronym for Virtual Reality Modeling Language, a file format that describes 3-D space on the Web.

A 2-D navigational structure can be mapped out in the planning stages of a project through the use of a flowchart or a program map. Maps that show function and approximate layout of visual components are particularly helpful if there are several people working on a project.

Sites can consist of simple linear slide shows or take the form of an inverted hierarchical tree structure. Grouped areas offer Web visitors choices. For example, the www.1996.com magazine consists of a tree structure that presents a home page followed by a table of contents. (See Figure 27.6.)

FIGURE 27.6.
*Tree diagram of
www.1996.com.*

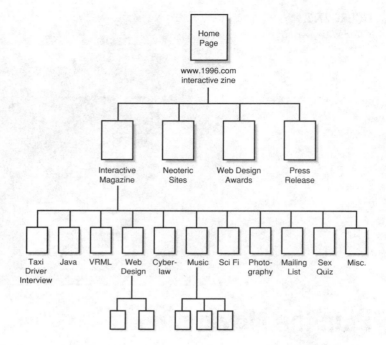

Linear Links

Linear links provide a simple structure for a simple Web site in which one page is equivalent to the next. However, in a site with a top-down structure, linear links tend to confuse the Web visitor. If you plan to use linear links in combination with a tree hierarchy, use a limited number of links that move ahead and back, because too many linear links will cause Web visitors to get lost.

In his interactive zine, Bill Murphy uses a navigation design that requires a Web visitor to return to the start before proceeding down another branch. (See Figure 27.7.) This method offers visitors choices or paths that may interest them without confusion.

Link to a Home Page or Fork

Always design a home page or button link to a recent fork. This takes a Web visitor back to a "starting point." Web page designers usually place this button at the bottom of a page, but some sites put this link at the top of a page, as shown in Figure 27.8.

FIGURE 27.7.

A "back to the magazine" link takes Web visitors back to a starting point so they don't get lost.

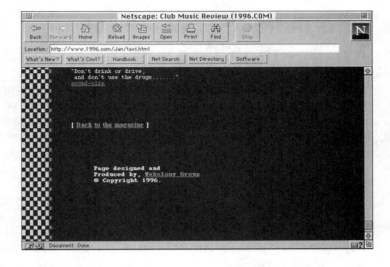

FIGURE 27.8.

A home page link in an upper-left corner.

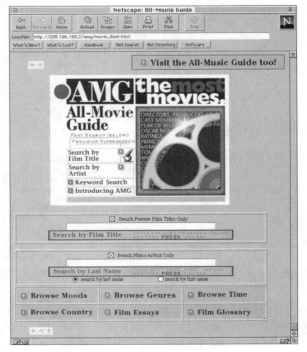

Determine the Source for Presentation Content

At the present time, many companies and individuals are transferring content that exists in print or some other medium to the Web. This process has been called "repurposing." Writers, graphic designers, videographers, and musicians are all experiencing a paradigm shift to a new medium that is unlike any other medium. As the Web evolves, the content will become unique rather than repurposed.

Text

Writers who create content for the Web need to learn about the Web's structure of hyperlinks. Weaving links into page content is what forms the basis of a "web." This is what the scientists who invented the Web had in mind: a latticework of resources in the form of text, images, and multimedia elements. When text is repurposed for the Web, links should be added so pages are not literal translations of print content. (See Figure 27.9.)

FIGURE 27.9.

Text with embedded links.

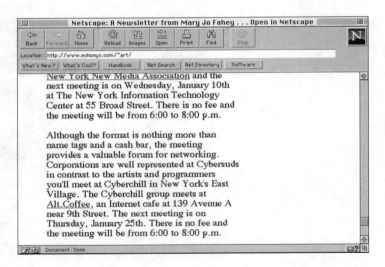

Links can either be designed to link to relevant information on the same site or to related information elsewhere on the Web. The research work to find related links on the Web can be done on the Web's large search engines. (See Figure 27.10.)

FIGURE 27.10.

Alta Vista, a search engine on the Web.

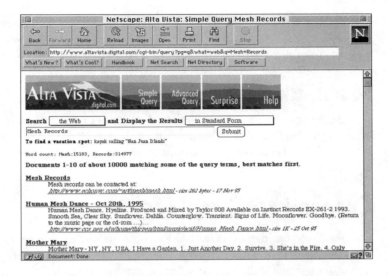

At the start of a project, consider what keywords best describe your project. All of the Web's search engines work on the principle of "keyword searches." Visit any one of the search engines at the following URLs and type your keywords into the field provided:

Search Engine	URL
Alta Vista	http://www.altavista.digital.com
Yahoo	http://www.yahoo.com
Lycos	http://www.lycos.com
Web Crawler	http://webcrawler.com/
Excite	http://www.excite.com
DejaNews	http://www.dejanews.com
Open Text	http://www.opentext.com/omw/f-omw.html

Images

As in print, images are obtained from illustrations, scans of original photography, or stock photos. As the prices of filmless digital cameras drop, it makes sense to gather original photographs without the intermediate step of film development. The low-end cameras produce images that are too low in resolution for print, but because the Web resolution is 72 ppi, digital becomes an attractive alternative to conventional photography.

For example, Apple's QuickTake camera is priced at $725. It stores 40 320×240 images or 20 at 640×480. It also includes a close-up attachment. Ken Hansen Imaging (KHI) in New York City rents the QuickTake for $60 a day. Although Kodak developed the QuickTake for Apple, they developed their own version that is slightly more versatile. Priced at $995, the camera can hold 99 images at 320×240 or 48 at 640×480. Telefoto, wide angle, and close-up lenses are available from third parties.

Sound

Sound has become a complex subject on the Web because there are now several different types of sound. Gathering original sound content is usually done with a traditional tape recorder that can then be connected to a computer with a soundboard and sound software for sound digitization.

Create the Graphics

The best Web page design is created by artists who have made a commitment to learn HTML, or the HyperText Markup Language. Figure 27.11. shows some text marked up with HTML tags. Although the skills learned for print graphics are beneficial, a Web artist needs to vary between an image editor like Photoshop and the Netscape page to try various effects. Other supplementary software programs may include an animation program, a sound editor, and a bit-depth reduction tool. See Chapter 21 for details on multimedia software tools for the Macintosh and Windows platforms.

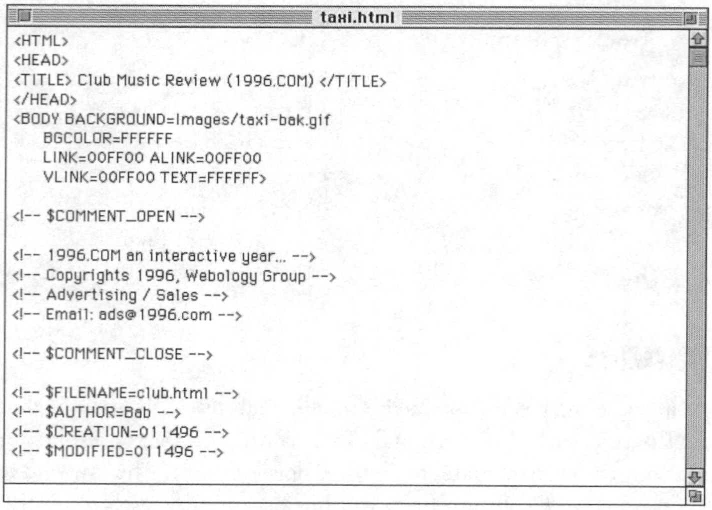

FIGURE 27.11.

Text marked up with HTML tags.

```
                                        taxi.html
<HTML>
<HEAD>
<TITLE> Club Music Review (1996.COM) </TITLE>
</HEAD>
<BODY BACKGROUND=Images/taxi-bak.gif
    BGCOLOR=FFFFFF
    LINK=00FF00 ALINK=00FF00
    VLINK=00FF00 TEXT=FFFFFF>

<!-- $COMMENT_OPEN -->

<!-- 1996.COM an interactive year... -->
<!-- Copyrights 1996, Webology Group -->
<!-- Advertising / Sales -->
<!-- Email: ads@1996.com -->

<!-- $COMMENT_CLOSE -->

<!-- $FILENAME=club.html -->
<!-- $AUTHOR=Bob -->
<!-- $CREATION=011496 -->
<!-- $MODIFIED=011496 -->
```

Image Editing: Creating the Taxi Checker Pattern

Although the famous checker trim on taxicabs no longer exists, the checker pattern will always be associated with taxicabs because of Morris Markin's famous Checker automobiles that existed from February 2, 1922 to July 12, 1982.

Here's how to create the checker pattern:

1. Select a foreground and background shade.

    To create the checkers he needed on his Web page, Bill Murphy selected foreground and background shades for painting in Photoshop. This is accomplished with a double-click on the Foreground and Background Control squares in Photoshop's Toolbox. The arrow tools next to the Foreground Background squares will rotate these two shades.

    Before making the foreground yellow, Bill rotated the black and white default shades to move black to the background shade. To select yellow, he double-clicked on the Foreground Control and then selected a yellow from Photoshop's Color Picker dialog box, pictured in Figure 27.12.

FIGURE 27.12.

Color Picker dialog box in Photoshop.

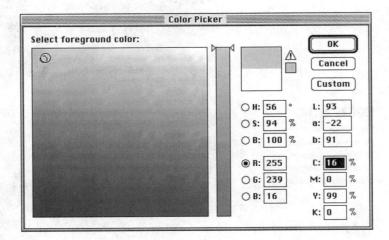

2. Use Photoshop's selection tool to draw a rectangular selection.

    Painting in Photoshop can be done in several ways. When a straight edge is needed, it is best to first use a selection tool and then fill an enclosed area with paint.

    The most straightforward approach to filling a selection rectangle is to use the Fill command on the Edit menu. However, a faster method is to make the desired shade the background color, draw the selection rectangle, and then delete the foreground shade with the Delete key. This uncovers or fills a desired area with paint.

3. Create one yellow rectangle on a black canvas.

    With Black set as the background color, Bill selected the white default canvas with Photoshop's Select All command and then pressed the Delete Key. This turned the canvas black. (See Figure 27.13.)

    On the black canvas he drew one rectangle with the rectangular selection marquee, changed the background shade to yellow, and pressed the Delete Key. (See Figure 27.14.)

FIGURE 27.13.

With Black selected as a background color, a Select All command followed by a Delete keystroke will turn the canvas black.

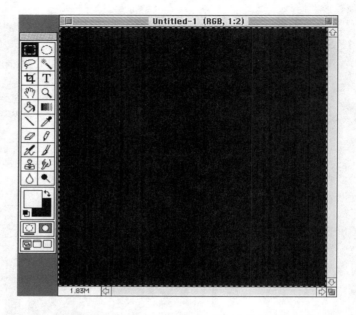

FIGURE 27.14.

With yellow as a background shade, a rectangular selection can be deleted to uncover the background color.

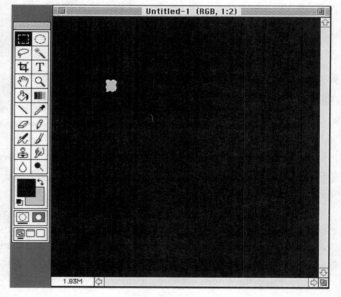

4. Duplicate the rectangle with Option-Drag.

   Since Bill wanted to create other rectangles with equal proportions, he duplicated the first rectangle by selecting Copy and then Paste from the Edit menu. This creates a second square element that overlays the original. Bill used the right arrow keys to move the second yellow square to the right until both squares lined up next to each other (see Figure 27.15). At this point, he continued to use the right arrow keys to move the yellow square but counted keystrokes this time. This provided a method to measure the distance he moved the yellow square. Using this same method, he made one more square. (See Figure 27.16.)

FIGURE 27.15.

Duplicating the squares can be done with the Copy and Paste commands on the Edit menu.

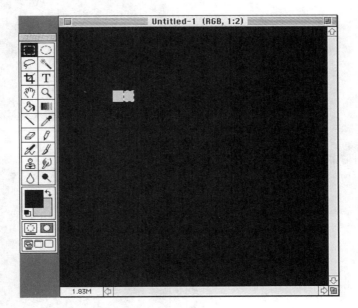

To make a second row in the checker pattern, Bill selected the squares that were complete, selected Copy and then a Paste from the Edit menu, and then used the same number of keystrokes to move the squares down. (See Figure 27.17.)

FIGURE 27.16.

The arrow keys on the keyboard move the squares and the number of keystrokes helps an artist record the distance.

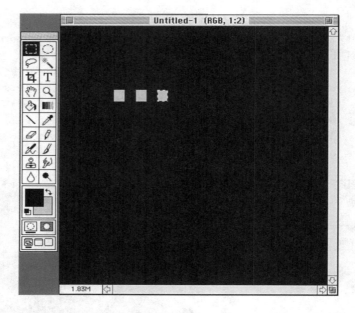

FIGURE 27.17.

Duplicate rows.

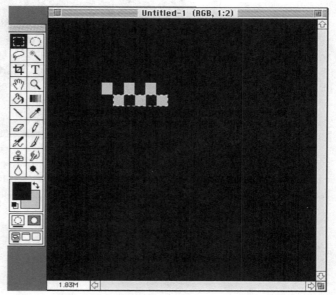

5. Reduce the bit-depth.

Lowering the bit-depth lowers the file size. First, select Indexed Color from the Mode pull-down menu. Next, select 3-bits per pixel under Resolution, Adaptive under Palette, and Diffusion under Dither. (See Figure 27.18.)

FIGURE 27.18.

Lower the bit-depth as much as possible to create a smaller file size.

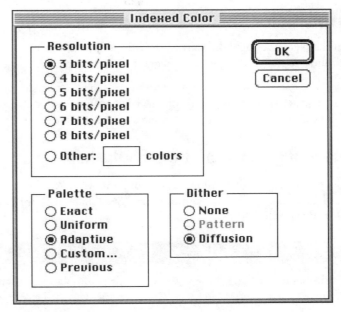

6. Save the checker pattern as a GIF file.

    Since the Netscape browser will read either GIF or JPEG files, Bill saved the checker pattern as a GIF image (see Figure 27.19). GIF images are read by more browsers, and by reducing the bit-depth, the file size is kept to a minimum.

FIGURE 27.19.

With Indexed Color selected on the Mode menu, the image can be saved as a GIF file.

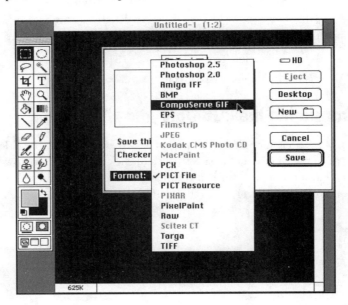

HTML Color

On the Netscape page, Bill wanted the color of the regular test to be white and the color of the text links to match the green in his graphic at the top of the page.

Two other shades would also have to be considered: a shade for an active link and a visited link. The active link shade is displayed when a Web visitor clicks on a link, and a visited link shade is displayed on text links that have already been explored.

Gathering RGB data from Photoshop

Bill used the BBS online color editor to obtain the HTML hexadecimal red-green blue triplets he needed for the body background tag. (See Chapter 21 for details about finding the BBS color editor online.)

> **NOTE**
>
> BBS has created an offline version of their color editor that is available for Windows.

With the yellow in the checker pattern selected as the foreground shade, Bill double-clicked the foreground square and obtained the RGB data he needed to input into the BBS color Editor. Photoshop displays the values on the Color Picker dialog box. The shades he collected had the following red-green-blue (0-255) values:

	R(ed)	G(reen)	B(lue)
Text link color (green)	255	239	16
Active link color (red)	181	9	5
Visited link color (dark green)	22	71	7

Translating the RGB Data into HTML Color

On the BBS color editor Web page, click to enter an *X* in the field labeled Input RGB value. Type in the RGB data for each shade and click on the Test it Now button. (See Figure 27.20.) The background will turn to the shade you're testing and the red-green-blue triplet will be displayed. For example, the red-green-blue triplet in Figure 27.21 is `#ffef10`.

FIGURE 27.20.

Note the Input data field and the RGB fields in the BBS Color Editor.

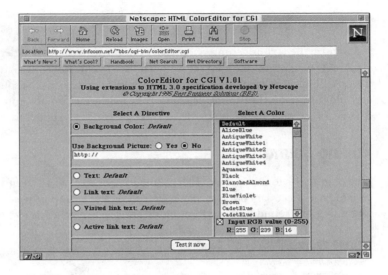

FIGURE 27.21.

Note the RGB triplet.

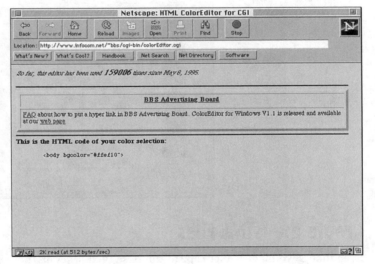

Create the Sound Files

Sound files are usually recorded with a tape recorder and then digitized. With the addition of a microphone, a notebook computer with sound hardware and software can be used to record sound into the computer's RAM memory.

Digitizing Sound

To digitize the taxi driver interview, Bill connected his tape recorder to the microphone jack on an AV Macintosh. He used the SoundEffects sound editor to digitize the sound and save it as an AIFF file. He then used the SoundApp utility to convert the sound to a WAV file and an AU file for use on the Windows and UNIX platforms. To accommodate Web visitors with IWave Sound players, he also used the IWave encoder to convert the files to an IWave format.

Editing Sound

The objective is to make sound files as small as possible, and a sound editor provides a means to remove unnecessary portions of a sound wave. For example, deleting a trailing silence at the beginning of a sound wave pattern significantly reduces the file size. (See Figure 27.22.)

FIGURE 27.22.

Deleting a trailing silence at the beginning of a sound wave.

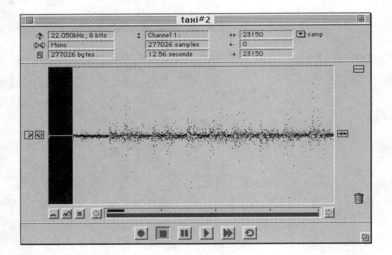

Create the HTML Files

Even though you'll need Netscape to compose Web pages, it's not necessary to compose pages while you're online. Although the Netscape program is designed to look for a network connection, it can be used offline in a mode that is similar to other software application programs.

A future version of Netscape called Netscape Gold will contain a built-in HTML editor; still, a separate text editor is necessary to compose HTML documents at this time. The HTML documents are ASCII text files that an artist saves with an `.htm` or `.html` extension.

Line Length and Paragraph Spacing

Graphics designers conventionally limit line length to make text easier to read. In typesetting, line length is referred to as a "measure." Since there is no HTML tag to limit line length, Bill improvised using the `<UL>`, `<DD>`, and `<BLOCKQUOTE>` tags. Similar workarounds were necessary to achieve his desired paragraph spacing. Although the `<P>` tag adds space between paragraphs on an HTML page, Bill used the `<PRE>` tag, which limited the font to Courier but retained the spacing he selected in his text processor.

Launch and Test the Presentation

The Web page launch occurs when the HTML documents are placed on the Web server. Although Web page composition offline in Netscape is adequate in the first stages of the project, the real test occurs when the documents are launched. For example, Bill discovered the taxi driver page looked slightly different in different versions of the Netscape browser. An earlier version of the browser squeezed the text to the left and caused the type to bump up against the checker pattern. Unfortunately, at this time, it's impossible to resolve the differences in browsers. Since an estimated 70 percent of people on the Web use the Netscape browser, many artists feel the best they can hope for is a good-looking page in the latest version of the Netscape browser. As the Web evolves, the differences in browsers will disappear.

Summary

Conventional graphic design principles used to arrange text and images on the printed page are useful for the Web artist who is learning to create Web pages for the first time. Examples can be found in print.

Before beginning your project, work on defining and refining your focus. Technology often affects the presentation content. For example, of the elements one might expect to see in a multimedia presentation on the Web, sound and video often need to be limited because the Web is a low-bandwidth medium. When you're planning your multimedia presentation, you need to consider the player(s) and hardware end-users will need. Then, building on ideas and resources presented here, put together text, images, and sound for your multimedia presentation.

PART

Looking Ahead

The Future of Web Publishing

28

by William Robert Stanek

IN THIS CHAPTER

Whether your Web publishing plans are large or small, 1996 is a year you won't want to miss. In 1996, the dozens of innovations that have been growing in development houses all around the world since the birth of the Web will hit the mainstream. Throughout the chapters of this book, you have read about most of these innovations, yet what you may not know is how these innovations will influence the future of Web publishing.

While 1993 marked the beginning of the marriage of the Internet and the Web, 1996 is the year the Web will swallow the remnants of the original Internet. Many probably won't even notice this event because the Web's dominance of the Internet will be a global information infrastructure that you will have to see to believe.

Fast Track to Electronic Commerce

One of the forces driving the dramatic changes taking place online is the global love affair with the Web and Web technology. Soon 50 million people will be wired in with full access to the Web and by the end of 1998, the number will grow to 100 million. In fact, in the time it'll take you to read this chapter, 5 to 50,000 consumers will become a part of the global online community. This tremendous audience of consumers is attracting a force that is changing the face of the Web forever: commercialism.

Commercialism has come to the Web in a big way, and it's here to stay, for better or worse. Web publishing, marketing, advertising, and technology development are multibillion dollar industries. Every major player in the world who understands that the Web is much more than a toy for Generation X is taking an active role in the electronic future of the Information Age. Those companies who are players now and aren't on the Net will be eating cyberdust in a contest where winners take all and losers fade away into obscurity.

Hundreds of companies around the world have set up shop to create home pages and Web sites. Some, like AT&T, are corporate conglomerates. AT&T is in a flat-out race to achieve dominance in the Internet service industry. Through its WorldNet division, AT&T is providing managed Internet services to businesses and consumers worldwide. These services include Internet access, Web hosting, and Web publishing.

In the Web's early days, most of the companies providing marketing and advertising services were Internet start-ups. Now, as the online world moves farther and farther into the mainstream, every major advertising agency in the world is preparing to dive into the game. Already dozens of traditional advertising agencies have stepped up to the plate and hit a few balls out into the stands. And why not? Some companies are already charging advertising rates that rival traditional mediums. A prime spot at Macmillan's busy site (`http://www.mcp.com`) will cost you $10,000. A prime spot at Netscape will cost $25,000+.

In 1995, we saw that Wall Street largely agreed that the future of cyberspace and electronic commerce is rosy. The stock for some Internet start-up companies soared to three to four times the price of the initial public offerings. The startling fact is that most of these IPOs were traded on dreams. Some stock, like Netscape's, rocketed to seven times the IPO, and the frenzy created by the media was largely responsible. This combination of consumer interest, media frenzy, and rugged commercialism are the driving factors in today's world of electronic commerce.

The lure of a fast track to new revenue is transforming the Web's dominant culture from one opposed to marketing to one that openly embraces it. My mailbox gets flooded with mail that less than a year ago would have caused thousands of Internet users to rise in protest and flame the offender back into the industrial age. You can see this change everywhere on the Web. Products that were once available freely are now commercial products and, in an ironic twist, sites that were once bastions of anti-commercialism now have a steady stream of advertisers due to their tremendous popularity. While some still wonder why there's little resistance now to the commercialism of cyberspace, many others know this commercialism is bringing with it all the technological wonders that computer enthusiasts have ever dreamed of.

Secure Money and Information Transfers

The future of true electronic commerce—where all your banking, shopping, and information needs can be met online—depends on universal standards for secure money and information transfers. The mechanism that will make true electronic commerce a reality for all online users already exists, and it's called Secure HTTP. S-HTTP enables secure transactions between Web clients and servers. The developers of S-HTTP set out to design an extremely flexible protocol that supports multiple encryption and authentication mechanisms, and S-HTTP is indeed the most versatile secure transfer protocol currently available.

S-HTTP is being developed by Enterprise Integration Technologies in cooperation with NCSA, RSA Data Security, and others. The protocol is based largely on Tim Berners-Lee's HTTP and on years of encryption technology research by hundreds of individuals and dozens of companies.

The business world, however, isn't rushing to embrace S-HTTP. The reason is that there are competing standards, and most businesses are waiting to see which one wins out before investing big money. A key concept with S-HTTP or any secure transfer protocol for that matter is that both the client and server must support the protocol. If a company invests in a server whose secure transaction protocol fades away into obscurity, the company will have to turn to another secure server at a cost of thousands of dollars.

One of the major competing standards is Netscape's Secure Socket Layer (NSSL) protocol. In December 1995, Netscape unveiled SSL Version 3.0 in the form of an Internet draft. SSL Version 3.0 is fully compatible with SSL 2.0. As a large part of Netscape's future as an Internet technology developer depends on SSL, the company is pulling out all the stops to ensure SSL is adopted as an industry standard for secure transfers. Those who thought Netscape would drop SSL in favor of S-HTTP may have to eat their hats.

Both S-HTTP and SSL can secure your transactions using encryption and authentication mechanisms. Encryption is the process of encoding information. When information is encoded, it cannot be read by normal means. Authentication is the process of ensuring that the receiver is the party for which the data was intended. The encryption and authentication processes are handled using a pair of keys.

The first key, called the public key, is used to encrypt the data. The second key, called the private key, is used to decrypt the data. If you want to send information to someone, you must obtain that person's public key and encrypt the information using this key. When the intended recipient receives the information, the private key—known only to the authentic recipient—is used to decrypt the information.

Although both S-HTTP and SSL get the job done, they differ in one extremely important way. S-HTTP is a protocol strictly designed for use in transferring information using the HyperText Transfer Protocol. SSL is a protocol designed to be layered on top of any reliable transfer protocol. This means SSL can be used with any existing Internet transfer protocol, including FTP, Gopher, HTTP, and telnet. Consequently, we may find that both S-HTTP and SSL become universally embraced standards in the near future.

You can read the current Internet draft regarding S-HTTP at

```
http://www.commerce.net/information/standards/drafts/shttp.txt
```

You can read the current Internet draft regarding SSL at

```
http://home.netscape.com/
```

Client-Side Everything

With the flood of new users coming to the Web every day, there is a great need to reduce the load on Web servers and the network backbone as well. As you saw in sections of this book pertaining to client-side image maps and client-side scripts, placing more of the burden on the client computer benefits everyone. Here is how:

> Client-side scripts reduce the load on the server and the network backbone by allowing the client to process inputs locally.

> Client-side scripts dramatically improve performance for the client because the client does not have to wait for responses from the server and can process inputs immediately.

> Client-side scripts simplify the design and implementation process by reducing the interaction to a single source document.

Reducing the load on Web servers and simplifying complex processes in Web publishing is a goal of client-side specifications. Early Web applications did not make full use of the resources available on client computers and relied primarily on the server to do most of the processing.

In an age when the computer sitting on your desktop is as powerful as the mainframes of yesteryear, it makes sense to use that power whenever possible. Yet other factors are driving this change as well.

With server-side handling of scripts, Web publishers must rely on the server to process inputs and return results. There are two major problems with this. First, the server must support the CGI specification. Second, you must have access to CGI. If your server does not comply with the CGI specification or your Internet service provider does not allow you to use CGI, you cannot use gateway scripts. To free Web publishers from a reliance on CGI, Web technology developers introduced client-side specifications.

Not only are innovations such as client-side image maps and client-side scripts redefining the way browser and server applications interface, they are redefining the way information is published on the Web. Client-side image maps greatly simplify the process of creating and using image maps. As the publisher, you don't have to rely on CGI, gateway scripts, and image maps files to enable your image maps. To enable client-side image maps, all you need are an image and definitions mapping out actions for the image in your HTML document.

Similarly, client-side scripts greatly simplify the process of creating dynamic documents. As the publisher, you don't have to rely on CGI, access to the cgi-bin directory, or gateway scripts to create extremely dynamic documents. All you have to do is insert your script into the HTML document. Currently, there are several competing client-side scripting languages, but the one with the most potential is JavaScript. JavaScript is discussed briefly in Chapter 12, "Form and Image Map Creation and Design."

In the near future, you can expect to see greater support for client-side image maps and client-side scripting. In fact, you may see a trend to client-side everything. If you think there is nothing left to redefine using a client-side model, consider this: A rather obscure browser from NCD called the Mariner automatically saves every file you find during an Internet session. When you are done with your work online, Mariner lets you work with the resources offline.

Depending on your viewpoint, this function can seem like a small step forward or a colossal innovation. After all, almost every browser since the Netscape Navigator has used client-side caching of files to improve performance. However, no one—until now—created a Web browser that enabled you to use these files offline in a seamless fashion.

Mainstream Integration

Ask people how to find things on the Web, and they'll probably tell you to point and click. Yet the conversation may come to a screeching halt when you ask for advice on using multimedia. To preview video, you need a video player. But what type of player—an MPEG player, a QuickTime player or a Video for Windows player? To listen to sound, you need a sound player. But what format is the sound file in and does your player support the format?

If you read Chapter 10, "HTML Toolkit: Browsers, Editors, and Converters," you know the answers to these questions, yet most Web users don't know AVI from MOV or WAV from MOD. This means many users miss the multimedia feast the Web provides. To make it easier for Web users to use external multimedia sources, many Web browser developers package their browsers with helper applications. The most basic packages include a sound player with the browser. More advanced packages include an image viewer, a sound player, and a video player.

Yet if you've used any of these integrated packages, you probably know that you often have to download a new player or viewer because your old viewer or player doesn't support the file format you want to use. When I looked at the number of helper applications I had downloaded to make my Web surfing experience surreal, I found that I had 27 of them:

> 3 HTML browsers
> 2 VRML browsers
> 1 SGML browser
> 1 PostScript/PDF viewer
> 3 image viewers
> 2 sound players
> 4 video players
> 2 e-mail programs
> 2 newsgroup programs
> 1 IRC program
> 6 miscellaneous utilities

All right, maybe I went a little overboard, but this doesn't even take into account the tools I use for research and development. Most Web users—myself included—simply want to be able to use the same program to browse the Web, send e-mail, access newsgroups, chat on IRC, and preview multimedia presentations no matter their format. In answer to this, we are starting to see the mainstream integration of browsers and helper applications. This mainstream integration is taking the form of inline support for video and sound, plug-ins for various file formats including PDF and PostScript, and even browsers with IRC-like chat capabilities.

Mainstream integration of every imaginable file format and helper application function is a trend that will continue for years to come. Web users want simplicity and ease of use as they surf the Web. After all, one of the reasons the Web is so wildly popular is that you can surf from New York to Hollywood to Zaire at the touch of a button.

Live Documents in Realtime

Direct support of multimedia, plug-ins, Java, and VRML are making live multimedia publications on the Web a reality. Behind this first wave of inline multimedia capabilities is a second wave carrying more advanced capabilities. This new wave of technology is bringing with it the capability to create live documents that either execute in realtime or update in realtime.

Using inline multimedia, you can create documents with full-motion video and sound tracks. Innovations such as RealAudio enable you to create sound tracks that begin playing almost as soon as they are accessed. Plug-ins enable browsers to incorporate features from advanced multimedia tools, such as the Macromedia Director plug-in available for the Netscape Navigator.

The next major release of the Java programming language is more powerful and versatile than existing Java specifications. A key focus of the latest version of the Java Developer's Kit is to make it easier to create inline applications in this advanced object-oriented programming language that is poised to storm the application's development marketplace like no other programming language before it. In the coming months, you will find that if a browser developer wants to be taken seriously in the race to develop the ultimate browser, the browser will have to support Java. Web users will demand this simply by the choices they select as their favorite destinations.

The hottest innovation for VRML is the live application engine. Using a live application engine, you can transform static 3-D worlds into worlds filled with live animation. While pointing and clicking in 3-D environments was fun, nothing compares to entering a 3-D world with spinning, moving, and flying objects that race by and, based on your actions, intelligently interact. If you want to create live VRML documents, Microsoft's ActiveVRML is a must-see.

While Microsoft based ActiveVRML in the current VRML 1.0 specification, VRML is specifically designed to meet the needs of Web publishers who want to create multimedia interactive animation. ActiveVRML enables you to use existing programming languages, such as Visual Basic, Java, and C++, to create modules for handling file system management, network protocols, and intensive numerical computation. As ActiveVRML communicates with programs written in these general programming languages, you can use modules written in a variety of languages. For example, since Java is ideal for inline applications, you could create a Java module to handle an inline application. Since C++ is good for number crunching, you could use C++ to handle numerical computations. Since Visual Basic is great for creating buttons and other objects with associated functions, you could use Visual Basic to handle functions that aren't inherent to VRML.

To support complex actions and spontaneous interaction, ActiveVRML allows for two communication paths between ActiveVRML and program modules:

1. ActiveVRML can originate events by notifying the program module that an event has occurred.

2. Program modules can originate events by notifying ActiveVRML that an event has occurred.

Using these two basic mechanisms, you can simulate other forms of communication, including real-time events. To simulate real-time events, you can send data to a program module with time-stamps. If your program module is designed to handle time-constrained events, the module will tell ActiveVRML how to behave and what events to execute based on the time-stamped input. If all this sounds complicated, consider the following example.

A visitor to your VRML world is racing toward a black hole you've created in the center of your cybergalaxy. Your VRML world file feeds data to the appropriate program modules according to the speed and direction they are traveling. Using this input, you can vary the sounds the visitor hears as he or she speeds up or slows down. You can decrease the intensity of celestial bodies as the visitor begins to enter the black hole's gravitational field, and so on.

Using these same live functions, you could create a live cybermall populated by the visitors to the mall. Here, your real-time world would change as visitors move around the mall. Doors could open and close. Visitors could chat with each other. They could interact with information desk personnel to find the products they are looking for.

If the VRML cybermall just described seems far off, consider browsers like the Sesame Navigator from Ubique that let you invite friends to cybersurf with you. While Sesame Navigator uses HTML to create what it calls Virtual Places, it is only a matter of time before someone integrates this capability into VRML. (Chapter 10 includes a review of Sesame Navigator.)

You can learn more about ActiveVRML by visiting Microsoft:

`http://www.microsoft.com/`

Hot Innovations

The Web is swallowing the Internet, there is no doubt. If you've visited an FTP or Gopher site lately, you've probably noticed that many of these sites are being transformed into HTTP-FTP or HTTP-Gopher hybrids. Increasingly, FTP and Gopher sites expect you to use a Web browser to visit the site, and often HTML documents contain the only documentation available. Other FTP and Gopher sites are directing visitors to Web sites that provide direct and easy access to the file archives. Yet ease of access isn't the only reason file archive sites are directing users to Web sites. HTTP uses fewer system resources than other protocols, making it possible for a less powerful computer to serve more customers.

Replacing FTP and Gopher functions with HTTP is more than a trend, it is the wave of the future in a world that wants consolidation and simplification of complex tasks. Some file archive sites have completely replaced their FTP and Gopher server functions with HTTP server functions. The way these sites do this is by relying on the client to know what to do with a particular file type. Clients know how to handle files based on the MIME content-type of the file. If a document is formatted with HTML, an HTML browser will display the document. If a document is in the Macintosh Binary Hexadecimal format, an HTML browser will usually provide a prompt asking if you want to save the file to disk. This means you can place any type of file in a `public_html` directory and link it to your documents just as you would link any other document.

Other innovations that you will want to keep an eye on include Hypermail, Hypernews Hyperchat, and Hyperphone.

Hypermail

Hypermail integrates the best qualities of e-mail with the hypertext capabilities of browsers. URL referencing is the most basic hypermail function. Several leading e-mail applications enable you to click on URLs referenced in e-mail messages and launch a browser to retrieve and display the referenced document. The next step in hypermail is full support for HTML markup and interaction capabilities.

Netscape Corporation has been developing a hypermail application for some time now. The latest version of Netscape Mail is fully hypermail capable. If you downloaded Netscape 2.0 Beta 4 or later versions, you found the message displayed in Figure 28.1 waiting for you. This message uses the MIME Content-Type `text/html` to tell Netscape Mail to display the message as an HTML document.

FIGURE 28.1.

Netscape Mail is fully hypermail capable.

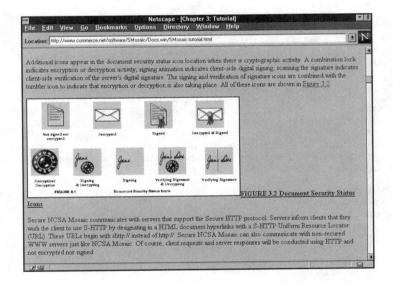

Listing 28.1 presents the complete source for this quirky message from the developers at Netscape.

Listing 28.1. mailnets.htm.

```
From: Mozilla <info@netscape.com>
Date: Wed, 2 Aug 1995 22:38:26 -0700 (PDT)
MIME-Version: 1.0
Content-Type: text/html
Subject: Welcome!
Message-ID: <30208F41nsintro@netscape.com>
X-Mozilla-Status: 0001
```

continues

Listing 28.1. continued

```
<HR SIZE=4 WIDTH="50%">
<CENTER>
<FONT SIZE="+1">Welcome to<BR></FONT>
<FONT SIZE="+2"><B>Netscape Mail</B><SUP><FONT SIZE="-1">(TM)</FONT></SUP></FONT>
</CENTER>
<HR SIZE=4 WIDTH="50%">

<P>Some day soon this message will contain a brief overview of the mail
interface, some demos of the features, and pointers to the manual.
Or something.  But for now, boys and girls, gather round and uncle Mozilla
will tell you a little story.  This story is called

<P><TABLE>
<TR><TD>
<CENTER>
<FONT SIZE="+2">The Troubled Aardvark</FONT>
<FONT SIZE="+1"><BR>by Tom Annau</FONT>
</CENTER>

<P>Once upon a time, there was an aardvark whose only pleasure in life
was driving from his suburban bungalow to his job at a large brokerage
house in his brand new 4x4.  He hated his manipulative boss, his
conniving and unethical co-workers, his greedy wife, and his snivelling,
spoiled children.  One day, the aardvark reflected on the meaning of
his life and his career and on the unchecked, catastrophic decline of
his nation, its pathetic excuse for leadership, and the complete
ineffectiveness of any personal effort he could make to change the
status quo.  Overcome by a wave of utter depression and self-
doubt, he decided to take the only course of action that would bring
him greater comfort and happiness: he drove to the mall and bought
imported consumer electronics goods.

<P><I>Moral of the story:</I> Invest in foreign consumer electronics
manufacturers.
</TD>
<TD>
<CENTER>
<IMG SRC="about:logo" ALT="N E T S C A P E">
</CENTER>
</TD></TABLE>
<P><HR SIZE=4 WIDTH="80%">
```

As you can see from the HTML markup, Netscape mail supports the features and elements that the Netscape Navigator supports. This integrated approach for e-mail and hypertext is the wave of the future.

HyperNews

HyperNews integrates the best qualities of Usenet newsgroups with the hypertext capabilities of browsers. This innovation developed by Daniel Laliberte enables you to directly access discussion groups with your browser. LaLiberte implemented HyperNews using the basics of

CGI and gateway scripts to create interactive discussion groups directly accessible from your browser.

A lot of effort went into ensuring that the marriage of hypertext and newsgroups is seamless. As you can see from Figure 28.2, hypernewsgroup messages are similar to Usenet newsgroup messages. Hypernewsgroups are maintained by HyperNews administrators. Although there is no current method for accessing all existing hypernewsgroups from a single source, it is only a matter of time before this feature is available. Primarily, this feature relies on coordination between HyperNews administrators and setting up automated jobs to pass new messages to HyperNews servers.

FIGURE 28.2.

Using HyperNews in your Web browser.

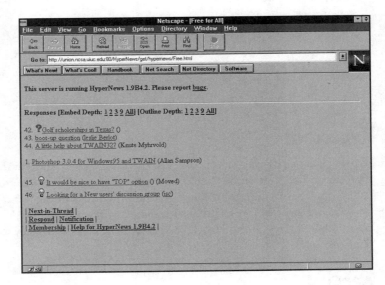

Each HyperNews message contains a message header, a message body that can be formatted with HTML, and links to actions the user can take. These actions are shown at the bottom of Figure 28.2. Clicking on the Next-in-Thread link enables you to see the next message in a thread. Clicking on the Respond link enables you to reply to a message. Clicking on the Notification link enables you to subscribe to any or all messages in the current thread. When a new message is posted to the thread, you will be notified by e-mail. Clicking on the Membership link enables you to become a known member on the HyperNews server. When you become a member, you have additional privileges. Clicking on the Help link brings you to a page with helpful pointers for using HyperNews.

HyperNews is designed to complement your existing Web server. Setting up a HyperNews server and becoming a HyperNews administrator is easy. The first step is obtaining the HyperNews source code, which at this time is freely available for UNIX systems. You can obtain the source from

```
http://union.ncsa.uiuc.edu:80/HyperNews/get/hypernews/source.html
```

Once you obtain the source, you will want to unarchive the source in the Web server's `cgi-bin` directory. The only file you need to update is `hnrc`, the HyperNews configuration file. Following the comments in the configuration file, update the configuration file as appropriate for your system. Following the directions in the README file, create your first hypernewsgroup.

> **NOTE**
>
> HyperNews depends on Perl-optimized system libraries. If Perl is not installed on your system, you may need to install it and execute the Perl utility h2ph as follows from the `/usr/include` directory:
>
> `h2ph * sys/*`
>
> This command tells h2ph to convert all files ending in `.h` to `.ph` files. This effectively converts your existing system library files written in C to Perl-optimized system library files. These Perl-optimized files will be stored in your Perl library directory. You will want to check file permissions on the resulting `.ph` files.

Hyperchat

Hyperchat integrates the best qualities of Internet Relay Chat with the hypertext capabilities of browsers. This innovation enables you to directly access live chat groups with your browser. Using hyperchat facilities, you communicate with others through text-based means. You type in words and those you are chatting with answer with words. Hyperchat has been implemented in a number of ways on the Web. The next sections looks at two key ways: WebChat and IRC W3 Gateway.

WebChat

WebChat is a CGI application that enables you to access multiple chat rooms, create your own conference rooms, and more from the comfort of your Web browser. Much like traditional IRC, WebChat enables you to see the messages you input and the messages of others. After you enter a message and submit it, your message is displayed for others to see. Your messages can contain HTML markup, images, and sound. WebChat uses client-pull technology to automate the update process. Using the fill-out form shown in Figure 28.3, you can update the refresh rate so you can chat in near realtime.

The WebChat is easy to install on your Web server. The first step is obtaining the WebChat source code, which at this time is freely available for UNIX systems. You can obtain the source from

`http://www.irsociety.com/webchat/code.html`

FIGURE 28.3.
Using WebChat.

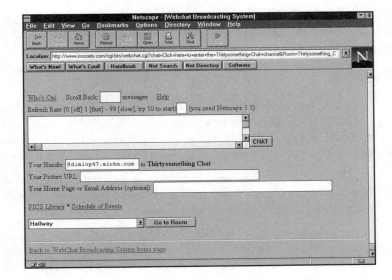

Once you obtain the source, you will want to unarchive the source in the Web server's `cgi-bin` directory. The WebChat package is very simple and consists of only a few files. You will need to update two files of these files: `nph-client` and `init_transcript_file`. These files are the gateway scripts that handle the live chat process. The package also includes several GIF images and an HTML document containing a fill-out form. You should move these files to the appropriate directory on your system. You can customize the look of WebChat simply by updating the images and form document.

IRC W3 Gateway

Like WebChat, IRC W3 Gateway is a CGI application. Using the IRC W3 Gateway, you can access multiple chat channels, find out who is on the current channel, and more from the comfort of your Web browser. Unlike WebChat, IRC W3 gateway is not intended to replace or be a substitute for IRC. IRC W3 Gateway interfaces with the existing IRC structure, channels, and servers.

While the IRC W3 Gateway has the look and feel of a traditional IRC, you are required to reload the page to see updates. This should change quickly when the developers implement client-pull or a similar technology. You can learn more about the IRC W3 Gateway at

```
http://hplyot.obspm.fr:8001/irc
```

Hyperphone

The rising popularity of Internet phones may one day put long distance phone companies out of business, and this section is going to tell you why. While hyperchat is a text-based means of communicating with others, hyperphone is a way of communicating with others using audio and sometimes audio and video. Thus, hyperphones work just like your telephone or video phone and allow you to integrate these functions into your Web browser. Currently, the only Web browser that lets you communicate with others using audio and video is Ubique's Sesame Navigator.

To do this, Sesame Navigator takes advantage of the Internet's multicast backbone called the MBONE. The MBONE is such a complex and fascinating topic that it is the subject of several books. While the MBONE opens the door for endless multimedia possibilities, similar functionality can be achieved using the existing structure of the Internet and the Web.

One of MBONE's key concepts is multicasting, or the capability to do many things simultaneously. The capability to send and receive many types of information simultaneously—such as text, audio, and video—is extremely important to the future of communication.

Your telephone is a simple device that can send and receive information at the same time. Generally though, one person is talking and another person is listening. Early Internet phone applications took advantage of this and operated in a mode called half-duplex. In half-duplex mode, one person could talk and the other person could listen. When the speaker paused, the other person could begin speaking. If both parties tried to talk at the same time, the message got garbled. This was a basic solution for long distance communication over the Internet that current Internet phone applications have improved upon.

Current Internet phone applications can operate in a mode called full-duplex that allows for simultaneous send and receive. The key difference between an Internet phone and a traditional phone is in the features and in the cost of a long distance phone call. Internet phones generally have all the same features as your phone, yet are more intuitive in the way you can use these features. For example, most Internet phones maintain a database of every number you call, and you can call these numbers at the touch of a button without having to memorize key combinations, such as star-8 to reach Aunt Agnes.

But best of all, with an Internet phone you can call anywhere in the world free of charge. The only monthly bill you have to pay is to your Internet service provider. If your ISP charges a flat fee for unlimited access, you've got the world's least expensive phone system.

Several versions of Internet phones are available: Internet Phone, Net Phone, and CU-SeeMe.

Internet Phone

For Windows and Windows 95/NT systems, you will want to try Internet Phone. Internet Phone is capable of full-duplex audio conversations and using a unique voice compression algorithm to reduce the amount of network bandwidth it uses. To use Internet Phone, you need the following:

- At least a 486SX PC with 25MHz and 8MB RAM running Windows 3.1.
- A standard TCP/IP Internet connection. The minimum connection recommended connection is an SLIP/PPP connection at 14,400 baud.
- A standard Windows-compatible audio board, a microphone, and a speaker.

As Internet Phone sends and receives audio directly from the user to whom you are speaking, Internet Phone is a very safe way to communicate. Internet Phone software can also connect to the IRC network, allowing you to chat one-on-one with others and join topic threads if you wish. If you want your privacy, you can have private and unlisted conversations. Access to the IRC network also lets you find other Internet Phone users.

While the current version of Internet Phone requires the user to whom you are speaking to use the Internet Phone software, future versions of Internet Phone should be more flexible. You can download a free trial version of Internet Phone from

```
http://www.vocaltec.com/
```

NetPhone

For Apple Macintosh and PowerPC systems, you will want to try NetPhone. NetPhone is the first full-duplex Internet phone to enable you to make conference calls. Using the NetPhone encoder-decoder or GSM audio, you can reduce the amount of network bandwidth NetPhone uses. To run NetPhone, you need

- Any Macintosh from the IIsi to the PowerMac.
- System 7 or later revisions.
- Sound Manager 3.*x* or later versions. (System 7.5 includes this utility.)
- MacTCP and an Internet connection. The minimum connection recommended connection is a SLIP/PPP connection at 14,400 baud.
- A microphone.

NetPhone is compatible with other Internet phones, including VAT and CU-SeeMe. This enables you to talk to people on Windows and UNIX systems. Although NetPhone does not have access to IRC, the makers of NetPhone, Electric Magic, have created a unique server device called NetPub. As the name implies, a NetPub is a place you can visit and talk with other NetPhone users. NetPubs are located worldwide. When you connect to a NetPub, you see a list of everyone connected to that NetPub, and they see that you've joined them.

The features included with NetPhone are some of the best available. The caller ID feature tells you the name of the person calling, the person's IP address, and his/her host name. The multiple active calls feature enables you to have multiple call windows open at once. The Web integration feature enables you to make phone calls by clicking on URLs.

You can download a trial version of NetPhone from

```
http://www.emagic.com/
```

CU-SeeMe

CU-SeeMe is a full-blown video conferencing solution for the Internet. Using CU-SeeMe, you can conduct a real-time conference with video, audio, and written messages. While CU-SeeMe is designed to work over LANs and WANs, it can be used over the Internet to video conference with other computers using CU-SeeMe or compatible software. The software requires no special hardware and can be used with inexpensive video cameras.

Using software compression algorithms, CU-SeeMe enables anyone with a standard TCP/IP connection to the Internet to use the full video, audio, and text capabilities of the software. However, the developers recommend that you have at least a 28.8Kbps modem.

To hold group conferences, you need an add-on application called Reflector. Reflector accepts multiple CU-SeeMe connections and directs the video, audio, and text to all participants in the conference. Currently, Cu-SeeMe and Reflector run only on UNIX systems.

CU-SeeMe is undoubtedly the most powerful and versatile free communications program ever produced. WhitePine, the developers of CU-SeeMe, are busy creating an enhanced version that will be distributed as a commercial product for UNIX, Mac, and Windows systems. The commercial version of CU-SeeMe will have many advanced features, including the capability to integrate with the Web.

You can download the current version of CU-SeeMe from White Pines:

```
http://www.wpine.com/cuseeme.html
```

Summary

The future of Web publishing is being defined right now. In fact, most of the innovations that will carry us into the year 2000 are already in development. The wonderful thing about 1996 is that these innovations will begin to hit the mainstream and when they do, the Web will swallow the Internet and at the same time be transformed into a medium that you will have to see to believe. So what are you waiting for? Join the revolution that is redefining the future of the Information Age!

An HTML Reference

This appendix is a reference to the HTML tags you can use in your documents, according to the HTML 2.0 specification. Tags in common use that are either HTML 3.0 or Netscape extensions are noted as such. Note that some browsers other than Netscape may support the Netscape extensions.

> **NOTE**
>
> A few of the tags in this section may not have been described in this book. If a tag is mentioned here that you haven't seen before, don't worry about it; that means that the tag is not in active use or is for use by HTML-generating and -reading tools, and not for general use in HTML documents.

HTML Tags

These tags are used to create a basic HTML page with text, headings, and lists.

Comments

<! ... >

Creates a comment.

Structure Tags

<HTML>...</HTML>

Encloses the entire HTML document.

Can Include: <HEAD> <BODY>

<HEAD>...</HEAD>

Encloses the head of the HTML document.

Can Include: <TITLE> <ISINDEX> <BASE> <NEXTID> <LINK> <META>

Allowed Inside: <HTML>

<BODY>...</BODY>

Encloses the body (text and tags) of the HTML document.

Attributes:

BACKGROUND="..." (HTML 3.0 only) The name or URL for an image to tile on the page background.

BGCOLOR="..." (Netscape 1.1) The color of the page background.

TEXT="..." (Netscape 1.1) The color of the page's text.

LINK="..." (Netscape 1.1) The color of unfollowed links.

ALINK="..." (Netscape 1.1) The color of activated links.

VLINK="..." (Netscape 1.1) The color of followed links.

Can Include: <H1> <H2> <H3> <H4> <H5> <H6> <P> <OL> <UL> <DIR> <MENU> <DL> <PRE> <BLOCKQUOTE> <FORM> <ISINDEX> <HR> <ADDRESS>

Allowed Inside: <HTML>

<BASE>

Indicates the full URL of the current document.

Attributes: HREF="..."; The full URL of this document.

Allowed Inside: <HEAD>

<ISINDEX>

Indicates that this document is a gateway script that allows searches.

Attributes:

PROMPT="..." (HTML 3.0) The prompt for the search field.

Allowed Inside: <BLOCKQUOTE> <BODY> <DD> <FORM> <HEAD> <LI>

<LINK>

Indicates a link between this document and some other document. This is generally used only by HTML-generating tools. <LINK> represents document links to this one as a whole, as opposed to <A> which can create multiple links in the document. Not commonly used.

Attributes:

HREF="..." The URL of the document to be linked to this one.

NAME=... If the document is to be considered an anchor, the name of that anchor.

REL="..." The relationship between the linked-to document and the current document, for example, "TOC" or "Glossary."

REV="..." A reverse relationship between the current document and the linked-to document.

URN="..." A Uniform Resource Number (URN), a unique identifier different from the URL in HREF.

TITLE="..." The title of the linked-to document.

METHODS="..." The method with which the document is to be retrieved; for example, FTP, Gopher, and so on.

Allowed Inside: <HEAD>

<META>

Indicates metainformation about this document (information about the document itself); for example, keywords for search engines, special HTTP headers to be used for retrieveing this document, expiration date, and so on. Metainformation is usually in a key/value pair form.

Attributes:

HTTP-EQUIV="..." Creates a new HTTP header field with the same name as the attributes value, for example HTTP-EQUIV=Expires. The value of that header is specified by CONTENT.

NAME=... If meta data is usually in the form of key/value pairs, NAME indicates the key, for example, Author or ID.

CONTENT=... The content of the key/value pair (or of the HTTP header indicated by HTTP-EQUIV).

Allowed Inside: <HEAD>

<NEXTID>

Indicates the "next" document to this one (as might be defined by a tool to manage HTML documents in series). <NEXTID> is considered obsolete.

Headings and Title

All heading tags have the following characteristics:

Attributes:

`ALIGN=CENTER`: (HTML 3.0 only) Centers the heading.

Can Include: `<A>` `<IMG>` `<BR>` `<EM>` `<STRONG>` `<CODE>` `<SAMP>` `<KBD>` `<VAR>` `<CITE>` `<TT>` `<B>` `<I>`

Allowed Inside: `<BLOCKQUOTE>` `<BODY>` `<PRE>` `<ADDRESS>` `<FORM>` `<TH>` `<TD>`

<H1>...</H1>

A first-level heading.

<H2>...</H2>

A second-level heading.

<H3>...</H3>

A third-level heading.

<H4>...</H4>

A fourth-level heading.

<H5>...</H5>

A fifth-level heading.

<H6>...</H6>

A sixth-level heading.

<TITLE>...</TITLE>

Indicates the title of the document.

Allowed Inside: `<HEAD>`

Paragraphs

<P>...</P>

A plain paragraph. The closing tag (`</P>`) is optional.

Attributes:

`ALIGN=CENTER` (HTML 3.0 only) Centers the paragraph.

Can Include: `<A> <IMG> <BR> <EM> <STRONG> <CODE> <SAMP> <KBD> <VAR> <CITE> <TT> <B> <I>`

Allowed Inside: `<BLOCKQUOTE> <BODY> <DD> <FORM> <LI>`

Links

<A>...</A>

With the `HREF` attribute, creates a link to another document or anchor; with the `NAME` attribute, creates an anchor which can be linked to.

Attributes:

`HREF="..."` The URL of the document to be linked to this one.

`NAME=...` The name of the anchor.

`REL="..."` The relationship between the linked-to document and the current document, for example, "TOC" or "Glossary." Not commonly used.

`REV="..."` A reverse relationship between the current document and the linked-to document. Not commonly used.

`URN="..."` A Uniform Resource Number (URN), a unique identifier different from the URL in HREF. Not commonly used.

`TITLE="..."` The title of the linked-to document. Not commonly used.

`METHODS="..."` The method with which the document is to be retrieved; for example, FTP, Gopher, and so on. Not commonly used.

Can Include: `<IMG> <BR> <EM> <STRONG> <CODE> <SAMP> <KBD> <VAR> <CITE> <TT> <B> <I>`

Allowed Inside: `<ADDRESS> <B> <CITE> <CODE> <DD> <DT> <EM> <H1> <H2> <H3> <H4> <H5> <H6> <I> <KBD> <LI> <P> <PRE> <SAMP> <STRONG> <TT> <VAR> <TH> TD>`

Lists

<OL>...</OL>

An ordered (numbered) list.

Attributes:

TYPE="..." (Netscape only) The type of numerals to label the list with. Possible values are A, a, I, i, 1.

START="..." (Netscape) The value to start this list with.

Can Include: <LI>

Allowed Inside: <BLOCKQUOTE> <BODY> <DD> <FORM> <LI> <TH> TD>

<UL>...</UL>

An unordered (bulleted) list.

Attributes:

TYPE="..." (Netscape) The bullet dingbat to use to mark list items. Possible values are DISC, CIRCLE, SQUARE.

Can Include: <LI>

Allowed Inside: <BLOCKQUOTE> <BODY> <DD> <FORM> <LI> <TH> TD>

<MENU>...</MENU>

A menu list of items.

Can Include: <LI>

Allowed Inside: <BLOCKQUOTE> <BODY> <DD> <FORM> <LI> <TH> TD>

<DIR>...</DIR>

A directory listing; items are generally smaller than 20 characters.

Can Include: <LI>

Allowed Inside: <BLOCKQUOTE> <BODY> <DD> <FORM> <LI> <TH> TD>

<LI>

A list item for use with <OL>, <UL>, <MENU>, or <DIR>

Attributes:

TYPE="..." (Netscape) The type of bullet or number to label this item with. Possible values are DISC, CIRCLE, SQUARE, A, a, I, i, 1.

VALUE="..." (Netscape) The numeric value this list item should have (affects this item and all below it in <OL> lists).

Can Include: <A> <IMG>
 <EM> <STRONG> <CODE> <SAMP> <KBD> <VAR> <CITE> <TT> <B> <I> <P> <OL> <UL> <DIR> <MENU> <DL> <PRE> <BLOCKQUOTE>

Allowed Inside: <DIR> <MENU> <OL> <UL>

<DL>...</DL>

A definition or glossary list. The COMPACT attribute specifies a formatting that takes less whitespace to present.

Attributes: COMPACT

Can Include: <DT> <DD>

Allowed Inside: <BLOCKQUOTE> <BODY> <DD> <FORM> <LI> <TH> TD>

<DT>

A definition term, as part of a definition list.

Can Include: <A> <IMG>
 <EM> <STRONG> <CODE> <SAMP> <KBD> <VAR> <CITE> <TT> <B> <I>

Allowed Inside: <DL>

<DD>

The corresponding definition to a definition term, as part of a definition list.

Can Include: <A> <IMG>
 <EM> <STRONG> <CODE> <SAMP> <KBD> <VAR> <CITE> <TT> <B> <I> <P> <OL> <UL> <DIR> <MENU> <DL> <PRE> <BLOCKQUOTE> <FORM> <ISINDEX> <TABLE>

Allowed Inside: <DL>

Character Formatting

All the character formatting tags have these features:

Can Include: `<A>` `<IMG>` `<BR>` `<EM>` `<STRONG>` `<CODE>` `<SAMP>` `<KBD>` `<VAR>` `<CITE>` `<TT>` `<B>` `<I>`

Allowed Inside: `<A>` `<ADDRESS>` `<B>` `<CITE>` `<CODE>` `<DD>` `<DT>` `<EM>` `<H1>` `<H2>` `<H3>` `<H4>` `<H5>` `<H6>` `<I>` `<KBD>` `<LI>` `<P>` `<PRE>` `<SAMP>` `<STRONG>` `<TT>` `<VAR>` `<TH>` `TD>`

<EM>...</EM>

Emphasis (usually italic).

<STRONG>...</STRONG>

Stronger emphasis (usually bold).

<CODE>...</CODE>

Code sample (usually Courier).

<KBD>...</KBD>

Text to be typed (usually Courier).

<VAR>...</VAR>

A variable or placeholder for some other value.

<SAMP>...</SAMP>

Sample text.

<DFN>...<DFN>

(Proposed) A definition of a term.

<CITE>...</CITE>

A citation.

<B>...</B>

Boldface text.

<I>...</I>

Italic text.

<TT>...</TT>

Typewriter font.

Other Elements

<HR>

A horizontal rule line.

Attributes:

SIZE="..." (Netscape) The thickness of the rule, in pixels.

WIDTH="..." (Netscape) The width of the rule, in pixels.

ALIGN="..." (Netscape) How the rule line will be aligned on the page. Possible values are LEFT, RIGHT, CENTER.

NOSHADE="..." (Netscape) Causes the rule line to be drawn as a solid black.

Allowed Inside: <BLOCKQUOTE> <BODY> <FORM> <PRE>

A line break.

Attributes:

CLEAR="..." (HTML 3.0) Causes the text to stop flowing around any images. Possible values are RIGHT, LEFT, ALL.

Allowed Inside: <A> <ADDRESS> <B> <CITE> <CODE> <DD> <DT> <EM> <H1> <H2> <H3> <H4> <H5> <H6> <I> <KBD> <LI> <P> <PRE> <SAMP> <STRONG> <TT> <VAR>

<NOBR>...</NOBR> (Netscape)

Causes the enclosed text not to wrap at the edge of the page.

Allowed Inside: <A> <ADDRESS> <B> <CITE> <CODE> <DD> <DT> <EM> <H1> <H2> <H3> <H4> <H5> <H6> <I> <KBD> <LI> <P> <PRE> <SAMP> <STRONG> <TT> <VAR>

<WBR> (Netscape)

Wrap the text at this point only if necessary.

Allowed Inside: <A> <ADDRESS> <B> <CITE> <CODE> <DD> <DT> <EM> <H1> <H2> <H3> <H4> <H5> <H6> <I> <KBD> <LI> <P> <PRE> <SAMP> <STRONG> <TT> <VAR>

<BLOCKQUOTE>... </BLOCKQUOTE>

Used for long quotes or citations.

Can Include: <H1> <H2> <H3> <H4> <H5> <H6> <P> <OL> <UL> <DIR> <MENU> <DL> <PRE> <BLOCKQUOTE> <FORM> <ISINDEX> <HR> <ADDRESS> <TABLE>

Allowed Inside: <BLOCKQUOTE> <BODY> <DD> <FORM> <LI> <TH> TD>

<CENTER>...</CENTER>

All the content enclosed within these tags is centered.

Can Include: <A> <IMG>
 <EM> <STRONG> <CODE> <SAMP> <KBD> <VAR> <CITE> <TT> <B> <I>

Allowed Inside: <BLOCKQUOTE> <BODY> <DD> <FORM> <LI> <TH> TD>

<ADDRESS>...</ADDRESS>

Used for signatures or general information about a document's author.

Can Include: <A> <IMG>
 <EM> <STRONG> <CODE> <SAMP> <KBD> <VAR> <CITE> <TT> <B> <I>

Allowed Inside: <BLOCKQUOTE> <BODY> <FORM>

<BLINK>...</BLINK> (Netscape)

Causes the enclosed text to blink irritatingly.

Font Sizes (Netscape)

<FONT>...</FONT>

Changes the size of the font for the enclosed text.

Attributes:

SIZE="..." The size of the font, from 1 to 7. Default is 3. Can also be specified as a value relative to the current size, for example, +2.

Can Include: <A> <IMG>
 <EM> <STRONG> <CODE> <SAMP> <KBD> <VAR> <CITE> <TT> <B> <I>

Allowed Inside: <A> <ADDRESS> <B> <CITE> <CODE> <DD> <DT> <EM> <H1> <H2> <H3> <H4> <H5> <H6> <I> <KBD> <LI> <P> <PRE> <SAMP> <STRONG> <TT> <VAR>

<BASEFONT>

Sets the default size of the font for the current page.

Attributes:

SIZE="..." The default size of the font, from 1 to 7. Default is 3.

Allowed Inside: <A> <ADDRESS> <B> <CITE> <CODE> <DD> <DT> <EM> <H1> <H2> <H3> <H4> <H5> <H6> <I> <KBD> <LI> <P> <PRE> <SAMP> <STRONG> <TT> <VAR>

Images

<IMG>

Insert an inline image into the document.

Attributes:

ISMAP This image is a clickable image map.

SRC="..." The URL of the image.

ALT="..." A text string that will be displayed in browsers that cannot support images.

ALIGN="..." Determines the alignment of the given image. If LEFT or RIGHT (HTML 3.0, Netscape), the image is aligned to the left or right column, and all following text flows beside that image.

All other values such as TOP, MIDDLE, BOTTOM, or the Netscape only (TEXTTOP, ABSMIDDLE, BASELINE, ABSBOTTOM), determine the vertical alignment of this image with other items in the same line.

VSPACE="..." The space between the image and the text above or below it.

HSPACE="..." The space between the image and the text to its left or right.

WIDTH="..." (HTML 3.0) The width, in pixels, of the image. If WIDTH is not the actual width, the image is scaled to fit.

HEIGHT="..." (HTML 3.0) The width, in pixels, of the image. If HEIGHT is not the actual height, the image is scaled to fit.

BORDER="..." (Netscape only) Draws a border of the specified value in pixels to be drawn around the image. In the case of images that are also links, BORDER changes the size of the default link border.

LOWSRC="..." (Netscape only) The path or URL of an image that will be loaded first, before the image specified in SRC. The value of LOWSRC is usually a smaller or lower resolution version of the actual image.

Allowed Inside: <A> <ADDRESS> <B> <CITE> <CODE> <DD> <DT> <EM> <H1> <H2> <H3> <H4> <H5> <H6> <I> <KBD> <LI> <P> <SAMP> <STRONG> <TT> <VAR>

Forms

<FORM>...</FORM>

Indicates a form.

Attributes:

ACTION="..." The URL of the script to process this form input.

METHOD="..." How the form input will be sent to the gateway on the server side. Possible values are GET and POST.

ENCTYPE="..." Only one value right now: application/x-www-form-urlencoded.

Can Include: <H1> <H2> <H3> <H4> <H5> <H6> <P> <OL> <UL> <DIR> <MENU> <DL> <PRE> <BLOCKQUOTE> <ISINDEX> <TABLE> <HR> <ADDRESS> <INPUT> <SELECT> <TEXTAREA>

Allowed Inside: <BLOCKQUOTE> <BODY> <DD> <LI> <TH> <TD>

<INPUT>

An input widget for a form.

Attributes:

TYPE="..." The type for this input widget. Possible values are CHECKBOX, HIDDEN, RADIO, RESET, SUBMIT, TEXT, or IMAGE.

NAME="..." The name of this item, as passed to the gateway script as part of a name/value pair.

VALUE="..." For a text or hidden widget, the default value; for a check box or radio button, the value to be submitted with the form; for Reset or Submit buttons, the label for the button itself.

SRC="..." The source file for an image.

CHECKED   For checkboxes and radio buttons, indicates that the widget is checked.

SIZE="..." The size, in characters, of a text widget.

MAXLENGTH="..." The maximum number of characters that can be entered into a text widget.

ALIGN="..." For images in forms, determines how the text and image will align (same as with the <IMG> tag).

Allowed Inside: <FORM>

<TEXTAREA>...</TEXTAREA>

Indicates a multiline text entry widget.

Attributes:

NAME="..." The name to be passed to the gateway script as part of the name/value pair.

ROWS="..." The number of rows this text area displays.

COLS="..." The number of columns (characters) this text area displays.

Allowed inside: <FORM>

<SELECT>...</SELECT>

Creates a menu or scrolling list of possible items.

Attributes:

NAME="..." The name that is passed to the gateway script as part of the name/value pair.

SIZE="..." The number of elements to display. If SIZE is indicated, the selection becomes a scrolling list. If no SIZE is given, the selection is a pop-up menu.

MULTIPLE Allows multiple selections from the list.

Can Include: <OPTION>

Allowed Inside: <FORM>

<OPTION>

Indicates a possible item within a <SELECT> widget.

Attributes:

SELECTED With this attribute included, the <OPTION> will be selected by default in the list.

VALUE="..." The value to submit if this <OPTION> is selected when the form is submitted.

Allowed Inside: <SELECT>

<FRAMESET>...<FRAMESET> (Netscape 2.0 and up)

The main container for a frame document.

Attributes:

COLS="column_width_list" The size of the frame's columns in pixels, percentages, or relative scale.

ROWS="row_height_list" The size of the frame's rows in pixels, percentages, or relative scale.

<FRAMES> (Netscape 2.0 and up)

Attributes:

MARGINHEIGHT="value" The height of the frame, in pixels.

MARGINWIDTH="value" The width of the frame, in pixels.

NAME="window_name" Naming the frame enables it for targeting by link in other documents. (Optional)

NORESIZE A flag to denote the frame cannot be resized.

SCROLLING="yes¦no¦auto" Indicates (*yes/no/auto*) whether a frame has scrollbars.

SRC The URL of the document displayed in the frame.

<NOFRAMES>...<NOFRAMES> (Netscape 2.0 and up)

Creates frames that can be viewed by non-frame browsers only. A frames-capable browser ignores the data between the start and end <NOFRAMES> tags.

Tables (HTML 3.0)

<TABLE>...</TABLE>

Creates a table, which can contain a caption (<CAPTION>) and any number of rows (<TR>).

Attributes:

BORDER="..." Indicates whether the table should be drawn with or without a border. In Netscape, BORDER can also have a value indicating the width of the border.

CELLSPACING="..." (Netscape only) The amount of space between the cells in the table.

CELLPADDING="..." (Netscape only) The amount of space between the edges of the cell and its contents.

WIDTH="..." (Netscape only) The width of the table on the page, in either exact pixel values or as a percentage of page width.

Can Include: <CAPTION> <TR>

Allowed Inside: <BLOCKQUOTE> <BODY> <DD> <LI> <FORM>

<CAPTION>...</CAPTION>

The caption for the table.

Attributes:

ALIGN="..." The position of the caption. Possible values are TOP and BOTTOM.

<TR>...</TR>

Defines a table row, containing headings and data (<TR> and <TH> tags).

Attributes:

ALIGN="..." The horizontal alignment of the contents of the cells within this row. Possible values are LEFT, RIGHT, CENTER.

VALIGN="..." The vertical alignment of the contents of the cells within this row. Possible values are TOP, MIDDLE, BOTTOM, and BASELINE (Netscape only).

Can Include: <TH> <TD>

Allowed Inside: <TABLE>

<TH>...</TH>

Defines a table heading cell.

Attributes:

ALIGN="..." The horizontal alignment of the contents of the cell. Possible values are LEFT, RIGHT, CENTER.

VALIGN="..." The vertical alignment of the contents of the cell. Possible values are TOP, MIDDLE, BOTTOM, and BASELINE (Netscape only).

ROWSPAN="..." The number of rows this cell will span.

COLSPAN="..." The number of columns this cell will span.

NOWRAP Do not automatically wrap the contents of this cell.

WIDTH="..." (Netscape only) The width of this column of cells, in exact pixel values or as a percentage of the table width.

Can Include: <H1> <H2> <H3> <H4> <H5> <H6> <P> <OL> <UL> <DIR> <MENU> <DL> <PRE> <BLOCKQUOTE> <FORM> <ISINDEX> <HR> <ADDRESS> <TABLE>

Allowed Inside: <TR>

<TD>...</TD>

Defines a table data cell.

Attributes:

ALIGN="..." The horizontal alignment of the contents of the cell. Possible values are LEFT, RIGHT, CENTER.

VALIGN="..." The vertical alignment of the contents of the cell. Possible values are TOP, MIDDLE, BOTTOM, and BASELINE (Netscape only).

ROWSPAN="..." The number of rows this cell will span.

COLSPAN="..." The number of columns this cell will span.

NOWRAP   Do not automatically wrap the contents of this cell.

WIDTH="..." (Netscape only) The width of this column of cells, in exact pixel values or as a percentage of the table width.

Can Include: <H1> <H2> <H3> <H4> <H5> <H6> <P> <OL> <UL> <DIR> <MENU> <DL> <PRE> <BLOCKQUOTE> <FORM> <ISINDEX> <HR> <ADDRESS> <TABLE>

Allowed Inside: <TR>

Internet Explorer 2.0 Tags

<BODY>

You can add BGPROPERTIES=FIXED to the <BODY> tag to get a nonscrolling background. <BODY BACKGROUND="mybackground.gif" BGPROPERTIES=FIXED>

<TABLE>

Internet Explorer 2.0 fully supports tables as specified in the HTML 3.0 draft standard. Using the ALIGN=RIGHT or ALIGN=LEFT attributes, you can set the alignment of your tables. Using the BGCOLOR=#nnnnnn attribute, you can specify a different color for each cell in a table.

<IMG>

You can add video clips (.AVI files) to your pages with a string of new attributes to the <IMG> tag, most notably the dynamic source feature, DYNSRC=URL. You can integrate video clips in such a way as to not exclude viewers without video-enabled browsers. If your browser supports inline clips, you see the video; if not, you see a still image.<IMG SRC="earth.gif" DYNSRC="spinearht.avi">

You can use START=FILEOPEN or START=MOUSEOVER and a variety of LOOP commands to gauge when and for how long the clip is played.

<BGSOUND>

You can now use soundtracks for your web pages. Samples or MIDI formats are accepted. <BGSOUND SRC="whistle.wav">

You can use LOOP features to specify the repetition of the background sound.

<MARQUEE>

As you might guess, this new tag offers your pages a scrolling text marquee. Your text can appear using different attributes, such as ALIGN=RIGHT and can have behaviors of SLIDE, SCROLL (the default), and ALTERNATE.<MARQUEE ALIGN=MIDDLE>Buy Low, Sell High!<MARQUEE>

Character Entities

Table B.1 contains the possible numeric and character entities for the ISO-Latin-1 (ISO8859-1) character set. Where possible, the character is shown.

> **NOTE**
>
> Not all browsers can display all characters, and some browsers may even display different characters from those that appear in the table. Newer browsers seem to have a better track record for handling character entities, but be sure and test your HTML files extensively with multiple browsers if you intend to use these entities.

Table B.1. ISO-Latin-1 character set.

Character	Numeric Entity	Character Entity (if any)	Description
	&#00;–&#08;		Unused
	&#09;		Horizontal tab
	&#10;		Line feed
	&#11;–&#31;		Unused
	&#32;		Space
!	&#33;		Exclamation mark
"	&#34;	&quot;	Quotation mark
#	&#35;		Number sign
$	&#36;		Dollar sign
%	&#37;		Percent sign
&	&#38;	&amp;	Ampersand

continues

Table B.1. continued

Character	Numeric Entity	Character Entity (if any)	Description
`	&#39;		Apostrophe
(	&#40;		Left parenthesis
)	&#41;		Right parenthesis
*	&#42;		Asterisk
+	&#43;		Plus sign
,	&#44;		Comma
-	&#45;		Hyphen
.	&#46;		Period (fullstop)
/	&#47;		Solidus (slash)
0–9	0–9		Digits 0–9
:	&#58;		Colon
;	&#59;		Semi-colon
<	&#60;	&lt;	Less than
=	&#61;		Equals sign
>	&#62;	&gt;	Greater than
?	&#63;		Question mark
@	&#64;		Commercial at
A–Z	A–Z		Letters A–Z
[	&#91;		Left square bracket
\	&#92;		Reverse solidus (backslash)
]	&#93;		Right square bracket
^	&#94;		Caret
_	&#95;		Horizontal bar
`	&#96;		Grave accent
a–z	a–z		Letters a–z
{	&#123;		Left curly brace
|	&#124		Vertical bar
}	&#125;		Right curly brace
~	&#126;		Tilde

Character	Numeric Entity	Character Entity (if any)	Description
	&#127;–		Unused
¡	&#161;		Inverted exclamation
¢	&#162;		Cent sign
£	&#163;		Pound sterling
¤	&#164;		General currency sign
¥	&#165;		Yen sign
¦	&#166;		Broken vertical bar
§	&#167;		Section sign
¨	&#168;		Umlaut (dieresis)
©	&#169;		Copyright
ª	&#170;		Feminine ordinal
‹	&#171;		Left angle quote, guillemet left
¬	&#172;		Not sign
	&#173;		Soft hyphen
®	&#174;		Registered trademark
¯	&#175;		Macron accent
°	&#176;		Degree sign
±	&#177;		Plus or minus
²	&#178;		Superscript two
³	&#179;		Superscript three
´	&#180;		Acute accent
µ	&#181;		Micro sign
¶	&#182;		Paragraph sign
·	&#183;		Middle dot
¸	&#184;		Cedilla
¹	&#185;		Superscript one
º	&#186;		Masculine ordinal
›	&#187;		Right angle quote, guillemet right

continues

Table B.1. continued

Character	Numeric Entity	Character Entity (if any)	Description
1/4	¼		Fraction one-fourth
1/2	½		Fraction one-half
3/4	¾		Fraction three-fourths
¿	¿		Inverted question mark
À	À	À	Capital A, grave accent
Á	Á	Á	Capital A, acute accent
Â	Â	Â	Capital A, circumflex accent
Ã	Ã	Ã	Capital A, tilde
Ä	Ä	Ä	Capital A, dieresis or umlaut mark
Å	Å	Å	Capital A, ring
Æ	Æ	Æ	Capital AE dipthong (ligature)
Ç	Ç	Ç	Capital C, cedilla
È	È	È	Capital E, grave accent
É	É	É	Capital E, acute accent
Ê	Ê	Ê	Capital E, circumflex accent
Ë	Ë	Ë	Capital E, dieresis or umlaut mark
Ì	Ì	Ì	Capital I, grave accent
Í	Í	Í	Capital I, acute accent
Î	Î	Î	Capital I, circumflex accent
Ï	Ï	Ï	Capital I, dieresis or umlaut mark

Character	Numeric Entity	Character Entity (if any)	Description
Ñ	&#209;	&Ntilde;	Capital N, tilde
Ò	&#210;	&Ograve;	Capital O, grave accent
Ó	&#211;	&Oacute;	Capital O, acute accent
Ô	&#212;	&Ocirc;	Capital O, circumflex accent
Õ	&#213;	&Otilde;	Capital O, tilde
Ö	&#214;	&Ouml;	Capital O, dieresis or umlaut mark
¥	&#215;		Multiply sign
Ø	&#216;	&Oslash;	Capital O, slash
Ù	&#217;	&Ugrave;	Capital U, grave accent
Ú	&#218;	&Uacute;	Capital U, acute accent
Û	&#219;	&Ucirc;	Capital U, circumflex accent
Ü	&#220;	&Uuml;	Capital U, dieresis or umlaut mark
Ý	&#221;	&Yacute;	Capital Y, acute accent
Þ	&#222;	&THORN;	Capital THORN, Icelandic
ß	&#223;	&szlig;	Small sharp s, German (sz ligature)
à	&#224;	&agrave;	Small a, grave accent
á	&#225;	&aacute;	Small a, acute accent
â	&#226;	&acirc;	Small a, circumflex accent

continues

Table B.1. continued

Character	Numeric Entity	Character Entity (if any)	Description
ã	`&#227;`	`&atilde;`	Small a, tilde
ä	`&#228;`	`&aauml;`	Small a, dieresis or umlaut mark
å	`&#229;`	`&aring;`	Small a, ring
æ	`&#230;`	`&aelig;`	Small ae dipthong (ligature)
ç	`&#231;`	`&ccedil;`	Small c, cedilla
è	`&#232;`	`&egrave;`	Small e, grave accent
é	`&#233;`	`&eacute;`	Small e, acute accent
ê	`&#234;`	`&ecirc;`	Small e, circumflex accent
ë	`&#235;`	`&euml;`	Small e, dieresis or umlaut mark
ì	`&#236;`	`&igrave;`	Small i, grave accent
í	`&#237;`	`&iacute;`	Small i, acute accent
î	`&#238;`	`&icirc;`	Small i, circumflex accent
ï	`&#239;`	`&iuml;`	Small i, dieresis or umlaut mark
u	`&#240;`	`&eth;`	Small eth, Icelandic
ñ	`&#241;`	`&ntilde;`	Small n, tilde
ò	`&#242;`	`&ograve;`	Small o, grave accent
ó	`&#243;`	`&oacute;`	Small o, acute accent
ô	`&#244;`	`&ocirc;`	Small o, circumflex accent
õ	`&#245;`	`&otilde;`	Small o, tilde
ö	`&#246;`	`&ouml;`	Small o, dieresis or umlaut mark
÷	`&#247;`		Division sign
ø	`&#248;`	`&oslash;`	Small o, slash
ù	`&#249;`	`&ugrave;`	Small u, grave accent

Character	Numeric Entity	Character Entity (if any)	Description
ú	&#250;	&uacute;	Small u, acute accent
û	&#251;	&ucirc;	Small u, circumflex accent
ü	&#252;	&uuml;	Small u, dieresis or umlaut mark
ý	&#253;	&yacute;	Small y, acute accent
ÿ	&#255;	&yuml;	Small y, dieresis or umlaut mark

Netscape and
Internet Explorer
Extensions

B

Background Sounds and Documents with Sound Tracks

`<BGSOUND>` adds a soundtrack to a document.

The `<BGSOUND>` tag has the following attributes:

> SRC specifies the source audio file.
>
> LOOP specifies the number of times the video plays.

To loop as long as the reader is on the page, set the value to: LOOP=INFINITE or LOOP=-1.

LOOPDELAY defines how many milliseconds the video waits before looping.

	HTML 3.0	Netscape 1.0	Netscape 2.0	IE 1.0	IE 2.0
`<BGSOUND>`	no	no	no	no	yes

Blinking Text

To make text blink, you use the `<BLINK>` tag. For example:

`<BLINK> Text that blinks on and off</BLINK>`

	HTML 3.0	Netscape 1.0	Netscape 2.0	IE 1.0	IE 2.0
`<BLINK>`	no	yes	yes	no	no

Body Tag Extensions

The main part of an HTML document, the body, is defined as

`<BODY> The body section of the document </BODY>`

These extensions are added to the `<BODY>` tag:

> BACKGROUND specifies an image to be used as the background for the document, such as `<BODY BACKGROUND="concrete.gif">`.
>
> BGCOLOR="#rrggbb" specifies a color for the background.
>
> BGPROPERTIES adds a special background to a document called a watermark. It is used with this value:
> BGPROPERTIES=FIXED
>
> TEXT="#rrggbb" specifies the color for normal text.

`LINK="#rrggbb"` specifies the color for links that are unvisited.

`ALINK="#rrggbb"` specifies the color for active links.

`VLINK="#rrggbb"` specifies the color for visited links. Internet Explorer enables you to specify a color name instead of a hexadecimal value.

`BGCOLOR="name"` specifies the color for the background.

`TEXT="name"` specifies the color for normal text.

`TEXT="name"` specifies the color for normal text.

`LINK="name"` specifies the color for links that are unvisited.

`ALINK="name"` specifies the color for active links.

`VLINK="name"` specifies the color for visited links.

	HTML 3.0	Netscape 1.0	Netscape 2.0	IE 1.0	IE 2.0
ALINK=#rrggbb	yes	yes	yes	yes	yes
ALINK=name	no	no	no	yes	yes
BACKGROUND=image.gif	yes	yes	yes	yes	yes
BGCOLOR=#rrggbb	yes	yes	yes	yes	yes
BGCOLOR=name	no	no	no	yes	yes
BGPROPERTIES=FIXED	no	no	no	yes	yes
LINK=#rrggbb	yes	yes	yes	yes	yes
LINK=name	no	no	no	yes	yes
TEXT=#rrggbb	yes	yes	yes	yes	yes
TEXT=name	no	no	no	yes	yes
VLINK=#rrggbb	yes	yes	yes	yes	yes
VLINK=name	no	no	no	yes	yes

Centering Text

To center text, you can use these tags:

`<CENTER> This text is centered</CENTER>`

`<P ALIGN=CENTER>A better way to center paragraphs of text.</P>`

`<H1 ALIGN=CENTER>A better way to center headers</H1>`

`<DIV ALIGN=CENTER> A better way to center text and objects in a section</DIV>`

	HTML 3.0	Netscape 1.0	Netscape 2.0	IE 1.0	IE 2.0
`<CENTER>`	no	yes	yes	yes	yes
`<DIV>`	yes	no	yes	no	no
`<P ALIGN=CENTER>`	yes	yes	yes	yes	yes

Dynamic Sources to Create Inline Motion Video

DYNSRC enables you to specify an SRC image and a DYNSRC video.

The value you assign to the DYNSRC attribute is the URL to your video, such as

`<IMG SRC="SUNSET.GIF" DYNSRC="SUNSET.AVI">`

The following attributes for the `<IMG>` tag are to be used with dynamic sources:

> CONTROLS adds a basic set of user controls below the video frame.
>
> LOOP specifies the number of times the video plays. To loop as long as the reader is on the page, set the value to LOOP=INFINITE or LOOP=-1.
>
> LOOPDELAY specifies how many milliseconds the video waits before looping.
>
> START sets the video so it will play automatically. The two values for this attribute are
>
>> START=FILEOPEN—Start automatically when the file is fully opened.
>>
>> START=MOUSEOVER—Start automatically when the user moves the mouse over the video.

	HTML 3.0	Netscape 1.0	2.0	IE 1.0	IE 2.0
`<IMG DYNSRC=VIDEO.AVI>`	no	no	no	no	yes

Embedded Multimedia Objects and Plug-ins

`<EMBED>` specifies plug-ins and embedded multimedia objects.

The attributes for this tag are defined by the plug-in you are using. The primary attribute SRC is used as follows:

`<EMBED SRC="AFILE.PDF">`

	HTML 3.0	Netscape 1.0	Netscape 2.0	IE 1.0	IE 2.0
<EMBED>	no	no	yes	no	no

Font Enhancements

Both the Netscape Navigator and the Internet Explorer support many useful font enhancements. The next sections provide an exploration of all of them.

Base Font

You use the <BASEFONT> tag to define a base font size and can later change the font size relative to the base font. Use the SIZE attribute to specify relative size values between 1 and 7. The relative size 3 is the size of normal text. Size 1 is the smallest text. Size 7 is the largest text. For example:

```
<BASEFONT SIZE=7>  .  .  .  </BASEFONT>
```

Font Characteristics

To define the characteristics of fonts, you use the <FONT> tag. While both begin and end FONT tags are specified, you generally only use the end tag when you want to set an area of text to the characteristics specified. The <FONT> tag has the following attributes:

COLOR specifies font color.

FACE specifies font typeface.

SIZE specifies font size.

Font Color

Using the COLOR attribute for the <FONT> tag, you can set the font color with a predefined color name, such as

```
<FONT COLOR="name">
```

The currently defined color names are the following:

Aqua
Black
Blue
Gray
Green
Lime
Maroon
Navy

Olive
Purple
Red
Silver
Teal
White
Yellow

Hexadecimal values are used to represent the red, green, and blue content of the color. The basic form of the value is preceded by a number sign:

```
<FONT COLOR=#rrggbb>
```

Here are the hexadecimal values for the defined color names:

Color	Hexadecimal Values
Black	00 00 00
Blue	00 00 FF
Brown	99 66 33
Cream	FF FB F0
Cyan	00 FF FF
Dark Blue	00 00 80
Dark Gray	80 80 80
Dark Green	00 80 00
Dark Purple	80 00 80
Dark Red	80 00 00
Dark Yellow	80 80 00
Grass Green	C0 DC C0
Green	00 FF 00
Light Gray	C0 C0 C0
Medium Gray	A0 A0 A4
Purple	FF 00 FF
Red	FF 00 00
Sky Blue	A6 CA F0
White	FF FF FF
Yellow	00 FF FF

Font Face

You define the precise fonts to use with the FACE attribute of the <FONT> tag. The Internet Explorer browser tries each font face in turn and uses, if available. If none of the specified font faces are available, the default font is used. You can specify multiple font types as follows:

```
<FONT FACE="Arial Narrow","Lucida Handwriting","Times New Roman">
```

Font Size

To define the font size relative to the base font, you can precede the size value by + or − to indicate a relative change to the base font size, such as

```
<BASEFONT SIZE=3>
<P>Text is displayed in font size 2.
<FONT SIZE=-2><P>Text is displayed in font size 1.</FONT>
<FONT SIZE=+2><P>Text is displayed in font size 5.</FONT>
```

	HTML 3.0	*Netscape 1.0*	*Netscape 2.0*	*IE 1.0*	*IE 2.0*
`<BASEFONT>`	no	yes	yes	yes	yes
`<FONT COLOR=#rrggbb>`	no	no	no	yes	yes
`<FONT COLOR=name>`	no	no	no	yes	yes
`<FONT FACE=fontname>`	no	no	no	yes	yes
`<FONT SIZE=n>`	no	yes	yes	yes	yes

Frames

Frames enable you to create documents with multiple windows.

	HTML 3.0	*Netscape 1.0*	*Netscape 2.0*	*IE 1.0*	*IE 2.0*
`FRAMESET`	no	no	yes	no	no
`FRAME`	no	no	yes	no	no

Individual Frames

`<FRAME>` is used to specify the attributes of a frame. Attributes for the `<FRAME>` tag include

> `MARGINHEIGHT` defines the top and bottom margin size for the frame. The minimum margin size is 1.
>
> `MARGINWIDTH` defines the left and right margin size for the frame. The minimum margin size is also 1.
>
> `NAME` names a frame so you can target it from other frames on the page.
>
> `NORESIZE` turns off the resizing feature.
>
> `SCROLLING` displays the frame with or without scroll bars. The three attributes are
> ```
> SCROLLING=AUTO
> SCROLLING=NO
> SCROLLING=YES
> ```
>
> `SRC` specifies the source document for the frame.

NOFRAME Area

<NOFRAME> denotes a section of a document that will be used by browsers that cannot use frames. Normally this area contains the full text of your original document.

Setting the Frame

<FRAMESET> denotes a section of a document that will be used by frame-capable browsers. The only valid tag within the <FRAMESET> tag is <FRAME>. Valid attributes are

> ROWS defines the number and size of the rows to display in your browser window. The vertical size of a row is expressed as an absolute or relative value with multiple row assignments separated by a comma. The number of rows is equal to the number of items in the comma separated list.

> COLS defines the number and size of the columns to display in your browser window. The size of a column is expressed as an absolute or relative value with multiple column assignments separated by a comma. The number of columns is equal to the number of items in the comma-separated list.

Column and row size can be defined in three ways:

1. As an absolute value in pixels
2. As a relative value in percentage of window width
3. As a relative value following the CALS table model syntax

In the example below, the window is divided into two columns. The first column is divided into three rows. The second column extends the full length of the window. The first source assignment fills the frame in the first frame in column one, which is in the upper-left corner. The second source assignment fills the frame in the middle of column one. The third source assignment fills the frame in the bottom column one.

```
<FRAMESET COLS="25%,75%">
<FRAMESET ROWS="25%,25%,50%">
<FRAME SRC="titlepage.htm">
<FRAME SRC="subtitlepage.htm">
<FRAME SRC="menu.htm">
</FRAMESET>
<FRAME SRC="homepage.htm">
</FRAMESET>
```

Targeting Frames

Target the frame called MAIN as follows:

```
<A HREF="subpage.html" TARGET="MAIN">
```

Assign a base target for all links in a document as follows:

```
<BASE TARGET="MAIN">
```

The NAME and TARGET attributes can be used to establish the current document's relationship to other documents as follows:

_blank—Load this link into a new, unnamed window.

_self—Load this link over yourself.

_parent—Load this link over yourself and reset the window.

_top—Load this link at the top level.

Horizontal Rules

<HR> inserts horizontal rule. These extensions have been added:

ALIGN aligns a horizontal rule the left margin, right margin or center of the page with the values:

ALIGN=RIGHT

ALIGN=LEFT

ALIGN=CENTER

NOSHADE defines rules without shading.

SIZE defines the size of a horizontal rule in terms of pixels.

WIDTH defines the length of the horizontal rule in pixels or as the percentage of the browser's window width:

<HR WIDTH=10>—horizontal rule 10 pixels long

<HR WIDTH=5%>—horizontal rule 5 percent of the screen width

	HTML 3.0	Netscape 1.0	Netscape 2.0	IE 1.0	IE 2.0
<HR SIZE>	no	yes	yes	yes	yes
<HR ALIGN=LEFT>	no	yes	yes	yes	yes
<HR ALIGN=RIGHT>	no	yes	yes	yes	yes
<HR ALIGN=CENTER>	no	yes	yes	yes	yes
<HR WIDTH>	no	yes	yes	yes	yes

Image Tag Enhancements

<IMG> inserts inline images into your publication. The ALIGN attribute is used to position images in the page and has these values:

ALIGN=TOP
ALIGN=BOTTOM
ALIGN=MIDDLE
ALIGN=LEFT
ALIGN=RIGHT

```
ALIGN=TEXTTOP
ALIGN=ABSMIDDLE
ALIGN=ABSBOTTOM
ALIGN=BASELINE
```

Additional attributes include

BORDER indicates the pixel size of the border to be drawn around an image.

HSPACE increases the pixel size of the horizontal margins around the image.

VSPACE increases the pixel size of the vertical margins surrounding the image.

LOWSRC is a low-resolution image to display before a high-resolution image is displayed.

	HTML 3.0	Netscape 1.0	Netscape 2.0	IE 1.0	IE 2.0
`<IMG ALIGN=ABSBOTTOM>`	no	yes	yes	no	no
`<IMG ALIGN=ABSMIDDLE>`	no	yes	yes	no	no
`<IMG ALIGN=BASELINE>`	no	yes	yes	no	no
`<IMG ALIGN=BOTTOM>`	yes	yes	yes	yes	yes
`<IMG ALIGN=LEFT>`	yes	yes	yes	yes	yes
`<IMG ALIGN=MIDDLE>`	yes	yes	yes	yes	yes
`<IMG ALIGN=RIGHT>`	yes	yes	yes	yes	yes
`<IMG ALIGN=TEXTTOP>`	no	yes	yes	no	no
`<IMG ALIGN=TOP>`	yes	yes	yes	yes	yes
`<IMG BORDER>`	yes	yes	yes	yes	yes
`<IMG HEIGHT>`	yes	yes	yes	yes	yes
`<IMG HSPACE>`	yes	yes	yes	yes	yes
`<IMG LOWSRC>`	no	yes	yes	no	no
`<IMG VSPACE>`	yes	yes	yes	yes	yes
`<IMG WIDTH>`	yes	yes	yes	yes	yes

Line Break Extensions

Both Netscape Navigator and Internet Explorer support line break extensions.

Line Breaks

`<BR>` enables you to break a line without adding a space between the lines and has the attribute CLEAR.

The CLEAR attribute is extremely useful when you want to clear the left, right or both margins after placing an image on the page. Both Netscape and Internet Explorer support the values of

```
<BR CLEAR=LEFT>
<BR CLEAR=RIGHT>
<BR CLEAR=ALL>
```

Nonbreaking Lines

<NOBR> ensures a line of text is displayed as a single line with no line breaks. For example

```
<NOBR> Don't break this line of text no matter what.</NOBR>
```

Word Breaks

<WBR> inserts soft word break into the line of text; the browser will break the line of text at the point you inserted the <WBR> tag if necessary.

	HTML 3.0	*Netscape 1.0*	*Netscape 2.0*	*IE 1.0*	*IE 2.0*
<BR CLEAR=ALL>	yes	yes	yes	yes	yes
<BR CLEAR=LEFT>	yes	yes	yes	yes	yes
<BR CLEAR=RIGHT>	yes	yes	yes	yes	yes
<NOBR>	no	yes	yes	yes	yes
<WBR>	no	yes	yes	yes	yes

List Enhancements

Lists are enhanced with two key attributes: TYPE and START.

List Type

TYPE defines the shape of bullet to use for unordered lists and the style of lettering or numbering to use for ordered lists.

For unordered lists you can use these values with the unordered list tag:

<UL TYPE=CIRCLE> specifies an open circle for the bullet.

<UL TYPE=SQUARE> specifies a square for the bullet.

<UL TYPE=DISC> specifies a solid circle for the bullet, which is the default.

For ordered lists, you can use these values with the ordered list tag:

<OL TYPE=A> specifies capital letters for the ordered list elements.

<OL TYPE=a> specifies lowercase letters for the ordered list elements.

<OL TYPE=I> specifies Roman numerals for the ordered list elements.

<OL TYPE=i> specifies lowercase Roman numerals for the ordered list elements.

<OL TYPE=1> specifies numerals for the ordered list elements, which is the default.

List Start

START sets items in an ordered list to start at specific value.

The following list will start with the Roman numeral III:

<OL TYPE=I START=3>

	HTML 3.0	*Netscape 1.0*	*Netscape 2.0*	*IE 1.0*	*IE 2.0*
<UL TYPE=name>	no	yes	yes	yes	yes
<OL TYPE=x>	no	yes	yes	yes	yes
<OL START=n>	no	yes	yes	yes	yes

Marquees

Text within a <MARQUEE> tag pair with no attributes will scroll continuously from the right to the left.

<MARQUEE> Text you want to scroll </MARQUEE>

The attributes for this tag are

ALIGN specifies how text around the marquee will be aligned. The three values that enable you to align text around the marquee with the top, middle, or bottom of the marquee are
    ALIGN=TOP
    ALIGN=MIDDLE
    ALIGN=BOTTOM
BEHAVIOR specifies the behavior of the text when it moves. The three values you can use are
    BEHAVIOR=SCROLL
    BEHAVIOR=SLIDE
    BEHAVIOR=ALTERNATE
BGCOLOR ="name" specifies a color for the background of the Marquee.

BGCOLOR ="#rrggbb" specifies a color for the background of the marquee.

DIRECTION controls the direction the marquee scrolls in. The two values you can use are
    DIRECTION=LEFT
    DIRECTION=RIGHT

HEIGHT specifies the height of a marquee as an absolute value in pixels or as a relative percentage of screen height. Be sure to include a percent sign after the relative value:

```
HEIGHT=5%
```

HSPACE indicates the amount of horizontal space between the area reserved for the marquee and surrounding text and objects.

LOOP specifies how many times a marquee should loop. The value you assign to LOOP is normally a positive value. However, the values LOOP=INFINITE or LOOP=-1 cause the marquee to loop indefinitely.

SCROLLAMOUNT specifies the number of pixels the marquee moves each time it is drawn on the screen.

SCROLLDELAY specifies the wait in milliseconds between each successive redraw.

VSPACE indicates the amount of vertical space between the area reserved for the marquee and surrounding text and objects.

WIDTH specifies the width of a marquee as an absolute value in pixels or as a relative percentage of screen width. Be sure to include a percent sign after the relative value:

```
WIDTH=50%
```

	HTML 3.0	*Netscape 1.0*	*Netscape 2.0*	*IE 1.0*	*IE 2.0*
\<MARQUEE\>	no	no	no	no	yes

Tables

Table support is shifting to the current definition of tables as specified in the HTML 3.0 draft. You specify the basic components of a HTML 3.0 table as follows:

```
<TABLE>
<THEAD>
Header Information
<TBODY>
Data Set 1
<TBODY>
Data Set 2
<TBODY>
  . . .
<TBODY>
Data Set N
<TFOOT>
Footer Information
</TABLE>
```

Common Table Attributes

Attributes common to most table elements include

CLASS specifies a subclass for a tag. CLASS is normally used to display a tag in a different style based on a class type you've specified in a style sheet.

DIR specifies the direction for text layout. While English text is read from left to right, some Asian languages are read from right to left. Using DIR with the LANG attribute, you can specify the text layout as left to right by setting a value of DIR=LTR or right to left by setting a value of DIR=RTL.

ID labels an element with a keyword. If you activate a hypertext reference containing a keyword that matches the element's ID, the browser will jump to the section of the document containing the ID.

LANG specifies the language to be used for the element. You can use this attribute with the optional DIR attribute if the language is read from right to left instead of left to right.

UNITS specifies the type of unit for all numeric values in the associated tag. The implied default is UNITS=PIXELS. You can also specify en units with UNITS=EN.

	HTML 3.0	*Netscape 1.0*	*Netscape 2.0*	*IE 1.0*	*IE 2.0*
CLASS	yes	no	no	no	no
DIR	yes	no	no	no	no
ID	yes	no	no	no	no
LANG	yes	no	no	no	no
UNITS	yes	no	no	no	no

The <*TABLE*> Tag

Valid attributes for the begin table tag <TABLE> include the following:

BORDER specifies the width for framing around the table.

CELLPADDING specifies the spacing within data cells.

CELLSPACING specifies the spacing between data cells.

COLS specifies the number of columns in a table. If you do not specify the number of columns, the browser will read all table data before displaying any portion of the table.

FLOAT controls the alignment of the table. The two values for this attribute are

```
FLOAT=LEFT
FLOAT=RIGHT
```

FRAME indicates the style of the frame around the table. By default, tables do not have a frame.

You specify the type of framing for a table with these values:

FRAME=NONE—No frame around the table, the default.

FRAME=TOP—Put a frame only on the top of the table.

FRAME=BOTTOM—Put a frame only on the bottom of the table.

FRAME=TOPBOT—Put a frame on the top and bottom of the table.

FRAME=SIDES—Put a frame on the left and right side of the table.

FRAME=ALL—Put a frame on all four sides of the table.

FRAME=BORDER—Put a frame on all four sides of the table, which is the same as the value ALL.

RULES specifies the type of horizontal and vertical lines to display within a table. The values for the RULES attribute are

RULES=NONE—No horizontal or vertical rules separating rows and columns.

RULES=BASIC—Separate the header, body, and footer elements with a horizontal rule.

RULES=ROWS—Separate all rows in the table with horizontal rules and some browsers may add a thicker line to the header, body, and footer elements.

RULES=COLS—Separate all columns in the table with vertical rules and adds horizontal rules between header, body, and footer elements.

RULES=ALL—Separate all elements in the table with horizontal and vertical rules. Some browsers may add a thicker line to the header, body, and footer elements.

WIDTH—the width in units or as a percentage of the current window size. The default WIDTH is the current window size.

	HTML 3.0	Netscape 1.0	Netscape 2.0	IE 1.0	IE 2.0
BORDER	yes	yes	yes	yes	yes
CELLPADDING	yes	yes	yes	yes	yes
CELLSPACING	yes	yes	yes	yes	yes
COLS	yes	no	no	no	no
FLOAT	yes	no	no	no	no
FRAME	yes	no	no	no	no
RULES	yes	no	no	no	no
WIDTH	yes	yes	yes	yes	yes

Table Captions

Add a caption to a table as follows:

```
<CAPTION> . . . </CAPTION>
```

The placement of table captions is specified using the ALIGN attribute as follows:

ALIGN=TOP places the caption above the table.

ALIGN=BOTTOM places the caption below the table.

ALIGN=LEFT places the caption on the left side of the table.

ALIGN=RIGHT places the caption on the right side of the table.

	HTML 3.0	Netscape 1.0	Netscape 2.0	IE 1.0	IE 2.0
ALIGN=TOP	yes	yes	yes	yes	yes
ALIGN=BOTTOM	yes	yes	yes	yes	yes
ALIGN=LEFT	yes	no	no	no	no
ALIGN=RIGHT	yes	no	no	no	no

Table Sections

The main sections of any table are the head, body, and foot elements. The <THEAD>, <TBODY>, and <TFOOT> tags can be used with the following attributes:

ALIGN specifies the horizontal alignment of all cells in the section. You can use these alignment values:
```
ALIGN=LEFT
ALIGN=RIGHT
ALIGN=CENTER
ALIGN=JUSTIFY
ALIGN=CHAR
```
CHAR is used to specify the character you are aligning the cells on, such as CHAR=,.
CHAROFF specifies an offset for the character you are using for alignment.
VALIGN specifies the vertical alignment of all cells in a section. You can use these alignment values:
```
VALIGN=TOP
VALIGN=MIDDLE
VALIGN=BOTTOM
VALIGN=BASELINE
```

Tag Support

	HTML 3.0	Netscape 1.0	Netscape 2.0	IE 1.0	IE 2.0
<THEAD>	yes	no	no	no	no
<TBODY>	yes	no	no	no	no
<TFOOT>	yes	no	no	no	no

Alignment and Attribute Support

	HTML 3.0	Netscape 1.0	Netscape 2.0	IE 1.0	IE 2.0
ALIGN=LEFT	yes	yes	yes	yes	yes
ALIGN=RIGHT	yes	yes	yes	yes	yes
ALIGN=CENTER	yes	yes	yes	yes	yes
ALIGN=JUSTIFY	yes	no	no	no	no
ALIGN=CHAR	yes	no	no	no	no
CHAR	yes	no	no	no	no
CHAROFF	yes	no	no	no	no
VALIGN=TOP	yes	yes	yes	yes	yes
VALIGN=MIDDLE	yes	yes	yes	yes	yes
VALIGN=BOTTOM	yes	yes	yes	yes	yes
VALIGN=BASELINE	yes	yes	yes	yes	yes

Table Columns

<COL> specifies general rules for all the columns within the table.

You can use these attributes with the <COL> tag:

ALIGN specifies the horizontal alignment of cells in a column. You can use these alignment values:

```
ALIGN=LEFT
ALIGN=RIGHT
ALIGN=CENTER
ALIGN=JUSTIFY
ALIGN=CHAR
```

CHAR is used to specify the character you are aligning the column on, such as CHAR=,.

CHAROFF specifies an offset for the character you are using for alignment.

SPAN specifies the number of columns the <COL> tag applies to. The default is one.

VALIGN specifies the vertical alignment of cells in a column. You can use these alignment values:

```
VALIGN=TOP
VALIGN=MIDDLE
VALIGN=BOTTOM
VALIGN=BASELINE
```

WIDTH specifies the relative or absolute width of a column. Values for this attribute can be specified in the current unit as a percentage of window size or using the CALS table model.

	HTML 3.0	*Netscape 1.0*	*Netscape 2.0*	*IE 1.0*	*IE 2.0*
`<COL>`	yes	no	no	no	no

Table Rows

All tables must contain one or more rows of data cells. Table rows are defined with the `<TR>` tag. You can use these alignment attributes:

ALIGN specifies the horizontal alignment of cells in a column. You can use these alignment values:

```
ALIGN=LEFT
ALIGN=RIGHT
ALIGN=CENTER
ALIGN=JUSTIFY
ALIGN=CHAR
```

CHAR is used to specify the character you are aligning the column on, such as CHAR=,.

CHAROFF specifies an offset for the character you are using for alignment.

VALIGN specifies the vertical alignment of cells in a column. You can use these alignment values:

```
VALIGN=TOP
VALIGN=MIDDLE
VALIGN=BOTTOM
VALIGN=BASELINE
```

By making assignments in a table row, you override the defaults, column assignments you made with the `<COL>` tag, and the section assignment you made with the `<THEAD>`, `<TBODY>`, or `<TFOOT>` tags.

	HTML 3.0	*Netscape 1.0*	*Netscape 2.0*	*IE 1.0*	*IE 2.0*
`<TR>`	yes	yes	yes	yes	yes
`<TD>`	yes	yes	yes	yes	yes
`<TH>`	yes	yes	yes	yes	yes

Table Cells

<TD> defines data cells that are displayed in normal type.

<TH> defines heading cells that are displayed in bold type.

Table cells use these attributes:

> ALIGN specifies the horizontal alignment of cells in a column. You can use these alignment values:
> > ALIGN=LEFT
> > ALIGN=RIGHT
> > ALIGN=CENTER
> > ALIGN=JUSTIFY
> > ALIGN=CHAR
>
> AXIS labels one cell with a keyword (not displayed).
>
> AXES labels row and header attributes that pertain to the cell (not displayed).
>
> BGCOLOR ="name" specifies a color for the background of the marquee.
>
> BGCOLOR ="#rrggbb" specifies a color for the background of the marquee.
>
> CHAR is used to specify the character you are aligning the column on, such as: CHAR=,.
>
> CHAROFF specifies an offset for the character you are using for alignment.
>
> VALIGN specifies the vertical alignment of cells in a column. You can use these alignment values:
> > VALIGN=TOP
> > VALIGN=MIDDLE
> > VALIGN=BOTTOM
> > VALIGN=BASELINE
>
> COLSPAN—Creates cells that span two or more columns.
>
> ROWSPAN—Creates cells that span two or more rows.
>
> NOWRAP—Disables the automatic wrapping of text.

By making assignments in a table cell, you override the defaults and column assignments you made with the <COL> tag, the section assignment you made with the <THEAD>, <TBODY>, or <TFOOT> tags, and the row assignment you made with the <TR> tag.

	HTML 3.0	*Netscape 1.0*	*Netscape 2.0*	*IE 1.0*	*IE 2.0*
ALIGN=LEFT	yes	yes	yes	yes	yes
ALIGN=RIGHT	yes	yes	yes	yes	yes
ALIGN=CENTER	yes	yes	yes	yes	yes
ALIGN=JUSTIFY	yes	no	no	no	no

	HTML 3.0	Netscape 1.0	Netscape 2.0	IE 1.0	IE 2.0
ALIGN=CHAR	yes	no	no	no	no
AXIS	yes	no	no	no	no
AXES	yes	no	no	no	no
BGCOLOR	no	no	no	no	yes
CHAR	yes	no	no	no	no
CHAROFF	yes	no	no	no	no
VALIGN=TOP	yes	yes	yes	yes	yes
VALIGN=MIDDLE	yes	yes	yes	yes	yes
VALIGN=BOTTOM	yes	yes	yes	yes	yes
VALIGN=BASELINE	yes	yes	yes	yes	yes
COLSPAN	yes	yes	yes	yes	yes
ROWSPAN	yes	yes	yes	yes	yes
NOWRAP	yes	yes	yes	yes	yes

SGML

C

If Chapter 19, "Should You Upgrade to SGML?" piqued your interest in SGML, this appendix is a good starting reference for you. It provides several tables of information on SGML tags and attributes, as well as sample SGML element and attribute declarations.

An SGML document is actually composed of three parts: the SGML declaration, the Document Type Declaration (DTD), and the marked-up document (containing the content).

SGML Declaration

The SGML declaration defines the character set that is to be used, as well as delimiters used for the markup. It is used by the system to determine whether or not a document can be processed without additional modification by the system receiving the processing request.

SGML classifies characters as follows:

Type	Description	Character
Non-SGML characters	All UNUSED or SHUNNED characters, except FUNCTION characters	in ISO 646: 0-8, 11-12, 14-31, 127
SGML characters	FUNCTION characters that have purpose	RE, RS, SPACE, TAB, SEPCHAR
name	characters that can be used in a name	A-Z, 0-9, .,-
delimiters	characters that cause the text to be interpreted as markup instead of data	See Delimiter Table
data	all other characters	#PCDATA

When you create SGML documents, you should always follow the syntax rules. By following these rules, you will ensure your document displays properly and is portable to other platforms. In general, SGML defines syntax in terms of

- Concrete SGML syntax
- Reference concrete syntax

Concrete SGML Syntax

Defining a concrete SGML syntax is assigning a character to a particular role. This includes *delimiter roles, control characters, naming rules, reserved names,* and *capacities.* For example, the start-tag open delimiter STAGO is normally defined as the less than symbol (<). This means that whenever a tag is inserted in the text, the first character that signals that this is *markup*, not *data*, is the <.

The concrete syntax can also describe the following elements:

Delimiter roles.

FUNCTION classes for character sets, special characters, syntax, and capacities.

Naming rules—If special characters, such as #, %, or & are not allowed in names, you can define these rules.

Quantities—You can limit the number of characters allowed for the title of a column in a table.

Reserved names and keywords.

Delimiter Roles

The SGML language uses *delimiter roles* to define its syntax. This causes text to be interpreted as markup instead of data. For example, if you were not to define delimiters for the start and end characters for a tag, the contents of the tag would be printed as text in your document. This is what is known as an abstract syntax.

Each delimiter is identified by a name in the *abstract syntax* and defined by a character string in the concrete SGML syntax. Table C.1 identifies the standard delimiters used in SGML.

Table C.1. Standard delimiters in SGML.

Glyph	Delimiter Role	ISO 646 #	Abstract Name
&	and connector	38	AND
- -	comment start or end	45 45	COM
&#	character reference open	38 35	CRO
]	declaration subset close	93	DSC
[	declaration subset open	91	DSO
]	data tag group close	93	DTGC
[	data tag group open	91	DTGO
&	entity reference open	38	ERO
</	end-tag open	60 47	ETAGO
)	group close	41	GRPC
(	group open	40	GRPO
"	literal start or end	34	LIT
'	literal start or end (alternative)	39	LITA
>	markup declaration close	62	MDC
<!	markup declaration open	60 33	MDO
-	minus; exclusion	45	MINUS
]]	marked section close	93 93	MSC
/	null end tag	47	NET

continues

Table C.1. continued

Glyph	Delimiter Role	ISO 646 #	Abstract Name
?	optional occurrence indicator	63	OPT
¦	or connector	124	OR
%	parameter entity reference open	37	PERO
>	processing instruction close	62	PIC
<?	processing instruction open	60 63	PIC
+	required and repeatable; inclusion	43	PLUS
;	reference close	59	REFC
*	optional and repeatable	42	REP
#	reserved name indicator	35	RNI
,	sequence connector	44	SEQ
<	start-tag open	60	STAGO
>	tag close	62	TAGC
=	value indicator	61	VI

When changing delimiter definitions, remember:

1. The delimiter must be different from any other delimiter that may be recognized in the same mode to avoid ambiguity problems.

2. Avoid using name start characters or numbers in a delimiter string. For example, using <s as the start-tag open would make it impossible for you to have any elements whose name begins with the *s* character.

3. Delimiter strings must be less than NAMELEN characters in length.

You could change any delimiter in the reference concrete syntax after the DELIM keyword as follows:

1. Give the abstract name for the delimiter.

2. Follow the abstract name with a numeric character reference.

EXAMPLE: To change the delimiter for end-tag open from </ to :/, enter the following:

```
DELIM GENERAL SGMLREF
    ETAGO    "&#58;&#47;"    -- ":/" --
```

NOTE

If the previous reference looks like Greek, you may want to look back to Chapter 19, "Should You Upgrade to SGML?," and review the basics of SGML. Sometimes it helps to break down SGML references and declarations into parts. Here's how the previous reference is broken down:

```
DELIM GENERAL SGMLREF                              The first line of the
reference states that you are creating a general SGML reference for a
delimiter.
ETAGO    "&#58;&#47;"    -- ":/" --            The second line states
that the delimiter you are defining is the end-tag open delimiter.
```

The second line of the reference can be further broken down as follows:

```
"&#58;&#47;"                                     The first character to
be used for the delimiter, the colon, is specified by the numeric entity
&#58;. The number 58 corresponds to the colon character in the standard ISO
character set. The second character to be used for the delimiter, the
forward slash, is specified by the numeric entity &#47;. The number 47
corresponds to the forward slash character in the standard ISO character
set.
-- ":/" --                                       The double hyphen
indicates the start or end of a comment. Here, the SGML author is making a
comment that the numeric entities translate to :/.
```

Function Classes

Declarations for character sets and special characters can loosely be grouped together as function classes. You will find the declarations listed in Table C.2 are extremely useful when specifying character sets and related information such as capacity, scope, and syntax.

Table C.2. Function classes for defining character sets.

Declaration Keyword	Parameter	Description
CHARSET	Document character set	Begins description of a document character set
BASESET	Public identifier for character base set	Base character set for document
DESCSET	0 9 UNUSED	Documents base character set, in terms of the base set
CAPACITY	Public identifier	Limits not to be exceeded by document
SCOPE	DOCUMENT	Syntax applies to DTD as well as document

continues

Table C.2. continued

Declaration Keyword	Parameter	Description
SYNTAX	Public identifier	Syntax used by document. The reference concrete syntax can be used. If the reference concrete syntax is modified, it is referred to as a variant concrete syntax.
FEATURES	Start of features	Describes features used, such as EXPLICIT, MINIMIZE
APPINFO	NONE	Application-specific information that is applicable to the document

If no application-specific information is entered in the declaration, the default of NONE is used.

In SGML, you can use and define the meaning of special characters in many ways. One important way to define special characters is with function classes, such as those shown in Table C.3.

Table C.3. Function classes for defining special characters.

Name	Description/Definition
FUNCHAR	Identifies characters that may have some significance to the system but that have no SGML function defined.
MSOCHAR	Identifies characters that inhibit the recognition of markup (markup scan out) in the data that follow. The MSICHAR function character is used to restore markup recognition.
MSICHAR	Identifies characters that restore markup (markup scan in) recognition when it was suppressed by the use of a character defined as a MSOCHAR character.
MSSCHAR	Identifies characters that inhibit the recognition of markup (markup scan suppress) for the character that immediately follows the function character in the same entity.
SEPCHAR	Identifies characters that are allowed as separators (like RE, RS, and SPACE) and will be replaced by SPACE in all contexts in which RE is replaced by SPACE. TAB is often defined as a separator character.

Naming Rules

Naming rules are another important part of SGML syntax. When you specify naming rules, you set how SGML elements, entities, and attributes are named. You can change or set the naming rules using the naming rule category declarations shown in Table C.4.

Table C.4. Naming rules.

Category	Description
LCNMSTRT	Lowercase name start characters. These characters are considered lowercase and may be used as the first character in a name.
UCNMSTRT	Uppercase name start characters. These characters are considered uppercase and may be used as the first character in a name. Characters may occur multiple times in this definition to allow different lowercase characters to map to the same uppercase character. For letters that do not distinguish between lower and uppercase, the same character is used in both LCNMSTRT and UCNMSTRT.
LCNMCHAR	Lowercase name characters. These are considered lowercase and may be used within a name.
UCNMCHAR	Uppercase name characters. These are considered uppercase and may be used in names.
NAMECASE	Used to determine the extent of uppercase substitution during markup processing.
	Used to determine whether case may be used to differentiate entity names, attribute names, etc.
	If using this category, you must declare Yes or No for each specification in the declaration.

The NAMECASE specifications are

GENERAL—Determines whether all names, name tokens, number tokens and delimiter strings will be converted to uppercase.

ENTITY—Determines whether all entity names and references will be converted to uppercase.

Quantity Sets

Quantities are a set of limits placed on markup constructs. This can be very important when using a parser. The quantity set on a particular item (such as NAMELEN) will determine the size of the buffer in which the parser will store the output. Table C.5 lists the declarations associated with quantity sets.

Table C.5. Quantity set declarations.

Name	Value	Description
ATTCNT	40	The number of attribute names and name tokens in an attribute definition list

continues

Table C.5. continued

Name	Value	Description
ATTSPLEN	960	The normalized length of a start-tag's attribute specifications
BSEQLEN	960	The length of a blank sequence in a short reference string
DTAGLEN	16	The length of a data tag
DTEMPLEN	16	The length of a data tag template or pattern template (undelimited)
ENTLVL	16	Nesting level of entities
GRPCNT	32	Number of tokens in a group
GRPGTCNT	96	Grand total of content tokens at all levels of a content model
GRPLVL	16	Nesting level of model groups (including the first level)
LITLEN	240	Length of a parameter literal or attribute value literal
NAMELEN	8	Length of a name, name token, number, and so on.
NORMSEP	2	Used instead of separators when calculating normalized lengths
PILEN	240	Length of a processing instruction
TAGLEN	960	Length of a tag
TAGLVL	24	Nesting level of open elements

To change a quantity set specification, enter the variant in the declaration as follows:

```
QUANTITY   SGMLREF
           NAMELEN    32
           TAGLVL     30
```

The presence of the SGMLREF is a reminder that unspecified quantities will default to their value in the reference concrete syntax.

An example of an SGML declaration follows, with explanations for the various sections provided in bold italic text:

```
<!SGML    "ISO 8879:1986"
```

```
CHARSET
```
The CHARSET begins the description of the character set to be used for a document. If using IBM mainframes, the character set is called EBCDIC. However, in most cases, ASCII is the character set used. You can map ASCII characters to EBCDIC characters in the DESCSET portion of the declaration

```
BASESET   "ISO 646-1983//CHARSET
 International Reference Version (IRV)//ESC 2/5 4/0"
```
The BASESET defines the public identifier description for the character set you expect to use (or your "base" character set). This must be something that can be used by a receiving system, such as a public text owner identifier (which is shown in this example.)

```
DESCSET
    0     9   UNUSED
    9     2   9
         11     2   UNUSED
         13     1   13
         14    18   UNUSED
         32    95   32
        127     1   UNUSED
        128   128   "High-order characters"
```

The DESCSET provides mapping for the document character set character number being mapped. For example, if you want to map the upper case "A" for both ASCII and EBCDIC, you would provide the mapping information in this section. Also, the number of characters being used is defined here. You must define the mapping for ALL characters that exist in the document character set. In addition, if there are characters which must be used in the document, but are not defined in the public text owner identifier, you would declare them in this section.

```
CAPACITY SGMLREF
    TOTALCAP     200000
    ENTCAP        35000
    ENTCHCAP      35000
    ELEMCAP       35000
    GRPCAP       150000
    EXGRPCAP      35000
    EXNMCAP       35000
    ATTCAP        50000
    ATTCHCAP      35000
    AVGRPCAP      35000
    NOTCAP        35000
    NOTCHCAP      35000
    IDCAP         35000
    IDREFCAP      35000
    MAPCAP        35000
    LKSETCAP      35000
    LKNMCAP       35000
```

Capacities are a "rough" measure of the memory needed to store the results when a parser is used on an SGML DTD. This is used to provide a baseline for conformance for SGML systems. That means that any document that does not exceed the reference capacities and conforms in all other respects must be processed by an SGML system that conforms to the norms.

Capacity sets are calculated using capacity points. One capacity point is equal to one byte. Since these can occasionally generate error messages which are difficult to debug, setting these capacities to maximums you feel are sufficient should resolve this issue. Or, a formal public identifier can be specified which references a file with common capacity specifications.

The SGMLREF is a reminder that undefined elements will default to the values in the reference concrete syntax.

```
SCOPE      DOCUMENT
```

Scope indicates what data are managed by the delimiters and other parts of the syntax which were defined there. This allows the concrete syntax used in the DTD to be different from the syntax in the document instance. This allows users to have a document that uses a local variation, while the public DTD uses the reference concrete syntax. Select scope by choosing DOCUMENT or INSTANCE.

Select **DOCUMENT** to indicate that the DTD and the document instance both use the declared syntax. This means that the SGML declaration always uses the reference concrete syntax, and that the entire SGML document must use the defined document character set.

Select **INSTANCE** if only the document instance is usig the syntax being defined. Remember, the SGML declaration must use the reference concrete syntax.

SYNTAX
Use SYNTAX to signal the start of the syntax definition to define character mapping to delimiter roles, control characters, naming rules, reserved names and quantities used in document markup. You can either use a public syntax by referencing a public identifier, or you can use a full syntax specification, like the one shown below.

```
     SHUNCHAR 0 1 2 3 4 5 6 7 8 9 10 11 12 13 14 15 16 17
            18 19 20 21 22 23 24 25 26 27 28 29 30 31 127
```

SHUNCHAR refers to SHUNNED CHARACTER NUMBER IDENTIFICATION which specifies the characters that should not be used in any document character set using the syntax defined.

```
BASESET  "ISO 646-1983//CHARSET
         International Reference Version (IRV)//ESC 2/5 4/0"
```

BASESET refers to the public identifier description of the character set being used as a base. This description must be in a format that can be recognized by the receiving system, such as a public text owner identifier.

```
DESCSET  0     128    0
         128   128    "High-order characters"
```

DESCSET identifies the document character set character number being mapped, the number of characters being defined and the base set character number which corresponds to the document character set number of the same entry. It may also be used to define non-SGML characters, or it may be the literal which describes the character that exists in the document character set, but not in the base set.

```
FUNCTION    RE    13
            RS    10
            SPACE  32
            TAB    SEPCHAR  9
```

Characters that represent important function characters are declared in this section. Note that the special function character TAB has been declared using the function class SEPCHAR. Special function classes are described in this book in a separate table.

```
NAMING    LCNMSTRT ""
          UCNMSTRT ""
          LCNMCHAR "-."
          UCNMCHAR "-."
          NAMECASE GENERAL YES
               ENTITY  NO
```

Naming rules are declared in this section. These allow you to specify characters to be used in names and as name start characters, as well as rules for upper case usage. This is described in a separate table in this book.

```
DELIM    GENERAL SGMLREF
         SHORTREF SGMLREF
```

Any delimiters defined will be declared in this section. See the delimiter table for a list of default delimiters.

```
NAMES      SGMLREF
```
*This declaration notifies you (by using the SGMLREF keyword) that the reserved
names and keywords to be used will default to the reference concrete syntax. See
the section on Reserved Names for further information.*

```
QUANTITY SGMLREF
        ATTCNT        100
        ATTSPLEN      960
        BSEQLEN         960
        DTAGLEN          16
        DTEMPLEN      16
        ENTLVL          16
        GRPCNT         100
        GRPGTCNT      96
        GRPLVL          16
        LITLEN         800
        NAMELEN         32
        NORMSEP         2
        PILEN         1024
        TAGLEN         960
        TAGLVL          24
```
*The limits on markup constructs are defined in this section. Again, the SGMLREF
notifies you that any undeclared component defaults to the quantity specified in
the reference concrete syntax.*

```
FEATURES
```
*This is the section in the SGML declaration that allows optional features to be
defined by the user.*
```
MINIMIZE DATATAG NO    OMITTAG  YES   RANK     NO    SHORTTAG YES
LINK     SIMPLE  NO    IMPLICIT NO    EXPLICIT NO
OTHER    CONCUR  NO    SUBDOC   NO    FORMAL   YES
APPINFO NONE>
```

Reserved Names and Keywords

Reserved words have a specific role that is identified by its name in the SGML syntax. While SGML enables you to make substitutions in some cases, none of the reserved names used in the SGML declaration may be replaced. Table C.6 lists names and keywords reserved in SGML.

When defining a variant concrete syntax when allowed, the keyword SGMLREF is required. Remember: Unspecified reserved names default to their values in the reference concrete syntax.

Table C.6. Reserved names and keywords in SGML. All keywords that can be changed by defining a variant concrete syntax are noted with an asterisk (*).

A - E	E - M	M - R	R - Z
AND	ETAGO	MSICHAR	RNI
ANY (*)	EXCLUDE	MSOCHAR	RS (*)
APPINFO	EXGRPCAP	MSOCHAR	SCOPE
ASN1	EXNMCAP	MSSCHAR	SDATA (*)

continues

Table C.6. continued

A - E	E - M	M - R	R - Z
ATTCAP	EXPLICIT	NAME (*)	SDIF
ATTCHCAP	FEATURES	NAMECASE	SEPCHAR
ATTCNT	FIXED (*)	NAMELEN	SEQ
ATTLIST (*)	FORMAL	NAMES (*)	SEQUENCE
ATTSPLEN	FUNCHAR	NAMING	SGML
AVGRCAP	FUNCTION	NDATA (*)	SGMLREF
BASESET	GENERAL	NET	SHORTREF (*)
BSEQLEN	GRPC	NMTOKEN (*)	SHORTTAG
CAPACITY	GRPCAP	NMTOKENS (*)	SHUNCHAR
CDATA (*)	GRPCNT	NO	SIMPLE (*)
CHANGES	GRPGTCNT	NONE	SPACE (*)
CHARSET	GRPLVL	NONSGML	SRCNT
COM	GRPO	NORMSEP	SRLEN
CONCUR	ID (*)	NOTATION (*)	STAGO
CONREF (*)	IDCAP	NUMBER (*)	STARTTAG (*)
CONTROLS	IDLINK (*)	NUMBERS (*)	SUBDOCK (*)
CRO	IDREF (*)	NOTCAP	SWITCHES
CURRENT (*)	IDREFCAP	NOTCHCAP	SYNTAX
DATATAG	IDREFS (*)	NUTOKEN (*)	SYSTEM (*)
DEFAULT (*)	IGNORE (*)	NUTOKENS (*)	TAGC
DELIM	IMPLICIT	O (*)	TAGLEN
DELIMLEN	IMPLIED (*)	OMITTAG	TAGLVL
DESCSET	INCLUDE (*)	OPT	TEMP (*)
DOCTYPE (*)	INITIAL (*)	OR	TEXT
DOCUMENT	INSTANCE	OTHER	TOTALCAP
DSC	LCNMCHAR	PACK	UCNMCHAR
DSO	LCNMSTRT	PCDATA (*)	UCNMSTRT
DTAGLEN	LINK (*)	PERO	UNPACK
DTD	LINKTYPE (*)	PI (*)	UNUSED
DTEMPLEN	LIT	PIC	USELINK (*)
DTGC	LITA	PILEN	USEMAP (*)
DTGO	LITLEN	PIO	VALIDATE
ELEMCAP	LKNMCAP	PLUS	VI
ELEMENT (*)	LKSETCAP	POSTLINK (*)	YES
ELEMENTS	LPD	PUBLIC (*)	
EMPTY (*)	MAPCAP	QUANTITY	
ENDTAG (*)	MD (*)	RANK	
ENTCAP	MDC	RCDATA (*)	
ENTCHCAP	MINIMIZE	RE (*)	

A - E	*E - M*	*M - R*	*R - Z*
ENTITIES (*)	MODEL	REP	
ENTLVL	MS (*)	REQUIRED (*)	
ERO	MSC	RESTORE (*)	

Basic SGML Document Syntax

Basic SGML documents are easier to exchange between systems than custom SGML documents. Because every conforming SGML syntax must support the reference concrete syntax or the core concrete syntax, it is desirable to use this syntax wherever possible to provide maximum portability for your documents. The *core concrete syntax* is the reference concrete syntax with NONE as the value for SHORTREF. This means that no short references are allowed.

A document is known as a basic SGML document if it uses the following throughout:

> Reference concrete syntax
> Reference capacity set
> System declaration with only the SHORTTAG and OMITTAG features

Reference Concrete Syntax

The SGML declaration must use the *reference concrete syntax*. The reference concrete syntax is a defined concrete syntax used in the SGML declaration to define other syntaxes. The components of the reference concrete syntax are listed in Table C.7.

There are 31 delimiters defined in the reference concrete syntax. Whenever these characters are to be used in the text as data, you should use entity references. For example, if you want to use the less than sign (<) in your text, and you want to be sure it is not mistaken for an open tag, use the entity reference <.

Table C.7. The components of the reference concrete syntax.

Keyword	*Parameter*	*Explanation*
SYNTAX		Signals the start of the concrete syntax portion of the SGML declaration. This can be followed with a public identifier for a public syntax, or a full syntax specification.

continues

Table C.7. continued

Keyword	Parameter	Explanation
SHUNCHAR	CONTROLS 0 1 2...	Defines control characters that are to be ignored by the parser.
		Shunned characters may be used to represent markup or minimum data characters, but should not be used for ordinary data characters.
		If CONTROLS is used as a keyword, you are indicating that any character number that is used as a control character in the system character set is also a shunned character.
BASESET	Public Identifier	Represents the base character set of the concrete syntax.
		This is identical to the specification of the document character set used under BASESET as part of the defined components of the declaration.
DESCSET	0 128 0	The concrete syntax character set, in terms of the base set.
		This is identical to the specification of DESCSET used as part of the defined components of the declaration.
FUNCTION	RE 13, RS 10, SPACE 32...	Characters that perform a special function, in addition to being recognized as markup. Markup characters can be data, if they are not specified as markup.
		There are five additional function classes that you can use to define special function characters. You must define a name for the function and assign a function class and a character number. These functions are described in the table immediately following this one.

Keyword	Parameter	Explanation
NAMING	LCNMSTRT ""	Lowercase name start characters are a-z.
		There are five categories that may be defined.
DELIM GENERAL	SGMLREF	General delimiters are from reference concrete syntax.
NAMES	SGMLREF	Reserved names are from reference concrete syntax.
QUANTITY	SGMLREF	Quantity set values are from reference concrete syntax.
		The values set determine the size of the buffer that the parser uses to store this information.

Reference Capacity Set

Capacities are a rough measure of the memory needed to store the results when a parser is used on an SGML DTD. This is used to provide a baseline for conformance for SGML systems. That means that any document that does not exceed the reference capacities and conforms in all other respects must be processed by an SGML system that conforms to the norms.

Capacity sets are calculated using capacity points. One capacity point is equal to one byte. Since these can occasionally generate error messages that are difficult to debug, setting these capacities to maximums you feel are sufficient should resolve this issue. Or, a formal public identifier can be specified that references a file with common capacity specifications. Table C.8 lists the reference capacity set for basic SGML systems.

Table C.8. The reference capacity set.

Name	Maximum Value	Points per Unit	Units for which points are counted
TOTALCAP	35000		Grand total of individual capacity points
ENTCAP	35000	8	Each entity defined
ENTCHCAP	35000	1	Each character of entity text
ELEMCAP	35000	8	Each element defined
GRPCAP	35000	8	Each content token at any level of a content model

continues

Table C.8. continued

Name	Maximum Value	Points per Unit	Units for which points are counted
EXGRPCAP	35000	8	Each exceptions group
EXNMCAP	35000	8	Each name in an exceptions group
ATTCAP	35000	8	Each attribute defined, plus 8 for each occurrence in an entity declaration of a notation name
ATTCHCAP	35000	1	Each character of an attribute value defined as a default value, or explicitly defined in a data attribute specification
AVGRPCAP	35000	8	Each token defined in an attribute value name group or name token group
NOTCAP	35000	8	Each data content notation defined
NOTCHCAP	35000	1	Each character in a notation identifier
IDCAP	35000	8	Each id attribute specified in the instance
IDREFCAP	35000	8	Each IDREF attribute specified in the instance
MAPCAP	35000	8	Each short reference map declared, plus 8 for each map per short reference delimiter defined

The System Declaration

A system declaration is provided as part of the documentation with whatever SGML product is installed on a system. It specifies the features, concrete syntaxes, character set, and data content notations that the system supports. It appears similar to the SGML declaration, except that the parameters refer to system capability, rather than documents.

If you are using different systems, review the system declaration to identify which character sets are used as base and described character sets. Also, be aware of which features are used by the system and the maximum capacity set used by the system. Only SHORTTAG and OMITTAG features are needed for basic SGML documents.

Document Type Declaration (DTD)

The DTD defines the rules the system should use to mark up a specific document or set of documents. For example, if you want all interoffice memos to begin five lines from the top of a page, and you want the date of the memo to be displayed in italics, these rules would be defined in the DTD. The DTD is always written in SGML.

The DTD manages the following:

Document Structure—The number of blank lines between paragraphs, display features of tables within documents, and so on

Different types of documents—All types of document, such as books, manuals, interoffice memos, and letters

Since the DTD can be stored in a separate directory from the document being edited, it is important for a writer to be familiar with which DTDs are available and which DTD is appropriate for the type of document being created.

DTD Naming Conventions

When the document has been analyzed, and you have decided on the classes/types of documents you will require, select names for these classes that are descriptive, such as manual, memo, or help. Be sure that your names do not violate any of the SGML naming conventions described under SGML declarations.

In addition, DTD names cannot exceed eight characters.

Listing DTD Elements

After analyzing the document, you should have a list of elements, attributes, and entities. Some basic document elements are listed in the following minitable, which uses a memo as the sample document:

Name	Description
MEMO	Contains the entire memo
TO	Contains the name of the addressee
FROM	Contains the name of the sender
SUBJECT	Contains a description of the subject of the memo
BODY	Contains the text (data) portion of the memo
CLOSE	Contains the name of the person signing the memo

The BODY element could contain these subelements:

PARA   Contains the text of a paragraph

TABLE   Contains a table of information

Some important issues to remember when defining the elements in a document are

1. Are these elements going to be incorporated into a database?
2. Does this particular element need to be distinguished from others?
3. Will this element have multiple uses? Does this structure allow for multiple uses?

During the analysis, you will also need to decide whether the data is an element or an attribute.

> An *element* is a specific part of a document, such as a paragraph or a chapter. You can also consider an element as an object whose presence is required. For example, the name of the sender of a memo would be an element.
>
> An *attribute* can be defined as a qualifier indicating a property of an element, other than its type or content. If the data describes the content, it could be classified as an attribute. However, attributes should not be used to describe the way the data looks.

Element Declarations

A DTD must include element declarations for each identified element in the document. An SGML ELEMENT declaration consists of two parts: a name and a description of the contents of the element. The basic form of this declaration is

```
<!ELEMENT element_name (subelement1¦subelement2¦...¦subelementX)>
```

You could create a sample DTD for a memo. In the document, the following elements are identified: MEMO, TO, FROM, SUBJECT, BODY, and CLOSE. Therefore, the DTD should contain element declarations for each one of these identified elements. This is done by introducing sequence connectors and occurrence indicators into model groups (See Table C.1. for a description of these delimiters). You could declare elements in your DTD for memos as follows:

```
<!ELEMENT MEMO - - (TO+ FROM, SUBJECT* BODY, CLOSE?)>
<!ELEMENT BODY (PARA+ TABLE*)>
```

Table C.9 breaks down the parts of the first element declaration.

Table C.9. Parts of an element declaration.

EXAMPLE: `<!ELEMENT MEMO - - (TO+ FROM, SUBJECT* BODY, CLOSE? )>`

Order	Part	Description	Abstract Name
1	<!	markup declaration open delimiter	MDO

Order	Part	Description	Abstract Name
2	`ELEMENT`	declaration type keyword	
3	`MEMO`	element's generic identifier	`GI`
4	`- -`	omitted tag minimization	
5	`(TO+ FROM, SUBJECT* BODY, CLOSE? )`	elements that may appear in the document, the special characters are delimiters that describe how the elements can be used in the document	`CONTENT MODEL` or `DECLARED CONTENT`
6	`>`	markup declaration close delimiter	`MDC`

To put this example in perspective, once you fully define the elements and their related attributes and entities, you can create a memo using your DTD. The following is an example of the markup your SGML formatted memo could contain:

```
<MEMO>
<TO>Mr. SGML</TO>
<FROM>Mark S.</FROM>
<SUBJECT>SGML isn't so bad after all</SUBJECT>
<BODY>
<PARA>You're right. Learning SGML is easy once you know HTML
and understand the syntax.</PARA>
<PARA>Thanks for the help.</PARA>
</BODY>
<CLOSE>Mark S.</CLOSE>
</MEMO>
```

The contents of an element are described via either a *content model* or *declared content*. Both are used to markup valid SGML characters. However, include non-SGML data (such as bitmaps) by using an external entity declaration.

Content models—This specifies the model group that defines the allowed content of a specific element.

When working with elements that do not contain subelements (such as TO and FROM), the reserved name #PCDATA is used inside markup declarations to indicate zero (0) or more parsed data characters for a content model without subelements. PCDATA stands for *parsed character data*. This means the parser needs to determine if the data contains other markup, such as start tags. The number sign (#) is the reserved name indicator, or RNI. This distinguishes parsed character data from elements with the name PCDATA, as PCDATA without the number sign is a legal name that can be used by anyone for anything. In the following example, the model group TO can contain valid SGML data. Also, note the implicit optional and repeatable occurrence indicator, *.

```
<!ELEMENT TO    - O    (#PCDATA)*    >
```

Included elements—These are used to include elements that can occur in all subelements of a given element. This is done by using an *inclusion delimiter*. For example, in the following code line, a footnote (FN) element is allowed anywhere within the element MEMO:

```
<!ELEMENT MEMO    - -    ((TO & FROM), SUBJECT, BODY, CLOSE?) + (FN)    >
```

You could also have included a model group following the inclusion delimiter (PLUS), as long as only one type of connector is used.

Excluded elements—These are used to exclude elements from occurring in all the subelements of a given element. Use the minus sign (-) before the element name (FN) to prevent unwanted occurrences of an element. However, the following rules apply:

1. An element can *only* be excluded if it is *optional, repeatable,* or if it occurs in an "or" group, such as the group (CLOSE|FN).

2. The required or optional status of an element *cannot* be changed by an exclusion group.

3. Inclusions and exclusions may occur in the same document element. *If an element is excluded as well as included, the exclusion takes precedence.*

4. Exclusions should be used to prevent recursion of an inclusion, or when a part of a DTD is an external, unmodifiable DTD.

Declared CONTENT and ANY content—Giving an element declared content enables you to command the parser to treat text in a special way. When you include graphics, for example, you want the parser to be aware that this text is handled differently from markup delimiters, which may be composed of the same characters. There are three types of declared content:

Declared Content Type	Description
CDATA	Character data.
	May contain only SGML characters. All markup characters or delimiters are ignored, except for ETAGO (</) delimiters or valid null end tags (/).
	No reserved name indicators needed.
	Ignored markup includes entity references, character references, markup declarations, and processing instructions.

Declared Content Type	Description
RCDATA	Replaceable character data.
	Similar to CDATA except that entity references and character references are recognized.
	Ignored markup includes markup declarations and processing instructions.
EMPTY	An element without any content. For example, a table of contents is marked up by the empty `<TOC>` tag.
	No other elements are allowed inside these elements.
	End tags must be omitted because there is no content; therefore the element doesn't need to be closed.

Other markup allowed—The additional markup that may be contained in an element are as follows:

1. Entity references
2. Character references
3. Markup declarations
4. Processing instructions

Attribute Declarations

Attribute lists are used to declare a list of attributes associated with a previously defined element. The basic form of an SGML ATTLIST is

```
<!ATTLIST element_describing attribute_name attribute_value
(associated_attribute1¦associated_attribute2¦...¦associated_attributeX) default>
```

Attributes can be used to assign specific values to certain variables within an element. For example, suppose that you had two types of memos; interoffice and confidential. You would declare these memo types as follows in your DTD for memo documents:

```
<!ATTLIST MEMO TYPE (inter-office¦confidential)>
```

You could then create SGML documents that use the TYPE attribute for the `<MEMO>` tag:

```
<MEMO TYPE="interoffice">
<TO>Frank</TO>
<FROM>John</FROM>
<SUBJECT>Meeting 3:00pm Friday</SUBJECT>
<BODY>
<PARA>You're scheduled to give presentation on
the new product line. Don't let me down.</PARA>
</BODY>
</MEMO>
```

or

```
<MEMO TYPE="confidential">
<TO>Frank</TO>
<FROM>John</FROM>
<SUBJECT>Meeting 3:00pm Friday</SUBJECT>
<BODY>
<PARA>You're scheduled to give presentation on
the new product line. Don't let me down.</PARA>
</BODY>
<CLOSE>John Smith</CLOSE>
</MEMO>
```

Since the parser checks the values of attributes, once you declare attributes for "interoffice" and "confidential" in the attribute definition list for the element MEMO, each type of memo, when defined by the writer, will have the attributes required for each.

The parts of an attribute declaration are shown in Table C.10.

Table C.10. Parts of an attribute declaration.

EXAMPLE: `<!ATTLIST MEMO interoffice NMTOKEN INTEROFFICE >`

Order	Part	Description	Abstract Name
1	<!	markup declaration open delimiter	MDO
2	ATTLIST	attribute definition list declaration keyword	
3	MEMO	name of the element to which the list belongs	GI
4	interoffice	name of the attribute	NAME
5	NMTOKEN	declared value of the attribute or keyword	NOTATION, NAME, or a keyword
6	INTEROFFICE	default value of the attribute, or keyword	
7	>	markup declaration close delimiter	MDC

Because attribute names are case-insensitive, the preceding example has deliberately mixed the case used. The following rules apply:

You can define as many attributes as you need for any element, as long as there is only one list per element.

The length of any token in an attribute's declared value may not exceed eight.

ID and NOTATION may appear only once per element.

A token may not occur more than once per list.

An ENTITY declared value means that this attribute must have as a value the name of a data entity or the name of an SGML subdocument entity.

All spaces, record ends and separator characters are replaced by a single space, with the exception of CDATA attribute values.

All spaces between literal delimiters are retained. CDATA is the only declared value that may have an empty string as default.

Table C.11 lists the value descriptors for attribute lists, and Table C.12 lists the attribute default values.

Table C.11. Attribute list value descriptors.

Descriptor	Explanation
CDATA	Character data and can contain zero or more valid characters that can be letters, numbers, punctuation, spaces, and special characters.
ENTITY	Specifies a declared entity name.
ID	A unique identifier such as an account number.
IDREF	A reference value to a unique ID.
IDREFS	A list of references values to unique IDs.
NAME	A string of up to eight characters. The first letter of the name must be an alphabetic character. The remaining characters can be combinations of alphabetic characters, periods, and hyphens.
NAMES	A list of NAME strings; each NAME string must be separated by one or more tabs, returns, or spaces.
NMTOKEN	A name token that is a string of up to eight characters that can include and begin with letters, numbers, periods, or hyphens.
NMTOKENS	A list of NMTOKEN strings; each NMTOKEN string must be separated by one or more tabs, returns, or spaces.
NOTATION	Provides a way to process special information in your SGML documents.
NUMBER	A string of up to eight numeric characters.
NUMBERS	A list of NUMBER strings; each NUMBER string must be separated by one or more tabs, returns, or spaces.
NUTOKEN	A string of up to eight characters that begin with a number and can include letters, numbers, periods, or hyphens.
NUTOKENS	A list of NUTOKEN strings; each NUTOKEN string must be separated by one or more tabs, returns, or spaces.

Table C.12. Attribute default values.

Keyword	Description
#FIXED	Keyword is followed by the attribute's value.
	The attribute *always* has this value; it is not user-supplied.
#REQUIRED	Attribute must always be given a value.
	The user must supply a value on the *first occurrence* of a tag; tag may be used multiple times with the same value.
#CURRENT	Value is the most recently specified one.
	The user must supply a value on the *first occurrence* of a tag; tag may be used multiple times with the same value.
#CONREF	Value is for cross references.
	To avoid unresolved references while processing text elements contained in a separate part of a document, assign the *unique identifier attribute* to this default value. (See explanation after this table.)
	If the attribute is given, the element's content can be empty. However, when there is no attribute, an element can have content.
#IMPLIED	Value need not be given; the processing system chooses a default.

Unique identifiers are used to distinguish elements from each other. To do this, declare the attribute value as ID in the ATTLIST statement. It is a good practice to give all unique identifiers in a DTD the same name, such as ID. They also require the following:

They must have a declared default of either #REQUIRED or #IMPLIED. If the value of ID is not provided for an #IMPLIED element, the element is not available for referencing.

Only one attribute with a declared value ID may be defined per element.

To provide unique identification capability for an element for cross-referencing, give an attribute the declared value of IDREF. To link a paragraph reference to a paragraph, give the REFID attribute the same value as the previously defined value of ID.

Entity Declarations

An *entity* is an object that can be substituted into an SGML document based on a declaration. The object can be a text string or any type of file. The object to be substituted could be text that occurs between quotation marks after the declaration, as shown in the following code:

```
<!ENTITY entity_name "The text to substitute">
```

The object could also be instructions for loading a file to place into the document, as shown in the following code:

```
<!ENTITY yourfile SYSTEM "/docs/sgml/file2.sgm" SUBDOC>
```

The entity named yourfile contains two important directives. The first directive, SYSTEM, is a reserved keyword that means the referenced external entity is a file. The second directive, SUBDOC, is a reserved keyword that means the file contains formatted SGML text with its own document declarations. The formatting declarations in the subdocument will be used instead of declarations in the current document.

In your SGML document you describe entities by typing an entity name preceded by an ampersand and ending with a semicolon.

Notation Declarations

The NOTATION declaration provides a way to process special information in your SGML documents. Using notations, you can process mathematical equations through a program that will display it in a formatted output. You can create pointers to graphic files that are displayed via a drawing application.

The basic form of a notation is

```
<!NOTATION notation_name reserved_word "Identifier">
```

You can use notations with entity declarations. The entity declaration can include a pointer to the data contained in the notation. The keyword NDATA, or notation data, is used to identify a pointer to a previously declared notation. A pointer could be used as follows:

```
<!NOTATION gif SYSTEM "zgv">
<!ENTITY sunset SYSTEM "/images/sunset.gif" NDATA gif">
```

The gif notation declares that a program called zgv, a UNIX image viewer, can be used on the system. The second declaration names an entity called sunset. The keyword SYSTEM means the external entity sunset is contained in a system file. The parameter between quotation marks gives the location and name of the file containing the data. The keyword NDATA creates a pointer to the notation name that follows. Through the NDATA pointer, the system knows there is a link between the notation gif and the entity sunset. The presence of the link informs the system that in order to display the sunset.gif image, it must be displayed via the zgv viewer.

Sources for Additional Information

Haven't had enough yet? In this appendix you'll find the URLs for all kinds of information about the World Wide Web, HTML, developing Web presentations, and locations of tools to help you write HTML documents. With this list you should be able to find just about anything you need on the Web.

> **NOTE**
>
> Some of the URLs in this section refer to FTP sites. Some of these sites may be very busy during business hours, and you may not be able to immediately access the files. Try again during non-prime hours.
>
> Also, some of these sites, for mysterious reasons, may be accessible through an FTP program, but not through Web browsers. If you are consistently getting refused from these sites using a browser, and you have access to an FTP program, try that program instead.

Collections of HTML and WWW Development Information

Yahoo's WWW Section
Linkname: Computers: World Wide Web
```
http://www.yahoo.com/Computers/World_Wide_Web/
```

The Virtual Library
Linkname: The Web Developer's Virtual Library
```
http://WWW.Stars.com/
```

The HTML FAQ
```
http://www.umcc.umich.edu/~ec/www/html_faq.html
```

The Developer's JumpStation
Linkname: OneWorld/SingNet WWW & HTML Developer's JumpStation
```
http://oneworld.wa.com/htmldev/devpage/dev-page.html
```

The Repository
Linkname: Subjective Electronic Information Repository
```
http://cbl.leeds.ac.uk/nikos/doc/repository.html
```

The Home of the WWW Consortium
Linkname: The World Wide Web Organization
```
http://www.w3.org/
```

Netscape's HTML Assistance Pages
Linkname: Creating Net Sites
`http://home.mcom.com/assist/net_sites/index.html`

The Spider's Web Pages on the Web
Linkname: (BOBAWORLD) World Wide Web
`http://gagme.wwa.com/~boba/web.html`

The HTML Writer's Guild
Linkname: The HTML Writer's Guide Website
`http://www.mindspring.com/guild/`

Web Directories

ALIWEB, a great Web index
Linkname: ALIWEB
`http://web.nexor.co.uk/public/aliweb/aliweb.html`

An Index of Indexes
Linkname: Web Indexes
`http://www.biotech.washington.edu/WebCrawler/WebIndexes.html`

Galaxy
Linkname: TradeWave Galaxy
`http://www.einet.net/galaxy.html`

Point
Linkname: Point Communications Corporation
`http://www.pointcom.com/`

W3 Virtual Library
Linkname: The World-Wide Web Virtual Library: Subject Catalogue
`http://www.w3.org/hypertext/DataSources/bySubject/Overview.html`

Yahoo
Linkname: Yahoo: A Guide to WWW
`http://www.yahoo.com/`

Web Search Tools

CUSI
Linkname: CUSI (Configurable Unified Search Interface)
`http://Web.nexor.co.uk/susi/cusi.html`

excite
Linkname: excite Netsearch
`http://www.excite.com/`

InfoSeek
Linkname: InfoSeek Net Search
`http://www2.infoseek.com`

Lycos
Linkname: The Lycos Home Page: Hunting WWW Information
`http://www.lycos.com/`

Web Crawler
Linkname: The WebCrawler
`http://webcrawler.cs.washington.edu/WebCrawler/`

Browsers

A general list
Linkname: WWW Client Software products
`http://www.w3.org/hypertext/WWW/Clients.html`

Netscape (Windows, Windows 95, Mac, X)
Linkname: Download Netscape Software
`http://home.netscape.com/comprod/mirror/index.html`

Microsoft Internet Explorer 2.0 (Windows 95)
Linkname: Download Microsoft Internet Explorer 2.0
`http://www.msn.com/ie/ie.htm`

NCSA Mosaic (X, Windows, Mac)
Linkname: NCSA Mosaic Home Page
`http://www.ncsa.uiuc.edu/SDG/Software/Mosaic/NCSAMosaicHome.html`

Lynx (UNIX and DOS)
Linkname: About Lynx
`http://www.cc.ukans.edu/about_lynx/`

WinWeb (Windows)
Linkname: EINet WinWeb
`http://www.einet.net/EINet/WinWeb/WinWebHome.html`

MacWeb (Macintosh)
Linkname: EINet MacWeb
`http://www.einet.net/EINet/MacWeb/MacWebHome.html`

Arena (X)
Linkname: Welcome to Arena
http://info.cern.ch/hypertext/WWW/Arena/

Emacs-W3 (for Emacs)
Linkname: The Emacs World Wide Web Browser
http://www.cs.indiana.edu/elisp/w3/docs.html

NetCruiser
LinkName: NetCruiser HomePort
http://www.netcom.com/netcom/cruiser.html

Web Explorer (OS/2 Warp)
ftp://ftp.ibm.net/pub/WebExplorer/

Cello (Windows)
Linkname: FAQ FOR CELLO (PART 1)
http://www.law.cornell.edu/cello/cellofaq.html

Specifications for HTML, HTTP, and URLs

The HTML Level 2 specification
Linkname: HTML Specification Review Materials
http://www.w3.org/hypertext/WWW/MarkUp/html-spec/index.html

The HTML+ 3.0 draft specification
Linkname: HTML+ (Hypertext markup format)
http://www.hpl.hp.co.uk/people/dsr/html/CoverPage.html

The HTTP specification
Linkname: HTTP: A protocol for networked information
http://info.cern.ch/hypertext/WWW/Protocols/HTTP/HTTP2.html

Netscape's Extensions to HTML 2.0
Linkname: Extensions to HTML
http://home.netscape.com/assist/net_sites/html_extensions.html

Netscape's Extensions to HTML 3.0
Linkname: Extensions to HTML
http://home.netscape.com/assist/net_sites/html_extensions_3.html

Mosaic Tables
Linkname: HTML Tables in NCSA Mosaic
http://www.ncsa.uiuc.edu/SDG/Software/XMosaic/table-spec.html

Pointers to URL, URN, and URI information and specifications
Linkname: UR* and The Names and Addresses of WWW objects
`http://www.w3.org/hypertext/WWW/Addressing/Addressing.html`

Java and JavaScript

The Sun Microsystems Java home page
Linkname: Java: Programming for the Internet
`http://java.sun.com/`

A Java Applet Directory
Linkname: Gamalan
`http://www.gamelan.com/`

Yahoo Java Directory
Linkname: Yahoo - Computers and Internet:Languages:Java
`http://www.yahoo.com/Computers_and_Internet/Languages/Java/`

Netscape information about Java
Linkname: Java Applets
`http://home.netscape.com/comprod/products/navigator/version_2.0/java_applets/`
`index.html`

Netscape information about JavaScript
Linkname: JavaScript
`http://home.netscape.com/comprod/products/navigator/version_2.0/script/`
`index.html`

Tools for Images

Some good information about transparent GIFs
Linkname: Transparent Background Images
`http://melmac.harris-atd.com/transparent_images.html`

giftrans
Linkname: source for giftrans
`ftp://ftp.rz.uni-karlsruhe.de/pub/net/www/tools/giftrans.c`

LView Pro for Windows (at the OAK Simtel Mirror)
`ftp://oak.oakland.edu/SimTel/win3/graphics/lviewp1b.zip`

LView Pro for Windows 95 (at the OAK Simtel Mirror)
`ftp://oak.oakland.edu/SimTel/win3/graphics/lviewp1c.zip`

Graphic Converter for Macintosh (at the HyperArchive sumex-aim Mirror)
URL:http://hyperarchive.lcs.mit.edu/HyperArchive/Archive/
grf/util/graphic-converter-212.hqx

GIF Converter for Macintosh (at the HyperArchive sumex-aim Mirror)
http://hyperarchive.lcs.mit.edu/HyperArchive/Archive/grf/
util/gif-converter-237.hqx

Transparency (Macintosh)
ftp:// med.cornell.edu/pub/aarong/transparency
http://hyperarchive.lcs.mit.edu/HyperArchive/Archive/grf/
util/transparency-10b4.hqx

GIFTool (UNIX)
http://www.homepages.com/tools/

Sound and Video

SOX (UNIX and DOS sound Converter)
http://www.spies.com/Sox/

WAVany (Windows sound converter)
ftp://oak.oakland.edu/SimTel/win3/sound/wvany10.zip

WHAM (Windows sound converter)
ftp://gatekeeper.dec.com/pub/micro/msdos/win3/
sounds/wham133.zip

SoundAPP (Macintosh sound converter)
http://hyperarchive.lcs.mit.edu/HyperArchive/Archive/snd/util/sound-app-
151.hqx

FastPlayer (Macintosh Quicktime player and "flattener")
ftp://ftp.ncsa.uiuc.edu/Mosaic/Mac/Helpers/fast-player-110.hqx

QFlat (Windows QuickTime "flattener")
ftp://venice.tcp.com/pub/anime-manga/software/viewers/qtflat.zip

Sparkle (MPEG player and converter for Macintosh)
http://hyperarchive.lcs.mit.edu/HyperArchive/Archive/gst/
mov/sparkle-243a.hqx

XingCD (AVI to MPEG converter)
Send mail to xing@xingtech.com or call 805/473-0145

AVI-Quick (Macintosh converter for AVI to Quicktime)
http://hyperarchive.lcs.mit.edu/HyperArchive/Archive/gst/mov/avi-to-qt-
converter.hqx

SmartCap (Windows Quicktime and AVI Converter)
ftp://ftp.intel.com/pub/IAL/Indeo_video/smartc.exe

The MPEG FAQ
Linkname: MPEG Moving Picture Expert Group FAQ
http://www.crs4.it/~luigi/MPEG/mpegfaq.html

Information on making MPEG movies
Linkname: How to make MPEG movies
http://www.arc.umn.edu/GVL/Software/mpeg.html

Servers

CERN HTTPD
Linkname: CERN Server User Guide
http://www.w3.org/httpd_3.0/

NCSA HTTPD
Linkname: NCSA httpd Overview
http://hoohoo.ncsa.uiuc.edu/docs/Overview.html

NCSA HTTPD for Windows
Linkname: NCSA httpd for Windows
http://www.city.net/win-httpd/

MacHTTP
Linkname: MacHTTP Info
http://www.biap.com/

Web Providers

An index from HyperNews
Linkname: Leasing a Server
http://union.ncsa.uiuc.edu/HyperNews/get/www/leasing.html

Gateway Scripts and the Common Gateway Interface (CGI)

Yahoo's CGI List
Linkname: Yahoo - Computers and Internet:Internet:World Wide Web:CGI - Common Gateway Interface
http://www.yahoo.com/Computers_and_Internet/Internet/World_Wide_Web/
CGI___Common_Gateway_Interface/The original NCSA CGI documentation

Linkname: The Common Gateway Interface
`http://hoohoo.ncsa.uiuc.edu/cgi/`

The spec for CGI
Linkname: The Common Gateway Interface Specification
`http://hoohoo.ncsa.uiuc.edu/cgi/interface.html`

Information about CGI in CERN HTTPD
Linkname: CGI/1.1 script support of the CERN Server
`http://www.w3.org/hypertext/WWW/Daemon/User/CGI/Overview.html`

A library of C programs to help with CGI development
Linkname: EIT's CGI Library
`http://wsk.eit.com/wsk/dist/doc/libcgi/libcgi.html`

An index to HTML-related programs written in Perl
Linkname: Index of Perl/HTML archives
`http://www.seas.upenn.edu/~mengwong/perlhtml.html`

An archive of CGI Programs at NCSA
Linkname: CGI sample scripts
`ftp://ftp.ncsa.uiuc.edu/Web/httpd/Unix/ncsa_httpd/cgi`

Un-CGI, a program to decode form input
Linkname: Un-CGI Version 1.2
`http://www.hyperion.com/~koreth/uncgi.html`

Forms and Image Maps

The original NCSA forms documentation
Linkname: The Common Gateway Interface: FORMS
`http://hoohoo.ncsa.uiuc.edu/cgi/forms.html`

Mosaic form support documentation
Linkname: Mosaic for X Version 2.0 Fill-Out Form Support
`http://www.ncsa.uiuc.edu/SDG/Software/Mosaic/Docs/fill-out-forms/overview.html`

Image maps in CERN HTTPD
Linkname: Clickable image support in CERN Server
`http://www.w3.org/hypertext/WWW/Daemon/User/CGI/HTImageDoc.html`

Image maps in NCSA
Linkname: Graphical Information Map Tutorial
`http://wintermute.ncsa.uiuc.edu:8080/map-tutorial/image-maps.html`

Some Perl scripts to manage forms
Linkname: CGI Form Handling in Perl
`http://www.bio.cam.ac.uk/web/form.html`

Mapedit: A tool for Windows and X11 for creating Imagemap map files
Linkname: mapedit 1.1.2
`http://sunsite.unc.edu/boutell/mapedit/mapedit.html`

WebMap (Macintosh map creator)
`http://hyperarchive.lcs.mit.edu/HyperArchive/Archive/text/html/`
`web-map-101.hqx`

HTML Editors and Converters

A list of converters and editors, updated regularly
Linkname: Tools for WWW Providers
`http://www.w3.org/hypertext/WWW/Tools/`

A better list of converters
Linkname: Computers:World Wide Web:HTML Converters
`http://www.yahoo.com/Computers/World_Wide_Web/HTML_Converters/`

A great list of editors
Linkname: Computers:World Wide Web:HTML Editors
`http://www.yahoo.com/Computers/World_Wide_Web/HTML_Editors/`

Other

Tim Berners-Lee's style guide
Linkname: Style Guide for Online Hypertext
`http://www.w3.org/hypertext/WWW/Provider/Style/Overview.html`

The Yale HyperText Style Guide
Linkname: Yale C/AIM WWW Style Manual
`http://info.med.yale.edu/caim/StyleManual_Top.HTML`

Some good information on registering and publicizing your Web page
Linkname: A guide to publishing on the World Wide Web
`http://www.cl.cam.ac.uk/users/gdr11/publish.html`

VRML Resource
Directory

E

General VRML Information

VRML Repositories on the Web

The VRML Repository at the San Diego Supercomputing Center (`http://www.sdsc.edu/vrml/`) includes information on various VRML tools, software, and example applications. This is the most up-to-date repository.

An archive of the VRML e-list is one thing you'll find at `http://vrml.wired.com/`.

FAQ (Frequently-Asked-Questions) Web Pages

The main VRML FAQ is maintained by Jan Hardenbergh and is located at `http://www.oki.com/vrml/VRML_FAQ.html`. The FAQ includes information on configuring your HTTP server to transmit the MIME types for VRML and compressed VRML.

VRML Specification

The Version 1.0 Specification for Virtual Reality Modeling Language is at `http://www.hyperreal.com/~mpesce/vrml/vrml.tech/vrml10-3.html`.

A VRML-enabled version of the spec is at `http://www.virtpark.com/theme/vrml/`.

A version of the spec is available in Japanese at `http://tje12.is.s.u-tokyo.ac.jp:10000/~takuya/vrml/vrml.html`.

VRML Browsers

WebFX from Paper Software runs on Windows PCs (`http://www.paperinc.com`).

Webspace is a VRML browser available on various machines. (SGI version: `http://webspace.sgi.com`, others: `http://www.tgs.com`).

InterVista's WorldView VRML browser runs on Windows PCs (`http://www.intervista.com`).

VRScout from Chaco is available on Windows PCs (`http://www.chaco.com`).

WhurlWind is available on PowerMacs running QD3D (`http://www.info.apple.com/qd3d/Viewer.HTML`).

Virtus Voyager is available for Macintosh and Power Macintosh (`http://www.virtus.com/voyager.html`).

SDSC (the San Diego Supercomputer Center) is developing a VRML browser for SGI/UNIX machines, with source code available free for noncommercial use at `http://www.sdsc.edu/EnablingTech/Visualization/vrml/webview.html`.

VRWeb is available on UNIX machines, and the source code is also available at `http://hyperg.iicm.tu-graz.ac.at/vrweb/`.

Newsgroups

The e-list had a huge discussion about what a VRML newsgroup should be named. When all the votes came in, `comp.vr.vrml` was the most popular. However, it may take some time to get this newsgroup set up, as it requires the creation of the `vr` subhierarchy in the `comp.` realm. There is a chance it will end up being `comp.lang.vrml`.

`alt.lang.vrml` exists but has low propogation and low traffic. The FAQ for `alt.lang.vrml` is at `http://www.virtpark.com/theme/vrmlfaq.html`.

E-Lists

The main e-list for discussion of VRML is the unmoderated www-vrml list. Expect a minimum of 30 messages a day on this list; it's not for the faint-hearted. Hope springs eternal for a good newsgroup to complement the e-list! For information, e-mail `majordomo@wired.com` with the message `info www-vrml`. A digest version also exists, which concatenates the daily messages into one message. E-mail `majordomo@wired.com` with the message `info www-vrml-digest` for more information. Because of the volume of postings to the www-vrml list, please read the list for several days before posting, so you can get a feel for what's discussed. And if you have questions like "when will such-and-such browser be available?," please try the VRML Repositories mentioned in this section first. If you have problems with a VRML browser, e-mail the relevant company.

Two other VRML e-lists exist. They are the vrml-modeling and vrml-behaviors lists. The VRML-behaviors list is starting to get busy as people propose ideas for behaviors in VRML 2.0. For information e-mail `listserv@sdsc.edu` with the message `info vrml-modeling` or `info vrml-behaviors`.

An e-list about business applications and models for virtual worlds is vworlds-biz. E-mail `listserv@best.com` with the message `info vworlds-biz`.

Software

QvLib parser is a program that parses VRML files. An SGI version is at `ftp://ftp.sgi.com/sgi/inventor/2.0/qv1.0.tar.Z`. Old versions corresponding to Pre-1.0 VRML Specification drafts are available for LINUX, IRIX, Sun, NT and Mac at `ftp://ftp.vrml.org/pub/parser/`.

Authoring Tools

Webspace Author is a new authoring package for SGIs from SGI (`http://webspace.sgi.com`). The nice thing about Webspace Author is that it has good support for VRML-specific features, such as LOD (level of detail) editing, WWWInlines, and optimizing file sizes.

Home Space Builder is a VRML-compatible authoring tool for PCs from Paragraph (`http://www.us.paragraph.com/whatsnew/homespce.htm`). It works well once you understand the interface, though the file sizes can be large.

Fountain is a VRML authoring tool for PCs from Caligari, `http://www.caligari.com`. It builds nicely on Caligari's experience developing Truespace, a 3-D modeler, and can act like a VRML browser, too.

Create your own simple VRML home world out of 3-D fonts using Aereal Phonts at `http://www.virtpark.com/theme/phonts.html`. Aereal Phonts creates very small files (around 4K) because it uses VRML primitives. Aereal Phonts also enables you to have your simple home world automatically hosted by Aereal's Web server, so that you can instantly have your own VRML URL.

Portal (`http://www.well.com/user/jack/`) is a tool for building VRML worlds from Inner Action Corporation, running on Microsoft Windows operating systems.

WRLGRID from the SDSC generates tile or grid geometries in VRML format (`http://www.sdsc.edu/EnablingTech/Visualization/vrml/`).

Radiance software is developing Ez3d-VR, a VRML authoring tool (`http://www.radiance.com/~radiance`). Ez3d has several modules, has VRML-specific features, and is available on several platforms.

Converters

Keith Rule has added VRML output support to his popular freeware converter, wcvt2pov. You can find it at `http://www.europa.com/~keithr`.

DXF2IV converts DXF files to Open Inventor (what VRML is based on). It's available at `ftp://ftp.sgi.com`. (You can use `iv2vrml` to finish the conversion.)

INTERCHANGE for Windows from Syndesis Corporation (`syndesis@beta.inc.net`) is a commercial format translator that supports more than 30 3-D file formats, including VRML.

OBJ2WRL and TRI2WRL convert Wavefront obj (object) files and Alias tri (triangle) files to VRML; from the SDSC at `http://www.sdsc.edu/EnablingTech/Visualization/vrml/`.

Java/VRML Companies

Aereal (`http://www.aereal.com`) develops Java/VRML/database content sites.

Construct (`http://www.construct.net`) creates high-end VRML Web sites, including Java-enabled VRML.

Dimension X (`http://www.dnx.com`) has developed Liquid Reality, a Java-based VRML browser.

Paper Software (`http://www.paperinc.com`) has developed a Java API for its WebFX VRML browser.

Sun Microsystems is working with SGI and other companies on bringing 3-D to Java. The Java page is at `http://www.javasoft.com`.

Silicon Graphics (`http://webspace.sgi.com`) is developing a Java API for its 3-D software, including its VRML offerings.

WorldMaker (`http://earth.path.net/worldmaker`) is developing software for advanced Java/VRML behaviors and multiuser VRML.

Interesting VRML Web Sites

The Interactive Media Festival's home is at `http://vrml.arc.org/`.

Proteinman's Top Ten VRML Sites is a top ten list of VRML sites that can be accessed in VRML (`http://www.virtpark.com/theme/proteinman/home.wrl.gz`) and HTML (`http://www.virtpark.com/theme/proteinman/home.html`).

`http://www.vrml.org/vrml/` contains simple VRML models.

`http://www.lightside.com/3dsite/cgi/VRML-index.html` contains lots of VRML-related links.

The CAVE is at `http://www.ncsa.uiuc.edu/EVL/docs/html/CAVE.overview.html` and `http://jaka.eecs.uic.edu/dave/vrml/CAVE/`.

Build your own cell membrane at `http://bellatrix.pcl.ox.ac.uk`.

Step-by-Step Origami is at `http://www.neuro.sfc.keio.ac.jp/~aly/polygon/vrml/ika`.

Aereal Serch is a database of VRML links, viewable in VRML (`http://www.virtpark.com/theme/serch/home.wrl.gz`) and HTML (`http://www.virtpark.com/theme/cgi-bin/serch.html`).

An interactive application that lets you move around objects through the use of HTML forms and CGI is at `http://andante.iss.uw.edu.pl/viso/vrml/colab/walk.html`.

Fractal lovers can check out a page on VRML fractals at `http://kirk.usafa.af.mil/~baird/vrml`.

The Inter-Galacticum (`http://www.virtpark.com/theme/cgi-bin/ig.wrl`) is a bunch of worlds created online by users of Virtual World Factory (`http://www.virtpark.com/theme/factinfo.html`).

Kahlua, a Java wrapper for Open Inventor 2.0 (which is similar to VRML 1.0) running on SGI and Solaris platforms, enables you to write Inventor programs in Java. It's at `http://www.cs.brown.edu/people/jsw/kahlua`.

INDEX

SYMBOLS

& (ampersand symbol), 60, 414
@ (at) symbol, 59
: (colon) character, 58
// (double slash marks), 58
{} (ending braces), 672
= (equal sign) symbol, 59
/ (forward slash), URLs, 127
<! ... > HTML tag, 780
% (percentage), 58
+ (plus sign) symbol, 59
# (pound sign), internal hypertext
   links, 130
? (question mark) symbol, 59
"" (quotation marks), 697
/ (slashes), 54, 58
~ (tilde symbol), 58, 694
* (wildcard) notation, 661
3-D modeling, 634
    Fountain, 635-643
       adding color, 637-638
       adding hyperlinks, 641-642
       lettering, 638-640
       navigation modes, 635
       object movement, 635-636

J-K

Jacobs, Karl, interview with, 627-628
JASC, Web site, 323
Java, 652-656
applets, 46, 653-654
alpha versions, 655
code for marquee applet, 658-661
color values of Marquee, 665-66
compiling, 672-673
creating, 656-672
embedding in HTML, 673-674
initializing, 663-666
painting, 667-669
parameters for marquee applet, 657-658
threads, 670-672
capabilities, 655-656
classes, importing, 661-662
code, comments, 661
compilers, 653
defining classes, 662
HotJava, 654
HTML extensions, 87-88
initializing, 664-666
innovations, 769
object-oriented programming, 654
robustness, 655
security, 655
VRML, 618-627
companies, 865
interview with Mike McCue, 628-629
interview with Mitra, 629
interviews, 627-630
Liquid Reality, 619-622
Mark Pesce, 630
paper software, 622-627

JAVAC program, 672
JavaScript, 383
writing CGI scripts, 342-343
Jewels, 14
JFIF (JPEG File Interchange Format), 543
JIF files, 543-544
JPEG File Interchange Format (JFIF), 543
JPEG files (Joint Photographic Expert Group), 194, 211-212, 543-544
FAQ, Web site, 212
images, 567
saving images as, 567
JPEGView, 320
JPG files, 543-544
Jughead, 14
justifying figures, 208

<KBD> HTML tag, 125, 787
key combinations, 468
keyboard input text, displaying in Web pages, 125
keywords, 411, 748-749
KHz (kilohertz), 554
kidsofwais.pl gateway script, 398
kilohertz (KHz), 554
Kodak, Web site, 219
Korn shell scripts, 339

L

labeling
cells in Web page tables, 279
Web page elements with identification keywords, 148
LAN (Local Area Network), 448

<LANG> HTML tag, 184
LANG attribute
<A> HTML tag, 161
<ADDRESS> HTML tag, 167
<BODY> HTML tag, 160
HTML tags, 148
<TABLE> HTML tag, 268-269
language specifications
anchors, 161
tables, 268
Web page body, 160
Web page elements, 148
Web page text, 184
languages
C/C++, 340-341
Caml, 308
client-side scripting, 382-386
comparing markup to page layout applications, 98-101
HTML (Hypertext Markup Language), *see* HTML (Hypertext Markup Language)
Java, 13, 652-656
applets, 653-654
capabilities, 655-656
defining classes, 662
importing classes, 661-662
initializing, 663-666
object-oriented programming, 654
robustness, 655
security, 655
JavaScript, 342-343
page definition, 18
Perl, 341-342
Python, 304
selecting CGI scripts, 337-343

Teach Yourself the Internet in a Week, Second Edition

— Neil Randall

The combination of a structured, step-by-step approach and the excitement of exploring the world of the Internet make this tutorial and reference perfect for any user wanting to master the Net. Efficiently exploring the basics of the Internet, *Teach Yourself the Internet* takes users to the farthest reaches of the Internet with hands-on exercises and detailed instructions. Completely updated to cover Netscape, Internet-works, and Microsoft's Internet Assistant.

Price: $25.00 USA/$34.99 CDN   User Level: Beginner-Inter
ISBN: 0-672-30735-9   622 pages

Tricks of the Internet Gurus

— Various Internet Gurus

Best-selling title that focuses on tips and techniques that allow the reader to more effectively use the resources of the Internet. A must-have for the power Internet user, *Tricks of the Internet Gurus* offers tips, strategies, and techniques for optimizing use of the Internet. Features interviews with various Internet leaders.

Price: $35.00 USA/$47.95 CDN   User Level: Inter-Advanced
ISBN: 0-672-30599-2   809 pages

Teach Yourself More Web Publishing with HTML in a Week

— Laura Lemay

Ideal for those people who are ready for more advanced World Wide Web home page design! The sequel to *Teach Yourself Web Publishing with HTML, Teach Yourself More* explores the process of creating and maintaining Web presentations, including setting up tools and converters for verifying and testing pages. Teaches advanced HTML techniques and tricks in a clear, step-by-step manner with many practical examples. Highlights the Netscape extensions and HTML 3.0.

Price: $29.99 USA/$39.99 CDN   User Level: Inter-Advanced
ISBN: 1-57521-005-3   480 pages

The Internet Business Guide, Second Edition

— Rosalind Resnick & Dave Taylor

Updated and revised, this guide will inform and educate anyone on how they can use the Internet to increase profits, reach a broader market, track down business leads, and access critical information. Updated to cover digital cash, Web cybermalls, secure Web servers, and setting up your business on the Web, *The Internet Business Guide* includes profiles of entrepreneurs' successes (and failures) on the Internet. Improve your business by using the Internet to market products and services, make contacts with colleagues, cut costs, and improve customer service.

Price: $25.00 USA/$39.99 CDN   User Level: All Levels
ISBN: 1-57521-004-5   470 pages

Teach Yourself Netscape Web Publishing in a Week

— *Wes Tatters*

Teach Yourself Netscape Web Publishing in a Week is the easiest way to learn how to produce attention-getting, well-designed Web pages using the features provided by Netscape Navigator. Intended for both the novice and the expert, this book provides a solid grounding in HTML and Web publishing principles, while providing special focus on the possibilities presented by the Netscape environment. Learn to design and create attention-grabbing Web pages for the Netscape environment while exploring new Netscape development features such as frames, plug-ins, Java applets, and JavaScript!

Price: $39.99 USA/ $47.95 CDN   User Level: Beginner-Inter
ISBN: 1-57521-068-1   450 pages

Teach Yourself CGI Programming with Perl in a Week

— *Eric Herrmann*

This book is a step-by-step tutorial of how to create, use, and maintain Common Gateway Interfaces (CGI). It describes effective ways of using CGI as an integral part of Web development. Adds interactivity and flexibility to the information that can be provided through your Web site. Includes Perl 4.0 and 5.0, CGI libraries, and other applications to create databases, dynamic interactivity, and other enticing page effects.

Price: $39.99 USA/$53.99 CDN   User Level: Inter-Advanced
ISBN: 1-57521-009-6   500 pages

Teach Yourself Java in 21 Days

— *Laura Lemay and Charles Perkins*

The complete tutorial guide to the most exciting technology to hit the Internet in years—Java! A detailed guide to developing applications with the hot new Java language from Sun Microsystems, *Teach Yourself Java in 21 Days* shows readers how to program using Java and develop applications (applets) using the Java language. With coverage of Java implementation in Netscape Navigator and Hot Java, along with the Java Development Kit, including the compiler and debugger for Java, *Teach Yourself Java* is a must-have!

Price: $39.99 USA/$53.99 CDN   User Level: Inter-Advanced
ISBN: 1-57521-030-4   600 pages

Presenting Java

— *John December*

Presenting Java gives you a first look at how Java is transforming static Web pages into living, interactive applications. Java opens up a world of possibilities previously unavailable on the Web. You'll find out how Java is being used to create animations, computer simulations, interactive games, teaching tools, spreadsheets, and a variety of other applications. Whether you're a new user, a project planner, or developer, *Presenting Java* provides an efficient, quick introduction to the basic concepts and technical details that make Java the hottest new Web technology of the year!

Price: $25.00 USA/$34.95 CDN   User Level: All Levels
ISBN: 1-57521-039-8   207 pages

Netscape 2 Unleashed

— Dick Oliver, et. al.

This book provides a complete, detailed, and fully fleshed-out overview of the Netscape products. Through case studies and examples of how individuals, businesses, and institutions are using the Netscape products for Web development, *Netscape Unleashed* gives a full description of the evolution of Netscape from its inception to today, and its cutting-edge developments with Netscape Gold, LiveWire, Netscape Navigator 2.0, Java and JavaScript, Macromedia, VRML, Plug-ins, Adobe Acrobat, HTML 3.0 and beyond, security and Intranet systems.

Price: $49.99 USA/$61.95 CDN   User Level: All Levels
ISBN: 1-57521-007-X   Pages: 800 pages

The Internet Unleashed 1996

— Barron, Ellsworth, Savetz, et. al.

The Internet Unleashed 1996 is the complete reference to get new users up and running on the Internet while providing the consummate reference manual for the experienced user. *The Internet Unleashed 1996* provides the reader with an encyclopedia of information on how to take advantage of all the Net has to offer for business, education, research, and government. The companion CD-ROM contains over 100 tools and applications. The only book that includes the experience of over 40 of the world's top Internet experts, this new edition is updated with expanded coverage of Web publishing, Internet business, Internet multimedia and virtual reality, Internet security, Java, and more!

Price: $49.99 USA/$67.99 CDN   User Level: All Levels
ISBN: 1-57521-041-X   1,456 pages

The World Wide Web Unleashed 1996

— December and Randall

The World Wide Web Unleashed 1996 is designed to be the only book a reader will need to experience the wonders and resources of the Web. The companion CD-ROM contains over 100 tools and applications to make the most of your time on the Internet. Shows readers how to explore the Web's amazing world of electronic art museums, online magazines, virtual malls, and video music libraries, while giving readers complete coverage of Web page design, creation, and maintenance, plus coverage of new Web technologies such as Java, VRML, CGI, and multimedia!

Price: $49.99 USA/$67.99 CDN   User Level: All Levels
ISBN: 1-57521-040-1   1,440 pages

Teach Yourself Web Publishing with HTML in 14 Days, Premier Edition

— Laura Lemay

This book teaches everything about publishing on the Web. In addition to its exhaustive coverage of HTML, it also gives readers hands-on practice with more complicated subjects such as CGI, tables, forms, multimedia programming, testing, maintenance, and much more. CD-ROM is Mac- and PC-compatible and includes a variety of applications that help readers create Web pages using graphics and templates.

Price: $39.99 USA/$53.99 CDN   User Level: All Levels
ISBN: 1-57521-014-2   804 pages

Teach Yourself Web Publishing with HTML 3.0 in a Week, Second Edition

— Laura Lemay

Ideal for those people who are interested in the Internet and the World Wide Web—the Internet's hottest topic! This updated and revised edition teaches readers how to use HTML (Hypertext Markup Language) version 3.0 to create Web pages that can be viewed by nearly 30 million users. Explores the process of creating and maintaining Web presentations, including setting up tools and converters for verifying and testing pages. The new edition highlights the new features of HTML, such as tables and Netscape and Microsoft Explorer extensions. Provides the latest information on working with images, sound files, and video, and teaches advanced HTML techniques and tricks in a clear, step-by-step manner with many practical examples of HTML pages.

Price: $29.99 USA/$34.95 CDN   User Level: Beginner-Inter
ISBN: 1-57521-064-9   518 pages

Web Page Construction Kit (Software)

Create your own exciting World Wide Web pages with the software and expert guidance in this kit! Includes HTML Assistant Pro Lite, the acclaimed point-and-click Web page editor. Simply highlight text in HTML Assistant Pro Lite, and click the appropriate button to add headlines, graphics, special formatting, links, etc. No programming skills needed! Using your favorite Web browser, you can test your work quickly and easily without leaving the editor. A unique catalog feature allows you to keep track of interesting Web sites and easily add their HTML links to your pages. Assistant's user-defined toolkit also allows you to add new HTML formatting styles as they are defined. Includes the #1 best-selling Internet book, *Teach Yourself Web Publishing with HTML 3.0 in a Week, Second Edition,* and a library of professionally designed Web page templates, graphics, buttons, bullets, lines, and icons to rev up your new pages!

PC Computing magazine says, "If you're looking for the easiest route to Web publishing, HTML Assistant is your best choice."

Price: $39.95 US/$46.99 CAN   User Level: Beginner-Inter
ISBN: 1-57521-000-2   518 pages

HTML & CGI Unleashed

— John December & Marc Ginsburg

Targeted to professional developers who have a basic understanding of programming and need a detailed guide. Provides a complete, detailed reference to developing Web information systems. Covers the full range of languages—HTML, CGI, Perl C, editing and conversion programs, and more—and how to create commercial-grade Web Applications. Perfect for the developer who will be designing, creating, and maintaining a Web presence for a company or large institution.

Price: $49.99 USA/$53.99 CDN   User Level: Inter-Advanced
ISBN: 0-672-30745-6   830 pages

Web Site Construction Kit for Windows NT

— Christopher Brown and Scott Zimmerman

The Web Site Construction Kit for Windows NT has everything you need to set up, develop, and maintain a Web site with Windows NT—including the server on the CD-ROM! It teaches the ins and outs of planning, installing, configuring, and administering a Windows NT-based Web site for an organization, and it includes detailed instructions on how to use the software on the CD-ROM to develop the Web site's content—HTML pages, CGI scripts, imagemaps, and so forth.

Price: $49.99 USA/$67.99 CDN   User Level: All Levels
ISBN: 1-57521-047-9   430 pages

Add to Your Sams.net Library Today
with the Best Books for Internet Technologies

ISBN	Quantity	Description of Item	Unit Cost	Total Cost
1-57521-007-X		Netscape Unleashed	$45.00	
1-57521-041-X		The Internet Unleashed, 1996	$49.99	
1-57521-040-1		The World Wide Web Unleashed, 1996	$49.99	
0-672-30745-6		HTML and CGI Unleashed	$39.99	
1-57521-039-8		Presenting Java	$19.99	
1-57521-030-4		Teach Yourself Java in 21 Days	$39.99	
1-57521-009-6		Teach Yourself CGI Programming with Perl in a Week	$39.99	
0-672-30735-9		Teach Yourself the Internet in a Week	$25.00	
1-57521-004-5		Teach Yourself Netscape 2	$35.00	
1-57521-004-5		The Internet Business Guide, Second Edition	$25.00	
0-672-30595-X		Education on the Internet	$25.00	
0-672-30718-9		Navigating the Internet, Third Edition	$22.50	
1-57521-005-3		Teach Yourself More Web Publishing with HTML in a Week, SE	$29.99	
1-57521-014-2		Teach Yourself Web Publishing with HTML in 14 Days, Premiere Edition	$29.99	
1-57521-072-X		Web Site Construction Kit for Windows 95	$49.99	
1-57521-047-9		Web Site Construction Kit for Windows NT	$49.99	
		Shipping and Handling: See information below.		
		TOTAL		

Shipping and Handling: $4.00 for the first book, and $1.75 for each additional book. If you need to have it NOW, we can ship product to you in 24 hours for an additional charge of approximately $18.00, and you will receive your item overnight or in two days. Overseas shipping and handling adds $2.00. Prices subject to change. Call between 9:00 a.m. and 5:00 p.m. EST for availability and pricing information on latest editions.

201 W. 103rd Street, Indianapolis, Indiana 46290

1-800-428-5331 — Orders   1-800-835-3202 — FAX   1-800-858-7674 — Customer Service

A VIACOM  SERVIC·E

The Information SuperLibrary™

| Bookstore | Search | What's New | Reference | Software | Newsletter | Company Overviews |

| Yellow Pages | Internet Starter Kit | HTML Workshop | Win a Free T-Shirt! | Macmillan Computer Publishing | Site Map | Talk to Us |

CHECK OUT THE BOOKS IN THIS LIBRARY.

You'll find thousands of shareware files and over 1600 computer books designed for both technowizards and technophobes. You can browse through 700 sample chapters, get the latest news on the Net, and find just about anything using our massive search directories.

All Macmillan Computer Publishing books are available at your local bookstore.

We're open 24-hours a day, 365 days a year.

You don't need a card.

We don't charge fines.

And you can be as **LOUD** as you want.

The Information SuperLibrary

http://www.mcp.com/mcp/   ftp.mcp.com